P9-CBG-523

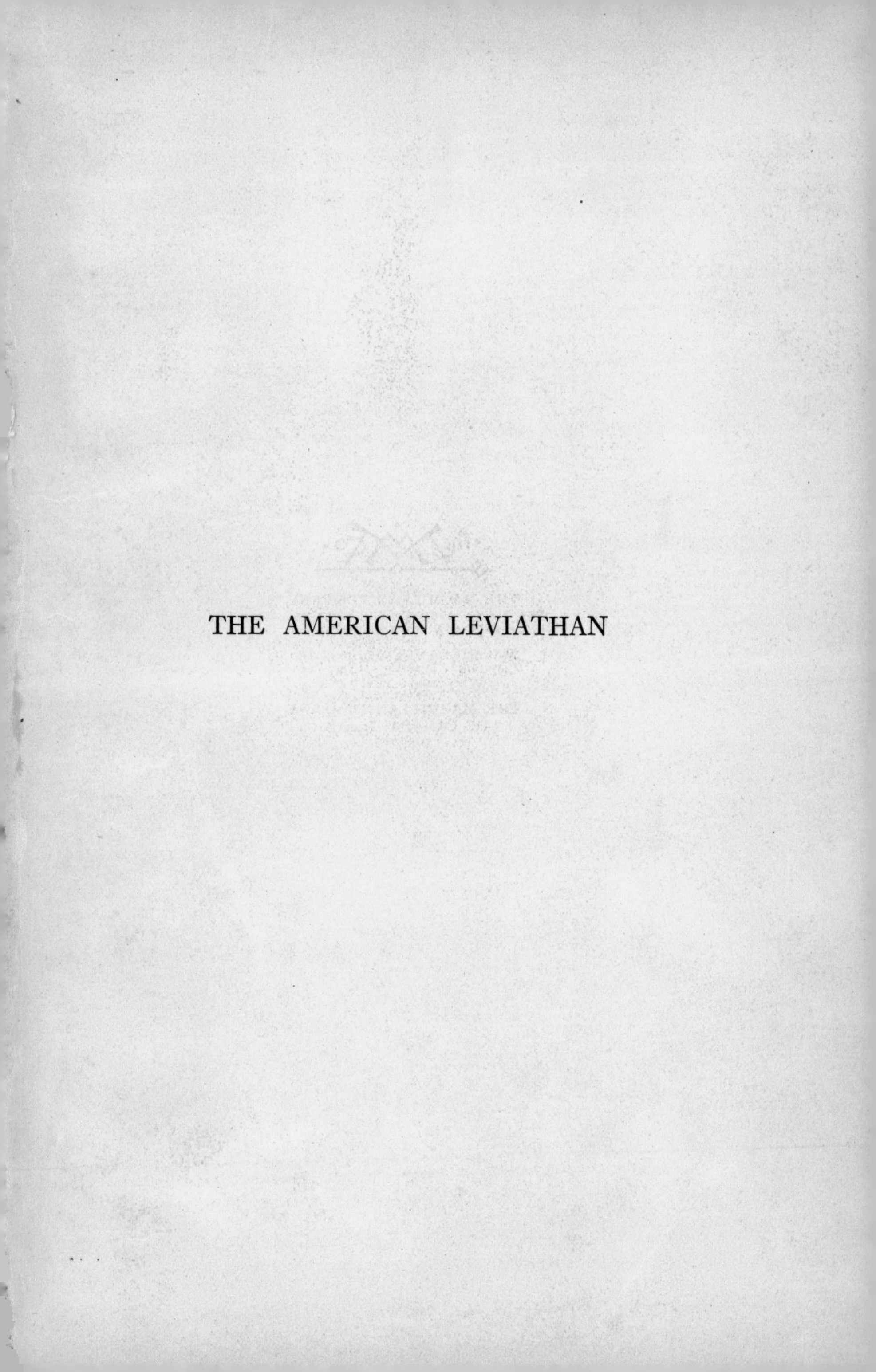

THE AMERICAN LEVIATHAN

THE MACMILLAN COMPANY
NEW YORK · BOSTON · CHICAGO · DALLAS
ATLANTA · SAN FRANCISCO

MACMILLAN & CO., LIMITED
LONDON · BOMBAY · CALCUTTA
MELBOURNE

THE MACMILLAN COMPANY
OF CANADA, LIMITED
TORONTO

Courtesy of the United States Coast Guard

A Coast Guard Vessel on Iceberg Patrol Discovers a Floating Monster of the North in an Atlantic Shipping Lane (*See* P. 397).

THE AMERICAN LEVIATHAN

THE REPUBLIC IN THE MACHINE AGE

BY

CHARLES A. BEARD

SOMETIME PRESIDENT OF THE AMERICAN POLITICAL SCIENCE ASSOCIATION

AND

WILLIAM BEARD

B.S., MASSACHUSETTS INSTITUTE OF TECHNOLOGY

NEW YORK

THE MACMILLAN COMPANY

1930

Set up and electrotyped. Published November, 1930.

. PRINTED IN THE UNITED STATES OF AMERICA .

Dedicated to the thousands of men and women who loyally serve the public on land and sea under the auspices of the Government of the United States

PREFACE

THIS volume is the result of an effort to unite politics, government, and technology as reflected in the federal system of the United States, with emphasis on the newer functions created under the pressures of the machine age. In organization and treatment, it is directed to the general reader, not the specialist or practitioner. Several sections on the more formal aspects of government have been taken from Beard's *American Government and Politics,* but they have all been recast and rewritten to bring them in line with recent tendencies.

When Thomas Hobbes, one of the greatest political thinkers of all times, searched for a title to crown his work on the State, published in 1651, he could imagine no name so appropriate to this powerful and bewildering Titan as the term *Leviathan*—a half-mythical giant uniting in one person a whole multitude. By universal admission, his choice of symbols betrayed amazing grasp and penetration. After surveying the American Federal Government—a huge complex of wealth, political institutions, military engines, economic undertakings, and technological activities looming fatefully on the horizon of the ages,—we could discover no better device to characterize it. Hence we have borrowed our title from Hobbes, in this act of pillage paying such tribute as we can to the immortality of his achievement.

For materials and advice we are indebted to many members of Congress and federal officials, and we wish to acknowledge our obligations collectively, without making any person appear responsible for shortcomings in our work. We are also under obligations to the Editors of *Harper's Magazine* and the *New Republic* for the right to reprint certain pages which have appeared in their columns.

C. A. B.
W. B.

NEW MILFORD, CONN.,
OCTOBER, 1930.

CONTENTS

CHAPTER PAGE

I. GOVERNMENT IN A TECHNOLOGICAL SOCIETY . . 3
Government a Cultural Complex, not a Machine . 3
The Technological Drive in Politics . . . 5
Technology and the Democratic Basis of Government 9
Competence and Intelligence in Modern Politics . 12
Proposed Government by Competence Groups . . 15

II. THE CONSTITUTION OF THE UNITED STATES . . 20
The Constitution as a Document . . . 21
Who Interprets the Constitution? 23
Interpretation of the Constitution by Reference to the Will of Its Makers 26
Interpretation by the Rational Method . . . 30
The Psychological Method of Interpretation . . 33
The Amending Process 39
The Nineteen Amendments 43

III. FUNDAMENTAL PRINCIPLES OF THE FEDERAL SYSTEM 52
The Doctrine of Limited Government . . . 52
The Doctrine of Delegated and Supreme Power . 64
The Separation of Powers 67
The Supremacy of the Judiciary in Matters Involving Persons and Property 71
Citizenship and Suffrage 73

IV. PARTIES AND OPINIONS 82
The Causes of Party Divisions 82
American Political Parties 84
The Nature of Party Organization 87
The Roots and Sources of Party Strength . . 89
Money in Politics 95
The Party and Public Opinions 103

CHAPTER		PAGE
V.	THE FEDERAL JUDICIARY	109
	Constitutional Position of the Federal Courts	109
	The National Judicial Power	111
	The Structure and Business of the Courts	113
	The Great Writs and the Rights of Citizens	121
	The Power of Passing upon the Constitutionality of Statutes	123
	Political Controversies over Judicial Decisions	127
	Law Enforcement	135
	Federal Prisons	141
VI.	THE STRUCTURE OF CONGRESS	145
	The House of Representatives	146
	The Senate	155
	Constitutional Provisions Governing Privileges of Members and the Organization of the Houses	163
	The Sessions of Congress	168
	The Two Houses Compared	170
VII.	CONGRESS IN OPERATION	173
	The Shadow of the Constitution	174
	The Nature and Mass of the Business before Congress	177
	Party Conferences in Congress	180
	Leadership	183
	The Committees of Congress	190
	The General Course of Procedure	197
	Rules for Expediting Business	201
	Information for Legislative Action	207
	Pressures and Lobbies	212
VIII.	THE NOMINATION AND ELECTION OF THE PRESIDENT	220
	The Composition of the National Convention	221
	The National Convention at Work	224
	The Presidential Campaign	232
	Casting and Counting the Electoral Votes	238
	The Inauguration	243
IX.	THE OFFICE OF PRESIDENT	246
	The Executive in the American System	246

CHAPTER		PAGE
	The President and Social Forces	250
	Recent Growth of Executive Prerogative	255
	The President at Work	257
	The President's Cabinet—Its Rôle as a Council	261
	The President as Director of the Administration	264
	The President's Power of Appointment and Removal	267
	The President and Foreign Affairs	273
	The War Powers of the President	279
	The Pardoning Power	282
	The President and Legislation	282
	The President's Privileges and Rights	287
	Legislative and Executive Ties	288
X.	Administrative Organization and Practice	295
	The Heads of Departments	296
	Departmental Organization	301
	The Independent Agencies	305
	Administrative Organization	307
	The Employees of the Federal Government	314
	Employment Methods	317
	Partisanship and Political Activities	323
	Administration and Its Social Environment	327
	Congress and Administration	330
XI.	Taxation, Finance, and Supplies	333
	Taxation	333
	The Purposes and Nature of Taxation	339
	The Enactment of Revenue Laws	344
	Tax and Debt Administration	348
	Appropriation Methods—the Budget System	350
	Money and Banking	360
	Supplies and Buildings	370
XII.	Transportation	376
	Water Transportation—Inland and Coastal	377
	Water Transportation—the Foreign Trade	386
	Land Transportation—Railways, Express, and Pipe Lines	398
	Highways and Motor Transportation	408
	Aviation	413

CHAPTER		PAGE
XIII.	COMMUNICATIONS	420
	Postal Services	421
	Wire Communication	433
	Radio	437
XIV.	THE PROMOTION OF BUSINESS ENTERPRISE	447
	American Political Economy	449
	The Protective Tariff	452
	"Unfair" Foreign Competition and Bounties	459
	Anti-Trust Legislation	462
	"Unfair" Domestic Competition	464
	Trade-marks, Copyrights, and Patents	469
	Promotion of Foreign Commerce	474
XV.	LABOR AND IMMIGRATION	484
	Immigration and Employment	485
	Working Conditions	497
	Industrial Disputes	502
	Research Work	511
XVI.	AGRICULTURAL INTERESTS	513
	Increasing Production	514
	Fighting the Farmer's Foes	521
	Financial Assistance to Agriculture	528
	Agricultural Marketing	533
XVII.	NATURAL RESOURCES	546
	Waste and the Conservation Movement	546
	Federal Lands—Parks and Minerals	549
	Forests	553
	Wild Animal Resources	562
	Water Power	568
	The Lands and Rights of Indians	573
XVIII.	PUBLIC HEALTH, SAFETY, AND MORALS	578
	Health	578
	Public Safety	593
	Public Morals	602
XIX.	MEASUREMENTS AND PLANNING	615
	Standards	617
	Surveying and Mapping	623

CHAPTER PAGE

Federal Statistics—Population 628
Statistics of Industry and Agriculture 633
The Dissemination of Information 634
Coördination and Planning 639

XX. FEDERAL RELATIONS WITH THE STATES . . . 645
The Theoretical Boundaries 645
Specific Federal Limitations on States 648
Federal Protection of Private Property 652
Federal Coöperation with the States 663
Interstate Relations 676

XXI. TERRITORIES AND EMPIRE 679
The Legal Powers of the National Government Over Its Possessions 680
The Government of Districts, Territories, and Possessions 682
Protectorates 687
Problems of Imperial Policy 690

XXII. NATURE AND CONDUCT OF FOREIGN RELATIONS 700
The Revolution in Diplomacy 700
Leadership in Foreign Affairs 705
The Department of State 708
Diplomatic and Consular Representatives in Foreign Countries 712
The Development of the Personnel for the Foreign Service 718
The Treaty-making Power 720
The Negotiation of Treaties 723
Secret Diplomacy 729
American Foreign Policies 732
International Government 743

XXIII. THE WAR MACHINE 750
Relation of Civil and Military Authority . . 759
The Peace Footing 763
The United States on a War Footing 767
The Care of Veterans 775

BIBLIOGRAPHICAL NOTE 781

INDEX 799

LIST OF ILLUSTRATIONS

A Coast Guard Vessel on Iceberg Patrol . . *Frontispiece*

FACING PAGE

Technical Competence at Work 12
The Government's "Great Brass Brain" for the Automatic Prediction of Tides 13
A View of St. Mary's Falls Canal 38
The American Shoal Lighthouse 39
Federal Scientists Unearthing Tricks of the Smuggler's Trade 136
Prohibition Officers Discover 3000 Cases of Liquor . . 137
Radio Enters Politics 236
Manufacturing Propaganda by the Ton 237
A Signpost of the Waves 394
A Practical Demonstration in Water Transportation . . 395
Delivering Mail in the Mountains 424
Army Engineers Laying the Military Cable Between Seattle and Alaska 425
The Government in Business: Logging in a National Forest . 470
A Patent Complexity 471
Immigration Examination at a Port of Entry . . . 492
Training in Mine Rescue Work 493
The Quest for New Plants 514
Reclaiming the Desert 515
Slaking Thirst on the Fire Fighting Line in a Federal Forest . 554
A Phase of Forestry under Private Enterprise . . . 555
Federal Agents Coöperating in Rescue Work . . . 600
A Coast Guard Cutter Saving Life at Sea 601
A Field Party from the Geological Survey Mapping in the Grand Canyon 618
Bureau of Standards Equipment for Testing Railway Scales . 619
An Agricultural Extension Agent at Work in the South . 670
A Case for Federal Highway Aid 671
United States Marines Train Native Constabulary in Santo Domingo 688
The Insular Building in Manila 689
Preparing for War in the Machine Age 774

THE AMERICAN LEVIATHAN

THE AMERICAN LEVIATHAN

CHAPTER I

Government in a Technological Society

Natural science and machinery have set a new and complex stage for the operations of government, imposed additional functions upon it, and lifted it to a new rôle in the process of civilization. No longer can it be correctly considered as a mere group of legal authorities set apart from private citizens to make and enforce simple rules of law. The election, terms, salaries, and duties of public officials—the staples of formal politics—are all incidents in a larger strategy. Even the most learned discussion of them throws little light on the social origins of government, the deeper causes of its form, policies, and tactics, or its place in the unfolding of national destiny and international relations. Philosophically surveyed it appears as a product and organ of world movements—more than a collection of mechanical devices for getting work done in limited time and space.

Government a Cultural Complex, not a Machine

Every national government, at least, has associated with it a vast and complicated heritage of geographical subdivisions, ideas, slogans, loyalties, and apparatus evolved in centuries of political development. Even the Government of the United States, though theoretically framed in the year 1787, was based on the pre-existing thirteen states, which in turn had grown up in the course of nearly two hundred years of experience. Moreover, in searching for the explanation of numerous colonial practices it is necessary to explore centuries of English history, going in some cases far beyond the Norman conquest of 1066. For example we are told by competent scholars that in a quest for the beginnings of jury trial we must inquire into the administrative methods of the Roman Empire. The oldest utterance of English law, the fountain of American common law, we are informed by the commentator Maitland, contains Greek words, and an effort to understand them carries us back to Babylon, into the very beginnings of Mediterranean civilization. Unquestionably, and this is the most significant fact in the case, nearly all the fundamental ideas and institutions of modern politics—universal suffrage, representative government, courts, executives, cabinets, and taxation, for instance—originated in the age of stage coaches, tallow candles, and wooden sailing vessels.

Heavily laden with a cultural heritage, government operates in a given social order which largely determines its functions, problems, and methods. In the industrial era of Herbert Hoover, engineer and economist, the Government of the United States, unchanged in general form, presents aspects radically different from those prevailing in the agricultural era of Andrew Jackson, warrior and planter. Why? The answer is implicit in the statement of fact itself: the social environment of that Government has been revolutionized by steam, electricity, machinery, and science. New economic facts produce new political facts, evolve novel concepts or variant applications of old ideas.

Great statesmen of all times have recognized the intimate connection between economics and government, between industry and property on the one hand and the structure, activities, and procedures of government on the other. From first to last the framers of the federal Constitution took into account the geared association of economics and politics. A distinguished heir to their traditions, Daniel Webster, once went so far as to say that the form of government in America was determined by the abundance of land, its cheapness, and the wide distribution of ownership. Those who do not accept Webster's extreme views will doubtless concede that there is a close reciprocal relation between government and its cultural environment, which must be examined in any serious consideration of the subject.

The Technological Drive in Politics

Hence it follows that a searching treatise on American government must reckon with the technological revolution wrought by science and machinery since the federal Constitution was drawn up more than a century ago. For the old congeries of provincial societies, founded principally on agriculture and local commerce, which made up the United States in 1787, machine industry and the various means of rapid communication have substituted a Great Society, based on national and international markets. Railways, telegraph lines, airplanes, and the radio override historic political boundaries, weld this country into a single economic organism, and steadily weave it into the web of world civilization. To speak of government merely in the political language of the eighteenth century is like talking of travel in the terms of gigs and schooners.

This technological revolution has thrust itself into all the institutions and practices of government. It has emphasized as never before the rôle of government as a stabilizer of civilization. In an agricultural age anarchy could rage without disrupting far-spread networks of industry, commerce, and intercourse. For a thousand years feudal Europe, divided into hundreds of kingdoms and principalities, managed to survive but our modern technological society simply cannot operate unless governments are able to maintain order over wide areas of the earth's surface. The cutting of a single railway line by bandits or revolutionists may bring starvation to people hundreds of miles away. When government collapsed in China in 1912, even though the economy of that country was still rather primitive, social disaster befell whole provinces. Only a hunter in the wilds can wring a living from nature if the rest of the world is in turmoil; people dependent on technical processes for their subsistence perish when the bonds of production and exchange are broken by violence and confusion.

While re-emphasizing the importance of government in maintaining social equilibrium, technology makes highly complex the environment in which it functions. For a simple order of farmers and merchants it substitutes a highly specialized society composed of engineers, machinists, bacteriologists, electricians, and the masters of a thousand or more professions, crafts, and arts. If all are theoretically equal and alike in the eyes of the state, the members of each group possess capacities, habits, and sentiments peculiar to their occupation. In bringing about this amazing differentiation among citizens, the technical revolution has at the same time created new and bewildering forms of property, which find sharp repercussions in the governing process. James Madison, the father of the Constitution, spoke of a landed interest, a manufacturing interest, a commercial interest, and the few minor interests which operated in politics in his era; to them have since been added railway, oil, public utility, sugar, rubber, and a hundred other powerful interests represented by active and highly paid agents in Washington. This is not all. Technology devises more efficient instruments for the distribution of their "information" and propaganda—the telegraph, rapid printing presses, the radio, the television, and the talking picture—instruments which facilitate the moulding of public opinion; in other words, the intellectual climate in which governments make and execute policies.

Besides reaffirming its significance and creating a complicated environment for it, technology multiplies the burdens of government. Inventions are continually introducing unexpected conflicts and confusions into society. To cite an illustration, the number of radio stations which can be put in operation is limited by the very nature of the device and chaos would prevail "on the air" if the Federal Government did not intervene to regulate its use throughout the country. Technology brings new perils in its train: falling aircraft, the pollution of streams, and dangerous explosives.

It makes possible new forms of law violation: safe-blowing, machine gun banditry, wire-tapping, and submarine smuggling. It offers to government striking opportunities to serve the common good: bacteriology reveals to it responsibilities in public health never dreamt of in the days of Franklin and Washington when yellow fever was fought by smudge fires. It is accompanied by hazardous industries which increase the number of injured and defective for whom provision must be made. It penalizes old age by demanding energetic youth for its machines, raising the grave problem of technological unemployment and old-age dependency. If governments tried to cling to the functions assigned to them in the eighteenth century, modern societies could scarcely escape disaster.

Under the pressure of these new forces, government itself has become an economic and technical business on a large scale. It comes into daily contact with all industries, sciences, and arts. As a purchaser of goods in a bewildering variety for its normal needs, government must deal with such involved matters as chemical composition, physical properties, and durability. An operator of battleships, dirigibles, canals, and wireless stations, it faces technical questions of the highest complication. A regulator of railways, telegraph lines, and other means of transportation and communication, it must command, for effective work, abilities equal to those of corporation managers, certainly greater than those of stockholding owners. A promoter of shipping, industry, and aviation, through direct or indirect subventions, it inevitably deals with the mechanics of these enterprises, unless forsooth it is to subsidize obsolescence and inefficiency at public expense. Even in taxing—that ancient function—it must classify, analyze, and evaluate thousands of products flowing from machines, upon which it imposes duties and excises. As an employer of agents to carry on its intricate activities, government draws into its service representatives of all the professions, sciences, and arts known to technology.

Few indeed are the duties of government in this age which

can be discharged with a mere equipment of historic morals and commonsense. Whenever, with respect to any significant matter, Congress legislates, the Courts interpret, and the President executes, they must have something more than good intentions; they must command technical competence. The situation is not changed in the case of so-called moral issues. Ethical aspirations in government—the enforcement of prohibition, for example—constantly run into technical questions; one of the chief difficulties in the way of suppressing the traffic in intoxicating liquors springs from the use of alcohol in various industries and from the necessity of denaturing and controlling that product. The airplane and radio also enter the prohibition process, for both instrumentalities are used in smuggling. Twist and turn as they will politicians cannot escape the necessity of reckoning with science and machinery.

Fortunately in introducing these bewildering complexities into government, technology has brought with it a procedure helpful in solving the problems it has created; namely, the scientific method. In principle this method is likewise opposed to the instinctive, emotional, rule-of-thumb operations of historic politics. It is essentially analytical and rational. It calls for the collection of pertinent facts, the formulation of conclusions on the basis of facts, and the execution of policies in accordance with the requirements of the fact situation. Though undoubtedly limited in its application, the scientific method promises to work a revolution in politics no less significant than that wrought in society at large by mechanics. It punctures classical oratory—conservative as well as radical—and offers to explore worlds unknown to politicians of the archaic school. Recognizing the demands of a new order, a United States Senator, Elmer Thomas, of Oklahoma, has proposed an official re-examination of our whole traditional system of government in the light of the changed situation. It is certainly not too much to say that science and machinery have set an intricate stage for the operations of government in the twentieth century.

Technology and the Democratic Basis of Government

Inevitably these new conditions have drawn in question the very basis of modern government—democracy with its insistence on the doctrine of equality and the popular election of all high public authorities. Yet nearly everything that has been said recently in criticism and defense of the idea is old in substance and obsolete in application. Like democracy and its forms of government, the arguments on both sides antedate in spirit and origin the era of science and machinery. Technology itself has not made a single important contribution to the philosophy of government. That philosophy is still heavy with age, as it already was when James Watt split the world open with his steam engine.

Disputes about democracy, therefore, creak with rust. In the eighteenth century when our Government was founded, as at the present moment, they turned on intelligence, not competence—on some mysterious mental quality of the masses. In championing democracy, Thomas Jefferson contended that the common people had as much, if not more, capacity than so-called superior persons. "We believed," he said in speaking of his party, "that man was a rational animal, endowed by nature with rights, and with an innate sense of justice; and that he could be restrained from wrong and protected in right, by moderate powers, confided to persons of his own choice." With reference to ethical questions, Jefferson once exclaimed: "State a moral case to a plowman and a professor. The former will decide it as well, and often better than the latter, because he has not been led astray by artificial rules."

Opposition to democratic government has likewise been based on certain ancient considerations respecting the nature and training of the masses. In every nation, said John Adams, a large proportion of the people "take no rational and prudent precautions to preserve what they have, much less to acquire more." They are indolent and without genius for grand political enterprise. These are the common people—

laborers, mechanics, and merchants—"without any knowledge in liberal arts or sciences." Opposed to this vast majority is a minority of "gentlemen." The latter are "more intelligent and skilful," and usually have received "a liberal education, an ordinary degree of erudition in liberal arts and sciences." As a rule intelligence and capacity to govern go with wealth. "Generally," Adams continued, "those who are rich and descended from families in public life will have the best education in arts and sciences." Politics he regarded as a contest between knowledge and ignorance; both classes, gentlemen and commoners, were predatory, he thought, and ready to rob each other. Hence, though the former had intelligence, a check on both was necessary in the shape of an independent executive and judiciary. In the absence of such a curb, greed would rule.

Adams' great contemporary, Alexander Hamilton, on the other hand, put a generous trust in the wisdom of "the rich and well born." According to his creed, "the people are turbulent and changing; they seldom judge or determine right." Although Hamilton did not flatly say in this connection that intelligence was monopolized by the rich and ignorance by the poor, the conclusion was implicit in his verdict. With many of his Federalist colleagues he doubtless thought that the well-born few were rich because they were wise, while the poverty of the masses was due to their inherent folly.

Along with the ineptitude of the masses, imagined the conservative Fathers, went a propensity of the commoners to despoil the rich by attacks on property through legislation if not by violence. A few eighteenth century philosophers, John Adams and Gouverneur Morris, for example, thought that the rich showed an equal tendency to fleece the poor, but most of them were particularly alarmed about democratic dangers to accumulated wealth. All through their writings ran a note of distrust: unless the masses are checked by strong government they will attack the vested interests of the minority. And this division into classes and masses they usually ascribed to innate differences in mentality: the intelligent and virtuous collect property; the ignorant and improvident remain poor and seek to despoil the prudent. Madison believed that men had "different and unequal faculties of acquiring property," that the rights of property sprang from "diversity in the faculties of men," that the masses would usually be poor, that government was primarily concerned with regulating various and interfering economic interests, and that rule by the majority, unless countered by other forces, would end in ruin to the public good and private rights.

Modern critics of democracy take a similar tack with other ends in view. The Bolsheviki insist in effect that the people at large are not intelligent; owing to their ignorance they are deluded by the religious and political teachings of the dominant classes and cannot attain power through the machinery of popular government. They can rule, if at all, only through a proletarian dictatorship operating in their name. Italian Fascists, on their part, while holding kindred theories with respect to popular discernment, substitute a "dictatorship of capacities," that is, of politicians, journalists, and the middle classes. Fascism, explains a distinguished advocate, Signor Rocco, with the express sanction of Mussolini, "proclaims that the great mass of citizens is not a suitable advocate of social interests for the reason that the capacity to ignore individual private interests in favor of the higher demands of society and of history is a rare gift and the privilege of the chosen few." It may be difficult to determine who are "the chosen few" but, beyond question, the fundamental Fascist criticism of democracy rests on a conviction that the ruling minority is "wise" and the multitude is "ignorant."

This concept of democracy has been given a certain vogue in the United States, consciously or incidentally, by the "intelligence testers." Although there is diversity of opinion among them as to the meaning of the term "intelligence" and as to the wider significance of their inquiries, a general thread of argument is discernible in their writings: intelligence can be tested by their devices; the sheep may be separated from the goats; and the number of intelligent persons is relatively small. One calculator of this persuasion estimates that the entire population of the United States embraces only about two hundred thousand people entitled to membership in the select upper circle. This is discouraging enough, no doubt; but as if to darken the outlook some of the testers contend that intelligence is, in the main at least, the product of heredity, not of education; it is a quality of mind, not a competence composed of acquired knowledge. Presumably if we had an enlightened electorate, democracy might work, but since intelligence is confined to a few and is hereditary—not subject to increase by education—the case of popular government must seem hopeless to such sponsors of mentality measurements.

Competence and Intelligence in Modern Politics

There is one significant aspect of the subject, however, to which neither writers on government nor psychologists have given sufficient attention. In dealing with politics both have adhered on the whole to the ideas of the agricultural age which preceded the advent of machine industry and applied science. It is true that Robert Michels, in his work on political parties, shows how the complexities of modern society make exceedingly tenuous, if not impossible, popular control over administration, especially by the ordinary rank and file without technical knowledge. Other critics have made similar observations—usually with the conclusion that perhaps the problems of modern government could be solved if the participation of the people were limited to the choice of representatives to do their thinking for them or if the whole business were handed over to aristocracies, dictators, or monarchs possessing, presumptively, superior intelligence.

In reality such thinking does not go to the heart of the matter at all, for the simple reason that an ever larger area of government, as well as industry, is being occupied by machinery and science; the operations of public administration become increasingly technical in character, involving a knowl-

Courtesy of the United States Bureau of Standards

TECHNICAL COMPETENCE AT WORK: TESTING AN AIRSHIP GIRDER AT THE UNITED STATES BUREAU OF STANDARDS (*See* P. 373).

Courtesy of the United States Coast and Geodetic Survey

THE GOVERNMENT'S "GREAT BRASS BRAIN" FOR THE AUTOMATIC PREDICTION OF TIDES IN ALL PARTS OF THE WORLD (*See* P. 396).

edge of chemistry, physics, and higher mathematics in their several branches. Hence the problems they present cannot be solved by intelligence, no matter how superior, unless it is factually informed. Power to deal with such realistic issues is proportioned to technical competence, not merely to degrees of natural understanding.

In the presence of an intricate question respecting the hydraulics of river improvement, the physics of hull design and the water resistance of ships, or tide prediction, the most sagacious and highly educated lawyer or editor in America is about as helpless as the most ignorant laborer. Jefferson's plowman and professor stand on the same footing. Hamilton's rich and well-born and his despised mass of the people are in the same boat. It is true that the person with "natural" intelligence can more readily master the details of some particular field, but his life is too short to span the whole range and in the best of circumstances his technical competence is accordingly limited to a small segment of engineering. And even technology is far from infallible within its proper domain.

A concrete example—one of the simplest in a vast array—will illuminate the problem. The Jones Merchant Marine Act of 1928 is designed to afford shipping companies a financial support which will enable them to build vessels equipped with "the most modern, the most efficient, and the most economical engines, machinery, and commercial appliances." If such aid is not to be granted blindly, thus subsidizing ignorance and fatuity, then the Federal Government is under obligations to see that certain standards of scientific measurement are applied. Leaving aside the difficulties of choosing commercial routes and securing cargoes, the technical questions of ship construction which arise in connection with the execution of the law are bewildering enough to stagger all the "two hundred thousand persons of superior intelligence in the United States," except a few marine engineers, who may or may not be in that fortunate class. Even their brethren in other departments of engineering are, in this relation, almost as helpless as Jefferson's professor and plowman. If "intelligence" alone actually governed the country, its collective wisdom would not necessarily produce correct conclusions respecting the efficient execution of the Jones Merchant Marine Act. Who among the most intelligent are able to choose competent technical administrators?

Even in dealing with the broader aspects of the shipping question, the case for mere intelligence is scarcely improved. Should any financial assistance be given to ship owners or should they be left to win in the competitive race on the strength of their own talents? No one would pretend for a moment that all intelligent citizens favor ship subsidies and that only the ignorant are to be found among the objectors. It is difficult to discover a single public question of significance on which wisdom and vacuity are diametrically opposed—assuming for the moment that these are really entities in the psychological world. Not even the most fanatical partisan contends that his group contains every bit of brains in the country.

Passing from issues of domestic policy, which call for technical qualifications of high order, we encounter similar difficulties in the sphere of foreign relations. They are present in all divisions of trade and finance. They are especially obvious in matters of national defence. Under modern conditions, war is founded on technology; and "adequate preparedness," whatever it may mean, certainly involves engineering designs, calculations, and operations of the most intricate character. Admitting for the sake of argument that the next foe or combination of foes can be determined in advance—an alignment depending on the foreign policy of the Government and the "accidents" of history—how can any military or naval expert determine with any degree of accuracy the exact mechanical and chemical equipment that will prove effective under the incalculable conditions in which it may be employed? Doubtless there are many "experts" who speak as if they were sure of their "facts" but the lessons of the World War have warned the public against childlike reliance on the correctness of their judgments and inferences.

Proposed Government by Competence Groups

So grave are the problems of technology in government that many critics, doubting the ability of the populace, propose to substitute for political legislatures, chosen by the head-counting process, composite organizations made up of agents representing industrial, technical, and professional groups, supposed to embody the subtlety and understanding of their several specialties. The idea is not new. Pelatiah Webster, in his suggestions for a federal constitution published in 1783, proposed to associate a national chamber of commerce with the Congress of the United States. Nor is it academic. The legislature of Italy was reconstructed on a corporate basis by the dictator Mussolini, and the German constitution provides for a system of economic councils. Within limits the theory and the experiments may be useful.

But the notion that any professional group, however successful it may be in solving problems of detail in its own field, is equally capable of meeting the issues arising from its relations to other groups and the totality is without support either in logic or experience. For example it is scarcely to be assumed that a gild of coal operators, while thoroughly able to administer its own property, is also equipped to decide with dogmatic precision all collateral cases such as taxation of mines, wages of labor, transportation of coal, and conservation of natural resources—to mention a few.

A government composed solely of federated groups would be more likely to fall to pieces from violent differences of opinion over general questions than to attain permanent unity through a reciprocal exchange of decisions expertly made by particular interests. Transcending the peculiar questions of each specialty are the interrelations of all the specialties; and the kind of knowledge or intelligence necessary to deal with these interrelations is not guaranteed by proficiency in any one sphere. Hence, if uninformed intelligence is barred from large areas of government by technical difficulties, the mere power to deal with them may be in its turn futile in other fields no less important to the welfare and destiny of peoples.

Beyond the technology of government lie fateful questions of great policy to which all other things are subordinate. Ruling classes, and sometimes their nations, have been destroyed by wrong decisions or guesses concerning duties, responsibilities, and activities. It is not necessary to cite any illustrations from the crowded pages of history. If it is said that ruling classes are likely to have more genius for government than the masses, then it must be admitted that their advantages have not always saved them from destruction. If they have in fact possessed all the wisdom in the past and have been overcome by ignorant multitudes, then we are driven to the conclusion that the verdicts of history are generally wrong and that the universe in which we live is founded on folly and stupidity.

If it is so constituted, intelligence and competence are enslaved to a Sisyphian task—eternally rolling a heavy stone up hill only to have it roll down again. The facts of history drive us to no such pessimistic thesis. At least if they lend color to it, they also give support to an opposite conclusion. History affords innumerable cases of sound judgments springing from the opinions of the nameless and unknown, given voice through leaders from their ranks, and resulting in actions afterward approved by the arbitrament of mankind, beyond which there is no appeal in earthly affairs. Those who arrogate intelligence to themselves are not always wise; nor are those to whom ignorance is ascribed always foolish.

In a machine age, at least, when informed competence, rather than "native intelligence," is such an important factor, no division of society into the politically wise and the foolish is possible. Nor can any permanent classification of the people into sharp economic and technical groups be effected; if it could be made at a given moment, it would soon be smashed by the flooding cross-currents of our rapidly changing industrial processes. Even if it could be brought to pass for the purposes of representation in government and administration, it would only assure efficiency in tight compartments, not the super-efficiency which could correlate all specialties. Moreover, in an era of mass production by the masses and for the masses—when the poor and bad-born work in the whole industrial structure from bottom to top, the people themselves bear heavy burdens of civilization and they are as likely to discover through their skins, if in no other way, what is politically feasible and desirable as are the rich and well-born through their superior powers of divination. History-making in a machine age is a mass process rather than the operation of a small aristocracy of conquest.

Hence we are forced to the conclusion that in any working scheme of modern government, provision must be made for bringing to a focus of power the opinions of the multitude as such. Most of these views may be foolish, as alleged by the "intelligent," but, springing from the very heart of the productive organism, they cannot be ignored by persons who imagine themselves directing the drama. A division of the population into classes for representation in legislation and administration could have only limited, though perhaps highly valuable, uses. American citizens, are no doubt, already well-organized into "pressure groups" which function powerfully within certain boundaries. But there is no reason for expecting any automatic solution of the problems of government by the mere legal incorporation of these gilds within the framework of its departments. Beyond the technical specialties there is unity—a unity which must be dealt with by a divination transcending that of particular experts.

Since this appears to be true, then as Mr. Walter Lippmann has pointed out, a frank recognition of the nature and rôle of private associations in government, not a recasting of political machinery along group lines, is the better hope for efficient government. Let the organization of economic and technical societies continue. Let them raise their standards.

Let the departments of administration and the committees of Congress take advantage of their counsel and advice. Let research unearth and philosophy illuminate the social data of technological evolution. Let the business of government proceed on the basis of the fundamental facts of our technological age. Effect an ever wider distribution of knowledge respecting the transformation which technology has made in human affairs. In themselves these new attitudes imply a revolution in the study of government, in the approach to the subject, and in the methods of research, calculation, and deduction employed. To the historic verbiage and tactics of politics such an operation would be fatal. If these are not the correct inferences, then what are the alternatives?

Light can be thrown upon this finding from the experience of Germany as described in Arthur Rosenberg's remarkable book on *Die Entstehung der Deutschen Republik*. The head of the German Army in 1914 was not selected by any process savoring of democracy—by a parliament or an elected president; he was chosen by the German emperor on the basis of "competent" advice from military specialists. And yet when the test came, he failed. The early breakdown of the German forces in the West is to be largely ascribed to his errors of judgment and his failure to keep in close touch with the progress of events at the front. The German army was technically proficient; it lacked a technically proficient leader. Choice by the élite had not produced him. Democracy could have done no worse. At all events the war was won by the countries in which military affairs were constantly interfered with by the "democratic politicians" so generally scorned by "experts." In war as in peace there are other elements involved besides machines. There are human factors that defy chemical analysis or statistical computation, and a government that does not take them into account is as unscientific as one that ignores mechanics, physics, and chemistry.

From the above survey it is apparent that government carries into our technological age a cultural heritage from the ancient agricultural order and yet finds its environment and functions revolutionized by science and machinery. It must now command expertness in all fields of technology and at the same time its work calls for a super-competence able to deal with the interrelations of the various departments. It must also reflect "the hopes and energies, the dreams and consummation, of the human intelligence in its most enormous movements." Constantly it faces large questions of choice which cannot be solved by the scientific method alone—questions involving intuitive insight, ethical judgment, and valuation, as of old. Science and machinery do not displace all cultural considerations. They complicate these aspects of life; they set new conditions for social evolution but they do not make an absolute break in history as destiny and opportunity. The problem before us, therefore, is that of combining the noblest philosophy with the most efficient use of all the instrumentalities of the modern age—a challenge to human powers on a higher level of creative purpose. Its long contemplation lights up great ranges of sympathies and ideas, giving to many deeds that appear commonplace a strange significance and elevation.

CHAPTER II

The Constitution of the United States

All the work performed by the Government of the United States—Congress, the President, the courts, and executive authorities high and low—is done under the sanction of a written instrument—the Constitution. Nay, more. The states, cities, counties, and all local agencies are limited in their powers and activities by the specific and general restraints imposed by this document. The American Government, therefore, stands in sharp contrast to the British Parliament—King, Lords, and Commons—which, to use the language of the commentator, Blackstone, "hath sovereign and uncontrolled authority," and can "do everything that is not naturally impossible." This fact colors all political life in America. Great public issues are not debated here solely on their merits, in relation to public welfare, convenience, necessity, or efficiency.

With respect to every one of them the question is asked, "Is it constitutional, is it sanctioned by the historic document handed down by the Fathers?" If a proposal involves an amendment of the Constitution deep sentiments are aroused, especially among opponents of the suggestion; it is felt that something transcending the practical needs of practical life is at stake, something almost sacred. Indeed the American Bar Association reports that every true American citizen should declare, "The Constitution of the United States ought to be as actual a part of my life and my religion as the Sermon on the Mount." While other citizens might hesitate in placing the clauses of the Constitution on a parity with the "divinely inspired teachings of Jesus," nearly all would doubtless agree that it is not to be treated lightly or to be altered without great deliberation.

The Constitution as a Document

Hence there are substantial, as well as sentimental grounds for asking, What is this marvellous instrument—the Constitution of the United States? Perhaps nine good citizens out of ten who know a little American history have a ready answer. The Constitution of the United States is a written document. The original instrument was drafted at Philadelphia in 1787 by a convention of delegates chosen by the legislatures of twelve states, and it was ratified by conventions chosen by the voters of the several states for that express purpose. It took the place of the Articles of Confederation formed during the turmoil of the Revolution. It was the product of a sharp conflict between the commercial and financial interests on the one side and the agrarian and debtor interests on the other. Under the Articles public debts had remained unpaid, private property had been attacked by state legislatures, the currency had been inflated by worthless paper, industry had gone without protection against foreign competition, business enterprise had been hampered at every turn, and a social dissolution had been threatened. To put the country on a secure basis, the Fathers established a government composed of three departments—legislative, executive, and judicial, strong enough to defend the nation on land and sea and endowed with ample powers to collect taxes for the payment of its bills, to regulate interstate and foreign commerce, provide a sound currency, and restrain the states in their propensities to violate property rights by devious measures. In this written document, it will be said, the fundamental principles of the federal system are set forth in a style so simple that school children can understand them and the wayfaring man though a fool cannot fail to grasp them.

Unquestionably the record is clear. Unquestionably also many passages of the Constitution are so plain as to admit of no uncertainty. "No person shall be a Representative who shall not have attained to the age of twenty-five years. . . . The Senate of the United States shall be composed of two Senators from each state. . . . [The President] shall hold his office during the term of four years. . . . The Congress may determine the time of choosing the [presidential] electors and the day on which they shall give their votes; which day shall be the same throughout the United States." If all the clauses of the Constitution were so precise and transparent, so definite and mathematical in terms, then it might be said with some warrant that a citizen who has a copy of the Constitution before him is in the presence of the whole instrument and can entertain no doubts as to what it is that confronts him. If this were true the present chapter might well stop here.

But unfortunately for any simple answer to the question, "What is the Constitution?" many of its provisions are not clear or, at all events, are composed of words susceptible of more than one interpretation. It is a lesson in humility to take the famous document and extract from it all the clauses that are not self-evident, that call for extrinsic aids in explanation. For instance, the Preamble announces among other purposes a design "to establish justice . . . promote the general welfare, and secure the blessings of liberty to ourselves and our posterity." Article I stipulates that "direct" taxes must be apportioned among the states according to their respective population and that duties, imposts, and excises shall be "uniform" throughout the United States. Article IV says that "the citizens of each state shall be entitled to all privileges and immunities of citizens in the several states." The Fifth Amendment declares that no person shall be "deprived of life, liberty, or property, without due process of law," that is, by Congress; and the Fourteenth Amendment adds that no state shall "deprive any person of life, liberty, or property, without due process of law."

What are direct taxes? What are the privileges and immunities of citizens in the several states? What is due process of law? Can intelligence, no matter how profound, can "natural reason," no matter how keen, find the answers to these questions in the Constitution? Decidedly, no. Such passages are meaningless in themselves; they can only be understood by reference to a great body of knowledge and practice outside of the Constitution. More than this, they are vague and indefinite and may be fairly and honestly interpreted in different ways by authorities equally competent and equally sincere in their quest for the truth in the matter.

If for practical purposes a large part of the Constitution is meaningless except when authoritatively explained elsewhere, the explanation itself must become in some organic way a part of the language of the Constitution when it is read; otherwise it is, in its indefinite provisions, a collection of empty formulas. In any case it is not a printed document at the end of a textbook that controls the political authorities in the discharge of their duties; it is a printed document explained by judicial decisions, precedents, and practices and illuminated by understanding and aspiration. In short, the real Constitution is a living body of rules carried into effect by living persons according to their convictions.

Who Interprets the Constitution?

Who, then, makes the Constitution an instrument of control, by answering the thousands of questions which it leaves unanswered? According to the formula of the child's book in civics, it is the Supreme Court of the United States, or at least a majority of the judges, that "interprets" the Constitution. But even a superficial examination of the instrument itself reveals a fatal weakness in this contention. Federal courts have no monopoly over the business of exposition. They are given a field of work, a jurisdiction, and it extends only to cases in law and equity arising under the Constitution, the laws of the United States, and the treaties made under its authority, and certain other enumerated cases.

Now, all problems arising under the Constitution cannot be formulated into cases, or actions between parties, and carried before the Supreme Court. Moreover, the Court has repeatedly ruled that some cases are political in character and lie outside its jurisdiction. If for the sake of argument, however, it be admitted that the Supreme Court in final analysis answers all questions arising under the Constitution, then it is proper to ask, What Supreme Court? Judges die. Times change. New Presidents are elected and nominate new judges to fill vacancies on the bench. The Court under Chief Justice Marshall, an ardent Federalist, is not the same Court as that under Chief Justice Taney, an ardent Democrat. Sometimes new judges reverse the opinions of their predecessors, give an opposite meaning to the Constitution. Since this is so, it follows that nothing is settled definitely by saying that the Constitution is the document as expounded by the Supreme Court.

And as we have said, that is not the whole truth. It is the duty of Congress also to interpret the Constitution. The Supreme Court has declared as a fixed principle that it will show great respect for the interpretations of Congress and will overrule them only when they are clearly and palpably wrong. Furthermore, it has on more than one occasion cited a long line of laws enacted by Congress in support of its own opinions, to prove that the Constitution means what Congress has assumed it to mean. With reference to many other matters which do not get into the form of cases in law and equity presented to the federal courts, Congress makes its own interpretation of the Constitution and establishes precedents of great weight. All the provisions of federal laws—thousands of acts that have never been brought before the courts, or if brought before them have been sustained—present interpretations of the Constitution. And when a law of long standing is attacked in the courts, judges are loath to impugn its constitutionality. Its very age may turn the balance in the minds of doubtful judges and give it the sanction of a correct interpretation. Again and again bills assailed as unconstitutional in the House and Senate by lawyers of undoubted competence have been passed and made the law of the land. When we ask, therefore, Who interprets the Constitution?

we must answer, Congress also in part—that changing body of members elected by popular vote.

Likewise, in his sphere, the President of the United States by his decrees, orders, and actions gives meaning to the Constitution. Many of his interpretations are "political" in character; and the Supreme Court will not inquire into their legitimacy. Others are discretionary, and these, too, the Court has said, must be left to his judgment. Does the Constitution authorize the President to have a cabinet and to consult its members as a collective body? The written document is silent. Precedents stretching from Washington's time to our own settle that point in the affirmative. May the President, on his own motion, send troops out of the United States and wage war? Very explicitly the Constitution vests in Congress the power to declare war. Yet President Wilson sent American soldiers as far away as Russia in 1918, and in effect, whatever the theory, they waged war on the Bolsheviki, against whom Congress had not declared war. Many times Presidents have dispatched troops to Caribbean regions and to distant parts of China to wage war or to be in a posture to wage it without any express authorization from Congress. These precedents form an important interpretation of the provisions of the Constitution respecting the President's powers, and it is not likely that they will be challenged by the Supreme Court in any case of law or equity.

Strange as it may seem, the Constitution is given meaning also by men and women who hold no office in the Federal Government—by the leaders of political parties. Indeed, political parties are important interpreters of that document. Innumerable examples may be cited. The Constitution states that the House of Representatives shall choose the speaker; in fact, it merely ratifies the choice made by a caucus or conference of the party having a majority of members in that body.

A still more striking illustration is that of the election of the President. It seems clear beyond doubt that the framers of the Constitution intended that the presidential electors, chosen as the legislatures of the several states may decide, should actually choose the President. Hamilton in the *Federalist* frankly said that it was desirable "that the immediate election should be made by men most capable of analyzing the qualities adapted to the station, and acting under circumstances favorable to deliberation." He added that "it was also peculiarly desirable to afford as little opportunity as possible to tumult and disorder" in connnection with elections.

Yet, as everybody knows, in spite of what seems to be the plain intention of the framers, the electoral system did not function as the Constitution contemplated, after the retirement of President Washington; the electors have been reduced to mere dummies, without any will of their own, who vote for the candidate of their party for President, the candidate nominated by a party caucus or convention wholly outside the Constitution. Nor is it likely that this historic interpretation by political parties will be overturned by a ruling of the Supreme Court. Who decides what the party interpretation of the Constitution shall be? Those who look to the written document for illumination on this point will not find any.

Interpretation of the Constitution by Reference to the Will of its Makers

Since many parts of the Constitution admit of more than one interpretation, and since public authorities and party leaders in their practices must determine in fact what the Constitution really is as a living instrument, it follows that, in adjusting their operations under the Constitution, they must seek the answers to many questions. What does it authorize? Is this or that action forbidden, commanded, sanctioned, or permissible? And, in their searching, how do the interpreters find the answers where the way is uncertain? By taking the words of the Constitution and consulting a dictionary? Although a justice of the Supreme Court has said that even the spirit of the Constitution "is to be collected chiefly from its words," the difficulty is not cleared up. The adverb "chiefly" leaves a great gap to be filled by some process other than a search for definitions of the words. It is true that the Court has on more than one occasion used Webster's dictionary in hunting for clues to the cabalistic symbols of the Constitution, but the enlightenment to be attained by that device is limited. Those whose business it is to interpret the Constitution have other and more important methods at hand—methods sanctioned by high authority and long usage.

Among the controlling rules of interpretation recommended by reason and custom is the theory that the "intention" of those who made the Constitution should govern. No other doctrine seems more rational and inevitable. It is expounded with great cogency by Chief Justice Marshall in the celebrated case of Marbury *vs.* Madison, and runs as follows: "The people have an original right to establish, for their future government, such principles as, in their opinion, shall most conduce to their own happiness." This, he says, is the basis on which the whole American fabric has been erected. "This original and supreme will organizes the government, and assigns to different departments their respective powers." Then, in dealing with the issue at hand, the authority conferred upon the judiciary, the Chief Justice asks about "the intention of those who gave this power." Although he speaks in another connection of what "the framers" of the Constitution contemplated, the underlying theory of his argument is that it is the "original and supreme will" of the people which is to be discovered and given effect in interpreting the Constitution. In American political reasoning nothing appears more axiomatic.

Yet in applying this controlling principle to an interpretation of the Constitution disconcerting difficulties arise. A search for "the will of the people who made the Constitution" leads into a Serbonian bog. Under this head must be included all the members of the national convention who drafted the Constitution in 1787, the members of the thirteen state conventions who ratified it, and the voters who elected the delegates to these ratifying conventions.

In their heroic efforts to disclose "the intention of the makers of the Constitution," judges of the Supreme Court have frequently, if not generally, limited their inquiries to the "intention of the framers," the aims of the men who drafted it in Philadelphia. The Constitution, declared Chief Justice Taney in the Dred Scott case, "speaks . . . with the same meaning and intent with which it spoke when it came from the hands of its framers."

If the inquest be limited narrowly to the intention of the framers of the Constitution the solution of the problem is not easy. Of course at the outset all the clauses, indeed many fragments of clauses, must be treated separately and taken as items voted on in the constitutional convention. Some of them were carried by a narrow majority, and in such cases it is the intention of the particular majority that comes in question. Now, no stenographic minutes were made of the debates in the convention; our information as to what the members said about the various clauses is limited to fragmentary notes taken by James Madison and a few other members. On none of the clauses did all the members speak; on few if any did a majority speak. Since we do not know what all the speakers said on the respective issues it is impossible to discover what their "intention" was.

With respect to some propositions the members who framed them differed as to their meaning. This is especially true of the sections dealing with the judiciary. As a matter of fact, Gouverneur Morris, in speaking of his work in shaping up the language of the Constitution, distinctly states that, owing to conflicting opinions in the convention over the subject of the judiciary, he found it necessary "to select phrases which, expressing my own notions, would not alarm the others or shock their self love." This is not all. Over the most fundamental of all rules of construction, two members of the convention who favored the Constitution took diametrically opposite views as to the intention of the framers, within two years after it went into effect. In discussing the constitutionality of the first Bank, Hamilton held that the document should be construed liberally with reference to great ends; Randolph with equal tenacity maintained that it should be construed strictly with reference to its express language.

Nevertheless, those who are called upon to expound the Constitution continually speak with confidence about "the intention of the framers" and cite speeches, letters, and papers to prove one interpretation or another, even though their constructions are frequently opposite in upshot. Undoubtedly light can be thrown on the meaning of the Constitution by reference to the writings of the Fathers; but the intention of the collective framers, as to points susceptible of various meanings, remains about as mysterious as the Delphic oracle.

If reference is made to "the will of the men who ratified the Constitution," the mystery deepens. What, for example, was the intention of the hundreds of delegates composing the thirteen state conventions called to ratify the Constitution? In some cases only the most fragmentary notices of speeches made in those conventions have come down to us. In none of them were all the indefinite phrases of the Constitution fully expounded and agreed upon. What the majority in each case may have thought about many of these phrases, whether they thought about them at all is not known, can never be known.

When this quest is extended to the will or intention of "the people" the twilight deepens almost to stygian darkness. For various reasons about three fourths of the adult males did not participate in electing delegates to the several conventions. In some cases, New York, for example, a majority voted against ratifying the Constitution as submitted by the framers. How many of the people who did vote had read the Constitution and made up their minds as to their "intention"? History is silent. What was the intention of the people who voted against the Constitution and yet saw their elected delegates ratify it in spite of their "will"?

It is useless to pursue this inquiry further. Those who are given to exactness in the use of language will be chary about speaking of "the intention of the people who made the Constitution."

So far we have spoken of the Constitution as if it were merely the original instrument which was drafted at Philadelphia in 1787. In a strict sense, of course, it includes all the amendments adopted at different times between 1791 and 1920. Matters of "intention," therefore, involve the will of the several Congresses which passed the amendments and the state legislatures which ratified them. In all such cases equally stubborn difficulties arise. The Fourteenth Amendment, for instance, was interpreted by the Supreme Court in two ways within twenty-five years after its adoption, and the second view seems to be nearer the truth than the first. Again, just how far did the "people" who made and ratified the Prohibition Amendment expect Congress and the states to go in suppressing the liquor traffic? Most of those who framed it and approved it are still living, and yet great differences of opinion are honestly entertained as to the precise limitations imposed by it, especially on private rights. Who can define beyond dispute the intention of those who enacted it into law?

Interpretation by the Rational Method

Whatever the strict theory respecting the intention of the framers of the Constitution, it remains a fact that the courts, the President, Congress, party leaders, and the laymen called upon to decide what the document really means are not absolutely controlled by the results of a quest for intention. When seeking to discover what can or cannot be done under the Constitution, they do not confine their studies to the words and purposes (if known) of the men who made and ratified the document. They also resort to processes of reasoning, to psychological devices, and to a bewildering assortment of historical claims, assertions, and inferences.

They cite history, both oral and written; they refer to their memory of what was done or intended. They make use of dictionaries, quotations from the Bible, and illustrations from preceding judicial decisions, acts of Congress, speeches by statesmen, and official documents by authorities presumed to be competent. In practice, therefore—and it is practice that counts—the Constitution is interpreted by psychological processes, which can be understood only through a study of the human mind, its nature, its laws, and its workings, and the interpretations are verbalized by the use of extracts from an ocean of printed pages and a maze of oral traditions.

Among the mental processes useful in discovering the meaning of the Constitution that of "logical reasoning" has been perhaps most commonly employed. At all events it is most prominent in the great decisions of the Supreme Court. Chief Justice Marshall was noted for his use of this mental instrument. He was sparing in his citation of precedents and speeches to prove his points. Nowhere is his method better illustrated in its strength and weakness than in the case of Marbury *vs.* Madison. Though he speaks of the intention of the framers and the people from whom the Constitution emanated, he does not cite long statements from them to prove his proposition that the Supreme Court has the power to set aside acts of Congress when it deems them unwarranted by the Constitution. He uses logic. "It seems only necessary to recognize certain principles," he says, "supposed to have been long and well established, to decide it." Here in brief is his syllogism:

Premise: The people have made the Constitution, established the departments of government, and assigned powers to each of them, and this Constitution is declared to be the supreme law of the land.

Premise: The Supreme Court has taken an oath to uphold the Constitution.

Conclusion: When an act of Congress (admittedly inferior law) conflicts with the superior law, the Supreme Court cannot enforce it but must declare it null and void.

On its face, nothing seems simpler, but critics of the decision from Jefferson's day onward have been unable to accept it as inescapable. The logic of their interpretation may be formulated in this fashion:

Premise: The people have made the Constitution, established the departments, and assigned powers to each of them, and this Constitution is declared to be the supreme law of the land.

Premise: The President has taken an oath to uphold the Constitution.

Conclusion: When a decision of the Supreme Court (admittedly inferior to the Constitution itself) conflicts with the superior law, the President cannot enforce it but must declare it null and void.

Hence it would appear that this "logic" which is so frequently employed in discovering the meaning of the Constitution is in reality not an instrument which inevitably finds truth, but is a two-edged sword which cuts both ways. Indeed the experts in logic differ violently among themselves as to what their subject is. Some hold that it is merely concerned with words; others contend that it is an instrument of knowing or a way of discovering truth; still others maintain that it is concerned with both the form and the matter of thought and cannot be separated from either. Whatever the upshot of their debate, it is certain that "logical reasoning" is only one mode of discovering truth, at best a dubious mode, and not the way most effectively used by science in making its amazing triumphs. Powerful minds, equally logical and, for practical purposes, equally informed, often arrive at different ends by the logical method. Hence, its frailty as a reed of reliance.

Its inadequacy as an instrument of acquiring knowledge concerning the meaning of the Constitution has been recognized by the courts and other authorities called upon to expound that document. Judges of the Supreme Court, in explaining the instrument, have frequently referred to the "nature of the system," "the spirit of the Constitution," and its "general spirit." Marshall remarked in the Dartmouth College case, with respect to a certain contention, that the framers of the Constitution "could never have intended to insert in that instrument" an idea "repugnant to its general spirit." Long afterward another judge maintained that there are some limitations, not clearly expressed in the Constitution, "which grow out of the essential nature of all free governments." A dissenting judge protested against this allegation, saying, "Courts cannot nullify an act of the state legislature on the vague ground that they think it opposed to a general latent spirit supposed to pervade or underlie the Constitution, where neither the terms nor the implications of the instrument disclose any such restriction." Other dissenting judges have filed similar protests, but still it remains a custom for those who undertake to interpret the Constitution to derive meaning from its "nature" and "general spirit."

Like the logical method, however, this process is beset with perplexities because two minds equally conversant with the nature and spirit of the Constitution may arrive at opposite conclusions as to what the nature and spirit authorize. In practice judicial reflections coming under this head embrace fragments from acts of Congress, groupings of several related provisions of the Constitution in one bracket with a view to making many phrases illuminate the particular point in question, extracts from the *Federalist* and other writings of the Fathers, and similar materials, more or less controversial, verging in the direction chosen by the expounding judge or authority.

The Psychological Method of Interpretation

Since, under all these methods of exposition, men of great logical powers and wide information often arrive at opposite conclusions respecting the meaning of the Constitution, it seems to follow that their conflicting judgments are due to something inside of their minds, that is, do not flow inexorably from the plain language of the instrument itself. What, then, is this mental force or substance that inclines the mind to one side or the other? Out of deep knowledge and long judicial experience, Justice Holmes made a satisfactory answer when he said, "General propositions do not decide concrete cases. The decision will depend on a judgment or intuition more subtle than any articulate major premise." This removes the explanation of differences of opinion concerning the indefinite clauses of the Constitution from the realm of exact science, which ordinarily proceeds by drawing conclusions from observing external things that have weight, form, and mass capable of precise description. According to Justice Holmes, constitutional interpretation is primarily emotional in character—a matter of feeling and sympathy.

Thus we are led to inquire, Whence springs the intuition or sympathy which inclines the mind to one side or the other? Is it inherited with the flesh and blood? Are babies from birth narrow or liberal constructionists by heredity? Or are these intuitions and sympathies acquired from associations—political, economic, and cultural? If the issue is concretely considered there can be no doubt of the answer. With reference to interpretations of the Constitution by the President, Congress, and political leaders, it is openly admitted that inclinations are connected with partisan sources—using the term in no invidious sense. Roger B. Taney, a Democrat from the slave-holding state of Maryland, thought that the Constitution did not confer upon Congress the power to abolish slavery in the territories; President Lincoln, a Republican from the free state of Illinois, with equal sincerity, thought that it did. At one time a political party that believes in the strict construction is in power; at another time, a party that advocates the liberal construction. Thus the Constitution means one thing in one season; another in the next. With a change in parties comes a change in its nature. And shifts in parties depend on variations in public opinion, in the conditions and beliefs of the people, or at least of the thinking and articulate section of the population.

Although none will deny that partisan considerations deeply affect, if they do not control, interpretations of the Constitution by the political departments of the Government, many contend that the judicial branch, in its operations, is not, or ought not to be, influenced by any such considerations. But this raises some interesting speculations. Judges are chosen by political branches of the Government, by the President and Senate. Do the appointing authorities, in selecting a judge, ignore his previous career, the decisions he has rendered, if he has been a judge in a lower court, the views which he has advocated as a lawyer at the bar? The correct reply is that they do not. The history of appointments, as far as it is recorded, makes this answer emphatic. It is true that Theodore Roosevelt once indicated that there was a large element of chance in the selection of judges, which is unquestionable. When asked whether it would be possible in the United States to pass a tax law as radical as the Lloyd George budget of 1909 in England, he replied laconically, "It would depend upon whether a Judge of the Supreme Court came down heads or tails." But in making appointments as President he took no such anarchic view of federal jurisprudence.

In a long letter to Senator Henry Cabot Lodge, written in 1902, with reference to filling a vacancy on the Supreme Bench, President Roosevelt explained the considerations which governed him in making the appointment and which, he thought, should always be controlling in such cases. "In the ordinary and low sense which we attach to the words 'partisan' and 'politician,'" said the President, "a judge of the Supreme Court should be neither. But in the higher sense, in the proper sense, he is not in my judgment fitted for the position unless he is a party man, a constructive statesman, constantly keeping in mind his adherence to the principles and policies under which his nation has been built up and in accordance with which it must go on; and keeping in mind also his relations with his fellow statesmen who in other branches of the government are striving in co-operation with him to advance the ends of government. Marshall rendered such invaluable service because he was a statesman of the national type, like Adams who appointed him, like Washington whose mantle fell upon him. . . . The Supreme Court of the sixties was good exactly in so far as its members fitly represented the spirit of Lincoln. . . . The majority of the present Court who have, although without satisfactory unanimity, upheld the policies of President McKinley and the Republican party in Congress, have rendered a great service to mankind and to this nation."

With this preliminary out of the way, President Roosevelt then turned to the character of the man under immediate consideration for appointment, Oliver Wendell Holmes, of Massachusetts. "Now I should like to know," he said, "that Judge Holmes was in entire sympathy with our views, that is with your views and mine, and Judge Gray's, for instance, just as we know that ex-Attorney General Knowlton is, before I would feel justified in appointing him. . . . I should hold myself as guilty of an irreparable wrong to the nation if I should put in his [Gray's] place any man who was not absolutely sane and sound on the great national policies for which we stand in public life." Then President Roosevelt added in a postscript, "I should know about Judge Holmes as soon as possible. How would it do, if he seems to be all right, to have him come down here and spend a night with me, and then I could make the announcement on the day that he left, after we have talked together?"

Besides taking this broad view of the function of federal judges as statesmen, President Roosevelt also referred to a particular matter—the attitude of the Court toward modern social legislation. Judge Holmes' "labor decisions," he remarked, "which have been criticized by some of the big railroad men and other members of large corporations, constitute to my mind a strong point in Judge Holmes' favor. The ablest lawyers and greatest judges are men whose past has naturally brought them into close relationship with the wealthiest and most powerful clients, and I am glad when I can find a judge who has been able to preserve his aloofness of mind so as to keep his broad humanity of feeling and his sympathy for the class from which he has not drawn his clients. I think it eminently desirable that our Supreme Court should show in unmistakable fashion their entire sympathy with all proper effort to secure the most favorable possible consideration for the men who most need that consideration." If "necessary" this letter was to be laid before Mr. Holmes. In due time, Mr. Holmes was appointed and in his decisions took the liberal course, although he did not always conform to President Roosevelt's "policies."

In seeking for judges in general harmony with their views of large public questions, Presidents have often found it necessary to choose men from their own political party. The Federalist President, John Adams, appointed to the post of Chief Justice, John Marshall, an ardent Federalist who had served his party as a member of Congress and as Secretary of State. His successor, Roger B. Taney, a Democrat who had held the post of Secretary of the Treasury, was chosen by a Democratic President, Andrew Jackson. When Taney died in 1864, the Republican President, Abraham Lincoln, put in his place, Salmon Chase, who had been head of the Treasury Department and was an aspirant for the Republican nomination for President in the very year of his appointment. Chief Justice Taft was a Republican President of the United States before he was elevated to his high judicial post by President Harding, a member of his political party. President Hoover selected his Republican colleague, Charles E. Hughes, to fill the vacancy created by the retirement of Chief Justice Taft in 1930. Exceptions serve to prove the rule; if President Taft gave the chief justiceship to Edward D. White, a Democrat, he chose a man whose public record presented no violent opposition to the general policies of the party in power.

After all, is it conceivable that the appointing authorities would select a judge who would so interpret the Constitution as to declare null and void significant measures of Congress which they deemed vital to the welfare of the country? In this there is nothing invidious. The fact that they espouse these measures is evidence that they believe in their constitutionality as well as their utility to public welfare. To work for them, and then choose judges to defeat them would be a strange procedure.

Indeed high and responsible political leaders have more than once taken the position that it is proper to use the appointing power to secure new judges who will reverse the decisions of their predecessors on fundamental issues, re-read the Constitution, discover that it does not mean what it has been interpreted to mean. "We think the Dred Scott decision is erroneous," said Lincoln, shortly after the Court had rendered its opinion. "We know that the Court that made it has often overruled its own decisions and we shall do what we can to have it overrule this." And the Democratic party, in its platform of 1896, criticized the decision of the Supreme Court nullifying the income tax law of 1894 and declared that it would be the duty of Congress to make use of the power which may come from a reversal by the Court "as it may hereafter be constituted," with a view to enacting legislation similar to that recently invalidated by this tribunal.

It was after reviewing such indubitable facts that the great commentator, Judge Cooley, came to the conclusion that the Constitution is not a mere written document with a determinate meaning that never changes. "We may think," he says, "that we have the Constitution all before us; but for practical purposes the Constitution is that which the Government in its several departments and the people in the performance of their duties as citizens recognize and respect as such; and nothing else is. . . . Cervantes says: 'Everyone is the son of his own works.' This is more emphatically true of an instrument of government than it can possibly be of a natural person. What it takes to itself, though at first unwarrantable, helps to make it over into a new instrument of government, and it represents at last the acts done under it."

If this statement by Judge Cooley is true, and the authority

Courtesy of the Corps of Engineers, United States Army

A VIEW OF ST. MARY'S FALLS CANAL, OWNED AND OPERATED BY THE FEDERAL GOVERNMENT.
"The power to regulate commerce does not give a power to . . . dig canals . . ."—*Thomas Jefferson.*

Courtesy of the United States Bureau of Lighthouses

THE AMERICAN SHOAL LIGHTHOUSE: A FEDERAL AID TO SHIPPING.
"The utility of the thing has sanctioned the infraction [of the Constitution]."
—*Thomas Jefferson.*

for it is unimpeachable, then the theory that the Constitution is a written document is a legal fiction. The idea that it can be understood by a study of its language and the history of its past development is equally mythical. It is what the Government and the people who count in public affairs recognize and respect as such, what they think it is. More than this. It is not merely what it has been, or what it is today. It is always becoming something else and those who criticize it and the acts done under it, as well as those who praise, help to make it what it will be to-morrow. Indeed an eminent authority, Frank J. Goodnow, recalling how difficult it is to amend the Constitution and how the courts show a tendency to block changes made imperative by new conditions, contends that criticism of the backward-looking decisions of the Supreme Court is necessary to force the continuous readjustment of the Constitution to new requirements. "In these days of rapid economic and social change," he says, " . . . it is on this criticism, amply justified by our history, that we must rely if we are to hope for that orderly and progressive development which we regard as characteristic of modern civilization." And criticism is authorized by the Constitution, for that instrument makes clear provision in Article V for its own amendment by regular political processes. This contemplation of change is a criticism, a partial repudiation, or a confession that the original falls short of the ideal, at least the ideal always in the process of becoming.

The Amending Process

Even the written words of the Constitution, therefore, are not fixed for all time. They may be lawfully altered in accordance with shifts in public sentiment. Article V, as we have said, provides a formal method for changing the instrument handed down by the Fathers. A proposition to amend may be adopted by Congress, with the approval of two thirds of both houses, and may be ratified by the concurrence of the legislatures, or of conventions, as Congress provides, in three fourths of the states. On the other hand, states may take the initiative, for, on the application of the legislatures of two thirds of them, Congress must call a national convention for the purpose of drafting amendments, which go into effect when ratified by conventions, or by legislatures, in three fourths of the states. The composition of the national and state conventions, the procedure to be followed by the legislatures in passing upon proposals, and numerous other questions are left unsettled by the Constitution, but presumably Congress may make such reasonable provisions as it deems fitting.

In practice only one method has been employed, namely, proposal by a two thirds vote in Congress and ratification by the legislatures of at least three fourths of the states. In adopting resolutions in this connection, Congress has been very brief in its provisions. A suggested amendment is usually submitted in the following form: "Resolved by the Senate and the House of Representatives of the United States of America in Congress assembled, two thirds of both houses concurring, that the following article be proposed to the legislatures of the several states as an amendment to the Constitution of the United States which when ratified by three fourths of the said legislatures shall be valid as part of the said Constitution." The state legislatures are then left to their own devices in approving or rejecting the article laid before them. Congress merely directs that "Whenever official notice is received at the Department of State that any amendment proposed to the Constitution of the United States has been adopted, according to the provisions of the Constitution, the Secretary of State shall forthwith cause the amendment to be published in the newspapers authorized to promulgate laws, with his certificate specifying the states by which the same may have been adopted, and that the same has become valid, to all intents and purposes, as a part of the Constitution of the United States."

Ordinarily no time limit is placed on ratification by the

states. To the resolution submitting the Eighteenth Amendment, however, Congress attached a condition that the article should be inoperative unless ratified within seven years. On its face, this presents a problem of constitutionality, yet unsettled. So, too, does the action of a state in withdrawing ratification after making it in due form. This issue, likewise, has not been finally determined but certain precedents illustrate the probable outcome, if the question is judicially raised. Although Ohio and New Jersey rescinded their approval of the Fourteenth Amendment, they were counted by the Secretary of State among the ratifying states. Hence the question may be said to be open, with a departmental ruling serving as a guide.

Owing to the fact that hundreds of amendments were proposed between 1803 and 1865 and between 1870 and 1913 only to meet defeat through failure to secure the requisite two thirds vote in Congress, there arose at the opening of this century an extensive criticism of the amending process itself. It was noted that only three amendments—the Thirteenth, Fourteenth, and Fifteenth—had been adopted in the course of a hundred years and that those had been carried as the result of a civil war. In short, it seemed impossible to amend the Constitution in the regular course of things, owing to the large majority required for initiation by Congress, to say nothing of ratification by three fourths of the states. Some radical changes were then proposed in the amending process itself, and they were under discussion when the spell was broken by the adoption of the income tax amendment in 1913 followed shortly by three others establishing the popular election of Senators, prohibition, and woman suffrage.

Very soon, however, the subject of alterations in the Constitution again came under severe scrutiny largely on account of the prohibition amendment itself. Two fundamental objections are urged against the existing method. Both of them rest on the ground that states—geographical districts—rather than population are the preponderant element in the ratification of proposed changes. On the one hand, the system is attacked as too conservative; approval by three fourths of the states is necessary to give sanction to an amendment laid before the Union for consideration. That means that thirteen states can hold up the entire country in an effort to make even the slightest modification in the scheme of government. Now if we take thirteen of the least populous states—Nevada, Wyoming, Delaware, Arizona, Vermont, New Mexico, Idaho, New Hampshire, Utah, Montana, Rhode Island, South Dakota, and North Dakota—we find that they have a combined population less than that of the single state of New York. In other words, about one tenth of the people of the nation, distributed in the right geographical districts, can prevent nine tenths of the people from effecting innovations in their system of government. Of course it does not necessarily happen that opposition to amendments falls only in the least populous states, but the requirement of an extraordinary majority both to initiate and to approve a new proposition makes the process very difficult in ordinary times.

On the other hand, it is urged that the same rule makes it possible for three fourths of the least populous states which are rural in character to force an amendment on the twelve largest states with their accumulated masses concentrated in cities—twelve states containing about one half the people of the United States. This argument is frequently heard in connection with discussions of prohibition, but in fact it was not the agricultural states alone that drove through the Eighteenth Amendment. It is true that the great commonwealths of New York and Pennsylvania with nearly one fifth of the inhabitants of the country did not ratify it until after the requisite majority had been won for adoption. At the same time among the three fourths that had already ratified were Massachusetts, Michigan, Ohio, Illinois, and California, which stand high in the numerical scale. Moreover, it takes two thirds of the members in each house of Congress to initiate an amendment and the Representatives in the lower chamber are apportioned among the states according to their respective population.

Another and perhaps more vital objection to the existing amendment process is that ratification can be effected by a relatively small number of persons who happen to be in the state legislatures at the time a proposition is submitted. In all there are about seventy-five hundred members in the forty-eight bodies combined. If we group the thirty-six states with the smallest assemblies together we find that approximately two thousand members properly divided between the upper and lower houses can carry or defeat a resolution of amendment laid before them by Congress.

The number of persons taking part in the ratifying operation is not as significant as the fact that they are only incidentally concerned in it as legislators. They are elected for other purposes. Their main duty is to make laws for the states. Often they are chosen previous to the passage of a proposed amendment by Congress, and are thus asked to decide a matter which was not even before the public when they were candidates. Moreover the type of man found in the legislature is usually not as high as that generally elected to state constitutional conventions. Many people of great ability are willing to serve in a convention for a short period, who would not think of spending any time in the business of ordinary legislation. It is, therefore, not merely the political arithmetic of the amending system which invites criticism. It is to be criticized because it is casual in its nature and does not provide for that special and searching consideration which a change in the supreme law of the land deserves.

The Nineteen Amendments

Under the sanction afforded by Article V, nineteen amendments have been added to the Constitution as it left the hands of the framers. Considered in relation to the circumstances of their adoption they fall into three rather distinct groups. The first ten were passed so soon after the ratification of the original instrument and were so obviously intended to meet objections raised against it that, for practical purposes, they may be almost considered a part of the document itself. Another group of amendments, especially those arising out of the Civil War, sprang from crises of one kind or another, small or large, and finally a few were made by what may be considered "the normal method of popular agitation and education." Besides throwing light on the meaning of the Constitution, the historical circumstances connected with the formulation of these amendments illustrate the functioning of American democracy in making innovations in its fundamental law.

The first ten articles of amendment were designed to conciliate an opposition that appeared during the struggle over the ratification of the Constitution. While the battle was raging it appeared that a great deal of criticism was founded on the absence of express provisions safeguarding personal liberty and private property against the action of the Federal Government. Jefferson, who was in Paris at the time the convention finished its work, wrote to a friend in Virginia that he wished four states would withhold ratification until a declaration of right could be annexed, stipulating "freedom of religion, freedom of the press, freedom of commerce against monopolies, trial by jury in all cases, no suspensions of habeas corpus, no standing armies." Most of the state constitutions already contained such limitations, and there was evidently a desire on the part of many, who otherwise approved the general plan of the new federal Constitution, to see the historic doctrines of private rights embodied in it. Seven of the ratifying state conventions even put their wishes in the concrete form of a total of one hundred and twenty-four articles to be added to that instrument.

In response to this evident dissatisfaction with the original Constitution, Congress adopted by two thirds vote, in 1789, the year of Washington's inauguration, twelve articles of amendment and submitted them to the states for their consideration. These articles were accompanied by a resolution stating that they had been proposed for the purpose of extending the grounds of public confidence in the Government and insuring the beneficent ends of its institution. Two of the propositions failed to receive the approval of the requisite number of states but ten of them were duly ratified and became effective in December, 1791. Thus various grounds for objection, especially among citizens who shared Jefferson's views respecting individual liberty, were removed. The operation caused no great excitement for it seems to have been generally regarded as a kind of finishing touch to the document drawn at Philadelphia in 1787.

For more than a hundred years every additional amendment attached to the Constitution was the product of critical circumstances. The Eleventh Amendment, proposed by Congress in 1794 and ratified in 1798, was the outgrowth of a violent controversy raised by a hearing of the Supreme Court in the case of Chisholm *vs.* Georgia—a case involving the question whether a state could be sued by a private citizen. Alarmed by the spectre, champions of states' rights stoutly insisted that federal intervention was a violation of the Constitution and an outrage besides. The Court, however, said that it possessed full jurisdiction in the matter, directed the service of papers on the governor and attorney-general of Georgia, and ordered that, unless the state appeared in due form, judgment should be entered by default. In short, it proposed to proceed with the case.

This ruling instantly aroused a popular agitation. Two days after it was made a Senator introduced into Congress an amendment prohibiting suits of this character against states. Within a short time the Massachusetts legislature declared the power exercised by the Supreme Court "dangerous to the peace, safety, and independence of the several states and repugnant to the first principles of a Federal Government;" and the Georgia house of representatives passed a bill providing that any official who attempted to enforce the decision should be declared guilty of felony and suffer death without benefit of clergy by being hanged. The proposed amendment, which was sent to the states by Congress in 1794, received the requisite approval, and went into force in 1798.

Little more than two years had elapsed after the ratification of the Eleventh Amendment when a serious crisis in connection with the election of 1800 called for a modification of that section of the Constitution which deals with the balloting of the electors for President. The original provision stipulated that the presidential electors chosen in each state should cast their ballots for two persons, without designating which was to be President or Vice President; and then added: "The person having the greatest number of votes shall be the President, if such number be a majority of the whole number of electors appointed; . . . after the choice of the President the person having the greatest number of votes of the electors shall be the Vice President."

In the contest of that year, Jefferson and Burr, candidates for President and Vice President respectively on the Republican ticket, received seventy-three electoral votes each, and the latter, willing to defeat what he knew to be the real wishes of his party, hoped to win the presidency by gaining Federalist support in the House of Representatives where the election was thrown on account of the tie. Fortunately his design was frustrated; Jefferson was chosen; but the outcome of the struggle and the low intrigue which accompanied it revealed the necessity of requiring the electors to designate the persons for whom they cast their ballots as President and Vice President.

Accordingly an amendment designed to effect this change was introduced in Congress in February, 1802. Although evidently deserving approval on its merits, the resolution met with stout opposition in some quarters. Certain Representatives contended that it was a good thing to have the election transferred to the House where each state had one vote in such cases and the small states stood a chance to secure one or both offices. More valid than this argument was one to the effect that the original system guaranteed that both the President and Vice President would be men of substantially equal ability, as illustrated in the case of the first elections. In spite of the arguments against it, the proposal received the requisite majority in Congress and then went to the states in December, 1803; it was promptly ratified and declared in force on September 25, 1804, as the Twelfth Amendment.

An eventful half century now passed before any further alterations were made in the letter of the Constitution. Vast territories stretching to the Pacific were acquired; nearly a score of states were added to the Union; the development of industries and the extension of railways began to work a marvelous transformation in the economic system of the country; state constitutions were remodeled over and over, showing at each successive decade an advance in democratic ideas of government; practices of every kind stretched beyond recognition many of the original terms of the written instrument. And yet no changes were made in the formal rules of the document itself until, in the hot struggles of the Civil War, the whole federal system was thrown into the melting pot.

In a strict sense the decade of the Civil War was a revolutionary period. Several states were temporarily out of the Union, or at least were not represented in Congress. The war power of the President overshadowed his civil authority; and in exercising it he emancipated slaves although the Constitution gave the Federal Government no right to interfere with them in any state. The act of emancipation, the determination of Republican leaders to confer the vote on Negro men, the necessity for novel measures dealing with the states formerly in arms against the Union, and the rise of new economic issues called for radical departures from the letter and spirit of the Constitution, and in an abnormal time.

In such circumstances three amendments were adopted, or perhaps it would be more correct to say "put through." The Thirteenth, sealing Lincoln's proclamation of emancipation, abolished slavery. The Fourteenth was designed to confer civil and political rights on Negroes, to provide certain conditions for the formal restoration of the confederate states to the Union and to subject all states henceforward to stricter control by the federal judiciary. The Fifteenth was intended to make more effective provisions for Negro suffrage. But in the Congress that passed these amendments, several of the states were not represented at all, for they were in arms against the Federal Government or had not yet been brought back into regular relations with it. Moreover it was impossible to secure ratification by the requisite three fourths of the legislatures without bringing pressure to bear on some of the Southern states.

This anomalous state of affairs was the subject of long debates at the time. When, for example, the Thirteenth Amendment was before the House of Representatives, a member contended that in the circumstances the article could not be legally adopted. "It is impossible," he declared, "that the amendment proposed should be ratified without a fraudulent use—I select the term advisedly—without a fraudulent use of the power to admit new states or a fraudulent use of the military power of the Federal Government in the seceded states. There are thirty-five states. Twenty-seven are necessary to ratify this amendment. There are nineteen free states. Suppose you get them all, where do you get the others? . . . Will the gentlemen call on the Southern states to furnish the requisite number? If these states are to vote in their present condition, it would be a broad farce, if it were not a wicked fraud."

The difficulties to which the Representative referred were especially revealed in connection with the Fourteenth Amendment. At the time of its submission the war had come to a close but several of the states were under military government controlled from the Capital and had not recovered their right of representation in Congress. Even in these conditions nine Southern states rejected the amendment when it was submitted and the defeat of the measure seemed inevitable. Thereupon Congress, by law, made the ratification of the Amendment a condition of the restoration of these states to the Union. Confronted by the choice of accepting the bitter medicine or remaining indefinitely out of the Union, some of them yielded. When in 1868 the Secretary of State announced the formal completion of the process, he declared that the Fourteenth Amendment had been ratified by the legislatures of twenty-three states and "by newly constituted and newly established bodies avowing themselves to be and acting as the legislatures" of six Southern states. So great was the necessity under which the directors of the Federal Government labored in securing the adoption of the "Civil War amendments."

More than forty years passed before another amendment was added to the Constitution, in spite of the fact that a large crop of proposed modifications was produced in every Congress during the intervening period. It was not until 1909 that a two thirds majority could be secured in both houses in favor of any change in the fundamental law. In that year there culminated a long struggle over the taxation of incomes by the Federal Government. During the Civil War such a tax had been laid by Congress and sustained by the Supreme Court, which declared it to be an indirect tax and hence not subject to the rule of apportionment among the states on the basis of their respective population. In 1894, after a sharp political fight, a Democratic Congress, driven by populistic forces, enacted another income tax law, which was declared unconstitutional in its principal parts by the Supreme Court during the following year. The Southern and Western states had deliberately sought to shift a large part of the burden of federal taxation to the accumulated fortunes of the Northeast, and the Supreme Court by a five to four decision had blocked their effort. Undaunted, the sponsors of the income tax kept up their fight and at the end of fourteen years they won enough Republicans and Democrats to carry through both houses a resolution providing that Congress shall have power to "lay and collect taxes on incomes, from whatever source derived, without apportionment among the several states and without regard to any census or enumeration." The Sixteenth Amendment was duly ratified and proclaimed in effect on February 25, 1913. In time, the income tax, which seemed so revolutionary to some in 1895, became an established part of the federal system of taxation.

Closely connected with the progressive movement which carried through the income-tax amendment was the effort to bring about the election of the United States Senators by direct vote. This proposal, warmly advocated by all populistic parties, was brought up in Congress many times and more than once it secured the requisite majority in the House of Representatives, only to be blocked by the Senate. In the meantime state legislatures, one after another, called upon Congress to summon a constitutional convention to effect the reform and also enacted primary laws ordering the nomination of Senators by popular vote, in fact instituting popular election by subterfuge. At length in 1912 there were enough Senators chosen by that process to work a revolution in the upper chamber, and the proposed constitutional amendment was passed by both houses. It was duly ratified by the states and put into force on May 31, 1913.

Somewhat in the same way, the Eighteenth Amendment prohibiting the manufacture and sale of intoxicating liquors for beverage purposes was finally adopted. Shortly after the Civil War a Prohibition party arose and started up a lively agitation throughout the country. Amendments establishing prohibition were introduced repeatedly in Congress, but without any appreciable effect. All the while prohibition advocates carried on their propaganda and actually secured the adoption of their program, county by county and state by state, until by 1920 thirty-three states and large sections of other states were legally "dry." In December, 1917, Congress finally approved a prohibition amendment; it was speedily ratified by forty-six states and proclaimed in January, 1919; and one year later it went into effect.

A similar process is to be observed in the history of the woman suffrage amendment. As early as 1868 that proposition was laid before Congress amid much derision. From year to year its supporters pressed the cause upon the attention of the national legislature without apparent effect. Discouraged at Washington, they turned to the states, winning one after another in a long and arduous campaign of agitation. By 1917 twelve states had adopted woman suffrage for all elections and many others had accepted it for certain local and special elections. Then the issue became general. Candidates for the presidency could not ignore it and political parties were compelled to give heed to it. On June 4, 1919, Congress adopted the Nineteenth Amendment providing that no citizen of the United States shall be denied the right to vote on account of sex. On August 26, 1920, Tennessee, the thirty-sixth state ratified the Amendment and it was immediately declared to be in effect.

There is a great deal of significance in the methods by which the last two amendments were adopted. Both of them were before Congress for a long time and were repeatedly rejected. The advocates of the two propositions kept at work in the states, carrying one after another until they made the issues inescapable at Washington. It would seem therefore that if we seek to divine the future of the Federal Constitution we must study the tendencies in the states. Indeed that eminent observer of American institutions, Lord Bryce, regarded our states as laboratories of experimentation in politics—laboratories in which many devices can be tested before they are applied to the whole country.

Although nineteen amendments have been added to the Constitution since 1789, it is to be noted that nearly all of them merely impose restraints on the Federal Government or on the states. A few make changes in the suffrage and in election methods. Only one, the Sixteenth, enlarges the enumerated powers of Congress to legislate substantially and positively, and that simply overcomes the effect of a decision of the Supreme Court. None alter the primary framework set up by the Fathers. The most important phases of the nation's growth are not reflected, therefore, in the letter of its fundamental law.

CHAPTER III

Fundamental Principles of the Federal System

Although the Constitution, as demonstrated in the previous chapter, is a highly flexible instrument, changing with time and circumstances, it provides the foundations on which the whole American system of government rests. It establishes the framework of the Federal Government—legislative, executive, and judicial—and confers specific as well as general powers on each of these branches. All that follows in this volume is in some respects merely an expansion of this statement in the form of description and commentary. Besides organizing the Federal Government, the Constitution takes powers away from the states, imposes limitations on the exercise of the authority they enjoy, and lends the color of sanction to coöperation between the national and state governments. The Constitution does more. Directly and by implication it enunciates certain broad principles which may be said to form the very essence of the American political philosophy. These principles will be considered here before descending into details.

The Doctrine of Limited Government

In contradistinction to all despotisms and dictatorships, the Constitution of the United States establishes limited government by imposing positive restraints on the Federal Government and the states. In some matters the individual is protected against the Federal Government, in others against the state, and in still others against both. These limitations are not mere political theories or vague declarations of rights; they are rules of law expounded and applied by the courts, enforced by proper executive authorities, and respected as a creed.

Ignorance of these principles constantly leads to many incorrect assertions about "the rights of American citizens." For example, the police of a city forbid a Socialist parade or break up a street corner meeting; immediately there appear in the newspapers letters from indignant citizens denouncing the police for preventing the exercise of the "rights of free speech guaranteed by the Constitution of the United States." An examination, however, of the clause to which they refer shows that it is *Congress* which is forbidden to make any law abridging the freedom of speech, the states and municipalities being left largely to their own devices in dealing with this matter.

It is not only ill-informed citizens who make these errors. Such a serious and responsible body as the Republican national convention of 1860 asserted in its platform, "That the maintenance of the principles promulgated in the Declaration of Independence and embodied in the federal Constitution—'that all men are created equal; that they are endowed by their Creator with certain inalienable rights; that among these are life, liberty, and the pursuit of happiness; that to secure these rights, governments are instituted among men, deriving their just powers from the consent of the governed'—is essential to the preservation of our republican institutions." Of course every student of history and law knows that the Constitution does not embody any such principles, and that the Federal Government is controlled only by rules of law imposed by the written instrument itself.

The fundamental character of these rules may be best illustrated by a comparison with the English system. Any law passed by Parliament—that is, by King, Lords, and Commons—must be enforced; it cannot be called into question by any court; the only remedy for the citizen is at the ballot-box when members of the House of Commons are elected. If the British Parliament should pass a law confiscating the land now owned by private persons, there would be no relief for the victims, unless the same Parliament or a succeeding one could be induced to repeal the law in question. If the Congress of the United States, however, should pass such a measure, it would be the duty of the courts on the presentation of the proper case to protect land-owners in their property rights by declaring the law null and void—in conflict with that section of the Fifth Amendment which provides that no person shall be deprived of life, liberty, or property without due process of law; and that private property shall not be taken for public use without just compensation. Likewise, if the legislature of a state should pass such a measure it would be the duty of the courts to protect the citizen under the Fourteenth Amendment forbidding any state to deprive a person of life, liberty, or property without due process of law—compensation being, under judicial interpretation, an indispensable feature of "due process."

The fundamental limitations laid down in the federal Constitution fall into two groups: those imposed on the National Government and those imposed on the states. The latter will be considered below in Chapter XX. The former are divided into two classes: (*a*) those designed to protect personal liberty against arbitrary interference on the part of the Government, and (*b*) those designed to protect private property against confiscation and any irregular action by federal authorities.

The limitations on behalf of personal rights which, under the Constitution, run against the National Government may be divided into several classes. In the first place, Congress cannot make any law respecting the establishment of a religion, nor can it interfere with the freedom of religious worship. This does not mean that any person has a right to commit an act, under the guise of a religious ceremony, which transgresses the ordinary law of the land. This point was discussed by the Supreme Court in a case involving the power of Congress to prohibit polygamy in the territory of Utah and penalize offenders who violate the law. A Mr. Reynolds, who was indicted under this statute for the crime of polygamy, set up by way of defense the contention that, under a religious sanction and according to a religious ceremony, he had married two wives. The Court replied that religion has to do with the relations of man to "an extramundane being," and that no citizen can claim a right, in the name of religious freedom, to violate a criminal statute.

Next to religious liberty the Constitution places freedom of speech and press by denying to Congress the power to abridge this historic right. As in the case of the other amendments it was said that this provision was unnecessary because Congress had no power to touch the subject at all, but men of Jefferson's bent were far from satisfied with the argument. They knew only too well the history of censorship and intellectual tyranny and were afraid that Congress, in the exercise of its undoubted authority over other matters, might suppress newspapers and punish critics. From this fear came their insistence on an express stipulation in favor of freedom. On the other side, Hamilton thought little of the project. He insisted that it was useless. "What is the liberty of the press?" he inquired. "Who can give it any definition that would not leave the utmost latitude for evasion?" Whatever declarations on the subject might be inserted in the Constitution, he thought, security of the press would depend altogether upon "public opinion and on the general spirit of the people and of the government." In short it was his view that if a people believed in liberty, they would have it and if they did not paper phrases would not give it to them.

Within a few years Hamilton's opinions were illustrated. The words forbidding Congress to abridge the freedom of the press and speech stood firmly in the First Amendment, but nevertheless in 1798 Congress passed the Sedition Act laying penalties on persons who published or said openly anything bringing or tending to bring the National Government or any of its officers into disrepute. Under this measure many American citizens were fined and imprisoned for what would be regarded to-day as harmless criticism of public authorities. Popular feeling against the Act waxed so strong that Jefferson, on becoming President, pardoned all prisoners held in jail under the law, and Congress later repaid the fines that had been collected. In the meantime Hamilton and Marshall warned their Federalist colleagues against this drastic legislation, but no court took advantage of any cases arising in connection with it to declare the statute unconstitutional. Nothing except the determined and almost revolutionary agitation of the Republicans against it prevented it from becoming a measure of fixed policy. As Hamilton had said, the people will have liberty if they want it, whatever fine declarations may be made on paper.

In theory the constitutional limits in behalf of freedom of press and speech all apply in war as well as in peace, for the amendment makes no discrimination as to circumstances. In practice, however, the National Government has imposed many restrictions on the exercise of such rights in time of war, and has been sustained by the courts. Speaking on this theme, Mr. Justice Holmes once remarked in the course of an opinion: "When a nation is at war many things which might be said in time of peace are such a hindrance to its effort that their utterance will not be endured so long as men fight and the Court could not regard them as protected by any constitutional right."

During the Civil War, the National Government suppressed newspapers, arrested and imprisoned editors, and punished speakers for criticizing its activities and advocating a stoppage of the war. When attacked by his opponents for "violating" the Constitution, President Lincoln replied that he had taken a solemn oath to support it and hence that he had the legal right to do all things necessary and proper to sustain the Constitution and the government founded upon it. "Must I shoot a simple-minded soldier boy who deserts," he asked, "while I must not touch a hair of the wily agitator who induces him to desert? The man who stands by and says nothing when the peril of his government is discussed cannot be misunderstood. If not hindered, he is sure to help the enemy." Although his critics insisted that by this line of reasoning he destroyed the Constitution and made himself "Caesar," President Lincoln was unshaken in his course.

During the war against Germany and Austria, when the danger to public safety was not so great as during the civil conflict, the National Government was even more severe in placing limitations on liberty of the press and speech, and was again sustained by the courts. In the Espionage Act of 1917 and the amending Sedition Act of the following year, Congress laid heavy penalties on all persons who said or printed anything that interfered with the operation or success of the armed forces of the country, or printed, wrote, or published any "disloyal, profane, scurrilous, or abusive language about the form of government of the United States, or the Constitution of the United States . . . or any language intended to bring the form of government of the United States, or the Constitution of the United States, or the military or naval forces of the United States, or the flag of the United States or the uniform of the Army and Navy into contempt, scorn, contumely, or disrepute." The second part of the above measure, it is evident from the language, was not directed as much against those who interfered with military affairs as those who criticized the form and operations of the National Government. It was hotly denounced during the debates on it in the Senate, Senator Johnson going as far as to say that it would "suppress the freedom of the press in the United States and prevent any man, no matter who he is, from expressing legitimate criticism of the present Government." Nevertheless it was adopted in the House with only one dissenting vote and in the Senate by a vote of forty-eight to twenty-six, and was sustained by the federal courts.

Under the law, hundreds were arrested and scores were sent to prison. As applied in practice, says Professor Zechariah Chafee, "it became criminal to advocate heavier taxation instead of bond issues, to state that conscription was unconstitutional, . . . to say that the sinking of merchant vessels was legal, to urge that a referendum should have preceded our declaration of war, to say that war is contrary to the teachings of Christ." Many who openly opposed the war or denounced it as a "capitalist" quarrel were sent to prison for long terms of years. One girl twenty-one years of age was sentenced to the penitentiary for fifteen years for taking part in issuing a circular severely attacking President Wilson's policy of intervention in Russia.

It was, moreover, with ample historical warrant that Charles E. Hughes, a man given to measured language, warmly protested in an address delivered in the summer of 1920 before the Harvard law alumni against inflammatory appeals to prejudice made by district attorneys and the browbeating of witnesses during trial by judges in every kind of court and in every part of the country. "We may well wonder," he exclaimed, "in view of the precedents now established whether constitutional government as heretofore maintained in this republic could survive another great war even victoriously waged." Evidently the liberties guaranteed by the Constitution hang upon a slender thread, especially in time of a crisis.

Those who have given the deepest thought to the subject have always warned us against assuming that mere legal rules provide definite assurances in the name of freedom. Liberty of opinion cannot be absolute, that is, no one can have the right to say anything he likes, anywhere, at any time. No government could tolerate a freedom of opinion that counsels direct attempts to overthrow it by violence or the murder of its officials. In ordinary criminal law the man who induces another to commit a crime by persuasion or promises also shares the guilt of the principal and is punished. So in the case of criticism of the government, conspiracies and attempts to overthrow it by violence are necessarily crimes; otherwise its foundations would be built on sand.

But it is difficult to draw the dividing line between spoken and printed words likely to lead to open violence and those that merely stir up a discontent which may eventuate in violence. Some of the courts have attempted to draw the line by saying that language which has "a reasonable and natural tendency to encourage resistance to the law" should be made criminal. This is a doctrine dangerous to liberty of opinion, for does not every criticism of a law have a "tendency" to encourage resistance to it? A perfectly innocent remark by a responsible citizen to the effect that some particular law, in his opinion, is unwise, unjust, or foolish may turn the scale in the mind of someone else and set him in motion to resist that law. A far sounder doctrine is that of Jefferson to the effect that only when criticism of the government immediately threatens to culminate in open resistance should the law intervene. In fact we have decisions of the courts all along the line from one of these extremes to the other and the whole problem in any concrete case becomes one of fact and inclination. Is there actual danger in the criticism? Should we lean on the side of repression or liberty?

At bottom everything depends upon the psychology of the people. Do they believe in liberty as a good in itself to which the dignity of human nature is entitled? Are they willing to allow to others the right of opinion which they claim for themselves? And in cases at law all depends upon the judge and jury. As an English writer once put it, liberty is what twelve grocers, bakers, and candlestick makers think it is, and little more. Into harsh law judges and juries may introduce moderation and grace. Out of high sounding proclamations in the name of liberty they can distill the essence of tyranny, slaying freedom in its own name. Even the most angular precedents become clay in their hands.

Besides religious liberty and freedom of press and speech, the Constitution guarantees to the people the right to assemble peaceably and petition the government for redress of grievances. This right is upheld against state governments as well as the National Government; but, of course, it does not secure to the petitioners the privilege of having their requests acted upon by federal authorities. Their documents may be presented and filed in the congressional waste basket. Indeed under a precedent now long buried—a rule adopted by the House of Representatives in 1836, petitions may be tabled without being referred to committees or receiving any further consideration. Perhaps, as John Quincy Adams maintained, the rule is unconstitutional, but neverthless it was in force for many years with respect to anti-slavery petitions.

Moreover the right of petitioning is, apparently, limited to requests for things lawful under Espionage and Sedition Acts. Under the Sedition Act of 1798 a man was indicted for demanding a repeal of the Act. During the World War, "twenty-seven South Dakota farmers were opposed to the draft and believed that an unduly high quota was exacted from their county. They petitioned various state officers, asking for a new arrangement, a referendum on war, payment of war expenses from taxation, and repudiation of war debts. As an alternative they threatened defeat to the officers, their party, and the nation. . . . The twenty-seven were sentenced to more than a year in prison."

Passing from the realm of opinion to that of crime, the Constitution imposes certain limitations on Congress in behalf of individual liberty. Congress is not authorized to define treason; it is defined in the Constitution: "Treason against the United States shall consist only in levying war against them or in adhering to their enemies, giving them aid and comfort." Congress cannot, therefore, vindictively declare to be treasonable any act which does not meet its approval.

In addition, the trial of persons accused of this high crime is carefully safeguarded. No person can be convicted of treason unless on the testimony of two witnesses to the overt act or on confession in open court. In the case of the United States *vs.* The Insurgents, the Court, interpreting a federal statute, ordered that the names of the jurors and a list of witnesses should be furnished the accused; and that a reasonable time be allowed for the defense to prepare its case after receiving this information. The Court, furthermore, declared that until the overt act of treason had been proved by the testimony of two witnesses, no evidence relating to the charges could be introduced.

While Congress has the power to provide the penalties for this grave offence, the Constitution expressly stipulates that no attainder of treason shall work corruption of blood or forfeiture except during the life of the individual thus condemned. In old English practice, corruption of blood meant the destruction of all inheritable qualities, so that any attainted person could not inherit lands or other hereditaments from his ancestors or retain those which he already possessed or transmit them to his heirs. But the constitutional provision mentioned above is designed to prevent the punishment of relatives; and accordingly no proceedings may be construed to work a forfeiture of the real estate of a traitor for a longer term than his natural life.

Likewise in the interest of individual liberty, proceedings against persons charged with crime under the federal law are controlled by several explicit provisions of the Constitution. Congress cannot act as a court by passing a bill of attainder condemning any person to death or to imprisonment or imposing any penalty whatsoever. Congress can pass no *ex post facto* law; that is, no law making an act a crime which was not a crime when committed, or adding new penalties after the commission of an act, or modifying the procedure in such a way as to make it substantially easier to convict a defendant already accused. Federal authorities have no power of arresting wholesale on general warrant; all warrants of arrest must be issued only upon probable causes supported by oath or affirmation and particularly describing the place to be searched and the persons and things to be seized. Indictment by grand jury and trial by jury are secured generally to all civilians charged with capital or otherwise infamous crimes except in the American insular possessions (p. 682). The writ of habeas corpus (p. 121) cannot be set aside except in case of rebellion or invasion, when suspension may be required by public safety; that is, under all ordinary circumstances any person held by federal authorities has the right to have a speedy preliminary hearing before a proper judicial tribunal. Excessive bail cannot be demanded by federal authorities; in other words, except in capital cases, federal courts must release prisoners on bail, and must not fix the amount at such an unreasonable sum as practically to deny the right. Finally, in general, the National Government must allow due process of law in all of its criminal proceedings: the trial must be open and speedy and in the state and district where the crime was committed; the defendant must be informed of the nature and cause of the charge against him; the witnesses against him must be brought face to face with him; he may force, by compulsory process, the attendance of witnesses in his favor; he cannot be compelled to testify against himself in any criminal case; and he has a right to have the assistance of counsel in his own behalf.

Such at least are the grand principles of personal liberty set forth in the Constitution. In actual practice, during American participation in the World War and for many months afterward, federal authorities played fast and loose with them—so fast and loose that a committee of eminent lawyers, among whom were two members of the Harvard Law School, made a public protest and filed a list of violations of law said to have been committed by the Government itself. It was alleged, and the allegation was well supported, that arrests had been made by federal authorities without proper warrants and on trivial and trumped-up evidence, that many persons were herded in jails and held for a long time without bail and without an opportunity to communicate with counsel or friends, that federal detectives actually stirred up meetings said to be seditious and then arrested participants, and that the Attorney General of the United States made improper use of his high office to pursue and punish persons accused of entertaining radical opinions. These charges were indignantly denied by the Attorney General, but no person should form an opinion on the subject without examining the evidence in the case. It is conservative to say that the constitutional limitations on behalf of personal liberty proved no barrier to the Federal Government in arresting and imprisoning persons charged with holding objectionable opinions. The officers of the law had a practically free hand in matters of personal liberty, and they were almost uniformly sustained by the courts of law.

In contrast to the provisions in defense of individual freedom, limitations on the National Government in behalf of property rights are few in number, but they are fundamental in character and easily enforced. The power to define property under our system is left to the state governments, subject to the one great restriction that slavery and involuntary servitude, that is, property in man, shall not exist. Congress has no power to legislate generally with respect to property except in the territories and districts not organized into states. Moreover, the Constitution lays explicit restraints on the power of the Federal Government to attack the property of private persons. Congress cannot impose taxes on articles exported from any state. Duties, imposts, and excises must be uniform, that is, must fall upon the same object with the same weight everywhere throughout the United States. In order to protect the tax-payer, it was prescribed in the Constitution that revenue bills must originate in the House of Representatives, which is composed of members chosen directly by the voters; but this formula is a dead letter in practice. The Constitution also stipulates that no money shall be drawn from the Treasury except under appropriations made by law; consequently the executive authority cannot on its own motion take money from the public chest.

It is not only by way of defining property and taxing it that the Federal Government can approach the material rights of citizens. It may regulate the use of property in various relations, but never in such a manner as to deprive any persons of property without due process of law—a term broad enough to embrace all tangible and intangible privileges of a substantial character, including earnings and most increments (p. 402). The Federal Government also enjoys the power of eminent domain; in other words, it may take private property for public use; but it must make just compensation to the owner. In determining what is just compensation, federal authorities must consider the purposes for which the property in question is suitable and pay due regard to the existing business or wants of the community and such as may be reasonably expected in the immediate future. The proceedings in ascertaining the value of property condemned for public use may be prosecuted before commissioners or special boards or the courts, with or without the intervention of a jury as Congress may determine. They must simply be conducted in some fair and just manner affording to the owner of the property in question an opportunity to present evidence as to its value and to be heard on that matter. While safeguarding private property against invasion by Congress, the Constitution protects it against all local governments by providing that no state shall deprive any person of property without due process of law (p. 654).

The Doctrine of Delegated and Supreme Power

Besides being limited by the positive restraints imposed on it by the Constitution, the Federal Government is broadly controlled by the principle that it possesses at most only delegated powers. States may do anything which they are not directly or indirectly forbidden to do by the Constitution or by the lawful exercise of authority under it on the part of the Federal Government; their powers are inherent, not granted or assigned to them by any written instrument. On the other hand the Federal Government enjoys only those powers which are actually conferred on it by the Constitution. The limited character of federal supremacy in this respect is apparent in nearly every line of the Constitution enumerating and stating the powers of Congress, the President, and the courts. And it is expressly enunciated by the Tenth Amendment which declares that "the powers not delegated to the United States by the Constitution, nor prohibited by it to the states, are reserved to the states respectively, or to the people."

Yet, as we have indicated in Chapter II, the point must not be too closely pressed, for the powers given to the Federal Government are often set forth in general terms; and Congress is specifically authorized to make all laws "necessary and proper" for carrying into execution the powers directly conferred—a blanket provision which takes some of the sting out of the word "delegated." Furthermore, as we shall see, especially in Chapter XX, there appears to be practically no limit on the purposes for which Congress may appropriate money and under that head it may do and has done many things not expressly covered in any other part of the Constitution.

Though the powers of the Federal Government are delegated, not inherent, federal law within its sphere is supreme over all state law. "This Constitution and the laws of the United States which shall be made in pursuance thereof, and all treaties made or which shall be made under the authority of the United States shall be the supreme law of the land." So runs the federal Constitution—apparently as clear as a statement of law can be—but it leaves unsettled the question as to the agency that shall decide what laws of the United States are duly made in pursuance of the Constitution and what state acts are in conflict with the superior laws. This question involves the very nature of the Union, and for more than half a century the famous controversy over states' rights raged around it.

On many occasions states declared that they themselves had the power to decide when acts of Congress violated the federal Constitution and that they could nullify such laws within their borders, no matter what the Supreme Court said. This was the doctrine of defiance and nullification announced from time to time by states, North and South, and made famous by the Kentucky and Virginia resolutions of 1798–99 and the Nullification Ordinance of South Carolina passed in 1832. On the other hand, the Supreme Court has consistently held to the principle that it alone is the rightful tribunal for determining what powers are in fact delegated to Congress and when they are lawfully exercised. Happily this question is now one of historic interest only. The Constitution and laws of the United States are supreme and the Supreme Court at Washington is the tribunal of last resort for deciding all controversies on this point.

The application of this principle may be illustrated by an example. Long ago Congress provided by law that when any civil suit or criminal prosecution was begun against a federal revenue officer in any court of a state in connection with some official act, the case should be immediately removed into the federal courts. Such an officer, in the discharge of his duty, killed a man in Tennessee, and his trial, against the protest of the state, was transferred to a federal court in due form. In discussing the constitutionality of this law, Mr. Justice Strong said of the Federal Government:

"It can act only through its officers and agents, and they must act within the states. If, when thus acting, and within the scope of their authority, these officers can be arrested and brought to trial in a state court for an alleged offence against the law of the state, yet warranted by the federal authority they possess, and if the General Government is powerless to interfere *at once* for their protection—if their protection must be left to the action of the state courts—the operations of the General Government may at any time be arrested at the will of one of its members. The legislature of a state may be unfriendly. It may affix penalties to acts done under the immediate direction of the National Government and in obedience to its laws. It may deny the authority conferred by those laws. The state court may administer not only the laws of the state, but equally federal law, in such a manner as to paralyze the operation of the

Government. . . . We do not think such an element of weakness is to be found in the Constitution. . . . No state government can exclude it from the exercise of any authority conferred upon the Federal Government by the Constitution, obstruct its authorized officers against its will, or withhold from it, for a moment, the cognizance of any subject which that instrument has committed to it."

The Separation of Powers

A third political principle, perhaps more widely known and celebrated than those cited above, is the doctrine that the powers conferred upon the Federal Government by the Constitution are divided among three departments: legislative, executive, and judicial. Congress makes laws, the courts interpret them, and the President executes them—a creed taught in the books on civics and almost as extensively circulated as the national anthem.

This doctrine is not expressly stated in a separate section of the federal Constitution, as in several state constitutions, but is embodied in the opening sentences of the three articles relating to the legislative, executive, and judicial power: "All legislative powers herein granted shall be vested in a Congress of the United States. . . . The executive power shall be vested in a President of the United States. . . . The judicial power . . . shall be vested in one Supreme Court and such inferior courts as Congress may from time to time ordain and establish." Thus, says the commentator, Kent, the Constitution has effected the separation of powers "with great felicity of execution, and in a way well calculated to preserve the equal balance of the government."

According to the traditional account, this doctrine came into our law and practice from the writings of the French philosopher, Montesquieu, whose treatise on the *Spirit of the Laws* was a veritable political text-book for our eighteenth-century statesmen, and it was derived by that distinguished author from an analysis of the English constitution. In point of fact, however, the theory was evolved by Montesquieu during a conflict between the judiciary and king in France in which he participated; afterwards he read the idea into his study of the institutions of England. As a principle of law and government, it is a part of that system of checks and balances and subdivisions of power by which statesmen have sought to prevent the development of the type of democracy that functions through simple legislative majorities. It was explained with great insight by Madison in the *Federalist,* and was thus eloquently defended by Webster: "The spirit of liberty . . . is jealous of encroachments, jealous of power, jealous of man. It demands checks; it seeks for guards; it insists on securities; it intrenches itself behind strong defences, and fortifies itself with all possible care against the assaults of ambition and passion."

Yet a close examination of the Constitution shows that the men who drafted it were unable to maintain the purity of the principle when they came to details. Indeed it was thoroughly understood by the framers that a complete separation of powers was impossible, save in the realm of pure theory. In commenting on the subject, Madison remarked that Montesquieu's doctrine "can amount to no more than this, that where the whole power of one department is exercised by the same hands which possess the whole power of another department, the fundamental principles of a free constitution are subverted." Madison then went on to show that the theory "does not require that the legislative, executive and judiciary departments should be wholly unconnected with each other." On the contrary he undertook to prove that "unless these three departments be so far connected and blended as to give each a constitutional control over the others, the degree of separation which the maxim requires as essential to a free government can never in practice be duly maintained."

Numerous illustrations of his contention are available. The appointing power of the President is shared by the

Senate. The treaty-making power—legislative in character—is divided between the President and Senate. Owing to the amount and variety of executive business, the President must function through departmental offices; these are created and to some extent controlled by Congress. On the other hand, the President shares in legislation through his veto power and his right to send as many messages as he chooses. Even the Supreme Court, which is created by the Constitution, lies at the mercy of Congress, for Congress may prescribe the number of the judges and fix their salaries subject to certain restrictions. It might, for instance, fail to create the requisite lower and intermediate courts, reduce the number of judges, and through the confirming power of the Senate secure pliant judges; and thus overthrow the prestige of the judiciary or make it subservient to the legislative branch.

Furthermore, political practice has shown that the influence actually exerted by a department of the Government depends not so much upon the legal authority which it enjoys in theory as upon the great interests which function through it in reality. For example, during the period of Reconstruction which followed the Civil War, Congress dominated the executive, overrode his exercise of the veto power, and through the Tenure of Office Act and other measures gathered into its hands almost the whole domain of federal authority. Throughout the entire course of American participation in the World War, leadership in legislation as well as administration went to the President as it had during the Civil War. All the great measures of law passed within that period were drafted under President Wilson's scrutiny, and many of them were forced through a recalcitrant Congress under the influence of his personality and prestige and power. Commenting on a bill presented to Congress by the executive department, a Senator complained: "If this bill passes, there would be only one more thing left for Congress to do, and that would be to make the President a king." Although there was partisan rancor in this lament, the bill became a law—another proof of the fact that President Wilson completely overshadowed and dominated Congress.

In this see-saw of political forces back and forth through the departments, the courts have seldom intervened on the simple ground that the doctrine of the separation of powers has been violated. It is true that the Supreme Court early applied it in Hayburn's case but that was with reference to an act of Congress authorizing judges of the circuit courts to receive and hear certain claims to pensions, subject to a supervisory review by the Secretary of War. Obviously the power thus conferred was not judicial in its nature, and the judges, therefore, declined to serve in the capacity required by the law. From time to time, usually in relation to matters of minor importance, the issue was raised in judicial tribunals and in 1929 it was involved in a decision of the Supreme Court setting aside an act of Congress requiring the approval of the Senate for the removal of certain federal officials (p. 272). Broadly speaking, however, it must be said that the occasions on which one branch of the Federal Government has by a law or order clearly trespassed upon the domain of another branch have been few indeed, and the Supreme Court of the United States has been loath to hold acts of Congress invalid on the general theory of the separation of powers.

The soundness of the theory as a practical working scheme of government has been rather severely criticized by two eminent publicists, Henry Jones Ford and Frank P. Goodnow. They hold that the functions of government are only twofold, the formulation and execution of public will—that is, legislative and executive—the judiciary being merely a branch of the law-enforcing agency. In their view the separation of powers creates friction in the government, divides responsibility, necessitates iron-bound party machinery outside the government to overcome the unwieldiness of the system, and altogether works for confusion and obscurity instead of simplicity and public scrutiny. They refer to the English system, in which the legislative and executive powers are fused under the direction of the Cabinet, the responsibility of the Cabinet is definitely fixed, and the judiciary cannot pass on the constitutionality of laws; they then express the opinion that the English parliamentary organization is a better machine for getting political work done expeditiously and efficiently.

In response to criticism of this type, John W. Burgess contends: "I think that we are upon the right line, and that those nations which have developed parliamentary government are beginning to feel, as suffrage has become more extended, the necessity of greater executive independence. Parliamentary government, *i.e.,* government in which the other departments are subject to legislative control, becomes intensely radical under universal suffrage, and will remain so until the character of the masses becomes so perfect as to make the form of government very nearly a matter of indifference. There is no doubt that we sometimes feel embarrassment from a conflict of opinion between the independent executive and the legislature, but this embarrassment must generally result in the adoption of the more conservative course, which is far less dangerous than the course of radical experimentation. . . . The feature *par excellence* of the American governmental system is the constitutional, independent, unpolitical judiciary and the supremacy of the judiciary over the other departments in all cases where private rights are concerned." This undoubtedly represents the prevailing view of American publicists and statesmen, and is at all events the fundamental doctrine of our law.

The Supremacy of the Judiciary in Matters Involving Persons and Property

Closely related to the separation of powers, with its check and balance system, is the supremacy of the federal judiciary over the other branches of the Government in matters relating to the privileges of persons and property. This judicial supremacy, says Professor Burgess, is "the most momentous product of modern political science. Upon it far more than upon anything else depends the permanent existence of republican government; for elective government must be party government—majority government; and unless the domain of individual liberty is protected by an independent, unpolitical department, such government degenerates into party absolutism and then into Cæsarism."

It is the Supreme Court, therefore, that stands as the great defender of private property against the attempts of popular legislatures to encroach upon its fundamental privileges. This fact has been so clearly and cogently demonstrated by Arthur T. Hadley that his statement deserves quotation at length. The theoretical position of property-holders, he says,—"the sum of the conditions which affect their standing for the long future and not for the immediate present—is far stronger in the United States [than in other countries]. The general status of the property-owner under the law cannot be changed by the action of the legislature, or the executive, or the people of a state voting at the polls, or all three put together. It cannot be changed without either a consensus of opinion among the judges, which should lead them to retrace their old views, or an amendment of the Constitution of the United States by the slow and cumbersome machinery provided for that purpose, or, last—and I hope most improbable—a revolution.

"When it is said, as it commonly is, that the fundamental division of powers in the modern State is into legislative, executive, and judicial, the student of American institutions may fairly note an exception. The fundamental division of powers in the Constitution of the United States is between voters on the one hand and property-owners on the other. The forces of democracy on one side, divided between the executive and the legislative, are set over against the forces of property on the other side, with the judiciary as arbiter between them; the Constitution itself not only forbidding the legislature and executive to trench upon the rights of property, but compelling the judiciary to define and uphold those rights in a manner provided by the Constitution itself.

"This theory of American politics has not often been stated. But it has been universally acted upon. One reason why it has not been more frequently stated is that it has been acted upon so universally that no American of earlier generations ever thought it necessary to state it. It has had the most fundamental and far-reaching effects upon the policy of the country. To mention but one thing among many, it has allowed the experiment of universal suffrage to be tried under conditions essentially different from those which led to its ruin in Athens or in Rome. The voter was omnipotent —within a limited area. He could make what laws he pleased, as long as those laws did not trench upon property right. He could elect what officers he pleased, as long as those officers did not try to do certain duties confided by the Constitution to the property-holders."

Citizenship and Suffrage

While nationalizing certain private rights of persons and property and laying down basic doctrines of government, the Constitution prescribes a number of fundamental principles covering citizenship and the suffrage. In international affairs, the term "citizenship" means membership in a nation, but when the American republic was established the word had no very definite connotation either in law or practice. The Constitution itself refers to "citizens of the United States" and "citizens of the states;" but a strict usage of the term would require us to speak of citizens of the United States and residents or inhabitants of the states, although this distinction might popularly be regarded as a species of pedantry. The state has no power to bestow or withhold citizenship, although it may confer many civil and political rights on foreigners. Citizenship is now guaranteed under the Constitution to all persons born on the soil of the United States, with certain exceptions noted below. Furthermore, the exclusive right to admit aliens to citizenship is given to the National Government by the clause authorizing Congress to make uniform rules of naturalization.

Citizenship in the United States, then, may be acquired by birth or by naturalization. According to the Fourteenth Amendment, all persons born in the United States, with a few exceptions such as the children of foreign diplomatic and consular officers, are *ipso facto* citizens of the United States. This is called citizenship by reason of birth in a particular place, *i.e., jure soli.* Yet in this relation it should be noted that certain insular possessions are not really parts of the United States within the meaning of this clause and children born there of native parents do not automatically obtain American citizenship (p. 697). To secure citizenship to American children born abroad, Congress has provided by law that all children born out of the jurisdiction of the United States, whose fathers are at the time of their birth American citizens, shall be deemed citizens of the United States. The rights of citizenship, however, do not descend to children whose fathers never resided in the United States.

Formerly an alien woman who married an American citizen became immediately an American citizen while an American woman who married an alien lost her citizenship in the United States. Driven by the modern feminist agitation Congress has abolished this ancient rule, by an Act passed in 1922 and liberally amended eight years later. The law now provides an easy method of naturalization for American women who were married before the passage of the first Act and for alien women who marry American citizens. It specifically adds that a woman citizen of the United States shall not cease to be a citizen by reason of her marriage to an alien eligible to citizenship (p. 75), unless she makes a formal renunciation of her citizenship before a court having jurisdiction over the naturalization of aliens; hence she automatically retains her citizenship or may voluntarily surrender it. Under the first of the Acts cited above, an American woman who married an alien and resided long abroad could be regarded as having surrendered American citizenship, but by the later modifying measure, approved July 3, 1930, even this clause relating to the presumption of loss of citizenship has been repealed, leaving no loophole. American women who wish to keep their American citizenship, regardless of their marriage ties, are at last authorized by American law to do so—a long delayed installment of simple justice. American women who marry aliens ineligible to citizenship, however, are still placed in a distressing position for they lose their birthright and cannot recover it again; even the exclusive immigration laws run against them.

Foreigners may be admitted to citizenship by naturalization, either collectively or individually. Collective naturalization may occur when a foreign territory and its inhabitants are ceded to the United States. The manner of this naturalization is generally stipulated in the terms of the transfer. For example, the treaty with France confirming the Louisiana Purchase provided that the inhabitants of the territory should be incorporated into the Union of the United States and admitted as soon as possible, in conformity with the principles of the federal Constitution, to the enjoyment of all the rights, advantages, and immunities of citizens of the United States.

The naturalization of individuals is subject, in all its details, to the laws of Congress. It is effected by judicial process in certain specified federal, state, and territorial courts. Only white persons and persons of African nativity or descent may acquire American citizenship by naturalization; foreign-born Chinese, Japanese, Hindus, and certain other Asiatics are entirely ineligible.

The general method of naturalization is as follows. At the outset the alien in quest of American citizenship, who must be at least eighteen years of age, files in the proper court a declaration of his intention to become a citizen. At the end of not less than two years and not more than seven and after at least five years' residence in the country, the applicant presents a petition signed by his own hand, stating that he is not opposed to organized government or a polygamist, and declares under oath his intention of renouncing his allegiance to his former country. His petition must be supported by the testimony of American citizens as to his residence and moral character. If it is made to a federal court, the judge may designate a naturalization examiner to inquire into the facts of the case. After ninety days have elapsed from the date of filing the petition, the appeal is heard by the court. On this occasion the applicant renews his adherence to the declarations made in the petition, and is then examined. The inquest may be formal or thorough and searching, according to the standards of the judge who conducts it. At all events he is required to satisfy himself that the provisions of the law have been complied with, that the applicant has behaved as a person of good moral character, can speak English, is attached to the principles of the Constitution, will defend it, and is well disposed to the good order and happiness of the United States. When the court is duly convinced the certificate of naturalization is issued. Evidently a large power of discrimination is conferred upon the judges, and may be employed to exclude from citizenship people who believe in political doctrines that appear objectionable to them.

In 1929, for example, Rosika Schwimmer, an alien woman forty-nine years of age, sought to secure American citizenship through naturalization. In the course of the proceedings, Mrs. Schwimmer declared that she "understood the principles of and fully believed in our form of Government" and had read and was prepared to take the oath of allegiance. She was asked the following question: "If necessary, are you willing to take up arms in defence of this country?" To this query she replied "I would not take up arms personally." She then amplified the statement by declaring that "If . . . the United States can compel its women citizens to take up arms in defence of the country—something that no other civilized government has ever attempted—I would not be able to comply with this requirement; . . . even men of my age—I was forty-nine years old last September—are not called to take up arms." Furthermore, she said, "I do not care how many other women fight, because I consider it a question of conscience."

With these facts before it the Supreme Court, to which the case had been taken by appeal, held that "the very conception of a just government and its duty to the citizen includes the reciprocal obligation of the citizen to render military service in case of need. . . . Whatever lessens the willingness of citizens to bear arms detracts from the strength and safety of the Government." While the Court declared that "a pacifist in the general sense of the word is one who seeks to maintain peace and abolish war" and that "such purposes are in harmony with the Constitution and policy of our Government," it also held that pacifism should not prevent one from fighting in a national emergency. In effect the Court refused citizenship to Mrs. Schwimmer on the ground that she would not agree to perform a hypothetical act never yet required of any American woman—namely, bear arms in case of need at the age of fifty. From the opinion of the Court, Justice Holmes dissented. He believed that the law requiring the support and defense of the Constitution should not be interpreted to mean that aliens must support and defend it in a manner not yet required of any citizens of the United States. "So far as the adequacy of her oath is concerned," said the Justice, "I hardly can see how that is affected by the statement, inasmuch as she is a woman over fifty years of age, and would not be allowed to bear arms if she wanted to."

The Schwimmer case has been used as an authority for a number of other decisions denying citizenship to aliens unwilling to agree to the assumption of duties not yet required of all American citizens. Thus a Quaker, Margaret Dorland Webb, was refused naturalization by a federal district judge on account of her unwillingness to fight, "if the law were changed compelling women" to do so. Again, a Russian priest was excluded because his religious convictions forbade him to carry arms—a situation expressly provided for during the World War when conscientious objectors with religious scruples were permitted to choose other than military activities even though they were American citizens.

Under the Constitution, of course, any terms may be exacted of aliens before extending the privileges of citizenship to them; indeed, Congress, as we have said, has flatly refused to grant citizenship to the members of certain races. In practice a peculiar legal tangle has been created, for there are now two groups of American citizens, one born in the country and entitled to the rights of a "tender conscience" and another consisting of naturalized aliens sworn to uphold principles not yet enacted into laws—principles which probably will never be placed on the statute books.

Although it might seem that the right to vote is on a level of importance with the privileges of citizenship, the original Constitution, owing to violent differences of opinion among the framers, contained no provisions defining the suffrage. It left the question to the states for solution by stipulating that voters for members of the House of Representatives should have the qualifications requisite for electors of the most numerous branch of the state legislature, and by authorizing the state legislatures to elect the Senators and to decide how presidential electors should be chosen. Thus matters stood until the close of the Civil War when the Republican party sought to make secure its supremacy and enable the newly emancipated Negro to protect himself against his former master by forcing the adoption of the Fourteenth and Fifteenth amendments.

These provisions, however, do not contain positive qualifications for the suffrage. They still leave the regulation of the franchise to the states but subject it to two conditions. The first declares that "when the right to vote at any election for the choice of electors for President and Vice-President of the United States, Representatives in Congress, the executive and judicial officers of a state, or the members of the legislature thereof, is denied to any of the male inhabitants of such state, being twenty-one years of age, and citizens of the United States, or in any way abridged, except for participation in rebellion, or other crime, the basis of representation therein shall be reduced in the proportion which the number of such male citizens shall bear to the whole number of male citizens twenty-one years of age in such state." Supplementing this indirect attempt at general male enfranchisement is a flat assertion in the Fifteenth Amendment to the effect that the right of citizens to vote shall not be denied or abridged on account of race, color, or previous condition of servitude. The negative character of federal suffrage provisions is also reflected in the Nineteenth Amendment providing that no citizen shall be denied the right to vote on account of sex.

Owing to the nature of such enactments, there is no uniform franchise throughout the United States. Various limitations have been established by Congress from time to time in the territories and insular possessions and at present more than one third of the states impose tax, educational, property, or other qualifications on the right to vote. In operation these restrictions exclude thousands of adult citizens, in the North no less than in the South. Massachusetts with an educational test or Pennsylvania with a tax qualification is legally quite as liable to a reduction of representation under the Fourteenth Amendment as any Southern state with a property or literacy bar in its constitution. Nevertheless, no serious attempt has yet been made to secure an enforcement of the Amendment. Threats to apply it are occasionally heard but they never pass beyond the academic stage. For all practical purposes this section of the Constitution is a dead letter, illustrating once more Judge Cooley's contention that the famous document is what the people respect and obey.

In connection with citizenship, consideration should be given to the position of aliens within the area of the continental United States. In law their rights are determined partly by the Constitution, acts of Congress, and treaties with foreign countries and partly by state legislation. At several points the Constitution specifically mentions *persons* rather than citizens. With reference to the enumeration required for the apportionment of representation and direct taxes, "the whole number of free persons" is to be taken into the reckoning. Again, the Fourteenth Amendment declares that no state shall deprive any person of life, liberty, or property without due process of law or deny to any person the equal protection of the laws.

Such provisions are supplemented by treaties with various countries guaranteeing a reciprocity of rights in specified cases, but the enforcement of these treaty agreements is generally entrusted to the states, with appeal, of course, to the federal courts for final determination respecting the validity of any particular local law or action. Undoubtedly Congress has the power to provide federal processes for enforcing treaty provisions; more than one President has recommended this step; but the opposition has always been too strong. Thus while the treaty rights stand squarely on the books, states may encroach upon them, subject only to judicial review in the courts of the United States. No machinery has been provided for the direct federal prosecution of individuals and mobs that violate them. Furthermore, Congress itself may discriminate against aliens in certain cases; it has, for example, denied Chinese, Japanese, and persons belonging to certain other non-caucasian races the right to become naturalized citizens, even though they are lawful residents of the United States.

By judicial rulings, particularly federal, the rights and disabilities of aliens have been authoritatively defined in various relations. It is unlawful under the Fourteenth Amendment for states to deny aliens the equal right to engage in certain callings, such as the laundry business, on the same terms as citizens; it is unlawful to tax employers for engaging alien laborers, or to compel employers having more than a fixed number of employees to hire a certain proportion of American citizens. On the other hand state legislation forbidding aliens not eligible to naturalization to buy or lease land for agricultural purposes has been sustained. Aliens may be denied the right to hunt and fish in public places, to enjoy the benefits of workmen's compensation legislation, to practice law, or to be employed on public works. In times of war, of course, the rights of alien enemies may be curtailed to the point of disappearance. Moreover the power of Congress to expel aliens for certain types of conduct and offences is broad, if not unlimited. Hence while a majority of alien residents enjoy nearly all the non-political rights of citizens, many of them labor under onerous disabilities. Vestiges of distant days when aliens were viewed by all countries of the world as rightless persons still remain here and there in American law, working grave injustices in individual cases.

CHAPTER IV

Parties and Opinions

A Constitution laying down general principles is not a government. It is only a plan or a body of rules for such an institution. Itself the product of a social conflict, it provides the legal frame within which the struggle is to be continued and constrained. In the present state of American evolution, the directive force of government is a body of men and women bound together by the ties of a political party. Realistically conceived a party is a union of people bent on getting possession of the organization authorized by the Constitution and employing its engines in making and enforcing laws which they hold to be just, expedient, or useful to their interests, as the case may be. Through the party their will to power is brought to a focus. Through government the party translates its policy into resolution and action. In beginning an exploration of modern politics, therefore, the sources, nature, and operations of parties must be examined.

The Causes of Party Divisions

In every civilized country not ruled by an absolute monarch or a single despotic class, that is, where some degree of freedom is allowed, political parties arise. Why is this so? Why do they spring up whenever liberty of opinion is permitted, to speak concretely, in the United States? Many answers have been made by philosophers in this field. One attributes partisanship to sound and fury, the tricks of demagogues who agitate the people and split them into contending groups for the love of high sport, coupled with a desire for power and the emoluments of office. Against this thesis may be brought the objection that it is too simple; it makes mere dupes of the masses—intelligent and unintelligent alike; above all it is not in accord with many stubborn facts in the situation.

A second explanation of party divisions falls back on "human nature:" innate qualities automatically divide the populace into parties. According to this theory, some people are instinctively conservative and want to leave things as they are; others are instinctively progressive and want to make changes. Or, to take a variant on this explanation, some are inherently aristocratic and sympathize with the "rich and well born"—are, therefore, Hamiltonian Republicans; while others are inherently democratic and sympathize with the masses—are Jeffersonian Democrats. This proposition also is countered by innumerable objections. It is a mere assertion that explains nothing. How does anyone know that these qualities are innate? If they are, whence did they come? Were they planted by the Creator in the first pair made for the Garden of Eden? If so, why are they not universal—in darkest Africa as well as in the United States? If not, then how and why were they acquired? In itself, the theory is in amusing discord with certain inescapable facts. For a long time the Democratic party was dominated by aristocratic slaveholders whose instinctive sympathy for the toiling masses, white or black, was nowhere in evidence. On the other hand, the so-called aristocratic party has as its idealized leader Abraham Lincoln whose faith in government by the people was simply beyond question. The instinctive solution of the problem is no solution—not even a faint clue.

Akin to this theory is another offered by distinguished authorities, including James Bryce, to the effect that some people believe in a strong federal government and are Republicans, while others cling to states' rights and are Democrats. Whence come the two beliefs? Should a satisfactory answer be made to this question, a disconcerting statistical memorandum would stand in the way of accepting the hypothesis. A study of the votes in Congress on measures strengthening the Federal Government or tending to exalt the states shows that the two parties have not consistently divided on any such issue. Thus the explanation of party origins on this basis disappears in a fog.

Far more realistic is the key to the riddle offered by James Madison, the father of the Constitution. Every civilized society, he says in the tenth number of the *Federalist,* is divided into groups and classes possessing various kinds and amounts of property—landed, mercantile, industrial, creditor, debtor, and labor interests, for example. From different possessions and economic conditions arise different sentiments driving the people into parties and factions, each bent on forcing government to do or abstain from doing something deemed advantageous or injurious as the case may be. Although too simple and open to many exceptions, Madison's explanation of party origins is nearer the realities of American political evolution than the rival offerings. At all events if farmers seeking relief, manufacturers demanding protective tariffs, munition makers, bankers, organized labor, railroads, public utilities, job-hunters, and other interests of a practical character were to withdraw entirely from American parties and politics, the substance of government would suddenly become very thin. Politics is not all economics, but it is better illuminated by reference to that science than to any other. Certainly without economics, politics is an utter mystery.

American Political Parties

Almost from the foundation of the National Government there have been two major political parties in the United States. Their names have changed but continuity in the measures and composition of each has rarely been broken. One of them is the Federalist-Whig-Republican party, associated with the names of Hamilton, Webster, Lincoln, McKinley, and Coolidge, and its center of economic gravity has been in the industrial and financial interests of the nation. Although it made a great combination with farmers in 1860, the chief sources of its economic strength have remained the same for nearly one hundred and fifty years. The second party is the Republican-Democratic organization, with Jefferson, Jackson, Davis, and Bryan as its sponsors. Its historic center of gravity has been in the agricultural interests of the country, although a large body of importing merchants and urban mechanics was early brought into its fold. This explanation of our party divisions does not mean that all industrialists have been in one camp and all tillers of the soil in the other, but that the predominating interests have been capitalistic and agricultural respectively.

If reference is made to the great issues involved in this party antagonism, it will be found that they have a distinctly economic bearing. Broadly speaking the Hamilton-Webster-McKinley combination has supported high protective tariffs for American industries, centralized banking, a sound currency based on the gold standard, ship subsidies, a strong navy, the promotion of internal improvements, commercial enterprise, and light taxation on great fortunes. In the main the Jefferson-Jackson-Bryan party has been aligned on the opposite side. Exceptions may be found, no doubt, in the long course of American history, but in the main the cleavage has been fairly clear, at least until recent times.

As American society has become more complex, however, the lines of the old party battle have become somewhat confused. Industry now overtops agriculture in the amount of capital employed and the proportion of the population engaged in it. It is no longer possible to reproduce the conditions of Jefferson's day when farmers and planters were in an overwhelming majority and the greater part of the actual wealth annually produced came from the soil. The tables are turned for all time. Large sections of the Middle West and the South, once the strongholds of agrarian Democracy, have become industrialized, with corresponding changes in attitude toward politics—the protective tariff for instance. On the other hand capitalism is divided against itself. New industries, such as the manufacture of automobiles, requiring no protection from foreign competition, have sprung up; a large part of the accumulated riches of the country is invested abroad and bankers in this field are interested in low tariffs rather than high.

So deeply have these changes run into American society that the Democrats in 1928 abandoned their slogan of "tariff for revenue only" and came out frankly for protection; while the Republicans long committed to high duties found themselves hopelessly divided for many months in their efforts to raise rates all along the line, after their success at the polls. Nor did the latter abolish the heavy taxes on incomes and inheritances previously imposed by the Democrats. A survey of the votes in Congress discloses the fact that there is scarcely a single issue in detail that brings about a clear-cut division between the members of the two parties. Indeed it might be safely said that the cleavage between the right and left wings of each is greater than the gulf between the parties themselves, especially in the Senate where the agrarian states are represented out of all proportion to their numerical strength. Yet in spite of periodical breaks in their ranks the Democratic and Republican organizations as such remain intact in battle array.

Although they have successfully avoided complete disruption, both parties have been periodically attacked on the left by agrarian and labor groups—dissatisfied farmers and industrial workers. Agrarian factions, called first Greenbackers, then Populists, and later Non-Partisan Leaguers, have kept up a steady fusillade on the "plutocracy." Appealing principally to urban labor, the Socialist party has been in the field since 1900 and the still more intransigent Communists, since the close of the World War. Occasionally one or another of these fragments has made great inroads on the old parties, polling at various times as high as a million votes. But none of them has ever succeeded in coming within gun-shot of political victory; most of the dissenting groups speedily perish or are merged with the Democratic or Republican organizations as left wings.

Still their operations have made a deep impression on the course of both the major parties. It has been claimed, with full historical warrant, that these intransigent factions have set most of the leading issues of the past fifty years—the income tax, regulation of railways, popular election of Senators, limitation on the use of injunctions in labor disputes, woman suffrage, and "farm relief" in all its manifold phases. Since the two traditional parties are on the whole rather evenly balanced, it is necessary for them to bid for votes among the independents, and to make concessions in return for ballots. No doubt this policy of trading, coupled with the enormous expense of constructing a new national political machine, is partly responsible for the failure of every third party to reach a dominating position. Danger from this direction is always allayed before it becomes too serious. Hence it happens that the Government of the United States is, and probably will be for an indefinite future, conducted alternately by two national political parties—the Republicans and Democrats, goaded and deflected by dissenters.

The Nature of Party Organization

Since this is true it becomes necessary to look somewhat closely at the structure of the political party and the sources of its strength. It is customary to regard such an association as composed of all those who support its candidates at the polls, but this is a very loose idea. Thousands who vote with a party at a given moment are independents or members of opposing parties, who for the time being favor its candidates and platforms. Additional thousands who regularly vote a given ticket bestow no thought or time on party debates and conferences, and could not give a fifty-word account of why they happen to belong to any particular organization. According to another definition, a "party" includes only those who are openly inscribed on its roster, as required by law or practice, and are thus entitled to participate in its primaries. Ordinarily this group consists of from thirty to eighty per cent of the party voters. In practice the number who actually go to the primaries and take a hand in electing party officers and nominating candidates is much smaller than the official party membership, ranging sometimes as low as ten per cent of the enrolled voters and not often higher than seventy per cent.

Among the fifty per cent of the members, more or less, who may be reckoned as taking some positive interest in the affairs of the party, only a minor fraction can be regarded as active and influential. There are at the center some loyal and zealous citizens who believe that the welfare and safety of the Republic depend upon the principles which they advocate—members who hold no office and may be disinterested. But we have no political micrometer for measuring the size of this element in each party. More constantly active, as a rule, are the regular and permanent officials of the party, such as the committee members and chairmen (national, state, and local), paid workers, office-holders dependent for their positions upon the party, would-be office-holders looking to it for preferment, editors of partisan newspapers, and representatives of various interests (real estate, commercial, industrial, labor, etc.), which expect favors at its hands.

Once established, the party institution becomes a kind of *imperium in imperio*—a state within the state. It has its constitution, officers, committees, laws, treasury, loyal subjects, and penalties for treason. No one can hope to rise in politics except through the regular channels of some party. An independent citizen who refuses to call himself a party member is looked upon as a "crank" or a "goody-goody." A person who leaves his party and joins another is treated with contempt and scorn by his former colleagues. The vilest words in our political vocabulary are reserved for this type of "deserter."

The spirit of partisanship was accurately reflected long ago in the Richmond *Whig's* editorial on the "no-party man." "We heartily join in desiring the extermination of this pestiferous and demoralizing brood, and will do whatever we can to effect it. . . . Let the Whigs and Democrats everywhere resolve that the gentry who are too pure to associate with either of them or to belong to either party, shall not use them to their own individual aggrandizement. Let them act upon the principle that the Whig or Democrat who has sense enough to form an opinion and honesty enough to avow it is to be preferred to the imbecile or the purist or the mercenary, who cannot come to a decision, or is ashamed of his principles, or from sordid considerations is afraid to declare them."

The party alignment, sharp enough before the Civil War, grew even sharper for a long time after that great crisis, so that political independence or sympathy with any "third-party" principles was regarded as a species of treason coupled with intellectual dishonesty. "The party," says Ostrogorski, "became a sort of church which admitted no dissent and pitilessly excommunicated any one who deviated a hair's-breadth from the established dogma or ritual, were it even from a feeling of deep piety, from a yearning for a more perfect realization of the ideal of holiness set before the believer."

The Roots and Sources of Party Strength

Why is it that party organization has become so minute in its ramifications and so powerful in the United States? To answer that question adequately, one would have to explore the structure of American society; but some of the more obvious reasons are agreed upon and may be enumerated here.

In the first place, the large number of elective offices makes it impossible for the mass of the people to take an active part in selecting candidates and running political machinery.

Wherever elective officers are provided for, devices for making nominations inevitably follow, with a long train of primaries, caucuses, conventions, and committees. Each new elective office adds to the weight, strength, complexity, and immobility of the machine. So party business of necessity falls into the hands of professional workers experienced in the art of managing primaries and elections. Laymen simply cannot direct it.

Even the very structure of our federal system makes party government and strong party organization indispensable if the will of the voters is to be realized. The legislative authority is divided between Congress and the states, so that when a party has a policy which requires action in the two spheres it must seek power in both. For example, if it wants an interstate commerce law, it must go to Washington; for a supplementary measure regulating commerce within the state in a consistent manner, it must turn to the state legislature. Any party which formulates a systematic and national program covering the important questions of our day relative to railways, utilities, labor, conservation, prohibition, and trust regulation must, therefore, include among its plans federal and state projects; and in order to accomplish its ideals completely, it should be strong enough to control state and national legislatures.

The legal separation of executive and legislative powers likewise serves to strengthen party organizations. It puts asunder the two great departments of government, while democracy or majority rule, as now understood, requires their coördination. To take a homely illustration from daily life: no businessman who has made up his mind that a certain thing shall be done would think for a moment of putting the execution of his design into the hands of an agent bitterly opposed to his plan; and yet this is exactly what may, and does often, happen in American politics. It frequently occurs that the legislature is Republican and the chief executive is a Democrat, or vice versa; that is to say, legislators are chosen to make laws which are to be enforced by an executive committed to a violent opposition to those very measures.

In order that popular government may freely and smoothly function, it is necessary that those who have decided upon a certain public policy should control not only the makers of the law, but also the principal officials charged with its execution. In England this fact is frankly recognized in the unwritten constitution; for the executive branch, that is, the Cabinet composed of the heads of departments, is usually selected from the party in the ascendancy in the House of Commons. The makers of the law and those charged with its execution are one. In the United States, however, this union of the legislature and the executive must be secured *outside* the written law; and the party system alone makes it possible. It is the party that assures the nomination of candidates who are in a fair degree of harmony with one another, and who, if elected, can work consistently together in legislative and executive positions to carry out the will of the voters expressed at the ballot box.

Passing outward from the structure of government, which in itself makes for strong party organization, we encounter the "spoils system" as a contributing factor. Civil service reform, of course, has materially reduced the proportion of offices filled by party workers, but there still remains an enormous number of federal and state positions to be divided among the victors. The political appointments subject to the President's orders have an annual value of millions. The multiplication of the functions of state administration has enlarged the appointing power of the governor and the state senate. Every state legislature has at its disposal many offices and positions adapted to partisan purposes, usually free from civil service control. For example, there are sergeants-at-arms and assistant sergeants-at-arms, principal doorkeepers, first and second assistant doorkeepers, journal clerks, executive clerks, index clerks, revision clerks, librarians, secretaries, postmasters, janitors, stenographers, and messengers to the various committees and assistants first and second, too numerous to mention. Then there are city offices, high and low, steadily multiplying in number, and, in spite of the civil service restrictions, within the gift of the political party that wins at the polls. Finally there are the election officers, a veritable army of inspectors, ballot clerks, and poll clerks for the primary and regular elections, who derive anywhere from $10 to $50 a year for their services. Every large city annually pays thousands of dollars to the officials who preside at primaries and elections.

Party machines are strengthened by huge levies on the candidates. Generally speaking, no one can hope to be elected to office to-day without being nominated by one of the political parties. The party organization wages the campaign upon which his victory hangs. What is more natural and just than the demand that the candidate shall help to pay the legitimate expenses of the undertaking? It is a regular practice, therefore, for party organizations, state and local, to collect tribute from candidates for nomination as well as from nominees to office—ordinarily in proportion to the value of the office they seek. There are in addition levies on office-holders after election, sometimes in spite of laws forbidding them. Office-holders do not always wait to be pressed by political managers in this matter. It is not expedient.

The construction of post offices, harbors, parks, school buildings, highways, and other public works yields revenues to the party organization which controls the official agencies in charge of letting contracts. High bids may be accepted on the condition that the surplus shall go to the war chest of the party or to its leaders. The capitol building and grounds at Albany cost New York nearly $25,000,000 and the plunder of the Pennsylvania treasury during the erection of the capitol at Harrisburg is a notorious chapter in history.

More important, as an economic factor, than the spoils of office are the large sums of money secured by party organizations from private interests and distributed by their officers and workers. Perhaps the most fruitful source of revenue for political treasuries during recent years has been contributions from business corporations—even though prohibited by federal law and by many states. They must all apply to some government, national, state, or municipal, for the right to come into existence in the first place, and for the right to extend their charter privileges in the second place. They are subject to constant regulation by municipal councils, state legislatures, or Congress (possibly by the three agencies); they may be compelled to do things which cost them large sums of money or to abstain from doing things which are highly profitable. In these circumstances, corporations often find it cheap to pay party "bosses" for favors and immunities. With a kindred concern for practical ends, industrial companies which thrive under protective tariffs often "insure themselves against free trade" by contributing generously to party war chests. Equally real though very elusive is the collection of party revenues in return for the official protection of gambling, liquor selling, and vice in various forms. The extent to which these sources of funds are exploited at any time by any party cannot, of course, be easily ascertained; but authenic documents show that in the not distant past huge tributes for political treasuries have come from government protection of those who violate laws.

Sometimes private interests affected by governmental action give money to parties to secure favors or prevent regulations really designed for public welfare. Sometimes they are forced to contribute, are "blackmailed," by party leaders under threats of punitive legislation if they do not "come across." On many occasions, they have given money to both the leading parties with a view to getting a "friend at court" without fail.

Leaving the economic realm for that of social psychology, we are on a less secure ground in searching for the secrets of party power, but here too are factors which contribute to the strength of political organizations. From the days of de Tocqueville to our own time, foreign observers have noted that the people of America are given to the formation of associations of every kind. There are in the United States literally thousands of lodges, orders, and fraternal societies; there are political, social, benevolent, religious, and reform organizations without number. It is a rare American who is not a member of five or six.

The causes of this zeal for association are obscure, but it may be attributed in part to the ferment of opinions in a democracy. Anyone who gets a new idea or a variant on an old one wants to start a society to spread it. The phenomenon has also been attributed by some acute foreign observers to the weakness of the individual and the power of the mass where theories of equality prevail. Since levelling doctrines are professed and no aristocracy is legally recognized, the individual who refuses to associate on equal terms with all other members of the community is an object of curiosity if not suspicion. If he must live by a trade or profession, he cannot hope to succeed as long as he refuses to join lodges and organizations.

Like a church or any other society, the political party may be used as a fellowship through which valuable acquaintances may be made and business, clients, or patients secured. This social power of the party organization enables it to entrench itself by drawing into its ranks the best energies and talents of young people who, though by no means devoid of idealistic motives, cannot be blind to the stern necessities of the struggle for existence. In some cities, it is well for the young lawyer practicing in certain courts to be known as a prominent worker in the party to which the presiding judges belong. A Democratic doctor in a strongly Republican district of a Northern city would doubtless find his rise in the world somewhat handicapped if he were overzealous in the support of his party, and a belligerent Republican lawyer in a Southern community might very well find his business limited to practice in federal courts. The subtle insinuations of party control are doubtless more powerful than the gross influences which appear on the surface.

Quite as elusive, and yet substantial, is the influence of the press and propaganda. Nearly all newspapers are partisan in their views; even the independent journals are usually controlled by men affiliated with parties. Most political editorials are written with a bias or a view to party advantage and the news itself is colored more or less by party opinions, for the emphasis given to events, the headlines, and the methods of treatment reflect particular interests. During campaigns especially, the political atmosphere is charged with propaganda—printed, written, and oral. Gossip, damaging or favorable to candidates, sweeps like a whirlwind through party clubs and organizations. With decided insight, someone has said that a party is "a great political whispering gallery."

Last, but not least, an effective practice contributing to party strength is the assistance given to voters by the machine. Political leaders and workers favor the poor by a thousand charitable acts. They give outings, picnics, clambakes, and celebrations for them; they help the unemployed to get work with private corporations or in governmental departments; they pay the rent of sick and unfortunate persons about to be dispossessed; they appear in court for those in trouble, and often a word to the magistrate saves the voter from the workhouse or even worse; they remember the children at Christmas; and, in short, they are the ever watchful charity agents for their respective neighborhoods. A kind word and a little money in time of pressing need often will go further than an eloquent sermon on civic virtue. Thus politics as it operates through party organization is a serious and desperately determined business activity; it works night and day; it is patient; it gets what it can; it never relaxes.

Money in Politics

Parties, as we have just seen, are and must be great economic organizations. Under our prevailing system of popular elections thousands and even millions of voters must be reached through various agencies—such as the press, meetings, post offices, telegraph, radio, and party workers. Huge expenditures are necessary even for legitimate purposes, to say nothing of bribery direct and indirect. To win party nominations for offices in large jurisdictions, individual aspirants and their supporters must make considerable outlays of money, and to win elections party organizations as well as candidates must do likewise, if they have any formidable competitors. Here the American theory of democratic equality absolutely breaks down in fact. Although it is not true that the longest purse is always victorious, it is certainly true that without a purse of some kind to aid him no citizen can expect to win the office of President or a seat in Congress.

Ordinarily, as we have said, money for such expenditures comes from four prime sources—disinterested persons of wealth, office holders, office seekers, and citizens engaged in economic undertakings which may be benefited by action or inaction on the part of the government. Attempts to raise large sums through petty contributions by the masses have never been crowned with success. Inevitably this brings about a concentration of immense power in the hands of a relatively small number of people with riches at their command. And many investigations, not to say scandals, have revealed a wide-spread use of money by individuals and groups in primaries and elections—money derived from donors economically interested and sometimes expended in a fraudulent manner. In recognition of such facts, the most advanced states have enacted elaborate campaign-practices laws and Congress has tardily but gingerly dealt with the subject. Federal legislation in this field is of four types.

First of all Congress has imposed certain limits on the collecting and giving of money in connection with elections. According to the terms of a law originally passed in 1883, no Senator, Representative, or federal officer may solicit or receive any contribution, subscription, or assessment from any officer, clerk, or other employee drawing a salary from the national treasury. Thus an effort was made to dry up one of the prime sources of political funds. Cut off from this assistance, political leaders came to rely more and more on the contributions of great financial and industrial corporations. To counter the new movement Congress has made it unlawful for any national bank or any corporation whatever to make any money contribution in connection with elections at which presidential and vice-presidential electors, Senators or Representatives are chosen; furthermore, candidates, political committees, and all other persons are forbidden to receive any direct financial aid from such sources.

While attempting to bar the collection of political funds from three interested groups in society—office holders, national banks, and all other corporations, Congress has placed limits on the amount which candidates for the Senate and House may spend in elections. In no case can they exceed the sum set by state legislation in this relation. In the absence of a state law fixing a smaller figure, a candidate for the Senate may spend $10,000 and a candidate for the House of Representatives $2,500. However, if the size of the constituency permits it, this amount may be increased —to a figure secured by multiplying by three cents the total number of votes cast at the last general election for all candidates for the position in question; that is, for Senator or Representative. Even then, no matter how large the vote, no candidate for the Senate may spend more than $25,000 and no candidate for the House more than $5,000.

But highly significant exceptions must be recorded. In summing up all his expenditures under the federal limit, a candidate may omit outlays for his necessary personal, travelling, and subsistence expenses. He may likewise leave out of the reckoning money spent for stationery and postage, for distributing circulars, and for telephone and telegraph services. Also excepted from the return are all assessments, fees, and charges levied on him under the laws of the state in which he resides.

Meagre as are the provisions of federal law on political

contributions and the amount of expenditures, they are still more meagre with respect to the purposes of outlays—the uses which may be made of money and other objects of value in elections. It is unlawful for any candidate for Congress to offer directly or indirectly any public or private employment in exchange for support or promise his influence to secure such employment on this condition. It is likewise unlawful to offer to make or to cause to be made any expenditures to any person with a view to inducing him to vote for or against any candidate or to withhold his vote. The acceptance as well as the tender of money for these purposes is also prohibited. In some measure, no doubt, the paucity of federal limitations on the uses of money is due to the fullness of state laws dealing with bribery and other corrupt practices in elections.

A further restraint on the collection and disbursement of money is supposed to be afforded by federal legislation providing for the publicity of campaign funds. Every candidate for Senator or Representative must file with the secretary of the Senate or the clerk of the House, as the case may be, both before and after election, statements showing in detail contributions received in support of his candidacy and itemized expenditures made by him or by any person with his knowledge and consent. And curiously enough he must add a statement of pledges or promises made by himself, or with his consent, relative to the offering of public or private employment in exchange for support.

Besides requiring candidates for Congress to file reports of their outlays, the law also prescribes publicity for political committees. Included within the scope of the statute is every committee, association, and organization which accepts contributions or makes expenditures for the purpose of influencing or attempting to influence the election of Congressmen or presidential or vice-presidential electors in two or more states. The law does not stop here. It also applies to every other committee, association, or organization engaged in influencing elections, whether it operates in more than one state or not, if it is a branch or subsidiary of a national committee, association, or organization—excluding duly constituted state and local committees of political parties. All political committees covered by this legislation must file periodically fully itemized statements giving receipts and expenditures. The list must show in great detail the purposes as well as the dates and amounts of the outlays.

After the above described federal legislation respecting the use of money in elections was consolidated and amended in 1925, some of the most extraordinary scandals in the long history of campaign funds occurred. Coupled with independent criticism from the outside, the discussion of these scandals in Congress raised anew the question of providing a complete national code regulating and restricting the use of money in politics. In this relation numerous deficiencies in the existing laws have been pointed out and remedial bills proposed.

Perhaps the greatest gap in federal legislation is the total exclusion of primaries from the scope of public control. The publicity law of 1911 covered them as well as elections, but the Supreme Court in the Newberry case in 1921 ruled that the power of Congress to regulate the manner of holding elections did not extend, at the time of the enactment in question, to senatorial conventions and primaries. Subsequently Congress, in consolidating the corrupt practices acts, expressly provided that the term "election" does not include a primary or convention of a political party. Yet it is doubtful whether this exception is now required by the Constitution. In the Newberry case just cited only four of the nine judges of the Supreme Court agreed that Congress had no jurisdiction over primaries. Another judge, who joined them in holding invalid a part of the law, called attention to the fact that it was passed previous to the adoption of the Seventeenth Amendment providing for popular election of Senators, and then reserved judgment as to whether the authority of Congress in this respect had not been increased by the later change in the Constitution. Hence the power of

Congress over primaries and political conventions is clouded with uncertainty.

And yet in a large number of cases it is the primary, not the election, that counts in the choice of Senators and Representatives. Whenever one political party continuously dominates a state, as for example the Democrats in Alabama or the Republicans in Pennsylvania, the real fight is over the nomination; the election is secure. It has been estimated that in a majority of the congressional districts the chief contest is the primary. It was in the primaries of Pennsylvania and Illinois that a large part of the enormous expenditure was incurred, which led to the exclusion of two men from the Senate on grounds of corruption or misuse of money. To clear the way for federal control over primaries, an amendment to the Constitution has been proposed, vesting in Congress supervision over nominations as well as elections.

A second criticism of the present corrupt practices legislation bears upon the clause which exempts from the limits fixed on expenditures money disbursed by candidates for stationery, postage, printing, personal uses and publicity in general (except for newspapers and billboards). Under this rule a candidate may spend as much as he pleases for effective campaigning—letters, telegrams, and circulars, for instance. Thus outlays for most of the purposes which may be called "legitimate" are in fact not at all restricted in amount and the man with a long purse is given a decided advantage.

Besides leaving the candidate absolutely free to spend as much as he likes for such publicity purposes, the law allows his friends to pour out money independently on his behalf without rendering any accounting whatever. It is in this connection that some of the worst abuses have arisen. Frequently it is not the candidate but some powerful economic interest behind him that is responsible for huge outlays in primaries and elections. As long as the candidate himself is not held personally responsible for all expenditures in support of his contest from start to finish and as long as the amount is not strictly limited, wealth has a decided advantage in every campaign.

Through another hole in the federal law money may creep. Political committees may have large deficits in their funds at the end of the campaign and may raise the money to meet these deficits long after the period for making public their accounts of the election has expired. As Senator Cutting once remarked: "A contribution made to a preëlection fund would have been in the nature of a gamble, but a contribution made to a deficit and particularly to a deficit of the party which had been successful in the election was simply putting . . . money over the counter and getting a return for the investment. That is a danger which is not dealt with under our present statutes at all." This practice was illustrated in connection with the campaign of 1920 when a big deficit in the Republican fund was covered by Mr. Harry Sinclair who was later charged with fraudulently obtaining oil leases from certain politicians assisted by his contributions. Mr. Sinclair stated at the time that he did not know whether he was a Republican or a Democrat, but at all events, for good and sufficient reasons, he staked his money on the winning horse.

In addition to having these defects the law is weak on the side of enforcement. The provisions for publicity are not effective. Statements of campaign receipts and expenditures are carelessly filed in irregular form, they are not published, and after a period of two years they may be destroyed. Most of them merely accumulate dust. Eager newspaper reporters may dig out certain figures that will make news or a sensation but as a rule candidates and committees can be fairly sure that little will be heard or known of their "public" statements. While the national committees of the great political parties report in detail, other political committees and associations and many candidates for Congress are, to say the least, extremely careless in making their returns. It is doubtful whether the news of their publicity statements often reaches their respective districts. In this relation the law has no teeth.

Furthermore, no agency is responsible for enforcing its terms. A defeated candidate may attack his opponent in the federal courts for some infraction, but there is no permanent machinery to investigate charges of irregularity. Committees on elections in both houses and special committees for inquiring into campaign expenditures do go into specific cases as they arise or make hurried searches when scandals break out, but they are almost always partisan in character and concerned primarily with immediate issues. It is not the business of any non-political federal officer or establishment to maintain constant scrutiny over the operations of the election laws.

From these criticisms it follows that any thorough-going revision of the corrupt practices acts should include primaries and conventions as well as elections within the scope of the law. It should fix limits to all expenditures, define the purposes for which they may be made, place full responsibility for disbursements on candidates and committees, and abolish exemptions in accounting for campaign outlays. If publicity is to be more than a farce then provisions must be made for giving effect to it in a form that will reach the voters. Deficits present a knotty problem but committees that incur them can be made accountable and conditions may be prescribed for meeting unpaid bills. With reference to the matter of enforcement, Senator Cutting has proposed the creation of an election commission to audit accounts, investigate credentials, deal with contested cases, serve as a fact finding body, and report the results of its inquiries to Congress for final determination.

If the defects in the present laws are cured by new legislation, the problem of money in politics will not be entirely solved. Indeed there are many observers who hold that it cannot be solved until the use of private money in primaries and elections is forbidden entirely. But this involves heroic action. Especially, it would throw upon the Federal Government the burden of providing machinery by which aspirants and candidates could present their claims to constituents on an even plane at public expense. It will take more thought than has yet been given to the subject to evolve a scheme that will place the long head on a parity with the long purse. Perhaps it can and may be done. But no matter what restraints the law might put on the use of money in elections it cannot by that process separate economics from politics.

The Party and Public Opinions

Powerful as it is, sustained by enormous funds, supported by a loyal press, fed by lust of office and domination, the political party is nevertheless sensitive to that elusive force known as public opinion. Since the rise of democracy, statesmen and writers have paid tribute to this "electric fluid." In one of his essays, Macaulay marvels at the way an idea arises in the brain of a single thinker, kindles the enthusiasm of a few disciples, spreads to a respectable minority, conquers a majority, and is finally accepted as a truth so universal that none ventures to question it. Employing a figure of his own Woodrow Wilson compared the forming of public opinion to a mountain spring that trickles out into a rivulet, widens with accumulations, and at length rushes forth like a torrent sweeping everything before its irresistible flood. Nor can it be said that these are mere allegories founded on no facts of experience. History is full of conforming illustrations—from the appearance of Christianity to the latest hour. And all the engines of modern civilization—the press, the telegraph, the cable, the radio, and compulsory education—serve to facilitate the process of disseminating opinions.

With religious fervor and assured faith in democracy, orators are wont to say that the voice of the people is the voice of God. If right is forever on the scaffold and wrong forever on the throne, exclaims the poet, still the scaffold sways the future and behind the dim unknown standeth God within the shadow keeping watch above his own!

Running counter to such divine optimism are numerous theories ranging from scorn to laughter. Thomas Carlyle never grew tired of expressing a low opinion of the masses—democracy with its agitations, caucusing, and ballot boxing. According to his philosophy, the people do not make history; that is the function of great men—leaders, warriors, thinkers, and writers—and the multitudes are mere pawns in the hands of Caesars and Napoleons. Since this was true, he argued, to collect the verdict of the English people, "mostly fools," at the polls was sheer nonsense—dangerous nonsense besides. Yet Carlyle himself preached "the golden gospel of silence," as John Morley said, "in thirty volumes" with a view to influencing the very millions he seemed to despise. Taking another tack, the British dramatist, George Bernard Shaw, applying his biting wit to the theme, once declared that falsehood, not truth, rules the world, that ideas are powerful in proportion to the error they contain; men are really not born free and equal but this doctrine from the Declaration of Independence rings around the world.

With a more scientific equipment, other writers, European and American—Prins, Christensen, Benoist, Michels, and Lippmann—subject public opinion to a merciless analysis with conclusions likewise critical if not devastating. In a composite view, drawn from the writings of this school the people are a mob, their theories are mainly delusions, and public opinion is a "phantom." Most of the time the masses are asleep; when they are aroused they are swayed by blind passions or crude doctrines and slogans. In reality they have no views of their own but are dominated by propaganda—the press, the radio, the pulpit, and a thousand other agencies in the hands of governments and powerful private interests. Two great dictators of the twentieth century, Lenin and Mussolini, started on the assumption that the masses are incapable of ruling and that democracy is a farce. In support of such findings it is common to cite the propaganda of the World War by which certain ideas—frequently falsehoods—were so firmly implanted in the minds of the populace that they became fixed "stereotypes" inspiring hatred, fury, and destruction.

Somewhat less pessimistic than other thinkers in this school of disillusionment, Walter Lippmann holds that after all the masses may play a limited rôle in the governing processes, although the public, which is supposed to direct the course of events, is a "mere phantom." The people are not without virtue or intelligence, he holds, but no one, not even the ablest, is omnicompetent, equipped with the insight and information necessary for wise decisions on all the complicated questions of government in our bewildering age of technology. With respect to these questions there is not one public, but many; some people are interested in one thing, others in something else. Hence ordinarily the affairs of government are run by a few adepts and manipulators. Only occasionally, and usually in a crisis, does a public, composed of a portion of the people thoroughly aroused, actually intervene—interfere with the specialists who are managing the game. "When power, however absolute and unaccountable, reigns without provoking a crisis, public opinion does not challenge it. Somebody must challenge arbitrary power first. The public can only come to his assistance. That, I think, is the utmost that public opinion can effectively do. With the substance of the problem it can do nothing usually but meddle ignorantly or tyrannically."

While rejecting "the public" as a "phantom," Mr. Lippmann allows limited functions to special groups formed from time to time. Public opinion, he says, is not the voice of God or of society, but of "interested spectators of action;" and the "opinions of the spectators must be essentially different from those of the actors." It is when men take a position in respect of the purposes of others, he continues, that they are acting as a public. "And the end of their action in this rôle is to promote the conditions under which special purposes can be composed." With direct reference to politics, "the public does not select the candidate, write the platform, outline the policy any more than it builds the automobile or acts the play. It aligns itself for or against somebody who has offered himself, has made a promise, has produced a play, is selling an automobile."

After stating this premise Mr. Lippmann goes on to add, "it is the function of public opinion to check the use of force in a crisis, so that men driven to make terms, may live and let live." To speak summarily, the business of the world is managed by men of affairs, interested groups, who often come into conflict with one another; the public is too distracted and too poorly informed to take an intelligent part in their disputes; but in a crash a special public may intervene to help effect a compromise or balance among the contestants, may in a word apply a kind of emollient to the points of friction to restore a workable harmony.

Without denying the force of the general indictment, it would be running counter to innumerable facts of experience to admit the whole case presented by the critics of the public and its opinions. When they assume, as some of them do, that a monarch or a ruling class is a better depository of wisdom than the masses, a caveat may be entered without any democratic bias. The fate of such monarchs and classes from the dawn of civilization in the Nile Valley to the latest hour would seem to indicate defects in their reasoning powers p. 16). After all, as the Germans say, world history is the world court—the tribunal of last appeal and its verdict on classes is as severe as its judgment on masses. It is even harsher, for whole classes are destroyed while the masses seem to go on forever.

If, to consider a variant on individual and class monopoly of wisdom, Carlyle's great-man theory of history is explored, other difficulties are encountered. Within recent times, at least, no dominant personality has been divorced from mass movements and opinions. Every high director or dictator embodies in some measure the *Zeitgeist*—the spirit of his age. Napoleon without the rush of the French revolution, Bismarck without the inner strivings of German millions for unity, Lincoln without the anti-slavery sentiment of his time, Lenin without the discontented proletariat and peasantry of Russia, Mussolini without the struggle of the Italian bourgeois against Bolshevism, would simply be unthinkable. All great figures of history whose opinions have come down to us have viewed themselves as the agents of destiny as well as the makers of events. Unless nameless thousands among the unknown masses cherish favorable inclinations and sentiments, the greatest man is powerless; Mahomet born in Indiana might be a plowman or a prohibition agent. Conceding for the sake of argument that the opinions of the "mob" cannot come to a focus without leaders, even so, the conclusion must be that the two factors in history-making are inseparable parts of the same thing. Hence arguments as to their respective merits and powers are a form of useless logomacy.

To a limited extent this conclusion applies to Mr. Lippmann's theory that a few inside manipulators nominate candidates, write platforms, and run governments, with occasional interferences, particularly in crises, by special publics. These manipulators—actors, he calls them—do not lift themselves into place by their bootstraps or operate in a vacuum after they are installed. Doubtless he is right when he says that there is no "public" as such, no unified "will of the whole people" but only special publics with reference to various problems and situations. Exceptions may be taken, however, to his contention that such publics intervene mainly in crises and then merely to help allay disturbances with a view to returning again to their former indifference.

Society is indeed made up of many publics, but they are operating more or less continuously. Their influences permeate the inner chambers where candidates are chosen, platforms are composed, bills drafted, and executive decisions taken. The wisest politician is one who knows when to yield or appeal, what he can "put across," what the marginal voters necessary to his triumph are thinking and feeling. Here again relations are reciprocal: the manipulator helps to make public opinion—on some matters he may make most of it, but at the same time historic opinions and present opinions, flooding in upon him, enter into the make-up of his mind and the course of his decisions. Nor is it wholly correct to say that public opinion may function best as a kind of soothing syrup to compose distresses and conflicts. It often swings powerfully to one side or the other and forces a revolution in affairs—in the Civil War in America for example. Moreover working underground and on the surface, creeping here, seeping there, it brings important ideas to fruition;—consider in this relation the movement of the special public opinion which forced the income-tax provision into the Federal Constitution and made that fiscal device a fundamental part of the American revenue system.

Undoubtedly many special publics fail to accomplish anything; many theories are defeated in the conflicts of the forum, though seldom without changing the attitude of the victors. But the opinions, patterns, stereotypes, illusions, and follies of multitudes, for good or ill, do condition very fundamentally the operations of all the chief actors in the political drama.

CHAPTER V

THE FEDERAL JUDICIARY

IN their literary arrangement of the Constitution, the Fathers relegated the judiciary to Article III, thus placing it after Congress and the President, but an economic and legal revolution has made a radical shift in the old balance of power. Although Chief Justice Jay thought the Supreme Court would never command the authority it deserved, that tribunal really stands now at the head of the Government of the United States. In a special sense it is the guardian of the whole federal system because on appeal in due course it may declare void acts of all other public agencies in the Union, low and high, from the village council to the Congress at Washington. Unlike the courts of most other countries it is not a creature of the Government but stands on an independent basis. Beyond its decisions there lies no appeal save to the cumbersome process of amendment.

Constitutional Position of the Federal Courts

The brief Article of the Constitution dealing with the judiciary makes only a slight reference to the number and structure of the federal tribunals. It merely states that the judicial power shall be vested in one Supreme Court and such inferior courts as Congress may from time to time ordain and establish. Thus Congress is given authority to determine the number of judges appropriate to the Supreme Court and to create additional tribunals. For the judges of all the regular courts, however, the Constitution seeks to maintain a high degree of independence by assuring them permanence of tenure during good behavior and a compensation for their services which cannot be diminished during their continuance in office.

Although the constitutional provisions respecting the judiciary are not self-executing, an imperative mandate is certainly laid upon Congress to carry them into effect. As a Senator once observed, it would be revolutionary for Congress to omit the organization of the Supreme Court and the construction of inferior courts. Indeed, in discussing the same topic, another Senator went so far as to say that the inferior courts are established as a public necessity and in pursuance of a policy outlined in the Constitution, and cannot be arbitrarily abolished. "Congress has power to create," he declared, "but has no power to destroy. Congress cannot destroy the judiciary any more than the judiciary can destroy Congress. . . . If to-day Congress should pass an act abolishing all the circuit and district courts of the United States without substituting other tribunals in their stead, can there be any doubt that the Supreme Court would declare the act to be unconstitutional and void?" It is difficult to see, however, what the Court could accomplish by holding such a law invalid if no money were forthcoming to pay the salaries of the judges thus released from all duties. Yet out of respect for the principle Congress, in putting an end to the Commerce Court in 1913, retained the members of that tribunal as circuit judges.

Still to some extent the federal courts are at the mercy of Congress. While it cannot abolish the Supreme Court at one stroke, cut the salaries of the acting judges, or remove any of them except by the process of impeachment, it may by a circuitous route effect a revolution in the composition of the Court. It may reduce the number of judges by providing that on the death or resignation of any of them the vacant post shall be abolished; then at the proper moment it may increase the number of judges to secure the appointment of men known to entertain certain views on the constitutionality of particular measures. As to the inferior courts, Congress has gone even further. In 1802, during Jefferson's administration, it repealed the law of the preceding year creating sixteen circuit judgeships which President Adams had filled with Federalists at the close of his term. Moreover, Congress can prevent certain classes of cases from coming before the Supreme Court by refusing to provide a system of appeals; this has been done on one occasion. It has even been suggested that Congress might require a vote of more than a mere majority of the judges to set aside a federal statute; but this idea has been assailed by lawyers as unconstitutional in itself. In the main we may say that, except in times of crisis, the federal judiciary enjoys a high degree of independence from legislative interference.

An additional guarantee is afforded by the method of selection. All federal judges are nominated by the President and appointed by and with the advice and consent of the Senate. With regard to the inferior courts, this rule is a matter of custom rather than of express command. The Constitution merely stipulates that the President and Senate are to appoint the judges of the Supreme Court and authorizes Congress to vest the appointment of such "inferior officers" as it thinks proper in the Presidnet alone, in the courts of law, or in the heads of departments. But by uniform practice, it is settled that the judges of the lower federal tribunals are not "inferior officers" whose appointment should be taken from the President and Senate and vested in some other authority. Unlike most other officers, federal judges can only be removed by impeachment.

The National Judicial Power

The jurisdiction of the federal courts as a whole is defined in the Constitution. It embraces two broad classes of cases; those affecting certain *parties* or *persons* and those relative to certain *matters*.

With reference to the former, federal jurisdiction covers all cases pertaining to ambassadors, other public ministers and consuls; controversies to which the United States is a party; controversies between two or more states, between a state and citizens of another state, between citizens of different states, and between a state or the citizens thereof and foreign states, citizens or subjects. To this generalization an exception must be made, namely, that the judicial power does not extend to any suit in law or equity commenced or prosecuted against any state in the Union by an American citizen or by a citizen of a foreign country. It must be noted also that, in actions coming within federal jurisdiction, corporations are citizens although for other purposes they may be deemed persons. When parties enumerated above are involved in actions at law their cases may come under federal judicial authority, even though the Constitution and laws of the United States are not at all drawn into controversy. So much for the jurisdiction of the federal courts over parties to actions at law.

Regardless of the parties involved, federal judicial power extends to certain *matters,* that is, to all cases in law and equity arising under the Constitution, the statutes, and the treaties of the United States and to admiralty and maritime questions. Under this head a proper case is made, says Story, "when some subject touching the Constitution, laws, or treaties of the United States is submitted to the courts by a party who asserts his rights in the form prescribed by law." But it need not always be taken into a federal court; state courts hear many cases involving federal law, subject to appeal.

Except with regard to two classes of cases, the Constitution does not say which of the federal courts shall have jurisdiction over any particular party or matter; it leaves to Congress the distribution of the judicial powers among the courts. The two exceptions, noted below, are cases affecting ambassadors, other public ministers, and consuls and those in which a state is a party. Evidently, therefore, Congress has a large freedom in determining what courts shall hear various classes of cases and in fixing limitations on the right of appeal from one to another.

The Structure and Business of the Courts

Under these constitutional mandates, Congress has created a hierarchy of federal tribunals. At the head is the Supreme Court composed of nine judges, a Chief Justice, paid twenty thousand five hundred dollars a year, and eight Associate justices with salaries of twenty thousand dollars. This Court holds its sessions usually from October until May in the chamber of the Capitol formerly occupied by the United States Senate—pending the construction of the new building for which Congress has made provision. Concerning the actual duties of the Supreme Court the Constitution says little. It confers on that tribunal original but not exclusive jurisdiction over all cases affecting ambassadors, other public ministers, and consuls and those in which a state is a party; that is, as far as the Constitution is concerned, such cases may be carried before it in the first instance without having been heard previously in a lower court. But in all other cases the jurisdiction of the Supreme Court is appellate, subject to such exceptions and regulations as Congress may see fit to make.

Hence it may be said that the language of the Constitution throws a very dim light on the actual jurisdiction of the Supreme Court—on the substance of the business which comes before it for decision. For information on this point it is necessary to examine the laws of Congress stretching back over more than a century to the great Judiciary Act of 1789. In general the later laws, especially the highly significant Judiciary Act of 1925, reveal a striking tendency to diminish the obligatory duties of the Court and to widen its discretionary authority. To speak concretely the classes of cases which can be carried up on appeal, as a strict matter of right, from state and lower federal courts are now limited mainly to matters involving the constitutionality of state and federal laws and the regulation of economic enterprises. It is the discretionary power of the Court which is broad and flexible. It has wide authority to hear petitions for the writ of *cer-*

tiorari asking it to call up, review, and determine cases tried or pending in lower courts for "special and important reasons" governed by "sound judicial discretion." Although the hearing of such petitions consumes a large amount of its time, the Court nevertheless, under legislation limiting its obligatory jurisdiction, escapes hundreds of cases and so is free to pick and choose the weighty matters upon which it wishes to pass. It occupies, therefore, a position somewhat analogous to a king in council who keeps high powers in his hands to be exercised whenever great issues are at stake.

In all this there is nothing theoretical. The effect of the narrowing of obligatory jurisdiction is statistically revealed in comparative tables presented by Frankfurter and Landis in their epoch-marking volume on the business of the Supreme Court. According to their figures, a noteworthy decline has occurred in the amount of ordinary private and common law litigation. On the other hand a great increase has taken place in cases involving state and federal control over trusts, railways, labor, and other economic matters and cases affecting the constitutionality of state and federal statutes, which are also frequently concerned with regulation of economic enterprises. For example the annual number of common law cases before the Court fell from eighty-one in 1875 to eleven in 1925; while cases calling for the construction of federal legislation rose from zero to twenty-nine and those touching the regulation of economic undertakings from zero to twenty in the same period. As these authors rightly conclude: "The Supreme Court is the final authority in adjusting the relationships of the individual to the separate states, of the individual to the United States, of the forty-eight states to one another, and of the states to the United States. It mediates between the individual and the Government; it marks the boundary between state and national action."

Now the exercise of the jurisdiction conferred upon the Supreme Court makes necessary two types of intellectual operations, one pertaining to large issues of public policy and the other to questions of technology. In the former instance the Court is controlled only by the general language of the Constitution which, as a judge once remarked of a particular clause, is characterized by "convenient vagueness" (p. 22). Speaking of problems under this head, the authors just cited remind us: "The words of the Constitution on which their solution is based are so unrestrained by their intrinsic meaning or by their history or by tradition or by prior decisions, that they leave the individual Justice free, if indeed they do not compel him, to gather meaning not from reading the Constitution but from reading life. It is most revealing that members of the Court are frequently admonished by their associates not to read their economic and social views into the neutral language of the Constitution. But the process of constitutional interpretation compels the translation of policy into judgment, and the controlling conceptions of the Justices are their 'idealized political picture' of the existing social order."

The second type of intellectual performance mentioned above, namely, that pertaining to technology, is invited in innumerable railway and utility cases. Frankfurter and Landis give a few illustrations. "What constitutes a 'spur track,' when public convenience justifies a railroad extension or abandonment, under what condition one railroad must permit use of its facilities by a rival, how far the requirements of a state for the abolition of grade crossings depends upon approval by the Interstate Commerce Commission, these and like questions cannot be answered by the most alert reading of the Transportation Act. Their solution implies a wide knowledge of railroad economics, of railroad practices and the history of transportation, as well as political philosophy concerning the respective rôles of national control and state authority." Even more complicated issues may arise in patent litigation forcing the Supreme Court to review the development of difficult technical processes and inventions and to pass upon matters that might well baffle the most skilled chemist, physicist, or engineer. Of such diverse materials is the business of the Supreme Court composed.

A case as presented to the Court is an action between two parties. It appears in the form of a statement of law and facts involved in the controversy, supplemented by briefs and arguments of attorneys supporting the contentions of their respective clients. When a case has been submitted, it is the duty of the justices to consider the issues and to apply the law. After each judge has examined the matter independently, a conference is held at which the various points are discussed at length and a decision is reached, if necessary by a majority vote. Thereupon the Chief Justice either prepares, or requests one of his colleagues to prepare, a document called "the opinion of the court," which contains a line of reasoning, citations of authorities, and the final order in the disposition of the affair. This "opinion" is subjected to careful scrutiny and, after revision, it is printed and placed on record. Any judge, who agrees with the decision, but bases his conclusion on other grounds than those put forward in the official argument, may prepare what is called a "concurring opinion," in which he explains how he arrives at the same end. In some instances, therefore, a majority of the Court may agree that a particular controversy shall be decided in a certain way, but each justice may assign different reasons for the judgment.

It is also the practice, if there is a diversity in views, for the judges who are not in accord with the ruling of the majority to file a "dissenting opinion," setting forth their reasons for believing that the case should have been decided otherwise. Occasionally each of the dissenters prepares his own statement; sometimes one of them writes an argument which is concurred in by his colleagues. Such protests, of course, are not law but they are by no means futile gestures. Often in the drift of time they are accepted by the majority of the Court and made the basis for reversing earlier decisions. At all events powerful nonconformist discourses, such as those of Justice Holmes and Justice Brandeis, are widely read by lawyers and enter into public consideration of federal jurisprudence—become a part of the thought of the land which in the long run affects the law of the land. Since many great cases are decided by a narrow vote of five to four, it can readily be seen that a slight change in the composition of the Court may transform a dissent into an official declaration.

All opinions rendered by the Supreme Court are published in the *United States Reports,* and at the present time the decisions for a single term of the Court may fill three or four volumes. They furnish a great authoritative source of information on the historical development and present status of constitutional law.

At the bottom of the regular judicial hierarchy is the federal District Court. To bring such a tribunal within easy reach of litigants, Congress has divided the country into numerous districts and provided a federal court for each of them. In the sparsely settled regions, a state may constitute a single district; but the larger and more populous states are laid out into two or more districts. New York, for example, has four. The number of judges assigned to a District Court also varies from place to place according to the magnitude of the business to be handled. If a district is very big it is in turn laid out into "divisions," and arrangements are made for holding terms of the Court in each of them at stated times of the year.

The matters which may be brought to trial in a federal District Court are so various in character and so complicated that they can only be successfully mastered by the practicing lawyer whose duty it is to discover the proper forum into which his client's business may be taken and reviewed. Among other things the jurisdiction of this tribunal embraces all crimes and offenses cognizable under the authority of the United States, cases arising under the internal revenue, postal, and copyright laws, proceedings in bankruptcy, and actions involving the laws which govern the immigration of aliens, contract labor, and monopolies in restraint of trade.[1]

[1] In addition to this regular hierarchy of courts, Congress has created from time to time special courts. There is a Court of Claims composed of a chief justice and four associate judges whose duty it is to hear claims against the Federal Government. If it decides that a certain amount of money is due from

Between the Supreme Court and the District Courts is a Circuit Court of Appeals in each of ten great circuits into which the United States is divided. Where the amount of litigation is large, the Circuit Court consists of four or five judges; in other places, of three. To each of the ten regions a Supreme Court Justice is assigned, but he no longer "rides the circuit" as in former times. As its position in the judicial system indicates, the prime function of the Circuit Court of Appeals is to provide for the review of appeals from the District Courts and to relieve the Supreme Court of a large mass of transactions that would otherwise glut its calendar.

To effect this purpose two fundamental arrangements are made by law. In the first place all appeals from District Courts, with a few substantial exceptions, must go to the Circuit Court of Appeals for the appropriate circuit. The exceptions are cases involving federal legislation against trusts and monopolies, the enforcement of the orders of the Interstate Commerce Commission, the validity of state laws, and a few other matters of special weight; only such controversies may be carried from District Courts directly to the Supreme Court of the United States. In the second place the decisions of the Circuit Court of Appeals in the ordinary run of things are final. However it may ask the Supreme Court for instructions on any point of law and under certain strict conditions causes may be removed from its forum to the highest court of the land. For example the Supreme Court may, on petition of a party affected, call up a case from a Circuit Court and decide the matter itself, just as if the issue had been brought before it by writ of error or on appeal; furthermore, whenever a Circuit Court decides against the validity of a state statute, an appeal may be taken to the Supreme Court. Thus by a sifting process,

the United States to any party, it cannot order payment, but must depend upon appropriations made by Congress. This Court partially relieves Congress of the great political pressure brought on behalf of private claims. Congress has also created a judicial system for the District of Columbia comprising a court of appeals, a supreme court, and minor courts. For special business there are a Court of Customs and Patent Appeals and a Board of Tax Appeals.

as we have said, the Supreme Court gets cases of high economic and constitutional significance.

For more than a century the several regular courts operated separately, and Congress was left largely to its own devices in discovering the needs of the judiciary as revealed by experience. Meanwhile judicial business increased in size and complexity, especially after the adoption of prohibition, taxing the strength and ingenuity of the judges to the limit. Perplexed with their tasks or overburdened with duties, they might respectfully address appropriate congressional committees in search for remedial legislation, but no system existed for coördinating the work of all the courts, making periodical reviews of the number of cases pending, and ascertaining their requirements in the interests of efficiency.

At last in 1922 Congress, in response to obvious necessities, authorized the establishment of a "judicial conference," to be called annually by the Chief Justice, or in case of his disability by the senior Associate Justice of the Supreme Court, and to be composed of one judge from each of the circuits, preferably the senior circuit judge. At these conferences, which are also attended by representatives of the Department of Justice, reports are heard from the several circuits on the state of their business; problems of improving judicial procedure are discussed; and suggestions are made for changes in statutes and court rules. In this way the Chief Justice and Congress may be kept informed respecting the questions and conditions of law enforcement throughout the Union. A further step has been taken in the improvement of judicial administration by an enactment authorizing the Chief Justice, in certain circumstances, to transfer district judges from one district to another temporarily to relieve congestion of business.

Attached to the federal judiciary, of course, is the ancient jury system, so long and so intimately associated with the development of personal liberty in England. The trial of all crimes, except in cases of impeachment, shall be by jury, runs the original Constitution; and to this stipulation are added three provisions in the way of amendment. No person shall be held to answer for a capital or otherwise infamous crime unless on a presentment or indictment by a grand jury, except in certain military cases; in all criminal prosecutions the accused shall have the right to a speedy and public trial by an impartial jury of the state and district in which the crime has been committed; and in suits at common law, where the value in controversy shall exceed twenty dollars, the right of trial by jury shall be preserved. According to statutory prescriptions, however, issues of fact in civil cases in any District Court may be tried without the intervention of jury whenever the parties or their attorneys of record agree to waive the jury by agreement made orally or in writing in due form.

Although the subject cannot be fully considered here it should not be dismissed without a hint as to the problems connected with indictment and trial by juries in the modern age. Issues of fact in civil cases in our technological society are frequently of the highest complexity—patent rights to intricate machinery, causes of death in industries, violations of civil law by industrial corporations, and questions of pure food and drugs, to mention only a few items. Highly trained judges, assisted by masters, referees, and other experts, are often at their wits' ends to discover the nature and merits of issues; and yet under the Constitution trial by a jury of uninformed laymen can nearly always be demanded by either party as a matter of right. With the multiplication of statutory offenses, frequently involving the use of technical apparatus, the delays necessarily imposed by indictment and trial by juries make the swift and efficient administration of justice well-nigh impossible. On all sides the evils of the system are recognized. Many remedies, ranging from minor modifications to abolition, are advanced but as yet there are few signs of change in the historic methods handed down from early centuries when life was simple and crimes were relatively few in variety and number.

The Great Writs and the Rights of Citizens

To aid them in the discharge of their functions, the federal courts may issue certain great writs which affect fundamentally the rights of citizens. First and most famous among them is the writ of habeas corpus, an instrument forged in the long battle over civil liberty in England. This writ is designed to secure to any person imprisoned an immediate preliminary hearing before a court for the purpose of discovering the reasons for his detention and whether they are sufficient in law. It is intended to serve as a protection against arbitrary arrest and imprisonment without full justification, to raise between the citizen and despotic executive authorities the shield of the judiciary.

Within their respective jurisdictions the judges of the various federal courts have the power to grant the writ of habeas corpus in order that inquiries may be made into causes of arrest. This does not mean, however, that a federal judge may issue the writ indiscriminately. He can only employ it when a prisoner is in jail under federal authority or for some act done or omitted in pursuance of a law of the United States or the order of some federal court or judge; or is in prison in violation of the Constitution or some law or treaty of the United States; or is a citizen of a foreign country claiming to be imprisoned for some act committed with the sanction of his government. In other words, a federal judge cannot issue a writ of habeas corpus on behalf of a person who merely claims that he is detained contrary to law in general.

An application for a writ of habeas corpus is made to the proper court by a complaint in writing, signed by the prisoner, setting forth the facts concerning his arrest and the reasons for his imprisonment, if they are known to him, and stating in whose custody he is held. It is the duty of the judge upon request in proper form to grant the writ, unless it is evident from the application itself that the prisoner is not entitled to it under the law. Within a certain time the officer to whom the writ is directed must make due return, bringing the prisoner before the judge and certifying as to the cause of his detention. The court or judge, thereupon, must proceed in a summary way to examine the facts, hear testimony and arguments, and either release the prisoner, if he is detained in violation of the law, or admit him to bail, or remand him for trial if there is warrant for holding him.

The second writ is the writ of mandamus which is employed against public authorities, private persons, and corporations for the purpose of forcing them to perform some duty required of them by law. The mandamus is properly used against executive officers to compel them to discharge a ministerial obligation. But where a duty is purely discretionary and performance depends upon the pleasure of the official or upon his own interpretation of the law, the courts will not intervene. In general, anyone seeking a writ of mandamus ordering a federal officer to fulfill an obligation must show that he has no other adequate legal remedy and that he has a clear, lawful right to have the act in question performed by the authority named. The writ is also often used to compel an inferior court to pass upon some matter within its jurisdiction, which it has refused to hear or decide.

The third great writ is the writ or bill of injunction, which may be issued when no other legal remedy is available. This instrument may be used for several ends. Sometimes it takes the form of a mandatory judicial decree directing some person or corporation to maintain a *status quo* by performing certain acts. Thus, for example, the employees of a railway may be ordered to continue handling the cars of a company which they wish to boycott; in other words, may be instructed to discharge their regular and customary duties while remaining in the service of their employer. Frequently the injunction takes the shape of a temporary restraining order forbidding a party to alter the existing condition of things in question until the merits of the dispute may be decided. Sometimes the writ is in the nature of a permanent injunction ordering a party not to commit a specified act, the results of which cannot be corrected by any proceeding in law. Owing to the frequency with which federal courts have applied the injunction in labor disputes, the problem of limiting its use has become a controversy of politics.

In connection with the exercise of their authority, federal courts, in common with courts in general, have the power to punish private parties for "contempt," entirely apart from labor disputes considered below (p. 507). According to one theory that power extends only to the right to punish for acts which are committed in the presence of the court or have the effect of interfering with the proper conduct of judicial proceedings. Such, indeed, seems to be the spirit of the federal law relative to the issue. In practice, however, judges do fine and imprison critics for spoken or written objections uttered outside the court room and merely casting some reflection on judges themselves. For example, on one occasion, the Comptroller of the City of New York published a letter passing certain more or less severe strictures on the conduct of a federal judge in that city in a particular case and was promptly sentenced to prison by the irate judge. The Comptroller was only saved from jail by a timely pardon issued by President Coolidge. Such cases, which are rather numerous, are responsible for a demand for the curtailment of the power of the courts to act as accusers, judges, and jurors in matters of contempt against themselves committed outside the court room, especially controversies involving criticisms of judicial policies and decisions, which in no way impede the course of justice. It must be remembered that judges, like other persons, have the right to sue people who slander them.

The Power of Passing upon the Constitutionality of Statutes

The jurisdiction of the federal courts extends not only to matters in law and equity in the strict sense; it also includes cases involving the constitutionality of state and federal acts. Nowhere, it is true, does the Constitution expressly provide that the federal courts may declare an act of Congress or of a state legislature invalid. Indeed, some writers hold that the framers did not intend to confer such a power over federal statutes, at least, upon the courts of the United States and that the judiciary has usurped its authority in this regard. Long ago, President Jefferson declared that it was the design of the Fathers to establish three independent departments of government, and that to give the judiciary the right to review acts of the other branches would make it supreme over Congress and the President.

Despite many claims made in their name, it is not possible to discover exactly what was the opinion of all the members of the convention at Philadelphia on this point. The issue was not laid before that body in the form of a definite proposition and was not the subject of a direct vote. Still, it is known that a few of the delegates were opposed to the idea of judicial control, for they expressed such a conviction incidentally while discussing other topics.

On the other hand many members of the convention, either before or after the adoption of the Constitution, indicated their belief that the federal judiciary, in the normal course, should exercise the power to pass upon the constitutionality of laws. Their side of the case was very plainly put by Hamilton in the *Federalist:* "The interpretation of the laws is the proper and peculiar province of the courts. A constitution is, in fact, and must be, regarded by the judges as a fundamental law. It must, therefore, belong to them to ascertain its meaning, as well as the meaning of any particular act proceeding from the legislative body. If there should happen to be an irreconcilable variance between the two, that which has the superior obligation and validity ought, of course, to be preferred; in other words, the Constitution ought to be preferred to the statute, the intention of the people to the intention of their agents." There is good ground for thinking that a majority of the prominent members of the convention took a similar view of the federal judicial power.

Whatever may have been the intention of the framers, Chief Justice Marshall, in the famous case of Marbury *vs.* Madison, decided in 1803, announced with an imperious wave that the Supreme Court, under the Constitution, possesses the power to hold federal statutes void when they conflict with the fundamental law (p. 31). Although there were some protests at the time from objectors, they made little stir, especially as the measure which Marshall declared invalid was of no great importance and the Court did not attempt to nullify another for more than fifty years.

In the early days of the controversy respecting the judiciary far more attention was paid to the power of the Court over acts of state governments. For a long time Marshall's practice of striking down state statutes was ardently resisted by Jefferson and other defenders of states' rights. They admitted the supremacy of the Constitution within its domain, but they argued that to give the Supreme Court the right to determine the validity of state laws would in fact enable the Federal Government to define its own sphere of sovereignty and reduce the states to mere administrative subdivisions. However, the leaders of this opposition party did not offer any adequate plan for amicably settling disputes between federal authorities and state governments over their respective limits of power. Nor did they advance any efficient scheme for obviating the endless complications that would arise from conflicting decisions in the state courts respecting matters of federal interest if no final tribunal of appeal gave uniformity to them. The logic by which the federal judiciary secures its right to pass upon the validity of state legislation is as compelling as that applied in the case of federal statutes.

At all events, Congress has provided by law various ways for testing in the federal courts the correctness of state actions. For example, a case may be taken to the Supreme Court of the United States from the highest court of a state having jurisdiction over the cause, whenever the latter denies the validity of a federal treaty or statute or any exercise of authority in the name of the Government of the United States. A case may also be taken to the Supreme Court whenever a state court of final jurisdiction declares that a state law or an act done under state authority does or does not violate the Constitution or laws of the United States.

To make the process of testing the constitutionality of a state statute clear, let us examine a concrete case. The legislature of New York once passed an act providing that no employees should be required or permitted to work in bakeries more than sixty hours a week, or ten hours a day. One Lochner, an employing baker of New York, claimed that this statute interfered with rights which he enjoyed as a citizen under the Constitution of the United States, and resisted its enforcement. His case was carried to the highest court in the state of New York, which upheld the measure in question. Since this ruling was against privileges which he claimed, Lochner appealed to the Supreme Court of the United States and won from that tribunal a favorable decision, holding the law in controversy void, as contrary to certain provisions of the federal Constitution.

In deciding against the validity of any statute, federal or state, the Supreme Court does not officially annul the measure in question; it merely declares it void and refuses to apply it in the particular case in hand. Thereupon, the executive department of the Federal Government, or of the state government, as the case may be, simply drops the enforcement of the law; and various officials and courts concerned take cognizance of the fact in due course.

All actions of the federal courts in this relation are in the nature of judicial proceedings. They take notice of the constitutionality of a statute only when the matter is brought to their attention in the form of a case involving the rights of parties to a suit. In no instance will federal judges consider the validity of a law in the abstract or render any opinion either to Congress or to the President on the constitutionality of a proposed measure. This rule was adopted early. In 1793 Washington sought the advice of the Supreme Court by laying before that body twenty-nine different questions, which the Court respectfully declined to answer on the ground that it could give opinions only in regular cases properly brought before it in the ordinary course of judicial proceedings. Federal practice in this regard, therefore, differs from that in some of the states.

Political Controversies over Judicial Decisions

In exercising the power to declare acts of Congress and laws of the states unconstitutional, the federal courts inevitably become involved more or less in political controversies. An important statute usually reflects the policies of a political party; often it is the fruit of a long and ardent agitation. If it is set aside by the courts, warm feelings are naturally aroused. Although the courts, in declaring an act void, seldom depart from the serene and austere logic of the law, they do in fact pass judgment upon the wisdom of the measure under scrutiny. Theoretically, they do not say what the law ought to be; they merely proclaim the Constitution as it is. Practically the matter is not so simple, for the language of the federal Constitution in some particulars, as we have said (p. 22), is very general. Phrases such as "necessary and proper," "due process of law," and "privileges and immunities" may be interpreted in many ways according to the theories, prejudices, and preconceptions of the judges. When a chemist resolves a substance into its elements, he performs an act about which there can be only one opinion; when judges look into the Constitution of the United States and try to discover whether it authorizes a state legislature to fix the hours of labor in a bakeshop at sixty per week or empowers Congress to regulate railway rates, they are dealing with a matter about which the good and true may rightly differ. In such cases the judges themselves often disagree; five think the Constitution means one thing and four think it means something else. What the judges really do in these circumstances, leaving all quibbling aside, is to say whether they believe a particular act of Congress or state law is wise and expedient or not—that is, wise according to their notion of the facts and contentions involved. No doubt the courts are a great conservative force in our government, and their decisions may be defended on conservative grounds; but the exercise of their powers necessarily raises political difficulties.

Broadly speaking these controversies fall into two classes. The first includes those arising out of cases in which the Supreme Court invalidates state laws. In recent times controversies respecting cases of this character have arisen over social and labor measures enacted by state legislatures and nullified by the Supreme Court, particularly under the "due process" clause of the Fourteenth Amendment (p. 661). In such disputes, it is the wisdom of the Court, rather than its power, which is usually drawn in question.

A second type of controversy has grown out of decisions of the Supreme Court setting aside acts of Congress. An exercise of this authority may involve large national questions, and on several momentous occasions it has dragged the Supreme Court into partisan hostilities. Perhaps the most famous of all these conflicts occurred in connection with the celebrated case of Dred Scott (1857), in which Chief Justice Taney, of Southern origin, sought to accomplish the impossible feat of settling the slavery issue by a judicial discourse. In principle Taney held that Congress had no constitutional warrant for abolishing slavery in the territories of the United States. But at the very moment, the new Republican party was staking its hopes and gaining strength on the contention that Congress had full power in the premises and should immediately exercise it.

Owing to the excitement over the slavery question which prevailed at the time, Chief Justice Taney's opinion precipitated a widespread and bitter struggle in the political forum. Naturally, Southern leaders accepted his dictum as final.

In the North, however, it aroused a storm of protest, and the legislatures of several states passed resolutions condemning his doctrines enunciated in the name of the Court. Maine, for example, expressed her views in the following legislative declaration:

Whereas, such extra-judicial opinion subordinates the political power and interests of the American people to the cupidity and ambition of a few thousand slaveholders, who are thereby enabled to carry the odious institution of slavery wherever the national power extends, and predooms all territory which the United States may hereafter acquire by purchase or otherwise to a law of slavery as irrepealable as the organic constitution of the country; and

Whereas, such extra-judicial opinion of a geographical majority of the Supreme Court is conclusive proof of the determination of the slaveholding states to subvert all the principles upon which the American union was formed, and degrade it into an engine for the extension and perpetuation of the barbarous and detestable system of chattel slavery: Therefore—

Resolved, that the extra-judicial opinion of the Supreme Court in the case of Dred Scott is not binding in law or conscience upon the government or citizens of the United States and that it is of an import so alarming and dangerous as to demand the instant and emphatic reprobation of the country.

Resolved, that the Supreme Court of the United States should, by peaceful and constitutional measures, be so reconstituted as to relieve it from the domination of a sectional faction. . . .

On reading Taney's epoch-making opinion, Lincoln, who was to wage war and sacrifice slavery to preserve the Constitution, at first regarded the decision with moderation, but he refused to accept it as the last word on slavery in the territories. Two or three months after it was rendered, he declared his belief in, and respect for, the judicial department of the Government, saying that its decisions should control the policy of the country until reversed by some lawful process. "We think the Dred Scott decision is erroneous," he declared to his neighbors at Springfield. "We know the court that made it has often overruled its own decisions, and we shall do what we can to have it overrule this. We offer no resistance to it." But in the heat of the fray he grew more belligerent. A year later, in a speech at Edwardsville, he exclaimed: "Familiarize yourselves with the chains of bondage and you prepare your own limbs to wear them. Accustomed to trample on the rights of others, you have lost the genius of your own independence and become the fit subjects of the first cunning tyrant who rises among you. And let me tell you, that all these things are prepared for you by the teachings of history, if the elections shall promise that the next Dred Scott decision and all future decisions will be quietly acquiesced in by the people."

Furthermore, Lincoln accepted without reserve the declaration of the Republican platform on which he stood for the presidency in 1860: "The new dogma that the Constitution, of its own force, carries slavery into any or all of the Territories of the United States, is a dangerous political heresy, at variance with the explicit provisions of that instrument itself, with contemporaneous exposition, and with legislative and judicial precedent; is revolutionary in its tendency and subversive of the peace and harmony of the country."

After he had been elected, he did not allow the case to rest. On the contrary, in his inaugural address, he presented a reasoned review of the issues involved and gave a clear intimation that the people were not irrevocably bound by the decision. To use his own words: "I do not forget the position, assumed by some, that constitutional questions are to be decided by the Supreme Court; nor do I deny that such decisions must be binding, in any case, upon the parties to a suit, as to the object of that suit, while they are also entitled to very high respect and consideration in all parallel cases by all other departments of the Government. And while it is obviously possible that such decision may be erroneous in any given case, still the evil effect following it, being limited to that particular case, with the chance that it may be overruled and never become a precedent for other cases, can better be borne than could the evils of a different practice. At the same time the candid citizen must confess that if the policy of the Government upon vital questions affecting the whole people is to be irrevocably fixed by decisions of the Supreme Court the instant they are made, in ordinary litigation between parties in personal actions, the people have ceased to be their own rulers, having to that extent practically resigned their Government into the hands of that eminent tribunal. Nor is there in this view any assault upon the Court or the judges. It is a duty from which they may not shrink to decide cases properly brought before them and it is no fault of theirs if others seek to turn their decisions to political purposes." In the end fate justified Lincoln and the Republican party. Slavery was abolished not only in the territories but also throughout the Union.

It was the Democratic party that was to raise the next serious controversy over a judicial action, nearly forty years after the Dred Scott case. In 1895 the Supreme Court, by a narrow vote of five to four, declared unconstitutional the fundamental parts of the federal income-tax law passed by a Democratic Congress during the preceding year—a law avowedly designed to shift a part of the burden of federal taxation from goods consumed by the masses to "accumulated wealth." When the Democratic national convention assembled in 1896, feelings ran high among the radical elements against the action of the Court, especially as it flatly reversed a previous opinion upholding Republican income-tax legislation. It was openly said that the Court had discriminated against the poor in favor of the rich. At the same time popular indignation was intensified by a conflict over the use of injunctions by the federal courts in labor disputes (p. 507). Profoundly stirred by these tendencies, leaders in the Democratic party, such as Governor Altgeld of Illinois, protested vehemently against the income-tax decision and the injunction, and carried their objections to the convention.

In response to their demands, Senator James K. Jones, as chairman of the committee on resolutions, brought in a platform containing two sharp attacks on the federal judiciary: "We declare that it is the duty of Congress to use all the constitutional power which remains after that decision, or which may come from its reversal by the Court as it may hereafter be constituted, so that the burdens of taxation may be equally and impartially laid, to the end that wealth may bear its due proportion of the expenses of the government." Then referring particularly to the recent railway strike in Chicago, the platform added: "We denounce arbitrary interference by federal authorities in local affairs as a violation of the Constitution of the United States and a crime against free institutions, and we especially object to government by injunction as a new and highly dangerous form of oppression by which federal judges, in contempt of the laws of the states and rights of citizens, become at once legislators, judges, and executioners."

In vain did Senator Hill of New York protest against these planks, denouncing them as foolish, ridiculous, unnecessary, revolutionary, and unprecedented in the history of the party. With fierce directness, William Jennings Bryan, in his "crown of thorns and cross of gold" speech, replied to Hill in defense of the party's position: "They criticize us for our criticism of the Supreme Court of the United States. My friends, we have made no criticism. We have simply called attention to what you know. If you want criticism, read the dissenting opinions of the court. That will give you criticisms. They say we passed an unconstitutional law. I deny it. The income-tax was not unconstitutional when it was passed. It was not unconstitutional when it went before the Supreme Court for the first time. It did not become unconstitutional until one judge changed his mind; and we cannot be expected to know when a judge will change his mind."

With this turn in fortune's wheel, Republican leaders now assumed the rôle of defenders of the Supreme Court. Democratic attacks on the decision in the income-tax case they denounced as assaults on fundamental American institutions. The proposal to reconstruct the Court and secure a reversal of the opinion they assailed as an attempt to drag the judiciary into the mire of politics. Although for a time after the victory of McKinley the sound of the conflict died away, the issue did not disappear. In fact the question remained open until the Sixteenth Amendment to the Constitution displaced by orderly procedure the opinion of the Court and gave to Congress the power which that tribunal had denied.

In our own day the position of the judiciary in the American political system was again drawn into controversy during a heated debate in the Senate in connection with the elevation of Charles E. Hughes to the Supreme Court early in 1930. While the high standing and personal integrity of the nominee was not denied by any opponents, it was said by his critics that the Court was already dominated by a majority of conservatives and that the appointment of Mr. Hughes would add another powerful weight to that side of jurisprudence. In taking this line of argument, Senator Norris declared: "No man in public life so exemplifies the influence of powerful combinations in the political and financial world as does Mr. Hughes. . . . During the past five years he has appeared in fifty-four cases before the Supreme Court. Almost invariably he has represented corporations of almost untold wealth. . . . During his active practice he has been associated with men of immense wealth and has lived in an atmosphere of luxury which can only come from immense fortunes and great combinations. . . . It is only fair to say that the man who lives this kind of life, whose practice brings him wealthy clients and monopolistic corporations seeking special governmental favor, it is reasonable to expect that these influences will become a part of the man. His viewpoint is clouded. He looks through glasses contaminated by the influence of monopoly as it seeks to get favors by means which are denied to the common, ordinary citizen. . . . Such men should not be called upon to sit in final judgment in contests between organized wealth and the ordinary citizen."

To arguments of this character, which were repeated with embellishments in detail, vigorous replies were made on the other side. In upshot, the defenders of Mr. Hughes, including by implication the Court, admitted that his clients had been, in the main, rich men and corporations, but insisted that the fact was not germane to the issue. "Mr. Hughes," said Senator Gillett, "attracted as clients the great business interests of the country. They are the ones that naturally demand the highest talent; that can pay for the highest talent; and every great lawyer necessarily has them as his clients . . . However, to say that he thereby accepts their business principles and that thereby his state of mind is so affected that afterwards he cannot sit as an impartial judge, I think, is a very mistaken conclusion. I do not agree that the arguments of a lawyer in a case which he is prosecuting is at all a guide as to his decisions upon the bench when he may have to pass upon similar cases. An advocate is compelled to present to the court his side of his case with all the strength of his talent, but when he is appointed to the bench, then he exercises his judicial temperament and passes upon the merits of the case." After a long dispute in these and similar terms, the Senate approved the appointment of Mr. Hughes, closing this chapter in the development of the judiciary. But within a few months another was written by the Senate in rejecting the nomination of Judge Parker of North Carolina to the supreme bench on various grounds including his alleged conservatism.

Some obvious conclusions come from a dispassionate review of the judicial conflicts which have occurred in our history. Criticism of the federal judiciary is not foreign to political contests. No party, when it finds its fundamental interests adversely affected by judicial decisions, seems to hesitate in expressing derogatory opinions; the wisest of our statesmen have agreed on the impossibility of keeping out of politics any decisions of the Supreme Court which are political in their nature. Finally, in spite of the attacks of its critics and the fears of its friends, the Supreme Court yet remains a very strong tower defending the American constitutional system.

Still, the exercise of the "judicial veto" continues to produce periodically a crop of suggested reforms, especially as the judges of the Supreme Court are so often divided in their opinions, five to four. The most radical scheme proposes to abolish entirely the power of the courts to pass upon the validity of acts of Congress—a project which calls for an amendment to the Constitution. A second plan is to provide by statute that the vote of six or seven out of nine judges be required to nullify a law; but it is highly probable that the Court would declare such a law void as invading its right to determine its own procedure; hence an amendment might be necessary in this case also. A third proposal, frequently discussed, is a constitutional measure permitting Congress to repass a law invalidated by the Court and give effect to it in spite of the adverse judicial decision. Thus a "judicial veto" would be treated very much as a presidential veto. While it is not probable that any of these schemes will be carried out, at least in the near future, the student of politics will always find judicial controversies among the staple issues of politics and should be prepared to understand them in their historic setting.

Law Enforcement

Upon the courts and their coöperating officials, especially in the Department of Justice, falls a large share of the responsibility for the enforcement of law; and their burdens in this connection are steadily increasing. Trials of offenders against legislation prohibiting the manufacture and sale of intoxicating liquors for beverage purposes crowd the calendars of the lower tribunals and important issues arising from this source are often carried on appeal even to the Supreme Court, adding to its perplexities. But this is merely a minor phase of the problem. The startling rapidity in technical development has multiplied the amount of business in hand and made it as complex as physics and chemistry. New devices, such as the radio and airplane, call for regulation, licensing, and inspection, and make it necessary for the courts to deal with intricate questions raised by enforcement and violations. Moreover, the task of upholding the standards imposed in the public interest with respect to an increasing number and growing variety of machines, appliances, and substances, including foods and drugs, is in itself nothing short of gigantic. Even a casual survey of the law books reveals hundreds of pages of federal statutes and executive orders dealing with technological operations in the terms of natural science and throwing upon the courts, in final analysis, the duty of interpreting and enforcing a huge volume of technological jurisprudence. Many of the chapters that follow illustrate the generalization in detail.

Significant as this is, it is only one side of the enforcement problem. The same technical development which has revolutionized government and business enterprise has placed at the disposal of criminals in the underworld new tools for the commission of old offenses and opportunities for the invention of odd crimes. Here we find in fact a regular race between law officers and offenders struggling for supremacy. The latter are constantly devising novel schemes for breaking through the net thrown around them by marshals, inspectors, and detectives. In smuggling, for example, the aim of the operator is to cross the border without detection. To the old methods, afoot, on horse, or afloat, technology has added others more romantic. The airplane is extensively employed in this sphere because it cannot be searched while in flight and by following a lonely course may elude the sharp eyes on the main paths. Indeed one convict released from prison almost penniless is alleged to have amassed a fortune of $5,000,000 in five years by using airplanes to carry on illegal activities in the liquor business. But the engineering staffs of the underworld have not been content with such easy exploits. Taking a hint from naval history, they recently fitted out on Lake Champlain a fleet of submarines for the purpose of smuggling goods between Canada and the United States. According to reports, the "submarine navy" served its owners well before a few mishaps led to its discovery and capture. Yet such spectacular undertakings represent efforts

Photo by Brown Brothers

FEDERAL SCIENTISTS UNEARTHING TRICKS OF THE SMUGGLER'S TRADE AT THE PORT OF NEW YORK.

Photo by Brown Brothers

The Climax of a Two Days' Search: Prohibition Enforcement Officers Discover 3000 Cases of Liquor under a Cargo of Coal.

in only one small corner of the underworld. Wire-tapping, machine-guns, photographic counterfeiting, these and many other "advances" show that technical "progress" has penetrated all strata of society. In any case, this development throws new burdens of enforcement on the courts and law officers.

The work of discovering offenders against federal law and bringing them before the courts is distributed among several distinct organizations of the Government with a personnel totalling more than 20,000. Only one of these agencies, the Department of Justice, has general authority to enforce the whole body of federal legislation. The head of this Department is the Attorney General of the United States, who is the chief law officer of the Federal Government. "He represents the United States in matters involving legal questions; he gives his advice and opinion when they are required by the President or by the heads of the other executive departments on questions of law arising in the administration of their respective departments; he appears in the Supreme Court of the United States in cases of especial gravity and importance; he exercises a general superintendence and direction over the United States attorneys and marshals in all the judicial districts in the states and territories; and he provides special counsel for the United States whenever required by any department of the government." In a strict sense, therefore, execution of federal laws depends in a large measure upon the activities of the Attorney General, or rather upon the policy of the President expressed by him.

Coöperating with the Department of Justice and subject to its general direction is a large corps of federal authorities scattered throughout the Union. Each judicial district has a United States district attorney, with one or more assistants, who represents the Government in the prosecution and defense of causes arising within his jurisdiction. Each judicial district also has a marshal and deputy marshals whose duty it is to arrest offenders against federal law, carry out orders of the courts, and otherwise aid in judicial administration.

Since these attorneys and marshals are appointed by the President and Senate and may be removed by the President alone, they too are subject to immediate direction from the center.

Besides local officials in every judicial district, the Department of Justice has a separate enforcement branch of its own, the Bureau of Investigation, with agents in all parts of the country, generally free from geographical ties. These scattered representatives report periodically to the central office where threads of evidence from various communities are compared to determine whether a case is merely a small infraction or an incident in a widespread plot. The Bureau does not work alone. It keeps in touch with other federal police agencies and it coöperates with various public authorities, both here and abroad, in the identification of fugitives from justice. Through a Division of Identification and Information it maintains a clearing house of data on criminals for the use of the police everywhere in the nation. More than two million one hundred thousand fingerprints, together with other valuable information on crime and criminal methods, are concentrated in the Division—a powerful aid not only to the Bureau but also to law officers, federal and local.

Supplementing the activities of the Department of Justice, as a rule independently, are several special agencies which concentrate their attention on the enforcement of particular laws and regulations or on certain types of offenses. An important phase of this policing is the patrolling of our national boundaries and seaports. The Department of Labor, for example, has many representatives assigned to the task of arresting aliens who attempt to enter the United States in violation of law. The Prohibition Bureau in the Department of Justice, in addition to its domestic duties, keeps men stationed on the borders to prevent the illegal entry of liquor; while the Customs Service, powerfully aided by the Coast Guard, performs a similar function in connection with the general smuggling of goods. Owing to the thousands of miles of sea line and land boundaries to be watched, the protection of the frontiers is an undertaking of almost staggering proportions.

In connection with its internal operations, the Federal Government also maintains a number of separate police forces. Thus the Treasury Department, through its secret service, is constantly engaged in suppressing the counterfeiting and forging of United States money and securities. Since enormous amounts and many varieties of paper currency, coins, Liberty Bonds, and other evidences of property are now in circulation, a technical knowledge of the appearance and contents of such issues is essential to law enforcement in this sphere. The Post-Office Department, too, through a staff of inspectors, not only keeps watch over the administration of its own affairs but seeks to apprehend offenders against the postal laws and regulations in detail. It is a part of their duty to arrest mail robbers, as well as persons using the mails for illegal purposes including fraud. In view of the complexities involved, these divisional police authorities, acquainted with the characteristic problems of a single service, are a useful adjunct to the general force. Ordinary law officers cannot be expected to have the skill and ingenuity necessary to deal with crimes that are highly technical in nature.

Nevertheless a continual dispute is waged over the relative merits of a general and special police. Offsetting the superiority of the latter in limited fields many practical disadvantages are cited. For instance, the secret service agents of the Treasury Department are not empowered to apprehend men who violate laws that do not concern that branch of the Government. With a criminal almost in his hands, an agent of the Department finds that forgery is not involved, that he has been shadowing a gangster who has robbed a post-office; then he must stop work and report to the police concerned with such offenses, perhaps discovering that in the meantime his prey has disappeared. Evidently here is a clear opportunity for coördination. By enlarging the powers of divisional police and permitting them to deal with border-line cases, the advantages of technical training and general authority might be combined.

Such issues, however, are subsidiary questions in the broad problem of law enforcement which, when examined closely, spreads out in every direction through the courts, agencies of detection, procedure in trials, and society at large. Recognizing the gravity and difficulties of the situation, President Hoover appointed in 1929 a National Commission on Law Enforcement and Observance, headed by George W. Wickersham, former Attorney General, and charged it with the duty of inquiring deeply into the whole subject. In a preliminary report made the following year, the Commission, besides advancing certain recommendations concerning prohibition, warned the public against a quick and easy solution. "To reach conclusions of any value," it said, "we must go into deep questions of public opinion and the criminal law. We must look into the several factors in the attitude of the people, both generally and in particular localities, toward the laws in general and toward specific regulations. We must note the attitude of the pioneer toward such things. We must bear in mind the Puritan's objection to administration, the Whig tradition of 'a right of revolution,' the conception of natural rights, classical in our policy, the democratic tradition of individual participation in sovereignty, the attitude of the business world toward local regulations of enterprise, the clash of organized interests and opinions in a diversified community, and the divergence of attitude in different sections of the country and as between different groups of the same locality."

In investigating forms and procedures, the Commission must deal with delays and evasions due to indictment by grand jury and trial by jury, to technicalities of trials, to endless appeals, to cumbersome judicial methods, and to the pressure of petty business as well as great interests on the courts. At the center of the discussion will be found a fundamental issue: how far is it possible to maintain in a technological age the individualism and the judicial practices appropriate to an era of agriculture and villages? Law enforcement is an integral part of the whole process of government sketched in this volume, and efficiency in that sphere, as elsewhere, depends largely upon the substitution of scientific for customary and traditional methods of operation.

Federal Prisons

To house the increasing number of offenders found guilty of violating federal law, the Government maintains several prisons, for example, at Atlanta and Fort Leavenworth, under the supervision of the Bureau of Prisons in the Department of Justice. The army of condemned is so large, however, that the federal institutions frequently cannot find room for all the grist ground out by the judges. In such cases, the surplus convict population is distributed among county and local jails and cared for under contracts with the communities in question. According to a report of the Superintendent of Prisons, approximately one thousand jails were used for this purpose in 1929. Certainly this is unfortunate. With federal penitentiaries overcrowded and hundreds of prisoners committed to the charge of local jailers, it was impossible for the federal authorities to establish and apply to the whole body of offenders under their jurisdiction the most advanced principles of penology.

Profoundly disturbed by this state of affairs, the Seventy-first Congress passed a series of bills designed to improve the facilities and management of federal prisons. One of these, signed on May 14, 1930, established a Bureau of Prisons in the Department of Justice, and made it responsible for controlling all federal penal and correctional institutions, except military prisons, and for providing "suitable quarters" for all civilians convicted of offenses against the United States. The head of the Bureau may contract with states and territories or their political subdivisions for the subsistence and care of federal convicts under definite conditions and, if he cannot secure suitable or sufficient quarters, he may select sites and authorize the erection of buildings for the confinement of prisoners. This measure was supplemented a few days later by another empowering the Attorney General to construct two new institutions of enormous capacity for male offenders. A third act in the series directed the Attorney General to build a new hospital for prisoners who are insane or afflicted with incurable or chronic degenerative diseases, making possible a more effective segregation. Thus it is hoped to eliminate many of the evils of overcrowding which have long plagued the Government.

In connection with the administration of federal prisons, the pressing question of the employment of inmates has naturally arisen. Here, as in the states, popular opposition, especially among trade unions, is encountered to "convict labor"—to the employment of prisoners in the manufacture of goods that come into competition with the output of free labor. The problem is thorny. To keep great bodies of men and women in total idleness is injurious to discipline and unfair to the victims. To employ them in making any kind of goods, even for prison use, throws them into conflict with workers outside of the institutions. To let them out on contract at low wages to employers engaged in general industry is to defeat the ends of justice in every direction. After considering all these difficulties, the Federal Government adopted many years ago the policy of utilizing convicts to produce supplies for its own purposes and then only on prison grounds.

As a part of its penal reform program mentioned above, Congress enacted in 1930 a comprehensive law governing the employment and training of federal prisoners. The new statute makes the Attorney General responsible for providing occupations for able-bodied inmates of federal penal and correctional institutions "in such diversified forms as will reduce to a minimum competition with private industry or free labor." He may make the services of such prisoners available to the heads of departments for building and repairing roads paid for by the Government, clearing and reforesting public lands, and constructing public works financed wholly or in major part from the Treasury of the United States. He may also establish industries in the several institutions for the manufacture of goods for sale to the departments and establishments of the Federal Government, but not for sale to the public in competition with private enterprise, or in such a way as to curtail production within the present limits of any navy yard, arsenal, or workshop of the Government. And in establishing these industries, the Attorney General shall give attention to employments which will afford a useful training to prisoners so that they may earn a livelihood more readily on their release. As an incentive to good work there may be a reduction of the term of sentence of each prisoner proportioned to the length of his employment in such government undertakings.

Imprisonment under any conditions has decided limitations as a means of enforcing law, protecting society, or reforming individuals. Hence federal authorities confront serious questions of administration in this sphere. Among the various devices adopted by them is a system of probation and parole under which convicts are released and permitted to live a normal life among their fellow citizens subject only to supervision. Until the completion of his sentence, an offender granted that privilege is expected to maintain good behavior and, failing this, he may be placed in prison. But the sound execution of the policy calls for constant watchfulness, requiring periodical visits to each person at large or at least frequent reports from him. If a careful check is kept, the custom is useful in practice, for it relieves the "housing load" on the jails and permits the gradual re-introduction of offenders to a normal routine instead of dumping them suddenly upon society at the close of their term. On the other hand, if the control is loose, the ends of punishment are defeated.

By action too long delayed it is now provided that federal judges having original criminal jurisdiction may place any offender found guilty of a crime not punishable by death or imprisonment for life on probation under such terms and conditions as they may see fit to impose. They may also appoint probation officers to look after men and women on parole, but such officers must serve without compensation except in special cases to be determined by the judge in question. As things stood in 1929 these agents were few in number and overburdened with work. One of them, for instance, had 1,738 cases under his care, and if he had tried to interview each of his charges once a month he would have been compelled to hold about sixty conferences a day—an obvious impossibility. Although the probation law passed by Congress the following year made no radical changes in the system already in force, it did provide for closer supervision by the Attorney General, and marks a step in advance on the way to an obligatory as distinguished from a largely voluntary scheme. The system is also strengthened by a collateral Act of 1930 creating a single Board of Parole to take over the functions formerly discharged by the Attorney General and various local boards in connection with parole administration. All in all the new penal legislation represents a decided awakening of public opinion to one of the outstanding social problems of our time.

CHAPTER VI

The Structure of Congress

Historical and practical considerations are responsible for the division of Congress into two chambers—the Senate in which each state in the Union has two members and the House of Representatives apportioned among the several states according to their respective numbers, counting all persons including aliens—except Indians not taxed. At the time the Constitution was framed, Rousseau's doctrine that all people are politically equal and alike and entitled to the same share in government was not generally accepted in the United States. It is true the Declaration of Independence announced that men are created equal and that governments derive their just powers from the consent of the governed; but this theory did not control the framers of the Constitution in devising the national legislature. They had to deal with a condition, not a theory, and the condition was not at all hypothetical in nature.

Under the Articles of Confederation, all states stood on an even footing in the Congress, and the delegates of the small states in the constitutional convention would not agree to a new plan of government unless their old status was preserved in one branch of the legislature. The adoption of the equality principle in the creation of the Senate was a result of their insistence. On the other hand, the movement for the formation of the Constitution was particularly sponsored by the larger states and they would not federate unless they were given a weight in the legislature proportioned to their numerical strength. Underlying this controversy were important economic facts. The more populous section of the country, the North, was commercial in interest, while the sparsely settled region, the South, was primarily agricultural. The division of Congress into two houses based on different principles of representation was, in part at least, the result of an effort to balance these economic powers in the Federal Government. Another consideration entering into the arrangement was the fear of majority rule which the Fathers entertained. It was their thought that a bi-cameral organization would act as a brake on hasty legislation, that the Senate would function as a conservative check on the "turbulence of democracy" likely to appear in the popular branch, the House of Representatives. Indeed attempts were made in the constitutional convention to have the Senate represent the wealth of the country but no agreement could be reached on any specific plan. Accordingly the Congress is based on population and on states as political entities.

The House of Representatives

Since the number of members in the House is related to population, a variable factor, it is not fixed by the Constitution. Its determination is left to Congress subject to two limitations, namely, that each state must have at least one member and that the total shall not exceed one for every thirty thousand inhabitants. Though apparently simple, agreement upon the exact figure is not a matter of theory because it is connected with the question of apportionment. In this relation the Constitution, as we have just said, provides that Representatives shall be distributed among the several states according to their population, including all persons except Indians not taxed. It also directs that the enumeration of the inhabitants shall take place every ten years and by implication that an apportionment shall occur after each census is completed. On principles of courtesy the territories and certain insular possessions of the United States are permitted to send delegates to the House of Representatives, who may speak on matters concerning their districts without enjoying the right to vote on measures in Congress (p. 684).

The membership of the first House was fixed at sixty-five

and the figure has been almost steadily increased until it now stands at 435. Even so, with the growth in the population of the country, the average number of inhabitants for each congressional district has risen from about thirty-three thousand in 1793 to more than two hundred and eighty thousand. When the time for reapportionment arrives, Congress is strongly tempted to add members to the already unwieldy assembly. Those states whose population has not increased object to having their quota of members reduced in order that the growing states may have the proportion due them under a fixed numerical rule.

After the census of 1920 the conflict over apportionment led to a deadlock which was not broken until the time for the next census arrived, thus resulting in a violation of the spirit if not the letter of the Constitution. In essence this dispute revolved around the mathematical rule to be applied in distributing members and several variables of a sectional and partisan nature. Strictly speaking, Representatives cannot be apportioned among the states according to population, unless by an impossible accident the number of persons in each state should happen to be exactly divisible by the quotient obtained by dividing the total population of the country by the number of members which Congress establishes. In every case, when the population of a state is divided by the quotient thus reached, there are fractions, large or small, left over which are not "represented."

During the ten-year controversy to which reference has been made many issues were injected into the discussion. The old question of applying the Fourteenth Amendment to the Southern states was raised anew. That Amendment provides that when any state denies the right to vote to any male citizen, otherwise qualified, in certain elections, its basis of representation in Congress "shall be reduced in the proportion which the number of such male citizens shall bear to the whole number of male citizens twenty-one years of age in such state." Under this rule the states which in fact disfranchise Negroes or other male citizens by property, literacy, or any tests whatever should have their representation proportionately reduced. A second scheme, advanced as a counterblast in the interest of the South, proposed the exclusion of aliens when counting the number of persons in each state for the purposes of assigning Representatives—a suggestion clearly unconstitutional, for the units of apportionment are "persons," not citizens. This, of course, struck at the industrial states of the North in which the foreign population is chiefly concentrated.

Both schemes failed. In providing for the census of 1930 Congress stipulated that for an indefinite future the existing number of members of the House, namely, 435, should remain unchanged. It also directed the President to report to the short session of Congress following the completion of each decennial census three projects for the allocation of seats. If the Congress fails to enact legislation for reapportionment in the short session, then one of the President's plans for the distribution of members—that based on the last preceding apportionment—automatically goes into effect commencing with the next Congress.

In the beginning of its history, Congress simply assigned to each state a quota of Representatives and left it free to decide whether they should be elected at large on a general ticket or should be distributed among districts within its borders. In 1842, however, this practice was abandoned. Every state having more than one Representative is now required by federal law to create a congressional district for each member allotted to it; all districts must be composed of "contiguous and compact territory containing as nearly as practicable an equal number of inhabitants;" and only one Representative is to be chosen in each district. Nevertheless if the state declines to carry out this provision with respect to new seats assigned to it after a reapportionment, the additional members to which it is entitled shall be elected at large.

Notwithstanding the clear intention of Congress to provide for substantially equal congressional districts, the state legislatures have succeeded in creating, principally for partisan purposes, gross inequalities. By this abuse of power, known as "gerrymandering,"[1] the political party dominant in the state at the time makes its vote go as far as possible in congressional elections and causes that of its opponent to count for as little as possible. To accomplish this design it masses the voters of the opposing party in a small number of districts, giving it an overwhelming majority in each, and so marshals its own voters that they can carry a large number of districts by slight majorities. Gerrymandering is responsible for some very curious political geography. In one of the Southern states there was once a famous "shoe string" district which ran through a large part of the state and counteracted the effect of the Negro vote. At another time there was an equally famous "saddle bag" district in Illinois, in which many Democratic counties were linked together in a strange assembly, assuring the Republicans safe majorities in the neighboring regions.

Gerrymandering is partly responsible for the great variation in the number of people for whom the several Representatives in Congress speak, but it does not account for other striking discrepancies. Limitations on the suffrage, especially in the South, and the exclusion of alien residents from the suffrage everywhere, make the differences in the number of voters—eligible and active—even more glaring than differences in population. For example, in 1924, the Representative of the second congressional district in Georgia spoke for 2217 voters while the Representative of the seventh district of Illinois spoke for 79,782 voters. It must be remembered, however, that the number of votes actually cast will vary according to the character of the contests; if one party normally has an overwhelming majority in a district, there may be no

[1] The term "gerrymander" originated in Massachusetts. It appears that Elbridge Gerry, a distinguished Democratic politician of his day, was instrumental in redistricting his state in such a way that one of the districts had the shape of a lizard. When an artist saw the map of the new district, he declared: "Why, this district looks like a salamander," and gave it a few finishing touches with his pencil. The editor, in whose office the map was hanging, replied, "Say rather a gerrymander," and thus an ancient party practice was given a new name.

spirited battle and the balloting may be light. On the other hand in evenly divided constituencies, party leaders may drag the most negligent citizens from their homes to the polls and swell the returns enormously.

As a result of gerrymandering and other operations, the House of Representatives is seldom an exact mirror of the political opinion of the country. Sometimes one party secures a majority of the popular vote, counting the congressional districts as a whole, and the other party obtains a majority in the House. There is always a large minority in each state which is not fairly represented; in 1920, for example, the Republicans cast one million one hundred fourteen thousand votes in the congressional elections of Pennsylvania and won thirty-five representatives, while the Democrats and the minor party voters, numbering about six hundred thousand in all, succeeded in electing only one Representative. On the other hand, in 1924, the Republicans received one million six hundred thousand votes in the congressional election in New York and carried only twenty seats while the Democrats with a vote of one million three hundred thousand in round numbers secured twenty-two Representatives. Nothing but a complete system of proportional representation can cure the evils of the gerrymander and the district system, but that reform is not at present within the realm of "practical politics." Perhaps, after all, in the long run, the discrepancies offset one another and a rough-hewn justice is attained.

According to the Constitution, the time, place, and manner of holding elections for Representatives may be prescribed by the state legislature subject to the restriction that Congress may by law make or alter such regulations. For almost a hundred years congressional elections were held at different times and in conformity with the requirements prevailing in the various states—the old system of viva voce voting being retained for a long time in some commonwealths. At length, by acts passed in 1871 and 1872, Congress provided that regular congressional elections must be by ballot and occur throughout the Union on the same day, that is, on the Tuesday following the first Monday in November; special elections are held only when a vacancy occurs for some reason. An exception to the rule allows Maine to hold its election somewhat earlier, according to the former custom. Subject likewise to federal law (p. 78), the states fix the qualifications for voters; apart from its negative clauses, the Constitution merely stipulates that those persons entitled to vote in each state for members of the lower house of its legislature shall also be entitled to vote within its borders for members of the House of Representatives.

Candidates at elections for the House of Representatives are nominated by the several political parties in accordance with regulations provided by custom and state legislation, and independents may present themselves to the public by filing with the proper officials petitions signed by a certain number of voters. In some of the states the candidates of each party are chosen at district conventions composed of delegates representing its membership in units of local government, such as counties in thinly populated regions and smaller districts in thickly settled areas. In a great majority of the states, however, the convention has been entirely abolished by law, and an official direct primary election has been substituted. Under the new régime any member of a party who wishes to be its candidate for Congress must have his name put on the party primary ballot by petition. Then at a subsequent primary election the party voters are given the opportunity to select their nominees from among the several aspirants on this ballot. Candidates for Representative-at-large are also nominated by state conventions or by state-wide primaries as the state law may require. The general direction of campaigns is entrusted to the national committees (p. 232) and to congressional committees made up of party members in the two houses.

No one can take a seat in the House of Representatives, of course, unless he has the qualifications required by the Constitution. A member of that body must be a citizen of the United States of at least seven years' standing; he must be not less than twenty-five years old and an inhabitant of the state in which he is chosen. He cannot be at the same time a military or civil officer of the United States; and nearly all the states, by special law or constitutional provision, have forbidden their officers to hold positions of trust under the Federal Government. Some states have gone further and provided that each Representative must be a resident of the district in which he is elected. Although this restriction is regarded by most lawyers as unconstitutional because it adds a qualification to those imposed by the federal Constitution, it is difficult to see how the prescription could be set aside by legal process.

At all events, it is an accepted rule that the member of the House must be a resident of his district. A few exceptions, as for example in New York, where down-town constituencies are sometimes represented by men residing in uptown quarters, merely confirm the normal rule. The reasons for the adoption of this general custom are thus summarized by James Bryce: local pride will prevent a district from seeking its Representative outside its own borders; the member of the House is relatively well paid, and the party machine does not want to waste the post on strangers, preferring to reserve it to strengthen the local organization; owing to the vast amount of party work required by our complicated system, it is necessary to have as many offices as possible to give to the workers; the Representative in Congress is expected to know local needs and to secure harbor and river appropriations, post-office buildings, special protection for industries, and other favors for his constituents; Americans regard the Representative as a spokesman of local interests rather than as a statesman, "formulating reason and justice into law." It is, therefore, highly improbable that any change will be made in this tradition, at least in the near future. Undoubtedly the custom excludes able men from Congress because talent is not distributed by nature according to congressional districts, but party affairs are not conducted on the basis of intelligence tests.

While the states theoretically cannot add qualifications to those imposed by the federal Constitution on members of Congress, it is conceded in practice that the House of Representatives may exercise its power as judge of the elections, returns, and qualifications of its members in such a way as to exclude persons on other grounds than those laid down in the Constitution. For example, in 1900, the House shut its doors to Brigham H. Roberts of Utah because he was a polygamist. The committee reporting in favor of this action contended: "Must it be said that the constitutional provision, phrased as it is, really means that every person who is twenty-five years of age and who has been for seven years a citizen of the United States and was when elected an inhabitant of that state in which he was chosen is eligible to be a member of the House of Representatives and must be admitted thereto even though he be insane or disloyal or a leper or a criminal? Is it conceivable that the Constitution meant that crime could not disqualify? The whole spirit of the government revolts against such a conclusion."

To this view a minority of the committee opposed a vigorous dissent: "The adding by this House alone of a disqualification not established by law would not only be a violation of both the Constitution and the law, but it would be a most dangerous precedent which could hardly fail to 'return to plague the inventor.' . . . What warrant have you, when the barriers of the Constitution are once broken down, that there may not come after us a House, with other standards of morality and propriety, which will create other qualifications with no rightful foundations? . . . It will no longer be a government of laws but of men. To depart thus from the Constitution and substitute force for law is to embark upon a trackless sea without chart or compass." This opinion was also held by those who claimed that the proper way of getting rid of Mr. Roberts was to admit him to membership and then expel him under the right to eject by a two-thirds vote; but the doctrine of the party of exclusion was accepted.

The same principle was applied long afterward to Victor

L. Berger, who was elected to the House in a Wisconsin district in 1918. Shortly after his election, Mr. Berger was tried under the Sedition Act and found guilty of obstructing and embarrassing the Government in the prosecution of the war against the Central Powers. He appealed his case and appeared in Washington to take his seat but he was quickly excluded by the House, only one member dissenting from the decision taken. A new election was then held and Mr. Berger was once more chosen, this time by a substantial majority. Once more the House, with little deliberation, denied him admission. In reporting against Mr. Berger, the chairman of the committee in charge of the matter did not rest the decision on the ground that the man had been convicted of a crime. On the contrary, he said: "The one and only issue in this case is that of Americanism." To this contention the former Republican floor leader, James R. Mann, one of the six men who voted this time in favor of giving the applicant his seat, replied: "Has it come to the point that a man who believes certain things cannot be heard? His people, his constituents, desire him to represent them. It is not our duty to select a representative from this congressional district. That is the duty of the people back at home. . . . To me the question is whether we shall maintain inviolate the representative form of government where people who desire changes in the fundamental or other laws of the land shall have the right to be represented on the floor of this House when they control a majority of the votes in a congressional district." Still, as things now stand it would seem that the House can exclude a person for conduct and views which it deems immoral or un-American. The qualifications on membership laid down in the Constitution have been so expanded as to lose their original precision.

In passing upon the election, returns, and qualifications of members, the House of Representatives exercises its own judgment. Unlike the Parliament of Great Britain it does not submit cases of dispute to the determination of an independent tribunal. Any person intending to contest the official results of an election is required by law to serve notice on the member whose seat he claims, and specify the grounds upon which he expects to rely. The member thus put in jeopardy must answer. Copies of the papers are transmitted to the House, and the clerk makes up the records of the case, which he lays before that body. These are referred by the Speaker to one of three regular committees on elections; testimony is taken; the contestants are given an opportunity to be heard and to be represented by counsel; on the basis of the evidence and pleading, the committee presents to the House a report, which is usually accepted. Inasmuch as each of the committees is composed of a majority of members from the dominant party, a disputed election is quite likely to be decided in the interests of that party, especially if the countervailing facts are not glaring enough to make trouble.

The term of the member of the House is two years—a brevity of tenure which has received so much criticism in our age that it is difficult to understand the reasoning that led the *Federalist* to apologize for the action of the Philadelphia convention in failing to provide for annual elections. It is a well-known fact that no Representative can secure a considerable influence in so short a time, since it requires a great deal of practical experience to master the mysteries of business procedure and get a hearing from the leaders in the chamber. On the other hand there is no provision for a dissolution of the House or a recall of members, and a long period of service might frequently result in a misrepresentation of the country.

The Senate

The Constitution prescribes that there shall be two Senators from each state, and that no state, without its consent, shall be deprived of equal representation in the Senate even by a constitutional amendment. Inevitably this rule of parity results in gross violations of the democratic theory that human beings, not geographical units, should be the basis of representation.

An examination of the statistics in the case reveals conditions which recall the "rotten borough" system of England in the days before parliamentary reform. For example, the state of Nevada with about ninety thousand inhabitants has the same weight in the Senate as New York with more than twelve million people. It now takes eighteen of the less populous states—Nevada, Wyoming, Delaware, Arizona, Vermont, New Mexico, Idaho, New Hampshire, Utah, Montana, Rhode Island, South Dakota, North Dakota, Maine, Oregon, Colorado, Florida, and Nebraska, with thirty-six Senators to their credit, to equal in population the Empire State with its two Senators. Ten states in the Union have within their borders more than half the people but command less than one fourth the total number of Senators.

In practice, however, the small states are not often aligned against the large states; social and economic factors work contrary to such a mathematical or geographical distribution of political forces. Nevertheless the system gives to the agricultural regions a strength in the Senate all out of proportion to their population, and this was the cause of bitter lament on the part of certain leaders from the industrial sections in 1929 when Senators of agrarian affiliations long delayed the tariff bill sent up by the House (p. 162).

The qualifications of the Senator are fixed by the Constitution. He must be not less than thirty years old, an inhabitant of the state for which he is elected, and a United States citizen of nine years' standing. The same question has arisen here as in the case of the House of Representatives, namely, whether the Senate, under its power to judge of the qualifications of its members, can add any to those fixed in the Constitution. The logical answer to this question seems to have been made by Senator Hopkins in a speech delivered in 1907 during a debate over the proposition to exclude Reed Smoot of Utah, on the contention that he was a polygamist. Mr. Hopkins said that neither the Senate, Congress, nor a state can add to the qualifications prescribed by the Constitution; that the power given to the Senate is not to create Senators but to judge whether they have the qualifications set forth in the Constitution; that the Senate has no authority to inquire into the antecedents and early career and character of a Senator who applies for admission with the proper credentials of his state; that no Senator has ever been denied a seat in the Senate of the United States because of any lapse of morals prior to his election; and that the Senate should content itself with the exercise of its power to expel a member for disorderly behavior whenever his conduct is such as to lower the standard of that body or bring it into disrepute. Mr. Smoot was accordingly given his seat and became one of the leading bulwarks of conservatism.

Although such were long the accepted principles governing the qualifications of Senators, there developed in the Senate after the World War a decided inclination to regard the expenditure of large sums of money in securing a nomination and election as sufficient reason for excluding a member-elect. If a date for the new doctrine must be fixed, it may well be 1922, when the Senate set an important precedent in this relation. It appeared that Mr. Truman Newberry, or rather friends on his behalf, had spent about $195,000 in his primary and election contests in Michigan, not fraudulently but lavishly in the ordinary course of the campaign. Thereupon the candidate was indicted for the violation of the federal law respecting the use of money in politics (p. 96), and convicted in a lower court—escaping punishment only because the Supreme Court of the United States declared a section of the statute in question unconstitutional. Attempts to exclude Mr. Newberry from his seat were also defeated but, as a kind of warning, the Senate resolved "that the expenditure of such excessive sums in behalf of a candidate, either with or without his knowledge and consent, being contrary to sound public policy, harmful to the honor and dignity of the Senate, and dangerous to the perpetuity of a free government, such excessive expenditures are hereby severely condemned and disapproved." In effect, Senator Norris contended, this resolution said to the applicant: "We will seat you this time, but we are going to give notice to the Senate, we are going to give notice to the country, we are going to given notice to the world, that we will never again seat anyone under such circumstances."

The dictum thus laid down was applied later in the exclusion of a Senator-elect from Illinois in whose campaign a large sum of money had been collected and spent, including contributions from wealthy men having an interest in matters likely to come before the federal administration. When the governor of the state then appointed the rejected applicant to fill the vacancy created by his own mishap, the Senate promptly shut him out again, apparently on the assumption that he was the same man after all. It did not contend that his second arrival was tainted by fraud or excessive use of money, but simply closed the doors in his face.

Shortly afterward, in the case of William S. Vare of Pennsylvania, the Senate followed this precedent. An investigating committee of that body reported that approximately three million dollars had been spent in the election, about seven hundred eighty-five thousand dollars on the part of the victor, and that there had been several instances of fraud in connection with his candidacy. Although it seemed that Mr. Vare had received a plurality of the lawful votes, the Senate nevertheless denied him the seat.

In vain was it argued that a member-elect who came with credentials of election sufficient in form and substance and who possessed the qualifications prescribed by the Constitution was entitled to admission. The argument was impatiently brushed aside. While some Senators voted against the petitioner on account of alleged frauds—not the expenditure of an enormous sum of money, it was evident in the debates that the mere fact of a huge outlay afforded justification for exclusion. It is true that the amount which a candidate may spend in the primaries or his friends may employ in his interests is not limited by federal law. Yet, judging by these precedents, the Senate may debar persons duly chosen and provided with credentials, on the ground that they have disbursed too much money in securing their nomination and election. Where is the line to be drawn? There is no answer in law. Hence the situation is anomalous.

Until the ratification of the Seventeenth Amendment in 1913, the Constitution provided that Senators should be chosen by the legislatures of the respective states, but even before that time the application of the direct primary and other devices to senatorial contests in a majority of the states had practically established popular election by a circuitous method. The Amendment in question, adopted after a long struggle, provides that the two Senators from each state shall be "elected by the people thereof for six years. . . . The electors in each state shall have the qualifications requisite for electors of the most numerous branch of the state legislature. When vacancies happen in the representation of any state in the Senate, the executive authority of such state shall issue writs of election to fill such vacancies: Provided that the legislature of any state may empower the executive thereof to make temporary appointments until the people fill the vacancies by election as the legislature may direct." Under this Amendment, it became necessary for the states to make provision for the nomination of Senators, and the direct primary or the convention system (p. 151) was adopted according to the policy of the state, the former being chosen in nearly all cases.

What has been the effect of popular election upon the composition and authority of the Senate? Perhaps no scientific answer can be made to this question, but still some facts pertinent to the matter may be brought under review. Since every candidate for the Senate under the new system must perforce make a state-wide campaign, the type of man who is most efficient in formulating programs which arouse public interest and in making speeches which evoke popular enthusiasm has an advantage over the more reserved and less resourceful leader. The quiet and thoughtful man of larger intellectual powers is likely to be overborne by a whirlwind campaigner or an astute manipulator of federal patronage. On the other hand the man with mere money or mere talent for slipping softly around and winning state legislators by one method or another probably has less chance under the present régime. He may buy huge publicity for himself and perhaps win an election, but he cannot escape altogether the necessity of making some statement as to his political ideas and opinions. There is also another point worthy of note, namely, that the Senator who desires reëlection must now take more time away from legislative business for the purpose of "nursing" his state—keeping his supporters in line and preventing someone from stealing a march on him while he is far off at the national capital. That has its good side as well as its bad side. It compels the Senator to keep more closely in touch with his constituents and to inform them about the policies and measures which he supports at Washington.

On other phases of the subject we speak with less assurance. There was a time when the Senate was, with a good deal of warrant, dubbed by journalists "a millionaires' club." That is no longer the case, but can we ascribe the change solely or even principally to popular election? The Senate was once regarded as the stronghold of great capitalistic interests representing railways, express companies, and protected manufacturers and blocking the more democratic and progressive House of Representatives. The great Senators who once spoke authoritatively for those interests have nearly all passed from the scene, and it now seems impossible for any newcomers to rival the powerful masters of the old order. Is the direct election responsible for this novel situation, or have other forces brought it about?

It was prophesied that the system of popular choice would make reëlection more difficult and that the practice of retaining Senators for long terms and drawing benefits from their experience would be abandoned. Events have hardly borne out the forecast. Changes come with variations in public sentiment, in the personal fortunes of individuals, and in the policies of parties; it takes a keen eye to discern the causes of reëlections to the Senate. Finally it was insisted by Senator Hoar, who stood like Horatius at the bridge fighting for the old system, that popular election would in the end overthrow "the whole scheme of the national Constitution as designed by the framers." For the present at least that Constitution still stands.

Frequently the contention is heard that popular election calls for expensive campaigns and makes the use of money a prominent factor in senatorial contests, but for every case of this kind during the past decade a match can be found during the period just previous to the adoption of the Seventeenth Amendment. Indeed the most flagrant instances of barter and sale in connection with elections were in the old days when state legislatures were sometimes bought outright by senatorial aspirants. If anyone is shocked by the size of the outlays made by and for Truman Newberry of Michigan in his famous contest with Henry Ford in 1918, let him remember the equally shocking example of Clark in Montana, Lorimer in Illinois, and Stephenson in Wisconsin, all of which occurred under the old order. The evidence against Lorimer was so conclusive that the Senate voted to expel him.

Whatever effects may justly be attributed to the system of popular elections, it became apparent, a few years after its adoption, that the character and proceedings of the Senate had been altered in certain fundamental respects. For some reason it was now impossible to construct a well-oiled machine dominated by a few powerful figures capable of controlling a majority of the members and marshalling them in solid ranks behind selected measures. Again and again the Senate carried resolutions, defeated bills, rejected presidential nominations, and made investigations against the wishes and efforts of "the Old Guard." Centralized leadership completely disintegrated. In 1929 it was so weak that a group of Republican Senators could unite with the Democrats and shatter the Republican tariff bill as reported on the basis of the measure sent up by the House of Representatives. In fact the special session of Congress, called by President Hoover to revise the revenue law, ended in such a complete deadlock that the tariff bill was carried over into the following year. Radicals in the Senate had long protested against "steam-roller" tactics on the part of the Old Guard; now it was the turn of the conservatives to protest against methods which hampered the transaction of business. Only by resorting to vote-trading behind the scenes was the Republican management able to overcome the results of the defection and finally assemble a narrow majority for its general tariff program.

In the course of the controversy over this chaotic state of affairs, the change was ascribed to the election of Senators by popular vote, but whether this was the cause or a symptom could not be discovered. Doubtless the national organization of each party did exercise a stricter control over the choice of Senators in the old days when selections were made in the secret caucuses of state legislatures. Perhaps a man who has fought his way up through a primary campaign is in a more independent position than a man picked by a small, unofficial political committee. Yet this alone does not account for the novel situation; the Senators aligned in the conservative ranks were also chosen in the same way. Hence it seems safe to say the method of choice does not automatically produce identical results in all states.

When probed to the bottom it appeared that the conflict which disrupted party leadership in 1929 was really a struggle between Senators from industrial states and Senators from agricultural states. With perfect frankness Mr. J. R. Grundy, President of the Pennsylvania Manufacturers' Association, later elevated to the Senate himself, stated the case. He attributed the breakdown of control entirely to Senators from "backward states," as he called them—the agricultural states of Arkansas, Georgia, Mississippi, North Dakota, Montana, and Idaho—and insisted that they should not be allowed "to throw the monkey wrench into the machinery twenty-four hours a day." He declared that equality in the Senate was a "misfortune," and that the states in which industries are more extensively developed and the tariff is best understood should really control the making of customs schedules. He said, in addition, that if "the volume of voice" of these agricultural commonwealths were reduced to the proportion of their tax contributions to the support of the Government, some of them would need an amplifier to be heard at all. If this is a correct analysis of the situation, and it seems to be, then the divisions in the Senate that cut across party lines and shatter party leadership must be ascribed primarily to divergences in economic conditions in the country at large, not to election machinery.

The term of the Senators is fixed at six years and in practice they are frequently reëlected. A service ranging from twelve to twenty-four years is by no means uncommon. Additional solidity is given to this chamber by the arrangement which provides that the terms of all the Senators shall not expire at the same time but that one third shall go out automatically every two years, thus making the body continuous. At the first session in 1789 the Senators were divided by lot into three classes, the seats of the first class to be vacated at the expiration of the second year, of the second class at the end of the fourth year, and of the third class at the close of the sixth year, assuring a biennial renewal of one third of the membership. As new states were admitted to the Union their Senators were likewise distributed by lot among the three groups, care being taken to give different terms to the Senators from each commonwealth.

Constitutional Provisions Governing Privileges of Members and the Organization of the Houses

Members of both houses of Congress are entitled to certain privileges by virtue of their position. First among these may be reckoned payment for their labors. The Constitution prescribes that Senators and Representatives shall receive a compensation for their services, to be ascertained by law and paid out of the treasury of the United States. Except for a brief period it was the custom until 1855 to give each of them a certain per diem allowance; but in that year a salary of $3,000 per annum was voted; and by various increments the amount has been raised to $10,000—to which is added a sum for clerk hire, stationery, and travelling expenses.

The second privilege enjoyed by members of Congress is exemption from arrest during attendance on the sessions of their respective houses, and in going to and returning from the same, in all cases except treason, felony, and breach of the peace. This privilege frees Representatives and Senators from many processes which involve imprisonment as a penalty for disobedience. That is, a Congressman, during the period mentioned above, cannot be compelled to testify in a court, serve on a jury, or respond to a civil action brought against him. The term "breach of the peace," however, extends to "all indictable offences, as well as those which are in fact attended with force and violence as those which are only destructive to the peace of the government;" therefore, the member of Congress really enjoys no exemption from the ordinary requirements of the criminal law. In going to and coming from the Capital he is allowed reasonable delays and deviations from the nearest course.

A third privilege conferred on Congressmen is freedom of speech during the course of the discussions in their respective chambers. According to an express provision of the Constitution, they shall not be questioned in any other place for any speech or debate in either house. This famous right, regarded by some persons as merely a guarantee for the full and free discussion of public matters, is really derived from the practices of the English Parliament where it was formerly invoked to safeguard members against arbitrary arrest for criticism of the king. In the opinion of Professor Henry Jones Ford, it was placed in the American Constitution to relieve Senators and Representatives from responsibility to their constituents. However that may be, the effect of the concession is to give them immunity from all liability to prosecution for libel or slander for anything said in Congress, in committees, in official publications, or in the legitimate discharge of their legislative duties. Apparently also it allows them to circulate their speeches at will, not only among their own constituents, but anywhere throughout the United States.

In special as well as general sessions members of Congress are free to determine the nature of the business to be transacted. In practice, to be sure, they are often instructed by state legislatures in formal resolutions to bring up for discussion, or to support, certain propositions, but all such orders have no binding force. A state legislature cannot compel a Congressman to resign or place any penalties on him for disobeying its requests. No provision in the Constitution warrants actions of this character. Indeed it is held by many American publicists that a Representative, though chosen in a geographical district, is in reality a member of a national assembly bound to act on broad national grounds. Since, however, every Congressman is sensitive to the wishes of his constituents, or at least the local party leaders, he ignores at his peril communications from below. If he does not heed them he may be retired. Moreover in regions where party contests are close and a few marginal voters hold decisive power, every demand of any significance carries weight in Washington.

With respect to their internal organization both houses of Congress are limited in certain fundamental matters by explicit provisions of the Constitution. The Vice President of the United States is made the presiding officer of the Senate with a vote only in case of a tie; neither house can expel a member for a breach of its rules except on a two-thirds vote. a quorum being present; each chamber must keep a journal of its proceedings and publish the same from time to time, except such parts as it may deem necessary to keep secret; if one fifth of the members present in either body demand a record of the yeas and nays upon the journal with regard to any question, that vote must be taken by roll-call. Subject to these conditions, each house has the right to elect its own officers, compel the attendance of members, and prescribe rules of procedure and discipline.

Nothing in the Constitution requires the houses of Congress to hold their sessions in public. Indeed it is implied that they may, if they wish, transact their business behind closed doors for, as we have just said, they can except from publication such parts of their journal of proceedings "as may in their judgment require secrecy." Shortly after the House of Representatives assembled in 1789, it threw open its meetings and has only departed from that practice occasionally on account of very special circumstances in time of war. The Senate, on the other hand, during the first four years of its life, kept everything secret and issued no official reports of its debates. Only under great pressure from within and from without, did it begin to hold public meetings in 1793. Moreover it later decided that all sessions dealing with treaties and nominations presented by the President should be secret. It also provided for the expulsion of any Senator who divulged information respecting its confidential transactions.

Under rules still in effect at the opening of 1929, "executive sessions" on presidential matters were automatically closed, unless the Senate, by a two-thirds vote, on rare occasions by majority vote, resolved to open them to the public. As a matter of fact, however, news of the debates and proceedings in the secret meetings usually leaked out and spread broadcast through the press, mingling rumors, guesses, and truth. At length after an acrimonious controversy, the historic arrangement was modified.

According to a new rule adopted in 1929, the Senate must transact all business openly unless, in a closed session and by a majority vote, it decides in favor of secrecy. Even then the injunction of secrecy may be removed as to all or part of any proceedings in an executive meeting by the action of a mere majority. Furthermore it is specifically provided that any

Senator may make public his vote cast in a closed executive session. Under this ruling it appears that a Senator may give out a statement revealing his decision on any matter handled in confidence, but cannot add the reasons assigned for it in debate, unless the Senate permits him to do so by special resolution removing the bar in that connection.

The quorum necessary for lawful operations in each house is fixed by law and practice at a majority of all the members legally chosen, living, and officially sworn, but a smaller number may adjourn from day to day, and may compel the attendance of absentees. This is no formal matter. It is necessary to make the quorum large in order to prevent "snap" legislation by minorities, and yet the stipulation is often attended by serious inconveniences.

For a long time it was a common practice for the minority party in the House of Representatives, whenever it desired to delay business, to refuse to answer the roll-call, and thus compel an adjournment on the ground that a quorum was lacking. To stop such "filibustering," as dilatory tactics were called, Speaker Reed, in January, 1890, held that members actually in the House who declined to answer should be counted as legally present in determining the question of a quorum. Shortly afterward the House embodied this principle in a rule authorizing the clerk, on demand of a member or at the suggestion of the Speaker, to record as present Representatives who are in the chamber and yet refuse to respond when their names are called.

A brief extract from the *Congressional Record* illustrates the rapid-fire methods now employed in marshaling a quorum and handling delinquents.

MR. WILLIAMS: Mr. Speaker, I make the point of order that there is no quorum present. . . .

THE SPEAKER: The Sergeant-at-Arms will close the doors and bring in the absentees, the clerk will call the roll, and those in favor of the passage of the bill will, as their names are called, answer "aye," and those opposed will answer "no," and those present and not voting will answer "present." . . .

Assistant Sergeant-at-Arms Pierce: Mr. Speaker, in accordance with the rules of the House and the warrant of the Speaker, I present at the bar of the House, under arrest, Mr. Buckman and Mr. Rucker.

The Speaker (*pro tempore*): The gentlemen will be noted as present and discharged from arrest.

. . . Does the gentleman from Minnesota desire to vote?

Mr. Buckman: I vote "aye."

The right of Congress, in the course of its proceedings, to interfere with private citizens is clearly limited by the Constitution: neither house has any general authority to punish outsiders for contempt, for such a power is judicial in its nature. If, however, the examination of private citizens is necessary to the performance of its regular legislative duties, Congress may require their attendance as witnesses and compel them to give testimony (p. 210). Each house may also punish its own members for disorderly behavior and, with the concurrence of two thirds, expel a member; but the Supreme Court has ruled that the power to penalize is confined to the session in which the condemnation occurs and cannot extend beyond imprisonment during the remainder of the session.

The Sessions of Congress

Congress must meet annually on the first Monday in December unless, by law, it appoints some other day. Each Congress, therefore, normally has two sessions. The first, known as the long session, begins in December of each odd year and extends theoretically until the following December, though as a matter of practice adjournment usually occurs sometime in the spring or summer. In a few instances it has continued at work until the opening of the next session. The second session of each Congress, known as the short session, begins in December of each even year and extends until the fourth of the following March. Hence an incoming President always has a new Congress available at the opening of his administration.

According to this arrangement, a member of the House of Representatives does not take his seat until more than a year after his election, unless the President calls a special session; that is, he is elected in November of an even year and does not ordinarily begin work until December of the next odd year. Thus it happens that an expiring House lasts for about four months after a new House has been chosen, and important measures may be passed by a party which the country has repudiated at the polls. "Under the present law," as a former member of the House has said, "a Representative in Congress who has been turned down by the people legislates for that people in the second regular session. A man who has been defeated for reëlection is not in a fit frame of mind to legislate for the people. There is a sting in defeat that tends to engender the feeling of resentment, which often finds expression in the vote of such members against wholesome legislation. That same feeling often produces such a want of interest in proceedings as to cause the members to be absent nearly all the second session. . . . It is then that some are open to propositions which they would never think of entertaining if they were to go before the people for reëlection. It is then that the attorneyship of some corporation is often tendered, and a vote is afterward found in the *Record* in favor of legislation of a general or special character favoring corporations."

Special sessions of Congress may be called by the President under his power to convene either house or both of them on extraordinary occasions—the Senate in particular to confirm appointments or ratify a treaty. Unlike those of many states, however, such sessions are not limited to the consideration of any particular matters. As a rule, of course, the President only summons the national legislature to deal with some pressing issue of high importance and usually he announces his purpose in his proclamation or message. Thus the attention of Congress and the country is sharply directed to the problems in hand. But since he has no power to adjourn the houses after they are called, he can in fact place no restraints on their transactions.

The Two Houses Compared

The difference in the organization of the two houses makes it necessary to say a few words by way of comparison. The Senate is the smaller body, being composed of ninety-six members, as against 435 in the House of Representatives. Generally speaking, it includes in its fellowship statesmen older in years and wider in political experience. Frequently Senators have served for years in some branch of state government or in the House of Representatives. As their term is longer and the chances of reëlection greater, they are usually more expert, better acquainted not only with the problems of law-making but also with the inner workings of the federal administration.

The influence of Senators, due to age and experience, is augmented by their position as party leaders within their respective states. Through their right to pass on many presidential nominees, they have a large power over appointments to federal offices; sometimes they are able by this means to construct political machines of extraordinary strength. They usually have great weight in selecting delegates to national party conventions, and in fact they are often responsible for the predominance of the office-holding element in those assemblies. Such command over party resources within their states enables the Senators to bring more or less pressure on the members of their party in the House of Representatives. When the state organization, in close touch with its Senator or Senators, adopts a policy, it is usually wise for the members of the lower chamber affected by it, if they expect further party favors, to fall in line with instructions.

There was a time, shortly after the opening of the twentieth century, when political leadership, especially in the Republican party, was mainly in the hands of Senators who were masters of the party machinery in their respective states. Among these powerful captains of politics were Hanna, of Ohio; Platt, of New York; Quay, of Pennsylvania; Aldrich, of Rhode Island; and Lodge, of Massachusetts. They made and unmade governors and minor officers at home, controlled legislation at Washington, and were powerful figures at national conventions. They were to be found among the influential members of the platform committee and the national committee. It seemed for a time as if senatorial leadership was an established institution, but appearances were deceptive. As the old directors of policy withdrew or died, they left no successors able to wield such high authority. It is not possible now to find three Senators comparable in political power to Hanna, Platt, and Quay. By the irony of fortune, the senior La Follette of Wisconsin, who in his early days so bitterly assailed the dominion of these men, during the later years of his life came nearer than any other Senator to asserting such sovereign dominion in the councils of his state.

If it possesses fewer leaders of the old type, the Senate still holds a whip hand over federal legislation. Owing to the almost unlimited freedom of debate in that chamber each member can block some bills indefinitely and force the consideration of others. In such circumstances the "steamroller" tactics of the House cannot be so effectively applied. Although the Constitution provides that revenue bills must originate in the lower chamber, the Senators, in practice, pay little attention to that mandate (p. 345). Their technical skill, their long experience, and their legal talents give them a superior position in strategy. Seldom does a debate in the House or its action on a bill attract the attention of the press throughout the country, but senatorial discussions on vital questions frequently break into front-page news. Besides making use of its ordinary legislative prerogatives, the Senate may employ its power over presidential treaties and nominations in circuitous ways to bring pressure on the Representatives. Whether on its merits or not, it completely overshadows the House in both government and politics.

Once the Senate was looked upon as the bulwark of conservatism. Such, the Fathers thought, would be its historic function. But comparison of the votes of the House and

Senate on those measures which may be called radical or progressive makes the former, as often as the latter, appear to be the seat of conservatism. It was only in the Senate that an effective protest was made in the name of American traditions of liberty against the harsh and unnecessary Sedition Bill of 1918, which flagrantly violated the spirit if not the letter of that liberty. There is more independence in the Senate. More Senators are willing to snap the chains of party bondage and speak their minds and hearts freely upon party measures.

CHAPTER VII

Congress in Operation

Congress is not a simple organization working easily in a vacuum under its own momentum; and a comprehension of its operations cannot be derived from a mere study of its form, records, and daily proceedings. At every session, its business is highly complicated, owing to the technical aspects of the problems before it—problems involving all branches of science and engineering, all industries, and all arts and crafts. Its functioning is very largely determined by the Constitution of the United States, by statutes for its own government, by the political character of its members, and by the forces which impinge upon it from the outside. Indeed, since its actions affect every department of American life, its members are under continual pressure from all the powerful social, economic, and professional groups in America—and some in foreign countries—a pressure quickened and intensified by modern means of transportation and communication. When in session, it is constantly confronted by citizens and agents representing particular interests, arriving by train and airplane with demands and protests, and is bombarded by telegrams, radiograms, and telephone messages without ceasing. There is not an important class in the country that does not look to it for legislative action of some kind—scarcely an individual active in politics who does not call upon its members for something—to find jobs, public or private, to support certain measures, to oppose others, to speak at celebrations, or render favors large or small. Under the Constitution and amid the endless whirl of a vast social system, Congress must conduct its inquiries, formulate its policies, enact laws, and scrutinize their enforcement. Not until the citizen has grasped certain fundamental facts in this relation can he hope to view the work of this body with a reasonable degree of understanding.

The Shadow of the Constitution

Congress can proceed only in accordance with the terms of the Constitution. Whenever it takes up any important matter touching life and property it must face the question of constitutionality. Unlike the British Parliament it cannot begin at once to deal with the merits of the case. If a constitutional issue does not appear obvious to all, it is certain to be raised by some member. A measure may be wise, expedient, and even necessary, but if it is clearly outside the powers of the legislature, it is useless to discuss it. If there is any doubt at all as to the validity of a bill, it surely will be the subject of searching inquiry and exposition on the part of the skilled lawyers in Congress. Some of the greatest legislative discussions in our national history, including the celebrated Webster-Hayne debate on Foote's Resolution, have arisen in this connection. In fact it often happens that the original proposal itself is lost to sight in the tortuous windings of historico-legal speculations, as was the case in the controversy just mentioned. The tendency to long-winded disquisition is especially marked in the Senate, where debate is less restricted and where there are more attorneys of distinction than in the House.

These discussions are often of a high order and of undoubted value in expounding the terms of the Constitution, but they are also quite as often mere displays of black-letter lore or personal vanity. More than once the country has been impatient at such diffuse lucubrations, rightly suspecting that many opposing members had first come to their conclusions on the merits of the bills under consideration, and then sought constitutional objections to them. More than once, also, these debates have only added confusion to what seemed perfectly clear and simple. "If we must wait until the great constitutional lawyers agree upon any subject," exclaimed

Bourke Cockran in the House long ago, "it is plain that we would never take a step in any direction. We would stand paralyzed at the threshold of every legislative enterprise, amazed and bewildered—puzzled to distinguish amid the din of their vociferation how much of it is advice to us and how much of it is denunciation of each other. I defy any man to define Congress itself according to the constitutional lawyers, after he has read three of their speeches."

Broadly speaking, there are three views of the Constitution which have been taken by members of Congress in deciding controverted questions. The first of these is known as "strict construction"—a concept that would restrain the powers of Congress to the bare letter of the written instrument, and confine the means of carrying its powers into execution to those absolutely and imperatively necessary. This theory of interpretation was applied by Jefferson in his opinion on the constitutionality of a national bank, and was later used with great acumen by his party as a moral justification for its opposition to the Federalists. During the long controversy over slavery, it was the chief reliance of Southern statesmen in resisting the Northern pressure on Congress urging it to make full use of its authority in blocking the spread of slavery to the territories. Since the disappearance of this question, there have not been many occasions to call the strict construction doctrine into party service with such consistency. Both parties, it is true, sometimes appear to oppose "encroachments" of the Federal Government, but their constructive legislative proposals are seldom in keeping with a narrow conception of the Constitution.

A second position respecting the powers of Congress, originally taken by the Federalists and held at various times by all parties, as their interests have required, is that of "liberal construction." Adherents of this school deny that there is any warrant whatever in the Constitution for applying astringents to it, and lay great stress on that clause which authorizes Congress to make all laws necessary and proper for carrying into execution the powers expressly enumerated.

They give a generous exposition to all the powers named, and then interpret the words "necessary and proper" to mean "highly useful and expedient." Under this construction, a national bank was created, paper money issued, American industries have been protected, national highways built, provisions made for lending money to farmers, subsidies granted from the federal treasury to the states, and irrigation, reclamation, and other large schemes of public improvement undertaken. Only under this conception of the Constitution has the authority of the Federal Government been made adequate to the exigencies of a national system of economy.

The third view of the proper attitude to be assumed by Congress in considering the constitutionality of any legislative proposition, and one which has been quite generally held, consciously or unconsciously, by liberal constructionists, was thus formulated by Bourke Cockran, during a debate in the House: "It seems to me that the duty of Congress is to examine closely the condition of the country and keep itself constantly informed of everything affecting the common welfare. Wherever a wrong is found to exist with which the nation can deal more effectively than a state, it is the business of Congress to suggest a remedy. . . . Our first step must be in the direction of legislation. The only way we can ascertain definitely whether a law which we believe will prove effective is constitutional or unconstitutional is not by abandoning ourselves to a maelstrom of speculations about what the Court may hold or has held on subjects more or less kindred, but to legislate, and thus take the judgment of the Court on that specific proposal. We can tell whether it is constitutional or unconstitutional when the Court pronounces upon it and not before. Even if the Court declares it unconstitutional, its decision will not reduce us to helplessness. When it drives us from establishing a remedy by legislation, it will, by that very act, direct us to propose a remedy by constitutional amendment. Having framed a suitable amendment and proposed it to the legislatures of the states, our duty will have been accomplished. The final step toward full redress will then be with the bodies most directly representative of the people affected by the wrong."

The Nature and Mass of the Business before Congress

With the question of constitutional interpretation duly considered, the next important fact to grasp is that the business before Congress is intricate in character and enormous in amount. It involves every phase of political economy and international relations. Taxation in all its branches, the administration of the post-office, natural resources, and other property, technical questions of defense (guns, battleships, and airplanes), the regulation of railways, the government of the city of Washington—these and a hundred other matters equally complex are constantly pressed upon the attention of the members. The demand for new legislation from every quarter is steady and insistent. Large problems in policy and problems minutely special in nature continually call for judgment of the highest order and knowledge deep and wide-reaching.

In sheer bulk the business is immense. Each Congress in the course of its life is confronted by twenty or thirty thousand bills, joint resolutions, concurrent resolutions, simple resolutions, and reports. Any member may introduce as many proposals as he likes by handing them to the clerk if they are of a private nature (such as a bill conferring a pension on some person) or to the presiding officer if they are public in character. He does not have to secure the permission of anyone in advance or assume any responsibility for them even if they carry a charge upon the treasury. As a matter of fact many are introduced "by request" just to please this or that group of voters and without any thought of enactment into law.

It is not enough to say that thousands of bills are laid before each Congress; the character of these measures must be analyzed, for it has a close relation to leadership in both houses. Some of the measures are general in nature; these we may call "public bills." Others pertain to particular persons, localities, or claims; these are "special bills." For every important public bill there will be hundreds of special propositions laid before Congress.

The significant public bills affect vital economic interests throughout the country such as railways, manufacturing, shipping, and farming; they concern the whole nation as well as special groups. Over them the more serious political divisions occur. It is mainly in carrying such public bills through Congress that the leaders of the majority must bring pressure to bear on the rank and file. It is in this connection that cleavages between the right and left wings of each party appear and threaten the disruption of the regular organization. Illustrations abound on every hand, especially in the debates and votes on railway bills and ship subsidies.

Great as may be the interest of the ordinary member in the fate of general bills, his own political fortunes are likely to be closely bound up with obscure special measures making appropriations for post-office buildings, river and harbor improvements, and pensions in his district. The local party machine and active citizens among his constituents expect him to get all he can out of the federal treasury for his section. On seeking reëlection he must be in a position to "point with pride" to the amount and importance of the favors he has secured for "his people." If he fails to obtain advantages for them they will turn against him and support some more energetic and pushing person. Law making of this character is called "pork-barrel legislation," a term reminiscent of plantation days. It was an old custom on Southern estates to allot periodically a certain amount of pork to the slaves; at the appointed time the pork-barrel was rolled into view, the head knocked in, and the contents distributed among eager beneficiaries. The applicability of the figure of speech to the legislative process described above needs no elucidation. In fact such a public bill as a tariff measure may well be placed under this head also because even advocates of low duties "in principle" are usually found voting for high rates in detail on goods produced in their districts and making "trades" with other members to secure local favors.

If the member does not "get his pork" from the treasury, he is generally regarded as a failure by his constituents. And to get it he is ordinarily compelled to do two things. In the first place, he must secure the consent of his party leaders who control legislation, and in return he must usually vote as he is told on other bills. Thus he may have to sell his birthright for a "mess of pork." In the second place he must coöperate with his colleagues bent on the same enterprise. Such coöperation is called "log-rolling." In olden times pioneers on the frontier helped one another to cut trees and pile up logs for cabins or for burning—a process known as "log-rolling." Like the term "pork-barrel," the phrase affords a homely but accurate characterization of the legislative procedure to which it is applied. So when the member of Congress with his eager eye on special bills is not busy placating his party leaders, he is likely to be engaged in making trades with his friends.

If thirty thousand bills, resolutions, and reports were taken up in order and ten minutes were devoted to every one of them, five thousand hours would be spent by each house in the operation, that is, about eight hours every week day during the life of a Congress. Obviously, therefore, each measure cannot be brought up for review; there must be a selection from the enormous mass of business. Hence it follows that some person or group of persons must be made responsible for choosing the proposals to be discussed and passed upon. Since even then the time is limited, methods must be devised for putting an end to debates. Now, the power to select measures and to control proceedings is a fundamental power; it carries with it in effect full authority to decide what laws shall be passed and how they shall be passed. And since the laws go deep into the pocketbooks of the citizens or otherwise affect their property and liberty, dominion over the procedure of Congress touches the most vital interests in the country.

Party Conferences in Congress

The operations of Congress are largely determined by the existence of two political parties—one, a majority in control of one or both houses and regarding itself as responsible for the principal legislative policies; the other, a minority, in opposition, bound under ordinary circumstances to criticize and to vote against the measures advanced by the other group. In England, party organization is carried frankly into the House of Commons, where the majority and minority sit facing each other, and where the government is avowedly that of the dominant party—a government of men, not even theoretically of constitutional law. In the Congress of the United States, the party rules none the less, but its organization and operations are unknown to the formal law of the Constitution. It is true that the votes on propositions in Congress are by no means always cast according to party divisions, but it is likewise true that the principal achievements of each session are the work of the majority party, formulated by its leaders, and carried through under their supervision.

In connection with its directing machinery, each party has a separate conference or caucus of its members in each house, but definite statements about the organization and functioning of this body are difficult to make. Its meetings are irregular and its powers are informal. Yet we may safely say that, before the opening of a new Congress, the majority in the House of Representatives holds a caucus which chooses its candidate for Speaker, makes provisions for selecting the committees, and arrives at decisions respecting the rules of the House—adopting or modifying those previously in force. About the same time the minority also holds its caucus, agrees upon its candidate for Speaker, and arranges for the distribution of its seats on committees. From time to time other meetings are held to discuss matters of high importance, including bills and resolutions of evident party significance.

In the Senate similar partisan "conferences" operate behind the scenes.

Beyond this all else is formless, dependent upon the exigencies of politics. Frequently the caucus is a mere "rubber stamp" which approves projects and measures already formulated by a few leaders. Such was the state of affairs in the Senate near the opening of the twentieth century. The operation of the system in those days is tersely described by Robert M. La Follette, in a speech delivered in 1908: "I attended a caucus at the beginning of this Congress. I happened to look at my watch when we went into that caucus. We were in session three minutes and a half. Do you know what happened? Well, I will tell you. A motion was made that somebody preside. Then a motion was made that whoever presided should appoint a committee on committees; and a motion was then made that we adjourn. Nobody said anything but the Senator who made the motion. Then and there the fate of all the legislation of this session was decided. . . . Mr. President, if you will scan the committees of this Senate, you will find that a little handful of men are in domination and control of the great legislative committees of this body, and that they are a very limited number." Within ten years, however, this dominance by "a little handful of men" had disappeared. At the present moment there is no such concentration of power in the Senate. True, the party conference continues to function there and committees are chosen by a "committee on committees" named by the titular leader. But those who appear to direct things must resort to persuasion and the caucus is a kind of informal council in which efforts are made to reach an understanding by common consent. Senators are not bound to speak and vote for the measures agreed upon in this assembly, although naturally they must allow some weight to its decisions.

In the House of Representatives the party conference likewise presents varied aspects from time to time although the very size of that body makes more formality necessary. At the opening of the twentieth century the House caucus was also mainly a machine for ratifying decisions already reached by a handful of managers, including the Speaker, the chairman of the rules committee, and a few elder statesmen. But in the great progressive upheaval which soon followed, their iron rule was broken. On coming to power in 1911, the Democrats sought to give vitality to the caucus and to grant the individual members a larger share in formulating policies. Henceforward, they said, the Speaker and the committees will be chosen in a full and free council of the party members. The Speaker sank into the background; power and responsibility were widely diffused among the rank and file. But in these circumstances decisions were difficult to obtain and leadership was transferred in 1913 to President Wilson.

When Wilson passed from the scene and Harding came to the presidency, executive control over legislation was relaxed, giving more freedom to Congress. After a period of confusion, the majority, or Republican, caucus in the House of Representatives once more became rather formal in character, owing partly to the decline in the number of "insurgents" and partly to the renewed concentration of leadership in the Speaker, the chairman of the rules committee, the floor leader, and the chairman of the ways and means committee, "the four horsemen," as they were called in political parlance. As a matter of fact even when the caucus was supposed to be a council of freedom, its agenda had to be prepared in advance and it was usually the practice for a few managers to hold a "pre-caucus" for that purpose.

Whether acting under its own momentum or under the direction of a few powerful figures, the caucus must frequently override individual dissenters in the party. Meetings are held in secret. Although news of their proceedings usually appears in the papers, attempts to throw them open have been without avail. Many members may be absent and decisions in such cases will be made by a small portion of the party group. Since, according to the rules of the Republican caucus in the House, every member is morally bound to abide by its decisions—unless he has made contrary pledges to his constituents—a narrow vote in the conference may compel all party Representatives to support, on the floor, a particular bill or resolution. Again and again it has happened that the dissenters among the majority, if united with the opposition, could have defeated or carried a measure. In other words, the caucus makes possible legislation by a minority of the House.

Yet it would be a mistake to lay too much emphasis on it as a directing organization. Only a small part of the business before Congress is settled in advance in solemn caucuses; hence the party member enjoys a large degree of freedom with respect to most matters. Moreover from time to time experiments are made in cutting athwart caucus and party lines. For example in 1921, as a result of conferences attended by Senators and Representatives of both parties, a "Farm Bloc" was formed to speak for the agricultural interests of the country. After discussing the issues in hand, they agreed to act together on bills of common concern to the farmers. Again in 1929 agrarian Republicans and agrarian Democrats in the Senate for a time united in a war on the Republican tariff bill sent up by the House, without making a formal treaty of alliance.

Leadership

Under the most favorable circumstances, the caucus works only a partial concentration of power in the houses of Congress in the matter of selecting the propositions to be considered and passed. It is too large and miscellaneous in membership to act on all measures or even to discuss critically very many of them. Most of the technical decisions and recommendations presented to it by experienced committee chairmen it must accept on faith; it cannot pretend to expertness. If the caucus did in fact frequently attempt to reverse the decisions of committee chairmen, it would force their resignation and break down the working party organization.

In practice, therefore, a still smaller number of members

than is embraced in the party caucus must perforce assume the responsibility for choosing the measures to be considered, directing congressional procedure, and deciding what bills shall be finally enacted into laws. In England this power is vested by law and custom in the hands of the cabinet, composed of twenty or more persons (most of them members of Parliament) who are in theory at least chosen by a conference of the dominant party. Among the cabinet officers, the acknowledged leader is the prime minister. Indeed he is picked first and accepts as colleagues only those who can work with him in a fair degree of harmony. He is responsible before the whole nation for carrying into effect the principles of his party, and if he is defeated on a test measure of prime significance, it is his duty to resign or to bring about a new election.

In the United States neither law nor custom vests the open and avowed leadership in the House of Representatives or the Senate in any small body of men known to the public and held accountable for the questions debated and the laws passed. But in reality there is and must be leadership and a certain degree of centralization in power. As the authority of the rank and file of the members in the party caucus expands and contracts, so the leadership varies in character. With political changes, too, it shifts from one center to another. Now it is the Speaker and the rules committee in the House that direct policies; now the chairman of the ways and means committee occupies the dominant position. Wherever the leadership is, it is certain to be assailed by members who feel their interests neglected or their sense of importance offended. Attacks long continued are sure to work a dispersion of prerogative and new localizations of it in detail.

At the opening of the twentieth century, the directing power in the House was unquestionably concentrated in the Speaker, the majority members of the rules committee (of whom the Speaker was one), and the chairmen of the important committees. The positive leadership of these men and their responsibility were definitely recognized throughout the country. They were working toward something like an inner council of government; they formulated policies and brought the other party members into line under a régime of severe discipline. In this little group the Speaker was the outstanding figure. As a writer at the time observed: "The Speaker's control over legislation is now, under the rules and practices of the House, almost absolute. The people know this now. The time has passed when the Speaker could exercise his vast power unsuspected. Nor can he shirk his responsibility. No bill can pass the House without his passive approval, and that in effect is the same thing as active advocacy." He appointed all the members of all the committees and named the chairman of each; he and two of his party colleagues formed a majority in the committee on rules which could in fact (with the approval of the House, which was always given) decide what measures should be debated, when and how long they should be debated, and when the vote on them should be taken.

Against this system, the Democrats protested as a matter of course, for it destroyed their influence in the House; but their objections would have availed little if there had not arisen discontent among the newer Republican members, particularly among the more radical Representatives from the West. They disliked many measures which their own party leaders forced through Congress and they failed to get a hearing for their own plans. Moreover, the Speaker, Joseph G. Cannon, was harsh in his rulings and unconciliatory in conducting proceedings. At length, in 1910, the Democrats, aided by disgruntled Republicans, overthrew the Speaker; they enlarged the rules committee, provided that it should be elected, and ousted the Speaker from membership. When the Democrats, victorious in the election of that year, took possession of the chamber, they provided that all committees should be elected by the House. Thus the Speaker was shorn of his power over the appointment of committees and their selection was transferred to the party caucus—which indeed had always enjoyed more or less authority in the matter. Amid cheers for "the fall of the Czar" and the end of "despotism," a dissipation of leadership was effected.

The "revolution" did not, however, make the rank and file of the members equal or destroy leadership. Through all such changes a certain concentration of power has remained. As the shots at a target, wild though some of them may be, tend to group around the center, so attempts to build up directing management in the House are found grouped around five sources of influence: the Speaker, the rules committee, the chairmen of the important committees, the floor leader, and the "steering committee." This has long been true and is true to-day.

The Speaker of the House of Representatives, a party man chosen by a party caucus, cannot be simply a presiding officer, like the Speaker of the House of Commons in England. There the prime minister assumes responsibility for his party measures; at Washington the position of the Speaker is entirely different. In the beginning of our history, to be sure, he was regarded as a mere moderator, but as the House grew in size and the business to be transacted increased to enormous proportions, it became impossible for him to sit passively and see the measures advocated by his party delayed indefinitely or defeated by the dilatory tactics of the minority. Though he can no longer appoint the committees, his powers over procedure are great. He may refuse to put motions which he thinks designed merely to delay business; he may recognize or refuse to recognize anyone who wishes to debate a question or call up a measure for consideration; he may rule members out of order and decide questions of parliamentary law—subject, of course, to appeals from the decision of the chair. In spite of recent changes these powers yet remain. The Speaker, therefore, inevitably holds a sector in the line of influence. He is not as imperial in his sway as were Cannon and Reed in the old days, but he is no mere figurehead.

Closely associated with the Speaker, no more dominant than he, is the rules committee composed of twelve members, of whom a majority speak for the party that is supreme in the House. It has a right to be heard at almost any moment. It may bring in resolutions stating what measures shall be considered, how long they shall be debated, and when the vote shall be taken. Members of the party for which the rules committee acts may revolt and refuse to support such resolutions, but if they do they incur all the risks inherent in party "treason."

The third element of leadership in the House of Representatives is composed of the chairmen of the important committees in charge of the weightiest measures brought up for debate and action. The premier among them is the chairman of the ways and means committee which prepares tariff and tax bills. Indeed when the Speaker was stripped of his regal authority in 1911, his influence and prestige temporarily went to the head of this powerful committee. Next in order of precedence may be placed the chairman of the appropriations committee which, under the budget law of 1921 and the rules associated with it, exercises a material influence on decisions respecting the amount and purposes of expenditures. Then follow in uncertain order the heads of other great committees, ten or fifteen in all, with the minor men swinging off loosely on the edges of power.

Finally in considering the inner dominion of the House we must take account of the floor leader chosen by the party caucus. Each party has such an agent. It is his duty to keep in close touch with the rank and file of his colleagues, to learn their opinions, to understand their prejudices and ambitions, and whenever necessary to "line them all up" in support of some measure on which the party managers have reached a decision. The floor leader is influential in determining who shall speak on bills, because by conferences with party brethren he helps to make up the list of members whom the presiding officer will recognize. On important matters the majority floor leader will take counsel with the minority leader and reach an agreement as to the Representatives who are to be heard and the time to be allowed for debate before the vote is cast. In short, the majority floor leader has succeeded to many of the prerogatives formerly exercised by the Speaker; in terms of power perhaps he ranks next to that official; and if he is clever he may hope to rise to the honor of taking the chair himself. But he must be circumspect. His power is uncertain. He is subject more or less to the direction of a "steering committee," unknown to the rules of the House, chosen by the caucus, *i.e.,* by "natural selection," for the purpose of exercising a general supervisory authority over proceedings—an informal group of a few members who operate quietly behind the scenes. He must also deal gently with the independents, especially if their votes are needed to carry party measures. But by the exercise of tact and with the aid of his "whip," a member charged with helping to hold the party in step, he can keep the machine in smooth running order.

In the Senate, the problems of leadership are not so difficult to work out. The number of members is small. The majority in control seldom consists of more than fifty or sixty. Among them are always several men of experience derived from long service, who are marked for management. The presiding officer, under constitutional provision, is the Vice President of the United States who, though himself a partisan, is more of a moderator than a director. Often indeed he represents the minority, not the dominant group in the Senate. In such circumstances actual leadership falls largely to a few committee chairmen, among whom the head of the finance committee takes high rank. There is a party conference, of course; its power, like that of the House caucus, expands and contracts with passing events and is seldom if ever despotic. Floor leaders, whips, and steering committees also are to be found in the Senate; but their function is not dictation; their business is rather to secure party harmony or get work done by informal methods. The individual Senator, therefore, enjoys more weight in party councils and more independence of action on the floor than the member of the House.

There are in addition other practices and customs which work for a concentration of power on business in Congress. The President, through his prestige, his party leadership, and his control over appointments to office, exercises an immense influence on the work of the national legislature. In times of party crises, there may be informal conferences of the leaders in both houses and party officers and workers on the outside. But here we pass from the known to the unknown, out into the realm of complex social forces which press in upon Congress from every part of the country.

Leadership, once secured, thrives upon the meat with which it is fed. Every member of Congress, as we have seen, has schemes of his own relating to his district and demanded by the voters who elected him. So he must get a hearing. And in the press of things he cannot get it without the consent of one or more powerful committee chairmen. What can he give in return? His vote on the measures recommended by party leaders, his loyal support to the program as formulated by them. So the net is drawn tightly and power concentrates —until accumulated discontent dissipates it again. Thus centripetal and centrifugal forces alternate, but, whenever business is to be transacted, leadership must come into play. A Senator recently described the situation at the opening of Congress in a crude parody on Kipling's "Recessional":

> "The tumult and the shouting dies.
> The captains and the kings depart.
> And the steam roller is about to start."

What after all is the cause of the continual uproar over the organization of Congress? Why are there always insurgents raging against established leadership and demanding a redistribution of authority? What is it that they want? The answers are difficult to formulate, but an attempt may be made. Whenever any party has a long tenure of office, such as the Republicans enjoyed between 1897 and

1911, two things happen. The members of longer service gather in all the power they can, for men thirst after it for its own sake and for the loaves and fishes connected with it. In the meantime new men appear and there is discontent on the left wing of the triumphant party. That is natural and inevitable also.

Now, the new men will receive little or no recognition unless they obey orders; that means they will otherwise get no power and no spoils; their measures will be smothered in committee and never see the floor of the house. They usually want, therefore, two reforms: a wider dispersion of committee assignments and party authority, especially among the members of the majority, and some kind of rule which will permit a certain number, let us say one hundred, to call up any bill from the recesses of any committee and force a vote on it. Some even go beyond this, and demand that every bill introduced in each house shall be automatically brought out and put to a vote. In this way they hope to get a consideration of their own measures and to place the members on record for or against their propositions. Indeed there are a few reformers who would like to destroy the party machine in Congress entirely, and allow all members an equal share of authority in controlling procedure. It is not likely that such a utopian reform will occur soon; it is more probable that we shall witness the continuance of the old struggle with changes only in emphasis.

The Committees of Congress

Whatever happens to other pieces of political machinery, a very fundamental element in congressional leadership will always be found in the standing committees nominally chosen by each house but in fact by party managers, subject to more or less interference on the part of the caucus and to the principle of seniority—the precedence of members oldest in service. As the bills brought into Congress become more and more technical, with the advance of the industrial age, so the power of those who have special knowledge and experience in various fields must increase. This is inevitable. It is highly desirable. At all events, the legislative work of each house is done mainly by committees composed of members more or less expert in the several branches of law making. Each important committee is dominated by a majority representing the party which is supreme for the time being and its chairman is always a prominent leader. He has power and must be heard. The number of standing committees varies from time to time, but at present (in 1930) there are thirty-three in the Senate and forty-four in the House.

Each committee has a well-furnished office and many perquisites which are not despised by members of Congress; that is, it has an allowance for secretaries, stationery, and other purposes. Often members employ their wives or relatives as clerks and assistants. Undoubtedly a great deal of money is wasted in useless activities, especially in connection with the minor committees, but criticisms of the system fall on deaf ears. Several years ago when a member from Massachusetts, shocked by the careless expenditures for committees that never met, resigned his post by way of protest, his action was greeted by indifference or laughter. Although efficiency calls for pruning the outlays of committees, the necessity of having assignments for all members and jobs for their constituents makes economy in this relation well nigh impossible.

As already suggested, the standing committees vary greatly in importance. In the lower house, the leading committees are on ways and means, appropriations, rules, banking and currency, interstate and foreign commerce, rivers and harbors, military affairs, naval affairs, post-offices and post-roads, public lands, labor, and pensions. In the Senate, the committees on appropriations, finance, foreign relations, judiciary, military affairs, naval affairs, interstate commerce, and pensions take high rank. From time to time the standing committees are supplemented by select committees chosen for some particular function and dissolved when they have fulfilled their duties.

Formerly all standing committees of the House of Representatives were appointed by the Speaker, but the rule was changed in 1910-11 in favor of election by the House itself. After this "revolution" occurred, the Democrats adopted a new plan which displayed more sympathy for the rank and file in making committee assignments; at a caucus they named the Democratic members of the ways and means committee; they then authorized that group to act as a "committee on committees" for the purpose of nominating the members of the remaining committees, subject to ratification at another caucus. When the Republicans came back to power in 1919, there was an attempt to make the diffusion of authority even more mechanical; their caucus created a committee on committees composed of one member from each state having one or more Republicans in the House and gave each of them as many votes as there were Republicans in the delegation from his state. In short, an effort was made to mirror the entire majority in the agency formed to select its members of the standing committees. The recommendations of the committee on committees, no matter how constituted, are always submitted to party conferences for approval, and then laid before the House for formal confirmation.

Although the transfer of the appointing power from the Speaker to the House asserted the authority of the latter, the change in practice was more apparent than real. Since the beginning of the party system in the United States, the selection of committees in each house has been more or less in the hands of the party caucus; but that assembly, as we have seen, is not a conference of men equal in terms of service, wealth, abilities, or political power. It is generally under the dominance of a few members skilled in the arts of management. To borrow a term from economics, we may say, therefore, that the committee assignments are determined by a "higgling" of the market and that the various posts fall to members roughly according to seniority, their abilities, their power as leaders, their capacity for negotiation. This "higgling" begins long before a new Congress meets. Most of the important assignments are probably determined, in fact, if not in theory, before the party conference assembles, and the caucus only ratifies the decisions of preliminary meetings just as the houses ratify the work of the caucuses. The minority party chooses representatives on each committee, somewhat in the same manner as the majority party but they seldom count for much in the determination of policies and the framing of laws.

Among the practices or traditions which govern the choice of committees none is more noteworthy than the custom that distributes important assignments among members in accordance with the length of their service—the "seniority rule." It is only natural that the direction of affairs should fall to the most experienced. However, when one of the parties returns to power after a long season in the opposition, the new incoming members are sure to make a great outcry against allowing their older colleagues to monopolize all the choice posts. The progressives in both the parties, looking upon age as a sign of inherent and irremedial conservatism, regularly protest against the time-honored custom, but the principle of seniority is consistently applied, with occasional exceptions of course. Still, as an offset to the monopoly of leadership by experience, no Senator or Representative is ordinarily permitted to serve on more than two powerful committees. On the whole, in practice, every significant committee—consisting in the House of from twenty-one to thirty-five members and in the Senate of from twelve to twenty members—is a fair mirror of the chamber itself.

Thus each of the two houses has created miniature legislatures to which are assigned, in accordance with their subject matter, all bills and resolutions. For example in the House every piece of proposed legislation relating to the revenue and the bonded debt or purporting to raise revenue automatically goes to the committee on ways and means. The recommendations contained in the President's message are distributed among committees on the same principle. But a committee is not limited to suggestions from outside; it may and does itself originate bills and other measures relating to questions placed under its jurisdiction.

Thousands of the bills which go to committees are not considered at all. It is only the propositions which are to be reported to the house for action that receive a more or less severe scrutiny. In such cases papers and documents may be secured from the President or high officials; department heads or other administrative authorities may be requested to appear personally, expound their opinions, and answer questions. Friends and opponents of projects are frequently admitted to state their views; witnesses may be summoned to give testimony; and the committee may even travel about the country, hold hearings, and gather evidence.

In almost every instance the measures entrusted to a particular committee are scrutinized or formulated by a subcommittee (in which the minority members receive scant recognition if any at all), and the whole committee generally accepts its report. When a strict party question, such as the tariff, is on the carpet, the majority members of the committee in charge will fix up the bill. After it is completed, they may invite the minority in to vote on it as a matter of form or they may even overlook that courtesy. With regard to any proposition in hand, a committee may recommend its adoption, amend it, report adversely, delay the report indefinitely, or ignore it altogether.

Measures on which committees do not report favorably have a very slight chance of passing, and even a favorable report is not a guarantee of victory, especially in the Senate. In the House it rarely happens that a member is able to get action on a bill which the committee in charge opposes; only by securing the signatures of a majority of the Representatives can he bring on the floor a project "buried in committee." In the Senate, greater freedom is enjoyed in this respect, because it is easier for a Senator to obtain unanimous consent to a motion discharging a committee from the consideration of a measure and thus get it before the chamber for discussion.

Both procedures are rather exceptional. As a rule the committees really control the sifting, preparation, and report of bills for debate, and their final deliberations are secret. Moreover in the pressure of business, especially in the House of Representatives, important measures are often forced through exactly as they come from committees, without any serious examination or a single amendment. This practice, of course, vests an enormous authority in the committees and has almost changed the House from a deliberative into a ratifying assembly. At the other end of the Capitol, however, the Senators, fewer in number, can insist on subjecting projects laid before them by committees to more careful analysis and more searching review. In their chamber the committee holds no such power of life and death over bills and resolutions.

Owing to the high prerogatives enjoyed by committees, to the secrecy that surrounds their operations, and to the pressure of lobbies on them, a great deal of criticism has been directed against the whole system as a piece of legislative machinery. As early as 1880, the Independent National, or Greenback, party demanded "absolutely democratic rules" for the government of Congress and advocated taking away from the committees "a veto power greater than that of the President." In the House itself complaints are constantly made, especially by members of the minority. "You send important questions to a committee," once lamented a member, "you put into the hands of a few men the power to bring in bills, and then they are brought in with an ironclad rule, and rammed down the throats of members; and then those measures are sent out as being the deliberate judgment of the Congress of the United States when no deliberate judgment has been expressed by any man."

It would be idle to contend that the indictments brought against the committee régime are to be lightly dismissed. In the House of Representatives at least it certainly tends to break responsibility into thirty or more fractions and to reduce that chamber to the level of a "rubber stamp" for committee reports. Since debate on the floor is likely to be ineffective, the secrecy that surrounds committee proceedings is made all the more objectionable. An illustration of this was afforded by the history of the tariff bill of 1929–30 which passed the House of Representatives with amazing speed and was held up in the Senate for more than a year. Out of the discussion that ensued came an investigation of lobbies, which revealed how the economic groups interested in the measure had brought influence to bear on its formation. In this case argument and inquiry brought many changes in the House bill and gave the country an education in politics. Besides contributing to back-stairs legislation the system permits the committees to work on their respective measures with little or no regard for one another, each preparing its own bills without constant reference to kindred measures in other hands.

For the undoubted evils of the committee scheme two outstanding remedies are offered. One is the creation of the kind of unofficial leadership and direction which was built up by the Republicans in the early part of this century. The other is the adoption of the English cabinet system which openly vests control in the hands of a responsible group, the cabinet. The first has been tried and rejected as a form of "invisible government." The second, striking as it does at the very root of the congressional structure, receives little consideration outside academic circles. Less radical suggestions include a consolidation of committees, materially reducing their number, and changes in the rules of the House of Representatives establishing a larger freedom of debate—a freedom akin to that prevailing in the Senate. But these also appear to be more theoretical than practical.

The General Course of Procedure

At the opening of a new Congress the House of Representatives is brought to order by the clerk of the last House, who, finding a quorum present, announces that it is time to choose the Speaker. In response the majority and minority put forward their candidates already picked by the caucuses, and after the former's nominee is duly elected, he takes the oath of office administered by the member longest in continuous service. The roll is then called by the clerk, and the Representatives go forward to be sworn in. The other officers are chosen, and the President of the United States and the Senate are informed that the lower chamber is ready for business. A proposition to adopt the rules of the preceding House, with modifications perhaps, is threshed out, and carried in the face of traditional protests from the minority. In due time the names of the committeemen selected by the conferences of the parties are read, and approved by the House.

The Senate differs from the lower chamber, as we have said, in being a continuous body. At each Congress only one third of the membership is renewed. The presiding officer, the Vice President, as required by the Constitution, takes the chair. In case of his absence, the duties are performed by a president *pro tempore*. The names of the newly elected Senators are read by the secretary of the Senate; each in turn is escorted to the presiding officer's desk, usually by the colleague from his state, and there takes the oath of office. The President and House are notified, and the Senate also goes into action.

Bills are introduced in several ways. Each member may bring forward any measure he likes or he may present a petition for a project which will be referred to an appropriate committee for formulation. Propositions may also come from the White House, from the departments of the Federal Government, and from the other chamber. All really important bills, however, such as tariff and currency measures, are framed by the majority members of the committees in charge of the subject matter. Sometimes, the committees of the two houses in care of similar business coöperate informally in preparing drafts of law. If the question is very significant, the President of the United States may join them in drawing up a bill and prominent party leaders not in office may be consulted. Indeed a party caucus may be held on the scheme even before it is brought up for consideration.

On introduction in the House by a member, a bill is referred by the Speaker to the appropriate committee, which may hold hearings and give the matter any amount of attention it sees fit. As we have said, it may report the bill favorably, unamended; it may make changes and report a new form; or it may report unfavorably. Similar arrangements prevail in the Senate. When a bill is reported for passage it is placed on a calendar and, unless otherwise ordered, it comes up for discussion on the day when the particular calendar is reached under the rules. But the chief measures, such as appropriation bills and important projects sponsored by party leaders, have the "right of way" under various technical rules including the privilege of "unanimous consent," and they may be brought out on the floor at almost any time.

Debates in the House of Representatives are often perfunctory, seldom animated, and very rarely have material effect upon its conclusions. With respect to important bills before it, decisions have already been made by party leaders; accordingly there is little to be said on such measures by members of the dominant group, except by way of explanation. The opposition, of course, is allotted a certain amount of time as a matter of form, but no one expects criticisms from that quarter to produce any surprising results. On the other hand, in the Senate, where, as we have noted, debate is freer than in the House, arguments of great power are sometimes delivered, and may really alter opinions and votes.

Many speeches that appear in the pages of the *Congressional Record* are delivered to empty benches during sessions of the committee of the whole, or not delivered at all. Frequently they are directed to the constituents of the orator rather than members of Congress. Since the "leave to print" or to "extend remarks" is rather generously granted, Senators and Representatives may address the voters of their districts through speeches supposed to have been made on the floor, printed often at public expense, and sent free of charge through the mails. Even such entries as "Cheers," "Laughter," and "Prolonged Applause" have been inserted in preparing copy for the printer of the *Record*.

When a bill has passed either house, it is immediately transmitted to the other chamber for review. For example if it goes through the Senate, it is sent to the House; if it is carried there in its original form, the Senate is notified; it is then signed by the President of the Senate and the Speaker of the House and is handed to the President of the United States for his signature. If he approves the bill, he transmits it to the State Department and, in due course, the Secretary of State gives it official publication. If he vetoes the measure, he returns it to the house of its origin, with a statement of the reasons for his decision, unless that body has adjourned. Repassage by a two-thirds vote is necessary to carry a bill over the President's veto (p. 284).

Although the provisions of the Constitution are explicit to the effect that every order, resolution, or vote to which the concurrence of the Senate and House of Representatives may be necessary (except on a question of adjournment) shall be presented to the President, Congress has devised a scheme known as the "concurrent resolution," which, although it clearly has the effect of law, is not submitted to him for approval. The form of this resolution is as follows: *Resolved,* by the House of Representatives (the Senate concurring) that, etc.; or, *Resolved,* by the Senate (the House of Representatives concurring) that, etc. It is the uniform practice of Congress, however, to avoid incorporating in such measures any matter in the nature of legislation. Frequently the concurrent resolution is employed in ordering the publication of documents, in paying therefor, and in incurring and meeting other expenses, from money that has already been appropriated and set apart by law for the use of the two houses in their legislative work.

Whenever a bill originating in one house is altered in the other, it must be returned to the first for reconsideration, and for adoption or rejection as amended. If, at last, the houses are unable to agree upon it—a regular occurrence in the case of important measures—it is the practice for the presiding officer of each body to appoint representatives to a joint conference committee, as it is called, authorized to discuss the differences, to come to some conclusion on the disputed points, and report back to the respective houses their agreement, or their inability to come to terms. As a general principle the conference committee, in reaching an understanding, should introduce no new matter into the proposal which it has under consideration—that is, no provision that has not been already adopted by either the Senate or the House. It is not easy, of course, to determine whether new materials have been introduced into a long and complicated bill. Certainly the conferees are not limited in their action to a choice of clauses actually passed by one house or the other. They may and often do, effect a compromise, perhaps midway between the extremes, and in drafting it they may, in fact, change substantially the language of the two bills before them. When a conference committee report is submitted, each house adopts it, or rejects it as a whole, unless it is purposely divided into parts so that separate action can be taken on special items.

Such is the general course of procedure. An examination of actual transactions as reported daily in the *Congressional Record,* however, shows that in practice no mechanical system prevails. With unanimous consent almost anything can be taken up at any time, and unless the pressure of business is great the privilege is generally granted. Powerful committees, privileged to report projects whenever they are ready, may interrupt proceedings almost at any hour, especially in the House, and start them off on a new tack. When a bill is up for discussion, particularly in committee of the whole,[1] members may use their time in speaking on matters not germane at all to the subject in hand. Thus, for example, debates on the wool schedule of a tariff bill may include speeches on good roads, patriotism, or prohibition. It has been said that the rule of the Senate is to have no rules. Although there is a touch of exaggeration in this statement, the same generalization may be applied, with still more reservation, to the lower House. At all events in neither chamber does there prevail a rigid system which requires the consideration of measures in order of their importance or their appearance from committee rooms, holds debates to the topic until it is disposed of, and relegates all minor issues to particular days. The exceptions to the rules are so great as to give the appearance of chaos rather than order to the daily business of Congress.

Rules for Expediting Business

Given the immense mass of business before Congress and the practice of party leadership and responsibility, it is necessary for each house to provide a body of principles for expediting action. These principles are to be found in Jefferson's *Manual of Parliamentary Practice,* the standing rules of each chamber, and the vast number of precedents established during the history of Congress. Whoever finds sheer enjoyment in unraveling complicated problems of parliamentary custom has an unlimited field for self-indulgence in the eight bulky volumes of a thousand pages each, compiled by A. C. Hinds, former Clerk of the Speaker's Table, bearing the title of *Parliamentary Precedents of the House of Representatives.*

In addition to assuring a certain degree of regularity in procedure and providing the canons for governing exceptional

[1] The committee of the whole forms a convenient body for discussion and provisional voting on measures. In it, one hundred constitute a quorum and the Speaker's chair is taken by some other member. Measures approved in it are reported to the House for formal adoption.

actions, the rules of the House and Senate make it possible for leadership to direct, limit, and in a measure dictate action. They are a part of the system of control and their changes reflect the periods of concentration and expansion of power noted above (pp. 181ff.). At all times, however, certain regulations remain fairly fixed.

In the larger body, the House of Representatives, the Speaker is authorized, by a rule adopted in 1890 and still in effect, to refuse to put dilatory motions—that is, propositions designed merely to delay business. The rule is not applied, however, until the purpose of such a motion has become apparent, and the Speaker usually waits until a point of order is raised on the floor before he brings it into force. Even then the constitutional right of the member to call for yeas and nays cannot be denied although the object is evidently dilatory.

The immediate cause of the adoption of this rule against dilatory motions was the practice of "filibustering" by the minority or by small groups. In ordinary use, the term filibuster means to act as a freebooter or buccaneer, but in a parliamentary sense it is applied to the obstruction of legislation "by undue use of the technicalities of parliamentary law or privileges, as when a minority, in order to prevent the passage of some measure obnoxious to them, endeavor to tire out their opponents by useless motions, speeches, and objections." Frequently, the purpose of such interfering tactics is to call the attention of the country in an emphatic way to the policy of the majority, and often it is highly successful. In the Fiftieth Congress, on one occasion, the "House remained in continuous session eight days and nights, during which time there were over one hundred roll-calls on the iterated and reiterated motions to adjourn and to take a recess, and their amendments. On this occasion the reading clerks became so exhausted that they could no longer act, and certain members, possessed of large voices and strenuous lungs, took their places. If this was not child's play, it would be difficult to define it. Then, again, when a measure to which the minority objected was likely to pass, the yeas and nays would be ordered."

In the succeeding Congress, in which Thomas B. Reed was the Speaker, the Republicans had only a narrow majority, and it soon became clear that the opposition, by making dilatory motions and refusing to answer to the roll-call on a quorum, could prevent them from doing any business at all. It was under these circumstances that Speaker Reed flatly refused to put propositions which he regarded as merely designed to hinder proceedings. In this decision he was sustained by the House and later fortified by the rule we have just cited above.

In defense Mr. Reed made the following explanation: "The object of a parliamentary body is action, and not stoppage of action. Hence if any member or set of members undertakes to oppose the orderly progress of business even by the use of the ordinarily recognized parliamentary motions, it is the right of the majority to refuse to have those motions entertained and to cause the public business to proceed. Primarily, the organ of the House is the man elected to the speakership; it is his duty in a clear case, recognizing the situation, to endeavor to carry out the wishes and desires of the majority of the body which he represents. Whenever it becomes apparent that the ordinary and proper parliamentary motions are being used solely for the purposes of delay and obstruction; . . . when a gentleman steps down to the front amid the applause of his associates on the floor and announces that it is his intention to make opposition in every direction, it then becomes apparent to the House and the community what the purpose is. It is then the duty of the occupant of the Speaker's chair to take, under parliamentary law, the proper course with regard to such matters."

As a part of the program for expediting business in the House of Representatives, the Speaker is also authorized to count as present those members who are actually in the chamber but refuse to answer to their names on a roll-call for the purpose of compelling an adjournment on the ground of the absence of a quorum (p. 167). This principle was established by Speaker Reed about the same time as his verdict on dilatory motions, and has likewise been incorporated in the rules.

Besides putting a ban on filibustering, the rules of the House expedite business by limiting the time devoted to the discussion of propositions. They provide that no member shall occupy more than one hour in debate on any question in the House or in the committee of the whole. This restraint was imposed in 1841, and in commenting on it Senator Benton declared that it was "the largest limitation upon the freedom of debate which any deliberative assembly ever imposed upon itself, and presents an eminent instance of permanent injury done to free institutions in order to get rid of a temporary annoyance." But it is difficult to see how the House could meet the enormous pressure upon it, if any member could talk as long as he pleased on any project. Supplementing this hour rule is another forbidding a member to speak more than once on the same issue unless he is the mover, proposer, or introducer of the measure in hand, and not even in this case until the other members have finished. A member reporting on behalf of a committee, however, is allowed an additional hour for closing the debate on his proposal, if the discussion has extended beyond one day.

If he chooses, of course, a member may yield a portion of his time to colleagues who wish to speak, but not more than one hour. Furthermore when it goes into committee of the whole, the House fixes a time to be employed in discussion which cannot be extended by the committee; and in many other ways freedom of speech is arbitrarily limited. Then as a climax it is always in order to move "the previous question" and shut off debate in the House automatically.

Supplementing these restraints on dilatory tactics and time limits on debate are provisions which enable the leaders of the majority party in the House of Representatives to compel that body to give attention to their important measures whenever they see fit. This end is accomplished by rules which permit the leading committees to report on specified subjects practically at any time in the course of the proceedings, no matter what may be under discussion. When such a privileged report is made, the House must consider it subject to the above restrictions on delay and loquacity.

With respect to such restraints the Senate by contrast is singularly free. When its rules were revised in 1806, the right to move the previous question, and thus close debate summarily, was omitted, and all attempts to restore control failed until 1917. At the session convened in March of that year, the Senate found its business blocked in an apparently endless dispute. By a certain irony of fate the Democrats, who had always been ardent champions of free speech, were forced to insist upon some method of limiting it. Acting on the recommendation of a special committee composed of an equal number of members from both parties, the Senate then adopted a new rule providing that, on petition signed by sixteen Senators, a motion to cut off the discussion of any measure can be presented to the Senate. If approved two days later by a two-thirds vote, debate will come to an end, after each member has enjoyed the privilege of speaking for not more than one hour on the pending question; when such a closure has been approved, amendments to the bill under consideration can be made only by unanimous consent and dilatory motions are out of order.

In practice it has been found impossible to bring this rule into frequent use, and long filibusters have often blocked the business of the Senate since it went into effect. Exasperated by such "inefficiency," Vice President Dawes tried to launch a national campaign to force the adoption of an easier method of terminating argument. But the Senate has been obdurate and not without reason. As Lindsay Rogers cogently contends in his book, *The American Senate,* liberty of debate in that body acts as a salutary check on the administration, gives the minority the right to be heard, and assures at least one open forum in the country for the free consideration of issues which might otherwise be smothered.

After this survey of the devices by which the dominant party, especially in the House of Representatives, may control reports of committees and the discussion and passage of measures, it might be assumed that the minority is powerless to influence in any effective manner the course of legislative procedure. This view, however, is not strictly correct. By exercising certain constitutional privileges, the minority may hamper proceedings and go a long way toward forcing the majority to accept some policies it would not initiate on its own motion. The Constitution provides that on the request of one fifth of the members present, the roll of either house must be called on any question and the yeas and nays of the members entered upon the journal. It furthermore stipulates that no business shall be done unless a quorum is present. Therefore the minority, in the House or Senate, may insist upon one roll-call after another, thus consuming time and making delays. Finally, since a great deal of the legislative business is actually done under the rule of unanimous consent, the members of the minority can employ the threat of refusal as an engine of coercion.

More than once a leader of the opposition party has thrown down the gage to the directors of the majority and frankly informed them that unless certain measures were adopted the minority would exercise all its privileges for the purpose of obstructing business. In this way a few members may defeat or modify bills by threats or by delays continuing until near the end of the session. They sometimes even compel action on their own measures by announcing that they will refuse unanimous consent on all propositions and call for the yeas and nays on every bill and resolution until the majority capitulates and brings in the propositions which they demand.

Constitutional provisions safeguarding the rights of the minority in the House of Representatives are strengthened by an important rule in favor of individuals. Any member of that chamber may present to the clerk a motion in writing instructing a committee to report within fifteen days a public bill or resolution which has been referred to it at least thirty days previously. If a majority of the members sign the motion, it is entered in the journal. On the day fixed by the rules, it may be called up for discussion and the House must proceed to its consideration. In this way it becomes impossible for the directorate to smother a measure that is really desired by a majority. As a result the single member, if he can secure support among his colleagues, may theoretically at least obtain a hearing for his cause.

Information for Legislative Action

Although each house has standing committees to deal with the broad classes of issues which regularly come up for discussion, it frequently makes special provisions for securing information on economic, technological, administrative, and other complicated issues. Both chambers have limited allowances for this purpose and additional amounts may be set aside by resolution or law.

Generally speaking four types of agencies are employed in such work. The Senate or House may direct one of its standing committees to conduct an inquiry into a particular matter and supply it with funds to hold hearings and engage expert investigators and advisors. If the question is deemed of high significance by both chambers, they may unite in appointing a joint committee of inquest with similar powers.

A third type of exploring organ, occasionally created, consists of members of both houses and prominent citizens named by the President. For example in 1898 Congress instituted by special act an industrial commission consisting of five Representatives, five Senators, and nine persons appointed by the President—the last to be paid salaries. This commission was instructed to study questions pertaining to immigration, labor, agriculture, and business, to report to Congress, and to suggest desirable legislation in these fields. It made long and exhaustive researches, assembled a voluminous mass of testimony, and drafted many legislative proposals. A few years later, namely, in 1907, Congress set up a joint commission on immigration, consisting of three Senators, three Representatives, and three persons selected by the President—charged with the duty of making a full examination of the subject. Again in 1913 Congress established an industrial relations commission which inquired into labor and agricultural problems and startled the whole country by the radical character of its findings. Such committees are usually authorized to appoint expert assistants for the purpose of collecting data, making detailed analyses, and aiding in the formulation of policies.

The fourth type of agency used by Congress in developing information is a branch or division of the executive department. For example, on one occasion, by joint resolution, it instructed the Interstate Commerce Commission to scrutinize railroad discriminations and monopolies, and to report on the same from time to time. Congress has even required certain federal courts to compel witnesses to testify before the Commission, and the Supreme Court has sustained this action. In expounding its decision, the Court declared that it was clearly competent for Congress to vest in the Commission an authority to require the attendance of witnesses, the giving of testimony, and the production of books, papers, and documents relating to any matter legally committed to it for investigation. Sometimes an executive office or division may be authorized by law to carry on certain studies on its own motion and report its results to Congress. Such powers, for instance, are enjoyed by the Trade Commission (p. 464). Again, a federal establishment may be called upon by both houses or either of them to make a particular inquiry. An illustration of this practice is to be found in a resolution passed by the Senate in 1928 instructing the Federal Trade Commission to look into the operations of public utility corporations and affiliated concerns.

In ordering inquiries Congress is not limited to the affairs of private citizens and corporations. It may also pry into the working of federal departments and offices. Although the Constitution vests the executive power in the President, a long line of precedents establishes the right of Congress to scrutinize his enforcement of the law. In the early part of the nineteenth century, the House of Representatives asserted its authority in this respect, to find out whether any of the federal employees had conducted themselves improperly and to discover whether the money appropriated had gone into legal channels. Long afterward, during the winter and spring of 1923–24, more than forty congressional investigations were made into the "oil scandals," corruption in the Veterans' Bureau, and other seamy matters. Before the season closed two cabinet members were forced out, one prominent official sent to the penitentiary, and indictments formulated against certain alleged offenders. It was contended, and with some reason, that the investigations were partisan in character, but it must be conceded that until Congress acted a number of the offenses were unknown to the country and apparently to the President.

Notwithstanding these and many other precedents, it is still an open question how far Congress or either house may go in compelling the executive branch of the Government to yield. For example, in 1909, the Senate, by a resolution, instructed the Attorney General to inform that body whether he had instituted proceedings against the United States Steel Trust for absorbing the Tennessee Coal and Iron Company in violation of the Sherman anti-trust law, and if not, why not. With his customary bluntness President Roosevelt directed the Attorney General not to respond to the demand. The President further declared that "heads of departments are subject to the Constitution and laws passed by the Congress in pursuance of the Constitution, and to the direction of the President of the United States and to no other direction whatever." On some occasions executive officials have insisted that their communications should be secret or have declined to give certain documents and data to Congressional committees on the ground that such action was incompatible with sound public policy. Evidently there is a line beyond which Congress cannot go by mere resolution. But presumably by formal legislation it may proceed to almost any length which it deems necessary. Certainly the theory of the separation of powers does not mean that the moment an executive agency is created, it is subject to the President alone and is entirely emancipated from congressional scrutiny. It would be preposterous to say that Congress can organize and abolish departments and offices at will, and yet cannot freely inquire into their operations.

Although the power of Congress to investigate other branches of the Federal Government appears to be hemmed in by certain restrictions, its right to secure information from private citizens on matters germane to its work is now fully recognized. If there had been any doubt on the point, it was settled by the Supreme Court of the United States in the case of McGrain *vs.* Mally S. Daugherty, decided in January, 1927. The defendant in this case declined to appear before a select committee of the Senate engaged in investigating certain acts of his brother, Harry M. Daugherty, Attorney General, and was taken into custody under a Senate resolution directing the Sergeant-at-arms to bring him before the bar of the chamber. Shortly after he was arrested under this measure, the defendant was released by the Federal District Court at Cincinnati on the ground that the Senate had exceeded its authority. On appeal the Supreme Court reversed the decision of the lower tribunal and in the course of a long opinion held that the Senate investigation was ordered for a legitimate object, that the witness had wrongfully refused to appear and testify, that he had been lawfully attached, and that the Senate was entitled to require him to give testimony pertinent to its inquiry either at the bar or before the committee. Later the power of Congress in this connection was reënforced when a prominent leader in the oil industry was sent to prison for refusing to answer questions respecting alleged frauds in the granting of oil leases by the Federal Government.

Naturally the chief sources of information for legislative

purposes are the hearings and investigations conducted by the various standing committees of Congress. Each of them has commodious and well-equipped quarters in one of the magnificent office buildings constructed for the Senate and the House. It has a collection of materials bearing on the subjects referred to it and commands the extensive resources of the Congressional Library, with its division of Legislative Reference responsible for furnishing materials on all questions up for consideration. Committees may also call upon the legislative drafting service, headed by two counsel, one for the Senate and another for the House.

At this point the reader may reasonably inquire whether debates in Congress do not throw light on legislative issues. In the Senate it frequently happens that the addresses of members, particularly on constitutional law, really illuminate the problems before that body; but it cannot be said that the House derives much assistance from the desultory and partisan speeches delivered in that chamber. Bryce attributes this absence of enlightening discussion to the committee system, but it is partly due to the highly technical character of the business before Congress. A busy Representative or Senator simply cannot master such a complicated matter as the regulation of public utilities or radio communications by burning midnight oil for a week or two.

In fact, the average member of the House is absorbed in his own affairs and the work of the committees to which he is assigned. He is, therefore, strongly inclined, as a rule, to accept the results reported by the other committees. He assumes that they know more about their affairs than he does, and furthermore he hesitates to stir up trouble for himself by criticizing their work. The Senator, on the other hand, with his longer term and greater chances of reëlection, has more time in which to develop expertness. He also has more incentive; for, if he is well prepared, he receives better attention at the hands of his colleagues and the press. He knows that an able argument may produce changes in legislation and public opinion.

Pressures and Lobbies

So far we have spoken of Congress as if it were merely a determinate body of representatives working at a given spot —the national capitol. In reality this is an illusion. Congress is a part of the living organism of American society— united with that society not only on election day but throughout the whole course of its proceedings. Each of the 531 Senators and Representatives is a personality, with a cultural heritage of his own, possessing immediate associations, including economic affiliations, with his constituents. In the process of winning his seat he has made commitments and formed ties which bind him as a legislator. After he arrives at Washington, perhaps even before, he comes under wider influences. Indeed he may owe his election largely to funds furnished by the congressional campaign committee of his party—funds derived from sources outside of his district. Once in Washington he forms connections with his party in Congress, with an organization having national responsibilities and subject to forces operating on a national scale.

In the discharge of his duties the member of Congress is, therefore, under pressure from two directions—his constituents at home, particularly the local party leaders, and individuals and associations operating in Washington. And it must be remembered that various elements in his double constituency are themselves united by innumerable ties. The farmers, manufacturers, and trade unionists of his district have national affiliations, and national associations in their turn have local branches. All of them are welded into solid bodies by the post-office, the telegraph, and the radio. Theoretically the member of Congress represents free and equal heads—all animated by a common aspiration—the public good. In reality he is under constant surveillance by powerful groups linked in chains throughout the country.

Considered according to type those groups may be marshalled in four classes—economic, professional, reform, and religious. To the first belong the industrial and trade associations, organized on a national basis, numbering about one thousand, and including all important divisions such as railways, oil, steel, retail stores, and public utilities. To this class also belong the farmers' organizations—the National Grange, the Farm Bureau Federation and the Farmers Union. Under this head come organized labor, directed by the American Federation of Labor and the Railway Brotherhoods. Functioning both coöperatively and independently is the Federal Employees Union, concerned especially with the hours, wages, and conditions of work in the government service. Likewise partly economic in character, various professional bodies—lawyers, engineers, and architects for example—offer advice and counsel in technical matters. Not wholly disassociated from economic considerations is the American Legion, speaking for the veterans of the World War; for, besides its other activities, it is constantly concerned with appropriations for hospitals and pensions, conveying benefits to its members.

Acting as reform organizations not seeking economic legislation as such, at least directly, are literally scores of societies, large and small. Some of them lobby for bigger appropriations for the Army and Navy in the name of patriotism—the Daughters of the American Revolution, the Navy League, the Reserve Officers Association, and the American Legion. Incidentally munition makers and shipbuilders rejoice in their activities. On the other side are several peace societies—which are usually branded with socialism, anarchy, and Bolshevism by their critics. In the reforming class may be placed the National Popular Government League and the People's Lobby interested in developing popular government and in exposing the operation of powerful economic interests in politics. Militant in its views, the National Woman's Party demands a federal amendment putting women on a strict legal equality with men. Less feminist in its outlook and non-partisan is the

League of Women Voters which encourages the study of government and sponsors selected measures of legislation from time to time.

The fourth class includes numerous religious organizations—the Board of Temperance, Prohibition, and Public Morals; the National Catholic Welfare Council; and the Federal Council of the Churches of Christ in America. Although they deal primarily with religious and ethical questions, such associations occasionally take a stand on issues in other fields.

Several of these organizations maintain in Washington powerful staff agencies which concentrate their energies on advancing or blocking legislation. Without attempting to list them in order of importance, there is first the National Chamber of Commerce, a federation of the local chambers throughout the United States, with elaborate machinery for taking the opinion of American business men on measures arising in Congress. Not far away stands the large building which houses the American Federation of Labor, always indefatigable in its support of friendly legislation and its warfare on measures deemed inimical to labor's cause. Equally active are the three nation-wide farmers' associations. Ever on the watch and ever busy disseminating its views is the American Association of Railway Executives which speaks for the combined railroads of America. Then descending to details we find each one of the leading manufacturing and mercantile branches organized and prepared to bring powerful influences to bear on Senators and Representatives in season and out.

It is estimated that there are in all about one hundred fifty economic organizations (to say nothing of moral and religious reformers) represented in the lobbies of Congress. Among them, for example, are the spokesmen of the coal, leather, beef, silk, glove, fertilizer, cotton, banking, wire, steel, express, drug, advertising, lime, and beet sugar interests. To the more or less permanent bodies may be added temporary associations formed and financed to advocate or oppose specific measures pending in Congress. Such, for example, was the Cuban Sugar Lobby "exposed" in 1929 as operating against an increase in the tariff on imported sugar—in conflict with domestic sugar producers. All these interests have skillful and astute agents, paid large salaries, and granted generous expense accounts for entertainment and other purposes; one of them is said to receive as much as the President of the United States.

These experts in lobbying vary widely in their training, talents, prestige, and methods. Some of them are distinguished lawyers who are retained by corporations to file briefs with the committees of Congress, interview members, and otherwise make themselves useful to their employers. The activities of these gentlemen present new problems in "the ethics of the bar." Other lobbyists are former members of Congress or federal officials, of deep experience and wide acquaintanceship at the Capital, who may "practice law" in Washington or engage in some nominal vocation. More recently there has come upon the scene a third type—"the high powered publicity expert," the ex-journalist, who specializes in "putting stuff over" through the newspapers and in attempting to frighten Congressmen by threats of antagonism or revelations in the press. Still operating, in spite of the emphasis on the new psychology, are the quiet, firm agents of special associations, who are expert in the statistics and technology of their business and rely largely on "the correct presentation of their cases" to the committees and members of Congress.

Obviously the ramifications of the lobby are very complex, and only old veterans in Washington politics have any idea of their intricate affiliations. For example the most efficient representative of a powerful economic group in recent years is a former Republican member of Congress of long service; his son-in-law is an officer in the Treasury Department; his law partner was once a Democratic assistant in the Attorney General's office; and a brother-in-law of this law-partner was formerly a Republican member of the President's cabinet. Through a single family, so to speak, any interested parties can easily get into direct relation with official situations and important personalities. Moreover Washington "society" is divided into certain sets, in which women are powerful factors; to these sets belong high officials, army and navy officers, and significant members of Congress. Apparently innocent entertainments often turn out to be "social lobbies" with specific ends in view.

With respect to methods those who seek to direct governmental action seem to be masters of the science and art of influence. They appear formally before committees of Congress to present facts, briefs, and arguments. They form "personal contacts," directly or through the social lobby, with "key" officials, Senators, and Representatives. They promise lucrative employment to politicians about to retire—especially to "lame ducks," as they are called, Congressmen defeated for reëlection but still serving unexpired terms. They "build fires" behind recalcitrant members at home by instructing prominent constituents and local organizations, such as chambers of commerce, to deluge their representatives with telegrams and letters. They "release" to the press news "stories" designed to construct in the popular mind images known as public opinion.

A concrete illustration is worth a book of generalities. Under a Senate resolution adopted in 1928 the Federal Trade Commission investigated the organization and methods of public utility corporations with special reference to propaganda. This inquiry produced a series of volumes in sociology which describe political ideas in the making under the drive of highly dynamic economic interests. Besides dealing directly with governments, these propagandists sought to build up a solid body of favorable sentiment through the schools, colleges, and newspapers. With a view to teaching children "correct doctrines," they made surveys of the textbooks in civics and economics offered to teachers by writers and publishers. They branded as "bad" and "unfair" the works which did not meet their requirements—treatises by some of the outstanding authorities in the United States. They approached publishers and authors and succeeded in inducing some of them to make changes suitable to their purposes. Owing to their standing with school boards and editors, they were in a strategic position to force action. Hence when teachers take up a textbook in civics or economics they do not know to what extent vital parts of it have been "doctored" to suit private parties who expect to make profits out of "educating" the public to take their views of governmental policy. If they choose a book which in fact presents a fair and honest account of both sides of public utility problems, they may find a superintendent or school board who will prevent its adoption.

While supervising textbooks used in instruction, directors of the utility propaganda sent speakers of their own selection to address school children on public questions—often people of good standing bearing honorable names. Instead of going openly and frankly to educational authorities, the propagandists in one of our great states operated through the chamber of commerce in getting their representatives before the schools. Here is an extract from a letter written by the manager in charge. "More recently," he says, "we have adopted the plan of having a third party organization make the arrangements with the schools. In strict confidence the State Chamber of Commerce handled it for us during the last summer. We, of course, paid the bill. We try to keep away from announcing the talk to have anything to do with public utilities—our last talks being on Government and Business. In placing speakers before schools, the job is most complete when you make arrangements with the speaker, who should be an educator of the highest standing, well-known, and accepted throughout the state." Thus when teachers and students of the state in question listened to "educators of the highest standing" on "Government and Business," they heard propagandists with secret retainers' fees in their pocketbooks.

Adults as well as children were subjected to similar influences. The investigation to which reference has been made showed that newspapers in many parts of the country had printed as news and information thousands of columns of materials prepared by utility propagandists. In one state the amount of this stuff published, not as advertising, but as plain reading matter without any earmarks as to origin, was at least "sixty thousand column inches, or four hundred pages the size of the Boston *Herald*." By the same methods many newspapers, including some great metropolitan journals, were induced to print as editorials, presumably representing unbiased opinion, materials prepared by interested parties. All this work was in addition to influences exerted on Congress and key officials in Washington; in reality it was part of a far-sighted, long-term program for creating a permanent leaden stereotype of opinion to control legislative and administrative action on utilities throughout the country.

Congress must always work, therefore, amid a vast net of agencies, having large sums at their disposal to spend in agitation and in maintaining research bureaus to accumulate facts favorable to their special concerns—agencies equipped with all the mechanisms of modern society for bringing "pressure" to bear. Under the burning spotlight of their scrutiny, constantly bombarded by their pleas, threats, and promises, "gassed" by their publicity, the legislator who tries to see things as they are and as a whole and to do his full duty in the midst of clamor and perplexity, must have poise, discrimination, and courage. Once he was buttonholed in the lobby by a few interested parties; now the lobby has widened to the boundaries of the country—even beyond—and the business of lobbying has become a science and an art. As we have noted above, there are students of government who boldly advocate giving up the fiction of political equality and suggest the incorporation of manufacturing, labor, agricultural, and professional interests into Congress itself.

But as we have said there are very grave difficulties in

the way of creating a direct and legal representation of economic interests in Congress. It would involve radical changes in our form of government and is generally viewed as outside the range of practical action. Instead it is proposed that legislation should be enacted controlling lobbies. Several states have laws of this character and many bills of a similar nature have been introduced in Congress. Broadly speaking they give a definition to lobbying and require all who come under that head to be officially registered, to reveal the names of the parties for whom they are working, and to describe the purposes of their operations. One measure laid before the Senate declares that a lobbyist is "anyone who shall engage, whether for pay or otherwise, to attempt to influence legislation or to prevent legislation by the National Congress." It defines lobbying as any effort to "influence" the proceedings of Congress by distributing literature, appearing before committees, or interviewing individual members of either house. Obviously such a measure, in its sweeping terms, could in effect prevent nearly all citizen activities in connection with molding legislative measures. It might very well block legitimate efforts to make public sentiment and at the same time fail to suppress the more insidious forms of pressure and propaganda. No scheme will eliminate diversity of interests; government inevitably reflects them; and a general understanding of the situation is more likely to check undoubted evils than any type of legislation. Knowledge is the beginning of wisdom.

CHAPTER VIII

THE NOMINATION AND ELECTION OF THE PRESIDENT

THE spectacle of twenty or thirty million people going about the business of nominating and electing a chief executive to preside over them for four years is one of the most arresting pageants in the long course of political evolution. It is an operation of the first magnitude, putting at stake the ambitions of individuals, the interests of classes, and the fortunes of the entire country. Nearly everybody in America takes part in it, from the President in the White House, busy reëlecting himself or helping in the selection of his successor, down to boot-blacks and garage-boys, who discourse on the merits and demerits of candidates with as much assurance as on the outcome of the latest prize fight or horse race. The performance involves endless discussions, public and private, oratory, tumult, and balloting, the election of thousands of delegates to grand national conventions, the concentration of opinion on a few ambitious leaders, a nation-wide propaganda as the sponsors for various aspirants exhibit the qualifications of their favorites to the multitude, and the expenditure of millions of dollars in publications, meetings, "rounding up delegates," and "seeing that goods are delivered."

This thundering demonstration of democratic power occupying the better part of six months every four years springs from no design of the Fathers who framed the Constitution. They intended to remove the chief executive as far as possible from the passions of the masses; and to accomplish this end, they provided that he should be elected by a small body of electors chosen as the legislatures of the states might decide. They contemplated a quiet, dignified procedure about as decorous as the election of a college president by a board of trustees. Their grand scheme has been upset, however, by the rise of political parties. It is necessary, therefore, to preface a discussion of our quadrennial campaign by a consideration of the extra-legal organizations known as national conventions which present the candidates for whom the presidential electors are morally bound to vote.

The Composition of the National Convention

Although in theory the national convention is a representative assembly, the delegates who compose it are not apportioned among the states strictly on the basis of party strength.[1] The Democrats give to each state a number of votes in the convention equal to twice the number of its representatives in Congress—the House and Senate combined. In 1928 they allotted to every state two delegates for each of its members in the House of Representatives and eight delegates at large for the Senators but assigned only one half of a vote apiece to these eight delegates. Under this rule a state in the solid South in which the Democrats greatly outnumber the Republicans receives relatively no more weight than some Northern state in which they are in a hopeless minority.

A similar rule was formerly applied by the Republicans, thus giving the Southern members of the party a representation in the convention all out of proportion to their numerical strength. There are several states in the South which have only a handful of regular Republicans and seldom, if ever, cast an electoral vote for a Republican candidate. In these states, the leaders of the Republican machine are usually federal office-holders who are nominated and can be removed by the President of the United States. Consequently, whenever a Republican President is in the White House, he can handpick the delegates from the South. In this way he may almost dictate his own renomination or the choice of his

[1] A number of delegates is assigned to certain territories and dependencies as a matter of courtesy to party members, although the latter have no voice in electing the President.

successor, as the case may be. Roosevelt certainly used the Southern delegates to drive through the nomination of Taft in 1908; and four years afterward the latter employed them at Chicago on his own behalf.

As a result of protests against the evils of this system, the Republicans have adopted a compromise. As in former times they still recognize geographical units as such. They provided in 1928 that every state, without respect to its Republican strength, should have in the convention four delegates-at-large, one delegate for each congressional district, and two delegates-at-large for each Representative-at-large, if any. Then they took party membership into consideration. Every congressional district in which ten thousand or more Republican votes were cast at the previous election received an additional delegate. The balance was further corrected by giving each state which went Republican in that election three more delegates-at-large.

In spite of this change glaring inequalities in representation still exist, but too much stress should not be laid on political arithmetic. The vote for President fluctuates from decade to decade and the outcome of any one election is not always an exact criterion for estimating the probable poll in the next, as experience in the South in 1928 abundantly demonstrated. Moreover, the Republicans, always suffering from the burden of sectionalism, cannot safely destroy their skeleton organization in the regions of the far South where they have little or no influence at present. The future may be different from the past. At all events, something is to be said for giving the Southern states a considerable share of power in Republican conventions. The amount required by justice and expediency is not easily ascertainable.

For more than half a century the Democrats and Republicans prescribed different methods for the choice of delegates. The former, regarding the state as the unit of representation, provided that all the delegates should be chosen at a state convention or by the state committee. Professing another view of the Union, the latter ordered the election of the four delegates-at-large at the state convention and the remainder at congressional district conventions. But the appearance of the direct primary in various forms as a means of selecting delegates, of necessity, forced alterations in the traditional rules; and both parties finally acquiesced in the changes wrought in their procedure by such legislation. Many states now require the election of all delegates at primaries; some leave the choice to state conventions; and others combine a state convention with local congressional district primaries.

In addition to applying the direct primary to the choice of delegates to the national convention, more than a third of the states give their voters an opportunity to express their preference for the presidential nomination. Among them are California, Florida, Georgia, Illinois, Maryland, Massachusetts, Michigan, Montana, Nebraska, New Jersey, North Carolina, North Dakota, Ohio, Oregon, Pennsylvania, South Dakota, West Virginia, Wisconsin, and Vermont. Naturally the primary laws vary widely in character, but they provide two general methods in assuring the people a chance to voice their opinions on party contestants for the nomination. In some states, a list of the presidential aspirants is printed on the primary ballot of each party and the voter may readily indicate his choice at the polls. In others, candidates for the position of delegate to the convention may specify on the ballot whom they will favor for President if elected. Thus the voters may disclose their will indirectly. First used in the campaign of 1912, when Roosevelt and Taft waged a bitter contest to secure control of the Republican organization, the presidential primary has had an uncertain career.

At no election has it been a deciding factor. Never have enough ballots been cast in such a primary to reveal the real opinion of a majority in either party. More than once the aspirant receiving the highest vote at the polls has been rejected by the convention. Nor are there any signs of a marked drift in practice. The task of organizing and financing a presidential primary is stupendous, and it remains to be seen whether it can be so operated throughout the Union as to become an effective instrument for the nomination of candidates.

It is very easy to pick flaws in the presidential primary. Not half the states have the system, so that no truly national test can be made. The primaries are held at different dates, ranging through two or three months. There is confusion in the laws. There is no method for securing the submission of the names of all the prominent aspirants in all the states. Indeed aspirants may even refuse to lay their claims before the voters of those regions in which they believe their strength to be slight. Besides these objections, there is no way of binding delegates who pledge themselves to vote in the convention for the men preferred by the electors at the polls.

In fact, confusion reigns everywhere. Still the system is not abandoned. On the contrary, there has been some demand for federal legislation covering the subject and more than one presidential primary bill has been proposed in Congress. But the difficulties in the way of federal action in this sphere are almost insuperable. At the outset, it is of doubtful constitutionality, in view of the decision of the Supreme Court in the Newberry case (p. 99). If a separate national system for enrolling voters and holding primaries for the presidential election could be instituted, the cost of operating it would be enormous. If an attempt were made to lay a federal system upon local foundations there would arise the perplexing problem of adjusting it to the varying and conflicting laws of the separate states. So we seem to be between two worlds. It is impossible, in view of popular temper, to go back to ancient ways or forward to a nation-wide system of direct primaries for presidential elections. So we "muddle along."

The National Convention at Work

The national convention of each party assembles on the date—usually in June preceding the election—and in the place fixed by its national committee at a preliminary meeting called by the chairman. Before the convention is formally opened, the committee confers again, determines upon the program of proceedings, selects the temporary officers whose names are to be laid before the grand party conclave for its approval, and makes up a provisional roll of delegates from the returns sent in by the authorities under whose auspices the primaries or local conventions have been held.

The purpose of the national convention is threefold. It formulates the principles of the party into a platform on which an appeal is made to the voters during the ensuing campaign. It nominates candidates for President and Vice President, and appoints committees to notify both nominees. Finally it organizes a new national committee charged with carrying on the campaign and managing party affairs for four years.

The convention always assembles in some huge building; there the thousand delegates or more and perhaps ten or twenty thousand spectators are seated. Each delegation is arranged around the banner of its state, and has a chairman to direct its part in the play. Some of the more important delegations are accompanied by brass bands, and often carry curious symbols and transparencies. In the audience are usually gathered the most active politicians who are not serving as delegates, enthusiastic partisans from all over the country, and interested visitors attracted by the spectacular affair. Bands play popular airs; party heroes are greeted with prolonged cheering as they appear on the scene; wire-pullers rush here and there, making and extracting promises; all are apparently intoxicated with party zeal. It is, indeed, a cool-headed politician who is not swept off his feet by the excitement of the hour. As if to add to the emotional tension a radio hook-up is now made so that millions of listeners throughout the country may hear the speeches and the uproar as though they were physically present.

While procedure varies from time to time, a certain general course is pursued. The convention is called to order by the chairman of the national committee and before any business is transacted, prayer is offered. Even here discretion is necessary. Clergymen from different congregations are chosen for the several sessions, so as to avoid offending religious susceptibilities. After prayer, the first important action is the nomination of the temporary officers, who have already been selected in fact by the committee. Usually these nominations are accepted without question, for the function of the temporary organization is largely formal. The temporary chairman, it is true, makes an address appropriate to the occasion, which is often regarded as the "keynote" to the proceedings, but he is not called upon to make any important decisions from the chair which may affect either the platform of the party or its nominations. The first day's session is then concluded by calling the roll of the states and territories and securing from each of them the names of its members for the four great committees of the convention: on credentials, on permanent organization, on rules and order of business, and on resolutions or platform.

In due course, the reports of the various committees are heard, not necessarily in any fixed order. The committee on credentials, charged with the important work of passing upon disputes over seats, naturally must act quickly. All notices of contests are filed in advance with the national committee, which makes up the temporary roll. Documents relative to the several cases are transmitted to the credentials committee, which holds meetings, hears arguments, and prepares reports for the convention. Sometimes the conflicts are very exciting, as among the Republicans at Chicago in 1912; for the policy of the party on national issues and the fate of candidates may be decided by the admission or rejection of a few individuals. Generally speaking, however, the recommendations of the majority of the committee on credentials are accepted by the convention; if necessary to peace, two opposing delegations may be seated and each member given one-half of a vote.

The next important report is that of the committee on

permanent organization, which nominates the chairman, secretary, and other officers of the convention. Usually this report is also approved without debate, although, of course, the convention may, if it sees fit, refuse to confirm the names suggested by the committee. The permanent chairman is promptly installed, makes a long speech, and is presented with a gavel. The regulations, under which he controls the assembly, are drawn up by the committee on rules, and are, in principle, those of the House of Representatives with some modifications.

On the second or third day, the convention is ready to hear from the committee on resolutions, to which is entrusted the preparation of the platform. This committee begins its sessions immediately after its appointment, and ordinarily agrees on a unanimous report, but sometimes there is a minority dissent. The platform is not often a statement of the particular things which the party proposes to do if it gets into power; it is rather a collection of generalities which will serve to create good feeling and unite all sections around "the grand old banner." Custom dictates that it shall contain, among other things, references to the great history of the party, interspersed with the names of its leaders, and denunciations of the policies and tactics of the opposition. Owing to its elusive character, the program drafted by the committee on resolutions seldom meets opposition in the convention. It is only when some very contentious matter arouses deep feelings, such as free silver in 1896 and Progressivism in 1912, that there is likely to be a divided report or any serious discussion of its terms.

About the third or fourth day, the chairman announces that the next order of business is the nomination of the party's candidate for President of the United States, and the roll of the states is then called in alphabetical order. If the first state has no "favorite son" to offer, it may defer to another lower on the list. A representative of the delegation which gets the floor thereupon places a candidate before the assembly in a speech full of high-sounding phrases and lofty sentiments dealing with many subjects and ranging over a wide geographical area from "the rockbound coasts of Maine to the sunny shores of California." This opening gun may be followed by speeches seconding the nomination, delivered by "spellbinders" from various delegations scattered over the house, including as a rule at least one woman orator. After the way is opened the names of other aspirants are presented in a similar manner, with all the flourishes of popular declamation.

When the nominations are all made, the vote is taken by calling the roll of the delegations by states; and the chairman of each announces the choices of his group. Previous to the rise of the direct primary, every party followed its own rules with respect to balloting in the convention. The Republicans assumed in theory that each member could vote as he pleased, although in practice he was often instructed by his party organization at home to support a certain candidate. The Democrats on the other hand permitted the state organization in each state to authorize a majority of its delegation to decide that all its votes should be cast in one block. This practice, known as the "unit rule," was defended on the ground that the party machine of a state had greater weight when it could "swing" all its representatives at the national convention.

Now the direct primary and the presidential primary, wherever applied, have upset the historic practices of both parties. Delegates in the Republican convention may be bound to a certain extent by pledges made in their campaign for election or by preferences indicated by the party voters (p. 223). Owing also to obligations imposed by primary legislation, the Democratic state organization can no longer bind its delegation in every instance to follow the unit rule; so in some cases the individual member may be constrained to support a particular aspirant, or may be free to vote as he pleases, no matter what the majority of his state delegation may wish to do.

After all the delegations, subject to the various limitations imposed on them by law, custom, and pledges, have reported the results of their balloting to the convention, the total is announced. If any aspirant for President in the Republican assembly receives a bare majority of the votes cast, he is thereupon declared to be the party candidate. On the other hand, the Democrats have an inflexible rule that a majority of two thirds is necessary to choice. Long associated with the unit arrangement just described, this requirement in a way offsets some of its effects. If no one receives the requisite number of votes, the roll is called until that outcome is reached—sometimes for hours and even days should the contest be sharp and bitter. Immediately after the presidential candidate has been selected, the nomination for Vice President is made in the same manner and by the same majority—with less display of rhetoric.

When the convention has chosen its candidates, it appoints a special committee to convey to each of them a notification of his success. In due course the committee calls on the victor, and through an official spokesman announces the will of the party organ. Thus informed, the presidential candidate replies in a long address and sometimes supplements his remarks by issuing an explanatory letter. Often the acceptance speech is an important political document for the reason that through this medium the candidate may interpret the party platform in his own way, going even so far as to modify its spirit, if not its letter, thus injecting unexpected issues into the campaign. After all, it is his speeches, rather than the platform, that attract the attention of the country. It would be interesting to know how many voters ever saw a political platform.

What are the qualities that make men available for the presidency? What elements, personal, geographical, religious, and so on, enter into consideration? The problems raised by these questions are elusive, but a few notes may be set down for scrutiny. Bryce has a chapter devoted to inquiring why great men are not selected. One answer is that some of them have been chosen, but still it must be admitted that a number of mediocrities have also been elevated to that position. Another answer is that merits are difficult to assess. Was Clay greater than Jackson, Blaine than Garfield, Hill than Cleveland? Who in the Republican party was greater than Roosevelt in 1904 or in the Democratic party greater than Wilson in 1912? Friends of defeated aspirants like Clay, Webster, Sherman, and Bryan have been wont to lament the failure of the democratic process to choose the best, but on the whole not much gain can come from threshing out such propositions.

Yet it may be safely said that certain definite factors enter into the business of selection. Very often unknown men, "dark horses" as they are called, have been presented as candidates. This frequently happens when there is a spirited contest among a number of prominent party leaders, none of whom can command enough votes in the convention to win. An outstanding man whether great or not, a man who has seen long service and taken a positive position on one issue or another is sure to have foes, so many that election may be out of the question. Protestantism in religion seems to be one prerequisite, for America is predominantly a Protestant country—a historic rule reaffirmed in 1928 when Alfred E. Smith, a Catholic, was overwhelmingly defeated. Since the Civil War no resident of the South has been elected. Republicans for obvious reasons do not look in that direction. And the Democrats, knowing that it is "solid" anyway, can ignore its claims. Since 1860, the Democrats have been successful only with candidates from the East, Cleveland and Wilson; for, apparently, the conservative wing of the party distrusts Western radicalism. The Republicans, on the other hand, commanding for historic and practical reasons the support of Eastern conservatism, usually offer the nomination to the Middle West. Until 1928 all its successful candidates, save two, Roosevelt and Coolidge, were from Ohio, Indiana, or Illinois and in that year it presented Hoover, of California. And the two exceptions were both chosen in peculiar circumstances; they had first been elevated from the vice-presidency on the death of their chiefs. When the Republicans nominated Blaine from Maine and Hughes from New York, they were defeated.

What career leads to the White House? One thing is certain, it is not a straight and narrow road like that to the premiership in England—constant service in and out of power for many years and marked qualities of leadership among men. We have had many generals: Washington, Jackson, Harrison, Taylor, Pierce, Grant, and Garfield; two colonels, Monroe and Roosevelt, and one major, McKinley. So we might venture the suggestion that military service, often accompanied by no definite political opinions, is an element in availability. Men of marked power in the Senate are never chosen. Harding was a Senator but not among the dominant group in that body or widely known in the country for any service there. To carry a strategic state as a candidate for governor, as did Cleveland and McKinley, is to enhance one's value in the presidential field. Lincoln was somewhat unique in that, beyond a term in the House of Representatives, his political experience on the national stage had been slight. He was not widely regarded as a great man when he was elected, and had he been chosen in a time of unromantic peace he might to-day be reckoned among the insignificant occupants of the presidential chair. Law and arms are the professions to which parties have most often resorted in the past. Roosevelt, Wilson, Harding, and Hoover stand apart—the first was a gentleman of private fortune without any regular occupation, the second a university president, the third an editor of a newspaper, and the fourth an engineer who, after becoming famous for services in the World War, added to his laurels by eight years' work as Secretary of Commerce. There was a time when birth in a log-cabin was an asset to an aspirant, but in an age of bungalows and Ford automobiles that appeal has lost its charm. Still there is a dramatic feature in the story of the poor boy who works, rides, drives, and stumbles along the uncertain way that leads to Washington. Many who have deliberately set out in it have missed the goal, and others have been blown into it by the winds of fortune.

A word should be said about the nominees for Vice President. Since the sole function of that officer, in ordinary circumstances, is to preside over the sessions of the Senate, not much consideration is usually given to his qualifications for the presidency to which he may be called on the death of his superior. Two rules seem to be controlling in the choice of candidates for this office. The first is that he should not be from the same geographical district as the presidential candidate. If the latter is from the Middle West, the former will be from the East, and vice versa. Wilson was from New Jersey; Marshall from Indiana. Harding came from Ohio; Coolidge from Massachusetts. The second, by no means so strictly applied, is that the candidates for the two offices shall represent different wings of the party, right or left as the case may be.

The Presidential Campaign

The work of directing the party campaign is entrusted to the national committee composed of two members—one man and one woman—from each state and in some cases from possessions belonging to the United States. Although they are formally confirmed at the national convention, the committee members are in reality chosen at state conventions, by state committees, or at direct primaries, as local customs and laws prescribe. The principal officers of the national committee are the chairman, secretary, and treasurer. Since the business of the chairman is to conduct the campaign for victory, the wishes of the presidential candidate count heavily in his selection. Harmony between the two men is essential to success. If no capable and energetic organizer is found in the original committee, the chairman is taken from among party leaders on the outside. A similar practice is followed in the case of the treasurer. Owing to the importance of his position as the collector of funds, he must be capable of wielding a large financial influence and the most available man will be drafted wherever he may be found. It is, therefore, impossible to lay down any absolute rules with respect to the way in which officials of the committee are chosen, for the operation is not determined by any written or unwritten law. It is left for adjustment according to circumstances.

Immediately after the adjournment of the convention, the newly elected committee meets and proceeds with preparations for the campaign. Leadership in this great national contest is taken, of course, by the chairman, who disburses enormous collections made by the treasurer, directs the huge army of speakers, organizers, and publicity agents scattered over the Union, and as the day of election approaches surveys the whole field with the eye of an experienced commander, discovering weak places in his battle array, hurrying up reënforcements to the doubtful states, and, perhaps, pouring an immense sum of money into districts where wavering voters may be brought into line. The outcome of the campaign, therefore, depends in a great measure upon the generalship of the chairman of the national committee.

Fully as important as the high officer who leads the army in the field is the organizer of the department which furnishes the sinews of war. Consequently, in the political battle, the treasurer of the national committee takes a prominent place by the side of the chairman. It is his duty to discover innumerable ways of raising the millions of dollars required to wage the political contest.

The amount of money which a party must and can raise for the fray depends upon circumstances. If a serious attack is made during the campaign on the great banking and manufacturing interests of the country, the amount is likely to be large and the spending lavish. For example, in 1896 when the financial interests were alarmed by the menace of free silver, Mark Hanna, chairman of the Republican committee, made "a tour of the high places in Wall Street," his biographer tells us, and had no difficulty in raising huge sums. How much was spent in that campaign no one knows.

The figure has been placed at sixteen million dollars, but counting state and national expenditures it was probably not more than one third or one half that sum. The silver mine owners of the West, expecting to benefit from Bryan's doctrines if applied, made generous, though not princely, gifts to his fund.

Shortly after that memorable campaign a great hue and cry went up against excessive expenditures in politics, and much was said about "plutocracy's capture of the government." Reflecting this spirit Bryan announced in 1908 that he would not receive any single contribution in excess of ten thousand dollars and called upon loyal Democrats to give one dollar each. To his chagrin, however, the revenue from small contributors was pitifully inadequate, for it seems that the average party member's zeal was exhausted before he reached the point of sacrificing a dollar. Campaigns cost money. The rank and file of the people will not give generously; so rich men must pay the bills. Protests against lavish campaign outlays, however, have resulted in a large amount of legislation, state and federal, on the subject—to which reference has been made above (pp. 96 ff.).

Since the chief work of the national committee in carrying on the campaign is to influence the minds of the voters, its attention is given in a very systematic way to the preparation of campaign "literature." As soon as the issues of the contest are fairly well settled, each party publishes a campaign text-book, which usually contains the platform, notification and acceptance speeches, biographical sketches of the candidates, statistics on business, tariff, trusts, money, and other economic problems, addresses by eminent leaders, papers in defense or criticism of the administration, and the most cogent arguments which the party can advance in support of its position. Campaign text-books are sent out in large quantities, not to the public generally, but rather to the newspapers, speakers, and others in a position to win voters by argument. Besides this great document another text-book is issued for each party by its congressional committee (chosen by the party delegation in Congress) to furnish collateral information on the legislative "records" of the contestants and their policies.

These central pieces of campaign literature are supplemented by innumerable pamphlets, leaflets, posters, cartoons, and congressional speeches, printed in every language that is represented by any considerable number of voters. A regular bureau of printing and publication under the supervision of an expert directs this enormous "literary" output, which is distributed broadcast, partly through the state central committees.

A far more effective way of reaching the public at large is through the newspaper. Thousands of the uninteresting documents sent out by the national committee are doubtless thrown away unopened or unread, and there must be an enormous waste in this branch of its work. The newspapers, however, have regular readers and reach the public directly; accordingly the national committee makes extensive use of the established journals, from the great city daily with its huge edition down to the rural weekly with a circulation of five hundred run off on a hand-press.

In addition to the printed arguments addressed to the people, there are oral arguments. To manage this phase of its activity the national committee generally maintains a special bureau which prepares a list of available statesmen and "spellbinders." These orators are of every rank, from the person with the strong voice who can harangue a crowd on a street corner to the finished speaker whose very name will draw multitudes. Hundreds of them are directed from the national headquarters, while thousands of local volunteers are supervised by state and county committees, sometimes in consultation with authorities higher up. Itineraries are laid out, halls and bands engaged, parades organized, and every device utilized to give the greatest possible effect to campaign eloquence.

Generally the presidential candidate himself enters the lists. In 1896 Bryan toured the country in a private car and delivered at least four hundred reported speeches in twenty-nine different states—the greatest oratorical record of any candidate up to that date. Twelve years later Bryan equaled his first record, while Taft, his opponent, outdid him by traveling eighteen thousand five hundred miles and making 436 speeches in thirty states. On the other hand the candidate occasionally remains at home and addresses crowds that are brought to him from far and near by enterprising organizers and railway companies. When a President is nominated to succeed himself, he usually regards himself bound by the decorum of his office to conduct his campaign circumspectly from the White House.

A very efficient means of enabling candidates and their supporters to invade the homes of the people with party appeals and speeches is now afforded by the radio, an agency on which about two million dollars was expended by the two leading parties in the campaign of 1928. By overcoming distance, the radio makes it unnecessary for presidential nominees to spend so many days and nights on the train in order to reach voters in the strategic centers of the country. It triumphs over the laziness of the indifferent citizen who would rather sit under his own roof in a comfortable chair than fight his way through a struggling crowd for standing room to hear a politician in person.

Moreover by its very nature the radio has had marked effects on orators as well as audiences. To-day the speaker knows very well that his radio auditors, when the least bit bored by his eloquence, can shut it off merely by turning a dial—which is much easier than trying to escape from the middle of a crowded house. At an old-fashioned meeting a statesman could go on for hours—as long as the people would endure him. Under the radio régime, every minute is precious as well as expensive, for the time allowed for each speech is fixed in advance and when it has expired the wireless audience is cut off. Since most of the important addresses delivered in halls are also broadcast, the restraints of the new electrical device operate quite generally. An-

Photo by Brown Brothers

Radio Enters Politics—President Hoover before the Microphone.

Photo by Brown Brothers

Manufacturing Propaganda by the Ton.

other technical matter must also be noted. The radio orator must speak directly and clearly into the microphone in front of him; he cannot pace up and down roaring like a lion and gesticulating like a windmill. The time is short; he must stand at one spot; and he must hold his audience by saying something, for he can no longer rely on theatrical tricks.

Obviously all the conditions of political campaigning are being revolutionized by the radio. It is no longer necessary to have a period of three or four months between party conventions and the election in which to reach the voters. Within two or three weeks the candidates and their supporting orators can lay before twenty million radio owners every plea that they have to present on the merits of their respective causes. Subjected to the severe time limits of the radio, they must measure their words. Jokes, ridicule, and backslapping become less effective; brief, pointed, definite statements of facts, principles, and policies are imperative if the invisible audience is to be convinced. What future developments hold in store, especially in view of the possibilities of television, no informed person will venture to guess. A new and amazing instrument has been thrust into the business of forming political opinion with reference to elections.

Campaigns, of course, are not limited to oratory and the dissemination of political literature. A very practical and useful part of the national committee's work is the polling and direct supervision of the wavering states. Early in the contest a political census is usually taken of the regions in which the vote is known to vacillate or in which incipient revolts appear. Frequently this survey is minute in the extreme. Thus the party leaders find out exactly how many voters they can rely upon and obtain a fairly accurate list of the doubtful persons whose opinions may be changed by various methods. With the results of the census in its hands, the national committee is very much in the position of a military commander on the battlefield; it is acquainted with the strength and weakness of the opposing army and knows the lines of advance necessary to win the victory. Effective means for influencing the several categories of doubtful persons can then be immediately dispatched to the scenes of action.

It is indeed a marvelous contest that closes on the day when the ballots of about thirty million voters are cast for the presidential electors in the several states. By act of Congress that day is fixed, Tuesday following the first Monday in November.

Casting and Counting the Electoral Votes

The political activities described above, important as they are, are wholly unknown to the Constitution. That document, in fact, contains only a few clauses with regard to the actual choice of the President and Vice President. In the first place it contemplates a system of indirect election: the President and the Vice President are to be selected by electors, not by the people themselves. To make sure that these agents voice the opinions of the several sections of the country, each state is given a number of electors equal to the number of Senators and Representatives to which it is entitled in Congress. To remove the electors from direct contact with the Federal Government, it is provided that none of them shall be a Senator or Representative or a person holding any office of trust under the United States.

In the second place the electors of each state are to be chosen as the legislature thereof may determine. In the course of our history no less than three distinct methods have been tried. In the beginning, the state legislatures often elected them; but in time this practice was abandoned in favor of popular election. When the more democratic system was adopted it was frequently the custom at first to have two electors chosen by the voters of the state at large and the others, by congressional districts. It was discovered at length that a state's influence in national politics was greatly increased if all its electors were carried by one party or the other; consequently, the district system was abolished, and election of the entire list on a general ticket by popular vote (p. 78) throughout the state became the universal rule.

It is necessary, accordingly, for each party organization in each state to prepare a list of candidates equal to the total number of electors assigned to the commonwealth under the Constitution. In practice, the presidential electors are usually nominated by the state convention or state committee; very often the office is treated as a titular honor to be given to distinguished citizens or to partisans willing to make liberal contributions to campaign funds.

On election day, therefore, the voter does not cast his ballot directly for President and Vice President, although for his information the names of the candidates of all officially recognized parties appear on the ticket. On the contrary, he ordinarily votes for all the presidential electors put forward by his party in his state. There is no point at all in distributing his preferences among the various parties, unless a fusion occurs, such as existed, for example, several years ago in some of the Western states between the Democrats and Populists whereby the two groups were to share the electors according to a predetermined arrangement. What happens, then, on the election day is the choice in each state of a certain number of presidential electors—531 throughout the Union.

Normally the party which secures a plurality of the popular votes in any state is entitled to all the electoral ballots of that state for President and Vice President, no matter how large the opposition; very rarely is there a split in the tickets. No elector would dare to break faith with the party which placed him in nomination and support the candidates of any other party. Consequently, the deliberative, judicial, nonpartisan system designed by the framers of the Constitution has been overthrown by political custom.

It is sometimes held that through this party practice the popular election of President and Vice President has been established but, if by this is meant choice by majority or plurality vote throughout the United States as a whole, it has not been attained. Indeed, several of our Presidents have been elected by a minority of the popular ballots cast. Lincoln, for example, was chosen President in 1860 by a vote of 1,866,452 against a total of 2,815,617 polled by his opponents; the opposition being so distributed that it obtained only a minority of the presidential electors. Wilson's popular vote in 1912 was less by two million than the total poll of the other candidates, and yet he secured 435 out of 531 electoral ballots. Two Presidents, Hayes and Benjamin Harrison, did not receive even a popular plurality, that is, stood lower in the scale than their principal rivals.

This possible contingency of election by a minority of the popular vote cast is largely due to the fact that when a party carries a state, even by the smallest margin, it wins all the presidential electors to which that commonwealth is entitled. Therefore, a party that is victorious by narrow margins in enough states to obtain a majority of the presidential electors may in reality have a smaller number of votes to its credit than the opposing party which may have swept its states by enormous majorities. As a matter of fact, the system only works with a fair degree of justice because the voters are somewhat evenly divided between two great parties. The appearance of a strong third party or the multiplication of factions would frequently result in throwing the choice into the House of Representatives.

The practice of giving the entire electoral vote of a state to the party that is victorious at the polls, even by the slightest plurality, has another significant effect. It concentrates the campaign principally in the states that are counted as "close" and are liable to swing to either party in the election. To carry these doubtful strongholds campaign managers employ every art known to practical politics. For instance, the small plurality of 1149 votes in New York gave that state to Cleveland instead of Blaine in 1884, and changed the result of the whole presidential election. Remembering this lesson, the Republican national chairman in the next campaign threw a force of detectives into New York City to check false registration and illegal voting, with results which more than exceeded his expectations. Undoubtedly this concentration of the campaign in the pivotal states has many bad features, especially the lavish use of money for questionable purposes. It is notorious that in the regions where the rivalry between the parties is keenest, there is the largest amount of bribery. On the other hand, the system works for "cleaner" politics in states dominated by one party since no advantage can come from piling up votes.

The rules according to which the electors so chosen in each state shall meet and cast their votes for President and Vice President are prescribed in the Constitution and in federal and state statutes. It is provided by federal law that the electors of each commonwealth shall convene on the first Wednesday in January, immediately following their appointment, at such place as the legislature of the state may direct —in practice, the state capital. When they have assembled, the electors vote by ballot for President and Vice President, "one of whom at least must not be an inhabitant of the same state with themselves"—that is, for the two candidates nominated by their party; thereupon they make separate lists of the number of votes so cast, and sign, certify, seal, and transmit the documents to the president of the Senate of the United States. With the lists of their votes for President and Vice President, the electors must transmit their certificates of election as evidence of their power to act—evidence of crucial importance in case of contested elections. When they have cast their votes and dispatched their documents, the electors have performed their whole duty.

The counting of the total electoral vote polled throughout the United States begins in the Hall of the House of Representatives on the second Wednesday in February, following the meeting of the electors in their respective states. It is conducted in the presence of the two houses of Congress with the president of the Senate in the chair. Except in the case of a contested election, this count is, of course, merely an impressive formality, for the result has been known since the preceding November.

If no candidate for President obtains a majority of all the electoral votes cast, the House of Representatives thereupon chooses the President from the three candidates who have received the highest number of electoral ballots. In the selection of the President by this process, each state represented in the House is entitled to only one vote; a quorum consists of the members from two thirds of the states; and a majority of all the states is required for a choice. Necessarily, in such cases, the single vote of each state for the presidency is commanded by the majority of its Representatives. Should the House, in these circumstances, fail to reach a decision before the fourth of March following, it becomes the duty of the Vice President to act as President. Owing to the fortunes of American politics there have been only two instances of presidential elections by the House of Representatives—Jefferson in 1801 and J. Q. Adams in 1825.

If none of the candidates for Vice President receives a majority of all the electoral votes, the election is thrown into the Senate, and the Senators voting as individuals must choose from the two candidates standing highest on the list. Two thirds of the whole number of the Senators constitute a quorum for this purpose, and a majority of the entire body is necessary for a choice.

The legal qualifications for President are laid down in the Constitution. He must be a natural-born citizen, not less than thirty-five years old, and a resident in the United States for at least fourteen years. Identical rules apply to the Vice President. The term is fixed at four years, and so far as the Constitution is concerned, the President or Vice President may be reëlected indefinitely.[1]

[1] In case of the death or resignation of the President, the Vice President succeeds. By statute Congress provided, in 1886, that in case of the death or resignation of both the President and Vice President the following officers shall serve, in the order mentioned: Secretary of State, of the Treasury, of War, the Attorney General, the Postmaster General, the Secretary of the Navy, and of the Interior.

To the constitutional requirements, another has been added by political practice: no person is eligible to the office of President for more than two terms, at all events, in succession. This "third term doctrine," as it is called, is supposed to rest upon the example set by Washington in declining reelection at the expiration of eight years' service. Tradition has it that he acted on principle, but this seems to have slight historical foundation. He did not share Jefferson's ideas on rotation in office, and there is apparently no reason for believing that he objected to three terms or more. In fact, his Farewell Address contains excuses explaining why he in particular ought not to be charged with a lack of patriotism or neglect of duty in declining to continue longer in office.

Jefferson himself was for a time dubious on this point. He originally believed that the President should have been given a seven-year term, and then made ineligible for reelection. Later, however, he came to the conclusion that service for eight years with the possibility of removal at the end of four was nearer the ideal arrangement. By retiring in 1809, he followed the example set by Washington, and thus gave to the third term doctrine such high sanction that it became a political dogma almost as inviolable as an express provision of the Constitution. When the question was raised anew in 1912 in the case of Roosevelt, and his supporters urged that his candidacy was only for a second "elective" term, the Democrats made an issue out of the controversy. In their platform of that year, they bound themselves and their candidate to a single term and promised a constitutional amendment to that effect; but when safely in power they overlooked the pledge.

The Inauguration

The new President does not assume his official duties until about four months after the popular election, namely, on March 4th. This is a long delay and in case the outgoing and the incoming executives are committed to radically different policies it works for uncertainty and confusion. Its serious possibilities were illustrated in a marked fashion in 1860–61 when President Buchanan played a supine rôle during the fateful closing months of his administration. He permitted several Southern states to secede without taking any action in the matter, and left the country in chaos. To be sure, he could with some reason justify his conduct on the ground that it was not proper for him to involve his successor, Lincoln, in a desperate situation created by desperate measures; but this afforded his distracted countrymen no consolation. To obviate just such difficulties it has frequently been proposed that the President and the new Congress should take office immediately after the election. More than once constitutional amendments to effect this reform have been introduced in Congress, without avail. The only effective argument against the change is that ordinarily it is a good thing for a victorious party to have a few months "to cool off" before getting hold of the reins of power; and yet every effort to alter the system has been balked in Congress.

Formerly it was the practice for Congress, after the official count of the electoral ballots, to select a committee for the purpose of notifying the victor, but this was not uniformly followed, and has now been entirely abandoned. Curiously enough no official notice whatever is given to the President-elect. He is supposed to be well aware of his election himself, and on the fourth of March he appears to assume his responsibilities. He usually arrives in Washington a short time before, and calls upon the retiring executive to pay his respects. On the day of inauguration, the President-elect, in charge of a committee on ceremonies, is conducted to the White House, whence, accompanied by the President, he is driven to the Capitol. If the weather permits, the oath of office, administered by the Chief Justice of the United States, is taken in the open air on a platform built for the special purpose at the east front of the Capitol; otherwise it is taken in the Senate Chamber. Following the custom established by Washington, the new President then delivers an inaugural address. After the ceremony, he is driven back to the White House, where he surveys from a reviewing stand a long procession, which is usually hours in filing past. At last he is ready for work.

CHAPTER IX

The Office of President

With a certain air of grave finality our school books on civics inform us that it is the duty of the President to execute the laws made by Congress and interpreted by the courts. In this statement there is an element of truth—an elusive element. When the personality and practices of any particular President of great strength are drawn under scrutiny, such a neat theory of his office becomes a pale and partial shadow of the reality.

The Executive in the American System

As we have said in our section dealing with the separation of powers, the framers of the Constitution, while paying respectful tribute to the tradition, recognized the impossibility of any sharp division of government into legislative, executive, and judicial departments. Indeed they thought it undesirable and did not intend to establish it. As the greatest thinkers among them viewed the office, the President was to be one of the organs of government charged with responsibility for getting work done and in the exercise of his functions was to use executive, legislative, and judicial agencies for the purpose. If there is any doubt on this point it can be dispelled by reference to the debates in the convention and the *Federalist*.

What these thinkers intended, practice has realized. Presidents can and have employed their prestige, the veto, and their appointing powers for the purpose of compelling Congress to enact laws which it otherwise would not pass. To this extent they have been legislators. On its face the veto power, expressly vested in the President, is legislative, not executive, in character; that is, it has to do with the making of laws, not their application. Moreover statutes duly proclaimed have been often defeated by the refusal of the President to enforce them although their terms were plain; the Sherman Anti-trust Act of 1890 was for many years a dead letter owing to presidential neglect. On the other hand, Congress, even the Senate or House acting alone, has by threats and actual investigations compelled Presidents to dismiss their subordinates and has thus assumed the right to direct phases of administration. Like the President, the federal courts also help to "execute" laws by interpreting their meaning and issuing orders to executive as well as judicial officers; and the President, in selecting judges, can and has exercised his prerogative with a view to getting judicial support for specific types of legislation and particular modes of interpretation and enforcement (p. 35). The President of the United States is not a mere executive official; he possesses under the Constitution a vast governmental authority which cannot in truth be separated into clear-cut divisions of any kind.

While the adoption of the Constitution was pending, critics assailed it on the ground that it would make the President more powerful than the King of Great Britain, would vest in him the authority and pomp of an Oriental despot. Although Hamilton showed great skill in counteracting this impression in the *Federalist,* he took equal pains to explain that vigor and force in the President were necessary to the ends of government and that due provision had been made for this fundamental requirement. "Energy in the executive," he said, "is a leading character in the definition of good government. It is essential to the protection of the community against foreign attacks; it is not less essential to the steady administration of the laws; to the protection of property against those irregular and high-handed combinations which sometimes interrupt the ordinary course of justice; to the security of liberty against the enterprises and assaults of ambition, of faction, and of anarchy. Every man the least conversant in Roman story knows how often that republic was obliged to take refuge in the absolute power of a single man, under the formidable title of Dictator, as well against the intrigues of ambitious individuals who aspired to the tyranny and the seditions of whole classes of the community whose conduct threatened the existence of all government, as against the invasions of external enemies who menaced the conquest and destruction of Rome." In short the framers of the Constitution contemplated and provided for an executive endowed with immense general powers and competent to deal with every kind of social and political upheaval, potential and real—if need be, for a substantial dictatorship in time of crisis, such as President Lincoln exercised during the Civil War.

And what arrangements did they incorporate in the Constitution to attain their ends? First of all, they made the President politically independent of Congress—elected by a separate process and removable only with great difficulty by impeachment. Thus he draws effective support from people outside of Congress and can appeal to his own constituency over its head. In the second place, they vested the powers assigned to the executive in one man, not in a council; and they defended this arrangement on the ground that a collective body lacks decision, is likely to be weakened by internal conflicts, and is often paralysed by the jealousies and machinations of its members. One man acts or does not act; he cannot escape responsibility by hiding behind the vacillations of colleagues. In the third place, the Fathers gave a long and fixed term to the President—to avoid frequent changes and constant manipulations designed to expel one incumbent and to install another. Furthermore the President's salary cannot be reduced or cut off during the period for which he is elected. Independence, unity, fixed term, and financial security—these were the prime principles which they adopted as conducive to energy and strength in the executive.

And this system, it is to be noted, is based on principles

exactly opposed to those controlling parliamentary governments in Europe—governments which have so often culminated in dictatorships without responsibility. Under the parliamentary régime, the executive department does not stand outside of the legislature but is a creature and servant of that body; it is not one person but a council, often a coalition of political forces; it has no fixed term, but may be changed any hour, day or night, once, twice, three times a year, as the winds of opinion and passion blow; it has no financial security but must always look for its support to legislative discretion. Under this régime, the very characteristics feared by the founders of the American republic have been made fully manifest during the past hundred years; the law-making function has often been impaired by lengthy intrigues in the legislature connected with ousting and installing cabinets; both legislative and executive actions have been repeatedly paralyzed by personal disputes within ministries; and serious fluctuations in high policy have been brought about by continual changes in the executive department.

These are the very grounds now cited in many European countries to justify the overthrow of parliamentary government and the substitution of dictatorships. Throughout the literature of Fascism in Italy runs a complaint against the weakness, fitfulness, and indecision of parliaments and a plea for independence, unity, and long tenure in the executive department. No small part of the argument could be drawn from the *Federalist,* but one essential American ingredient is omitted, namely, responsibility to the people. "To seek to provide somehow for the exercise of popular sovereignty in connection with the choice of the executive," runs an official Fascist report, "is contrary to good sense and the public interest." It was to this doctrine of pessimism and tyranny that the founders of the Federal Government refused to subscribe. They sought to combine popular supremacy with unity, stability, and energy in the executive.

In summary, the executive of the United States has been

given some of the fundamental attributes of the dictator—independence of the legislature, unity, long term, and security of income—and for similar reasons: to avoid vacillation and timidity in government. And in addition to the authority which the President derives from these ingredients of his office, he enjoys in effect under the very language of the Constitution, immense executive, legislative, and judicial powers. Therefore as an agent for doing work, the President may become a Caesar if circumstances require, subject, of course, to the checks of the other departments of the Government and his responsibility through popular election. Herein lies the wisdom of the Fathers—foreseeing, as it were, with almost uncanny prevision the fate of the numerous parliamentary systems culminating in dictatorships without democratic control. Who can withhold from them or their handiwork a profound admiration or fail to place them at the very top among the statesmen of the centuries?

The President and Social Forces

What then is this implement of government, the chief executive of the United States? If we turn from the commentaries of lawyers and theorists to practice—at least to that which is open to observation or revealed in the intimate papers of chief magistrates now dead—we find that the President is both a social force and an agency of social forces. In his origins, his training, his affiliations, and his profession, he represents types of ethical aspirations and economic interests. Jefferson, the Virginia planter, Lincoln, the Illinois lawyer, Hoover, the cosmopolitan engineer, each carried with him into office a definite heritage destined to give direction to his activities. To assume that the President is a disembodied spirit controlled only by the Constitution and the laws is to imagine a fiction. Through his personality, complex energies come to a focus and function.

Besides feeling the urge of the social forces within him, he is influenced by the impact of social forces without; in large enterprises he is usually more or less their instrument. Though as frequently used, the phrase "social force" is vague, it in fact covers substantial realities. Its positive significance may be illustrated by particular references. In advocating and bringing to pass the adoption of a higher protective tariff for the benefit of American industry, William McKinley reflected the interests of manufacturers and their supporters who believed, for various motives, in the wisdom of that policy. If these groups had not been conscious and operating in politics, McKinley, even as President, would have been powerless to accomplish his fiscal designs, however strong his own convictions, however ingenious his proposals. Again, in virtually compelling a Democratic Congress to enact a law establishing an eight-hour day for trainmen, President Wilson was for the moment a political agent for the great railway unions; if they had not demanded the law and backed it with the threat of a strike, his personal support of the idea could scarcely have carried the bill through the national legislature. Perhaps he would not have thought of it, if its promoters had not brought the issue squarely to his attention.

If the letters and papers of Roosevelt and Wilson may be accepted as authority—and they certainly reveal experience—then among the highly dynamic social forces with which Presidents must constantly deal are organized capital and organized labor, although it would be a mistake to assume that either party is unified and has a single will. It is impossible to study Roosevelt's utterances without coming to the conclusion that he was primarily concerned throughout his administrations in opposing extremists in both of these groups and tried to function as the agent of what he called "the plain people" not actively affiliated with either side. "In their hearts," he wrote to Senator Lodge in 1906, "they [rich men] take the ground that to take legal proceedings against them when they violate the law and endeavor to have them pay their proper share of the taxes is as much an outrage as to excite the mob to plunder the rich." On the other hand he was alarmed by "a great growth of socialistic and radical spirit among the workingmen," and publicly and privately attacked those responsible for this tendency.

How these forces beat upon him in a concrete case is illustrated by the great coal strike in 1902 when the country was approaching a heatless winter. "I am feeling my way step by step," he wrote to Senator Lodge, "trying to get a solution of the coal matter. Most of my correspondents wish me to try to do something violent or impossible. A minor but very influential part desire that I send troops at once without a shadow of warrant into the coal districts or that I bring suit against the labor organization. The others demand that I bring suit against the operators, or that under the law of eminent domain, or for the purpose of protecting the public health, I seize their property, or appoint a receiver, or do something else that is wholly impossible." Such were the realities amid which the President had to make his way. It was as an instrument of the great coal-using public that he was finally able to bring the operators and strikers to accept the rulings of a commission appointed on his personal motion, without the authorization of the Constitution or of Congress.

Having convictions akin to those of Roosevelt, President Wilson was even more outspoken about the pressures on the chief executive. Referring to Taft's administration, he said: "The masters of the Government of the United States are the combined capitalists and manufacturers of the United States. It is written over every intimate page of the records of Congress, it is written all through the history of conferences at the White House, that suggestions of economic policy in this country have come from one source, not many sources. . . . Every time it has come to a critical question these gentlemen have been yielded to, and their demands have been treated as the demands that should be followed as a matter of course." Although he confessed that the representatives of great economic interests should be consulted in connection with governmental affairs, as a part of the public entitled to a hearing, President Wilson at first gave little heed to them and the complaint was made that he "was not seeing enough business men and was not talking to them . . . 'in their language.'" Later this defect was remedied somewhat, but to the end Wilson's attitude toward them was one of chilly aloofness rather than cordial coöperation.

Yet powerful as are the forces which beat on the President, giving form and direction to his activities, he is not an automaton. No precise calculation can be made of the drives and counterdrives to which he is subjected; and were such calculation possible, no inevitable result could be derived from it. The President is more than the bearer of a social heritage, an agent of powerful organizations, economic and ethical. He is a personality working within the shadow of long traditions and under a sense of grave responsibilities and opportunities. Our great Presidents—Lincoln, Roosevelt, and Wilson, for example—recorded their conviction that they were in some ways servants of a destiny not of their own shaping, but they also made fateful choices out of numerous possibilities in front of them. All Presidents stand in the presence of work that must be done, of potentialities that may be realized by little effort, and of imaginable achievements that may be accomplished by a heroic exercise of the will and intelligence.

Illustrations lie on every hand. President Roosevelt might easily have taken advantage of friction with Japan in 1907 and involved the country in a war in the Pacific. President Wilson might have kept the United States out of the World War, with consequences momentous to mankind. President Hoover could have allowed the naval rivalry with Great Britain to drift into dangerous channels—with an inevitable outcome of portentous significance. With respect to domestic affairs, choices and decisions of equal importance, if less spectacular, are always within the range of possibility. In the hands of a dynamic, creative personality the office of President may expand into realms of immense scope; in the hands of a routineer it may shrink within the compass of a politician's job.

Largely upon the character of the social forces focussed in his work and upon the nature of his personality will depend the President's views respecting the authority which he enjoys under the Constitution. If for any reason he does not wish to touch a bill pending in Congress or to assume responsibility for it, he may declaim on the separation of powers and his constitutional duty to avoid interference with the legislative branch of the Government. On the other hand if he wants a certain bill passed or defeated, as the case may be, he will let his wishes be known publicly or privately, or both, and will bring pressure to bear in Congress and outside to effect his purposes, saying nothing about the separation of powers in the process.

Examples of executive theories abound. President Buchanan thought that the Constitution did not authorize him to employ force to prevent states from leaving the Union; President Lincoln believed that the Constitution commanded him to wage war against secession. Grover Cleveland in general took the ground that he could only do those things authorized by the Constitution and laws; Theodore Roosevelt openly declared that a President could do anything for the public good not forbidden by the Constitution and the laws. If a President is pleased with a decision of the Supreme Court he may speak of "the respect due to the acts of that great tribunal;" if he does not like it he may say with Andrew Jackson, "Let the Chief Justice enforce it," or take care not to appoint to new vacancies judges likely to repeat it. Evidently a large variety of activities and word patterns is possible under the Constitution. Even in the affairs of the most strenuous Presidents the Supreme Court has seldom interfered; it may set aside acts of Congress with facility, but it is not likely to throw itself athwart the great lines of executive force.

Recent Growth of Executive Prerogative

To the historic office of President the technical developments of our age have added powers of undoubted significance—powers not mentioned, if theoretically contemplated, by the Constitution. The enormous increase in the number of federal employees, the growing complexity and scientific character of public administration, and the inevitable tendency of Congress to vest regulative functions in the President have added to the strength of the executive branch and to its weight in all departments of the Government. Since laws are frequently general in character and detailed extensions and applications are left to executive determination, a great deal of the pressure of interested parties, which formerly fell on Senators and Representatives, is transferred to the interpreting and enforcing officers. The legislature declines, at least relatively, and the executive fattens with the continual expansion of governmental enterprises into new fields.

Besides increasing the administrative weight of the executive, technology has thrust into the President's hands new instruments of power over the public opinion upon which he depends for support in making and carrying out policies. Through the radio he may address millions in person whenever he has a message to deliver or an appeal to make.

Like the radio, the telegraph and the press are at the President's service. Assembled in Washington is a corps of the astutest journalists the country can furnish, ever ready to catch the lightest word or the most significant announcement that falls from his lips or is smuggled out through "a White House spokesman." At any hour, day or night, he may break into first-page headlines in special editions. In an instant he may fix the attention of the whole country on a matter that otherwise would escape its notice. An excellent illustration of this power to transform an obscure incident into a national news sensation—with amazing influence on American and international opinion—is afforded by the "big navy scandal" of 1929.

In the summer of that year a small news item appeared in a back corner of a New York newspaper reporting that one W. B. Shearer had brought suit against certain shipbuilding corporations for a large sum of money alleged to be due him for "services" in connection with the Geneva arms conference of 1927. In itself this obscure notice was of the highest importance for it at least hinted that powerful companies financially involved in naval policy had been lobbying against a reduction in armaments. Apparently, however, the note attracted little attention until *The New Republic* referred to it in an editorial and expressed the hope that the incident would result in a thoroughgoing congressional investigation.

Still the matter was ignored by the press at large. Then suddenly President Hoover, in an address to the Washington correspondents, mentioned the affair and asked for light on it. Immediately the story burst into front-page news, capped with towering headlines, and millions were talking about it. Within a few days a senatorial investigating committee began a probe into the charges, which unearthed in a surprising fashion the methods of "big navy advocates." Moreover the exposure of the business raised the whole question of lobbies (p. 212) and led to a raking inquiry into the influence of "interests" on governmental policies. By thus stirring up a hornet's nest, the President gained public support for his program of arms limitation. If some of the framers of the Constitution could have foreseen the incident they probably would have deprecated it as an appeal to "popular passion." Certainly the Constitution is silent on publicity. Yet such are the potentialities of the President's office in an age of technology.

It is evident, therefore, that through the radio and the press the President may use his exalted position to appeal to national, sectional, group, or class interests; in this way he may distribute instantaneously his doctrines, his selection of facts, alleged facts, and political notions, giving them currency in the homes, streets, offices, factories, and fields of the whole country. Against his publicity, opposition in Congress or among citizens in general is handicapped from the outset. For example, in 1929, a fierce controversy arose over the question whether the new tariff should be "flexible," that is, whether the President should have the power to raise or lower the rates fixed by Congress—a species of legislative authority in reality, whatever the theory. When President Hoover insisted that Congress should give him that right, his appeal appeared on the first pages of the newspapers, but arguments made in the Senate against his demand, speeches of the highest quality and understanding, based upon careful study of the problem, received relatively little consideration. In fact the most searching of all these counterblasts attracted almost no attention at all.

The President at Work

When the work of the President is studied in the light of practice and of private papers, such as those of Roosevelt and Wilson, everything that has just been said about the range of his interest is reënforced by concrete illustrations. First of all it is evident from authentic documents that the President operates with reference to certain large policies—a general program of action involving legislative, executive, and judicial authority. Roosevelt, for instance, was deeply concerned about the development of the navy, the promotion of American trade in all parts of the world, the preservation of the overseas empire acquired under President McKinley, conservation of natural resources, the evolution of social legislation, and restraining extremists in the ranks of capital and labor. President Wilson, on the other hand, was rather indifferent to empire, lent countenance to the idea of ultimate withdrawal from the Philippines, relaxed support for American business in the Orient, and advocated a material reduction in the protective tariff, a reorganization of the currency and banking system, and a revision of the anti-trust law in favor of the smaller businessmen, with a view to a renewal of competition. Although these policies were nowhere formulated in a single document or statement, they appear implicitly and explicitly in the letters and papers of the two Presidents under consideration. In short both national leaders concentrated on a work program and made use of all agencies at hand in attaining their ends.

Naturally the two Presidents leaned heavily upon the chiefs of their respective parties in the realization of their policies. For this reason each displayed constant solicitude about keeping his party in line and winning at all important elections throughout the country. Appointments to the cabinet and to federal offices were made with an eye to uniting factions and bringing them into harmony with executive purposes. Wilson, for example, did not want Bryan as Secretary of State, but accepted him on account of his great influence over Democratic managers in Congress where the fate of the President's legislative projects—his career in fact—was to be determined.

In congressional elections held during their terms, both Presidents intervened. Each of them, on an important occasion, openly called upon the voters to return a majority committed to his measures. Roosevelt made a practice of writing letters in support of Republican candidates in strategic places and apparently his decision to drive coal operators and miners into a settlement, during the great strike of 1902, was made partly with a view to success in the congressional campaign of that year. Even in state and local contests both Presidents took an active interest. Roosevelt practically forced the nomination of Charles E. Hughes for governor in New York in 1906 on account of his fear of a Democratic victory in case a "regular" Republican was put up at that time. In connection with their renomination, Roosevelt and Wilson employed the various engines of their office, especially appointments, in securing the return of their own supporters to the party conventions; and the former practically selected his successor by presenting W. H. Taft to the public as the proper candidate, by engineering the choice of delegates, and by lending his personal and official support during the campaign. Immense, varied, extra-legal, and subtle are the activities of the President in the interest of his party, particularly the wing upon which he relies for the realization of his policies.

The private papers which describe these activities also show the President working all the time under the scrutiny and pressure of powerful interests in the country, to which we have already referred (p. 251). From first to last President Roosevelt was subjected to a deluge of telegrams, letters, appeals, and demands from interested parties and could not move to the right or left without taking into account the possibilities of support or defection. In the records of Colonel E. M. House a similar story is told of President Wilson. A great steel magnate, H. C. Frick, is disturbed by a prosecution of his corporation; he approaches the President through Colonel House with a view to a pacific settlement out of court. James Speyer, a New York banker, with wide railway affiliations, calls the attention of Wilson to "the seriousness of the financial situation" with respect to railways, to the delays of the Interstate Commerce Commission in raising rates, to the dangers of bankruptcy, and adds: "Something must be done and *done soon,* in a big and courageous way, to stop these attacks by government agencies both Federal and State, if disaster is to be averted. We need a practical and constructive policy and measures." A few months later, a Boston banker, H. L. Higginson, complains that the Government "is keeping business men on pins," and says, "If we can only have peace and nothing new, trust placed in railroad directorates and in other great concerns, we shall go on very well." He suggests that his points be laid before "influential men." During the preparation and passage of the Federal Reserve Act, bankers were in constant communication with the President, using Colonel

House as a medium, making complaints and proposals negative and positive.

Under the spotlight of other revelations the separation of powers simply disappears. Senator Lodge asks President Roosevelt to bring Speaker Cannon of the House of Representatives into line on legislative questions by using "oriental politeness." He also asks the President to push a bill then pending in Congress by giving it support in a message and suggests that he employ his Secretary of the Treasury in putting pressure on a member of the House in connection with the passage of a law. He urges the Secretary of State directly by telegraph not to sign a certain treaty until after election—on account of objections among his Massachusetts constituents. On the other hand, President Roosevelt invites Lodge to bestir himself in the Senate to win support for the executive battleship program, and coöperates with Senators in the passage of a railway rate regulation bill by seeing influential leaders, Democrats as well as Republicans, and arraying them behind his policies.

Affairs supposed to be purely executive in nature are made the subjects of common consideration. Roosevelt sends drafts of proposed messages to Senator Lodge and the latter makes suggestions for eliminations and additions. A crisis arises in Cuba; Senator Beveridge tells the President to take the island without more ado; Senator Foraker insists that he should wait on the action of Congress. The Russo-Japanese war and the subsequent peace negotiations involve American interests; President Roosevelt transmits to Senator Lodge copies of important papers bearing on the topic, giving him information not known outside of the White House and the State Department. The question of Anglo-American relations becomes acute; Roosevelt sends Lodge with a personal message to King Edward VII, indicating American willingness to coöperate. The fishing rights of the Senator's constituents off Newfoundland are in jeopardy; he asks the President for a small naval vessel as a gesture of interest. The World War is raging and the

United States hovers on the verge; President Wilson summons members of his party into conference and announces his program of intervention to them; although it is the business of Congress to declare war, he manages affairs in such a way as to make war inevitable; Congressmen who vote against his proposal he denounces to the country although they are clearly within their constitutional rights. The dividing line between executive and legislative departments is nowhere in evidence.

The President's Cabinet—Its Rôle as a Council

From the preceding pages it is evident that the President must personally carry the heavy burdens of a Caesar and must work constantly under the fierce light of public scrutiny. He cannot shift his responsibilities, either as political leader or general administrative director, to any other person or body. It is true that the heads of the great executive departments under his direction form a Cabinet or sort of council, but this is a matter of custom not of law, and the President cannot make it collectively accountable for his policies.

In creating the first departments in 1789, Congress did not even recognize the possibility that the chief officers would form a presidential council. Indeed, the act establishing the Treasury Department indicated a desire to bring the Secretary under congressional control in many ways. Apparently the Senate was then expected to serve as the President's advisory body for it shared with him the power of making treaties and appointments and was sufficiently small in size to meet the requirement.

Whatever may have been the view of Congress, however, Washington regarded the four chief executive officials, including the Attorney General, as his confidential advisers, though the term Cabinet was not immediately applied to them. He also exercised his constitutional right of requiring opinions from the heads of departments, and took them into his confidence in all important matters very soon after the first appointments were made. We have direct evidence of cabinet meetings as early as 1791, when Washington, having departed on a tour to the South, wrote to the three Secretaries: "I have expressed my wish, if any serious or important cases . . . should arise . . . that the Secretaries for the Departments of State, Treasury, and War may hold consultations thereon, to determine whether they are of such a nature as to demand my personal attendance." During his first administration, Washington, by a gradual process, welded the departmental heads into an executive council, and by 1793 the term Cabinet or Cabinet Council was applied to it.

Some Presidents have cabinet meetings regularly at stated times, but others merely call sessions when matters in hand seem to require common action. The meetings are usually secret, and no minutes are kept of transactions. As the special business of each department is discussed separately with the President by the appropriate officer, it is ordinarily affairs pertaining to the general policy of the administration that are brought up for consideration in the Cabinet. Only important pieces of legislation desired by the President or by a department head and about to be submitted to Congress are likely to be discussed in detail with a view to a positive conclusion. Votes are seldom taken on propositions, and they are of no significance beyond securing a mere expression of opinion. This is illustrated by an incident related of President Lincoln, who closed a grave debate in the Cabinet, in which he found every member against him, with the announcement: "Seven nays, one aye, the ayes have it." Nevertheless, cabinet meetings are of service to the administration, especially in maintaining harmonious coöperation among the departments and in formulating the executive policy. When, in 1919, President Wilson became seriously ill, it was reported that many questions were decided at cabinet sessions which he was unable to attend. Later, however, he repudiated the legality of the meetings and forced the resignation of the Secretary of State who had taken leadership in convening them.

In the ordinary course of things, it appears from such glimpses of cabinet affairs as we can catch in the letters and papers of former members, most of the sessions are of slight importance, especially under a dominant personality. This view is given in the records of F. K. Lane, who served under President Wilson as Secretary of the Interior. A few entries will illustrate the point: "To-day's meeting has resulted in nothing, though in Mexico, Cuba, Costa Rica, and Europe we have trouble. . . . Yesterday we had a cabinet meeting. All were present. The President was manifestly disturbed. For some two weeks we have spent our time at cabinet meetings largely in telling stories. Even at the meeting of a week ago, the day on which the President sent his reply to Germany . . . we were given no view of the note which was already in Lansing's hands and was emitted at four o'clock; and we had no talk upon it, other than some outline given offhand by the President to one of the cabinet who referred to it before the meeting; and for three fourths of an hour we told stories on the war and took up small departmental affairs. . . . Another cabinet meeting, and no light on what our policy will be as to Germany."

Clearly the Cabinet is merely the kind of an organization which the President wishes to make of it and is his own council in a very peculiar sense. Having no existence or warrant in law, it is not subject as such to congressional control. In the first administration of President Jackson this point was settled for all time. When the Senate requested the transmission of a paper supposed to have been read by him to the heads of the executive departments, he replied flatly: "The executive is a coördinate and independent branch of the government equally with the Senate, and I have yet to learn under what constitutional authority that branch of the legislature has a right to require of me an account of any communication, either verbally or in writing, made to the heads of departments acting as cabinet council. As well might I be required to detail to the Senate the free and private conversations I have held with those officers on any subject relating to their duties and my own." As a personality and a representative of social forces the President stands alone; his responsibility cannot be distributed among his colleagues; and Congress cannot hold them to account collectively for anything that they do.

The President as Director of the Administration

In addition to serving as a general political leader, the President assumes high technical responsibilities as the head of the national administration. It is his duty, among other things, to see that the Constitution, laws, and treaties of the United States and judicial decisions rendered by the federal courts are duly enforced throughout the country. In the fulfillment of this obligation, he may direct the heads of departments and their subordinates in the discharge of the functions vested in them by the acts of Congress. Some of the departments are placed, by law, more specifically under his control than others. For example, the Secretary of State, in the conduct of foreign affairs, is completely subject to the President's orders; and the Attorney General must give an opinion or institute proceedings if required to do so. On the other hand, when the Treasury was organized in 1789, it was definitely understood that Congress had a special control over the administration of that department (p. 293).

How far the President, in ordinary times, may go in controlling administrative officers is a matter of dispute among lawyers. Long ago the Supreme Court held that he is bound to see that an officer faithfully carries out the duties assigned to him by law, but is not authorized to direct the officer as to the ways and means to be employed in the operation. It is doubtful, however, whether this view of the issue would be taken to-day. Clearly, the President has the power to remove the head of a department who refuses to obey orders, and it is difficult to see why, in reality, he cannot determine, within the lines of the statutes, the steps to be taken by that officer. When President Jackson wanted government funds withdrawn from the United States Bank, he ousted, one after the other, two Secretaries of the Treasury, and finally appointed a third who was known to be subservient to his will. He had his way in the end.

Certainly the President's authority over the direct execution of the law, especially through the agency of the Attorney General, is very great. He may instruct the Attorney to institute an action against anyone suspected of violating federal statutes. Since the principles which control the proceedings of officers in arresting, holding, and prosecuting accused persons are general in character, the very spirit as well as the tactics of law enforcement can be shaped by the President. Laxness or severity is, therefore, largely within his discretion.

In the case of open resistance he may have recourse to the armed forces of the United States. Indeed this drastic stroke is not limited to such exigencies. If postal operations are obstructed or interstate traffic is seriously hampered by local disturbances, he may order out the troops. In 1894 President Cleveland, against the protest of the Governor of Illinois, sent soldiers to Chicago which was the scene of a great railway strike blocking the movement of commerce and the mails. President Wilson resorted to similar action on the occasion of a labor dispute at Gary, Indiana, among the steel workers, and President Harding turned to the Army in 1922 when a strike threatened to tie up the railways.

In the discharge of his administrative duties, the President enjoys a large ordinance power—that is, the authority to supplement statutes by regulations covering details often of great importance. He makes extensive rules for the Army and the Navy, the Patent Office, and the customs, internal revenue, consular, and diplomatic services. Sometimes he issues decrees under his general executive power; many army ordinances he promulgates as commander-in-chief. On other occasions he acts in accordance with express responsibilities conferred upon him by law. It has, for instance, become a practice for Congress to make the rates of tariff duties imposed upon foreign goods flexible, dependent upon certain conditions, and then to authorize the President, subject to definite restrictions, to vary them in application (p. 455).

During the war against the Central Empires, Congress took steps with regard to the organization of departments which may foreshadow new policies in time of peace when the work of government becomes still more complicated. In vesting immense powers over industries, shipping, food supplies, and other matters in President Wilson, Congress did not attempt to create all the boards, commissions, and other agencies necessary to the exercise of those powers; neither did it often prescribe the exact methods to be pursued. These important matters it left almost entirely to the determination of the President. Furthermore by the Overman Act, passed in 1918, it even authorized him, during the war and for six months afterward, to consolidate existing bureaus, offices, and agencies and to rearrange them and their functions in any way which might contribute to efficiency.

Though conceived in relation to special exigencies this legislation was in complete harmony with the tendency of Congress to enlarge what is called "executive discretion," by passing laws in general terms and entrusting the details to the President, department heads, and great agencies like the Interstate Commerce Commission. Indeed such a practice is made necessary by the growing complexity and fluidity of the social and economic matters with which Congress must deal. It cannot foresee all contingencies and provide for them; it must entrust great responsibilities to federal officers charged with the application of the principles of the law. To use the language of a witty French poet in relation to a similar state of affairs in his own country, Congress "must leave something to Providence." Concretely this means an immense increase in presidential power, for when Congress authorizes a federal officer to issue sweeping orders, it really transfers the formulation of definite policy to the President who appoints and removes him.

The President's Power of Appointment and Removal

In connection with his executive functions, the President chooses a large number of federal officers. This is significant from the point of view of politics, as well as administration. It is a power which may be employed to foster partisanship or to secure the efficient performance of public duties.

When considered in relation to the manner of their selection, the civil authorities of the United States—other than the President, Vice President, presidential electors, Senators, and Representatives—fall into two groups: officers whose appointment is entrusted by the Constitution or by act of Congress to the President and Senate; and "inferior" officers, whose appointment is vested by Congress in the President alone, the courts of law, or the heads of departments.

Between superior and "inferior" offices no clear distinction has ever been made. The right of Congress to decide, when establishing an office, that it shall be deemed "inferior" is not questioned, but no very consistent rule has been adopted for guidance. A few bureau chiefs of great importance are "inferior" officers in the view of the law because their selection is vested in the President alone or in the departmental Secretaries. On the other hand, many bureau chiefs, some relatively less significant with respect to their duties, are appointed by the President and Senate. In the main clerks and minor officers are chosen by departmental heads subject to the terms of the Civil Service Act (Chapter X).

The first, or superior group, embraces nearly all the important officers of the Federal Government—for example, the heads of departments, most of the bureau chiefs, judges of the federal courts, the civil service and interstate commerce commissioners, revenue collectors, and immigration chiefs. Taken together, they constitute an official army numbering thousands of persons, whose salaries amount to millions of dollars a year. In filling positions in this class, the President and Senate are unhampered except in some cases by statutes imposing such qualifications as citizenship, professional attainments, and the like. And as many of these officers serve only for a term of four years, under various acts or in practice, each President has at his disposal an enormous amount of patronage.

The officers appointed by the President and Senate may be divided into groups according to the degree of freedom which the former enjoys in exercising his own judgment.

Members of the Cabinet, that is, heads of departments, are usually the President's personal selection, although in this relation he is often bound by preëlection promises or by obligations incurred in gaining the support of certain prominent persons in his party. At all events, the Senate, even when it is in the hands of the opposition, does not seek to interfere with the appointments to these offices; it usually ratifies the President's nominations promptly and without objections. One exception in the course of thirty years or more—the rejection of a nominee for the office of Attorney General presented by President Coolidge—merely proves the rule. The choice of diplomatic representatives is also left largely to the President's discretion, as far as the Senate is concerned; although he always has many party obligations to consider in this connection. Military and naval appointments, especially in times of crisis, are principally subject to presidential determination, but political influences are by no means wanting here. Nominations to the judiciary are nearly always approved—although occasionally the subject of hot contests in the Senate (p. 133).

A group of local federal offices nominally filled by the President with the advice and consent of the Senate is subject largely to the control of the latter, as the result of a time-honored practice, known as "senatorial courtesy." Under its power to advise and consent, the Senate does not officially suggest names to the President, but it will ratify nominations to many offices only under certain conditions. If either one or both of the Senators from the state in which the offices under consideration are located belong to the President's political party, then executive freedom of choice almost disappears. If only one Senator is of the President's party, then his will is likely to prevail. If both Senators are party colleagues, the preferences of the senior member will probably decide the matter, especially if he is the stronger of the two, or a division of spoils may occur. At all events in such circumstances selections are made in fact, or at least approved in advance, by the Senator or Senators in question; otherwise the Senate, acting under the rule of senatorial courtesy, will reject the nominations.

The rule, however, is not always followed. President Garfield, for example, once refused to place before the Senate certain candidates for federal offices in New York suggested by Senators Platt and Conkling of that state. The latter feeling that their rights had been flouted thereupon tendered their resignations, but on asking vindication at the hands of the state legislature failed to secure reëlection. Here, again, it is not a matter of fixed principle but of time and circumstances—the character of the President, the Senators, and the aspirants themselves. In case the federal offices to be filled are located in a state which has no Senator of his party, the President has more freedom of action, but even here he is bound to consult the party leaders in the region concerned.

A third group of officers subject to presidential nomination is composed of minor authorities of the United States such as postmasters, revenue officers, marshals, and federal attorneys within congressional districts. In this relation it has become the custom to allow the Representative, if he is of the President's party, to name the appointees of his district; but if he is not of that persuasion, the patronage may go to a Senator, if there is one of the same political affiliation; unless for special reasons the President desires to make a "personal" appointment. The advice of the Representative is not always taken, but it has great weight, for as a rule such patronage is of considerable utility in maintaining the local party organization.

In selecting officers of the Government in localities, the President is compelled to rely more or less on persons familiar with local opinion. Speaking on the point, President Taft once remarked: "A member of a community remote from the capital . . . wonders that a President, with high ideals and professions of a desire to keep the government pure and have efficient public servants, can appoint to an important local office a man of mediocre talent and of no particular prominence or standing or character in the community. Of course the President cannot make himself aware of just what standing the official appointed has. He cannot visit the district; he cannot determine by personal examination the fitness of the appointee. He must depend upon the recommendations of others; and in matters of recommendations, as indeed of obtaining office, it is leg muscle and lack of modesty which win, rather than fitness and character. The President has assistance in making his selection, furnished by the Congressmen and Senators from the locality in which the office is to be filled; and he is naturally quite dependent on such advice and recommendation."

It is obvious that the appointment and removal of federal officers must consume a large share of the President's time, especially just after his inauguration. The rush of office-seekers in 1841 contributed to the illness and death of the first Harrison; the second Harrison declared that he spent about half his time for the first two years of his term haggling over patronage. Of course the task is made far more difficult by the necessity of consulting Senators and Representatives, hearing complaints from them, considering their suggestions, and allaying their grievances. It has been proposed, therefore, that nearly all the offices now filled by the President and Senate be placed under civil service rules (p. 316). This would require in some cases a constitutional amendment and in others changes in law calling for a self-denying ordinance on the part of the Senators.

It has been cogently argued that if the President could appoint without having to consult the Senate, the quality of the persons selected would be improved. The contention may be well founded but, on the other hand, the President could thus build up a political machine of his own. This is exactly what Republican Presidents usually do in the Southern states where they have no Senators of their party to placate with appointments. President Coolidge was not oblivious to the advantages of the system in seeking his own election in 1924; nor President Hoover in consolidating his forces after his inauguration in 1929. The elective system inevitably involves politics, and appointments will be made with reference to partisan exigencies as well as efficiency. For some social problems there is no mechanical solution; but no doubt it would be well to place a large number of the presidential offices under civil service rules.

The power of removal, so indispensable to the conduct of efficient administration, has long been one of the controverted points of American law. The Constitution itself makes no provision for removal except by impeachment—accusation by the House of Representatives and trial by the Senate acting as a court. On the general subject it is silent. With respect to officers chosen by the President in co-operation with the Senate, it was early agreed, however, that the President could remove them without asking for senatorial approval. At length, by a memorable act passed in 1867, during the long dispute between Congress and President Johnson, it was provided that in effect no person holding a civil office to which he was appointed with the ratification of the Senate could be removed by the President without the consent of that body. Although this sweeping provision was subsequently modified, Congress from time to time applied the same principle to certain classes of federal officers. For example, by a law enacted in 1876, it stipulated that first, second, and third class postmasters shall be appointed and may be removed by the President by and with the advice and consent of the Senate.

Fifty years later this provision came squarely before the Supreme Court in the case of Myers *vs.* the United States, and the Court ruled that the section in question "by which the unrestricted power of removal of first-class postmasters is denied to the President is in violation of the Constitution and invalid." Apart from certain historical arguments, Chief Justice Taft, who rendered the opinion, rested his conclusion mainly on the clauses of the Constitution which vest in the President the executive power, the duty of appointing officers (when it is not placed elsewhere by Congress), the duty of taking care that the laws be faithfully executed, and the responsibility for commissioning officers of the United States.

While clear as to the exact point decided, this case leaves a number of important questions hanging in the air. What restrictions, if any, can Congress place on the President's removal power? Can it stipulate that certain officers shall hold their positions for a fixed term of years and shall not be removed during that period except for specified causes? Strictly applied, the Myers case, by resting the President's removal authority on the Constitution, would forbid Congress to put any curb whatever upon it. What limits may Congress place on the removal of officers whose appointment it vests elsewhere than in the President? This point is not settled. Again, if Congress cannot impose restraints on the removal power of the President, what becomes of the Comptroller General? As the law now stands the President appoints him with the consent of the Senate; while Congress may dismiss him by joint resolution. Is the law valid? Judges of the Court of Claims hold office "during good behavior." May the President retire them at will for any reason he may deem proper? According to law, Federal Trade Commissioners may be removed for "inefficiency, neglect of duty, or malfeasance in office." Can the President oust them merely for dissenting vigorously from his policies? Apparently, yes. Under the Myers case it is difficult to see how Congress can, by a mere statute, hinder him from doing exactly as he pleases in such situations.

Perhaps, however, this is laying too much stress on legal formalities. Although it seems that Congress may no longer require the consent of the Senate to the removal of any officer whose nomination it ratifies, the upper chamber is not powerless. Its consent is still necessary to the appointment of the successor to any officer in this class unseated by the President. Hence it may serve informal notice on the latter that it will not approve any name suggested for the vacancy. This is not academic. Not many years ago a President ardently desired to get rid of an Interstate Commerce Commissioner whose term had expired and was taking steps in that direction. But his plan was blocked by underground news from certain powerful Senators to the effect that in case he did not reappoint the man in question he would have on his hands a vigorous fight in the Senate to secure the confirmation of any new person proposed for the place. After this subterranean passage-at-arms, the President yielded and renominated the Commissioner whose tenure was in dispute. What the law forbids, political custom may establish by other means.

The President and Foreign Affairs

Although foreign affairs are treated below in a separate chapter, the President's powers in this field are so great that, even at the risk of some repetition, they must be emphasized in the present review of his high office. It is true that in some respects he is controlled by the Senate and in others by Congress. The Senate may confirm or reject the treaties which he negotiates and has a similar jurisdiction over his nominations to diplomatic and consular posts. Congress alone can provide for American representation abroad and appropriate money for its support. In many instances also Congress must enact the special laws necessary to put treaty stipulations into effect. But while it may pass bills and resolutions, such as tariff and immigration measures, which deeply affect the attitude of other peoples, neither Congress nor either house can establish and conduct relations with any foreign country.

It is the President who acts as the official spokesman of the United States in international affairs and assumes primary responsibility for American foreign policy and its results. Under the Constitution, he nominates ambassadors, other public ministers, and consuls; he negotiates treaties; and he receives ambassadors and public ministers from abroad.

But his authority is not limited to the formal letter of the law. He may do many other things of vital significance in this sphere. He may dismiss an ambassador or minister of a foreign government for political as well as personal reasons, and, if on the former ground, he might embroil the country in a serious conflict. His power to receive foreign representatives authorizes him to recognize the independence of a new state, perhaps in rebellion against a legitimate sovereign, and thus he might incur the risk of war.

As head of the Navy, he may order a fleet or a single vessel to a foreign port under circumstances likely to raise difficulties; the ill-fated battleship *Maine* was sent to the harbor of Havana by President McKinley at a critical time when the action was regarded by many Spaniards, though not officially, as unfriendly. The result all the world knows. As Commander-in-chief of the Army he may move troops to a position on the very borders of a neighboring state and bring about an armed conflict. A notable instance of such a stroke occurred at the opening of the Mexican War, when President Polk directed American troops to enter disputed territory and, as soon as they were attacked by the Mexicans, declared that hostilities existed by act of Mexico.

Again, in his messages and notes the President may outline a foreign policy so hostile to another nation as to precipitate a diplomatic clash, if not more serious results.

This happened in the case of the Venezuelan controversy, when President Cleveland recommended to Congress demands which seemed offensive to Great Britain. Years later President Wilson, in his negotiations with Germany after the sinking of the *Lusitania* in 1915, followed a program destined to end in an open break. By his enunciation of principles, his notes to Germany, his dismissal of the German ambassador, his appeal to the nation to support his leadership, and other acts, he placed Congress in such a position that war was its only choice.

On the other hand, the negative attitude of a President may be of high significance in foreign affairs. The refusal of President Harding to take part in the numerous conferences held in Europe after the Great War kept the United States definitely out of the official international assemblies of the Old World. Had he participated in those councils he could have committed the country to responsibilities and obligations. By clinging to the doctrine of isolation he helped to fasten that historic dogma upon the nation more firmly than ever.

In directing foreign affairs the President is not compelled to incorporate every positive arrangement with another country in the form of a treaty. On the contrary he may make "executive agreements" on his own authority. Under the Constitution only treaties must have the approval of the Senate; while other types of international understandings are left by custom to presidential discretion. If this seems extraordinary at first glance, its reasons become apparent on second thought. It would be impracticable to embody the results of every little parley in a solemn convention to be ratified by the Senate. Indeed the number and variety of minor adjustments necessary to the smooth working of international relations make it impossible to employ the cumbersome treaty-making process in every case.

Taking this fact into account, Congress has recognized the existence of a distinction between agreements and regular treaties; for example, by empowering the Postmaster General to make "conventions" with foreign countries respecting the carriage of international mails, without asking for senatorial approval. Another class of compacts is covered by the term "identical note." Such an understanding is really an exchange of letters between the Secretary of State, acting under the President's immediate direction, and the representative of some foreign power. A remarkable illustration of that operation is afforded by the Lansing-Ishii Agreement of 1917 between Mr. Lansing, our Secretary of State, and Mr. Ishii, the Japanese ambassador, recognizing, so to speak, "by correspondence," among other things, the special position of Japan in the Far East—a sort of Oriental Monroe doctrine for that country. This was in reality a vital commitment with respect to American foreign policy which the Harding administration felt compelled to cancel in connection with the Washington conference.

The line between matters appropriate to a treaty and an executive agreement respectively is difficult to draw. Practice has established no rule. As a matter of fact a President may resort to the latter when he has been baffled by the Senate in an effort to make a treaty or believes that he could not obtain senatorial approval if he negotiated it. The shadowy character of the border between the two forms of international understanding is well illustrated by President Roosevelt's procedure with regard to Santo Domingo. In January, 1905, he signed a treaty with the Dominican government to the effect that the United States would maintain the integrity of that country, direct the administration of its finances, make provisions for the settlement of foreign claims, and generally assist in keeping order there. This treaty the Senate refused to ratify. Thereupon the President secured from the Dominican government the appointment of an American citizen to supervise its finances, undertook to impound a certain portion of the republic's revenues for the benefit of foreign creditors, and sent American battleships to the scene of action as a sign that he was in earnest.

For thus realizing the original plans which the Senate

had rejected, the President was, naturally enough, severely taken to task in that chamber. "The treaty has been practically carried into effect without consulting the Senate," contended a critic. "The appointment of an American agent as an official of Santo Domingo to collect its customs was simply a cover and an evasion. Under the principles of international law and the comity of nations, this government is morally bound for the proper custody of this fund, and would be liable in case of its waste or loss. . . . When you add to this fact that our warships are in the harbors of the island ostensibly for the purpose of protecting American interests, but in reality protecting the officials of the island against any menace from without and revolution from within, you have the establishment of a sovereignty or a protectorate without a word from Congress or the Senate sanctioning the same." Nevertheless the precedent stands. The President, under his authority to make executive agreements, may go to great lengths and effect arrangements with foreign governments far more serious in character than the matters often incorporated in formal treaties.

All the cases to which reference has just been made were publicly known, but the President is not limited to "open diplomacy." He may enter secret agreements with foreign powers and commit himself during his term of office to the pursuit of a specific policy. Through a high emissary sent to Tokyo in 1905, President Roosevelt came to terms with Japan on certain oriental affairs. On her part Japan undertook to respect American dominion in the Philippines; on the other side President Roosevelt agreed to accept the establishment of Japanese sovereignty over Korea (whose independence the United States had officially recognized). At the same time the President, acting through his agent in Tokyo, assured the Japanese premier that the people of the United States were in full accord with Japan and Great Britain in maintaining peace in the Far East, and that "whatever occasion arose, appropriate action of the government of the United States, in conjunction with Japan and Great

Britain, for such a purpose, could be counted upon by them quite as confidently as if the United States were under treaty obligations." When the news leaked out in Tokyo, a Japanese journalist close to the government exclaimed: "It is a Japanese-Anglo-American alliance!" Undoubtedly President Roosevelt personally favored such a concert of the three powers, but he knew that the Senate would not approve it and that, as he said, he "might as well strive for the moon." The whole affair was so quietly arranged that the American people knew nothing about it until Mr. Tyler Dennett found the documents in the private papers of the late President, after they had been made accessible in the Library of Congress, and gave them to the world in 1924.

Whatever the nature of the foreign business in hand, the President has a wide range of choice as to methods to be employed in negotiation. He may take up matters personally with the spokesmen of other countries either in Washington or, as in the case of President Wilson, in a foreign capital. If he employs agents, he has many possibilities open before him. The regular ambassadors, ministers, and consuls, of course, are at his command, but he is by no means limited to them. He may use a personal representative chosen and instructed at his pleasure, without reference to any act of Congress or the approval of the Senate. Hundreds of such representatives have been engaged by Presidents since the establishment of the Republic. More than once during his administrations, President Wilson sent a private citizen, Colonel E. M. House, to Europe—sometimes with a general roving commission to sound foreign governments and on other occasions with high and significant powers—virtually to speak with the same authority as the President himself. Again, the agent may be very secretly engaged; even the American ambassador in Tokyo did not know the purpose for which Roosevelt's agent visited Japan in connection with the affair mentioned above. If circumstances warrant, presidential representatives may be given high official rank. When President Wilson sent a mission to Russia in 1917, he assigned to the chairman the title of ambassador and to the other members that of ministers plenipotentiary. Yet they were not officers of the United States in a legal sense; they were merely executive agents. Evidently the President, endowed with a large freedom in the choice of instrumentalities, may carry on public and private investigations and negotiations in all parts of the world on his own authority and for his own purposes. So great are his powers in diplomacy.

The War Powers of the President

The President is Commander-in-chief of the Army and Navy and of the state militia when called into the service of the United States. He holds this power in peace and during hostilities. Since, however, Congress controls the equipment of the Army and Navy and possesses, nominally at least, the right to declare war, it may to a certain extent undertake the actual direction of military affairs. Indeed some publicists have even contended that Congress can require the Commander-in-chief to assign a particular officer to a specified division, and that in case a regiment has been dispatched to a given point by presidential decree, Congress can countermand the order. If this is true, Congress might practically assume charge of a campaign in a slow and cumbersome way. Still, it is argued on the other side, with more reason, that its power ends with providing and maintaining the Army and Navy and declaring war; and that the entire command of the military and naval engines is vested in the President, whose guidance, under the Constitution, is the law of nations and "the regulations of civilized combat," whatever this phrase may mean during a severe struggle.

The latter view of the issue is certainly supported by the provisions of law which empower the President to appoint military and naval officers by and with the advice and consent of the Senate—except in the militia—and in time of war to dismiss them at will. The practice of vesting the removal power in courts-martial during peace merely relieves the President of an unnecessary burden without diminishing his supreme authority.

In the actual conduct of hostilities the President is not limited to the direction of the armed forces; he may do whatever a commander-in-chief is warranted in doing under the laws of war to weaken and overcome the enemy. It was under this general power, inherent in his office, that President Lincoln, during our civil struggle, suspended the writ of habeas corpus in states that were not even within the theater of combat. It was under this authority that he emancipated the slaves in the sections in arms against the Union, arrested those charged with giving aid and comfort to the Confederacy, established a blockade of Southern ports, and, in short, brought the whole weight of the North, material and moral, to bear in the contest.

Even more extensive, if possible, was the high prerogative exercised by President Wilson in prosecuting the war against the Central Empires. By act after act Congress conferred upon him almost unlimited authority over the economic resources and the man power of the nation. It prescribed general principles and left their interpretation and application to him. Even the bureaus, offices, and other civil agencies already in existence were made as wax in his hands under the Overman law (p. 266). Subject to his direction and leadership drastic control over the expression of opinion—the most drastic in our history—was established by the Sedition Act of 1918. Still more extraordinary was the invasion of Russian territory without authorization of Congress. The country was at war, it is true, with the Central Powers, but previous to the Bolshevik revolution the United States had been an associate, not an enemy, of Russia. Nevertheless, in August, 1918, American troops were landed at Archangel and at Vladivostok in coöperation with certain of the Allied Powers. Nominally, war was not declared and the ostensible purpose of the expedition was to protect supplies and steady Russian efforts at self-government, but in fact American soldiers took part in fighting Bolshevik troops. The causes of this affair and its constitutionality are obscure questions. The precedent remains.

Indeed, the right of the President to employ the military and naval forces in actual fighting without a formal declaration of war from Congress has never been closely defined in practice. Many punitive excursions have been made into Mexico, the last in 1917 to capture the bandit Villa who had murdered and plundered on the American border. In 1900 the President coöperated with European and Asiatic governments in an armed expedition to rescue foreigners in Peking from the hands of the Boxer rebels. During Wilson's administration, American marines were landed in Haiti and Santo Domingo on presidential authorization, local skirmishes were waged, and American military supremacy was established over the two countries—without any declaration of war by Congress. Subsequently, under Harding and Coolidge, similar action was taken in certain Caribbean countries.

Under his war power, the President may govern conquered territory. He can appoint officers there, make laws and ordinances, lay and collect taxes of all kinds, and, in brief, practically exercise sovereign jurisdiction until Congress has acted.

At home the President may likewise use armed forces in executing federal law against resistance that cannot be overcome by ordinary civil process. The United States, under the Constitution, guarantees to each commonwealth a republican form of government, protects it against invasion, and, on application of the legislature or of the executive (if the legislature is not in session), defends it against domestic violence. By act of Congress, the President is authorized to send troops when aid is asked in due form by the authorities of a state struggling with an insurrection.

The Pardoning Power

Besides his administrative prerogatives, the President enjoys the power to grant reprieves and pardons (except in cases of impeachment) for offenses against the United States. He may remit a fine, commute a death sentence to a term of imprisonment, or give a convict complete freedom; but when forfeiture of office is one of the penalties imposed, he cannot restore the offender to his former position. A pardon may be issued before or after conviction.

In exercising this power, the President relies, of course, largely upon the conclusions of others. In each instance the application for executive clemency, with all the papers attached, is sent to the office of the Attorney General, where a pardon-clerk takes charge of preliminaries. Usually the judge and the district attorney under whose direction the case was first tried are asked to make a statement about the merits of the appeal. After the facts are carefully reviewed, the Attorney General endorses on the application his opinion as to the course of action which should be pursued, and transmits the documents to the President for final determination. "If the trial seems to have been fairly conducted," said President Harrison, "and no new exculpatory evidence is produced, and the sentence does not seem to have been unduly severe, the President refuses to interfere. He cannot weigh the evidence as well as the judge and jury. They saw and heard the witnesses, and he has only a writing before him. It often happens that the wife or mother of the condemned man comes in person to plead for mercy, and there is no more trying ordeal than to hear her tearful and sobbing utterances and to feel that public duty requires that she be denied her prayer."

The President and Legislation

The President's position as chief executive is so exalted and his powers in that respect are so extensive that his functions as legislator are often lost to sight. Yet the fame of most Presidents rests upon their success in writing policies into law rather than upon their achievements as administrators. In reality the Constitution itself contemplates their leadership in this relation. It requires the President to give Congress from time to time information on the state of the Union and to recommend such measures as he may deem necessary and expedient. The presidential message may be delivered orally in the presence of both houses or sent to them as a document. Washington and Adams adopted the former procedure; Jefferson discontinued the custom and substituted for it the practice of sending written messages. This was the rule for more than a hundred years, until President Wilson in 1913 with a somewhat dramatic gesture returned to the ceremony inaugurated by Washington and read his communications to the houses in joint session. For a time his successors followed in his footsteps. President Coolidge, with the aid of the radio, even read his first message to the general public as well as to Congress. But later he resumed the old practice of transmitting his message to Congress in the form of a state paper.

The nature and purpose of the message vary from time to time. Occasionally it is a formal document conveying definite information on some special issue. Again, particularly at the opening session of Congress, it may have great political significance. It may be a solemn declaration of party policies drafted in consultation with party leaders. It may be a bid for a reëlection in the form of a careful statement of the views entertained by its author. It may be an announcement to some other country, warning it against pursuing a certain course of action. It may contain a noteworthy statement of principles, such as the doctrine incorporated in Monroe's famous message of December, 1823, or the Fourteen Points in which Wilson summarized the war policy of the United States in 1918 and outlined a basis of peace to the enemy countries. Sometimes the message even goes into details and suggests specific laws.

Whatever may be its purport, the message is the one great public document of the United States which is widely read and discussed. Congressional debates receive scant notice, but the President's message is ordinarily printed in full in nearly every metropolitan daily, and is the subject of general editorial comment throughout the length and breadth of the land. It stirs the country; it often affects congressional elections; and it may establish grand policy.

The treatment which the President's recommendations receive at the hands of Congress varies, of course, according to circumstances. They may be accepted if it feels that they are sound in principle and that there is an effective demand for them in the country. If it is not convinced on such grounds, the President, by his party leadership or personal favors or the use of patronage, may in effect compel action. At all events, having set the issue by a proclamation to the country, he is in a strategic position to force favorable consideration.

Besides bringing pressure upon the national legislature to secure the adoption of policies which he favors, the President may veto acts of Congress which are out of line with his convictions. Every bill or joint resolution, except proposed constitutional amendments, concurrent resolutions, and questions of adjournment, must be presented to the President. If he signs, it becomes law; if he disapproves, he must return it to the house in which it originated, with a statement of his objections. The house in question must then reconsider it and a two-thirds vote of both chambers is sufficient to carry a measure over an executive veto. If the President fails to return a measure within ten days (Sundays excepted) after it is presented to him, it becomes a law without his signature, unless Congress prevents its return by adjourning. In this case it does not become a law if the President simply withholds his signature. When Congress adjourns leaving many bills on his desk, the President may quietly suppress those which he does not like—a procedure known as the "pocket veto." A search made by the Attorney General in 1928 disclosed the fact that more than 400 bills and resolutions had been killed by this operation.

The word "adjournment" in relation to the veto has been held by the Supreme Court to refer not only to the final dissolution of a Congress on the expiration of its term but also to an interim adjournment at the close of a session. In rendering its decision the Supreme Court said: "No return [of a bill by the President] can be made to the House when it is not in session as a collective body and its members are dispersed." Hence the adjournment of every session affords an opportunity for the use of the pocket veto.

Unlike the governors of several states, the President cannot veto single items in appropriation bills. Taking advantage of this situation, Congress has, on more than one occasion, attached other measures—disapproved by the President—to appropriation acts with a view to forcing his signature. Unwilling to block the wheels of the Government by cutting off supplies, he accepts the evil with the good. Fortunately, however, the practice of attaching "riders" to finance measures is somewhat discredited, so that Congress resorts to it only in exceptional circumstances.

On what grounds is the Chief Magistrate justified in employing the veto? According to the opinion of Hamilton, the right of negation was conferred on the President on account of the propensity of the legislature to intrude upon and absorb the powers of the other departments, and was designed to supply the executive with a means of defending his constitutional prerogatives. To this contention Hamilton also added: "The power in question has a further use. It not only serves as a shield to the executive, but it furnishes an additional security against the enactment of improper laws. It establishes a salutary check upon the legislative body, calculated to guard the community against the effects of faction, precipitancy, or of any impulse unfriendly to the public good, which may happen to influence a majority of that body."

On the question of propriety, Presidents themselves have

differed. Jefferson contended: "Unless the President's mind, on a view of everything which is urged for and against the bill, is tolerably clear that it is unauthorized by the Constitution—if the pro and con hang so even as to balance his judgment—a just respect for the wisdom of the legislature would naturally decide the balance in favor of their opinion." General Taylor held that the veto power should never be exercised "except in cases of clear violation of the Constitution, or manifest haste and want of consideration by Congress." On the other hand, President Jackson, whose relations to Congress were very different from those of either Jefferson or Taylor, thought that he could do as he pleased and besides he had his own opinion as to what the Constitution was; he even alleged unconstitutionality as one of the reasons for refusing to sign the Bank Bill, although such a measure had been clearly upheld by the Supreme Court. In vetoing a bill, President Grant assigned as his reason the fact that it was "a departure from true principles of finance, national interest, national obligations to creditors, congressional promises, party pledges (of both political parties), and personal views and promises made by me in every annual message sent to Congress and in each inaugural address." Taking broad grounds also Cleveland expressed his opinion that the veto power was given to the President for the purpose of inviting independent action on his part.

Naturally it is when the President is of one party and Congress of another that the veto most frequently comes into play. If the two branches are in the hands of the same political organization, differences of opinion on important issues are usually smoothed out in conferences and not brought to the attention of the country. There are exceptions, of course; for example, in President Coolidge's administration a Republican Congress enacted a bill granting a bonus to veterans of the World War and then repassed it over his veto. President Hoover had a similar experience with a Spanish-war pensions project. Sometimes it is understood among party leaders that a specific bill is to be vetoed by the President; thus members in Congress may carry out promises to their constituents knowing in advance that the President will kill the scheme at the White House.

Executive procedure in dealing with measures sent up for approval has been described in the following general terms by a former President, Benjamin Harrison. After a bill has been passed by Congress and signed by the president of the Senate and the speaker of the House, it is taken to the Executive Mansion. Usually it is referred to the head of the executive department to which its subject matter relates and, in case a question of constitutionality arises, the Attorney General is consulted. The bill then goes to the President with the departmental report upon it; if he approves he signs the bill, dates it, and transmits it to the Department of State for filing and publication.

Taken in connection with the message and the appointing power, the veto is an effective political instrument in the hands of the President. By threatening to use it on other measures, he may secure the passage of bills which he personally favors. By holding up appointments to federal offices he may bring additional pressure to bear on Congressmen. At all times, in considering important proposals, they must keep in view the possible action of the President, especially when a party question is involved and a correct attitude before the country is indispensable. Roosevelt once went so far as to warn Congress publicly that he would not approve certain projects then before that body, and raised a storm of protest from those who said that he should not veto a bill until it was laid before him. In reality the criticism was academic, for whenever a strong President is in office party leaders can discover his position in advance.

The President's Privileges and Rights

In the discharge of his duties, the President enjoys certain privileges and rights. No court of law in the land has any jurisdiction over him for any offense. He cannot be arrested for any crime, no matter how serious—even murder. Like other civil officers he may be impeached by the House of Representatives and tried by the Senate for treason, bribery, or other high crimes and misdemeanors, but until judgment has been pronounced against him, he cannot be in any way restrained in his liberty.

The President is entitled of right to payment for his services, for the Constitution provides that he shall receive at stated times a compensation which may not be increased or diminished during the term for which he is elected. He is forbidden, however, to receive any other emolument from the United States or from any state. The salary of the President was fixed at twenty-five thousand dollars in the beginning; it was increased to fifty thousand dollars in 1871; and to seventy-five thousand dollars in 1909. In addition to his personal compensation the President is furnished an Executive Mansion, administrative offices, and certain allowances for contingent expenses. In time of war huge sums may be placed in his hands by Congress to be expended at his own discretion.

Legislative and Executive Ties

As we have said, the framers of the Constitution, while paying tribute to the separation of powers, knew full well that there were large elements of fiction in the theory (p. 68). On this point the *Federalist* is clear and explicit. In addition the leadership assumed by Washington and Hamilton in drafting and supporting important measures of law demonstrated early in the life of Congress that they did not look upon the executive as a mere supine instrument charged with the duty of putting into effect acts of the legislature after they had been independently adopted.

As a matter of fact, from that time to this, it has been found impossible, even highly undesirable, to keep the departments isolated. Such separation would break the natural tie that should exist between the body which expresses popular will and the agency which carries that will into execution, assuming for the moment the feasibility of a sharp distinction. Accordingly there have been established through informal customs and official actions many close connections between the executive and legislative branches.

In the first place, the political tie, of necessity, binds the President and the members of his party in Congress. Although they may from time to time engage in controversies more spectacular than edifying, yet on fundamental matters of policy, they must come into a sort of working agreement. Furthermore, the President is regarded as the leader of his party, and it is to him, rather than to Congress, that the people look for the enforcement of specific promises contained in the platform or made officially during the presidential campaign. Congress cannot, therefore, ignore the leadership of the President, and, however much it may oppose his policies on occasion, it must give heed to those propositions on which he has unquestioned national support.

During the opening years of the twentieth century the nation recognized more clearly than ever the position of the President as a party director. Roosevelt was largely responsible for the policies which became national issues during his administration. In speeches delivered at different points throughout the country and in presidential messages, he advocated doctrines and measures which Congress was compelled to accept, even against its will, because it knew that he had behind him a powerful popular movement that could not be disregarded.

His successor, Taft, took a similar attitude in practice and publicly expressed his belief that it is a fundamental duty of the President to assume leadership in politics and government. "Under our system of politics," he said, "the President is the head of the party which elected him, and cannot escape responsibility either for his own executive work or for the legislative policy of his party in both houses. He is, under the Constitution, himself of the legislature insofar as he is called upon to approve or disapprove acts of Congress. A President who took no interest in legislation, who sought to exercise no influence to formulate measures, who altogether ignored his responsibility as the head of the party for carrying out ante-election promises in the matter of new laws, would not be doing what is expected of him by the people. In the discharge of all his duties, executive or otherwise, he is bound to a certain extent to consult the wishes and even the prejudices of the members of his party in both houses, in order that there shall be secured a unity of action by which necessary progress may be made and needed measures adopted."

A climax in executive leadership was reached during the six years of Wilson's administration (1913–1919) in which his party had a majority in both houses of Congress. He exerted a decided influence on the drafting and passage of every great measure of law enacted during that period. Some of them he forced through under the pressure of his prestige, his control over the patronage, and his appeals to the country. He very often went personally to the Capitol to consult Senators and Representatives; and in order to bring some issues forcibly to the attention of Congress and the nation he made them the subjects of special messages which he read to the members. His leadership and doctrines overshadowed the personalities and opinions of Congressmen. Since no dominant Democrat towered above the rank and file in the legislative branch President Wilson was really the master of the whole political scene. Finally in the election of Congressmen in November, 1918, he appealed to the country to choose Democrats, on the principle that divided councils were dangerous and that a return of a Republican majority would be interpreted in Europe as a repudiation of his program. The Republicans, he said, "have sought to take the choice of policy and the conduct of the war out of my hands and to put it under the control of instrumentalities of their own choosing. . . . It is well understood . . . that the Republican leaders desire not so much to support the President as to control him." His appeal failed. The Republican victory in the election which ensued marked a turn in the tide, for President Wilson afterward incurred stout opposition on all significant measures, especially the Versailles treaty submitted to the Senate for ratification. After a serious breakdown in health in the autumn of 1919, he lost his unquestioned ascendancy in the Federal Government.

On assuming Wilson's mantle, President Harding tried conciliation rather than dominance in dealing with Congress. The strength of the opposition even in his own party suggested caution and there was little that was dictatorial in his spirit. When President Coolidge succeeded Harding he took a firm stand on certain measures of economy and tax reduction and by repeated insistence drove Congress to accept them. If on other matters he was somewhat indifferent or inarticulate, there was no doubt about his command with respect to the fundamental policies of his party. Brought up in a different school of experience President Hoover seemed inclined during the early months of his service to pick his way with circumspection, but on several crucial issues, such as the World Court, reduction in naval armament, and a flexible tariff he announced his opinions in positive tones. With various fluctuations in efficiency, presidential leadership operates in Congress, while reciprocally the views of Senators and Representatives are forcibly expounded in the White House.

The mere party tie is by no means the only bond of union between the executive and legislative branches. By vesting the appointing power in a large number of cases in the hands of the President alone or subject to the sanction of the Senate, the law itself draws the two departments together. Naturally the extent to which the President may use his control over nominations to influence his party colleagues in Congress and the extent to which the Senate may employ its confirming authority in bending the President to its purposes, will depend upon circumstances; but it is perfectly clear that either may take advantage of the opportunity offered by this constitutional connection. More than one measure has been driven through Congress under "the whip of patronage." More than one President has been constrained to pursue certain policies by threats of Senators to hold up the confirmation of his nominees.

Another important bond of union between the executive and the legislature is formed by the practical necessity of co-operation in formulating and enforcing laws. Neither can function effectively without the aid of the other. Congress is constantly making demands upon the President for papers, documents, and special materials, and insofar as he regards these requests as reasonable and compatible with public interest he complies with them. As a matter of right, Congress may call upon him for information, but it has no sovereign power under the Constitution to compel him to yield to its wishes (p. 209).

Ordinarily, however, the eagerness of an administration to secure favorable consideration of its own measures in Congress leads it to grant legislative requests for assistance. Besides furnishing mere data, officials frequently appear before congressional committees to give testimony, answer questions, and support or oppose pending bills. This is as it should be, for those who have charge of the execution of statutes generally know more about the real conditions to which the laws must apply and their actual effect in operation than do the legislators themselves. Furthermore, it is desirable that officers who are called upon to enforce an act should understand the spirit and intention of the body that has passed it. Enforcement nearly always brings sharp repercussions in Congress.

The relation thus established is strengthened by the congressional practice of inviting the aid of departmental chiefs in framing bills. Often the Attorney General, who is supposed to be merely the legal agent of the President, is asked to give his opinion to a committee, either by letter or in person, or to advise members of Congress informally on particular issues before them for action. It sometimes happens that heads of departments draft complete measures, transmit them to Congress either through a friend in one of the houses, or directly, and even secure their reference to proper committees and ultimately their passage. It is a matter of common knowledge also that the President from time to time invites to the White House legislative leaders who may be of influence in securing the enactment of laws favored by his administration. On the other hand, Congress has in a number of instances even assumed the right to suggest, by a statute or by a resolution, that the President adopt some specified executive policy.

A highly important line of connection is formed between the executive and the legislature by the system for making appropriations. The Treasury Department is by law placed in a special relation to Congress; for the latter has the power to call directly upon it for financial information without going through the formality of making a request to the President. The first Secretary of the Treasury, Hamilton, claimed the right to report to Congress personally whenever he pleased on matters within his jurisdiction, although in practice his famous reports and recommendations were submitted to it only on request. While his demand for admission to the House of Representatives for the purpose of defending his policies was denied, he maintained close relations with his supporters in Congress throughout his term and directed legislative tactics especially with regard to the funding of the national debt and the assumption of state debts. In a letter to Jay he wrote: "'Tis not the load of proper official business that alone engrosses me, though this would be enough to occupy any man. 'Tis in the extra attention that I am obliged to pay the course of legislative maneuvers that alone adds to my burden and perplexity."

The relations between the executive and legislative branches in the matter of finance were made still more intimate by the national budget law of 1921. Under this act the President is directly responsible to Congress for the preparation of a balanced program of expenditures and revenues.

It also gives him more power over outlays of money, especially over those sought by members of Congress in the interests of their districts, and compels them to sue for favors at his door. The weight of his influence in legislative affairs pertaining to finance is correspondingly increased. Indeed the budget bureau has been called by a member of the House of Representatives, Albert Johnson, a kind of "fourth department of our government" serving and uniting in action both the executive and the legislature. Some of the congressional committees even venture to send to the budget office for scrutiny appropriation bills referred to them on introduction by private members and are often happy to have its disapproval. Significant developments are taking place in the growth of this system (p. 357).

Finally it should be noted that all, or nearly all, of the powerful pressure groups described above (p. 212) which operate on Congress also seek to influence the executive department as well as the legislature—to bring the two into harmony with respect to specific policies. Naturally the President is not as accessible to the public as are members of Congress, but he seldom ignores any important interest demanding the right to be heard. For example, during the tariff lobby investigation of 1929 it was disclosed that the sugar corporations highly exercised over certain rates of duty had placed their cases before President Hoover as vigorously, perhaps, as before Senators and Representatives. Pressure groups are not divided into executive, legislative, and judicial branches. Each is solidly bent on a particular program and insists on united action by all parts of the Federal Government. Hence the forces seeking to drive Congress in a given direction tend to swing the President into that line, to this extent drawing together in the same orbit the executive and legislative departments, whatever the constitutional theory as to the separation of powers.

CHAPTER X

Administrative Organization and Practice

The task of carrying into execution in detail the Constitution and acts of Congress is mainly entrusted to a large number of departments, boards, commissions, and other establishments. Three of them—the Congressional Library, the Printing Office, and the Botanical Garden, are directly under the supervision of Congress. In a sense the Comptroller General is also a legislative officer, certainly within the contemplation of the law; for, although he is appointed by the President with the consent of the Senate for a term of fifteen years, he can only be removed by a joint resolution of the two houses. All administrative organs except these are, in political theory at least, arms of the executive branch of the Federal Government. As such they may be divided into two classes: the first are grouped under the ten great departments headed by cabinet chiefs and the second are independent agencies standing outside of that hierarchy, such as the Civil Service Commission and the Interstate Commerce Commission.

Unlike the fundamental laws of most states, the federal Constitution makes no direct provision for departments and branches of administration. This fortunate omission, revealing the wisdom of the Fathers, leaves Congress free to create from time to time the establishments which seem appropriate to the discharge of specific functions undertaken by the Government. The Constitution evidently assumes that this will be done in due course, for it authorizes the President to require in writing the opinion of the heads of the executive departments, and also gives Congress power to vest in them the appointment of inferior officers. It is on this slender basis that the national legislature constructs departments, regulates the duties of their respective secretaries sometimes down to the minutest details, prescribes their internal organization, and sets forth the powers and duties of the chiefs even in the minor subdivisions. Only under the stress of the World War did Congress pass the Overman Act authorizing the President temporarily to organize, abolish, and transfer offices, bureaus, and other agencies of the Government at his own discretion.

It cannot be said that in the formation of the federal administrative structure any strictly logical principles have been followed. Certain agencies which might very well come within the scope of a regular department are given an independent status immediately under the President. Such, for example, is the Veterans' Administration. Others are associated with departments to which they have little organic relation in terms of similar activities. Even so, when attempting to get a broad picture of the federal administration, it is well to begin with the ten great departments—State, Treasury, War, Navy, Post Office, Justice, Agriculture, Interior, Commerce, and Labor.

The Heads of Departments

Standing at the head of each department is a secretary or chief official, appointed by the President and Senate. He is essentially a political officer who expresses the policy of the party in power in the White House. Although the President occasionally selects members of the opposition for one or more posts, even then he designates men who have been friendly to his cause or at least lukewarm in their opinions. As a rule he chooses from his own party, and its interests rather than experience or technical competence must often control his decisions. In any case all sections of the country and various factions must be represented in his Cabinet. Subject to such exigencies, he has a fairly free hand. His nominations, it is true, must be approved by the Senate but in practice that body nearly always accepts them as a matter of course. Rejections are sensations (p. 268). In general, therefore, it may be said that the President's "official family" is a group of political and personal associates upon whom he can rely for advice and counsel in making his administration a success.

With respect to political considerations in detail, two posts are generally filled for the President by strict party requirements. Custom, though not without variations, commands him to choose as Secretary of State the member of his organization who stands next to him in the esteem of the country. For example, Lincoln called to the State Department William H. Seward who had been his chief rival at the Republican convention in 1860. Wilson, in 1913, gave the position to William Jennings Bryan who had been three times the national nominee of the Democrats and was, excepting the President himself, the most influential person in the party. Harding likewise recognized this tradition by assigning the first honor in his Cabinet to Charles E. Hughes, the Republican candidate for President four years previously. On the other hand the Post Office Department usually goes to a prominent worker in the presidential campaign, partly on account of the patronage to be distributed through that agency. The place of Postmaster General was given by President Benjamin Harrison to John Wanamaker, the treasurer of the Republican committee during the election contest. Taft and Harding respectively rewarded with that department the chairman of the national party committee. As for the rest, the necessity of finding official compensation for party leaders, conciliating all factions, and securing harmony with Congress makes the business exceedingly delicate.

In such circumstances the head of a department is generally a layman. If he has had experience in politics, as is usually the case, it is experience that bears only a slight relation to the realities of his new position. He may have been a governor of a state, a former member of Congress, a candidate for President, or a "lame duck" defeated for reëlection to Congress, but not often has he demonstrated in actual administration any marked capacities for the particular place to which he is assigned in the Cabinet. It often happens that chairmen of important congressional committees who have served many years know more about the workings of his department than he does himself after he has completed his allotted time. If the federal administrative machine depended solely on the technical competence of cabinet officers in its daily operations, it would soon break down.

Although in a strict sense, the department head is a presidential appointee, his work is not prescribed minutely in executive orders, save in certain instances; it is defined by acts of Congress. He is responsible to the President for the faithful execution of the law; but the President cannot alter or diminish any of the duties laid down by the statutes, and cannot prevent Congress from imposing or taking away burdens or formulating them in such detail as to leave little leeway. "The President," once declared John Sherman, a former head of the Treasury Department, "is intrusted by the Constitution and laws with important powers, and so by law are the heads of departments. The President has no more right to control or exercise the powers conferred by law upon them than they have to control him in the discharge of his duties. It is especially the custom of Congress to intrust to the Secretary of the Treasury specific powers over the currency, the public debt, and the collection of the revenue. If he violates or neglects his duty, he is subject to removal by the President or impeachment, . . . but the President cannot exercise or control the discretion reposed by law in the Secretary of the Treasury, or in any head or subordinate of a department of the government."

Yet the President, as we have seen, has the power of removal, and may exercise it for the purpose of directing his subordinates. Accordingly in practice there are many variations from Sherman's apparently convincing legal theory, especially when a strong-willed President has a firm policy of his own which he is determined to carry out. Indeed, a logical application of the theory would amount to a complete decentralization of the administrative organization and a destruction of the President's responsibility.

While it is impossible to give here a full account of the duties of each secretary, it seems desirable to consider some matters which are common to them all.

A large appointing power to minor offices is conferred by law upon the departmental head, but this is now exercised under civil service rules which restrict his choice, for nearly all except the important positions, to candidates who have qualified by examination. Actually, therefore, he can select only his chief subordinates and even here he must often give heed to party requirements, including the demands of Senators and Representatives, rather than to his own wishes and technical considerations. The power of removal generally accompanies the power of appointment, although there are some striking exceptions by law and by executive order.

If materially limited in choosing his personnel, the head of a department enjoys a certain range of freedom in issuing orders pertaining to the administration of affairs under his charge. By a general act of Congress, he may "prescribe regulations, not inconsistent with law, for the government of his department, the conduct of its officers and clerks, the distribution and performance of its business, and the custody, use, and preservation of the records, papers, and property appertaining to it." And this broad provision is frequently supplemented by special legislation with reference to particular matters.

Each cabinet officer maintains a more or less definite relation to Congress. He must prepare annually a report on the work under his jurisdiction, but this is principally a formal compilation, for the matters of policy or detail covered in it have little or no influence in shaping legislation. Though department heads cannot be members of Congress, there is nothing in the Constitution excluding them from the right to sit and speak there. Custom has decreed, however, that they must bring their influence to bear in circuitous ways. They often appear before Senate or House committees to explain measures or to answer inquiries about legislation relating to their respective functions. They write letters to Senators and Representatives urging or opposing measures up for discussion. Indeed they sometimes transmit to Congress, on their own motion, elaborate drafts of bills which they wish to have enacted into law. And it is always the better part of wisdom for them to establish cordial relations with the chairmen of prominent committees, and thus obtain a friendly hearing for their policies, that might otherwise be denied to them.

Owing to the multiplication of the official duties connected with such matters as immigration, the transmission of mails, and taxation, it has been found necessary to give to the heads of certain departments high authority in hearing cases carried up from the lower administrative divisions under their control. For example, the immigration law provides that whenever an alien is excluded from the United States, the decision of the officers at the port of entry against his admission may be reversed by the Secretary of Labor on appeal. Again, the Postmaster General may hear causes involving a closure of the mails to persons and concerns engaged in fraudulent transactions, and his determination of the facts is final. In all these controversies, indeed, the ruling of a secretary is conclusive unless it becomes apparent that he himself has exceeded his jurisdiction or violated the law.

Thus, only administrative questions which raise a construction of statutes can be taken from a department into the courts. In upholding this doctrine, the Supreme Court said: "If the ordinary daily transactions of the departments which involve an interference with private rights were required to be submitted to the courts before action was finally taken, the result would entail practically a suspension of some of the most important functions of government. . . . It would practically arrest the executive arm of the government, if the heads of departments were required to obtain the sanction of the courts upon the multifarious questions arising in their departments, before action were taken in any matter which might involve the temporary disposition of private property. Each executive department has certain public functions and duties, the performance of which is absolutely necessary to the existence of the government, and it may temporarily at least operate with seeming harshness upon individuals. But it is wisely indicated that the rights of the public must, in these particulars, override the rights of individuals, provided there be reserved to them an ultimate recourse to the judiciary."

As may be imagined from what has been said, the departmental chief is not concerned with efficiency alone. Unlike the head of a business corporation, he is constantly subjected to demands and interruptions which have no immediate bearing on the correct discharge of his obligations. "Washington wishes to see evidence of democracy about the departments," says a former Secretary of the Treasury, Frank Vanderlip. "Neither Senator nor Congressman is satisfied to cool his heels in an ante-room for any length of time, nor are political leaders who come to the capitol on a mission likely to be pleased if the Secretary's engagements are such that an appointment cannot be made without notice or delay. . . . The Secretary of this great department must give heed to innumerable trifles such as would never reach the head of even a comparatively small business organization. Requests come from people of importance, and they must be taken up with the care which the position of such persons demands rather than with any thought of their importance in relation to the administration of departmental affairs."

Departmental Organization

On account of the lay character of departmental heads and the brevity of their tenure, as a general rule, it is necessary to have close to each of them a permanent official acquainted with all the work in hand. In England it is the custom to place this responsibility for technical competence on permanent undersecretaries who do not change with the fortunes of politics but hold office during good behavior. In fact some of them grow so powerful through their practical experience and wide knowledge that they, rather than the titular heads, are the real masters of the divisions in which they operate. History affords many examples of their ascendancy over political chiefs, even contrary to policies of the party for the moment in power.

For various reasons the institution of permanent under-secretaries has not taken root in the Federal Government. The so-called assistant secretaries, like their superiors, are generally temporary political appointees; thus the burden of preserving unity and continuity is ordinarily thrown upon subordinates of lower rank. Yet in each department is usually found one or more employees of long service who are acquainted with the machinery and functions of the branch in question and can keep it going even in the absence of the head. Such for instance was Alvey Augustus Adee who, after a brief career in the diplomatic service, was appointed an Assistant Secretary of State in 1882 and labored in that capacity until his death in 1924. He was a living repository of the business of the Department of State and indeed acted as Secretary on two occasions.

Within themselves the great departments are not organized in a strictly hierarchical form, with bureaus, divisions, offices, and personnel logically classified and called by names that have the same meaning throughout the service. There are "departments" within the War Department. Nearly all the ten departments have bureaus but these bureaus vary greatly in the importance of their work and the number of their personnel. Hence, when the term bureau is employed, it does not carry any definite significance. Nor is there any clear distinction between an office and a bureau; recently the title of Bureau of Education was changed to read the Office of Education, without making any drastic changes in the internal structure of that agency. In some departments the major portion of the business is distributed among bureaus; in others among assistant secretaries, offices, and services.

Most of the supervisory functions of the post office are divided among four assistant postmasters general, while those of the Labor Department are assigned to bureaus. In the Department of Commerce, functions pertaining to navigation are placed in charge of a bureau while steamboat inspection is given to a service.

For continuity in technical methods and for competence, the head of each department must rely mainly on the chiefs of the great divisions which, as we have just said, differ in name; some are known as departments, others, bureaus, and still others, offices. For the sake of convenience, these high subordinates are called here "division chiefs." Upon them falls the burden of keeping large branches of administration in constant operation amid all the fluctuations of politics and parties. A large number of them are appointed by the President with the consent of the Senate, without any material restrictions except that they must have had certain training and experience. Chiefs selected in this way may be regarded as spoilsmen, but even in the worst days they have not all fallen within this category. Some division chiefs are appointed by the President alone, and thus may come within the political sphere, but custom has made many of them permanent officials. Other chiefs are appointed by heads of departments, either subject to civil service rules or independent of such restraints, and in the latter case they may be political officers.

Whatever the law, the spoils system has never been as bad as its terms permitted. Even Andrew Jackson did not put coon hunters in charge of engineering work nor oust all expert public servants to make room for partisans; like Clive in India, he might have been surprised at his own moderation. A searching study of federal practice by Professor Arthur Macmahon shows that at the present time relatively few division chiefs are purely political appointees and that the number is declining. Conversely the divisions subject to the control of the merit system are increasing; and the chiefs in this class are selected by promotion within the service, or after competitive examination, or after having demonstrated their capacity in kindred work outside of the agency in question. Other divisions—the public health service, the coast guard, and the coast and geodetic survey—by departmental tradition and rule are also headed by officials who have risen through the hierarchy. In fact only about one fifth of the divisions are political—a class that now includes the office of education, the bureau of navigation, the land office, and the patent office. Almost all the great technical divisions—entomology, plant industry, forest, reclamation, chemistry, public roads, engraving and printing, and agricultural economics, for example—are now firmly established by law or practice on a merit basis. Moreover experience has shown that it is possible to devise general examinations and provide other tests of achievement and capacity which guarantee reasonably well the selection of competent administrators. It is not necessary to rely on "automatic promotion," which often brings dead wood to the surface; the discovery of ability is feasible without resorting to party politics.

How has this significant change been brought about in the upper ranges of federal administration? Not entirely by the adoption of civil service rules. The highly specialized character of government functions in the modern age runs against mere job-hunting politics; the worst spoilsman in the White House would not put a real estate agent in charge of research in fixed nitrogen. Then the very necessity of competence itself narrows the range of choice, and the selective process in the scientific world inevitably applies somewhat rigid standards. Besides, there is the pressure of engineering and other professional associations, organized outside of the Government, which operates steadily on appointing officers in favor of capacity as against mere partisanship. At the same time development of technical education makes available an ever larger supply of trained men and women for posts requiring proficiency. Finally the demands of industries and other enterprises that are regulated by the Government or make use of its various services tend to exclude politics from the selection of division chiefs entrusted with scientific functions. Hence technology by its inherent nature brings results which civil-service reformers could scarcely hope to accomplish on moral and patriotic grounds alone.

The Independent Agencies

For almost a hundred years, Congress in creating new agencies placed them within existing departments. It thus followed somewhat closely the principle that similar functions should be grouped in one organization headed by a single responsible officer who in turn is accountable to the chief executive. Except in some minor matters, the rule was well observed until 1883, when an independent Civil Service Commission of three members was set up to administer the new merit system. This precedent was followed four years later by the formation of the Interstate Commerce Commission charged with the regulation of railways. In the course of time other agencies were erected outside of the great departments until to-day we have twenty or more commissions, boards, and offices which are independent of cabinet secretaries and responsible directly to the President or to Congress. The major portion of these establishments, as we note below, either have regulatory functions, such as those vested in the Federal Trade Commission, or they have duties that are not readily assignable to any one of the historic departments.

It is the custom to regard these independent agencies, except those frankly placed under Congress, as arms of the executive branch of the Government and, as we have remarked above, theoretically perhaps, they may be so viewed. In practice, however, a distinction must be made among them. Many of these establishments, in particular, the commissions, are more than mere executive authorities charged with enforcing specific laws. Some of them are in effect legislative bodies, projections of Congress itself; the statutes governing them are general in character and it is their duty to amplify the laws, to supply details, to add provisions. In a strict legal sense, of course, if we care to split hairs, they are not subordinate legislatures, for the lawyer tells us that constitutional power cannot be delegated; but in reality they are. Since this is true, Congress may rightfully be more concerned about the way they fulfill their functions than even the President himself. As a matter of fact in creating these commissions or law-making bodies, it has sought to allow them a certain security over against the President by giving to their members terms longer than his, so that on coming to office he cannot automatically reconstruct them by filling vacancies with his own appointees. Members of the Federal Trade Commission and the Interstate Commerce Commission hold office for seven years, with overlapping terms, while members of the Farm Loan Board, except the Secretary of the Treasury, *ex officio,* serve for eight year periods, also overlapping.

Besides being executive and legislative bodies, some of these commissions exercise what is in substance judicial power. Legally, of course, they do nothing of the sort, for the Constitution vests all judicial power in the Supreme Court and such inferior courts as Congress may create from time to time. Hence for the sake of consistency it is the fashion of theorists to speak of certain functions discharged by regulatory bodies, such as the Interstate Commerce Commission, as merely "quasi-judicial" in character, that is, "almost" or "as it were" judicial. While leaving dust sifters to their own devices, we may safely say that some commissions have duties which are for practical purposes judicial in nature. They hear complaints, listen to arguments of counsel, read briefs, make decisions, and render opinions based on law and facts. And all their important rulings, especially those touching the rights of property, are subject to review by the federal courts; in other words, parties aggrieved by their orders and decrees may appeal to the courts, just as they may appeal from the findings of lower courts to the higher tribunals for reconsideration. Accordingly if there is any reason for taking the federal courts out of presidential politics and making them to some degree independent of the chief executive, there are also grounds for throwing similar safeguards around the quasi-judicial commissions.

These stubborn facts are recognized by law and practice. Whereas the heads of departments usually do not have fixed terms and their nomination is almost universally approved by the Senate without objections, appointments to the quasi-legislative and quasi-judicial commissions are for definite periods and are always carefully scrutinized before confirmation. More than once the President in making selections for such posts has been compelled to defer to the demands of critical Senators. While it now appears that he may remove them at will (p. 272), the consent of the Senate is necessary to the installation of their successors and may be employed against action to oust. Moreover committees and private members of both houses of Congress ordinarily keep a far stricter watch on the operation of these agencies than they do on authorities that may be deemed purely executive in operation. Indeed partly on account of the legislative and judicial functions involved in the business of the Federal Power Commission, composed of the heads of three executive departments under the Act of 1920, Congress has created in its place another independent body to deal with water power and certain related utility questions. All this merely illustrates again the difficulties which arise when efforts are made to split the work of government into executive, legislative, and judicial divisions.

Administrative Organization

In order that the student may have a bird's-eye view of the immense complex of departments and establishments of the Federal Government a tabular chart is included here. Even this bare outline is in itself illuminating and deserves careful examination. It gives a clue to the vast and complicated enterprises undertaken by the national administration.

When it is remembered that about half a million men and women are employed in these various agencies and that every science and art known to mankind is used by them in the service of the public, it dawns upon the mind that here is one of the most marvelous organisms in the history of human society. Here is work for the financier who knows how to handle billions of dollars, the chemist with his test tube, the expert in poisonous gases who goes down into the depths of the earth to safeguard the lives of miners, the postman who keeps his rounds in summer and winter, and a hundred other varieties of specialists all contributing their share in a huge association created for the common good. If in the reign of King John, of Magna Carta fame, some English prophet had foretold an immense democracy, without king or aristocracy, spread across three thousand miles of territory, governing itself and undertaking such complex services in the public interest, he would have been laughed out of court as a jester. Perfection, of course, or anything like it, is not to be ascribed to this organism; so while marvelling at the extent and variety of its functions, we must take account of its shortcomings.

For nearly thirty years rather severe criticisms have been advanced against the exact form given to the departments and agencies of national administration. President Roosevelt made the matter a subject of special consideration and created a commission to study the business methods of the Government. President Taft followed this example by the appointment of the Commission on Economy and Efficiency, under the direction of Frederick A. Cleveland, which carefully analyzed the structure of the federal administration and recommended the regrouping of many activities, the elimination of duplications, the integration of nearly all functions in certain departments, and the establishment of clear lines of responsibility from the President of the United States to the lowest subordinate. Again, in 1920, a Congressional Joint Commission on Reclassification of Salaries rather sharply criticized the "complex, indefinite, poorly designed organization; inadequate provisions for administrative control and supervision; apparent duplication between departments and within departments; conflicts of authority and overlapping of functions; overmanning; unstandardized procedure; unnecessary records; and other unbusinesslike methods."

The following year a Congressional Joint Committee on the Reorganization of Government Departments was established under the chairmanship of Walter F. Brown, representing the President; it prepared and published in 1923 a general scheme for reconstruction. A number of bureaus and agencies were to be consolidated or removed to new positions; the Departments of War and Navy were to be united in one Department of National Defense; and a Department of Education and Welfare was to be formed to discharge federal functions relating to education, public health, social service, and veteran relief. The main features of this plan, except that providing for the union of the War and Navy Departments, were endorsed by President Coolidge in his first message in December, 1923, when the whole project was laid before Congress for debate and action. Since that time the subject has been periodically discussed either in the Government or outside and a number of transfers and consolidations have been made in detail. But no thorough overhauling has been effected and decision on the larger issues has been indefinitely postponed.

Such plans are naturally based on a desire to bring together in one place, if possible, all the branches of the Federal Government dealing with a particular specialty. But due regard is not always paid to the fact that, while a consolidation may reduce the dispersion of certain activities, the very process itself may disrupt organizations primarily concerned with different tasks, and in effect increase rather than diminish the confusion of the Government considered as a whole. The question, then, is not whether a specified administrative concentration will clear up a given snarl but whether it will leave fewer loose ends in other quarters when completed and thus result in a substantial net gain.

The difficulty may be illustrated by a proposal put forward in 1921 by the American Association of Engineers favoring the combination of many non-military engineering activities of the Government under a Department of Public Works—a proposal which affords grounds for interesting speculation on the results of a general administrative reorganization along "logical" lines. Reasoning, for example, that "the heaviest expenditures for the forest service and for the national park service are for the construction and maintenance of roads, bridges, and buildings," the sponsors of the Association plan suggest the transfer of these agencies to their new department. Now it is true that large sums of money are spent for engineering work in the forests and marked advantages may be gained from integrating all federal road work, but there are other factors to be considered in this connection. To be concrete, the study of soils, the fighting of insect and fungous pests, the supervision of livestock grazing, and the all-important problem of raising tree crops in the forests are essentially agricultural in nature. Thus the forest service involves both engineering and agriculture. At present the agricultural side is recognized by placing the service in the Department of Agriculture, with road building as a "loose end" in charge of engineers in that Department. In its scheme the American Association of Engineers emphasizes its interest by making forest administration primarily an engineering enterprise, with its agricultural work as a "loose end" taken care of by agriculturists of a Department of Public Works. In other words each plan combines with one specialty work belonging to another specialty. And in this relation it should be remembered that it is not the technical character of the men employed which should control in an administrative set-up; it is the public policy to be effected by it. If forest administration is essentially agricultural in its ends, then the amount spent for road building and the number of engineers engaged in it are incidental not determining factors.

The truth of the matter is that no rigid classification of

the functions of the Federal Government can prevent overlapping. To say that any type of activity can be crowded into a departmental niche and cut off from connections or relations with other activities is generally to ignore the realities in the situation. In an organic society such as our technological civilization, reorganization should aim to group the various undertakings of the Government according to their major nature as indicated by the public policy to be realized by the various branches, leaving the minor and incidental duplications to be handled by other means, particularly by coöperation.

This fundamental fact is already recognized by many experts in the Federal Government. Indeed a most promising method has already been developed for cutting across office lines in dealing with activities which cannot all be placed in any "water-tight" compartment. The method is essentially that of effecting inter-office coöperation under the direction of a coördinating body, without making any substantial change in the legal individuality of the several establishments involved. In this enterprise the Bureau of the Budget has taken leadership by organizing a number of coordinating bodies. Generally speaking, their very names give the clue to their functions. The Federal Real Estate Board handles common land problems; the Permanent Conference on Printing deals with printing needs; the titles of the Interdepartmental Patents Board, the Federal Traffic Board, and the Federal Board of Hospitalization are similarly self-explanatory. These bodies consist of delegates from certain federal agencies interested in various aspects of over-lapping activities, together with a representative of the Bureau of the Budget in some cases.

Another phase of such coöperation under the Budget Bureau is area coördination. Naturally there is a wide geographical distribution of plant and personnel belonging to the numerous federal agencies scattered throughout the country. An army post and a weather station may represent the Government in one spot while not far away perhaps a post-office, a coast guard station, and a plant-quarantine unit may be located. Although their common needs for transportation, storage, printing, and other items cannot be readily supplied through a single Washington office, they are so similar as to permit an easy local coördination within a given region. Dealing with this situation there is a chief coördinator in the Bureau of the Budget, and under him are several area coördinators, each assigned to a specific district. Aiding the latter are many Federal Business Associations. Every Association is composed of representatives from the several federal organizations and agencies within the area, who give time and effort to effecting coöperation in their region, in addition to doing the regular work of their own offices.

A few brief statements showing the results of such activities and revealing a spirit of public service rather than individual pride illustrate the process—all taken from a report of the Bureau of the Budget:

"Lockmasters of the Army Engineers at eight dams in the Pittsburgh district are acting as river observers for the Weather Bureau." "The director's representative, eastern area, United States Veterans' Bureau, called upon the coördinator for one thousand cubic feet of storage space. The officer in charge, naval supply depot, furnished the needed amount of space without cost." "The Commissioner of Immigration continues his translation service for the Veterans' Bureau and other federal activities." "Frankford Arsenal cast an aluminum beam for the United States Mint." "The Naval Home, Philadelphia, loaned United States Veterans' Hospital No. 49 a concrete mixer and lawn mowers." Thus it is clear that the division of executive duties according to departmental lines need not hinder joint action for the common good whenever it is technically feasible.

Coördination is far from being a monopoly of the Bureau of the Budget. The Interdepartmental Board of Ocean Mail Contracts, for example, is intended to bring several groups together under one head without disrupting any existing establishment. It consists of three cabinet officers and the Chairman of the United States Shipping Board. The Department of Commerce, now entrusted with steamboat inspection and other functions pertaining to navigation, has a spokesman on it. Since vessels for which lucrative mail rates are sought must be approved by the Secretary of the Navy as potential naval auxiliaries in time of war, he also is added to the membership. Having charge of awarding mail contracts, the Postmaster General is naturally included, along with the Chairman of the Shipping Board which is not only responsible for operating federal vessels but controls the important loan fund made available by Congress to aid shipbuilders in planning and constructing ships for use in the carriage of mails.

Another striking illustration of this integrating process is furnished by the act of 1930 providing for the coördination of the public-health activities of the Federal Government. On request of the head of any executive department or establishment that is carrying on public-health work, the Secretary of the Treasury may detail officers or employees of the Public Health Service to coöperate in such activity. He is also authorized to establish additional divisions in the Hygienic Laboratory to aid in solving all public health problems and to supply facilities for coördinating research by public-health officials and other scientists. By the same measure the Surgeon General is empowered to detail personnel from the Service to educational and research institutions for special studies and to extend the facilities of his Service to health officials and scientists engaged in research. Besides promoting coöperation among the agencies of the Government, the law in question contemplates drawing outside experts into the general scheme by sanctioning the appointment of a National Advisory Health Council, partly *ex officio* and partly composed of representatives selected from the public-health profession. In other words there is to be a long step forward in bringing the science of public health to bear on health activities, federal, state, and local (p. 592).

The Employees of the Federal Government

In the discharge of their functions the departments, commissions, and agencies of the Federal Government have at their command more than half a million civil officers and employees ranging from highly skilled technicians—masters of all branches of science—to casual laborers.

Taking the nature of their work into consideration, the positions coming under the civil service acts of Congress are distributed among five great "classes," each containing a number of "grades." At the head of the list is the Professional and Scientific Service requiring for admission a special training equivalent to that represented by graduation from a college or university. It calls for the application of the principles of a profession or science in the performance of routine, advisory, administrative, or research work. Immediately below is the Subprofessional Service. As the name implies, places in this class carry with them duties connected with the work of the Professional and Scientific Service but of minor significance. Accordingly the equivalent of a college education is not demanded of its members. The third group is the Clerical, Administrative, and Fiscal Service. In this division are to be found all minor posts commonly associated with office, business, or financial administration. In the fourth class—the Custodial Service—are included occupations involving the care of public buildings, the transportation of persons and property, or the transmission of official papers. At the bottom of the scale stands the Clerical-Mechanical Service, embracing all positions, outside of recognized trades or crafts, which require skill and experience either in machine operation or in the inspection or verification of products in the Government Printing Office, the Bureau of Engraving and Printing, and the Mail Equipment Shops.

Respecting methods of appointment, offices and employments of the Government may be divided into those which are filled only by persons who have complied with the requirements of certain examinations or standards and those which are "political" in character. There was a time when all positions in the federal service were theoretically and to a large extent practically subject to the spoils system—that is, they were given to party workers without special regard for their competence and without any regular test of their abilities. After some tentative experiments in reforming the abuses, Congress at length passed in 1883 the Civil Service Act, which is still the fundamental law governing the occupations that come within the scope of the merit scheme. This Act provides for a Civil Service Commission composed of three persons, no more than two of whom shall be adherents of the same party, appointed by the President and Senate. They are charged with the duty of aiding the President, at his request, in preparing suitable rules for competitive examinations designed to measure the fitness of applicants for offices in the public service, already classified or to be classified by executive order under the Act or by supplementary legislation. In addition the Commission renders general assistance to the President in dealing with problems arising under the Act.

With a view to immediate application, the Civil Service Act itself ordered the Secretary of the Treasury and the Postmaster General to classify certain positions within their respective jurisdictions for transfer from politics to the merit régime. At the same time it provided that the heads of specified departments and establishments should, at the direction of the President, revise any existing arrangement of their employees and reconstruct it with respect to the new dispensation. In other words, the Act itself brought a few offices under the "merit system," and left the extension of the principle to the discretion of the President and Congress.

When the law went into force it covered only about fourteen thousand places then included in the classified service. The number has been steadily increased, however, mainly by executive orders. And as a result of executive and legislative action, more than three fifths of the entire executive civil service is now within the competitive scheme—the operations of which are described below.

Notwithstanding this extraordinary development thousands of federal officers and employees are still on a political basis, some of them, it is true, only nominally; that is to say, their appointment is not controlled by competitive examinations held under the jurisdiction of the Civil Service Commission. In a technical sense two groups of federal positions are exempt from the formal requirements for testing the abilities of applicants. One of them embraces a number of places actually within the classified service which are not put on the competitive list for various reasons. The second group lies entirely outside of the classified service and may be called "political" in the strict sense of the term. In its distinctions the federal appointment system is not severely logical.

There is indeed no uniformity of practice even in the case of the so-called political offices. In certain instances new men are chosen for partisan reasons whenever there is a change of administration and in others the incumbents really enjoy what amounts to permanent tenure by virtue of tradition and necessity (p. 304). This is due to the fact that federal employments have never been divided on any systematic theory into classes that are truly political—or policy-determining—in character and those that are professional and technical. Some high posts are under the merit system and some minor positions are not.

These facts are matters of common knowledge to publicists who have studied the federal service at first hand, and there is a constant demand that thousands of offices of the higher grade now on a political footing be placed on the merit basis—including many that are quite frankly in the "political group" and several in the classified service which are "exempt." Advocates of such a reform lay great emphasis on the practice of England in this respect. In that country some of the most important places ranking close to high cabinet offices are filled by competitive examination and promotion, so that able young men who enter the service know that an attractive career lies before them. As a rule English examinations are more difficult and more general than similar tests in America and are designed to secure persons of broad knowledge rather than specialists. The English system thus lays more stress on education and general ability and attracts university graduates of the highest caliber, whereas in the United States the federal civil service is not as a rule viewed with marked favor by college students.

Undoubtedly the exemption of purely administrative and technical positions from the operation of the competitive principle produces many unfortunate results, as Dr. Lewis Mayers points out in a study of the federal service. When the chief of a bureau or division is a political appointee, selected on account of his party views, it is almost impossible to exclude political considerations from the assignment of duties to employees and other matters of prime importance to efficiency. Even though the head sincerely desires to enhance the good of the service, his actions in regard to salaries and promotions are always open to the charge that he is controlled by ulterior motives. Being a political appointee he must of necessity give a certain amount of time to partisan affairs to the neglect of his official duties, and he is liable to be drafted into partisan work by a directing superior. Even more significant than these evils is the fact that the appointment of politicians to purely administrative and technical offices limits the career of faithful and ambitious subordinates who have entered by the merit route; no matter how hard and intelligently they work, they cannot hope to rise to the top. Political appointments also usually exclude outside experts who are not partisans.

Employment Methods

In applying the competitive idea to positions brought under its jurisdiction, the Civil Service Commission, at the direction of the President, prepares the large variety of examinations required to test the fitness of candidates for the different types of offices. To administer the system there has been established at Washington a chief examiner who has under his supervision several hundred local boards of examiners scattered among the states and territories. The law orders that these boards shall be erected at points reasonably convenient for persons in search of federal employment.

Examinations, according to the terms of the law, must be practical in character and, as far as possible, fairly measure the relative capacity of applicants to discharge the duties of that branch of the government service to which they seek admission. In preparing the examination papers it is the custom of the Commission to invite the coöperation of the various departments; if a technical position is to be filled, the department concerned usually notifies the Commission and indeed may furnish the specific questions.

Any citizen of the United States, except certain small classes such as those mentally or physically incapacitated, may offer himself for an examination if he can meet the preliminary conditions. For a long time, owing to lax methods, aliens were often admitted to government employment, but within recent years the requirement of citizenship has been rigidly enforced. Applicants for examination are not even charged a fee, in spite of the fact that the Civil Service Commission has several times recommended the establishment of a nominal charge for the purpose of excluding many thousand ill-prepared persons who try the tests in a gambling spirit—nothing to lose and possibly something to gain.

Through the periodical holding of examinations the Civil Service Commission must secure and maintain a list of eligibles for all the classes and grades of positions coming under the merit system, so that it can furnish candidates of the most diverse training and experience when called upon by the several departments. On the same day, there may be demands for accountants, stenographers, expert chemists, patent examiners, draftsmen, interpreters, and postal clerks.

When notified of a vacancy by an appointing officer, the Commission selects from the proper register and transmits to him the names of three candidates at the head of the roll, who are if possible residents of the state to which the appointment falls. From these three the appointing officer selects one and returns the other names to the Commission to be replaced upon the list. If he refuses to accept any one of the three, he must give satisfactory reasons for his action and is supplied with a new quota. The successful candidate is put on probation for a short period; then if his record is good he is given permanent tenure.

It should be noted in passing that there are important exceptions to the operation of the above rules. Preference is given to persons honorably discharged from the military or naval service. And appointments in the departments at Washington must be apportioned among the several states and territories and the District of Columbia on the basis of population. Naturally the latter principle cannot be strictly carried out in practice and it affords a pretext for constant clamoring on the part of candidates and Congressmen from states that do not happen to secure their share of places in the Government.

Promotions in, as well as appointments to, the federal service are to some extent based upon the competitive principle. Examinations are held to test candidates for advancement and a list of eligibles is kept. In fact, however, no reasoned system of advancement has yet been worked out to inspire the employees in the lower ranges to work harder and develop their latent powers with a view to rising in the scale. As a matter of practice the appointing officer has a right to decide whether he will fill a vacancy by open competition or by selection from within the service—a right contrary to good administration. In certain states and cities the local civil service commission can prescribe the method to be used and develop machinery for facilitating the transfer of competent persons from minor to higher positions. After a long study of the problem the Joint Commission on Reclassification, referred to below, even went so far as to recommend that open competition should be adopted only when it is impossible to secure three eligibles from among persons already employed by the Federal Government. The salutary effect of an orderly program of promotion upon the rank and file of the service is beyond question, and there is no doubt that such a scheme will be evolved under the influence of the new forces at work in civil service reform.

The process of removal from the federal service is a relatively simple matter. The law provides that a person may be discharged from a competitive position, "for such causes as will promote the efficiency of the service." When the President or head of an executive department (with respect to his own subordinates) is convinced that any person in the classified service is incompetent, he may oust such employee after giving due notice to him. While the power thus conferred is broad, a complaint is frequently made to the effect that incapable men are protected by the regulations against dismissal. Such contentions, the Civil Service Commission maintains, are groundless in fact. "On the contrary," it declares, "the power of removal for unfitness is with the head of the office. The appointing officer being responsible for the efficient performance of the work of his office, it rests with him to determine whether such cause exists as to require the removal of an employee in order to promote the efficiency or discipline of his office."

In short, the administrative head enjoys great freedom in this respect. As a rule the courts will not interfere with him in such matters. They take the position that the power of appointment involves the right of removal and that the Civil Service Act limits the right in only one instance—an employee cannot be dismissed merely because he has refused to give money or service to a political party. When, however, a large number of employees of the same political faith are discharged at the same time, partisan motives are suspected and the officer responsible for the action is required to convince the Commission that a just cause exists in each case; but even here the courts will not attack the discretion of directing officers.

The adoption of the principle of tenure during good behavior nearly half a century ago soon raised the question as to what should be done with government employees who had passed the period of usefulness and merely stood in the way of able men and women in the prime of life. For many years the subject was discussed in Congress and at length in 1920 a federal pension system was established to provide for all persons in the classified service and certain other divisions who on account of age or disability are unfit for "useful and efficient" labor. Under this scheme as modified by later amendments the age of retirement in the normal course is fixed at various points according to the nature of the work done. Everyone who benefits from the arrangement must contribute a small percentage of his salary to the pension fund, and on his withdrawal after a period of active employment he receives an allowance based on the length of his service and the amount of his compensation. In addition to being an act of tardy justice to old and faithful public servants, the project is also a contribution to efficiency in service. Previous to its adoption hundreds of old people were kept on federal pay-rolls by warm-hearted department heads because their discharge would be an act of cruelty. Work was thus entrusted to employees whose competence had departed, while young and ambitious subordinates, finding their careers blocked, left to seek better opportunities. In the new régime capacity rather than charity can furnish the criterion for the directors of the federal administration.

Notwithstanding all the efforts made after 1883 to place the civil service upon the merit basis, numerous abuses grew up in practice. To put the case in summary form: employees of similar experience and length of service and doing identical work were paid varying salaries; employees engaged in activities calling for widely different qualities and training received equal compensation; discriminations were made against women; the same title was frequently given to positions utterly unlike as to the duties required of the incumbents; and wage and salary schedules, in addition to being inconsistent and inequitable in themselves, were often far below those in effect in private business. The discovery of such conditions led to the appointment, in 1919, of a Congressional Joint Commission on Salaries and Grades which studied these problems in several important departments and framed constructive recommendations on employment policies.

After many months of acrimonious debate among experts and politicians, Congress adopted in 1923 the most significant installment of civil service reform devised since the great law forty years before. As amended in 1930, this measure, known as the Classification Act, created a Personnel Classification Board composed of a representative from the Civil Service Commission, the chief of the Efficiency Bureau (an independent agency of inquiry), and the Director of the Budget Bureau. It instructed this Board to make a logical classification of all civil servants in the District of Columbia (except certain skilled workmen), according to their duties, responsibilities, and titles. It swept away the tangle of irregular and unequal salary schedules established by various acts of Congress and prescribed, within certain general terms, the substitution of a consistent, uniform salary plan designed to prevent favoritism and to do justice to employees of similar talents and occupations. In this connection it laid down the rule of equal pay for equal work for both sexes. The Board was also instructed to survey the federal personnel in the field, that is, outside the District of Columbia, and report to Congress a scheme of classification for that portion of the service.

This law, defective as it was in details, revealed a determined effort on the part of Congress to place additional checks on the operations of the spoils system and at the same time apply sound employment principles to the government service. According to an experienced student of the subject, John M. Gaus, it likewise represented a new force in American politics, "the growing spirit of the dignity of the service, of a corporate life centered in the service of the nation, a changing attitude on the part of the finest citizens toward the service of the state." Furthermore, it was in harmony with the development of an efficient technical administration which, as Charles E. Merriam has pointed out, tends to reduce the influence of "spoils" in politics, and to concentrate the attention of parties on their true function of bringing popular will to a focus on issues and ideas. Unfortunately, in some respects, the execution of the new Act was hampered by discord in the Personnel Classification Board, and the completion of the work contemplated by it has long been delayed.

Partisanship and Political Activities

From decisions relative to promotions, removals, and reductions in rank it is very difficult to exclude all partisan considerations, but attempts are made through acts of Congress and presidential orders to protect employees in the classified service against such pressures, and also to prevent them from engaging in undue political activities. The original civil service law provides that no person in the employ of the Government is for that reason under any obligations to contribute to political funds or to assume any political duties, and that he shall not be removed or otherwise prejudiced for refusing to do so. Moreover, no one in the federal service has a right to use his authority to control the political action of anybody. No recommendation by a Senator or a member of the House of Representatives, except as to the character or residence of an applicant, can be legally received or considered by officials responsible for conducting examinations or making appointments under the

Civil Service Act. Members of Congress and executive, judicial, military, and naval officers are forbidden to seek or accept political assistance or contributions from employees of the United States. The practice of soliciting campaign funds in buildings occupied by agencies of the Federal Government is strictly prohibited. However, as far as the law is concerned, employees in the classified service may make contributions to persons or committees of persons who hold no office under the United States; in fact many of them do, either voluntarily or in compliance with assessments levied by political managers.

Other forms of partisanship were left by the Civil Service Act to the control of the heads of departments. And from time to time executive orders were issued for the purpose of eliminating specific abuses arising from the participation of inferior office-holders in party affairs. At length in 1907 political activity in the broadest sense was placed under the supervision of the Civil Service Commission by an amendment to the rules, adopted by the President, providing that "all persons who by the provisions of these rules are in the competitive classified service, while retaining the right to vote as they please and to express privately their opinions on all political subjects, shall take no active part in political management or in political campaigns."

This rule has been construed by the Commission to forbid the use of official positions for the benefit of any political party; and since its adoption it has been interpreted to prohibit the following types of political action: "Service on political committees, service as delegates to county, state, or district conventions of a political party, although it was understood that they were not 'to take or use any political activity in going to these conventions or otherwise violate the civil service rules;' continued political activity and leadership; the publication of a newspaper in the interest of a political party; membership in a club taking an active part in political campaigns and management; the circulation of petitions having a political object; service as a commissioner of elections in a community where it was notorious that a commissioner of elections must be an active politician."

Efficient administration must also take into account another phase of activity among federal employees, namely, the formation of unions, the federation of unions, and the participation of such organizations in politics to secure higher wages and better labor conditions generally. On this matter President Roosevelt took a decided stand by flatly forbidding them either individually or through associations to solicit an increase of pay or favorable legislation before Congress or any of its committees. But within a few years his executive orders were reversed by an act of Congress expressly proclaiming the right of federal employees and their organizations to resort to such tactics and forbidding any interference with their exercise of the privilege.

As may be imagined the issue had by that time become a matter of prime concern in administration. Skilled workmen in federal employment had long been members of trade unions affiliated with the American Federation of Labor and with increasing frequency, it seemed, were bringing pressure to bear on Congress through regular channels. In 1905 there appeared in the Post Office Department a new union of clerks which repudiated the mild methods of the older postal association and openly joined the American Federation of Labor. Some time later local unions of federal employees sprang up in various large cities. By 1916 there were at least fifty of them; and in that year they were brought together in the National Federation of Federal Employees which is now connected with the American Federation of Labor. Thus through direct organization and through affiliation with unionized labor outside of the service, federal employees can concentrate heavy forces upon Congress in support of legislation favorable to their interests. Indeed, the National Federation of Federal Employees boasts that it has been able to defeat unfriendly Representatives seeking reëlection to the House, to secure the passage of important laws, and to obtain the presidential veto of other measures. It tells federal employees that the way "to get on is to get together." Undoubtedly it was the most potent single force behind the reclassification bill of 1923, which was a tardy act of justice and reform.

Owing to its extent and ramifications, the authority enjoyed by the regular unions of federal employees raises many problems in politics and government. As yet these organizations do not proclaim the right to strike and tie up the government service; on the contrary their charters of affiliation with the American Federation of Labor expressly recognize their special obligations to the public. But their political activities are wide-reaching and may easily interfere, for good or ill, with the course of legislation and administration. Thus far, they have been able to remedy many evils, for it is notorious that in some respects the Federal Government has not always been a "model employer." If, on the other hand, they exert their power selfishly and come into open collision with the Government they may do a great damage to the morale and efficiency of the entire federal force. Their very existence raises a question whether there should not be instituted some formal system of coöperation between the Government and organizations of its employees with a view to a continuous and sympathetic adjustment of all controversies as they arise.

This leads inevitably into the larger aspects of personnel administration or employment policies. The movement for a scientific treatment of this question, which has already produced considerable effect in states and cities, has reached Washington. Traces of it are now to be found in the reports of the Civil Service Commission, the proceedings of committees of Congress, and debates on civil service measures. The technique of this science, still in a formative stage, is most highly developed in private industry, but its influence is now widely felt in governmental circles where it doubtless has a future of great significance.

Administration and Its Social Environment

Whatever is done by way of better organization and fairer practices to improve public administration, its nature and quality are to a large extent determined by the social environment in which it is carried on. The ideals, personnel, and performances of government cannot be separated from those prevailing among the private undertakings by which it is surrounded. Inevitably the type of the men and women who go in for official service is deeply affected by the opportunities open in other fields; while the spirit and loyalty of public employees are continually influenced by the inducements offered to them by business enterprises. Since the government, to an increasing degree, regulates and impinges upon great economic interests, it follows that the officers in charge of such functions are thrown into constant contact with corporate concerns from which attractive offers of employment may come. Circumspection in enforcing laws may result in their translation and advancement. Nothing invidious need be implied in this relation but it is a prime consideration in the conduct of public administration. The statesman cannot ignore the fact that government always operates in a social medium, which may be favorable or detrimental to efficiency.

Such generalizations may be illuminated by reference to varieties of human experience. In Europe those who enter politics generally expect to make a business of it, and the institutions associated with parliamentary government decidedly favor professionalism. In America, on the other hand, political life is more adventitious; for example, a man defeated in an election for either house of Congress cannot often go into another district or state and seek victory there. Nor do we have any arrangement, such as exists in Germany under proportional representation, for assuring the continuous return of distinguished party leaders whatever may be their fate in local constituencies.

In Europe careers are also open to talent in the upper ranges of the administration. In the United States they are possible; but the hazards are serious and only personal riches can supply the necessary insurance. Under the parliamentary system high executive opportunities are tied in with legislative work; each great department of government is assigned as a rule to someone who has previously been in that office or in a kindred position; even if new men are chosen for such posts they are usually parliamentary managers, not lawyers, businessmen, or labor leaders hastily "drafted" for the occasion. And when a political change turns a cabinet out of power, its members ordinarily go back to the opposition benches in parliament. In a word, institutions are shaped to provide unbroken opportunity; rising leaders are given progressive experience; the chief administrative posts go to outstanding and trained party directors; and occupants of the principal positions, while in power, are expecting to resume their political services at the end of their term rather than to seek a place somewhere in private economy. With careers are associated permanent honors, titles, decorations, and ceremonials—objects of desire for which large pecuniary sacrifices may be made.

In the lower ranges of public service in the Old World, the same professionalism obtains, for the whole administrative organization is founded on the assumption of continuity. A provision for permanent undersecretaries in the great departments of government (p. 301) assures stability in essentials and serves as a standing notice to clerks at the bottom that there are opportunities at the top. A scheme of gradation from the base to the apex, with promotions, increased emoluments, titles, and other attractions furnishes a definite ladder for youth. And owing to monarchical and feudal traditions, especially the close association of civil affairs with the profession of arms, service of the state is a coveted honor. Those who enter it usually intend to remain in it to the end of their days and to win their spurs by performance in it. Their eyes are fixed upon their superiors rather than upon possible chances to drop out and enter some lucrative private employment. In addition the more limited range of choices in business makes competition for admission to government service keener in Europe, while the social recognition accorded to it makes for contentment and emulation.

In the United States, on the other hand, service in the highest posts is not incidental to a parliamentary career. Heads of departments are not often taken from Congress. Generally speaking, as we have said, they are drawn from the legal profession, or business, or state politics. Still more important, however, is the fact that the cabinet officer does not as a rule intend to return to a political career if he has come from it. On the contrary he expects to go out into some important private enterprise or into the practice of law where his prestige will attract a rich and powerful clientele. His special knowledge of administrative functions and his personal acquaintance with federal employees make him a highly valuable adjunct to a corporation having legal or economic contacts with the Government. Even bureau chiefs and lower officials possessing permanent tenure may likewise look to the outside world as well as upwards in the service for opportunities to improve their economic status.

Thousands of illustrations crowd the pages of our political biographies. George B. Cortelyou, stenographer to President Cleveland, private secretary to McKinley and Roosevelt, Secretary of Commerce, and then Secretary of the Treasury, graduated from the public service to the presidency of the Consolidated Gas Company of New York and later assumed the chairmanship of the Joint Committee of the National Utility Associations. In the former position he has vital relations with state and municipal government in New York and in the latter with the Federal Government. His experience and standing are useful in both connections. Franklin K. Lane, Secretary of the Interior under President Wilson, and his colleague W. G. McAdoo, Secretary of the

Treasury, became counsellors to great oil concerns on leaving their official posts. Similar translations frequently occur from the lower divisions of federal service. A former employee of the Department of Commerce in charge of power matters was made executive director of the National Electric Light Association. After serving the Government for many years, a chief hydrographer of the United States Geological Survey entered private practice as a consulting engineer and soon appeared as an official of a power company. A solicitor of internal revenue who retired to practice law secured the United States Steel Corporation as a client and got it a tax refund of thirty-five million dollars from the Department in which he formerly worked. In an action at law it was revealed in 1930 that he claimed a fee of five million dollars for his "services." Such movements from public to private employment tend to make administration in America less perpendicular, less bureaucratic than in Europe, and to immerse it in the general medium of business enterprise which has its special economic opportunities and its own code of ethics. How far this practice makes for efficiency in the Government and for precision in law enforcement has not yet been subjected to scientific study; but undoubtedly it is a factor of prime importance in the development of federal administrative ideals and aspirations.

Congress and Administration

Attention has already been drawn to the special relation which Congress maintains with certain independent agencies in the Federal Government (p. 305), but it would be a mistake to assume that it does not have an interest in the execution of the law in general. To say that owing to the separation of powers it is not concerned with administration is to deny the traditions and practices of more than a century. The Constitution authorizes no such view. And certainly the exalted character of the President does not make him so immune to human frailties or guarantee to him so perfect a knowledge that Congress may safely rest content with passing acts for him to carry out at his discretion. Through incompetence or inadvertence, if nothing worse, Presidents may appoint dishonest and inefficient men to strategic positions and for various reasons may fail to discover their neglect of duties and even their betrayals of the public trust.

More than one scandal in the executive departments has smirched the Government and shocked the nation. During the years that followed the Civil War the "star route" and "whiskey ring" frauds made two administrations malodorous. Nor need we rely on ancient history for illustrations. President Harding appointed to the Veterans' Bureau a man who was soon convicted of corruption, and sent to the penitentiary for his rascality. Harding also selected for one cabinet post a former Senator who was later found guilty of fraudulent transactions, and for another a politician who was afterward charged with crimes, tried, and disgraced, although nominally cleared at law.

With respect to the two cabinet officers in question, it was not the President responsible for administration but Congress charged primarily with legislative duties that first moved to unearth the offenses against the laws and public decency. In the case of the Secretary who was convicted the evidence of his misconduct was not originally obtained by the Department of Justice, but by a senatorial investigating committee. The exposure began with a quarrel among oil interests over leases to federal lands illegally made by the Secretary—a dispute which broke into a Western newspaper. Rumors of the affair then spread in all parts of the country, but nothing was done in the White House about the uproar. Not until R. M. La Follette moved in the Senate and secured the creation of a special committee of inquiry was the lid taken off of the design to despoil the Government of property. Only after the committee disclosed the offenses did the President discover them and take steps to bring the guilty to book. Once more the difficulty of separating the power of government into executive, legislative, and judicial divisions was illustrated by experience. Once more it was made clear that Congress must maintain a constant scrutiny over the entire federal administration.

CHAPTER XI

TAXATION, FINANCE, AND SUPPLIES

THE power to lay taxes, coin money, make appropriations, and regulate currency and banking is one of the great forces of government. Its exercise affects the whole range of private economy—every branch of commerce and industry, the occupations of the people, their standards of life, even their amusements and enjoyments. It reaches beyond domestic boundaries and involves foreign intercourse. A tariff in the United States may cripple or paralyze industries in Germany or England. An inflation of the currency in France has actually reduced in value by three fourths the old domestic bonds of that country held by American citizens. A failure of public revenues in Mexico and China has in effect destroyed millions of dollars worth of property in the United States by cutting off the interest on their securities owned in this country. Indeed so closely interlocked are the financial structures and functions of all nations that a world super-bank, the Bank for International Settlements, has been erected, with representation from the central banks of the leading industrial powers, including unofficially the United States.

Taxation

Taxation, which normally means taking money from citizens for governmental purposes, involves more than merely raising funds to meet public expenditures. Like many other operations of government, it affects the distribution of wealth among the people and is hence entangled in the struggle of groups, classes, and particular interests in society. Its possibilities in this relation are illustrated by the variety of uses to which it may be put. In the shape of tariffs, taxation may be employed to regulate commerce and to protect domestic industries. In the form of retaliations against foreign discriminations it may be directed to the promotion of American trade abroad. In the guise of social legislation it may be deliberately utilized to bring about a more equitable distribution of wealth; taxes on unearned increment in land and on the incomes and inheritances of the rich fall, to some extent at least, within this category. Finally taxation may be applied to the prohibition of noxious articles such as opium.

Closely interwoven with the matter of purpose, the choice of objects for taxation raises controversial questions. Is a tax designed to bear primarily on land? Then it may discriminate against farmers and landlords in favor of capitalists engaged in commerce and industry. Does a tax fall primarily on manufacturing, transportation, or merchandizing? Then it may penalize these branches of economy as compared with agriculture. Does it take the shape of indirect imposts on imports, tobacco, the sale of goods, or theater tickets? In this case, it is often argued, an undue proportion is collected from the masses who are least able to carry the load, while the strongest are given a privileged position. Moreover the process is complicated by the fact that taxes on one class may be shifted to another. Those levied on business operations may be transferred to consumers. Those laid on lands and dwellings may be, within limits, passed on to tenants and renters. Indeed the very uncertainty as to the class which, in final analysis, pays any particular tax generally embitters the continual strife over the nature and incidence of taxation.

Running deeply into the interests and occupations of classes and masses, taxation is always at the very center of political conflicts in normal times, and it often becomes a major issue during those great social storms known as revolutions. No person or group enjoys paying taxes; all naturally seek to minimize the burden or transfer it entirely to some one else. Around taxation have been formed some of the most important political institutions of Western civilization;

representative government itself originated in the necessities of kings which led them to call upon their subjects for grants of revenues. Magna Carta, the Petition of Right, and the Bill of Rights are, among other things, tax documents imposing restraints on the powers of monarchs. It was the financial distress of Louis XVI which led him to summon the Estates General in 1789 and thus open the way to the first great French revolution. Taxation without representation was one of the causes of the American revolution.

And the purposes and forms of federal taxation have been involved in the strife of political parties from the days of Hamilton and Jefferson down to the latest tariff debate between the representatives of the industrial and agricultural states in Congress. Into the very causes of the Civil War in the United States entered a controversy over taxation. Although slavery loomed dramatically in the struggle, there was at bottom a fundamental collision between planters demanding low tariffs on imports and Northern manufacturers desiring high protection for their industries. Later, toward the close of the nineteenth century, the taxation of incomes and inheritances, laying special charges on the rich, figured prominently in the conflicts of parties and politicians.

Fully aware of the issues at stake and after a debate almost sulphurous in its acrimony, the framers of the Constitution granted to Congress a broad and general power "to lay and collect taxes, duties, imposts, and excises, to pay the debts and provide for the common defense and general welfare of the United States." Subject to certain rules, which we shall consider later, there is apparently no limit to the rate of any tax which may thus be imposed. On one occasion, Congress put a tax of ten per cent on state bank notes and drove them entirely out of circulation. In speaking of this drastic measure, the Supreme Court said that it was not within the province of the judiciary to prescribe to the legislative department limitations on the exercise of its acknowledged powers. If the taxing function is exercised oppressively, the Court declared, the remedy for the wrong rests with the people who choose the legislature. From this and other judicial decisions it appears that as long as Congress conforms to the restrictions mentioned below it can prescribe any rate of taxation—even one confiscatory in nature.

But on the taxing power so generously conferred, the Constitution imposes a number of express limitations. Three of them, which belong to a common group, are prohibitive in character and are intended to protect the states against discriminations. Congress cannot lay any tax or duty on articles exported from any state. In the regulation of commerce and revenue it must give no preference to the ports of one state over those of another; nor can it compel vessels bound to or from one state to enter, clear, or pay duties in another. Recalling poignantly their grievances against the British Parliament, the Fathers evidently sought to safeguard the states forever against all special legislation bearing heavily upon their respective products or business enterprises. Owing to the explicit nature of the restraints thus devised, there has been little debate as to their meaning and extent. They stand clearly written in the Constitution.

Unfortunately this cannot be said of two fundamental limitations of the Constitution respecting the taxes which Congress may lawfully lay. The first of them, dealing with what may be called "indirect taxes," provides that all duties, imposts, and excises shall be uniform throughout the United States. This leaves to the courts the task of deciding whether any particular tax comes within the class described or complies with the requirement of uniformity. As on other doubtful matters, the opinion of the Supreme Court has varied from generation to generation. At one time it held that a tax on income, gains, and profits by the year was in the nature of an excise or duty; but about thirty years later it declared unconstitutional nearly all the income tax schedules contained in the revenue act of 1894, on the ground that they were direct in character and not duties, imposts, or excises. Yet it is fairly well established that this class of indirect taxes includes customs or tariff duties imposed on goods coming into the United States, taxes on whiskey, tobacco, and other commodities, on the sale, transfer, or transportation of merchandise and on business transactions, on checks, mortgages, and other legal papers, on inheritances, and apparently on incomes not derived from real or personal property. However clear the Court may try to make the boundary around this type of taxes, border-line cases are constantly arising, especially as the changing nature of modern industry, commerce, and property gives new facets to the forms and substances of capital and wealth.

In attempting to fix such metes and bounds the Supreme Court, of course, must define the term "uniform." Generally speaking a uniform tax, according to the interpretations of that tribunal, is one which falls with the same weight upon the same object wherever found within the United States. For example, a duty levied on passengers coming from foreign countries into the United States was held to be uniform, although it was principally collected at a few ports. Again, an inheritance tax is uniform when it is imposed equally upon all inheritances of the same amount and character, though it may so happen that taxable estates of a given size may occur in only a few states of the Union.

The second fundamental limitation on the taxes which Congress may lawfully lay applies to direct taxes; the Constitution stipulates that capitation and other direct taxes, except on income, must be apportioned among the several states according to their respective numbers excluding Indians not taxed. What taxes are direct? In answering this question the Supreme Court has not adhered to the terms of the economists, whose views are themselves marked by differences of opinion. During the early years of the Federal Government it was generally understood that there were two kinds of direct taxes—a capitation or poll tax and a tax on land. In 1895 the term was widened; the Supreme Court held that taxes on *income* from real and personal property were also direct and therefore legal only when apportioned among the states as ordered by the Constitution. As the higher taxable incomes were concentrated mainly in a few states, it was obviously impossible to make such an apportionment; hence the decision of the Court amounted to a prohibition. After a long agitation over the matter, a constitutional amendment was adopted in 1913 authorizing Congress to lay taxes upon incomes from all sources without reference to any census or enumeration.

In addition to the express limitations laid down in the Constitution, there are two implied restrictions on the taxing power. In the first place, Congress cannot tax the instrumentalities or the property of any state. This doctrine has been applied in a number of cases. For example, during the Civil War, Congress levied a tax on the gains, profits, and income of every person residing in the United States; a judge in Massachusetts refused to pay the tax on his income derived from the commonwealth, and the Supreme Court of the United States upheld him in his refusal, declaring that the Federal Government was thus taxing a state instrumentality.

According to this principle the bonds of state and local governments are exempt from all federal taxes except on inheritances. When national taxation was light and mainly indirect in form, this condition of affairs called for little consideration, but it has become a subject of serious discussion now that federal expenses have mounted into billions annually and the income tax is used to bring enormous revenues into the Treasury. In practice, it is argued, rich people are induced to invest their money in tax-exempt bonds and thus escape a part of the federal burden. Especially is this true in the case of persons enjoying large incomes on which heavy and progressive surtaxes fall with great weight. It is also alleged that the exemption of state and local securities from federal taxation invites the withdrawal of capital from productive industry and stimulates public investments in roads, buildings, and other enterprises which yield no return in the form of profits or revenue. Owing to these circumstances, it is contended, an amendment should be added to the federal Constitution authorizing Congress to tax incomes derived from all new issues of state and local bonds; that is, in effect abolishing the privilege of tax exemption as to the future.

Probably, however, these arguments partake of the nature of good reasons rather than real reasons. An examination of the sources of such criticism seems to indicate that the most important motive behind it is to discourage states and cities from embarking on programs calling for large expenditures. The true point of the dispute, therefore, is whether a brake, in the form of bond taxation, should be placed on the tendencies of states and localities to adopt costly improvement projects.

The Purposes and Nature of Taxation

Far more controversial than any of the restraints discussed above is the question of purpose in federal taxation; here are involved grave matters of law and policy. The clause of the Constitution which gives Congress the power to lay and collect taxes, duties, imposts and excises adds the words: "to pay the debts and provide for the common defence and general welfare of the United States." Obviously this is a limitation in respect of purpose, but the term "general welfare" is so vague that it is difficult to conceive of any kind of a tax which could not come under that rubric. Yet vague as it is it disposes of an ancient contention that taxes can only be laid for the object of raising revenue—a theory long held by the Democratic party with reference to tariffs on imports.

As a matter of fact the Supreme Court has declined to hold that tax laws must always be written with a view to bringing income into the federal treasury. It has explicitly held to the contrary. When Congress in 1866 laid a tax of ten per cent on the notes of state banks for the purpose of destroying them and driving them entirely out of circulation—not with any idea of raising revenue, the Supreme Court sustained the law in a vigorous opinion. Again, when in 1902 in the interest of "dairy legislation," Congress imposed a high tax on oleomargarine colored as butter, to prevent its sale in such a guise, Chief Justice White, speaking for the Court, said that this was a revenue measure and that the Court would not go into the motives of Congress in passing it. A similar position was taken with regard to a law of Congress enacted in 1912 which laid a prohibitory tax on phosphorus matches found dangerous to health. A still more striking example is the Narcotic Drug Act of 1914 which subjected the sale of narcotics to close federal scrutiny in connection with a nominal tax on dealers. This Act was sustained by the Supreme Court but with four out of nine judges dissenting.

Reasoning from these judicial decisions Congress came to the conclusion in 1919 that it had the power to restrict child labor throughout the United States by imposing a tax on the owners of certain industries, who employed children under a fixed age limit. Here the Supreme Court, dismayed perhaps by the rapid advance in social legislation in the form of taxation or not in sympathy with the new law on principle, called a halt by declaring the act null and void as an improper use of the taxing power. Reversing in effect previous doctrines, it inquired into the purpose of the child labor law and said: "A court must be blind not to see that the so-called tax is imposed to stop the employment of children within the age limits prescribed. Its prohibitory and regulative effect and purpose are palpable." Then the Court went on to insist that taxes are imposed "in the discretion of the legislature on proper subjects with the primary motive of obtaining revenue from them and with the incidental motive of discouraging them by making their continuance onerous. They do not lose their character as taxes because of the incidental motive. But there comes a time in the extension of the penalizing features of the so-called tax when it loses its character as such and becomes a mere penalty with the characterization of regulation and punishment."

By many competent students this decision was greeted as a dangerous departure from a long line of precedents—a ruling that would make questions involving the constitutionality of taxes continually subject to judicial review as to motives. "The American people," says E. S. Corwin, "know something of their legislative history in this respect. They are fully aware that almost every customs revenue act which has been passed since the beginning of the Government has enacted whole schedules which were designed not for the purpose of raising revenue at all but for the purpose of excluding goods from the country. And yet are such duties any less 'duties'—and so 'taxes'—within the sense of the Constitution? If so, why are they subject to the requirement that they be 'uniform' throughout the United States?" If the motives of Congress may be called into question, why may not the motives of the Court be likewise scrutinized? A conflict of emotional views over right and wrong, over social expediency, is thus imminent. After a frosty survey of the reasoning of the Court, Mr. Corwin casts aside the language of jurisprudence and concludes that the opinion in this case "must be written down as a piece of grandmotherly meddling." But it stands. The Court will inquire into the purposes of taxes.

Whatever judicial comments the Supreme Court may make on the fiscal acts of Congress, fundamental motives other than that of raising revenue do enter into policies of taxation. Used previously in an emergency, the income tax appeared during the agrarian upheaval near the close of the nineteenth century as a measure deliberately designed to effect a more equitable distribution of wealth. As its advocates expressly declared, the income-tax section of the tariff act passed in 1894 was intended to shift a part of the burden of taxation from the consuming masses to the accumulations of wealth, especially in the East. On that assumption the issue was fought to a conclusion in Congress. On that assumption also Joseph Choate assailed the income tax in his argument against the law before the Supreme Court. When the Court, by a narrow margin, held invalid most of the income taxes imposed by the act, a long political debate ensued in which the question of the distribution of wealth was uppermost. And out of this debate came the Sixteenth Amendment.

Furthermore, nearly all the Presidents for a quarter of a century have recognized the social principle involved in income and inheritance taxes. In his striking message of 1907 Roosevelt defended them on the ground that they would help to bring equality of opportunity nearer to a correct realization. Wilson expressed similar views and early in his administration the first income tax was laid under the new amendment. While repudiating socialism, Herbert Hoover, as Secretary of Commerce, declared his belief that "the present inheritance, income and excess profits taxes tend to a better distribution of wealth;" and he also argued that the application of receipts from inheritance taxes to the extinction of the national debt or to reproductive expenditures in the improvement of national property was in harmony with conservative principles. Concerning the wisdom of such measures, however, Coolidge took the opposite tack, saying, "I do not believe that the Government should seek social legislation in the guise of taxation. If we are to adopt socialism it should be presented to the people of this country as socialism and not under the guise of a law to collect revenue." Yet if he personally would have rejoiced in shifting the burden of taxes from the receipts of the rich to the consumption of the masses, the policy once advocated by Populists alone had become so firmly imbedded in practice that it could not be uprooted. Though reduced, both inheritance and income taxes were retained.

For the purpose of realizing certain social and economic doctrines, as well as raising revenues, Congress has erected a complicated tax structure. In times of peace the system embraces four fundamental features.

Taxes on consumption occupy a prominent place. They include customs duties especially intended to protect American industry against foreign competition and internal excises such as the imposts on tobacco. But these two classes no longer bring in, as in former times, four fifths or more of the revenue of the Federal Government. During the year ended June 30, 1929, they accounted for only thirty per cent of the total returns to the Treasury.

The second part of the federal fiscal program embraces taxes on the incomes of persons and corporations, which yielded fifty-eight per cent of the receipts for the year just cited. In spirit and letter, the law laying taxes on individual incomes makes discriminations clearly based on assumptions respecting the distribution of wealth. At the outset the great mass of the people are entirely exempt from them—all unmarried individuals with fifteen hundred dollars a year or less and all married couples living together with thirty-five hundred dollars a year or less. A further provision permitting parents to withhold from their returns a certain amount for each of their children under a given age likewise reflects a social policy, akin to the tax imposed on bachelors in France and Italy. By express stipulation also a differentiation is made between those who derive their income from personal efforts—in the form of salaries, wages, and professional fees—and those whose receipts come from stocks, bonds, and other property; that is to say, rebates are allowed on "earned" as contrasted with "unearned" incomes. This is not all. There is a still more substantial distinction related to the distribution of wealth. While a low normal rate is imposed on small taxable incomes—after exemptions are deducted—the figure is materially increased on incomes in the higher ranges. A crowning discrimination is the surtax starting with a small percentage on incomes above ten thousand dollars and rising with rapid increments to twenty per cent of net incomes of one hundred thousand dollars or more a year.

On similar principles the federal inheritance tax law likewise makes distinctions pertinent to the distribution of wealth by varying the rate according to the size of the estates left by deceased persons. During the administration of President Coolidge special efforts were made to secure the repeal of this tax. Naturally heirs do not like to see their fortunes diminished and much was made of the argument that many of the states also impose inheritance taxes, thus creating a double burden. But Congress refused to yield; on the contrary it encouraged the states that do not have this form of tax to adopt it, for it eased the load by providing that the amount paid under any state inheritance tax law can be credited on the federal levy up to twenty-five per cent of the latter. More pointed than the double-burden argument is the contention of President Hoover that an inheritance tax may hamper the increase of capital necessary to industrial production by making large transfers of accumulated wealth to the Government, but this criticism he countered himself by saying that if the Government puts receipts from this source to productive uses the practice is socially defensible. At all events it requires no subtle analysis of the above tax structure to discover that it departs from the fundamental principle of classical political economy, namely, that under the prevailing system each factor in production—land, labor and capital—receives a return fairly proportioned to its contribution to the process and should not be deprived of it for the benefit of the others.

Besides customs duties and excises, income, inheritance, and miscellaneous taxes—besides imposts designed to produce revenue, to alter the "natural" distribution of wealth, or to protect business enterprise, Congress lays taxes for other purposes. For example, as we have seen above, by taxation it prohibits the manufacture of phosphorus matches, restrains the use of narcotics, and limits the sale of oleomargarine.

The Enactment of Revenue Laws

In theory all bills for raising revenue must originate in the House of Representatives and the Senate can merely propose or concur in amendments. The Constitution so provides. By a few words it summarizes a century of political conflict in England between the Crown, the House of Lords, and the House of Commons over fiscal prerogatives. As if making obeisance to Oliver Cromwell, the Fathers sought to vest the power to initiate taxes in the hands of that branch of the Federal Government nearest to the people on whom the burden must fall. To make known the reason for their action, the *Federalist* explained that "This power over the purse may, in fact, be regarded as the most complete and effectual weapon with which any constitution can arm the immediate representatives of the people, for obtaining a redress of every grievance and for carrying into effect every just and salutary measure."

In spite of what seems to be a clear prohibition, the Senate has in effect frequently originated revenue measures under the guise of making amendments to bills passed by the lower chamber. For example in 1871 it took a brief House project repealing certain duties—an act only two lines long—and transformed it into a general revision spread over twenty printed pages. Against this action, leaders among the Representatives protested vigorously. "It is clear to my mind," said James A. Garfield, "that the Senate's power to amend is limited to the subject-matter of the bill. . . . To admit that the Senate can take a House bill consisting of two lines, relating specifically and solely to a single article, and can graft upon that bill in the name of an amendment a whole system of tariff and internal taxation, is to say that they may exploit all the meaning out of the clause of the Constitution which we are considering, and may rob the House of the last vestige of its rights under that clause." Though forceful, such protests were without material avail, for the Senate was able to carry through most of its program.

More than once since 1871 the Senate has extended its right of amending to cover changes equivalent to a total reconstruction of House revenue bills—in effect the initiation of new measures. Nor is it likely that Senators will readily surrender their authority. With the concentration of industries in a relatively few states, the upper chamber has become the strong bulwark of agriculture. Since policies of taxation, as illustrated by the contest over the tariff in 1929–30, deeply involve the two great branches of American economy, it is evident that, although the House of Representatives theoretically enjoys the right to originate revenue bills, the Senate will insist on making terms of its own. In the drift of politics, therefore, the historic privilege of initiation has become a fiction of slight significance.

Even with respect to the preparation of revenue bills there is little distinction between the two chambers. When it becomes apparent that a demand for tariff revision is imperative, the House of Representatives instructs its committee on ways and means to gather pertinent information and prepare new schedules. As a general rule the Senate, about the same time, directs its finance committee to take similar steps; often the Senate has virtually finished its own program before the House bill arrives for consideration. Moreover both committees follow substantially identical procedure. Both hold hearings which are attended by interested parties—usually manufacturers or their agents seeking changes in customs duties. Both receive briefs and pleas in the same tenor. Consumers on whom the tax will mainly fall may appear, of course, but they are unorganized and can present no solid front like that of the manufacturers. Besides, their spokesmen, if there are any, usually do not have the special knowledge necessary to clinch their arguments before the committees.

After it is duly reported to the House of Representatives by the chairman of the committee on ways and means, a revenue bill is debated in the committee of the whole on the state of the Union. The discussion at first is rather free, so that practically every member who has anything to say about the proposal is given an opportunity to speak his mind. The general review is then followed by a limited debate on details which may result in many specific changes. From time to time as the argument proceeds, the committee on ways and means will report modifications in its original draft, for the chairman, as an astute party leader, is quick to perceive the points on which it is expedient to yield. Votes are taken by items and finally on the bill as a whole. In the former stage party members enjoy some latitude, for after all tariff schedules are "local issues" related to local industries; but at the end all good party men are expected to stand solidly for or against the completed measure.

When the bill reaches the Senate, it is referred to the committee on finance, which has, as a matter of fact, been busy on its own scheme and has watched with close scrutiny the progress of the discussion in the House. After making amendments or substituting practically a new project, the committee reports its bill to the Senate. In that body, as we have seen, debate is almost unlimited; agrarian opposition to high rates on manufactures is likely to be more effective; and as a rule the party yoke is lighter. Accordingly a revenue measure usually receives a more searching criticism in the upper chamber than in the House of Representatives.

After it has gone through the Senate, the bill, purporting to be the original measure with Senate amendments, is returned to the House, which naturally enough votes not to concur in the proposed changes and asks for a conference (p. 200) to settle the differences.

Frequently the conference committee takes into its confidence the President, whose views as party leader with regard to taxation cannot be neglected. Indeed it is at this stage of the proceedings that he can most wisely intervene, unless forsooth he is willing to incur the risks of undertaking to settle all the little party squabbles as they arise in the course of the debates in both houses. In any event he faces great hazards in dealing with a measure which runs so deeply into the economy of the nation. By leaning too far one way or the other, he may help to disrupt his party—as did President Taft in 1909. When at length the conference committee has come to an agreement, at least on the majority of items, its report—with perhaps a few appendices for independent action—is submitted to the House where it is passed without amendment and then it is sent to the Senate for similar action, unless for reasons of political strategy the process is reversed. Thereupon the bill goes to the President for his signature.

This method of adopting a revenue measure is obviously attended by serious drawbacks. No man or group can assume responsibility for it. The President, who has usually been elected on a platform favoring in vague language some kind of tariff revision, can do nothing more than exert the indirect influence which his party leadership gives to him. He may, of course, exercise his veto power, but with reference to a general revenue bill that would be drastic action, resulting in great confusion among the business interests awaiting a settlement and among the contestants in his own party. In Congress responsibility is divided between the two houses, and for this reason many important matters of controversy must be settled in the joint conference. So it may be said that the final word on tariff laws is pronounced by a committee unknown to the Constitution—not a permanent body but a temporary organization set up to arbitrate disputes. Its decisions are binding because both houses are in practice constrained to accept the measure which it reports, fearing to reopen a long and tedious debate and thus delay indefinitely the conclusion of the wrangle. The completed bill is, therefore, not an act which has received careful consideration at every point by an accountable legislature; it contains a series of compromises rushed through at the end without much deliberation. This, however, is the inevitable result of the system of checks and balances designed to break the force of direct majority rule.

Tax and Debt Administration

Revenues accruing to the Federal Government through the tax laws are collected under the auspices of the Treasury Department by two great services—one in charge of customs duties and the other, internal revenues. For efficient administration the country is divided into separate customs and internal revenue districts, each with its commissioner and force of inspectors, accountants, and other agents. To facilitate quick decisions on controversial points two special tribunals have been erected. The Court of Customs Appeals has power to make final rulings on questions involving the classification of imports and the rates imposed by customs officials—with appeal to the regular courts on problems of constitutionality and treaty provisions. Cases arising under legislation imposing income and inheritance taxes can be carried to the Board of Tax Appeals for review and settlement. Besides the returns from taxation, the Federal Government derives revenues from the post office, the sale of land, and other miscellaneous sources, which are usually collected by the special agency in charge and accounted for by its own officials.

The tax revenues received from various sources are kept in the Treasury at Washington and in banks belonging to the Federal Reserve System (p. 365) designated by the Secretary of the Treasury. Here they are held until paid out on warrants issued under congressional acts of appropriation. The safety of funds so deposited in banks is guaranteed by United States bonds and other prime securities placed in pledge. Although the distribution of federal receipts among banks appears to be a formality of administration, it may have a vital significance to private enterprise especially during financial panics. In allocating or withholding funds under his jurisdiction the Secretary may seriously affect the money market with wide-reaching repercussions in commerce and industry.

Until the declaration of war on Germany in April, 1917, the United States was one of the few fortunate countries in the world that were not staggering under the burden of a rapidly growing debt. In 1916 the total interest-bearing debt of the Federal Government was only $971,562,590 or $9.88 per capita. Three years later the figure stood at more than $25,000,000,000 or $203.06 per capita, not including in this sum about ten billion dollars then due from the powers affiliated with the United States in the World War.

By various agreements, the obligations of Great Britain, Belgium, Italy, France, and all our other debtors except Russia and Armenia have been funded and are to be repaid gradually over a long period of years. The terms vary. Great Britain came close to fulfilling the strict letter of the bond, but most of her associates were granted exceedingly low rates of interest and thus were allowed in reality to effect a material repudiation. Although the Government of the United States seems to regard these settlements as closed, many of the debtor countries resent the necessity that compels them to pay. From time to time official and unofficial overtures are made with a view to reopening the question. What will happen before the last installment falls due near the end of the twentieth century, no one can tell.

In connection with its management of the huge national debt, the Federal Government has consistently made periodical reductions in the principal since 1921. Under a fixed policy the Treasury has applied certain funds to this purpose and has besides devoted to the same end a portion of the surplus accruing from an excess of revenues over expenditures. Accordingly in 1929 it could announce that the gross debt then stood at sixteen billion eight hundred million dollars. Moreover, owing to fortunate economic circumstances, it has also been able to cut annual charges by refunding some of its bonds into obligations bearing a lower rate of interest. Yet in the pursuit of this policy of debt reduction the Treasury has not escaped criticism. In many quarters it is urged that the generation which fought the World War should leave a larger part of the bill of costs to coming generations. If attractive, the argument is easily offset by the contention that a wise government, unable to forecast the future, prepares for all possible contingencies by curtailing its burden of debt whenever conditions are favorable.

Appropriation Methods—the Budget System

No money can be paid out of the Treasury of the United

States except under the authority of an act of Congress. In the beginning of our history all appropriation bills laid before the House of Representatives were prepared by the ways and means committee, which also had charge of revenue legislation. Thus there was effected some coördination between the taxing and spending functions of the Government. In the course of time, however, appropriation measures were taken away from that committee and distributed among several different committees, each reporting a separate bill of its own. A similar dissipation of authority occurred in the Senate. As a starting point for their labors, these various committees had before them a book of estimates, compiled by the Secretary of the Treasury—a mere unedited collection of requests for funds.

Under this time-honored system neither house ever had in hand, while passing any one of the appropriation bills, a complete program of probable revenues and expenditures. Department heads and others seeking appropriations constantly besieged the doors of the committees. Every administrative interest was represented in the pressure for larger outlays. The moment a new bureau or agency was created it began to lobby for increased funds. Army and navy officers, loyal to their branch of the service, always presented insistent claims for additional money. Then there was the interminable list of demands made upon Congress by the log-rollers—for post offices, river and harbor improvements, naval stations, docks, and other public works.

Amid such circumstances an appropriation bill would be reported out of committee, debated, perhaps amended, sent to the other house, debated and amended, adjusted in a conference committee representing the two chambers, and finally sent to the President for his signature. Other bills followed at irregular intervals; not until the end of the session could anyone know how much money was being voted away.

Against this chaotic financial procedure, accompanied by extravagance and "raids on the treasury" for local benefits, protests were early heard in the country but not until about

1910 were they taken seriously. In that year, Congress granted to President Taft a large appropriation for an inquiry into the methods of transacting public business and authorized him to organize a Commission on Economy and Efficiency (p. 308). After an extended investigation the Commission recommended, among other things, the establishment of a national budget system, bringing the fiscal functions of the Federal Government into line with the practices of European states. With full warrant the work of this special agency may be said to mark the beginning of the widespread agitation which finally brought results in the Budget and Accounting Act of 1921.

This Act created a Budget Bureau in the Treasury Department, headed by a director appointed by the President without the necessity of senatorial approval. It imposes upon the President the duty of laying before Congress at the opening of each regular session a consolidated budget statement setting forth, among other things, the revenues and expenditures for the previous fiscal year, proposed revenues and expenditures for the coming year, and the condition of the public debt. If his budget shows a deficit then the President must recommend revenue measures to meet the difference; if it reveals a surplus, then he may make suggestions with respect to reductions in taxation. The data for the President's budget are assembled by the director of the Budget Bureau, who collects them from the various departments and other spending agencies.

Although the Budget and Accounting Act was supposed to mark a revolution in federal finances, it did not in itself make any important changes in the authority of the President. The preparation of estimates had long been required by law; and by an act of 1909 the President had been requested to review the estimates and make recommendations as to tax bills for meeting a deficit or reducing a surplus according to circumstances. Without any express warrant from Congress the President under his general powers could have done exactly what he is now authorized to do by the Budget Act.

The point is that he did not and Congress was not yet prepared for such a large installment of executive direction.

What the Act of 1921 really did, therefore, was openly to invite the President to assume leadership in organizing the budget, provide him with expert assistance from a new technical bureau, and prepare the country to expect executive action in shaping the fiscal program of the Government. Incidentally, it enabled the President to dramatize the budget each year at the opening of Congress and by means of the press to concentrate the attention of the nation upon financial policies and appropriation methods. Through the Budget Bureau, moreover, the various departments and agencies were brought into close coöperation in the preparation of estimates and the adoption of economies.

In practice preparation of the annual budget is a long process during which estimates of the funds needed by the several executive divisions of the Government for the coming fiscal year are assembled and revised in conformity with the President's policy, always with an eye to a proper balance between revenues and expenditures for the period in question. The work falls into two stages, the first being in the nature of a preliminary survey of requirements and the second a final adjustment previous to the publication of the budget document.

The first step begins with the sending of blanks by the Budget Bureau to the various departments and agencies, with instructions advising them to report all their money requests for the coming year. When these blanks, duly filled out, are returned to the Bureau, the proposed outlays are totalled and compared with the estimated receipts for the same period compiled jointly by the Treasury Department and the Bureau. Together the two groups of accounts present a picture of income and expenditures as drawn by the interested parties.

At this point a Bureau inquest begins. As a check on the individual agencies, it sends out special investigators who go over the figures submitted by the several divisions of the Executive Department and may recommend changes in them.

A Board of Estimates, composed of Bureau personnel, then reviews as a body the findings of the investigators, making adjustments as it sees fit. This review completes the analysis of the tentative estimates. Having scrutinized fiscal demands with reference to the President's financial policy, the Bureau now assigns a tentative maximum to the amount to be allotted to each agency at this stage in the procedure.

The second phase of budget making commences when the Budget Bureau distributes notices to the several departments, offices, and commissions advising them to cut their estimates to specified figures. In response the agencies proceed to prune their demands, using the limits set by the Bureau as their standards. Since it is possible, however, for the Bureau to err on the side of economy in issuing its orders relative to downward revisions, they are permitted to prepare "supplemental estimates," accompanied by supporting data, covering items which they feel should be included in addition to the totals as fixed. On reaching the Bureau, the new revised figures now go through much the same procedure as the preliminary estimates. Members of the Bureau staff are dispatched to various agencies for the purpose of inquiring into the soundness of the latest requests. Upon receipt of the recommendations from its investigators, the Board of Estimates of the Budget Bureau meets once more, this time holding hearings to which representatives of the spending authorities are invited. At these meetings the estimates are discussed at length and the agreements reached are incorporated in the budget document for presentation to the President.

As matters stand there is a long interval between the opening of the work on the budget and the date on which it goes into operation. Early each summer the Bureau of the Budget starts on a new program for presentation to Congress in December. At the winter session the budget is adopted for the year beginning with the following July 1st. Thus expenditures under the budget do not start until a full year after the preliminaries of preparation open.

The President's budget, presented to Congress with a

special budget message, is essentially a guide to the legislator. In composition and arrangement, the text is designed to simplify for Congress the task of handling the many annual bills authorizing expenditures. In its pages appropriations actually made for the current fiscal year and those suggested for the ensuing year are exhibited in parallel columns. Accompanying these figures indicating projected changes in outlays are descriptions of the appropriation acts already in force for each item. To facilitate legislative action, brackets and italics are employed in these descriptions showing just what modifications must be made in existing laws to bring them in line with the budget plan. In other words, the task of phrasing the new bills is performed for Congress and the proposed revision is supported by figures giving its financial effect in items and totals. The work is so thoroughly done that the budget could be passed with great expedition if there were no dissent or Congress had no policies of its own. With outlays fully covered one phase of the work is completed.

But expenditures present only one side of the story; they must be compared with income. Accordingly the receipts and expenditures for the proposed budget year and the current fiscal year are estimated, and the totals are supplemented by the balances struck at the close of the last two fiscal years already terminated. Thus is revealed a combined four-year picture of the nation's finances with an outline of the method by which the expenditures of the fourth year may be met.

From the above survey of the budget it is apparent that most of its contents would not interest the general reader, although the expenditures and revenues covered by it vitally concern even the average person. A penetrating summary of it is essential if the public at large is to be initiated into its mysteries. Consequently the President annually takes upon himself the task of writing a short sketch of the proposed fiscal plan and its implications in terms of policy to serve as a preface and a kind of proclamation to the country. In reality it is the President's message, and not the text of the budget, that strikes the attention of the people each year. Through the widespread publicity given to his financial statement in newspapers and magazines, the citizens of the United States, most of whom never see the document itself, may become acquainted with the fundamental principles of the new project.

While greater coördination in preparing the budget was being effected in the Executive Department, Congress took steps in the same direction. With a view to concentrating interest on the budget program of expenditures, the House of Representatives discontinued its custom of distributing appropriation bills among twelve or fourteen committees and consolidated them all in the hands of one committee on appropriations—itself divided into many subcommittees. This example the Senate soon followed.

In practice it is difficult to say just what the budget system has accomplished, for no searching scrutiny has ever been made of its actual operation. At the end of four years' experience, Martin B. Madden, chairman of the appropriation committee of the House, could state correctly that in none of these years had Congress authorized the expenditure of more money than the President had requested in his estimates. In contrast to their previous records, the House and the Senate had not added materially to the appropriation bills reported to them by their respective committees in charge of proposed outlays. With full justification also it may be said that the budget system has worked innumerable economies in detail, which make totals of respectable size. It has been particularly effective in curtailing the expansion of the social service agencies of the Government, especially those engaged in public health and general welfare activities. Under the new régime, however, expenditures for military and naval purposes increased enormously, causing President Hoover to declare in his first message to Congress, that " the total of our expenditures [for national defense] is in excess of those of the most highly militarized nations of the world."

Beyond all question the budget system has vested enormous powers in the committee on appropriations in the House of Representatives and has diminished the influence of other committees and of private members over expenditures and over legislation calling for outlays, large or small. In effect it has put a brake on law-making in general, for nearly all important bills carry with them, if only incidentally, charges on the Treasury.

This check has been imposed in the following manner. The Budget Act itself stipulated that no request or estimate for an appropriation, or for an increase in any such item, shall be submitted to Congress or any committee thereof by an officer or employee of any department or establishment unless on instructions from one of the houses. Extending this principle, President Harding issued a circular providing that no executive official shall send to either house or a committee a request or recommendation for legislation involving directly or remotely an appropriation of money until he has first laid it before the Director of the Budget. On receipt of such a proposal the Director must make recommendations respecting it to the President. If the President does not approve, it cannot be transmitted to Congress or the committee in question; if he approves, it goes with a memorandum to the effect that the President has given his consent. Furthermore whenever either house or a committee transmits a measure calling for expenditures to the head of an agency or department for comment or opinion, the latter must ascertain through the Director of the Budget whether the proposal "is in accord with the fiscal program of the President." In making his report to the house or the committee as the case may be, the official must include a statement indicating whether the particular measure in hand has or has not received executive sanction.

Under such a system it is easy for the chairmen of committees, especially when they do not like a bill proposed by a private member, to refer it to an executive officer and secure presidential dissent. Indeed for various reasons it is a common practice for committees to refer bills to the departments and bureaus for report. When a measure is brought out with an appendix showing that it is in accord with the President's fiscal program, its chances of passage are better. If it is branded with executive condemnation, its chances are materially reduced. Since in fact it is impossible for the President himself to scrutinize these matters in detail, the Director of the Budget becomes the real master of ceremonies.

Speaking on this point during a debate in the House, Albert Johnson, Representative from Washington, declared: "I have observed each year the increasing power of the Bureau of the Budget, until now I am inclined to believe that the Bureau of the Budget is developing into a third house of Congress with more power under certain conditions than the Senate and House. (Applause.) In my opinion, the Bureau of the Budget not only exercises a veto power prior to legislative action, but a power more formidable than the executive veto. I believe also that the Bureau of the Budget has turned down proposed constructive legislation not because such legislation is in opposition to the financial policy of the President, but because such bills of the House or Senate are repugnant to the views of the coördinating officers of the Bureau of the Budget. (Applause)."

As if to enlarge the dominion of the Director of the Budget, certain members of the House take the view that they must object to the consideration of every proposal involving an appropriation that is not accompanied by a formal report from him. And as a great deal of business must be done under the rule of unanimous consent, a penalty is likely to be attached to any bill that does not bear the budget-office stamp.

This is, of course, not always the case but no doubt in actual operation the system places in the hands of subordinates in the Budget Bureau an immense power over legislation carrying a charge on the Treasury—a development certainly open to criticism. "The legislating committee," said Robert Luce, Representative from Massachusetts, in the course of the debate cited above, "is to concern itself with policy and principle, the appropriating committee with prudence and proportion.

It is the appropriating committee that should consult the Bureau of the Budget." Although, as Martin B. Madden said in reply, a member does not have to consider the Budget Office at all but can carry his bills if he can get enough votes for them, the fact remains that significant measures of legislative policy may be readily blocked by mere reference to the Director of the Budget. Perhaps this is one of the incidents necessarily connected with attempting to graft on the American scheme a fiscal device taken from the parliamentary form of government in which the minister in control of the budget is himself responsible to the legislature that passes upon it.

Of equal importance, perhaps, with the sections providing for a budget, but less spectacular in its effects, is a second part of the Budget Act, which created a General Accounting Office. This Office is charged with the duty of prescribing forms for accounting in the several departments and agencies, scrutinizing their expenditures, and reporting its findings to Congress. It is under the direction of the Comptroller General, appointed by the President with the consent of the Senate for a term of fifteen years and removable only by impeachment or a joint resolution of Congress. Although intended to be a legislative instrument for auditing expenditures with respect to their legality, the Accounting Office has become an independent establishment in more ways than one. The Director's tenure is long and apparently the President cannot oust him for any reason (p. 272); Congress to which he is theoretically responsible has no organization to watch over him; and in fact his kingdom is practically autonomous.

Moreover under explicit provisions of law the powers of the General Accounting Office are large. It sees that all money accruing from revenues is properly deposited in the Treasury and that none is issued therefrom except as authorized by Congress. Besides acting thus as a watch-dog, it has full jurisdiction to settle finally and conclusively all ordinary claims for or against the Government arising under acts of Congress. It is true that the several departments and agencies disburse money as they believe proper but such expenditures are not closed transactions until they have been examined and approved by the General Accounting Office. If there is doubt about the manner in which a payment should be made, the Comptroller General can render a legal decision that binds the spending officer involved in the case. Although his right to control in a similar way the handling of receipts is still in question, he has vigorously asserted it on various occasions. Besides carrying on the work of auditing, the Office is empowered to set up a general system for the standardization of accounts among the many federal agencies —an undertaking not yet completed.

Already doubts have been expressed regarding the wisdom of the existing organization and procedure in the General Accounting Office. The usual practice in other governmental units within the United States is to create one agency to handle accounts while delegating to a separate officer, known as the comptroller or auditor, the power to review them. The latter officer, acting as a representative of the executive or the legislature, is merely supposed to make sure that money is being spent legally in the manner desired by the branch which he represents. The General Accounting Office in Washington, on the other hand, combines under one head the functions of accounting and auditing. It not only scrutinizes accounts but it also keeps them and makes vital decisions with respect to the legality of the actions of spending officers, subject to no superior control, except by the courts in contested cases.

Money and Banking

Modern civilization rests upon money economy. Primitive and backward communities can live by bartering goods for goods, but all great nations must depend upon the exchange of commodities for money and credits throughout the world. Theoretically money is merely a medium, a token of exchange, but practically the stability of commerce and the distribution of wealth among the various classes of society are materially affected by the exercise of the power to mint coin and issue bills. Hence the currency question is inevitably drawn into the conflict of interests which furnishes so much of the substance of politics. No scheme for a "scientific currency" can possibly take the monetary problem out of the forum into the laboratory. Nor can banks, even if denied the power to emit legal tender and other notes, be exempt from the government supervision necessary to enforce standards of efficient and honest management and to protect the public against frauds and defalcations.

What then are the institutions and practices connected with currency and banking which keep them within the scope of political controversies? First of all there is the problem of the volume or amount of money to be kept in circulation. How is the "proper" amount to be determined? No categorical answer is possible, but beyond doubt there are limits both ways. By an unrestrained inflation of the currency public and private debts may be practically wiped out as in Germany, Russia, and other European countries after the World War, and industry laid prostrate by financial chaos. On the other hand, if the amount of money afloat be too narrowly contracted, business may be paralyzed for the lack of cash and credit facilities.

Between the extremes there is a margin of manipulation which may be employed for the benefit of one class or another —without disaster to the whole social structure. A slight inflation raises prices and makes it easier for producers of commodities to pay their debts. If, for example, a farmer borrows one thousand dollars when wheat is a dollar a bushel he can pay his debt in the normal course with one thousand bushels; if however there is an inflation which raises the price of wheat to two dollars, he can discharge his obligation with five hundred bushels. Conversely, if there is a contraction of currency which reduces the prices of commodities, the holders of bonds and other paper drawing a fixed rate of interest profit from the operation. If, for instance, the drop in prices is fifty per cent then the farmer in the case cited above must furnish two thousand bushels of wheat instead of one thousand to square his account. In other words control over the monetary system may be employed to enrich one class and impoverish another, to transfer by devious devices money from the pockets of one group to the pockets of another. For more than twenty centuries conflicts of creditors and debtors involving currency problems have been storm centers of politics.

Closely connected with the volume of the currency is the question of its nature. Indeed the two problems are inseparable. Since civilized societies began there have been staunch advocates of restricting money to gold and silver coins. These metals, it is argued, are limited in amount, precious in themselves, and permanent bearers of value because people ardently desire them as objects of art or adornment if for nothing else. They cannot be inflated or contracted in amount, at least to extremes, by artificial means. Nobody—private banker or government official—can make gold or silver by operating a printing press and collect interest and profit from his manipulations. Here, therefore, it is said, are the "natural" materials for money.

But these contentions are countered by many facts. It is impossible to keep gold and silver on a parity in value owing to fluctuations in the amount of bullion arising from divergence in output. Moreover modern methods of discovery and extraction may and often do lead to a great influx of gold or silver into the world market, producing a certain degree of inflation akin to that caused by paper issues—with similar effect. In any case these increases in volume are dependent mainly on accident and bear no relation to the changing needs of agriculture or business. Finally there is the great argument of convenience. Immense and varied transactions in gold or silver are so expensive and dangerous as to clog the wheels of enterprise. Hence a purely specie or metallic currency is out of the question in modern civilization. Paper money is a necessity.

This being true, who is to issue it, governments or private

bankers? If the responsibility is to be given to a government, should it be vested in the states or in federal authorities? That is the rub. Advocates of private banking contend that no public officials can safely be entrusted with such power, because under political pressure they will favor one class or another by inflation or contraction and, in time of crisis, seek to avoid a resort to heavy taxation by printing large issues of notes to pay government expenses. On the other side it is argued that to allow private parties to emit bills is to permit them to give a fictitious value to worthless paper and lend it to borrowers at interest, thus enriching themselves in the process without adding anything of worth to society. Moreover, unless they too are controlled by higher authority they may likewise employ various forms of inflation; it has happened in the history of the United States and may well happen again.

Here then are the chief economic considerations involved in the development of currency and banking legislation and practice. A large part of the political history of the United States can be written in terms of this question. It was so troublesome in colonial times that Great Britain felt compelled to forbid the colonies to issue paper money. During the period of the Revolution the whole monetary system was thrown into chaos by huge emissions of paper sent out by the states and the Continental Congress. There was no term of contempt greater than "not worth a Continental." Among the many forces which led to the formation of the Constitution few were more significant than the deranged condition of the currency. Having suffered from the baneful results of inflation, the framers of the Constitution sought to put an end to it by depriving the states of the right to emit paper money and by vesting the power to coin money and regulate the value thereof in the Congress of the United States.

After the adoption of the Constitution the currency problem was one of the topics which split the country into contending parties, and from that day to this there have been broadly speaking two policies. The founders of the Federal Government were not opposed to paper money, but they did not want to have it floated under the auspices of the states where debt-burdened farmers were likely to be dominant. Reflecting the views of the commercial classes, in the main, they preferred to give the power to emit notes to a semi-private corporation organized under federal control, known as the Bank of the United States. On the other hand the opponents of this policy, usually agricultural in interest, wished either to confine the currency to gold and silver coins or, more generally, to permit the states to issue notes directly or through banks.

Such are the roots of centralized and decentralized finance so prominent in American political controversies. Under the former policy, it has been contended, a few great centers of commerce dominate and reap the rewards; under the latter the advantages and profits are more widely distributed in rural regions. From 1791 to 1836, except for a brief period, the party of centralized finance was supreme and operated through the first and second United States banks. From 1836 to 1863 the party of decentralized finance was uppermost. And owing to a curious interpretation of the Constitution by a friendly Supreme Court, the states, although themselves forbidden to issue notes, were permitted to charter banks of their own and grant them ample powers to emit bills of credit, with the result that the country was flooded with unsound paper money.

From 1863 to 1913, centralized finance was again dominant, functioning through the national banking system established in the former year. State banks of issue were taxed out of existence by a statute effective in 1866, and private banks, known as national banks, chartered under federal authority, were given a monopoly of bank note issues. During this period the coinage of silver dollars was stopped; gold was made the basis of all currency; the inflated paper issued in the stress of the Civil War was placed on a specie basis; and the policy of contraction rather than inflation was followed. But during these fifty years the currency question and the free silver dispute filled the political arena with the tumult of debate, the fortunes of men and parties hanging upon the outcome. At last the controversy culminated in the Federal Reserve Law of 1913 enacted by the party of Thomas Jefferson which was forced by an embattled opposition to compromise—to combine centralized finance with its traditional schemes for local control.

Every phase of the historic conflict involving finance, commerce, and agriculture is mirrored in the terms of the Federal Reserve Act of 1913—now the fundamental law of American banking and currency. Not a single one of its basic provisions can be understood without reference to this long struggle. Even the amendments added to the original Act bear the same marks.

In the construction of the federal agency which controls banking and currency are reflected the Hamiltonian creed of centralization and the Jacksonian notion of government monopoly, rather than private or mixed management. The Federal Reserve Board standing at the apex of the whole system is composed entirely of government officials. Theoretically at least bankers as such have no power over their selection or removal. Of the eight members two, the Secretary of the Treasury and the Comptroller of the Currency, serve *ex officio* and six are appointed by the President with the consent of the Senate. The conflict of interests which entered into the enactment of the law is recognized in the provisions governing the choice of the six appointive members. In selecting them "the President shall have due regard to a fair representation of the financial, agricultural, industrial, and commercial interests and geographical divisions of the country." The last named limitation is reinforced by the rule that no more than one shall be taken from any federal reserve district—a provision for decentralization which itself has economic significance.

Continuing the Hamiltonian tradition, the Act vests in this body high centralizing functions. The Federal Reserve Board chooses three of the nine members on the governing board of each subordinate federal reserve bank, described below, and may suspend any of its officers or directors. It exercises a rigid control over the issue of currency. It supervises the transactions of all banks under its jurisdiction. It scrutinizes their accounts, inspects their books and papers, and is responsible for the execution of the law to the minutest detail. In a word, within the limits of the Act, it controls the bank-note currency of the country and the entire federal banking system. If, however, the Hamiltonian concept of centralization prevails in the character and powers of the Federal Reserve Board, there is an element of old Jacksonian policy in the organization of the scheme of local banks. Under the law the country has been divided into twelve large districts each with its financial capital and a federal reserve bank at the head; and individual banks scattered throughout the districts are drawn into the general structure. All of the old national banks that wished to keep their charters had to become members and state banks were allowed to join the network by conforming to the requirements of the Act.

With respect to the administration of these local institutions a curious blend of historic traditions prevails. Government banking of the Jacksonian type, control by bankers themselves, representing the opposing school, and the conflict of economic interests are intermingled. Each member bank is managed by its own board of directors elected by the stockholders. Here immediate management by private financial interests is undisputed. On the other hand the federal reserve bank in each of the twelve districts is governed by a body composed of different classes of directors, numbering nine in all. Three of them, as we have said, are chosen by the Federal Reserve Board in Washington; three are elected by the member banks of the district to represent primarily finance; and the remainder are selected in the same way from among men "actively engaged in their district in commerce, agriculture, or some other industrial pursuit." In other words, banking and currency are not to be dominated wholly by financiers, but by a combination of public officials, bankers, and spokesmen of business and agriculture.

Likewise, with reference to the nature and volume of the currency, another compromise is effected. While the demand of the sound-money advocates for a gold underwriting is partly realized, the old populistic contention that gold is too narrow to serve as the sole base for paper issues is also distinctly conceded. In deference to the former, the provisions of the Act of 1900, which makes gold the foundation for the entire monetary system, are allowed to stand unimpaired in principle. Moreover, the law authorizes the emission of federal reserve bank notes, corresponding essentially to the old national bank notes resting on United States government bonds payable in gold.

But such paper is limited in amount and hence is "inelastic." To this currency, accordingly, is added a new type—federal reserve notes—which are issued to the member banks by the district reserve banks under the supervision of the Federal Reserve Board. This is an elastic currency. It is based fundamentally on prime short-term commercial paper, such as personal and corporate notes, drafts, bills of exchange, and acceptances, and—as a result of agrarian agitation—also on agricultural and live-stock paper of early maturity. Member banks in whose name these notes are issued do not have to keep to their credit a gold fund equal to more than forty per cent of their outstanding currency; that is, within the terms of the law, the volume of federal reserve notes may be two and one half times the metallic base upon which they rest. Theoretically, it is true, all these notes are government obligations and may be exchanged for gold, but in practice the amount of them in circulation is about twenty-five per cent above the total gold supply held against them. Thus a specie support gives an assurance of soundness while the underlying commercial and agricultural credits allow for elasticity. And to prevent this arrangement from producing a dangerous inflation, complicated provisions are made for the retirement of federal reserve notes surely and promptly. Inflation there has been and is, but a strong retaining wall confines it.

Finally there remains the question of distributing the profits arising from the issue of paper as money. According to accepted populist notions, the government in control, either federal or state, should garner in all the gains accruing from the operation. On the other side private bankers naturally regard themselves as the proper beneficiaries. Here again the Federal Reserve Act registers a compromise, with a decided leaning to the bankers. Member banks retain their earnings for the advantage of their stockholders. On the other hand the profits of the federal reserve banks are divided between them and the Federal Government. Theoretically they are not conducted primarily for gain. Their dividend is limited to six per cent; and after they have laid aside a surplus equal to their subscribed capital stock, ten per cent of their net income above the annual dividend requirements goes to surplus and the remainder to the Federal Government in the form of a franchise tax. A more complicated union of politics and economics could scarcely be imagined.

Still the struggle over banking and the currency continues. The debates in Congress respecting the Federal Reserve Act, the amendments proposed and defeated, and the endless protests against the operations of the system reveal dissatisfaction with it. After the collapse of war prosperity in 1920 discontent flamed out among the farmers of the West as it had in the days of the free silver battle. The price of wheat fell below a dollar per bushel and debt-burdened farmers could not meet their obligations. Immediately they concentrated their attacks on the federal reserve scheme as they had once on the currency itself. They alleged that it had enriched the bankers and that business men, not farmers, had benefited from the inflation of the currency under it. They accused the Reserve Board of favoring business instead of agriculture; and by act of Congress they forced the appointment of at least one agriculturist to membership on that body. A few years later, during the great stock market spurt of 1929, the system was vigorously assailed by some financiers for attempting to curtail feverish speculation, by others for failing to raise the discount rate and curb the boom before it burst.

Almost from the beginning the federal reserve system has also been criticized for imposing on its member banks certain restrictions as to the number and location of the branches which they may establish—restrictions conceived in the interest of decentralized finance. True, the requirements may be evaded to some extent by the gradual union of nominally independent units under a common company—the integration of scattered banks into a single federation. But this is quite a different operation from the expansion of a central nucleus through the creation of numerous feeders widely scattered over large geographical districts. It is the latter process, involving potentialities of a different sort, which is still hampered by law. And to get rid of such limitations a large school of financiers calls upon Congress to release members of the federal reserve system from all restraints which prevent them from organizing branches wherever they please. So the conflict over banking and currency goes on and must go on as long as civilization rests, as it must, upon money economy.

While the Federal Government is compelled to deal constantly with important questions pertaining to the nature and volume of the currency, it must also wrestle with other financial problems not quite so obviously entrusted to it by the Constitution. Various economic groups, looking with envy on the low rate of interest at which it can borrow from the public, press the Government to lend money to them at a figure below the general market. On the plea of shipowners it has created a fund out of which loans are made to certain shipping concerns at rates of interest close to those paid on federal bonds (p. 391). The farmers, too, have won a battle for similar consideration. In 1929, a Farm Board was established to furnish money to coöperative agricultural associations at favorable rates of interest—an institution supplementing the Federal Farm Loan Board already in existence in the money lending field (p. 528). Nor is this all. For the benefit of the cautious or timid, the Government has organized, under the auspices of the Post Office Department, a chain of savings banks in which citizens can deposit their money with full confidence that it will be perfectly safe (p. 425). Hence under the influence of interested parties the Federal Government has become a kind of banker as well as a regulator of banking and the currency.

Responsibility for the general management of federal finances is vested in the Secretary of the Treasury. He must oversee the receipt and expenditure of billions of dollars every year—a huge bookkeeping undertaking in itself. He must secure a fair and impartial administration of the customs which are irritating to importers in the best of circumstances and doubly irritating when administered in an arbitrary fashion. He must supervise the minting of coins and the printing of paper money, the issue of bonds, and the payment of the interest on the debt. He is head of the Farm Loan Bureau and must wrestle with baffling problems of agricultural economics. He must master theoretical and practical questions of finance in order to make recommendations to Congress and meet the demands of that body for expert advice. He is a big policeman, because he has under his jurisdiction the coast guard and the bureau of internal revenue, which are on watch against evasions of law. By a historical accident he is also head of the public health service (pp. 578 ff.).

Supplies and Buildings

The Federal Government is in the market for a far wider range of supplies than any other customer in the country. Everything from fountain-pen ink, through crowbars, eggplant, goggles, electric fans, and tacks, to all-metal dirigibles is to be found among its purchases. An attempt has been made, however, to restrict the number of items on this list, a huge one at best, to a reasonable working minimum by a careful standardization designed to eliminate needless varieties in size, shape, and quality. For a long time the several establishments of the Government formulated specifications for their own requirements, each one independent of the others, and even these limited efforts had a salutary effect in avoiding duplication within the particular units. But there are numerous supplies, such as ink, paste, or paper which are necessary to the work of many agencies. If every organization had its separate specifications for materials of common use, uniformity of stock throughout the entire service could not be effected.

In recognition of this fact, a Federal Specifications Board has been created, composed of members representing the different departments and independent branches. Operating as a coördinating body, with the assistance of the Bureau of Standards, the Board develops and adopts "United States Government Master Specifications" which, with few exceptions, become binding on all agencies that buy the commodities covered by them. As its name indicates, the master specification generally replaces the conflicting standards formerly adopted by the various units for their own purposes, thereby applying a single principle to the given commodity throughout practically all the federal offices.

The actual purchasing work of the Government, with specifications as a guide, is carried on by the component departments, establishments, and their subdivisions. As yet no central office has been organized to handle supplies for the Government as a whole nor is there just ground for supposing that highly centralized buying through a single agency is desirable under the present circumstances. Indeed, owing to the wide distribution of federal activities throughout the world, coupled with the extraordinary diversity in the types of commodities used, extreme centralization would scarcely add to efficiency in this field. Furthermore, where a bureau or office has need for a special object which no other agency requires, such for example as lenses for lighthouses, there is no convincing reason why it should not buy the article in question for itself.

But in the case of identical items used by many departments, the problem is quite different. Here coördination in purchasing can certainly serve the interests of economy. Taking into account the numerous possibilities in this connection, Congress has created the Federal Purchasing Board, consisting of representatives from the several establishments, together with a member of the Federal Specifications Board. In practice the Purchasing Board deals with every situation on its merits. It continues the former policy of permitting each agency to buy independently the specialities which it alone uses. But whenever several units of the Government need the same item of supply, the Board tries to get them to pool their purchases and encourages the most appropriate agency among them to buy stock for the rest, distributing it to the others as required. Although the Board can stimulate mutual aid in this fashion, it has no power to purchase materials itself nor can it compel the various establishments to follow a fixed course of action. Hence it must depend on the rationality of its plans to secure united action on their part.

While the Federal Purchasing Board acts as a coördinator for the entire Government, the General Supply Committee, operating under the Secretary of the Treasury, endeavors to secure coöperation in the buying of materials for use in Washington, where a large number of federal offices, many of them having similar needs, are crowded into a small area and furnish an ideal opportunity for an experiment in centralized purchasing. This body has more than advisory duties. It is actually empowered to buy the commodities necessary to meet the common requirements of federal establishments in the District of Columbia, certain field services outside, and the municipality itself. Such agencies must obtain their supplies through the General Supply Committee and reimburse it for its outlays. If the Committee had a generous revolving fund it could act as a merchant at large for the Government and buy supplies under the most favorable market conditions.

If genuine efficiency is to be attained in purchasing, then goods bought must be inspected and tested on delivery, to discover whether they comply with specifications. As a rule each unit of the Government performs this function for itself with respect to its own commodities, but here too beginnings have been made in coöperation. Whenever it appears feasible and advantageous the Purchasing Board makes arrangements to have the most appropriate agency examine goods for others. Thus the Department of Agriculture, besides its regular activities in this relation, inspects meat for some government hospitals as well as for the Army and Navy in a few places. Where local facilities are not adequate, samples submitted with bids and samples of actual deliveries made to any federal department or establishment or to the city of Washington may be sent to the Bureau of Standards for scrutiny. In such instances the Bureau conducts the necessary tests as a part of its regular work and submits its reports on results to the parties concerned.

The storage of purchases is left to the individual agencies, which maintain their own supply depots at strategic points. In certain cases, however, the area coördinators, operating under the Bureau of the Budget described above (p. 311) have effected large savings by promoting common action. Frequently it happens that one federal office can easily provide facilities for a number of neighboring establishments.

To house its numerous activities the Federal Government must construct and operate buildings at various points throughout the United States and in foreign countries as well. Efficiency in this function calls for strategy in the design, location, and management of structures. But often petty politics runs against economy. Every large town wants a handsome post office at a place that will adorn its "civic center" and enhance its real estate values. Whenever an important institution such as a veterans' hospital is to be established, many communities will seek the prize and bring pressure to bear on Congress (p. 178). Not only does the construction of the buildings provide work for artisans in the community but the supplies continually required in operation are business items not to be despised. Hence the distribution of "golden eggs" over the country in the form of federal buildings is an important phase of "practical politics."

In accordance with authorizations by Congress respecting locations and costs, various federal agencies build and maintain structures for their own use. Several branches of the Government with special functions to perform, such as the War Department and the Lighthouse Service, appropriately take charge of their own building programs. On the other hand great economies can be effected by coöperation in the construction and management of standard types of buildings and to reap the advantage of such opportunities the Office of Supervising Architect has been created in the Treasury Department to serve as a common agency. This Office now has jurisdiction over all matters pertaining to the erection and maintenance of certain classes of buildings such as court houses, customs houses, mints, quarantine stations, and marine hospitals.

Subject to the approval of the Secretary of the Treasury, the Office of Supervising Architect begins each project by engaging in the necessary real estate transactions. After it has selected and purchased a suitable site, giving due weight to the needs and requests of the services to be accommodated, it prepares plans for the structure, occasionally with the aid of outside architects called in as consultants. When the designs are finished and approved by the agency which is to use the building in question, contracts are let for construction. Upon the completion of the undertaking, the Office then supplies the furniture, rugs, safety deposit vaults, and similar equipment.

On the transfer of a building to the authorities who are to

occupy it, the work of the Supervising Architect does not come to an end. His Office looks after repairs, maintenance, and operation. It hires janitors, caretakers, and boiler, engine room, and char forces. It assumes responsibility for supplying heat, light, and power and provides for the upkeep of the grounds. In short, the Office continues to act as a kind of landlord for federal tenants and, since there are approximately one thousand six hundred buildings under its control, it is in fact one of the largest real estate managers in the country.

With respect to the actual construction work of the Federal Government, few generalizations are possible. A part of the building program it carries out directly through the agency of technical staffs and labor forces organized under its own auspices. This method has been applied, for example, in connection with the Panama Canal, the Alaskan Railway, various naval craft, and numerous river and harbor improvements. Indeed the army engineers in charge of the last group of enterprises maintain that unless they themselves occasionally build from start to finish they cannot secure exact information on methods and costs and thus exercise proper scrutiny over the portion of the work that is entrusted to private concerns. On the other hand a great deal of federal construction is done by contractors. In this case the appropriate authorities merely prepare plans, receive bids, let contracts, supervise, inspect, and make a final approval. But whether the work is undertaken immediately by the Government or by contractors, certain labor standards described below (p. 500) are enforced as provided by acts of Congress.

CHAPTER XII

Transportation

Except in the brief clauses relating to vessels and post roads, no mention is made in the Constitution of any specific means of transportation. True, authority for regulating interstate and foreign commerce is there but no details are given respecting the objects which come under this head. When the great document was written interest in interstate traffic was concentrated mainly on tariffs and other barriers which had been set up between several states. It was the transaction of selling and shipping goods rather than the wagon or vessel which hauled them or the rates charged for freight that engaged the concern of the Fathers. Transportation equipment, often home-made, was of slight value as compared with the commodities handled.

Since then a revolution has taken place. Commerce now involves vast railway systems, huge terminals, airplanes, expensive ships, steam boiler design, automatic block signals, the electrification of lines, grade-crossing elimination, and many other phases of engineering which have given an amazing significance to mere equipment and operation. Still the all-inclusive phrasing of the constitutional clause regarding commerce has made it possible to shift the emphasis of control, whenever necessary, from goods to carriers, enabling the Federal Government to bring every new means of transportation under its jurisdiction as fast as advances in the arts and pressures for regulation become effective. The railway, the steamship, the motorship, the pipe line, and the airplane have all in turn become subjects of federal surveillance. Words which once sanctioned the abolition of state tariff barriers are now quoted as authority for supervision over the design of steam boilers, the examination of airplane mechanics or pilots, and many other technicalities.

Water Transportation—Inland and Coastal

The Constitution is as silent as the Sphinx about the power of Congress to regulate navigation as such. Indeed, President Jefferson in 1802 thought it necessary to discover a special interpretation in order to build piers for the use of the Navy. In a letter to Albert Gallatin, then Secretary of the Treasury, he explained his line of reasoning: "Although the power to regulate commerce does not give a power to build piers, wharves, open ports, clear the beds of rivers, dig canals . . . yet a power to provide and maintain a navy, is a power to provide receptacles for it, and the places to cover and preserve it." Speaking of lighthouses, Jefferson said in the same communication: "I well remember the opposition . . . to the first act for building a lighthouse. The utility of the thing has sanctioned the infraction. But if on that infraction we build a second, on that second a third, etc., any one of the powers of the Constitution may be made to comprehend every power of the Government." If Jefferson were alive to-day and could see the Panama Canal, the long chain of federal lighthouses, harbor dredging, and iceberg patroling in the North Atlantic, to mention only a few things now approved by the courts or practice, he certainly would be alarmed at the elasticity of the simple prerogative under which most of this work has been accomplished, namely, the power to regulate commerce.

In the period of our history previous to the development of railways, water transportation was of special importance in interstate commerce. Despite Jefferson's misgivings about its legality, great attention was early given by the Federal Government to improving facilities for navigation. The dredging of rivers and lakes was supplemented by the construction of canals under state auspices or by private enterprise. But when railway lines were laid out in every direction, many water routes were abandoned and attention was concentrated mainly on transportation by land.

Once more, however, in our own time, the problem of inland water transportation comes to the front. During the past decade in fact it has taken on a novel aspect. Since our commerce is growing more rapidly than our railway facilities, the development of new routes has become a pressing concern. Carriage by water, especially of bulky freight, is in some circumstances cheaper than by rail and so may act as a regulator of freight rates. Moreover, when planned in relation to railroads, waterways may supplement them and play an important rôle in national economy. With a mileage of waterways in the United States equal to at least one fourth that of the railways and with only one half of it now in use, the urgent question of developing old routes and opening additional routes forms the subject of continual discussion on the part of the President, Congress, and business-men.

On the whole, administrative leadership in the improvement of rivers, lakes, and harbors is assigned to the War Department on the theory that waterways are essential to national defense and that the Army's experience in engineering affairs peculiarly fits it for this function. In carrying out the Government's program, as authorized by Congress, army engineers are constantly at work surveying new routes, supervising the deepening of old channels, and operating completed units.

At the present time the corps of army engineers is engaged in the creation and maintenance of channels in about 125 salt water ports on the Atlantic, the Gulf of Mexico, and the Pacific as well as approximately 70 ports on the Great Lakes. In 1929, at least three hundred projects for the development of inland rivers and other waterways, having a total length of approximately thirty thousand miles, were either completed or under way. Outstanding among these enterprises are the Panama Canal, the Mississippi River Improvement, and the Intracoastal Waterway along the east coast of the United States. The first connects the Atlantic and Pacific oceans through Central America; the second is intended to unite the Great Lakes with New Orleans; and the third designed to enable small craft to travel from Maine to Mexico with a minimum exposure to the sea.

Of the three main developments the Panama Canal, opened in 1914, is of course the most spectacular. By forty-two miles of waterway this canal shortens the distance by ship from New York to San Francisco thousands of miles. Constructed at a cost of three hundred sixty-seven million dollars, exclusive of arrangements for military defense, it stands as a monument to the army engineers who built it. A railway, repair shops, warehouses, drydocks, and other equipment are operated in connection with it, in large part by electricity generated on the spot by water power.

Before the Panama Canal had been open many years a discussion arose over the necessity for an additional channel to handle traffic when the system becomes unduly crowded. A second route, across Nicaragua, has been suggested and, indeed, a treaty between the United States and that country authorizes it; but actual construction has been postponed into the distant future. At the present time the Panama Canal is able to take care of all the ships that appear for transit; as a matter of fact its business is only about forty per cent of its capacity. And that capacity is now materially limited by the water supply available. Whenever a ship passes through the locks a large amount of water is lost in shifting it from one level to another. To meet this situation a new source is in process of development which will make it possible for the management to increase the number of vessels carried through the canal annually to such a point that, according to recent calculations, the normal demands for a hundred years can be met.

On all the various river, harbor, and canal improvements, it is estimated, at least one billion two hundred fifty million dollars was spent during the nineteenth century under the direction of the War Department. And since the beginning of the present century additional millions have been devoted to the same purposes. Notwithstanding this huge outlay and the fine promises of those who have espoused such enterprises, the amount of water-borne traffic is relatively small. In discussing conditions on a single river which had been improved at great cost President Harding publicly declared in 1923: "It is a very discouraging picture to contemplate the expenditure of fifty million dollars of public funds on an inland waterway when the tonnage on that waterway has diminished more than half, while the waterway itself is made better and better year by year. We have either wasted many hundreds of millions in blind folly or have been inexcusably remiss in turning our expenditures to practical account." Referring to the same point, the Secretary of War, John W. Weeks, added that "We should either have a demonstration of the possibility and economic practicability of the utilization of our navigable streams in the interest of the public, or we should stop spending huge sums of money indefinitely on what up to this time appears to be a chimerical project."

In response to such arguments, Congress has enacted legislation for the purpose of showing private citizens what they have missed by not making full use of the facilities furnished to them at such great expense. It has created the Inland Waterways Corporation under the management of the War Department and financed it by authorizing the purchase of fifteen million dollars' worth of stock through appropriations made from time to time, thus vesting outright ownership in the Federal Government. The Corporation operates fleets of vessels engaged in the carrying trade between Minnesota and the Gulf of Mexico as well as along the Gulf from Alabama to New Orleans. In every sense this is a business undertaking for the Corporation charges regular freight rates and maintains terminals as a part of its enterprise.

It was the hope of the promoters of internal improvements that barge operations would serve not only communities located on the shores of the waterways but also distant centers through a union with rail facilities. Thus freight could be delivered by rail to a barge terminal, hauled by boat to a second terminal, and there transferred to another railway for delivery. To insure the assistance of the railroads in developing such traffic, Congress passed a law which permits certain carriers by water to apply to the Interstate Commerce Commission for a certificate of public convenience and necessity requiring coöperation between the two forms of transportation. If the Commission finds the said service to be in the public interest, it must determine the joint rail-water rates between the specified points. The railroads and the water carriers concerned are then to confer for the purpose of deciding on the proportion of the total charge for the transportation of freight in combination which each is to have. If they fail so to agree within 120 days, then the Interstate Commerce Commission is empowered to make the division itself. Under this law the Inland Waterways Corporation is able to obtain rail connections in its pioneering undertaking, and certain private shipping concerns which may follow in its footsteps are assured similar consideration. In some cases the joint rail-water rates established by the Commission are as much as twenty per cent below the all-rail rates.

But if rail and water routes are to be placed on a truly comparable basis the costs of the respective rights of way and general upkeep should be taken into account. While railroads must pay for building and maintaining their tracks, carriers by water are granted free use of the elaborate system created by the Federal Government for their benefit. Congress has definitely provided that, with one exception, no tolls or charges whatever shall be collected from any vessel using federal canals, locks or other improvements in the interest of navigation. In keeping with this principle, the Cape Cod Canal, for several years in private hands, has been purchased by the Government and its former toll charges abolished. Vessels may now pass at will over this expensive route while the public foots the bill through taxation.

The one exception just mentioned is the Panama Canal. Few have ventured to suggest that this gigantic enterprise, built at public expense, should be free as the winds. But in this connection Congress is subject to a specific limitation. By the terms of the Hay-Pauncefote treaty with Great Britain in 1901, it was explicitly provided that there should be no discrimination against other nations in the matter of rates on that canal. Although, despite the treaty, Congress passed a bill granting lower rates to American ships, it was later induced by President Wilson to restore equality of charges.

While, as we have just seen, the waterways of the United States improved and managed by the Federal Government are free and are supported by national taxation, foreigners are not permitted to take easy advantage of the gift. Congress has reserved not only all the inland business but the entire coastwise trade as well to American vessels. It has expressly forbidden the carriage of freight between the ports of the continental United States by foreign ships. It merely permits them to stop at two or more American ports in succession for the purpose of discharging cargoes consigned from abroad or taking on supplies such as food and water. The carriage of passengers between points within the United States by foreign vessels is practically forbidden, because a fine of $200 for each person so transported makes the operation unprofitable. This is not all. The full protection of American shipping requires one more step. The ports of Cuba, Canada, and Mexico are in close proximity to our coasts and if it were legally possible for a foreign vessel to carry persons or goods from one United States port to another by a circuitous route touching some neighboring country, the American coastwise monopoly would be subject to considerable competition. This evasion Congress has forestalled by declaring it a violation of the above law for a foreign ship to carry passengers or freight from one United States port to another by way of any foreign port; for example, from New York to New Orleans *via* Havana.

As a direct outgrowth of the expansion of American shipping during the World War, Congress, through the Merchant Marine Act of 1920, widened the scope of the coastwise laws to include our insular territories and possessions. But as an offset the President of the United States was given power to permit, by proclamation, the transport of goods and passengers between these islands and the United States by foreign vessels until such time as American ships can offer adequate service. As things stood early in 1930 a vessel flying the flag of a country with which the United States had a commercial treaty could freely engage in carrying goods between our continental ports and the Philippine Islands, the Virgin Islands, and the Canal Zone. Even with these exceptions over fifty per cent of American tonnage is engaged in the coasting trade under the general protection afforded by the Government.

In connection with the improvement of waterways, the Federal Government must control all the works of man which might run counter to the interests of navigation. This activity is carried on by the War Department and involves supervision over the erection of dams, dikes, bridges, and causeways which span the navigable waters of the United States. Before construction can be started on such an undertaking, approval of the plans must be obtained from the Department and in the case of waterways which do not lie entirely in a single state Congress must add its consent. Although primarily concerned with preventing the obstruction of traffic by bridges built under its jurisdiction, Congress has seized the opportunity to regulate the use of these structures after completion. More specifically, it has reserved the right to fix tolls, construct telephone or telegraph lines, and even require a railroad to permit the trains of other companies to pass over its bridge. If the tolls charged are found to be unjust and unreasonable, the Secretary of War may change them.

While bridges and dams which span a waterway may entirely prevent the movement of vessels, a condition almost as bad from the standpoint of the navigator can be created by encroachments which merely narrow waterways. For the purpose of preventing anarchic growth of this character Congress has enacted special legislation. Excavations, the filling or alteration of channels, or the erection of piers, wharves, dolphins, booms, and other structures may be undertaken only in accordance with plans approved by the Chief of Engineers and the Secretary of War, supplemented by authorization by Congress. When he finds it necessary, the Secretary may even establish absolute harbor lines beyond which no piers, wharves or other obstructions shall extend.

Besides providing safeguards against fixed objects which interfere with navigation, the Federal Government takes other precautions to keep channels clear and safe. The dumping of any materials into navigable waters which may menace vessels is controlled by regulations of the War Department. Thus oil, which might be set aflame by a cigarette or lighted match and destroy ships in the neighborhood, cannot be discharged on coastal or inland waters except under special rules. Furthermore, the custom of floating logs down rivers to sawmills is supervised in a similar fashion.

Such regulations appear to be entirely reasonable if the interests of transportation are regarded as paramount. But there are other uses for water, and a well-rounded economy must take all of them into consideration if far-sighted planning is to occur. To obtain water for great cities, streams are often tapped far back in the hills, near their sources, and pipe lines carry millions of gallons daily to teeming multitudes. Thus the supply of lakes and rivers may be diverted, sinking their levels and halting the passage of boats. Which shall have precedence, shipping interests or a metropolis that must have more water for its expanding population? Here the industrial development of the country has brought about a clash of forces which cannot be dismissed with a wave of the hand.

That such conflicts are not mere fiction is illustrated by the controversy respecting the Great Lakes which has been a fruitful source of litigation and comment. To avoid the necessity of spending huge sums of money for a waste disposal plant, Chicago adopted many years ago the simple expedient of dumping its sewage into a drainage canal, there to be diluted by water taken from Lake Michigan. In time the withdrawal of enormous quantities of water from the Great Lakes for this process had far-reaching effects. According to the Master appointed by the Supreme Court to study the problem, Lake Michigan and Lake Huron were lowered six inches and Lake Erie and Lake Ontario five inches by the additional drain on their resources. As a result in a single year over four million tons of cargo had to be left behind by steamers on account of the decline in the water level. After tolerating this diversion for a while, seven American states and Canada at length raised a protest against the encroachment on their rights. Finally at the close of a long litigation the Supreme Court held that the interests of navigation should take precedence over the mere desire of a city to save expenses. Accordingly the Court issued a decree ordering Chicago to reduce the amount of water drawn from the lakes as soon as suitable plants for the disposal of sewage can be erected. Cases of this sort may be expected in increasing numbers as competition in the uses of water grows. It is evident even from this brief and imperfect survey that here is a problem for nation planning on a large scale—a problem involving the best use of water resources for transportation, domestic, agricultural, and industrial purposes.

And the subject should not be left without reference to the doubtful utility of many of the inland water projects. Beyond question hundreds of millions of dollars have been wasted in enterprises of this kind and few if any really pay their way in an economic sense, that is, if all construction and maintenance charges were reckoned in the fixing of rates. Why then are so many undertaken?

The answer is not simple but the activities of powerful interests account for some of them. Alleging the requirements of national defense and eager to keep in practice, Army engineers are usually ready to approve almost any kind of river and harbor improvement. Farmers, manufacturers, and other shippers, naturally seeking the lowest possible freight rates, regard waterways opened at public expense as a means of creating competition with railways and forcing them to reduce their charges for carrying goods. Chambers of commerce in towns and cities which are located on real or potential water routes lend vigorous support to federal activity in this sphere, for it means large outlays of money in their respective communities and brings additional transport facilities. Finally innumerable dredging companies, which make large profits from federal contracts, for obvious reasons insist that the good work should go forward. Under the impact of these forces, members of Congress vote for costly undertakings that never could be justified on mere grounds of practical economy.

If the whole question were approached on its merits, with an eye solely to national defense in the strict sense of the word and to securing efficient transportation at the lowest possible cost, all factors considered, then numerous projects now under way would doubtless be abandoned and few would be undertaken in the future. At all events the subject calls for a searching examination with respect to national requirements scientifically measured—a difficult task where so many interested parties are concerned in the outcome. But a beginning is being made by the War Department for it announced in the summer of 1930 that its Corps of Engineers, under authorization of Congress, was prosecuting with vigor a comprehensive study of nearly all the waterways in the country for the purpose of working out a complete national plan in this branch of transportation.

Water Transportation—the Foreign Trade

In the case of shipping on the high seas, as well as inland water transportation, other factors than mere economical freight rates and efficient services enter into consideration.

There was a time, in the days of wooden ships, when American shipbuilders and masters could hold their own with their rivals in every part of the world. And after the beginning of steam navigation, the Federal Government subsidized American vessels for a brief period to assist them in meeting foreign competition. But on the eve of the Civil War, under the pressure of agricultural interests, Congress abolished these aids to private enterprise and most of the carrying trade between the United States and other countries passed into foreign hands. In spite of insistent demands Congress long refused to renew the practice of giving public support to transoceanic shipping.

The World War, however, drew the Federal Government into a new and gigantic undertaking in this connection, one which expanded our vision from the narrow strip of waters along our shores to encompass the oceans of the globe and all its markets. When the great European conflict broke out, the United States found itself in the presence of a crisis —a dearth of ships to carry its produce to foreign markets. Thus it happened that farmers as well as manufacturers felt the pinch. Confronted by a real dilemma the Democratic party, which more than half a century before had helped to sweep the American flag from the high seas by withdrawing subsidies, laid aside its theories. In 1916 Congress created the Shipping Board and endowed it with enormous powers, including authority to purchase, construct, operate, and lease merchant ships. After America entered the war, the Emergency Fleet Corporation was established under the supervision of the Shipping Board and, with the aid of lavish grants from the public treasury, ships were built with a speed that astonished the world. Within a few years the merchant marine of the United States rivaled in tonnage that of Great Britain, the mistress of the seas.

When the war closed, leaving the Government with a huge fleet of idle vessels on its hands, American shipping interests saw an opportunity to expand their carrying trade on the high seas. "Ship under the American flag" became a battle cry for builders and operators alike. But private business apparently could not make it pay. Competing countries were taxing themselves in order to subsidize the ships of their nations, enabling them to steam to every continent loaded with freight and passengers, often on ventures which brought no true economic returns. During the period from 1880 to 1927, excluding war years and postwar programs based upon naval exigencies, the national governments of the United Kingdom, France, Germany, Italy, Japan, and Spain expended approximately nine hundred sixty million dollars out of public funds in various forms of support for merchant shipping. So, despite the evident opposition of popular opinion in this country to government subsidies, it was now insisted that the American shipper must either get help from the federal treasury or succumb to foreign competition. The aid was asked and finally received. It is true, direct grants in money were denied by Congress but other forms of assistance were given.

That Congress is now whole-heartedly in sympathy with the efforts of American shippers to establish the flag on the high seas is evident from the phrasing of the opening section of the Merchant Marine Act of 1920 which still stands as fundamental law. "It is necessary," runs the language of the Act, "for the national defense and for the proper growth of its foreign and domestic commerce that the United States shall have a merchant marine of the best equipped and most suitable types of vessels sufficient to carry the greater portion of its commerce and serve as a naval or military auxiliary in time of war or national emergency, ultimately to be owned and operated privately by citizens of the United States; and it is declared to be the policy of the United States to do whatever may be necessary to develop and encourage the maintenance of such a merchant marine."

From this declaration it is plain that Congress had two objects in mind when formulating its statement of policy. Federal aid to shipping is intended to promote both commerce and national defense. Now the needs of commerce are fairly tangible and may be roughly estimated; they call for a merchant marine sufficient to meet specific demands—a physical plant that can be constructed to somewhat precise calculations. But what about national defense? If crises like the World War should occur again, would the people of the United States be called upon once more to feed and munition many nations and to produce ships in such quantities that no other country could destroy them fast enough to cut the flow of American goods? Would American ships, instead of crossing merely three thousand miles of ocean, have to cross ten thousand miles? Are the American people to develop, for national defense, a merchant fleet of a size capable of coping with any eventuality, however grave, on the assumption that there is no other way to face the indefinite, unforeseen possibilities of the future? Must they keep this fleet plowing the seas with half-empty hulls in order to have it ready for any possible emergency no matter how remote? If that is the goal, can American taxpayers reach it without breaking their backs? At all events planning for the use of merchant ships in national defense involves preparation for an eventuality which cannot be measured. Hence in the last analysis it is not planning but guessing.

Whatever may be the conclusion under this head Congress, by the Merchant Marine Act of 1920, continued the Shipping Board and empowered that body to establish, after careful study, any pioneer lines, either foreign or domestic, which in its judgment would be in the best interests of American commerce. On these routes the Board was authorized to operate its own ships as a public enterprise. But in accordance with the general desire to "get the government out of business," it was provided that such undertakings should be eventually turned over to private capitalists. Whenever it seems practical to do so, the Board either sells its vessels outright or leases them to American companies that guarantee the maintenance of particular services. Only lines for which private capital will not assume the risk are kept under government operation, in other words, unprofitable ventures.

Since the ultimate withdrawal of the Government from the shipping business requires the actual sale of its fleet rather than leasing, its general methods of disposal must be noted. To prevent undue foreign competition the Board is forbidden to sell ships to aliens unless it is established that such vessels are unsuited to American needs and that no demand for the same is forthcoming from American citizens. Moreover the Merchant Marine Act of 1920 expressly stipulated that the sale of ships, whether to Americans or to aliens, must be "consistent with good business methods." In practice this has meant that the Shipping Board sells vessels at extremely low figures, partly with a view to offsetting the higher wages paid to American crews and enabling the owners to compete in the foreign trade. "We bought twenty ships from them at ten dollars a deadweight ton," declared a San Francisco shipping man, "while the British and Japanese purchased from their governments at about three times that price. So our interest charges have been only about one-third of theirs." Thus the Goverment assumed the burden of pioneering and then sold its lines cheaply whenever they showed profits attractive to private enterprise. The flag was put back on the sea but at a heavy cost.

Eleven years after the war had ended the Government was operating ships directly on a considerable scale. On August 21, 1929, the Shipping Board owned 250 vessels in active service on eighteen lines. Owing, however, to the mail subsidies authorized in 1928 (p. 392), it is taken for granted that these will pass with increasing rapidity into private hands. Besides its vessels in action, the Shipping Board on that date had the largest tied-up fleet in the world. Some of these idle craft have been burnt merely to get rid of them while others have been sold at nominal prices for junk. Of necessity the process of retiring from business an organization that controlled at one time or another 2,536 vessels is a slow one and in the circumstances expensive.

Notwithstanding the various favors received, the American concerns which bought vessels from the Shipping Board declared that they were still unable to hold their own in many instances, especially as traffic tended to flow heavily to foreign companies possessing more modern equipment. At a conference of American shipping men held in Washington resolutions were adopted to the effect that "our overseas merchant fleet is being rendered obsolete by the rapid march of science and invention, which has completely revolutionized the manner of vessel propulsion since our ships were built." But American construction costs were double those on the Clyde where a huge volume of tonnage was being steadily turned out for Great Britain. If American yards were to keep our merchant fleets up-to-date, it was contended, drastic action had to be taken.

To meet the new situation Congress, by the Merchant Marine Acts of 1920 and 1928, created a revolving loan fund amounting to two hundred fifty million dollars. This money the Shipping Board is authorized to lend as it sees fit, up to seventy-five per cent of the value of the work completed at any date, to American citizens for the construction of vessels equipped with "the most modern, the most efficient, and the most economical engines, machinery, and commercial appliances," or for reconditioning older vessels. Such ships must be intended for use on services which the Shipping Board deems desirable or necessary. Moreover to protect American interests conditions are attached which require the work to be done in American yards and the finished vessels to be kept under American registry for not less than twenty years. In addition, the loans continue at a low rate of interest only as long as the ships in question are employed in the foreign competitive trade; the moment they become idle or are transferred to the coastwise sphere, already an American monopoly, the rates of interest rise from approximately three and one half per cent to five and a quarter per cent or even higher.

Obviously the purchase of vessels from the Federal Government at a low price and the building of ships with the aid of favorable loans reduce the running expenses of American lines by cutting their annual interest charges. Still American shipowners insist that with this help alone they are not able to cope with their foreign competitors.

In order to assure them profitable operation, the Federal Government, with the passage of the Merchant Marine Act of 1928, began to follow in the footsteps of the other great maritime powers by offering lucrative mail agreements to American ships which meet certain standards. Under the new Act, the Postmaster General may award contracts to the lowest bidder for the carriage of mails to all ports except those covered by coastwise shipping laws (p. 382). But instead of paying a certain sum for each pound of mail carried, as formerly, he allows all vessels operating under such arrangements a fixed amount for every mile traveled on the outbound voyage from the United States regardless of the quantity of mail aboard. The maximum rates which may be granted vary with the tonnage and speed of the ship, running as high as twelve dollars per nautical mile. Provided in this manner with a definite guarantee, shipowners can compute in advance just how much money they will get for a certain number of voyages and need no longer worry about fluctuations in mail tonnage. According to Commissioner Poole of the United States Shipping Board, the contracts of 1929 offered the most lucrative mail subsidy in the world.

Certain conditions, however, limit the application of the law. Thus a vessel, to be entitled to a contract under its terms, must be built of steel and propelled by machinery. It must also be on the American registry and owned by American citizens during the entire life of the agreement. Beginning on February 1, 1928, all new eligible vessels must be ordered from American yards; but foreign-built craft in operation before that date are allowed the benefits of the law so that the owners of steamers taken from Germany during the war may not be excluded. A further significant provision requires that acceptable ships on which work has been started since the enactment of the measure must either be "constructed, according to plans and specifications approved by the Secretary of the Navy, with particular reference to economical conversion into an auxiliary naval vessel, or . . . be otherwise useful to the United States in time of national emergency."

As a supplementary aid to shippers, the Merchant Marine Act of 1928 permits any naval officer of the United States on the active list to volunteer for service on board vessels running under mail contracts. On an agreement with the owner or master he may be assigned to such a vessel by the Secretary of the Navy, receive half pay from the Government, and accept any additional sum which the shipping concern is willing to allow him. While on this duty he cannot be required to assume any responsibilities except in connection with the merchant marine. Besides thus offering assistance in paying the salaries of officers, the law provides that until 1932 only fifty per cent of the crew on merchant ships need be American citizens. In other words, for the time being, American shipping companies may employ cheaper alien labor, thus making a saving in wages which helps them in competing with foreign vessels that have the same class of seamen.

No matter how much time and effort are spent by Congress in the promotion of American shipping on the high seas, its work may largely be in vain unless some means is devised for preventing discriminations against American vessels on their arrival in foreign harbors—to which, of course, federal protection cannot extend. In extreme cases such discriminations may deny American ships the right to enter on any terms or require them to pay as the price of admission a "tonnage tax" all out of proportion to that laid on vessels of the same nationality as the port. As it happens, this is a game that two can play. Since the ships of any country which penalizes American vessels must ordinarily come into American waters, the Government of the United States may reciprocate by levying exorbitant duties on them. In fact Congress has authorized the collection of a tax for this purpose running as high as two dollars per ton on each ship entering an American port. It has, however, made the whole arrangement flexible by allowing the President full discretion in the matter. Thus our tonnage taxes on foreign ships may rise and fall in response to the treatment meted out to Americans in other waters.

So far we have studied the activities of the Government which relate to the creation of the physical plant employed in water transportation. There remains for consideration a further function—the expedition of business through aids to the navigation of vessels. By helping to make smooth the path of the mariner the Government pays big dividends in saving lives, ships, and time. It is to this phase that we now turn.

Waterborne traffic faces two problems in operation. In the first place, the river, lake, or ocean bed above which a vessel floats is entirely hidden from view, if the water is more than a few feet deep; and the navigator must feel his way much like a blind man, unless he has other guidance than that afforded by the surface over which he moves. Amid the best of circumstances there is always a possibility of stranding or running into some sharp object buried out of sight. In the second place, a delicate and swift manipulation of large vessels is impossible; they are clumsy and will not respond immediately to the wishes of the pilot. It is necessary, therefore, to map rocks, shoals, and other obstructions to navigation, which lie partly or wholly submerged, and mark them in such a way as to give vessels ample warning about perils lying in their path. If properly made, these signposts may serve to announce geographical positions as well as dangers ahead.

On American waters the Federal Government, through the Bureau of Lighthouses, has established many conspicuous markers for the use of navigators. These take the form of floating objects anchored in place or fixed towers, depending on local conditions. In the daytime they can be identified at long distances by their shape and color design. Just as the pedestrian becomes aware that a barber shop is near when he sees a pole with red and white spirals, so pilots and

Courtesy of the United States Bureau of Lighthouses

A SIGNPOST OF THE WAVES. THE NANTUCKET SHOALS LIGHTSHIP RIDING AT ANCHOR AS A GUIDE TO SHIPPING.

Courtesy of the Inland Waterways Corporation

A Practical Demonstration in Water Transportation: Boats of the Inland Waterways Corporation Plowing the Mississippi (*See* P. 380).

navigating officers recognize in certain types of government symbols the presence of submerged rocks, shallow waters, and deep channels leading into harbors. To the trained observer a sign may say in effect: "Welcome stranger, this is Diamond Shoals as plotted on your map. Pick up the string of buoys just beyond and follow them into port."

In darkness or in fog, however, markers cannot be readily discerned by the unaided eye. To overcome this difficulty the Lighthouse Bureau has placed lights at the more important positions. By employing various devices such as revolving or flashing lights, with different colors or timed to special schedules, it has established a code of signals through which each symbol may be distinguished from its neighbors at night. But lights will not always penetrate fog far enough to afford safety to the mariner. Then the ear is brought into play. Fog horns sending various combinations of long and short blasts through the air and submarine bells ringing underneath the surface of the water serve as announcers when the weather is "thick."

Having coped reasonably well with the difficulties involved in conveying warnings and information by day and by night, in clear weather and foul, to vessels near the coast, the Lighthouse Bureau then attacked the problem of supplying the same service to ships far out at sea. Owing to the curvature of the earth lights are of no avail for long distances. Sounds likewise are limited in range. But with the development of the radio-compass and the radio-beacon, the last great goal in providing guidance to navigators was reached. To-day ships may obtain their position at any time, anywhere, by directing a wireless inquiry to the radio-compass stations of the Lighthouse Bureau or the United States Navy or by picking up radio-beacon signals sent continuously as warnings to all mariners, day and night, in sunshine, fog, and storm. Slight indeed is the excuse if a navigator loses his way on the water in this age of scientific miracles.

It is not even necessary for the navigator to charge his memory with the significance of the various shapes, lights, sounds, and radio signals which guard the coast. For his convenience official guide-books and maps are prepared by the Coast and Geodetic Survey, the Navy, and the Lighthouse Bureau. In these publications he can readily find full descriptions of all marking and guiding devices, in every region, and their precise location and meaning. Thus with the aid of technical works a total stranger can soon become almost as much at home in American waters as the oldest sailor; tramp steamers have as much help as the finest ocean liners.

In its desire to furnish the mariner with every bit of information that he ordinarily needs, the Federal Government finds itself drawn out of the field of relatively easy operations, such as the mapping and marking of shoals, reefs, capes, or islands, into a realm of fluctuations where changing tides and shifting icebergs create uncertainty. Here the tides call for special attention on account of their place in the strategy of navigation. If the water-level in ports and channels remained constant throughout the year, government charts showing the mean depth of harbors would afford sufficient guidance to seamen. But the tides ebb and flow, lowering and raising the level. If a navigator had no advance knowledge of their movements, he would be unable to tell whether he could get into port and out again without the labor of making soundings and incurring the risk of stranding.

To supply this advance knowledge, the Coast and Geodetic Survey now prepares and publishes elaborate tables showing the estimated heights of tides in all the important ports of the world for given periods in the future. With this statistical aid shippers can plan ahead, arranging for their boats to come in or go out when the tide is most favorable. Once human beings labored with paper and pencil to make tide predictions, but now the task is performed by a machine called "the Great Brass Brain," developed and used by the Federal Government—a contrivance weighing approximately twenty-five hundred pounds, about eleven feet long, two feet wide, and six feet high, which takes account of thirty-seven factors. A massive robot with a labyrinth of cranks, gears, sliding frames, and precision chains, it is in reality a super-computing machine of wonder-working capacity. It not only indicates the time and height of high and low water on dials but, in addition, traces a curve showing the same facts on paper.

While tides may be predicted with reasonable certainty, the exact location of icebergs or derelicts cannot. In coping with these perils government vessels operated by the Coast Guard play a game of hide and seek that takes them over wide reaches of the Atlantic Ocean. In the spring and early summer, particularly, they cruise in the North locating icebergs and icefields that might menace navigation, reporting the drift and position of dangerous floes by radio. A direct outgrowth of the *Titanic* disaster of 1912—the foundering of a giant liner with frightful loss of life after a collision with an iceberg, this service is carried on by the American Government on the basis of an international agreement under which other nations engaged in sea commerce help to bear the expenses. Although the work is undoubtedly in the interests of safety, it must be remembered that vessels can steam south of the ice zone and avoid its perils if they wish. Such a course would merely lengthen the voyage and add to the running expenses. There is ample warrant, therefore, for regarding the ice patrol largely as an aid to commerce rather than a measure of safety. Besides keeping watch for icebergs Coast Guard vessels also search for derelicts for the purpose of destroying these floating monsters of the sea.

Since the present chapter is concerned primarily with the commercial aspects of transportation, the problems of security for life and limb arising out of the use of modern machinery lie outside its scope. Safety is a matter of such vital importance in connection with the growth of dangerous appliances that the activities of the Government in this relation deserve to be grouped in a separate place in order that their significance may be properly emphasized. To be sure, lighthouses, radio-compasses, and iceberg patrols present aspects which come under this head but their contributions to the promotion and expedition of commerce are so fundamental that they seem to be associated with harbor improvements and ship subsidies rather than with safety measures strictly considered. Other federal functions, such as the provision of scientific standards and the examination of vessels, lifeboat equipment, officers, and crew, carried on primarily with reference to safety, are described below (pp. 595 ff.).

Land Transportation—Railways, Express, and Pipe Lines

It is sometimes assumed by superficial thinkers that the Federal Government has made no great contributions to the development of railways, but merely interferes with them by regulating their rates and services. It is true that many lines, especially those along the Atlantic Seaboard connecting the larger cities, were built by private capital at its own risk, but to the railways of the West and Southwest the Federal Government and state and local governments made enormous gifts for promotion in the form of land, subsidies, underwritings, and special favors. To the Pacific railroad companies alone, Congress granted more than one hundred million acres of land along their tracks, the free use of timber and stone for construction, and financial support in federal credits running upwards of sixty million dollars. A high railway official once estimated that the value of the federal lands turned over by Congress to the Northern Pacific Company was sufficient "to build the entire railroad to Puget Sound, fit out a fleet of sailing vessels and steamers for the China and India trade, and leave a surplus that would roll up into the millions." On a conservative reckoning, the Federal Government had assigned to railway promoters previous to 1872 an area of land "almost equal to the New England states, New York, and Pennsylvania combined; nineteen different states had voted sums aggregating two hundred million dollars for the same purpose," to say nothing of the money supplied by municipalities. Moreover Congress to a limited extent lent collateral assistance by remitting duties on railway materials imported from abroad. While aiding in construction, the Federal Government and the state governments at first gave railroad proprietors a generous freedom in manipulating and operating as they saw fit.

In these circumstances numerous abuses appeared. Stocks and bonds were issued in enormous amounts often without any proper basis in material values; bankruptcies were frequent, ruining thousands of innocent investors and enriching inside speculators; in some cases it was more profitable to "wreck" companies than to operate railways. The highest possible rates were charged on the theory that the companies should collect "what the traffic will bear." There were also discriminations in many forms. Freight rates were made high to one shipper and low to another, enabling the beneficiary to ruin his competitor. Frequently the money paid in freight rates by favored shippers was returned to them in part in the shape of secret "rebates." Some shippers found it easy to obtain freight cars when they needed them; others met with delays and reports of "car shortages." There were differences in terminal charges for switching, storage, lighterage, and similar services. As the "long haul" was more profitable than the short one, railway companies sometimes charged less for carrying freight to distant cities than to those nearer at hand. There was constant complaint, often not well founded, that the railways favored certain ports or sections at the expense of others. To make matters worse, companies were competing and fighting among themselves, by no means always for the permanent good of the communities they were supposed to serve. Hence there arose transportation difficulties of great magnitude which demanded public consideration.

These abuses were widely known and advertised, but Congress did not move until after the states had begun to close in on the railways by stringent legislation fixing rates and charges. It was not until 1885, when the demand for reform forced action, that the Senate appointed a committee to investigate the whole railway situation. The report of this committee produced such a furor that two years later Congress enacted an interstate commerce law forbidding certain practices and providing for the regulation of others under the direction of an Interstate Commerce Commission. The original statute, the amendatory and supplementary measures, the Esch-Cummins Transportation Act of 1920, the decisions of the courts touching the subject, and the orders of the Commission constitute a formidable body of law which can only be briefly sketched here.

The administration of legislation respecting common carriers is vested in the Interstate Commerce Commission, which is entirely independent of all other agencies of the Federal Government. The Commission, consisting of eleven members appointed by the President and Senate for terms of seven years, is a quasi-judicial body in that it hears complaints, issues orders, and makes decisions. In conducting inquiries it is aided by a large staff of accountants, engineers, and expert investigators.

As things now stand federal control is applied to concerns engaged in transporting passengers and freight, or pumping oil through pipe lines, and to sleeping-car, telephone, telegraph, cable, and wireless enterprises (p. 434). All their business which is interstate in its nature comes within the purview of the Commission.

A part of the law is negative in character and a part is positive. Common carriers are forbidden to issue free passes except under severe restrictions; they cannot grant rebates, drawbacks, and special rates, thus making lower charges to some persons than to others for the same service; competing lines are forbidden to combine, pool their receipts, and distribute among themselves the profits of such an operation—save under the strict supervision of the Commission as provided in the Act of 1920. They cannot give any undue or unreasonable preference to any person, company, corporation, or locality. They are not allowed to transport any commodity in which they have a direct property interest, except timber and its products—a provision intended to prevent a combination of railways with manufacturing or mining corporations.

On the positive side, the law requires all rates for services to be just and reasonable. The accounts of common carriers must be kept according to uniform principles prescribed by the Commission. Companies must print and keep open for public inspection schedules showing rates, fares, and charges for transportation and they cannot change such rates without notice to the Commission. They must comply with the terms of the law respecting safety provisions, hours of labor for employees, and compensation for employees injured in the course of duty (p. 500). Finally they must render annual reports to the Commission showing their exact financial status and the nature of their operations.

In the enforcement of these principles the Interstate Commerce Commission exercises extensive powers. It is required to investigate the manner in which business is conducted by carriers coming under its jurisdiction; and on its request any district attorney of the United States must prosecute, in the proper court, offenders against the law. The Commission can summon witnesses and compel the production of books, papers, and other documents relating to matters under investigation. Any person, corporation, body politic, or municipal organization complaining of anything done or omitted by a common carrier, contrary to law, may apply to the Commission by a petition stating the facts, and the Commission must thereupon make an inquiry into the allegations. After a full hearing on such a complaint it may thereupon determine and prescribe just and reasonable rates and charges for the services rendered by the common carrier in question, as well as fair and proper regulations and practices. Without its approval railroads cannot isssue long-term securities, purchase or build extensions, or abandon old lines. Its orders are subject to review, however, by federal courts.

Exceedingly difficult in application is the provision that the rates of common carriers must be just and reasonable. What criterion is to be applied in passing upon the justice and reasonableness of any particular set of charges? Fundamental to the answer of that question is the stipulation of the Fifth Amendment of the Constitution to the effect that no person shall be deprived of life, liberty, or property without due process of law and that private property cannot be taken for public use without just compensation. Under repeated decisions of the Supreme Court, rates for transportation cannot be fixed by the Government at a point so low as to make it impossible for the carrier affected to earn a fair return on the value of its property. But what is that value? Cost of construction, cost of reproduction at present prices, amount of money put into the enterprise as a prudent investment, amount of stocks and bonds outstanding against it? For a long time no definite attempt was made to meet this issue, but finally in 1913 Congress instructed the Interstate Commerce Commission to make a physical valuation of the railways under its jurisdiction with a view to establishing a positive base for rate-making. The task has now been practically completed with respect to the major lines, but the results of its findings are in doubt.

This uncertainty is clouded by an opinion rendered in 1929 by the Supreme Court of the United States, in the O'Fallon rate case, which held that the Interstate Commerce Commission must take cognizance of many factors in the valuation of a railway, including reproduction cost, especially when attempting to recapture profits in excess of six per cent earned by any particular road (p. 405). In this decision no effort was made, however, to determine how much weight should be given to reproduction cost; indeed the Court held that such a determination "is not the matter before us." If, in a given case, the Interstate Commerce Commission should consider that reproduction cost is of little or no significance, would that be "due" weight? The only answer afforded by the ruling of the Court is that "no doubt there are some, perhaps many, railroads the ultimate value of which should be placed far below the sum necessary for reproduction." In other words, the whole question of valuation was left hanging in the air for the future to settle.

In illustrating the confusion thus created Mr. Justice Stone declared, in a dissenting opinion, that if full recognition were given to reproduction cost in making rates then "the railroads of the country having in 1919 a reproduction cost or value of nineteen billion dollars would now have a value of forty billion dollars and we should arrive at the economic paradox that the present value of the railroads is far in excess of any amount on which they could earn a return." This paradox appears all the more startling when it is remembered that, since the opening of the Panama Canal, the renewed effort to stimulate inland waterways, and the advent of the motor truck, railroads have often appealed to the Commission for the right to reduce rates to meet the new menaces. If even now competition is sharp enough to call for a cut in rail rates, then it is difficult to see how they can be raised to provide earnings on a valuation that includes high reproduction costs.

The problems confronting the Commission in the matter of rates are complicated by the fact that each state has the power to regulate railway rates and services *within* its borders. This is not a mere theory. All the states have enacted elaborate laws pertaining to railways and most of them have set up commissions with more or less drastic authority over intrastate business. Yet it is not easy to say when shipments are wholly within a state and when they affect interstate commerce. For example, can a state, through its railway commission, lower the rates on freight to some cities within its borders and raise them to other points still within its borders but close to cities in another state? A case of this character came up in 1914 involving the attempt of Texas to discriminate against Shreveport, Louisiana, in favor of Dallas and Houston; and in an important decision the Supreme Court of the United States declared that the federal Interstate Commerce Commission had the right to regulate even rates within a state when they clearly caused discrimination in interstate commerce.

Still more noteworthy was the case raised by Wisconsin, supported by forty-two other states, in 1922, dealing with the action of the Interstate Commerce Commission in increasing railway rates with a view to securing a "fair return" to the companies under the federal Transportation Act of 1920. Taking an independent position, Wisconsin declined to raise rates on intrastate business as ordered by the Commission. Clearly the purpose of the Act would be defeated if each state insisted on keeping rates down within its jurisdiction, because interstate travelers could buy new tickets on crossing state boundaries and many shippers could avoid higher federal rates by a careful routing of goods. Moreover, low intrastate charges would reduce the revenues of the railway companies and make necessary higher interstate rates to offset the loss. Accordingly under orders of the Commission and a decision of the Supreme Court, states were compelled to make their local rates conform to the schedules fixed under federal authority. In short, Congress can regulate local or intrastate rates insofar as they affect interstate business. Where is the dividing line? Questions of this kind, constant controversies between state and national authorities, the conflicting and confused regulations of states, and the increasingly national character of transportation have led to the demand that the railway system of America be made national in operation and control.

Although the railway problem has been in politics for half a century and law after law has been passed with a view to solving it, no satisfactory disposition of the issue has been reached. The question is constantly agitated. Some railway companies are earning a large return on a generous capitalization—on the whole there has been general improvement since 1920; some have paid no dividends for years; others are bankrupt and in the hands of receivers. Farmers and shippers occasionally clamor for still lower freight rates, and from time to time labor makes an appeal for higher wages. To make matters worse, many small companies, especially the subsidiaries to trunk lines, find it increasingly difficult to meet the competition of the automobile and motor truck.

In this state of affairs there is much difference of opinion among railway managers and their critics. The strong railroads that are making money want to be let alone; while the weaker concerns demand increased rates or financial support of some kind either from the Government or from the larger companies which they feed. Critics, on the other hand, assert that if the "water" were squeezed out of railway stocks and bonds and their capitalization reduced to an actual physical value then they could all earn a reasonable income without any change in rates. But little light can be obtained from such controversies.

Broadly speaking, two solutions of the railway problem are before the country. There is, in the first place, the prescription of government ownership; whether desirable or not, it is at present outside the sphere of practical politics. In the second place, there is the proposal to consolidate the various lines into a few great systems subject to government control and regulation.

For some time this has been the prevailing tendency. Indeed the Transportation Act of 1920 has given a decided impetus to the movement. It expressly authorized companies to pool their earnings from freight and divide the proceeds and to effect certain combinations among themselves under the supervision of the Commission. It also instructed the Commission to work out a plan for the union of all the great railways into a limited number of systems—an order fulfilled in 1929 by the presentation of a general program for consolidation. These provisions looking to unification were then supplemented by the so-called "re-capture clause" which stipulated that one half of the earnings of each company in excess of six per cent on its capital shall be placed into a revolving fund to be used by the Commission in making loans and otherwise furnishing financial assistance to railways. As a radical departure from previous concepts of policy, this requirement was attacked on constitutional grounds, but it was finally sustained by the Supreme Court. The way has been cleared, therefore, for unification, in spite of strong opposition, and the operation is in process.

While railway consolidation has been moving at a slow pace, unity has actually been attained in the railway express business. During the World War the four leading express concerns were combined into the American Railway Express Company, given a virtual monopoly, and placed under the supervision of the Director of Railways. When federal management was terminated after the return of peace, the Company was permitted to continue operation for a fixed period in accordance with a system of uniform contracts with the railroads. On the expiration of this term in 1929, the participating railway companies took advantage of an option to acquire the entire enterprise.

Under an arrangement then effected, the Railway Express Agency was formed by the leading railroads, with control over nearly ninety-eight per cent of the express traffic of the country. Each of the companies taking part in the scheme now holds stock in the new concern and receives a share of the earnings proportioned to the amount of express business which it transacts. Like the railways, the Express Agency is subject to regulation by the Interstate Commerce Commission, but its enormous power and the complexity of its activities make government scrutiny far from easy.

In dealing with the railway and express business we have considered those forms of land transportation which depend upon the use of wheeled vehicles. But that is not the only type subject to the Interstate Commerce Commission. Its jurisdiction also extends to a business in which such instrumentalities do not play a part. With the expansion of the petroleum fields during the past century, engineers early began to realize the possibilities that lay in the carriage of crude oil, and the allied product of natural gas, through pipes rather than by rail or truck. The development of the idea was highly successful, for by 1928 there were ninety thousand miles of line in the United States. The longest continuous system transports petroleum from Texas and, through numerous pumping stations, delivers it to Bayonne, New Jersey.

At first pipes were commonly owned or controlled by concerns engaged in the business of refining oil, which operated them in bringing petroleum from distant fields to their plants. Since the cost of transportation by this method was usually lower than by other means, the large refineries with lines of their own were soon able to under-cut the small independent oil companies that had to rely on railways for hauling their raw materials. Naturally the independents protested and demanded equal rights. In the end they won their case for in 1906 Congress took interstate oil pipes out of the class of private undertakings and declared them to be common carriers—leaving natural gas lines still unregulated. When in 1911 the Standard Oil Company was dissolved under judicial orders, the giant pipe-line concern controlled by it was separated from the parent company. Three years later the Supreme Court upheld the act of Congress which placed such enterprises in the category of common carriers and ruled that they must comply with the lawful orders of the Interstate Commerce Commission. Since that time they have been treated as parts of the general transportation system of the country under the Commission's authority as to rates and services.

In a technical sense the problems connected with federal supervision of pipe-lines are quite distinct from those associated with other phases of common carrying discussed elsewhere in this chapter. In the case of railway shipments, goods are boxed and addressed to specific consignees; containers are kept intact in transit and delivered as sent. With respect to transportation by pipe, of course, no separation of goods for different shippers is feasible. Crude petroleum is frequently delivered to a line by many different producers. These "shipments" are mixed and reach the receiving end in one stream of fluid. On their arrival each "addressee" takes a certain quantity of oil from the common supply and pays the shipper a price corresponding to the amount of oil poured in at the beginning to his account. In order that buyer and seller may deal with each other on definite terms, therefore, it is necessary that all the petroleum admitted into a given line be approximately of the same quality so that the mixture may be uniform. What oil fields should be favored in setting the standards of quality? What fraction of the oil is actually lost in transit and should be charged up to the users of the common system? These and other questions make the Commission's work of regulating pipe-lines as common carriers a highly complicated branch of oil engineering.

Highways and Motor Transportation

The advantages accruing to the public through highway construction have been so strongly emphasized in recent years that the casual observer may regard federal adventures in this field as a new development. While the coming of the motor car has dramatized them, they are by no means novel. As far back as 1806, long before the advent of the railway, the Federal Government was spending money on a road to connect the seaboard with the Mississippi Valley and it continued the policy of lending assistance in this field until steam cars began to take the place of stage coaches. But by the opening of the Civil War, enthusiasm for highway undertakings had declined and it remained almost dormant until the internal combustion engine made possible a return to the larger freedom of the open country. At length in 1916 Congress inaugurated a program of construction on an immense scale, this time with the support of the huge interests affected by motor transportation, and in a different form, namely, in close coöperation with the states (p. 671). Within a few years all previous efforts had been outdistanced and a new era, of amazing significance to the social life of the entire nation, had been inaugurated.

Through all the arrangements established by the Federal Aid Road Act of 1916 runs the coöperative idea. The Federal Government is committed to the promotion of a nation-wide net of arterial highways, embracing in 1929 approximately one hundred ten thousand miles in addition to the seventy-seven thousand miles already completed. It prepares specifications, supervises construction, and, except in the states in which it is the owner of a large public domain, pays fifty per cent of the costs, provided that its share shall not exceed twenty-five thousand dollars per mile on any road. Subject to federal approval the states initiate plans, carry out construction, assume the balance of the outlay, and take the responsibility for continual maintenance. In other words the Federal Government assures the application of standards and furnishes a part of the money while the states build and maintain according to uniform regulations.

With a view to avoiding the waste and favoritism connected with other forms of public improvements, Congress apportions the annual highway appropriation among the states on definite principles. One third of the sum is distributed among them on the basis of their relative area, one third on the basis of their relative population, and the remainder with reference to their relative mileage of post-roads—with special concessions to Western states intended to relieve them of a large part of the burden of building and operating highways across the national domain. An additional safeguard is supplied by the rule that federal funds are to be withheld until the states have signified their willingness to share the expenses and have furnished proof that the work for which financial aid is requested has been satisfactorily completed. To assure strict compliance with the terms of the law in detail there has been established in the Department of Agriculture the Bureau of Public Roads endowed with ample powers to supervise all federal-aid highway construction and enforce the provisions of the statutes applicable to it.

Within the several territories and possessions, for which it assumes direct responsibility, the Federal Government takes general charge of highway work. In Alaska it operates through a special road commission. In Hawaii it follows a different policy, granting assistance to these islands from the same fund and in the same manner as in the case of the several states. Going outside of its territorial jurisdiction Congress is now helping to build roads even in foreign countries. Under the Cole Act of 1929 money was placed in the hands of the Secretary of State for the express purpose of extending aid to Central and South American nations in making surveys for the proposed Pan-American highway—a route intended eventually to link together all the countries of the Western Hemisphere.

Having participated in the construction of a network of interstate highways so indispensable to the automobile, the Federal Government now faces the problem of regulating a new form of enterprise. According to an estimate of the Bureau of Public Roads, the highway transportation system and equipment of the United States, including motor vehicles as well as roads, represent a capital outlay of approximately twenty-six and one half billion dollars—a sum greater than the book-value investment in the tracks and rolling stock of the steam railways of the United States, not including switching and terminal companies. Thus motor transportation bids fair to outrank railway carrying in financial significance. Moreover this traffic is rapidly increasing. On January 1, 1927, the American Automobile Association reported, 2,468 busses were already engaged as common carriers in interstate commerce over 52,017 miles of route and since then expansion has been continuous. Besides regular motors there are other passenger vehicles which operate for hire. With respect to the extent of their interstate business, freight and passenger, it is well-nigh impossible to obtain exact figures, for many trucks make irregular runs, "tramp hauls," while only an uncertain fraction follow fixed schedules.

Already some of the old evils which plagued the early days of railroading have appeared in the interstate motor-transport field. In its report of 1928 the Interstate Commerce Commission describes a few of the existing difficulties. Among other things it says: "The equipment of 'wildcat' operators is sometimes represented by a single secondhand touring car purchased with a small down payment. Some sell round-trip tickets and fail to make the return trip. Misleading advertisements are placed in newspapers. Sometimes their cars break down and passengers are forced to seek other transportation without reimbursement. Accidents have occurred, with the operator having no liability insurance and being financially irresponsible. Passengers' property has been lost with no method of recovery for the loss. On some occasions where a breakdown has occurred, passengers have been required to furnish the operator with sufficient funds for the repair of the car in order that the journey might be continued. In other instances cars have broken down and the operator with little equity in the car has abandoned it and left the passengers stranded." Rate conflicts have also flared up. For instance the Commission, in discussing the Detroit-Chicago bus lines, says "the steam railroad fare is $9.81 from Detroit to Chicago. When the bus lines started operation between those cities, large touring cars were operated, the fare being $7.50. Later motor busses seating from 26 to 32 passengers were installed and the fare was reduced to $5. This was the standard bus fare from Detroit to Chicago until a rate war was started between bus lines, when, it is reported, the fare became as low as $2.50. At one time there were eight bus lines offering transportation between Detroit and Chicago."

In these circumstances, while the Federal Government delayed action, several states took steps to remedy the evils themselves by appropriate regulations. For a time their supervision of motor busses and trucks engaged in interstate commerce was partially effective, but at length the Supreme Court intervened and flatly declared that such control lay wholly within the province of the Federal Government. Thereupon, the country witnessed a breakdown of state surveillance without any substitution of federal administration to take its place. The condition of affairs now prevailing can be best described in the language of the Interstate Commerce Commission: "With no law regulating interstate commerce carried over the public highways, such commerce can be, and is, carried on by as many as desire, regardless of financial responsibility and free from the slightest control or regulation as to routes, fares, schedules, public convenience and necessity, and comfort or safety of passengers. Operators engaged in such business are not required to report to any authority and, save for the police regulations of states and municipalities, are subject to none. They may operate at their pleasure and may cease operation temporarily or permanently as they choose. There is nothing to prevent them from discriminating unduly and competing unfairly. The public using such lines have no governmental agency of any description to which they may appeal in the matter of rates, routes, schedules or safety in the use of public highways."

Naturally, therefore, the Interstate Commerce Commission believes that federal regulation of interstate motor traffic is desirable, especially since all authority in the matter is denied to the several states. The question, then, is one of terms and conditions. As a preliminary the Commission suggests that passenger busses be placed under federal control first, leaving to the indefinite future the thorny problem of "tramp" trucks engaged in carrying freight. With reference to the supervision of the passenger business, the Commission suggests that it should itself act as an arbitrator and board of appeals in questions involving the states directly. It furthermore expresses the opinion that the ownership and operation of bus lines by railway companies should be taken into account in considering their earnings.

Whatever is done with passenger busses the freight truck still remains a troublesome factor. Inasmuch as "tramp" motors pick up loads for haulage locally as well as to various points in other states, it would not be an easy task to discover the extent of their interstate business or to regulate them without providing for a swarm of inspectors. Railroads making use of tracks must operate over definite routes through sheer necessity. Furthermore their physical property employed in interstate traffic is definitely subject to federal jurisdiction. On the other hand when a motor truck passes through a town few know whence it came, where it is going, whether it is owned by a manufacturing concern or an irresponsible individual, or whether it is a common carrier at all. In short the motor truck is elusive game for public control at best. Under such circumstances it is not surprising that federal officials are inclined to avoid this thorny problem as long as possible.

Aviation

In the field of aeronautics the Federal Government is striving for the goal of safe and efficient planes, piloted and repaired by skilled personnel, flying over well-lighted, marked and equipped airways in accordance with uniform traffic regulations. Continuing the method which we applied to land and water transportation, we have relegated the licensing of planes and pilots, as well as accident inquests, to another chapter where it more properly belongs under the head of Safety (p. 597). In this section we propose to discuss only those phases of federal intervention which are primarily designed to promote the industry or smooth the path for flying.

With respect to providing facilities for the business, the Federal Government now assumes several responsibilities resembling its services to navigation on water. It marks and maintains regular airways for the guidance and general convenience of aircraft just as it renders analogous aid to the pilots of vessels. In fact the similarity between the two has been officially recognized, for the Lighthouse Service, once devoted solely to marine work, has been placed in charge of airway lighting. Furthermore, the aviation industry in the United States is receiving the benefit of public subsidies in the form of mail contracts, akin to those granted to the merchant marine. Here the analogy stops. While the Interstate Commerce Commission fixes certain water-borne freight rates, there is now no federal agency to perform a similar function in connection with the new common carrier—the airplane.

Between the landing fields at which the air mail makes its stops, airways are established and maintained by the Lighthouse Service and the Aeronautics Branch of the Department of Commerce in coöperation. These routes are marked and lighted so that they may be readily followed day or night and they are, in addition, supplied with emergency landing fields, to be used in case of trouble. In laying out airways the shortest feasible line is naturally chosen, for planes, unlike land or water craft, need not follow fixed contours. But it is not always wise to select a perfectly straight course because this may make it difficult for the aviator to see the important land-marks, such as railways or highways, or may take him over territory in which a forced landing might spell disaster or into regions where the atmosphere is unduly disturbed by mountains.

The marking of airways, as we have said, is designed to guide aircraft both day and night. For use in the daytime concrete arrows of large size are placed along the federal air lines at intervals of approximately ten miles. These symbols not only show the direction of the route but also, by means of figures painted on them, give the distance covered from the last airport. Inasmuch as the indicated speed of an airplane in the air does not always correspond with its actual speed over the ground, owing to the influence of head or tail winds, these mileage signs are essential to the maintenance of regular schedules. At night searchlights, located approximately at ten-mile intervals, replace the arrows visible by day. Besides giving the aviator direction, other course lights blink out for him the number of the beacon, which indicates roughly the distance from the last airport. To furnish additional guidance the emergency landing fields maintained by the Federal Government are provided with markers and are lighted at night.

As air and water navigation have day markers and night lights in common, so they likewise have the radio-beacon in common. Along the federal airways have been constructed wireless stations which enable aircraft to discover at any time whether or not they are on the right path to their destination. As on the water this service is of great value in time of rain, clouds, or fog. When commercial airplanes are developed to a degree of perfection that will permit their use in the most unfavorable weather in regular service, the utility of the radio-beacon will become even more apparent.

Again, as in the case of water navigation, it is not enough merely to establish markers, lights, and landing fields; for, unless the airman is familiar with the ground, he may have no idea where he is even though fixed symbols tell him he is over some airway. More specific geographical information is necessary, therefore, to efficient flying. In response to this need, in part, the Navy has published maps of seaplane routes along the coast and the Army has furnished other airway charts for certain inland regions. As often pointed out, however, by men engaged in flying over areas lying off the direct routes, complete air maps of the whole United States are needed. To meet the requirements of universal aviation, the Coast and Geodetic Survey, long engaged in making charts for ships, has been instructed to map all civil airways and in time, no doubt, the whole country will be thoroughly covered.

In this connection arise problems unlike those in any other field of transportation. On the wide ocean there is no need of detailed maps for purposes of navigation because the only "culture" visible is the rolling waves. True, rivers and coast lines must be charted but here specific regional maps are sufficient for guidance. In the case of air navigation, however, no single course need be followed; aviators are free to wander anywhere. Hence every important item of topography must be shown to make air maps generally serviceable—particularly to those who do not cling to the official routes.

While the Federal Government assumes the important functions just mentioned, it is specifically denied, by the Air Commerce Act of 1926, the right to establish commercial "airports" along the airways described above, that is, to carry on activities which might interfere with the profits of private enterprise. By the term "airport," as used in this relation, is meant a landing field where facilities are provided for the custody, repair, and fueling of aircraft. Of course the Army and Navy, as well as certain other federal agencies, have such equipment of their own but they cannot make it available to commercial craft save under exceptional conditions. Indeed the law expressly forbids federal airports to sell supplies or take any care of a private plane except insofar as "such action is by reason of an emergency necessary for the continuance of such aircraft on its course to the nearest airport operated by private enterprise." And the emergency landing fields established by the Federal Government along the civil airways are not to be classed as "airports" in a strict sense, for they are a burden, producing no revenues and serving merely as aids to safety.

Smoothing the path of the aviator by the maintenance of airways and the publication of charts is one thing but supplying him with an economic motive to fly at all is quite another. At present the Government makes no outright cash payments in the nature of subsidies to private concerns engaged in commercial aviation. Probably it is not yet politically feasible for Congress to authorize such grants in aid without requiring any services in return.

Other alternatives, however, present themselves. The

Federal Government stimulates American aviation by purchasing large quantities of planes for the Army and the Navy and it furnishes financial assistance to this branch of business enterprise in the form of air-mail contracts. The contract system was inaugurated to revive the aircraft industry after the slump following the decline in the demand for military planes at the end of the World War and it has annually resulted in a large deficit on the books of the Post-Office Department (p. 427). In fact it has been explicitly stated by the Postmaster General that the object in view has been the promotion of aviation in the United States and not the carriage of mails at cost. In this sphere, therefore, the Government has pursued a policy of indirect aid similar to that employed in developing the merchant marine and shipping in general.

Thus, as we have seen, the Government, at public expense, maps, lights, and marks the great airways. It provides emergency landing fields. It subsidizes planes carrying mails. It spends large sums on aeronautical research. But it does not regulate the charges made for the transportation of freight and passengers by air in interstate commerce. Already the question has been raised whether the public, which pays for these benefits, is not entitled to special consideration in return. On the basis of an inquiry into the subject, Senator Bratton stated in 1929 that the majority of the concerns engaged in the aviation industry were opposed to federal interference with rates and services. With this attitude, the Senator continued, the American nation is familiar; for seventy-five years the railways received huge grants from public treasuries but resisted regulation until their "pernicious practices" forced the Government to assume control in return. On the basis of an inquiry into the subject, Senator Bratton cited an example: "Two passengers riding in the same plane, with the same accommodations, pay different rates, one paying eight cents a mile and the other thirteen cents." Shortly afterward a representative of the Department of Commerce declared that federal rate regulation was bound to come, but could not be readily undertaken until aviation was sufficiently stabilized to warrant it. Naturally the industry prefers to receive aid from the Government without any "meddling" in the conduct of its business, and probably as in the case of railways the speed with which regulation comes will depend upon the extent of its "pernicious practices."

If the federal regulation of interstate air rates is finally brought about, what agency should be put in control? Should this responsibility be placed on the Interstate Commerce Commission, already heavily burdened with duties in connection with railroad, telephone, telegraph, and pipe-line rates? That arrangement is not promising. On the other hand if a new and independent agency is created for the purpose of dealing with air transport, a division of jurisdiction over subject matter would ensue, for joint air-rail services are now an established fact. Here, as in the case of water transportation, is another problem in general economy calling for planning on a national scale. When Congress takes the subject under consideration, it will confront not a simple matter but the whole question of transportation as a national service.

So far, the Government has had little to do with the promotion or regulation of lighter-than-air craft. Although the Army and Navy have developed dirigible services for their own designs, private capital has not yet entered the field on a large scale. If and when it does, interesting governmental questions will arise. For the sake of safety, it is important to have a non-inflammable gas to inflate the carriers, and helium is the only substance commercially available which will not burn and yet is lighter than air. Furthermore the production of this gas for the Army and Navy has become almost a complete monopoly of the Federal Government, because helium cannot be obtained economically except from certain natural gas fields in the United States. If, therefore, dirigible transportation is to advance rapidly it must be for some time at least under federal auspices.

But the matter of gas is only one of the problems associated with the development of such craft. Airships are very expensive to build; they require large crews to manage them and heavy passenger traffic to make them pay. Moreover huge sheds or terminals are necessary to house them. Finally a small army of men, as many as four hundred, are needed to pull large dirigibles to the earth and walk them to their mooring masts.

Evidently this phase of air navigation presents difficult issues. The cost of dirigibles, helium, and ordinary operation is so high that commercial success calls for handsome revenues. The case is concretely illustrated by a proposal for the establishment of a line from California to Hawaii. A single airship for this enterprise, it was stated, could not be built in less than two and a half years and would involve an outlay of four and a half million dollars. After making its calculations the promoting company declared that a profitable outcome could not be assured unless the Merchant Marine Act was extended to include dirigibles, thus furnishing lucrative mail contracts. Evidently dirigibles, unlike small planes, belong in the category of ocean ships with respect to size and cost and, in the present state of affairs, cannot be put into extensive use without public subsidies.

CHAPTER XIII

Communications

For very practical reasons governments have always had a vital interest in the transmission of messages, whatever the technical apparatus employed for the purpose. Originating in the middle ages as an agency for the dispatch of royal decrees in connection with civil and military administration, the post office has been traditionally regarded as a public monopoly. Even after postal authorities began to carry private as well as official messages and the new business completely overshadowed the old, governments continued to own and operate their respective systems. This was the case in the American colonies as in England from which they sprang. Such was the background when the federal Constitution was written and as a matter of course that historic document put post offices and post roads under congressional direction.

Thus in a single phrase the Fathers dismissed the communications problem of the young republic. They did not foresee the coming revolution to be wrought by technology. Not long after the last of them passed from the scene, the first rude clickings of the telegraph ushered in a new era, and in due course came the transatlantic cable, the telephone and wireless—each a marvel in its day—adding new questions to those already facing the National Administration. Should the Federal Government incorporate all these instruments of communication in the historic legacy of the post office or leave them in other hands? Here a compromise was effected in which private operation was accepted with certain safeguards to the public. Possessing a veritable Aladdin's lamp in its right to regulate interstate and foreign commerce, Congress has placed the new communication concerns on the basis of public utilities, and under its treaty-making power the Federal Government has established connections in this field with every part of the earth.

With control over the machinery for the transmission of messages has gone supervision over the words contained in them. In wartime especially Congress may make this scrutiny absolute by giving to national authorities an actual mastery over all the prime agencies for the spread of ideas. In short, it may direct the formation of public opinion upon which in final analysis the Government itself is supposed to rest.

Postal Services

The corner-stone of the federal postal system is the constitutional power of Congress "to establish post offices and post roads." Although the meaning of the term "post offices" has seldom been called in question, no agreement has been reached as to "post roads." The interpretation of the latter phrase was early drawn into controversy during a partisan debate over the power of Congress to build national roads—to make internal improvements; since then the development of new technical agencies of transportation has raised additional doubts on the subject. Advocates of a strict interpretation of the Constitution have contended that Congress, under its authority to establish post roads, can merely indicate the various routes over which mails shall be carried. With equal force opponents of this view have insisted that the National Government may build and operate them. As a matter of fact during the first half of the nineteenth century it did construct a number of roads, although only in part for the avowed object of facilitating the carriage of mails. And in our own times the improvement of the postal service has been one of the arguments put forward to support federal aid for highway construction and aviation even within the several states (p. 427).

Moreover there is high legal authority for the broad

theory illustrated by practice. Long ago the learned Justice, Story, declared that there was no reason why Congress could not build and operate roads for the purpose of carrying mails. "If it be the right and duty of Congress," he asks, "to provide adequate means for the transportation of the mails wherever the public good requires it, what limit is there to these means other than that they are appropriate to the end?"

Under this generous interpretation, may Congress make the railway, telegraph, telephone, or radio business a government monopoly? Professor John W. Burgess holds that the issue is not finally settled. Certainly in time of war it may take this drastic step, as was amply demonstrated after the opening of hostilities with the Central Powers in 1917, by the transfer of the whole system of transportation and communication to federal management. Furthermore in the Debs case, involving among other things the power of the Government over the mails, the Supreme Court declared that "The strong arm of the National Government may be put forth to brush away all obstructions to the transportation of the mails." If this doctrine is sound, Congress should be able to do anything necessary to keep the postal business in efficient operation, in peace and war.

Whatever the outcome of the dispute as to the power of Congress in other fields of communication, it enjoys an undoubted monopoly over the mails. This function is not only assigned to national authorities; its assumption by private parties is entirely forbidden. But what is the mail matter that comes within the scope of the federal monopoly? The Supreme Court has answered the riddle by saying in effect that it is limited to letters, papers, and other things so reckoned when the Constitution was written. And in practice Congress has narrowed its range by excluding from the mails certain written and printed matter considered objectionable on various grounds as well as firearms and dangerous chemicals (p. 604). Letters, papers, and articles thus denied admission may be carried, however, by private parties, unless forbidden by congressional regulations pertaining to interstate commerce.

Federal jurisdiction over the transportation of mails is not confined to the territory of the United States. Exercising its authority over post offices, post roads, commerce, and foreign relations, the Federal Government has established postal communications with all parts of the world. Previous to 1874 such connections were formed by direct negotiations with individual governments; by treaties and other conventions, arrangements were made for sending mails along various lines to foreign countries, each line having its own schedules of postage. But under this cumbersome system it was difficult for a sender to discover the quickest route for his letters or the combination of routes offering the lowest rates. In addition, as long as mail transmission was controlled by nationalistic interests, postal charges were high and the complications of bookkeeping bewildering and expensive.

To clear up this confusion, the leading governments of the world held a conference at Berne in 1874 and formed the Universal Postal Union which is still functioning. Since its establishment the Union has steadily expanded until to-day it covers almost the entire globe. The goal of the Union has been to establish low and uniform rates for the carriage of mail between the various parts of its vast empire on a basis similar to that prevailing within each individual country. Through international coöperation the rate on a one-ounce letter from the United States to New Zealand has been cut from two dollars and fifty cents to two cents and on a letter to France from seventy-five cents to the sum of five cents. By holding periodical congresses and maintaining a permanent headquarters in Switzerland for managing administrative details, the Postal Union makes continual readjustments in harmony with developments in technology and commerce.

Within the states, territories, and dependencies subject to its jurisdiction, the Federal Government has built up a vast and complicated system of services, progressively keeping pace with the requirements of American life. It began in 1789 with seventy-five post offices, one for every fifty thousand inhabitants, in round figures; at the close of the nineteenth century it was operating more than seventy thousand post offices or about one for every thousand people—a number later reduced to about fifty thousand, with the growth of the rural free delivery mentioned below.

Besides establishing post offices, the Government has brought its services to the very doors of citizens in nearly all parts of the country. In the old days, every person had to go to the post office to get his mail. At length in 1863 free delivery was instituted in cities of fifty thousand inhabitants and upwards. Steadily the figure was reduced. At the present time the law authorizes the establishment of this convenience in cities of at least ten thousand inhabitants and any other place in which the gross receipts of the post office amount to ten thousand dollars a year. Under a ruling of the Postmaster General, even a village of fifteen hundred inhabitants may have it providing the postal receipts reach the figure just cited and certain conditions respecting sidewalks, public lighting, and street signs are met by the local authorities. In 1885 the "special delivery" of mail was inaugurated; on the payment of a small sum a letter will be delivered by messenger immediately after its arrival.

In keeping with the expansion of its urban activities, the Post-Office Department inaugurated in 1896 free delivery in rural districts. In 1929 more than one million two hundred and fifty thousand miles, organized in about forty-four thousand routes, were covered by this service, reaching nearly twenty-five million people. Incidentally, the rural free delivery system, especially since the appearance of the automobile, has exercised a profound influence on country life. In addition to carrying letters to the gates of farm yards, it has been a powerful factor in the improvement of roads and in increasing the circulation of newspapers and books in backward regions.

While widening the range of its deliveries, the Post Office

Courtesy of the United States Post-Office Department

DELIVERING MAIL IN THE MOUNTAINS.

Courtesy of the Signal Corps, United States Army

ARMY ENGINEERS LAYING THE MILITARY CABLE BETWEEN SEATTLE AND ALASKA (*See* P. 445).

has steadily added to the number of its functions. In 1855 it provided for the registry of mail; now it is possible for anyone, by paying a small fee in addition to the regular postage, to secure the registration of a letter at every point in its journey, a return receipt from the addressee, and an insurance up to a certain amount, thus practically guaranteeing delivery. The registration of mail was supplemented in 1864 by a money-order system which now provides for the transmission of money throughout the vast territory of the International Postal Union.

If money as well as letters and papers can be carried by the post office at a low rate, why not parcels? For a long time this question was urgently asked. It is true that Congress early provided for sending books and small packages by post, but it imposed high rates on such matter and narrowly restricted its scope. With the great increase in the commerce of the country, however, the demand for special arrangements for carrying parcels at low rates grew in volume. Naturally it was opposed by the express companies, for obvious reasons, and by country merchants who feared the competition of the great department stores and mail order houses in the cities. But at last in 1912 Congress was forced by public opinion to establish a system for the transmission of packages at moderate rates. As anticipated by its sponsors, the scheme was immediately successful and was quickly expanded into an enormous business undertaking.

A still more radical departure was made in 1910 when Congress in response to a long agitation enacted a bill authorizing the establishment of savings banks in connection with post offices (p. 370). This proposition was strenuously attacked on the ground that it was unconstitutional, paternalistic, and injurious to private financiers. On the other hand, its defenders laid stress upon the encouragement of thrift, the importance of affording absolute security to small depositors, and the desirability of developing a market for government bonds. Within a short time after the opening of the first post-office banks, the large number of people who made use of the new facilities proved that Congress had responded to a real popular need.

In the discharge of its functions, the Post-Office Department operates partly by direct methods—buying and managing equipment and employing its own servants—and partly through contracts with railways, steamship companies, and other common carriers and private undertakings. In the case of some contracts competitive bidding is possible but in others the Government must make the best terms it can with virtual monopolies or enterprises occupying strategic positions. And in fact throughout its history, the Post-Office Department, in adjusting its outlays, has been compelled to reckon with other than strictly business considerations, in particular the promotion of highways, stage lines, railways, the merchant marine, and aviation. Not often has it been able to drive hard bargains with the concerns which render service to it. Hence on the expenditure side of its program, the Post-Office Department is made liable for many costs which should properly come under the head of subsidies, aids, and bonuses to private business.

With reference to charges made for the carriage of mails, it has been for years engaged in expensive litigation with railway companies. Frequently the decisions rendered by the Interstate Commerce Commission and the Court of Claims in such controversies run against the contentions of the postal authorities. For example, in 1928, the New England railroads, which demanded a forty-eight per cent increase in their rates, were granted fifteen per cent applied retroactively from the date of filling the request, three years before. About the same time many other railways won large additions to their allowances—the longer lines, fifteen per cent and the separately operated short lines, eighty per cent—four of the nine commissioners dissenting with respect to the retroactive feature. In the course of his opinion one of the dissenters, who also objected to the amount of the increase, laid special emphasis on the fact that "no effort is made by the railroads to increase the rates for passenger and express business although the mails make a better showing than they do."

If the rates levied by railway companies for the transportation of mails are not in reality higher than the charges made for similar services rendered by them to individuals and corporations, no such claims can be advanced in the case of air mail. In this division of postal activity, expenditures are frankly made for the purpose of promoting enterprise in aeronautics. For a time the air mail service, inaugurated between New York and Washington in 1918, was conducted in coöperation with the military branch of the Government. In order to help sustain the aviation industry when the demand for craft dropped at the close of the World War, the Post-Office Department expanded its fleet and continued to operate mail planes as a public undertaking. Gradually, however, it withdrew from the field and transferred the business to private concerns, surrendering the last link in its system on September 1, 1927. Now the Department confines its interest in the subject to making contracts with aviation concerns for the carriage of mails on terms that amount in fact to a bonus of substantial size.

Under the policy of promoting aviation by grants in the guise of postal bounties, the expansion of the air mail service was phenomenal—the mileage, with all transcontinental routes included, rising from four thousand in July, 1926, to eleven thousand and one hundred in July, 1928. In the meantime the Department made contracts for air mail connections with foreign countries, including arrangements for a line from Canada through the United States to Chile. In 1929 the Western Hemisphere had twenty-two thousand six hundred miles of air mail routes, tying into one complex North and South America and several islands of the Caribbean.

A kindred policy of subsidising private enterprises by special rates is also pursued in dealing with oceanic transport. Formerly the Post-Office Department paid for the carriage of mails by steamers on the basis of the number of pounds actually hauled, a procedure in keeping with normal business methods applied to other freight. In 1928, however, the practice was revolutionized by the Merchant Marine Act, supplementing a law passed eight years previously (p. 392). Under this legislation the Post Office has been compelled to grant large increases in the payments made to shipping concerns.

Thus the previous method of compensation founded on business principles has been superseded by one which assures to the ship-owners benefited a steady income no matter how little mail they carry. The intent of the new policy was illuminated in 1929 by Jefferson Myers, a member of the Shipping Board, when he declared that "government aid may be secured through long term mail contracts on a lucrative basis." In other words, the Post Office serves as an instrument for stimulating American shipping. Indeed the Postmaster General in his report for 1928 asserted that his department had been "made a principal agency" for the accomplishment of the purposes of the new law. Hence it may be said that the shipping interest is to receive, under the guise of postal favors, a substantial portion of the subsidy which it long sought in vain as a direct grant from the federal Treasury, and the increased expenditure so incurred must be met by higher postal rates or appropriations from Congress.

Even in the erection or renting of the structures necessary to its operations, the Post-Office Department is not always free to consider mere efficiency. As a rule, the moment a town begins to take on metropolitan airs, it demands a federal building appropriate to its pretensions, and its chamber of commerce immediately brings pressure to bear on the local Congressman to secure an allowance from the Treasury for the purpose. Inasmuch as these money grants are regarded as shares of the "pork" distributed among Senators and Representatives in return for party services (p. 178), they are not always made on the basis of strict postal requirements. An important step was taken in the direction of rationalization, however, in 1926 when Congress created public buildings machinery under the direction of the Post-Office and Treasury Departments, limited the yearly outlay to twenty-five million dollars, and ordered the Departments to work out annual construction programs based on detailed estimates as to needs. In the smaller towns and in cities where existing facilities are inadequate, the Post Office encounters the renting problem and is extremely fortunate if it can lease a building on sound economic principles without reference to politicians or to local manipulators bent on gouging the Treasury. Indeed this is one of the perennial sources of trouble in postal administration.

On the side of revenues, or charges for its services, no less than on the expenditure side, the Post-Office Department is subject to pressure from many directions and is unable to apply strictly business methods. Hence it cannot easily put its operations on a paying basis. As a carrier of "intelligence," it is expected to promote intelligence by doing its work at a low cost to the public. In 1792 its rate for handling an ordinary letter within the United States ranged from six cents for thirty miles to twenty cents for more than four hundred and fifty miles, but by various reductions the figure has been brought down to the nominal sum of two cents. Whenever it is proposed to raise this charge to cover more of the expenses, citizens object and businessmen protest that the increase will throw an unfair burden on correspondence and advertising.

Furthermore "to encourage the diffusion of knowledge among the people," Congress has fixed especially low rates for newspapers and periodicals and for journals issued by educational institutions, churches, fraternal orders, and certain social organizations not conducted for profit. It has even provided that all publications entered as second-class matter shall be carried free of charge within the county of origin, if delivered to the subscriber in person at his post office. In a similar spirit a reduction has been made in the postage on books sent by public libraries on loan to readers—

a concession "long sought by those interested in fostering the reading of good books." Although the poundage and zone rates on the "advertising portions" of periodicals are higher than on the "reading matter," the diffusion of knowledge has not yet been subjected to the simple principle of collecting full transportation costs.

This is not all. The Post-Office Department handles two large groups of mail matter without any charge whatever. The first group consists of letters, papers, and other materials pertaining to official business sent out by the officers, departments, and agencies of the Federal Government. The second group comprises special matter carried for private parties and certain state institutions. In the latter class fall literature for the blind which does not contain advertising, periodicals within the county of origin as indicated above, and publications sent out by agricultural colleges and experiment stations.

In volume the free mail is enormous. In 1928 the Postmaster General estimated that his Department carried for the Federal Government alone five hundred and twenty million pieces weighing eighty-one thousand tons and for parties and institutions in the second group just mentioned, thirty-seven thousand tons. At the usual rates, the official matter would bring in an additional revenue of seventeen million six hundred thousand dollars while the remainder would return perhaps one third of that amount. When the finances of the Post-Office Department are brought under review, therefore, account must be taken of the services which it renders for nothing.

Facing a huge deficit of one hundred and thirty seven million dollars in postal finances for the year ended June 30, 1929, President Hoover declared that the Department should be considered simply as a public service institution and that its cost of operation should be borne by those who use it, not by the taxpayers of the country. But in fact the Post Office, as we have seen, has been regarded from the beginning as a kind of educational agency for encouraging the spread of knowledge and its rates have never been based on a close calculation of outlays and income. If the Post Office were put on a severely economical footing, then the payments to railroads for carrying the mails would be exactly the same as those made by private parties for similar services and the indirect subsidies to the merchant marine and aviation would be entirely discontinued. The introduction of rigorous business methods into postal administration would, in short, work a revolution in historic policies.

Assuming that the revenues of the Department ought to balance the expenditures, including the collateral subsidies, it would not be easy for the postal authorities to discover the precise rates necessary to produce this result. If the amount of mail remained constant, of course, then raising the postage would automatically produce the additional revenue; but in practice an increase in charges may so diminish the volume of matter transmitted as to cause a loss rather than a gain in income. On the other hand, in the case of air mail, when rates were lowered in the hope of extending the business and bringing in a larger net return, the aim was not immediately realized. Involved with national economy as a whole, the problem of revenue-producing postal charges cannot be easily solved by statistical methods; the best conclusions are estimates with large margins for error in both directions.

In addition to its vast technical operations and perplexing financial problems, the Post-Office Department has to deal with many ticklish questions in business, ethics, and opinions. It is required by Congress to exclude from the mails the letters and papers of persons and corporations practicing fraud and deception on the public and also all indecent, libelous, immoral, and treasonable matter (p. 605). Whenever an individual or company attempts, by dishonest methods, to procure money or property through the use of the mails, the Department must intervene. It instructs the postmaster at the place where the imposture originates to stamp on all letters addressed to the offender the word "fraudulent" and to return them to the writers if their addresses are given, or otherwise to the Dead Letter Office. At the same time it serves notice on the person charged with violating the law, and informs him of the nature of the complaint. If the accused wishes to offer a defense, he must go to Washington and present his case. On issues of fact the decision of the Postmaster General in fraud order cases is not subject to judicial review; but the question whether any particular scheme is in reality fraudulent may be taken into the courts for final determination.

The exercise of this large power by the Postmaster General has been severely criticized by many champions of individual liberty, who hold that it is not the business of the Government to act as the paternal guardian of the citizens, protecting them from their own folly against the machinations of patent medicine fakirs and "get-rich-quick" swindlers; or guiding them as to literature proper for them to read. On the other hand, it is asked, with a good deal of plausibility, whether the Government should permit the commercial use of the mails by fraudulent concerns or for indecent purposes, and thus become a party to the deception or corruption of innocent persons.

In time of war, of course, the jurisdiction of the Post-Office Department over matters of opinion is even more extensive. Under the provisions of the espionage and sedition legislation enacted during the conflict with the Central Empires, the postal authorities were empowered in effect to exclude from the mails all periodicals suspected of "dangerous" tendencies and to open and read the letters of every person whom they distrusted. To assure the strict enforcement of the terms of the law a Draconian control over all postal services was vested in a censorship board. And in its exercise peremptory orders closing the mails to newspapers and magazines were issued by the Post-Office Department and sustained by decisions of the courts.

Wire Communication

Originating in the modern age of technology and having no historic association with government comparable to that of the Post Office, the telegraph has been developed in the United States by private enterprises. It is true that the first long distance line—between Washington and Baltimore—was built and operated at the expense of the Federal Government. When the inventor, Samuel F. B. Morse, was on the verge of despair, Congress appropriated thirty thousand dollars to aid him in making his experiments and an additional sum to maintain the line after it was opened for general use in May, 1844. Grateful for the assistance thus rendered Morse offered to sell the invention to the Government for one hundred thousand dollars. But the Postmaster General, finding the receipts from the line almost trivial in amount, rejected the proposition because, he said, he was not satisfied "that under any rate of postage that could be adopted the revenues could be made equal to the expenditures." Accordingly the promoters of telegraphy were compelled to rely mainly upon private capital for the construction of lines, and the business passed from the realm of public ownership and management.

When, about thirty years after Morse's epoch-making achievement, Alexander Graham Bell introduced the telephone, communications by telegraph had already been established by many companies on a nation-wide scale. Accordingly connections with those concerns rather than with the Government seemed more feasible to him. In fact Bell and his associates tried to sell their invention to the Western Union Telegraph Company. It was not until they received a reply from the president to the effect that his corporation could not use "an electrical toy," that they proceeded with independent financing by private enterprise. Within a few years every large city had its own telephone exchange; in the next stage came short lines between cities and in country districts; finally new devices made long-distance telephony possible and in 1915 telephone communication was opened between New York and San Francisco.

Although American telegraph systems have been developed on the whole as private undertakings, the Government has materially assisted in the process by favorable legislation. It, for instance, has authorized telegraph companies to construct and maintain lines "through and over any portion of the public domain of the United States, over and along any of the military or post roads of the United States which have been or may hereafter be declared such by law." In return for its favors Congress has required companies taking advantage of them to give priority to government messages at rates fixed by the Postmaster General. Furthermore it has reserved the right to purchase such lines at an appraised value. In addition, all railroad concerns to which the Government has granted aid in land or money must maintain telegraph lines, and coöperate with telegraph companies on certain conditions.

Since the more important telegraph and telephone lines cross state and international boundaries, this branch of communications comes within the power to regulate interstate and foreign commerce conferred on Congress by the Constitution. The actual function of regulation is delegated by law to the Interstate Commerce Commission subject to certain general principles laid down in the statutes. In the first place, charges for the transmission of interstate telegraph and telephone messages must be "just and reasonable"—a provision which permits a distinction to be made in rates with respect to different types of service such as day and night traffic. Discrimination between customers, within any one class of service, is expressly forbidden. When it appears that there has been unfair treatment or that unreasonable charges have been made, the Commission may hold hearings, prescribe rules, and fix new rates. In this connection it has access to the papers and maps of the various concerns for the purpose of valuation, and it requires each of them to file an annual financial report in the form which it has provided.

A second important function of the Interstate Commerce Commission is that of supervising the consolidation of telegraph and telephone companies into larger units. It is scarcely necessary to dwell upon the advantage of being able to step to a telephone and talk with users in every part of the United States or to send a telegraph message to any station in the country irrespective of company ownership. Nor need we emphasize the economies frequently arising from a combination of the telegraph and telephone, working for efficiency in transmission and delivery. Some communities, however, are served by two telephone companies and where this condition of affairs exists citizens are either compelled to install both systems or suffer great inconvenience. It may also happen that the telegraph company whose office is nearest at hand has no station in the city to which a message must be sent.

The unification of telegraph and telephone systems, however, introduces the element of monopoly—and runs against competition which is commonly supposed to be an automatic regulator of charges and services. In foreign countries it has generally been achieved under government ownership and operation. In the United States, on the other hand, it is being accomplished under the pressure of private initiative by the elimination of small concerns through mergers and consolidations. This process, though accompanied by delays and litigation, promises in the end to bring about at least unity within the telegraph and telephone systems if not a combination of the two. According to the official reports for the year 1927 the American Telephone and Telegraph Company controlled thirteen million seven hundred and twenty-six thousand 'phones while all its independent competitors taken together operated only four million seven hundred ninety-seven thousand.

When interstate business is involved, that is, when one or both parties to the action are or will be engaged in interstate transmission, the consolidation of telephone and telegraph companies by purchase or merger must have the approval of the Interstate Commerce Commission. In the case of telephone companies special provisions of law govern the transaction. Upon application from such concerns for authority to unite, the Commission grants public hearings to interested parties, including the governors and public service commissions of the states affected, and it only gives its permission when it finds "that the proposed consolidations, acquisition, and control will be of advantage to the persons to whom the service is rendered and in the public interest."

Cable lines to foreign countries are supervised by the Federal Government under legislation enacted by Congress in 1921. No submarine cable directly or indirectly connecting the United States with any foreign land or one portion of the United States with another through waters beyond its boundaries can be brought to shore or operated without a license issued by the President. He may withhold or revoke cable licenses, after due notice and hearing, whenever "such action will assist in securing rights for the landing or operation of cables in foreign countries or in maintaining the rights or interests of the United States or of its citizens in foreign countries or will promote the security of the United States." In granting licenses the President cannot confer any exclusive privileges and must take care to assure "just and reasonable rates and service."

A single example will illustrate the application of this principle. In 1920 the All America Cables, Inc., of New York, an American concern, proposed to open cable communication with the coast of Brazil. At the same time the Western Union Company wished to land in Florida a line which was to connect, through the Barbadoes, with a British wire to South America. Here was a clear case of foreign competition in part, and accordingly the Western Union was denied entrance to the United States with its portion of the system. In making this ruling the Government took the position that since an American concern was already planning a direct connection with South America, the admission of a cable permitting a British company to handle traffic in competition would not be to the best advantage of our nationals. Obviously such a policy may in the future bring about a considerable expansion of American cables at the expense of those owned in other countries.

In addition to regulating telephone, telegraph, and cable companies, the Government has installed certain wires of its own, mainly for official purposes. For example, the Coast Guard manages more than twenty-six hundred miles of telephone line which forms a communication net tying together its widely scattered stations. The Army also operates a long cable from Seattle to Alaska. While traffic over such wires is primarily intended to aid the Government in performing its duties, private citizens may make use of them for regular commercial messages, subject to the priority of public business, at rates prescribed by the federal agency in charge of the particular system.

Radio

Owing to its peculiar physical nature radio communication presents difficult, and for practical purposes inescapable, problems to the Government. Indeed, these problems transcend all geographical boundaries and raise issues which can only be met by international coöperation. Accordingly it is necessary to give attention to certain technical aspects of the art that make government regulation imperative and at the same time baffling in complexity.

A radio transmitting station sends out electrical waves in widening circles which spread over the earth in every direction, ignoring all man-made boundaries. Although nations have divided the surface of the globe and erected barriers along their borders to prevent visible objects from crossing, save at their pleasure, they cannot stop at their frontiers an invisible wave which has no bones, flesh, or substance, a wave that passes through the walls of houses, the very bodies of sentries, the offices of presidents and kings, and invades the redoubts of the strongest fortresses. With these spreading electrical waves governments cannot cope by setting up city, county, state, or national guards. The problem is international and such it must remain. Obviously, if there is to be control, it must be at the sending stations. So much for the radio and political geography.

Government regulation is complicated by other technical difficulties. Radio communications are dispatched by sending stations in the form of electric waves of different sizes. In the present state of the art the number of wave-lengths which can be readily separated and heard by receivers is limited. If two or more stations of high power use the identical wave-length simultaneously in the same region, confusion arises so that clear reception becomes impossible. On the other hand if low power is employed waves of the same size may be used by stations far enough apart in space without causing disorder. Aside from other technicalities too difficult to explain briefly, these fundamental circumstances condition the radio business. In short the number of stations operating at the same time without creating interference in a given area has physical limits, and unless chaos is to result from competition the Government must determine who is to have the privilege of transmitting and under what stipulations as to power and time of operation.

Another technical feature of the radio creates issues respecting property rights and the dissemination of information and propaganda—both of which involve government control. It is a legal offense to tap a telephone line and listen to conversations passing over it. In this case actual contact is made with a wire which is the property of another, and the secrecy of a private conversation is violated. On the other hand, radio waves roll out freely to the world. When two persons are talking to each other over a radio telegraph in Ohio, let us say, the conversation may spread over Canada, Mexico, and Bermuda. In this case the communication leaves private property, passes beyond the control of the participants, and is open to all who care to give ear. If a receiver "listens in" on this conversation is he violating property rights and the secrecy of messages? Can he employ the findings of such "listening in" to his own profit and the injury of the senders? Is there anything criminal in just happening to hear something extremely important, merely incidentally while searching the air for music or song? Then what about international propaganda in peace and war? How can a government censor something which is not secret, which cannot be caught, put in jail or shot, when that intangible something comes from another country?

Finally, owing to its flexible nature the radio may be put to multifarious purposes. Certain concerns exploit it to compete with the regular wire telegraph, telephone, and cable lines in the carriage of commercial messages. Others use it to send still or moving pictures, including photographs of Chinese characters, legal documents, and signatures. The radio is devoted to broadcasting entertainment, French lessons, lectures, news episodes, prize fights, cigarette and car-polish advertising, and innumerable other items. It is employed by the police in sending out warnings concerning criminals. In the form of the compass and beacon it directs ships and aircraft on their journeys. It calls for help when a steamer is in distress. It makes possible the operation of ships and automobiles without any human hand at the wheel. It recently appeared as a means for geophysical explorations in search of oil. In short its applications are wider than those of any other known means of communication while at the same time it is more intangible and technically more difficult to regulate.

Yet, perplexing as are the problems presented by the physical nature of the radio, the Federal Government is simply forced to give attention to them—to make rules for its use and to devise measures of control. At first there was room for all who desired to enter the field of radio communication, for the air was not crowded. At this stage the Government was chiefly concerned with routine inspectional work. As the possibilities of the radio unfolded, however, a large number of individuals and companies wished to establish sending stations and as soon as the available wave-lengths were taken up, several concerns began to use the same wave-length in such a way that the whole system commenced to crumble. Chaos, interference, and ill-will reigned in the industry and private interests were unable to straighten out the tangle amicably by agreement among themselves. A mediator was needed. At that point the Government stepped in to assume the function of arbiter and controller.

Among the leading questions confronting the Government in connection with its new duties is that of adjusting wireless relations with foreign countries. A large number of radio plants are now engaged in sending out signals which either travel far beyond the bounds of the nation in which they originate or at least interfere with the reception of foreign signals by neighboring stations. To meet this condition international agreements are absolutely necessary. In 1927 a great International Radiotelegraph Conference, representing seventy-nine governments, was held in Washington, D. C., to devise rules covering the use of the radio within and between countries. Building on principles laid down at a previous convention held in 1912, this conference agreed that certain bands or ranges of wave-lengths should be employed throughout the world exclusively by specified services. Thus, for example, all broadcasting stations, regardless of nationality, are now required to operate on definite wave-lengths while all aircraft and ships are limited to other wave-lengths. Hence the ranges of wave-lengths for given purposes are made uniform for all countries ratifying the agreement.

While assigning bands of wave-lengths to particular services, the International Radiotelegraph Conference left the various nations free to divide the wave-lengths within each band among their nationals. Under this rule, therefore, the Federal Government might have allotted all the wave-lengths in the broadcast range to stations within the United States and attempted to monopolize the air in North America. It did not, however, take this grasping attitude but instead called conferences composed of representatives from

Canada, Cuba, Mexico, and the United States for the purpose of deciding how many wave-lengths within the broadcast band each of the four countries was to use within its jurisdiction. Then the Federal Government in turn distributed the wave-lengths allocated to it for broadcasting services among its own nationals applying for such privileges. This somewhat complex arrangement is perhaps the best possible compromise between man-made boundary systems and the invisible and irresistible radio.

For the purpose of exercising jurisdiction over the radio within the United States, Congress has created two agencies: the Radio Service of the Department of Commerce and the Federal Radio Commission, organized in 1927. The former conducts routine inspections of radio sending equipment to make sure that it complies with the terms of the licenses under which it is permitted to operate. This work includes checking wave-lengths, detecting illegal transmitters, determining what stations are exceeding their legal powers, and similar duties.

In addition to discharging its domestic functions the Radio Service acts as an international agency. Since radio stations are scattered widely over the surface of the earth and on the waters of the sea, the adjustment and distribution of toll charges for the messages which they handle present knotty problems. So, to aid them in the rapid settlement of their debits and credits, the various governments of the world have set up central clearing houses. In the United States it is the Radio Service which acts in this capacity. To its office American stations send periodical reports covering the amounts due from, or owed to, foreign stations. With this information in hand it then "squares" accounts with the corresponding national agency in each of the several coöperating countries—a rapid and efficient transaction which is a great boon to the radio business.

To the Federal Radio Commission Congress has entrusted full authority to license sending stations, limit the hours during which they may operate, fix their wave-lengths, and determine the amount of sending power they may use. In choosing among applicants the Commission is to be guided by public interest, convenience, and necessity and by evidence bearing upon the way in which these ends may be served by the parties desiring permission to establish stations. The number of hearings that must be held, the deluge of letters which pours in upon the Commission, and the multiplicity of controversies show that the task is by no means an easy one.

In accordance with the old theory that competition is advantageous to consumers in forcing lower rates and better service, the Radio Commission has licensed several stations to operate communication nets by radio in direct rivalry with land wire telegraph lines. While this development may, at first sight, appear to be in the public interest, the matter is not so simple. As we have already seen, there is not room on the air for everybody and in consequence numerous applicants must be denied the privilege of radio communication. Since this is the case, one theory of government policy holds that the radio should be employed primarily for services which cannot be duplicated by wire and that preference should be given to them in assigning wave-lengths. On this assumption radio nets competing with wire telegraph systems would be ruled out in favor of such uses as the radio-compass or communication between distant points not yet connected by wire or between aircraft and land stations. The first or competitive theory has been championed by the United States and the second by her next door neighbor—Canada.

Closely connected with the distribution of wave-lengths among applicants and the determination of the commercial uses to which the radio may be put is the thorny task of passing upon the opinions, political, religious, and economic, which may be broadcast by licensed stations. Are there to be limits on "freedom of speech" in the radio world?

This question is handled in different ways by various governments. Japan supervises broadcasting by placing a censor in charge of each station with power to cut it off the air at any moment if the program appears to present "dangerous thoughts." The United States, on the other hand, exercises no such official control; broadcasting stations in this country may send out whatever they wish provided that it is not unduly profane or obscene.

Nevertheless the problem of "censorship" is not so easy as this statement seems to imply. In granting licenses, the Radio Commission may and does take into account the purposes of the several applicants for transmitting rights. In choosing from among them the Commission must be governed, runs the law, by considerations of public interest, convenience, and necessity. What type of service complies with these requirements? What religious, political, or economic opinions come under this head? Can a station be deprived of its broadcasting privilege because it is guilty of using phonograph records instead of musicians in sending out programs? Can the right of a company to operate a radiotelegraph system be denied because the concern does not appear to be financially sound? Since the terms of the original Act are vague almost any number of interpretations is possible.

Fully aware of the difficulties the Federal Radio Commission has proceeded circumspectly for the avowed purpose of avoiding the establishment of restrictive precedents too serious in character. For example, it granted renewals of licenses to stations which were accused by the National Food Products Association of broadcasting "insidious" cigarette advertising. In making this decision the Commission took the ground that it was not prepared to act as a censor and refuse licenses "in the public interest" to organizations which broadcast ideas that did not suit its taste. On the other hand it revoked the license of a station in 1930 for permitting the use of obscene, indecent, and profane language in broadcasting attacks on chain stores and individuals connected with them.

Among the other questions associated with the radio is that of taxation. In this relation the governments of the world have adopted various policies. Germany, for instance, requires all persons using broadcast receivers to pay a license fee; and the revenues from this source are divided between the government and the broadcasting stations which offer programs of entertainment and information. Thus the listener, instead of relying entirely on advertisers, helps pay for the service he enjoys. Under such a system, of course, it is possible to escape the tax by "hooking on" to the air surreptitiously, but this is controlled more or less by inspection. In the United States receivers are unlicensed. The cost of radio broadcasting is borne by advertisers who pay for the programs they sponsor or by other interested parties, such as political organizations, desirous of reaching the public. Whether the listener would rather pay a small annual fee, which might amount to the cost of a new tube for his set, or whether he would prefer to endure or enjoy occasional announcements of goods for sale is a moot question. Under a licensing scheme advertising can be eliminated but under the American arrangement it is an essential part of the radio business. If all the receivers in the United States were taxed at the average rate prevailing in those countries which follow that custom, the returns would net the Federal Government about thirty-eight million dollars yearly—enough to pay for many excellent programs.

Besides supervising the private use of the radio, the Government employs this modern agency of communication for the benefit of its own departments and agencies. To the President of the United States has been given the power to set aside wave-lengths by executive order for the use of the Government, and his decrees take precedence over assignments to individuals and companies. In practice, for example, the lighthouse service operates radio-compass stations enabling ships at sea in dense fogs to determine their position; and the coast guard vessels in the North Atlantic use the radio to warn ships of icebergs that have been sighted near the regular traffic lanes. As the art advances such governmental operations increase in number.

As a phase of national defense, of course, the Government has constructed many radio plants. Besides, in all parts of the United States and its possessions, the Army Radio Net performs important functions in handling correspondence for the various branches of the national administration. Outstanding among the enterprises of the Army is the communications web for Alaska. This system included in 1929 a cable between Seattle, Washington, and Seward, Alaska, a telegraph line from Seward to Fairbanks, Alaska, and thirty-four radio stations throughout the territory—twenty-five of them equipped with radio telephone apparatus.

In places where the Federal Government has found it necessary to establish communications projects for national defense the question arises as to whether these facilities should stand idle when there is no official business to be handled. With respect to this issue the Government has definitely committed itself to the policy of keeping its personnel in training and rendering service to the civilian public by opening its plants, within certain limits, to private commercial traffic. Both the Army Radio Net and the Naval Communications System are employed for this purpose. For example, over eighty per cent of the business done by the Army chain in the Alaskan Service during the fiscal year ended in June, 1928, consisted of private messages.

Moreover by specific act of Congress the Secretary of the Navy has been authorized to use all radio apparatus belonging to the Navy for handling American press dispatches, communications between ships and between shore and ship, and messages within Alaska or between Alaska and the United States. In case, however, privately owned and operated equipment is available and can take care of the entire volume of traffic, the Navy must terminate the use of its facilities for such purposes in the locality concerned. The rates of toll and the conditions under which the Navy service is carried on are prescribed by the Secretary of the Navy, subject to review by the Interstate Commerce Commission whenever complaint is made that they are not just and reasonable. In any case its charges are not to be less than those made by private concerns for the same traffic, except for service between the Pacific Coast, Hawaii, Alaska, Philippine Islands, and the Orient generally and between the United States and the Virgin Islands.

From the above review it is apparent that the rapidly developing technology of the radio must sooner or later involve fundamental readjustments in the relation of the Government to the whole apparatus for the transmission of information. Wire and wireless instrumentalities are employed in many identical services. The possibilities of combination, obviously immense, are illustrated by the more recent inventions which provide for "radio" broadcasting through electric light lines. "These interrelated functions must be combined," declared Senator Watson in 1929; yet at that moment the regulatory functions of the Federal Government were distributed among the President, the Interstate Commerce Commission, the Federal Radio Commission, and the Department of Commerce. Furthermore, owing to its preoccupation with railroad affairs, the Interstate Commerce Commission, according to Senator Couzens, was not "doing any work on the telephone and telegraph." At all events its annual reports revealed very limited activities in this sphere. Largely on account of the confusion then reigning Senator Couzens introduced in that year a bill to create a Communications Commission with jurisdiction over all branches—wire, wireless, and cable. Though widely discussed the proposal failed to pass.

CHAPTER XIV

The Promotion of Business Enterprise

The individualistic theory of English classical economy left no room for political interference with "the natural and normal course" of business enterprise. It branded as unsound and wasteful all government promotion of private undertakings by subsidies, bounties, and discriminating tariffs. In sweeping terms it denounced paternalism in every form. Society, ran the argument, is composed of individuals, each struggling to avoid pain and to secure pleasure-giving possessions. Where legal freedom of contract and of movement exists, the individual applies his talents and capital to the work for which he is best fitted. The very processes of nature guarantee the survival of those who render economical services at the lowest cost. Every purchaser of goods knows what is best for himself and can avoid adulterations and frauds; while competition and rent automatically regulate for him prices, profits, and wages. By the pressure of population wages are kept near the cost of subsistence, and the unfailing improvidence of the poor assures an abundant labor supply. Each person is the surest judge of his own situation and by trusting to his instincts and reason will find the place in society to which his merits entitle him. Therefore attempts to control prices, wages, and the quality of goods are interferences with "natural laws," bound to fail and to injure those for whose supposed benefit they are made.

The freedom which operates so perfectly within the country, continues classical economy, works equally well in foreign commerce. Under a régime of free trade, a nation produces the commodities for which it is best adapted by climate, resources, and skill; and an unobstructed exchange of goods among states results in the widest benefit for all, the parties to such transactions receiving the most desirable things at the lowest price. Building up industries by tariffs and bounties is like trying to make water run up hill. To be sure, bananas could be grown in hothouses in the icy north, but it is cheaper to import them from the warmer regions where they grow naturally, and so forth.

From this system of ideas it follows that there should be no interference with the freedom of capitalists to buy, manufacture, and sell. Yet, if private monopolies attempt to fix prices, they run contrary to natural law, and should be dissolved by the government. If trade unions make a similar effort to determine wages, they too violate natural law and should be dissolved. In short, it is the duty of the government to protect private property and to keep order, allowing the economic machine to function freely under its own momentum—the profit-making-passion and the struggle for existence. In this way wealth will be "naturally" and "justly" distributed among the productive factors of society—land, capital, and labor, for each will receive from the annual national income a share nicely adjusted to its contribution, that is, its deserts.

Although this individualistic theory long dominated the writings of the classical economists, it was not strictly applied, even in its native land. No doubt it had a great vogue in England because industrialism won its first triumph over agriculture in that country and for a long time needed no protection against foreign competition in manufactures; but statesmen never succeeded in bringing about the ideal state of affairs outlined in the books. France flirted for a few years with free trade and so did Germany, but neither of them adopted the thoroughgoing doctrines of the Manchester school. Indeed Germany, for peculiar economic and military reasons, retained a great deal of the historic paternalism inherited from the feudal age and developed it into a kind of state socialism—government ownership and interference on a large scale.

American Political Economy

Nor did the United States ever take over the classical theory in its pure and logical form. It is true that the American republic was born in revolt against British interference with American business enterprise. It is true also that under the Articles of Confederation from 1783 to 1789 the general government had little or no power over commerce of any kind. But from the ratification of the Constitution forward, the policy of political interference with private affairs to promote economic undertakings, particular and general, made steady gains in spite of occasional setbacks more apparent than real. In fact the demand for such a policy was a prime, if not the chief, cause for the institution of the new form of government. Daniel Webster was certainly right when, on an examination of the writings of the Fathers, he found it "everywhere held up as the main reason for the adoption of the Constitution that it would give the general government the power to regulate commerce and trade"—in short, a permanent repudiation of the doctrine of non-interference with "the natural and normal course" of business.

In a strict sense, Alexander Hamilton's scheme of state was based on the conviction that the Federal Government should foster, protect, and even initiate economic enterprises by providing bounties, subsidies, tariffs, and discriminating legislation. It was a distinct denial of the axiom that men, if let alone, will make the wisest and best use of their material opportunities and effect a just and beneficial distribution of wealth. Only for a short time in the history of the United States was his system in peril of destruction. That was near the middle of the nineteenth century when Congress, under the direction of cotton planters, abandoned ship subsidies and veered sharply in the direction of free trade. But their régime was short lived. It was rejected in the campaign of 1860 and overthrown during the Civil War. After that crisis opened, the program of Hamilton was renewed and extended, with such remarkable results that even the Democratic party, long associated with opposition to it, was finally forced to accept in substance at least its principles and applications. As a matter of fact, the growth of manufacturing in the old planting states of the South made that party's *laissez faire* doctrines untenable, at all events in their pristine purity.

Although this statement of historic facts cannot be successfully denied, no slogan has been more popular in recent times, particularly among chambers of commerce, than the cry: "Less government in business and more business in government." While the idea, upon analysis, appears far from simple, at least in the minds of its proponents it has very definite connotations. It means a repudiation of those phases of government interference which take the form of regulating the rates and charges of business undertakings, controlling prices directly with a view to reduction, prosecuting trusts, taxing profits, and so on. On the other side, the slogan means strict economy in the employment of officials, the purchase of materials, and the letting of contracts. In short it calls for efficiency in all government work undertaken. At first glance this program seems obvious as well as attractive to its sponsors and advocates.

But a distinction must evidently be made. The new creed does not imply that all government activities pertaining to business should be abandoned, for in that case protective tariffs, ship subsidies, bounties, the improvement of waterways, and the construction of canals would go into the discard. These are all interventions in the "natural and normal course" of private enterprise. A tariff interferes with the undertakings of importing merchants; they are businessmen. Discriminations against aliens in our coastal waters (p. 382) deprive American manufacturers of the right to ship their goods by foreign vessels within the jurisdiction of the United States, often at rates far below those charged by domestic concerns. High duties on woollen goods, by curtailing the sales of importers, may divert profits from traders to spinners and weavers. To tax industrialists who sell their output mainly in the home market for the purpose of maintaining a navy to protect those who dispose of their products abroad is an interference with the distribution of wealth, with one kind of business in favor of another. To build a tariff wall between the United States and Europe is to hamper the operations of investment bankers who earn commissions on foreign loans. And so on down through a long schedule.

Moreover, on close inquiry it becomes clear that most varieties of government interference with private enterprise do not spring from the theories of politicians, the plaints of farmers, or the clamor of the consuming public, but from the demands of businessmen themselves. Each particular intervention usually originates in the desire of one group to promote its own prosperity by regulating some branch of economy. Manufacturers as well as farmers call for government control of railway rates and services. Shipbuilders and owners advocate federal invasion of the shipping sphere—subsidies to the American marine and the exclusion of aliens from coastwise traffic. One class of manufacturers who use chemicals in their processes, for example, will favor free trade in those commodities as against chemical producers who insist on protection against foreign competition. It is unnecessary to burden the record with more illustrations. If the Federal Government were to abandon all interference with private enterprise that can be attributed to the insistence of businessmen and is actively supported by them, its operations would shrink to small proportions—proportions so small in fact that it would make little difference to national economy whether public expenditures were extravagantly managed or not.

If attention is given to the other side—more business efficiency in government—the matter is not so simple either. A very large part of the corruption and waste in public administration is connected with the purchase of supplies, the making of contracts, and the letting of leases. From all these operations businessmen generally derive profits. Politicians do not always devise the objectionable processes that arise in this connection; even if they did, capitalists who come in as beneficiaries must bear their full share of responsibility. Certainly to no small extent, the lack of frugal methods in government is due to the persistent and continuous, and sometimes fraudulent, activities of men engaged in private enterprise. Hence the introduction of real efficiency into public management would exclude many of them from transactions now highly lucrative.

Furthermore, of the great army of federal employees, so often cursed as a bureaucracy, a large number are engaged in functions instituted and maintained in response to the demands of businessmen themselves. Relatively few civil servants are "political appointees," selected without reference to talents and the necessities of state. And if business methods are to be applied to their employment, it may be asked quite properly: "Whose business methods?" Those of the executive who ruthlessly "hires and fires" solely with respect to immediate profits, leaving society to maintain his discarded wrecks in public institutions? Or those of the far-sighted leader who allows his employees to buy stock in his concern, maintains a pension system for them, takes pride in a low labor turnover, and otherwise follows a humane social policy? The problem of government and business is not so simple as sometimes imagined.

The Protective Tariff

One of the prime purposes of the Fathers in framing the Constitution was to afford protection and assistance to American commerce and industry. This proposition has been often denied; for more than half a century the Democratic party held to the view that customs duties could be levied for revenue purposes only, that a discriminating tariff designed to safeguard manufacturers against foreign competition was unconstitutional. When it was dominated largely by cotton planters, who needed no protection and wanted free trade with England, it actually steered in the direction of low tariffs designed especially to produce an adequate income for the Government. But as a matter of fact the Democratic party, in its long history, never made a purely revenue tariff; if its duties were sometimes very moderate, they were generally laid for the avowed object of favoring particular industries and economic interests. Moreover, in its platform of 1928, that party abandoned its historic opposition to protection as such and announced that henceforward it would sponsor tariff legislation based on "the maintenance of legitimate business and a high standard of wages for American labor." On the other hand the opponents of the Democratic party—Federalists, Whigs, and Republicans—have consistently maintained that a protective tariff is constitutional and represents sound American policy.

After the Democratic party surrendered its earlier doctrines on this subject, the chief questions remaining were: What industries shall be protected? How high shall the tariff be on each class of articles? Who shall control the making of schedules? Shall Congress or the President fix the rates?

With reference to the first two of these questions, attempts have been made to formulate definite answers. Once it was contended that customs duties should be merely high enough to protect "infant industries," those in an initial stage of development and not yet able to meet the competition of old and established foreign concerns. As a general rule the judgment of the owners of such industries prevailed in Congress when revenue bills were formulated. But in our times this historic doctrine and this practice have been expanded. It is now urged that all industries, old, young, and in the process of establishment, should be protected and that the rate of tariff in each case should be determined by "the difference between the cost of production at home and abroad." According to this hypothesis the tariff is simply designed to put the American manufacturer on an equal footing with his foreign competitor; rates are not matters of opinion but can be automatically fixed when the difference in manufacturing costs is discovered by scientific inquiry.

This new creed was set forth in the Republican platform of 1908 and was endorsed in effect by the Democrats twenty years later. But collaterals were attached to what seemed to be a matter of mathematical calculation. In announcing the novel dogma, the Republicans added an important proviso, namely, that the tariff duties should also insure "a reasonable profit to American industries." And in accepting the general principle in 1928 the Democrats appended conditions of their own: "legitimate" business and high wages must be maintained.

Subject to these material, if vague, limitations, "a scientific tariff" is to be based on the difference between the cost of production at home and abroad. By way of a beginning the Republicans created in 1909 a board of tariff experts who devoted themselves to the collection of data showing the respective manufacturing costs in the United States and foreign countries. When the Democrats formed their tariff bill in 1913, however, they rejected the difference-in-cost dogma and went on the assumption, to use the words of President Wilson, that "the object of the tariff duties henceforth laid must be effective competition, the whetting of American wits by contest with the wits of the rest of the world." But later the Democrats agreed with the Republicans on the desirability of having a fact-finding agency and created a tariff commission to serve in that capacity. And, as we have said, in 1928 they also incorporated the cost-of-production theory in their party platform.

Though simple on its face, this concept is beset with perplexities. Costs in industry depend on many variable factors, such as ingenuity in management, the size of the plant, and the modernity of the machinery. Moreover what shall be included under that head? Interest on unwise investment and overcapitalization? Expenses for lobbying, publicity, high freight rates, unproductive advertising? Assuming that these questions could be correctly answered, the Federal Government, in applying the new theory to tariffs, would have to command almost superhuman talents, the combined wisdom and understanding of all American businessmen. If it is not to encourage sloth and inefficiency, to tax the American people to pay profits to bad managers, it must discover what efficiency in manufacturing really is, and that is more than some of the greatest corporation directors in the world actually know. Undoubtedly there is such a thing as scientific management, but the core of its truth is surrounded by a gas of uncertainty. Hence the cost-of-production hypothesis does not automatically furnish a basis for determining the rate to be charged on each article or class of articles imported into the United States. In spite of all efforts to "take the tariff out of politics," it is still entangled in problems of human judgment, interest, desire, and hence in politics.

Since there is a wide margin for conflicts of opinion over true costs of production, the question as to whether Congress or the President should determine the rates becomes of high political significance. At first glance, perhaps, the query seems absurd: a tariff measure is a law and Congress alone can make laws. But practice shows interpretations and distinctions. By the McKinley Act of 1890, the President was empowered to levy special duties on certain commodities imported into the United States whenever, in his opinion, any country from which such commodities came imposed "unjust and unreasonable" charges on American goods. Opponents of this scheme for a "flexible tariff" contended that in effect it transferred a taxing power from Congress to the President, but they were overborne in the political battle. The principle was established that for practical purposes Congress can delegate to the President the power to lay customs duties, at least within limits.

A still wider application was given to it by the tariff measure of 1922. Under that law, whenever the President found that the rates fixed by Congress in the act did not "equalize the said differences in cost of production in the United States and the principal competing country," he could by proclamation increase or decrease any duty, not more than fifty per cent, with a view to realizing the cost-of-production doctrine. As a check on the President, however, it was provided that he should make no such changes in rates until the Tariff Commission had first investigated the issues in question; but since the President appointed and removed the members of that body the restraint was relative, not absolute.

And the President made extensive use of his authority by introducing frequent changes in the rates established by the Act of Congress, usually in an upward direction. Accordingly, when the revision of the tariff was again under consideration in 1929–30, a combination of Democrats and Independent Republicans in the Senate, opposed in general to higher duties, tried to strike the "flexible provision" from the bill but were countered by vigorous protests from President Hoover. In the course of the debate over the proposal, critics contended that under the flexible rule protected interests had brought continuous pressure to bear on the President for increases in duties and had secured numerous favors at his hands. They also insisted that it kept the tariff continually in politics, transferred the tariff-making power from Congress to the President, and deprived the agricultural states of the influence which they enjoyed in the Senate over the making of revenue bills.

Clearly then in spite of all efforts to put it on a scientific basis, the protective tariff still remained highly controversial. Although the Act of 1922 was presumably based on the cost-of-production doctrine and the President was empowered to make readjustments keeping the rates on this foundation, it could hardly be said that the system produced satisfactory results. If it had the new tariff law of 1930 would have been theoretically unnecessary. In fact when the issue came up again at that time, the methods employed in revamping the rates did not differ from those in vogue for more than a century.

Representatives of industrial groups—lawyers, publicity experts, and professional agents—in quest for higher duties crowded the lobbies of Congress. Senator Bingham, desirous of knowing what the manufacturers of his state wanted in the way of reconstruction, appointed as his secretary an employee of the Connecticut Manufacturers' Association and introduced this official into the secret councils of the Senate finance committee in charge of the revenue bill. Although censured by the Senate for his action, Mr. Bingham saw no impropriety in it. About the same time, J. R. Grundy, President of the Pennsylvania Manufacturers' Association, declared before a congressional committee engaged in investigating lobbies that industrialists had contributed money to help elect President Hoover, that the country had approved the protective principle, and that the representatives of the manufacturing states in Congress should in effect control the making of rates. Later Mr. Grundy won a seat in the Senate and powerfully aided in putting his ideas into force.

During the debates on the tariff bill of 1930, it was made evident that the "difference between the cost of production at home and abroad" was not often the controlling principle in reaching decisions. Representatives and Senators from agricultural states demanded lower rates on the commodities which farmers had to buy and higher rates on competing agricultural products imported from foreign countries. In support of their contentions they cited the huge profits of certain manufacturing corporations already enjoying protection and portrayed the depressed state of American agriculture. On the other side Congressmen from industrial states, while referring frequently to the "cheap labor" of Europe and lower production costs there, did not usually confine their arguments to proofs bearing on such differentials. More often they cited corporations that had paid no dividends recently, referred to unemployment that would result if certain industries were not better safeguarded, and used the briefs of manufacturers in support of increased duties.

The process is well illustrated by the following colloquy which took place while Senator Deneen of Illinois was demanding protection for the manufacturers of escalators:

> MR. WHEELER: . . . They are afraid somebody will start in and manufacture them over in Germany and ship them into this country.
>
> MR. DENEEN: It is not a mere theory. They know it.
>
> MR. WHEELER: How do they know it?
>
> MR. DENEEN: Europeans have been here making contracts.
>
> MR. WHEELER: There has not been one sold in this country. . . . I am asking the Senator if he knows of one they have sold here?
>
> MR. DENEEN: I have stated that I do not know anything about it. I am accepting the information in the brief [filed by the Company asking for protection].

On another occasion, when Senator Bingham, seeking a higher tariff on meat choppers, cited "one manufacturer who had been unable to pay any dividends at all during the past three or four years," Senator Norris called attention to "thousands of people who have been tilling the soil and sweating blood between the plow handles for the last six or seven, or eight or nine or ten years, who have not made any money." Arguments in this vein prevailed at the moment, for Senator Bingham was the only member who voted in favor of his meat-chopper proposal.

When the smoke of debate cleared up and the tariff act of 1930 was given final form, the flexible provisions of the previous law were adopted with modifications. Under the new measure more power is given to the Tariff Commission and less to the President—at least on the face of things. Apparently it is to be a kind of judicial body charged with the duty of making suggestions relative to raising and lowering rates. It consists of six members, not more than three from the same political party, appointed by the President and the Senate, for overlapping terms of six years. Like its predecessor it has extensive powers of investigation into industry and the costs of production at home and abroad.

In applying the law it is to proceed upon request of the President, upon resolution of either or both houses of Congress, upon its own motion, or in its judgment upon application from an interested party. When it finds that a particular duty fixed by statute does not equalize the difference in the cost of production of the domestic article in question and like or similar foreign articles as produced in the principal competing country, the Commission is to report such increase or decrease in the rate (not more than fifty per cent either way) as it deems necessary to make up for the said difference. If it thinks this process insufficient it may specify an ad valorem rate based upon the American selling price of the domestic article. After inquiry, the Commission sends its recommendations to the President and if he approves they are made law by proclamation. In other words, the President cannot raise rates on his own authority but must act through the Commission. Since, however, he appoints and removes the members his relations with it are certainly more than Platonic.

Such is the latest scheme for "taking the tariff out of politics." But the ink had scarcely dried on the bill when a resolution was passed by the Senate calling upon the Commission to investigate certain items with a view to a reduction in rates, and it is likely that similar propositions will be laid before one or both houses with insistent regularity. Whereas once tariff revision came every six or eight years in a general upheaval and was settled for a brief period at least, it is now a continuous process. And pressures once brought to bear on Congress periodically will now be trained on the Commission without ceasing, and its recommendations, whether approved by the President or not, will doubtless be subjected to a constant discussion in Congress. Whether the new scheme will work better than the old, time alone can tell.

"Unfair" Foreign Competition and Bounties

It is not merely against lower costs of production abroad that American manufacturers are protected; the law throws up in front of them a screen against "unfair methods of competition," and "unfair acts" in the importation of commodities. All such importing methods and acts, the effect or tendency of which is to destroy or injure substantially any industry efficiently operated in the United States, are unlawful and may be countered by retaliatory executive action. It is the duty of the Tariff Commission to investigate complaints coming under this head, affording the accused parties an opportunity to be heard. If convinced that the objections are well founded, the President may suspend the importation of the articles drawn into controversy. Should a foreign nation make any "unjust discriminations" against commodities imported from the United States, the President may raise the rates (not to exceed fifty per cent) on its goods coming into this country or in special circumstances prohibit the entry of any or all of them.

Among the methods of competition frequently employed by the industrialists of all countries is that of "dumping" merchandise on foreign markets at very low prices, either to get rid of surplus stocks or to secure a foothold in new trading centers. Although the practice is not regarded as strictly unfair, provision is made to protect American businessmen against it in our tariff legislation. They may dump abroad, but they are not to be subjected to such hazards at home. Whenever the Secretary of the Treasury finds that an industry in the United States is prevented from being established, is injured, or is likely to be injured by the importation of any kind of foreign goods to be sold at less than fair value, he may make his discovery public. If the importer's sale price is less than the foreign market value or, in the absence of valuation, cost of production, then the Secretary may impose a special "dumping duty," in addition to the rate, if any, already laid; and the said dumping duty shall be equal in amount to the difference between the importer's selling price and the foreign market value or cost of production as the case may be. Since he is in charge of customs appraisals, valuations, and collections, the Secretary of the

Treasury is in a strategic position to keep watch on foreign merchants likely to engage in attempts to flood the American market.

To aid the President and American manufacturers in enforcing the protection afforded to industry by law, the Tariff Commission is given full power "to investigate the tariff relations between the United States and foreign countries, commercial treaties, preferential provisions, economic alliances, the effect of export bounties and preferential transportation rates, the volume of importations compared with domestic production and consumption, and conditions, causes, and effects relating to competition of foreign industries with those of the United States, including dumping and cost of production."

The Commission is also instructed to study the cost of production at home and abroad with reference to articles imported into the United States, to select, classify, and describe groups of commodities imported into this country, and to ascertain the facts respecting the selling prices of such goods in the chief manufacturing, producing, and merchandising centers. It must coöperate with the Treasury Department, the Commerce Department, the Federal Trade Commission, and other federal establishments in developing information. In the discharge of its duties it may summon witnesses, call for papers, and take testimony under oath. It must report to the President, the ways and means committee in the House of Representatives, and to the finance committee of the Senate with respect to subjects on which they wish enlightenment. If the Commission or any other agency fails to satisfy an American manufacturer, he may appeal to the Secretary of the Treasury against appraisals of imported goods which he deems too low. No loophole seems to be left open.

The promotion of American business enterprise by political policy has not been limited to the imposition of customs duties discriminating against foreign competitors. Congress has also the power to render aid by making direct appropriations of money from the Treasury in the form of bounties on commodities. For example, the McKinley tariff law of 1890 provided that for a term of fourteen years the Government would make a grant of two cents a pound on all sugar produced in the United States. Against this action lively protests were filed at the time, on constitutional as well as economic grounds, and on the return of the Democrats to office two years later political war was declared on the whole system. In fact, in their tariff law of 1894 they completely abandoned the sugar subsidy. However, when the Comptroller of the Treasury declined to pay the amounts already due under the old law, on the theory that they were not warranted by the Constitution, the Supreme Court upheld the McKinley measure. On the other hand when capitalists, who had invested money in the sugar industry on the expectation that the bounty would run for the full term promised by Congress, protested against the repeal four years after its adoption, they were informed that the pledge was not a contract and that they must assume all the hazards of fluctuation in political opinion. Perhaps for this reason business enterprise prefers assistance in the form of high duties on imports rather than bounties.

Anti-Trust Legislation

While tariffs, bounties, retaliation, and other devices are unquestionably designed to encourage American industry directly, laws against combinations and conspiracies in restraint of trade are supposed to accomplish that end indirectly by stimulating domestic competition. But a review of their history, enforcement, and efficacy raises doubts on this point. When the Sherman Anti-trust Act was passed in 1890 a great deal was said about reëstablishing competition and cutting prices for consumers whether good for industry or not—a contention especially emphasized by representatives from the agricultural states. Other advocates supported it on the simple ground that the dissolution of great industrial corporations would enable small businessmen to enter the race or stay in it, notwithstanding the handicaps of petty capital and limited operations. This argument was elaborated by President Wilson into a system for stimulating industry; it was the chief refrain in his speeches delivered during the campaign of 1912, now incorporated in a volume entitled *The New Freedom*. Business, he insisted, should be encouraged and promoted by emancipating it from the powerful capitalists, by restoring it to the basis of individualistic competition, by making it easier for new men to start up for themselves. On such theories was founded the Clayton Antitrust Act passed during the second year of his administration.

The first of these measures, the Sherman Act, is broad and general in its sweep. It forbids all contracts and combinations, in the form of trusts or otherwise, in restraint of trade or commerce among the several states, in the territories and District of Columbia, and with foreign nations; it declares them illegal, subject to penalties of fine or imprisonment or both. It lays open to punishment all persons who monopolize or attempt to monopolize, or combine or conspire to monopolize such commerce. Property in transportation under a contract or a conspiracy to restrain trade is liable to seizure by the Federal Government. By the terms of a law passed four years later, similar principles are applied to contracts and combinations in restraint of the import trade. While, as we shall see, under the Webb Act of 1918, American businessmen engaged in exporting are released from the restrictions of the anti-trust legislation, those who employ their talents in bringing goods into the country enjoy no such privileges.

With great elaboration in detail, the Clayton Anti-trust Act of 1914 extends the scope of the Sherman law respecting the same spheres of commerce. It forbids discrimination in the prices charged to different purchasers of identical commodities, that is, discrimination not based on variations in quality, grade, and quantity. Likewise prohibited are concessions in the form of special reductions to customers on condition that they do not use, or deal in, the goods of a competitor, where the effect of such an arrangement is "to substantially lessen competition or tend to create a monopoly in any line of commerce."

In addition, efforts are made to prevent interlocking relations among banks, industrial corporations, and common carriers. Recognizing the fact that banks, in financing industries on a large scale, may control their management, the Clayton Act stipulates that no person may serve as a director, officer, or employee of more than one bank organized under the laws of the United States and having above five million dollars in capital, surpluses, and undivided profits. No corporation may acquire stock in another concern where the acquisition lessens competition or restrains trade. No person may serve as a director in two or more competing corporations (excepting banks, trust companies, and common carriers) that have a capital, surplus, and undivided profits of more than one million dollars. To prevent restraint of trade through unions of manufacturers and common carriers, specific clauses of the law provide for separating their directorships and controlling large purchases of supplies by the latter. Any person injured by acts proscribed by the anti-trust measures may bring suit and recover threefold the damages sustained. The enforcement of these laws is entrusted to judicial process, the Federal Reserve Board, the Interstate Commerce Commission, and the Federal Trade Commission.

"Unfair" Domestic Competition

Among the activities of the Federal Government connected with the promotion and rationalization of business enterprise, the work of the Federal Trade Commission, composed of five members appointed by the President and Senate, assumes increasing significance. In itself it is a unique institution with extraordinary potentialities, for in its purposes and operations it marks a radical departure from the classical doctrines of political economy and from the anti-trust theory that the Government should endeavor to maintain competition among businessmen by suits at law and penalties. To be sure, the Commission must, as a part of its obligation, apply the drastic provisions of the Sherman and Clayton Anti-trust Acts, and seek to prevent monopolies and the restraint of competition among business concerns. But it was understood at the time of its creation in 1914 that one of the Commission's functions would be to substitute regulation for the indiscriminate prosecution of large corporations. The Sherman Anti-trust Act had then been in existence for twenty-four years and the general futility of attempting to destroy or check the formation of gigantic combinations had been demonstrated, if not popularly recognized. It was with particular reference to this situation that the Senate insisted on widening the powers of the Commission as proposed in the federal trade bill passed by the House of Representatives. In the end the new agency was given a general authority to prevent "any unfair method of competition in commerce" by advisory and administrative methods, reserving actions in the courts of law for exceptional cases.

Besides supplementing the judicial processes for enforcing the anti-trust laws, the Trade Commission Act lays down two fundamental principles respecting interstate and foreign commerce, excepting banks and common carriers which are otherwise subjected to federal control. The first is that "unfair methods" of competition are unlawful and are to be prevented. If its complaints, orders, and advice pertaining to such methods are ignored or disobeyed, the Commission may resort to compulsory procedure and the proper courts may take cognizance of the matter. The second principle stipulates that the organization, finances, practices, and management of corporations are matters of public concern and are open to investigation, description, and report by the Commission. If the second principle was justified by law-makers as necessary to the realization of the first, it outruns its origin in significance. In application it takes a major portion of the manufacturing and trading operations of the country out of the sphere of simple private undertakings and places them practically on the footing of public utilities with respect to accounting and reporting. Since banks and common carriers were already put in that position by earlier legislation (p. 401), the greater part of the nation's economy is thus open to official scrutiny.

Broadly speaking the activities of the Federal Trade Commission fall into three divisions. Primarily, of course, it is interested in the formulation and application of standards governing trade practices. Since it cannot make definitions of "unfair methods" out of thin air, it must evolve its interpretations of the law in connection with business itself. Consequently the Commission encourages the directors of each great group of enterprises—fur, heavy sheet glass, golf ball, wax paper, and varnish, for example—to hold conferences representing the individual concerns and to work out fair-trade rules for the industry in question, to be executed by self-discipline. Sometimes the Commission calls such conferences on its own motion. In any case it is always prepared to coöperate with trade conventions in devising their canons of economy. More than that; it stands formidably in the background, ready to enforce regulations relative to fair practices whenever any particular group is unable to secure obedience to its own constitution of government. Under explicit statutory authority, the Commission can reach out and compel recalcitrant members to abide by the rules of the game. Naturally the very existence of this power gives vigor to the codes adopted by the several trades; and seldom, speaking relatively, is the authority of the Commission invoked in the form of coercion. According to these principles and under official aegis, great branches of industry and commerce have been organized into associations, resembling the merchant gilds of the middle ages, with minute ordinances prescribing the practices which members may follow.

The second department of the Commission's work embraces investigating and reporting on the organization, management, and results of commercial undertakings. In this field it carries on continuous researches on its own authority and on instructions from the President, the Senate, or the House of Representatives. Inquiries undertaken on its own motion may result in the suggestion of remedial legislation to Congress or in the discovery of unfair practices, leading to appropriate process against guilty parties. Since its foundation in 1914, the Commission has surveyed most of the great industries in the country, producing economic information of the highest value for public and private purposes and laying bare the general forms and methods of American business enterprise. Perhaps its most significant venture in this connection was the vigorous investigation into the financial structure and publicity methods of public utilities, initiated by a resolution of the Senate in 1928. The mere fact that an inquiry may come at any time serves as a check and a corrective influence on trade practices.

To its coöperative and research activities, the Commission adds the stern business of law enforcement. It uncovers, hears, and examines complaints against particular persons and corporations, alleging that they are guilty of unfair methods or are otherwise violating the anti-trust legislation or the Trade Commission Act. When it discovers good grounds for moving against an offender, it explains to him the abuse or abuses with which he is charged and issues an order commanding him to desist from the objectionable conduct named in the bill. For example, certain lumber companies advertise as "Philippine mahogany" wood which is not mahogany at all but merely has its general appearance; a protest is filed against the practice; an inquiry is made; and in conclusion the companies are ordered to cease their misleading and deceptive publicity. Again, a security house engaged in selling the stocks of dubious oil concerns is accused of making false representations respecting their resources, assets, and financial conditions; after examining the facts in the case, the Commission instructs the defendant to stop issuing such fraudulent statements.

If a party does not obey its orders, the Commission may apply to the appropriate federal court for a judicial mandate to enforce its decision. On the other hand, any individual or concern may take exceptions to its edicts and carry the controversy into court for review and judgment. In all judicial cases, the Commission is represented by counsel and endeavors to establish the legality and correctness of its decrees. Frequently, however, it is overruled and its commands are set aside. At best this process is tedious and cumbersome, owing to the appeals and delays, but it is deemed necessary to protect private parties against arbitrary actions.

Of high importance to business enterprise, if not always with special reference to mere promotion, are many acts of Congress more fully covered in other parts of this volume, especially in connection with transportation and communication. Though strongly supported by farmers, especially in the beginning, the laws regulating railway rates and practices vitally affect manufacturing for both domestic and foreign markets. Freight costs enter into prices and influence sales, in the long run at least; rebates and other discriminations give privileges to favored shippers to the injury of those not enjoying such benefits. Under the head of business promotion also may be placed the activities of the Federal Government in the development of inland waterways, which open up new channels and may cut transportation charges. Under this caption likewise belongs federal aid to highways expediting deliveries by trucks and reducing expenses for short hauls. While the interests of manufacturers in general are recognized in legislation bearing on freight rates, those of shipbuilders and shipowners are advanced by acts of Congress restricting coastwise traffic to American vessels and allowing subsidies in the form of advantageous mail contracts and loans in support of the American merchant marine on the high seas. And of course the whole structure of business enterprise rests on currency and banking laws assuring stability, regularity, and a certain flexibility in the extension of credits for commercial and industrial purposes.

Besides looking to the Government normally for specific aid in the form of tariffs, bounties, and subsidies, businessmen turn to it for help during industrial depressions. This is a relatively new development. Until recent times periodical panics were regarded as natural phenomena, very much like earthquakes and cyclones. Production, it was thought, ran inevitably through a cycle of expansion, explosion, and contraction—repeated with striking regularity. But in the opening years of the twentieth century, doubts were expressed about the hypothesis and a quest was begun for ways and means of avoiding rhythmic disasters. The search had not gone very far when it was discovered that a solution of the problem involved governmental action in speeding up the construction of public works, such as highways and buildings, and in bringing about coöperation among the great branches of private economy—manufacturing, agriculture, labor, railways, and utilities (p. 642).

Trade-marks, Copyrights, and Patents

In another important relation the substantial rights of businessmen come under federal guardianship. Large industries have been established by creating a demand for products bearing a distinctive label. The buying public, for example, has learned to associate the names Kodak, Uneeda, and Ford with definite objects sold by particular concerns. If there were no legal protection for such intangibles unscrupulous manufacturers would place these valuable symbols on their own products to take advantage of the market built up through the efforts of others. It is easy to see that such piracy would lead to a general collapse of popular confidence, should it be widely practiced. Fortunately, however, under its power to regulate interstate commerce Congress has enacted legislation affording protection to trademarks, consisting of words, signs, and characters by which goods are normally distinguished. Since most commodities of consequence are sold in more than one state the federal statutes furnish, on the whole, a generous security.

As the law now stands, any person employing a trade-mark in interstate or foreign commerce may register it with the Patent Office in Washington on specific conditions. First of all the adoption of certain symbols, such as the American flag, is forbidden. Secondly an application for registration must not conflict with any device already in legal use on goods of the same description. To prevent duplications the Patent Office makes searches into prior rights and claims and in case it discovers no reason for refusing the request the proposed trade-mark is published in its *Official Gazette.* Any person who feels aggrieved by this tentative approval may lodge a protest against it. If there are no objections or if on appeal they are overruled the trade-mark in question is duly registered.

The possessor of a registered trade-mark is protected for a period of twenty years against all infringements and is entitled to an indefinite number of renewals. He may sell it or transfer it, thus making sure that an honorable name may be employed to protect goods as long as they are produced. If his rights are invaded by American competitors, he may resort to the courts in their defense, demanding an injunction, damages, and the seizure of unlawful labels. Still more expeditious is the procedure through which the importation of foreign goods bearing conflicting symbols is prevented. Under the law any trade-mark registered in the Patent Office may be filed by its owner with the Treasury Department. After this step is taken all goods manufactured in other countries, which carry this trade-mark, are excluded by the Government from entry into the United States and if they gain admittance are liable to forfeiture.

Owing to controversies arising in international commerce over trade-mark rights and the obvious desirability of reciprocity, the United States has joined several other nations in signing a general convention dealing with this subject. In accordance with the terms of the agreement an inter-

Photo by K. D. Swan, Courtesy of the United States Forest Service

THE GOVERNMENT IN BUSINESS: LOGGING IN A NATIONAL FOREST.

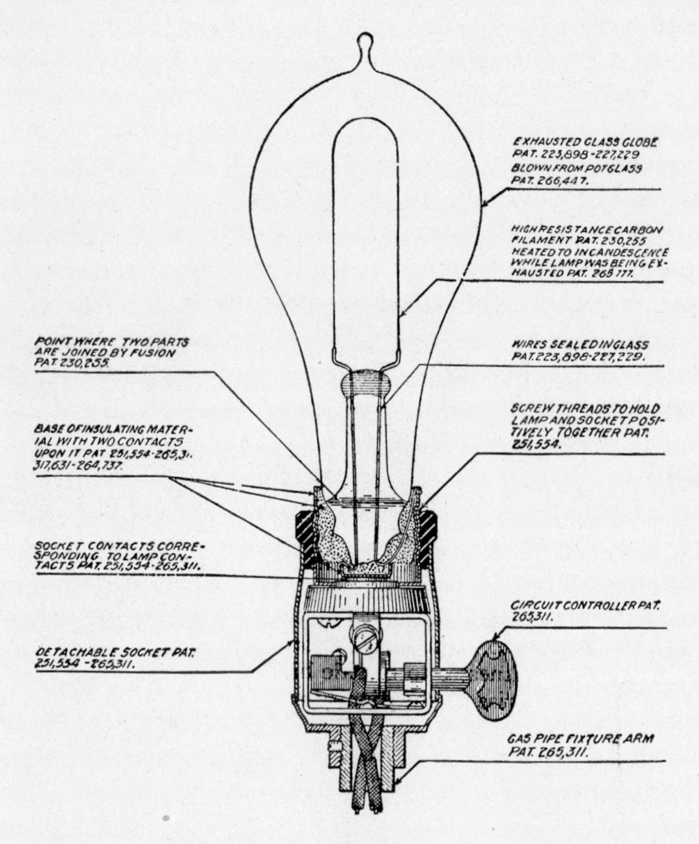

By permission, from "Edison, His Life and Inventions," by Frank L. Dyer and Thomas C. Martin, Harper and Brothers

A PATENT COMPLEXITY: NINETEEN GRANTS ON A SIMPLE DEVICE.

national bureau of registration has been established to render to all the signatories a service akin to that performed by the Patent Office in Washington for our own country. At this bureau any citizen whose government is affiliated with it may register a trade-mark and thereafter claim protection against infringements by concerns operating within the territory of the associated powers.

Equally, if not more, vital to the stability of the industrial structure of the United States is the patent system established by the Federal Government for the purpose of assuring to inventors broad rights covering their discoveries and contrivances. Under that system any person believing himself to be the original inventor of a machine, process, design, or certain living plants may apply to the Patent Office for a virtual monopoly over exploitation for a number of years. Upon receipt of an application the Office makes a search of previous records and if it finds that the claims of the petitioner are really novel it will grant him a patent. When formally sealed this document confers on the holder an exclusive privilege to make, sell, and use the object described throughout the United States for a period of seventeen years. The advantages thus obtained may be enlarged by a registration in foreign countries under international agreements for an exchange of courtesies, to which the United States is a party.

But patents duly granted are not absolute. The holder may be sued at law by any competitor claiming an infringement of prior concessions. Since, in technical matters, it is often difficult to distinguish a genuine novelty from earlier machines and designs, an inventor who breaks into an established line of industry is likely to find himself involved in expensive litigation even after the Patent Office has approved his device. Other circumstances also conspire to make his lot an unhappy one. Many valuable patents are held by powerful corporations with unlimited funds at their disposal and on slight provocation they are likely to hale an intruder into the courts and wear him out in an exhausting campaign in which the long purse has a decided preponderance. For these and similar reasons it is highly important that the Patent Office should be adequately supplied with funds and competent examiners, thus making its decisions and rulings more certain and less open to attack by skilled lawyers in the courts.

On various grounds the present patent system has been subjected to criticism. No doubt substantial inducements are useful in stimulating invention, but is the grant of a monopoly the best form of enticement for genius? A patent does not require the possessor to manufacture the article covered by it. On the contrary he may secure the parchment for the mere purpose of suppressing the idea and keeping his present plant running on obsolete patterns to the detriment of the consuming public. If he does set to work immediately turning out the product, his strategic position enables him to charge any price the traffic will bear. Evidently here are grounds for reasonable objections. Yet the way out is not easy. Perhaps the most feasible solution is the suggestion that any patent not put to use should be liable to forfeiture under rigorous safeguards and that all patents should be open to development by any manufacturer on payment of a fair return to the holder, which is the rule, as we shall see, in the case of copyrighted songs. Another proposition, incorporated in a bill introduced in the House of Representatives in 1930, recommends that any inventor sued for infringement may offer as complete defense the contention that the plaintiff is using his patent in violation of federal laws against combinations, agreements, and contracts in restraint of trade or in violation of the Clayton Act or the Federal Trade Commission Act. Still the difficulties in the course of any such arrangement are admittedly immense and cannot be lightly disposed of by legislation.

Literary and artistic products as well as machines, processes, and special commodities are protected by the Federal Government. Under the Constitution Congress has power to grant to authors an exclusive title to their respective works. In the exercise of this prerogative Congress has authorized the issue of copyrights vesting in the possessors the sole right to reproduce their books, sermons, dramas, articles, works of art, music, photographs, maps, and similar objects. Additional privileges are conferred at the same time, covering adaptations, translations, and use in public entertainments for profit. In only one field is a complete sovereignty denied. Any person may obtain, on the payment of a fixed fee of two cents a copy, a license to reproduce, by mechanical processes, musical compositions duly copyrighted—an incentive to large scale production at low prices which is absent in the case of patents, trade-marks, and other monopolistic concessions. In general, a copyright runs for twenty-eight years, with the possibility of one renewal.

Here, as in other matters, arrangements are made for the exchange of international civilities. For a long time American publishers "pirated" English and other foreign books, that is, issued them without asking the consent of the authors or paying any royalties. In return, of course, foreign publishers exercised the same freedom in dealing with American works. At last, however, Congress by special legislation provided that alien authors and proprietors shall be entitled to the substantial benefits of American copyright privileges if the countries to which they belong confer similar favors on American citizens. In various respects these statutory arrangements are amplified by treaties between the United States and foreign powers, thus throwing up fundamental safeguards throughout the republic of letters. As a concession to American printers, however, it is expressly stipulated by law that all books in the English language must be produced in American plants in order to enjoy the benefits of copyright. If, on its face, this seems fair to domestic industries, it often works hardships for the American publisher, because it is frequently difficult for him to tell in advance whether to import copies of an English book, incurring the hazard of pirating by competitors, or to risk the expenses of a separate printing on this side of the water. But whatever their shortcomings the new arrangements assure a certain degree of reciprocity and equality in literary and artistic exchanges.

Promotion of Foreign Commerce

From its foundation the United States has promoted, in a more or less methodical fashion, the foreign trade of its citizens. By an act passed in 1791 Congress extended extraordinary favors to Americans engaged in commerce with the Orient. The suppression of the Barbary pirates, the War of 1812, and the opening of China and Japan to American trade all gave signs of the Government's solicitude for the advancement of economic enterprise. One of the real reasons assigned by President McKinley for annexing the Philippine Islands was the development of new business opportunities. "Incidental to our tenure in the Philippines," he said, "is the commercial opportunity to which American statesmanship cannot be indifferent. It is just to use every legitimate means for the enlargement of American trade."

With the passage of time, the activities of the Federal Government on behalf of foreign trade have become more insistent, elaborate, and systematic. As manufacturing increases in importance, far above agriculture in the value of its capital and the number of people employed, the pressure of businessmen on the Government for assistance in commercial promotion is augmented from every direction. Indeed, since the opening of the twentieth century a veritable economic revolution has taken place. American manufacturers have fairly saturated the domestic market with goods and they are searching feverishly for additional outlets in all quarters of the globe, multiplying their demands on the Government in the quest. Moreover the United States is now a great creditor nation which lends money by the billions to Europe, Asia, South America, and Australia. As a result diplomatic and political intervention in support of American undertakings abroad has been organized into a fine art. Every year sees new statutes expressing this policy or new strokes of state illustrating its development. As a result of a cumulative process, almost every conceivable activity calculated to enlarge and sustain foreign trade is carried on by the Federal Government and nearly all its departments are involved directly or indirectly in the operation.

A prerequisite to the promotion of American commerce abroad is, of course, an accurate knowledge of the economic conditions prevailing in foreign lands, the compilation of such pertinent information in convenient form, and the timely distribution of it among interested businessmen in the United States. This information must perforce embrace materials bearing on natural resources, commodities in use or in potential demand, wages or buying power, costs of manufacturing, the methods of foreign competitors in their own markets, tariffs, bounties, subsidies, railway rates, and other aids to local enterprise, commercial legislation respecting alien traders and their agents, facilities for the collection of debts, various national tastes, borrowing capacity, and commodities offered in exchange for American goods. In short the advancement of trade calls for accurate, detailed, continuous pictures of every foreign country in which American goods are, or may be, sold. And these pictures are now provided by the Federal Government. Indeed the work is done so well that its official reports on the economic conditions of many countries are more complete and contemporaneous than those provided by their own governments. Perhaps it is fair to say that the most microscopic survey of world economic resources and potentialities is to be found in the statistical collections published or made available by the Government of the United States.

Innumerable statutes provide directly or indirectly for the collection of these data. Even the tariff acts, designed to promote domestic industry by affording protection against alien competition, thrust American scrutiny into the very centers of foreign manufacturing. The theory that rates should be based on the difference between the cost of production at home and abroad requires for its realization an examination on the spot into the wages, materials, manufacturing conditions, government subsidies, and all other factors entering into prices. In administering the sections directed against foreign dumping on American shores (p. 460), the Secretary of the Treasury, through agents in other countries, may search the factories, accounts, and methods of capitalists engaged in turning out goods for the American market. Moreover in their application the stringent terms of the revenue law, regulating the valuation of imports and permitting American manufacturers to protest against appraisals of the customs officers, throw a fierce glare of light on the kind of competition which American exporters must meet in foreign trade. In other words the very measures which defend American manufacturers at home reveal to them the nature of the operations necessary when they go afield.

But the Federal Government depends upon no such incidental processes in its continuous quest for light on foreign economic conditions. Its consular officers are in effect agents for the promotion of American business enterprise. They are required by law to make reports on the commerce and agriculture of the countries to which they are accredited, as instructed by the Department of State. Moreover by explicit statutory provisions they are ordered to furnish quarterly statements on the market prices of various articles of export and import in their respective regions, to supply information showing where and through what channels markets may be opened for American products and manufactures, and to transmit data respecting the local rates of wages paid to skilled and unskilled labor. To their general obligations are added particular duties. The Secretary of State forwards to consuls requests of the Department of Commerce for light on topics in which the latter is interested and transmits to it pertinent returns relative to its work. As an aid to publicity a special materials edition of the Daily Consular Reports is supplied to the Department of Commerce for publication and nation-wide distribution through its offices and agencies.

In spite of the strategic position of the consular officers for securing information and the excellent work done by them in this field, the Department of Commerce has not been satisfied with their findings. So, largely on the initiative of Secretary Hoover, Congress created in 1927 a great world-wide organization of special agents, paid unusually attractive salaries, for the sole purpose of assisting in the advancement of American trade. As a part of the scheme, a new division known as the Foreign Commerce Service was established in the Bureau of Foreign and Domestic Commerce, and a staff of trained officers was recruited for action at home or abroad on the command of the Secretary. Under his direction, their prime duties are to stimulate and forward business enterprise in the United States by investigating and reporting on commercial and industrial activities in foreign countries which may be of interest to American producers. At his request, the State Department must attach any officer of the new service to the diplomatic mission of the United States in the country to which he is sent, thus giving him a favorable ranking and better point of vantage. In accordance with these arrangements trained investigators have been dispatched to all parts of the earth to search out openings for trade and transmit the glad tidings to Washington. Although in a measure they duplicate the work of consuls and create some friction, increasing emphasis is laid on their activities by the Department of Commerce.

The collection and distribution of information respecting commodity markets are merely one phase of commercial promotion on the part of the Government. Through diplomatic and other channels it abets and facilitates the winning of opportunities to lend American capital abroad; for foreign loans also mean the export of American goods. "The consistent purpose of the present administration," said President Taft in 1912, "has been to encourage the use of American capital in the development of China." Then turning to the Caribbean region, he added: "The United States has been glad to encourage and support American bankers who were willing to lend a helping hand to the financial rehabilitation of such countries." The policy may be illustrated by a concrete example. When the news arrived in Washington in 1909 that French, German, and British bankers were arranging with the Chinese Government to lend it money for railway construction, the State Department tried by diplomatic hints to secure a share of the issue for American financiers. After it became evident that this strategy would fail, President Taft telegraphed directly to the Prince Regent at Peking, saying: "I have an intense personal interest in making use of American capital in the development of China as an instrument for the promotion of the welfare of China." With the powerful backing of the President of the United States, American bankers won the right to participate in the venture. In such ways the Federal Government contributes to the expansion of American capital, the forerunner of trade.

Similar patronage is given to American citizens seeking openings to develop natural resources, especially in the so-called backward places of the earth where there are no independent local governments strong enough to resist the encroachments of foreign powers. A sheaf of illustrations can be gathered from the papers of the State Department. One incident throws light on the process. After the World War, Great Britain was given a mandate over rich oil regions in Mesopotamia and British interests were on the point of getting a monopoly, with minor concessions to France. Against this whole business the Government of the United States made pointed objections and then espoused the claims of American oil interests to operating rights in coveted districts. After a sharp battle in the form of a diplomatic exchange, it obtained for them a share in the development under discussion. Kindred tactics have been followed by the Federal Government in the Caribbean regions, where issues of national defense as well as the prosperity of American trade are at stake. Whether far or near, on the frozen steppes of Siberia or under the tropical skies of Java, opportunities to unearth resources or sell goods are seldom neglected by the Government. If perchance one of its numerous agents should fail to see them, interested citizens will call its attention to the emergencies, perhaps by a lively protest to the State Department.

The solicitude of the Government in this relation is by no means confined to backward places where economic affairs may be highly irregular; it extends also to regions with established institutions. With a view to forcing foreign governments to provide a fair field for American business within their respective jurisdictions, the Tariff Act contains several thorny provisions. Whenever any nation makes "unjust discriminations" against the importation or sale of American goods the President may retaliate (p. 460). Again, if it puts charges or limitations on the import or sale of American commodities which are not equally imposed on like articles from other foreign lands, or places the commerce of the United States directly or indirectly at a disadvantage as compared with that of other competitors, the President may also take counter measures. This is not an idle gesture. American consular and foreign service officers are always on the watch for discriminations and American merchants may reach the Federal Government with complaints through many channels. Finally it is the duty of the Federal Trade Commission to be informed of, and to investigate, any and all obstructions raised against the foreign commerce of the United States.

While protecting American exporters against embarrassments abroad, the Federal Government assists them at home in organizing for the prosecution of their enterprises. By the Webb Act of 1918, Congress has exempted all combinations formed for the promotion of the export trade from the hobbles of the anti-trust laws, provided they do not restrain the business of any domestic exporter or interfere unduly with competition inside the United States. Associations formed under this Act vary from loose confederations of concerns bound together by temporary agreements to great consolidated incorporated companies. "One of the primary purposes of the law," reports the Federal Trade Commission under whose jurisdiction these establishments come, "was to enable American exporters to operate on an equal footing with foreign combines. This has been accomplished through coöperative agreements stabilizing export prices, reducing selling costs, standardizing grades, contract terms and sale conditions, improving the quality of the products exported, and assuring buyers of prompt and efficient service in the filling of orders. The Webb law association is also in a position to present a solid front to the buying combines which might otherwise play one exporter off against another and beat the price down to an unprofitable basis." In short, all the advantages of monopoly are thus offered to American businessmen engaged in foreign commerce—huge capital accumulations, the economies of mass production, and the privileges of price cutting and price fixing for operations abroad. Furthermore, in connection with its supervision of combinations formed under the Webb Act, the Trade Commission maintains a continuous study of unfair competition and restrictive laws in foreign countries, which may affect adversely the undertakings of American exporters.

Going beyond protests and diplomatic notes abroad, retaliations and legal assistance at home, the Government of the United States clothes its policy of supporting foreign commerce in the visible and outward signs of power. Subsidies to the American merchant marine, in the form of mail grants and loans on favorable terms, are designed to aid in furnishing the material means for keeping American commerce afloat on the waters of the seven seas. They also have another object. The trading ships built under this stimulus form an auxiliary arm of the American navy. And that navy is itself an instrument for assisting in the promotion of business—obtaining new markets and concessions and entrenching established enterprise. It is employed for this purpose not only in waters nearby, such as the Caribbean, where direct problems of national security are involved, but also far away in Turkey and China where the interests at stake are primarily economic. Huge appropriations for war craft are continually demanded by the Secretary of the Navy and admirals on the ground that additions are necessary to defend distant undertakings, not the shores of the United States. One Secretary has gone so far as to say that wherever an American dollar is invested, protection by the armed forces of the Government must extend.

This declaration is not pure hyperbole. The reality which it covers is illuminated by a statement issued by the United States Bureau of Naval Intelligence with reference to practical services rendered to American business along the shores of the eastern Mediterranean. "We have extensive interests in the Near East," runs the report, "especially in tobacco and petroleum. Early in 1919 several American destroyers were ordered to Constantinople for duty in the Near East. . . . The possible development of the economic resources of this part of the world were very carefully investigated by representatives of American commercial interests. These representatives were given every assistance by the Navy, transportation furnished them to various places, and all information of commercial activities obtained by the naval officers in their frequent trips around the Black Sea given them. . . . The Navy not only assists our commercial firms to obtain business, but when business opportunities present themselves, American firms are notified and given full information on the subject. . . . One destroyer is kept continually at Samsun, Turkey, to look after the American tobacco interests at that port. . . . The American tobacco companies represented there depend practically entirely on the moral effect of having a man-of-war in port to have their tobacco released for shipment." As a matter of fact an important concession in that region was won for American capitalists by an American naval officer, who after his retirement devoted himself largely to the promotion of the company in which he was interested. If the enterprise turned out badly, it was not his fault. Though few admirals and captains thus combine the art of making money with the development of trade, their concern for American advantages is none the less keen and effective.

Occasionally mere demonstrations of armed force pass into active military operations in other lands. Numerous cases of armed intervention "to safeguard American rights, maintain order, and uphold the honor of our country" have arisen in Caribbean regions since the opening of the twentieth century (p. 688). If similar incidents have not frequently occurred in other places further removed from the United States, the fact is due to local circumstances, not to absence of power or policy. Sometimes a mere threat is sufficient to produce results. Of course such hints must be made with discretion, but illustrations of their effectiveness are not wanting. When Mexico issued in 1918 a decree deemed injurious to American oil concerns operating in that country, the Secretary of State, in protesting against it, suggested serious consequences: "It becomes the function of the Government of the United States most earnestly and respectfully to call the attention of the Mexican Government to the necessity which may arise to impel it to protect the property of its citizens in Mexico divested or injuriously affected by the decree above cited." Veiled language could not be more explicit.

As an important supplement to its program for promoting and protecting American interests, the Government has adopted a policy of supervising loans made abroad. In 1922 the President directed the Department of State to publish a circular requesting financial houses that wished to sell foreign bonds in the American money market to furnish information concerning their projects to the Department, with a view to discovering whether any objections were forthcoming. Under this order many issues have been floated with the official sanction of the State Department, real or apparent, involving certain obligations on the part of the United States. For example, the bankers who bought out a block of securities for the Dominican Republic in that year announced in an advertisement that "the issue of these bonds has received the approval of the United States Government," and included a memorandum by the Secretary of State to the effect that the acceptance and valuation of this paper by Santo Domingo was guaranteed by the military government of that country—in effect his own Government. Moreover the text of the bonds contained a declaration that they were secured "with the consent of the Government of the United States." On other occasions, more or less officially, the State Department has intervened in proposed flotations, to give its approval or indicate its displeasure. For example, an important oriental loan was blocked by the Department in the interest of commerce as against banking. The extent to which sanction implies obligation is, however, one of the veiled mysteries of the future.

In forwarding the interests of American foreign commerce, many branches of the Federal Government are employed, as made apparent by the above record. This is one of the chief duties of consuls, commercial attachés, foreign commerce service officers, and other special agents. It is a fundamental part of the work of the Department of Commerce. Even naval and military attachés are supposed to report any trade and investment opportunities that come to their ken. The President and the Secretary of the Treasury, in enforcing tariff, anti-dumping, and anti-discrimination provisions, are laid under heavy responsibilities. An ever increasing share of the diplomatic work carried on by the State Department pertains to trade, investments, and concessions. The Department of Agriculture, through special agents, looks after the sale of farm produce overseas. The Navy, a mobile force always at the command of the President, is both an advance agent and a police officer for foreign business. Hence, when the various federal functions and establishments coming under this head are viewed collectively, it becomes evident that the promotion and protection of American business enterprise abroad constitute a primary concern of the Federal Government. Nothing, it seems, that ingenuity can devise is neglected. Whether it is "government interference with business" or "business interference with government" may be left to the debates of theorists.

CHAPTER XV

Labor and Immigration

Like many other functions assumed by the Federal Government, those pertaining to labor, organized and unorganized, have grown out of economic and technical developments rather than express authorizations of the Constitution. When that instrument was framed, mechanics and artisans in certain trades had formed unions in some of the leading cities, but these little groups were not yet federated on a national scale. In the main, their activities were confined within state boundaries and were subject to state jurisdiction. At that time, furthermore, labor did not play a continuous and important rôle in public affairs, even locally. Hence its existence is not even mentioned in the fundamental law of the land, except perhaps in the provision for the return of runaway servants. Only after the construction of long railway lines and the formation of huge industrial corporations on a nation-wide basis did labor take the continent for its sphere, by creating associations of the local unions in the great industries such as boot and shoe making, iron, steel, and brick laying. Not until 1886, following several tentative experiments in that line, was a general fusion of crafts firmly effected by the establishment of the American Federation of Labor.

Yet in all of its undertakings designed to raise wages, reduce hours, and improve working conditions, organized labor early found points of direct contact with the ordinary powers and functions of the Federal Government. In its efforts to uphold American standards of living, it encountered the immigration question, subject entirely to federal jurisdiction. In dealing with railways and other concerns engaged in enterprises extending beyond the boundaries of a single state, particularly in carrying on strikes, labor came within the scope of those clauses of the Constitution which confer upon Congress the power to regulate interstate commerce, to establish post offices and post roads, and to provide agencies, including troops, for the enforcement of federal law. Since, moreover, the Federal Government has always been a large employer of labor itself, its own standards of hours and wages naturally fell within the sphere of trade union interests. Finally, Congress can appropriate money for purposes not specifically mentioned in the Constitution—the promotion of business enterprise, agriculture, and education, for example; so, taking advantage of this opportunity, organized labor appealed for assistance in various forms, especially the collection of data and statistics bearing on wages, employment, and other industrial matters. In various ways, and for divers reasons, therefore, scarcely foreseen by the framers of the Constitution, the Federal Government has assumed many responsibilities and exercises many powers immediately related to the organization, methods, and welfare of American labor.

Immigration and Employment

It is not necessary to go very far into American history to discover that the prime force in the movement for the restriction of immigration has been organized labor. It has not been alone in its activities in this relation but it has been persistent and effective in its exactions. And the reason is not hard to find. The raising of wages by concerted efforts and the maintenance of standards depend very largely on control over the number of applicants available for employment. Within limits the law of demand and supply operates here with precision. Hence, whenever organized labor started a large-scale operation to increase wages or prevent reductions, it learned at once that its measures could be easily defeated by a huge influx of foreign workers willing to accept almost any wages they could get. Again and again labor leaders built up strong unions only to find their fences broken and their projects nullified by a new wave of immigration.

But for nearly a hundred years the Federal Government, instead of restraining immigration, actually fostered it by throwing wide the gates of the nation to all comers. Manufacturers, hoping to keep wages down, and land speculators, seeking farmers to buy their holdings, approved and supported the open-door policy. Indeed in 1864 Congress by law authorized the importation of laborers in large masses bound by contract to work for specific employers. And under this legislation profit-making corporations were formed to collect workers in Europe and the Orient for the American market. Although the law was soon repealed the practices sanctioned by it were long continued.

Against this free and easy immigration program American trade unions began to make vigorous protests shortly after the Civil War. With growing determination they called for the abolition of the contract labor system, the total exclusion of Orientals, and the limitation of immigration from the Old World. In time other citizens, for various reasons, demanded a restriction of immigration, and as a result of unremitting agitation, bill after bill was enacted by Congress. In their present form these consolidated statutes entirely exclude from the United States five classes of immigrants.

In the first place, contract laborers are denied admission. This class embraces all persons "who have been induced, assisted, encouraged, or solicited to migrate to this country by offers or promises of employment, whether such offers or promises are true or false, or in consequence of agreements, oral, written or printed, express or implied, to perform labor in this country of any kind, skilled or unskilled; persons who have come in consequence of advertisements for laborers printed, published, or distributed in a foreign country." The terms of the law, however, do not apply to domestic servants, members of learned professions, ministers, nurses, or entertainers such as singers and actors, even though they come to America under contract. Also, contract laborers needed in the preparation or operation of exhibits at fairs and expositions are allowed entry. And the Secretary of Labor is empowered to permit the immigration of skilled artisans bound by agreements if all similar workers in the United States are employed, that is, when the domestic supply is inadequate.

The second group of immigrants to whom the gates of the country are absolutely closed are persons from large specified regions of Asia and adjacent islands, including Chinese, Japanese, East Indians, Hindus, and many other races or nationalities. This measure of prohibition applies not only to laborers but all classes except "government officers, ministers or religious teachers, missionaries, lawyers, physicians, chemists, civil engineers, teachers, students, authors, artists, merchants, and travelers for curiosity or pleasure," and their legal wives and children under sixteen. If any member of the exempted group fails to maintain the status which entitles him to residence here, he may be deported. Although this exclusion of Orientals is based on various grounds, the laws providing for it were enacted largely as the result of pressure brought to bear by organized labor, particularly on the Pacific Coast. They sprang mainly from conflicts over standards of hours and wages—into which of course racial elements entered.

A third class of immigrants totally barred out embraces illiterates of all nations, otherwise admissible. An act of Congress passed in 1917 denies admission to all aliens over sixteen years of age, physically capable of reading, who cannot read the English language or some other language or dialect, including Hebrew. There are a few saving exceptions, but on the whole the test is rigidly applied. Like the legislation against Orientals, this measure was powerfully supported by the American Federation of Labor although its leaders insisted at the time on still more stringent provisions.

Shifting from actions directly involving the labor market to the realm of opinion, Congress has excluded immigrants who harbor "dangerous thoughts." In this category come anarchists and all people who advise, advocate, or teach opposition to organized government, or who are affiliated with any association or society devoted to that kind of propaganda. Likewise rejected are aliens who write or distribute, or belong to associations engaged in publishing and circulating, printed matter advocating opposition to organized government, or the overthrow by force or violence of the Federal Government or all forms of law, or the unlawful assault and killing of officers of any established government or the unlawful injury of property or sabotage. While these measures of prohibition are also generally endorsed by employers and by other persons outside of trade unions, the American Federation of Labor has ardently supported them as a part of its war on the "Reds" and other "disruptive forces" within its ranks.

Based on special considerations but still limiting the immigration of low grade labor are the provisions of law which lump together and debar, as undesirable, aliens who have certain physical and moral disabilities or are paupers. To the first division belong all persons afflicted with epilepsy, tuberculosis, or any loathsome or dangerous contagious disease or who are of unsound mind, together with those possessing other physical or mental defects likely to affect adversely their power to earn a living. Aliens shut out on moral grounds include criminals, habitual drunkards, polygamists, and prostitutes.

Not content with the exclusion of contract laborers, Orientals, illiterates, and revolutionists, the American Federation of Labor continued to press for still more drastic cuts in the volume of immigration, especially after the World War. In such efforts it was now aided more zealously than ever by citizens interested in Americanization, in preserving "the purity of the Nordic strain," in rejecting people inclined to be hostile to American institutions, and in holding down the growth of the population. As a result of pressure from many directions Congress enacted in 1924 the most sweeping immigration law in the history of the country. The new measure places a definite limit on the total number of immigrants from Europe and certain parts of the Americas who may enter the United States annually. As finally determined when the new system was inaugurated in 1929, the figure for each year was fixed at 153,714.

In distributing this number among the various countries entitled to send emigrants, Congress provided an elaborate quota system. With certain broad exceptions the total population of the continental United States for 1920 was divided into classes according to their respective "national origins." Although the task was in fact impossible, it was done—in a way. On this basis an estimate was made showing the proportion which the people of English, German, Italian, and other national descent in the United States respectively bear to the whole number of inhabitants included in the above census reckoning.

Thereupon each of the countries from which emigrants are allowed was assigned an annual quota. This figure is the number bearing the same relation to one hundred fifty thousand which the number of inhabitants of the particular national origin in the United States bears to the total population enumerated as just indicated—with the exception that no quota is to be less than one hundred. For example, the inhabitants of German descent in the country constituted about one sixth of the total population in 1920, and hence the annual quota of immigrants allotted to Germany is about one sixth of one hundred fifty thousand, or approximately twenty-five thousand. In effect, therefore, the tendency of the new system is to make the stream of immigration conform to the composition of the American population in 1920, with some exceptions. In other words one of its purposes is to preserve the "balance of power" among the various races represented in our polyglot nation.

Before passing from the subject, however, certain important exceptions or collaterals must be noted. Two classes of aliens are admitted without reference to the numerical restriction. One group, defined as non-immigrant, is composed of government officials with their families and assistants;

aliens, including seamen while on duty, temporarily visiting the United States or in continuous transit through it; legally admitted aliens who find it necessary to pass through a foreign country while in transit from one part of the United States to another; and aliens carrying on trade provided for by existing treaties. The other group, defined as "non-quota immigrants," is composed of unmarried minor children and wives of citizens of the United States and husbands of American citizens married previous to June 1, 1928; lawfully admitted immigrants returning from a temporary visit abroad; ministers and professors, together with their wives and unmarried children under eighteen years of age, who have already followed their calling for two years abroad and intend to continue doing so in the United States; students over fifteen years old entering the country for study at an institution approved by the Secretary of Labor; former women citizens who lost their citizenship by marriage prior to September 22, 1922, but who are now unmarried.

Entirely outside of the quota system also are all immigrants born in Canada, Newfoundland, Mexico, Cuba, Haiti, the Dominican Republic, the Canal Zone, or an independent country of Central or South America and their wives, and unmarried children under eighteen. In spite of the strong demand for additional limitations these may enter the United States freely in any number.

It is evident from such legislation that America is firmly resolved to maintain its standard of life against the pressure of the ever-multiplying populations of Europe and Asia. The wide-open door of "the asylum for the oppressed of all nations" is definitely closed, marking a new stage in the economy of the world. It is also evident that the immigration quotas favor Great Britain and Ireland above all and then Germany, for according to the present allotment these countries have about two thirds of the immigrants admissible under the rule fixing the normal annual number at 153,714. From figures available in 1926, it was reckoned that in central and eastern Europe alone there was a demand for 625,979 admissions against a quota of 13,870. Judging from long experience the total immigration would now exceed a million a year under an open-door policy whereas it actually amounted to 279,678 for the year ending June 30, 1929, including quota and non-quota contingents.

If there remains any doubt about the close affiliation of immigration restriction with labor interests, it can be cleared up by reference to the fact that the general supervision of the whole system of control is vested in the commissioner-general of immigration in the Department of Labor; and this Department has been headed, since its establishment in 1913, by a Secretary taken from trade union ranks. Subject to the terms of the law, the commissioner-general may establish rules, prescribe forms of reports, and issue any orders which he may deem useful in carrying out the provisions of the immigration acts and in protecting aliens from fraud and loss. It is his duty, from time to time, to detail officers from the service to make investigations into the number of aliens detained in penal, reformatory, and charitable institutions throughout the United States, and to look after the deportation of aliens who have become public charges or who are not lawfully entitled to be in this country. At each port of entry, there is a commissioner of immigration who has under him a staff of inspectors and other officials.

Formerly the work of examining immigrants was conducted entirely at American ports, with the result that great hardships were inflicted on people who had to be sent back as legally unqualified. Here was an evil which cried out for a remedy and finally the Government attacked it in 1925 by stationing special officers at its consulates in Great Britain and Ireland for the purpose of making preliminary inquiries into the fitness of applicants for admission. Proving successful in these instances, the practice was extended to several other countries, particularly in northern Europe. As an outcome there has been a substantial reduction in the number of immigrants rejected on arrival in the United States.

After running the gantlet of inspectors in his native land

and a scrutiny of his papers at the entry port, the immigrant is questioned with regard to his probable usefulness as a citizen of the United States. "The modus operandi at all government stations," says a former New York commissioner of immigration, "is to place every individual applicant for admission to these shores on the defensive and to make it incumbent upon him . . . to show why he should be admitted; but to do it in a humane spirit and treat each applicant with becoming consideration, without for a moment losing sight of the object that Congress had in view in limiting admission to these shores to those who are sound in body and mind and who are without question likely to find support without depending in whole or in part on public or private charity."

Aliens about whose qualifications an inspector is doubtful are held for examination before the board of special inquiry at each port charged with hearing such cases. From an adverse decision of this board an appeal may be carried through the commissioner of the port and the commissioner-general of immigration to the Secretary of Labor. All persons who are excluded must be returned to their homes by the steamship companies which brought them.

Immigrants who find themselves debarred by the numerous regulations discussed above do not always give up the struggle for entry. Seeing the doors shut in their faces they often try some ingenious scheme for worming their way into the United States. Sometimes they make use of "loopholes" in the law; for instance, that proviso which permits alien seamen to go ashore while their vessels are in port. Once on land sailors bent on settling in the United States simply try to "disappear" by mingling in the multitude. Not all aliens, however, can successfully pose as seamen, students, ministers, or other privileged immigrants for purposes of taking advantage of some quirk in the statutes. But such invaders may break in by resorting to one of the many devices now employed in smuggling. Owing to the long Canadian and Mexican borders, the leagues of sea-coast, and the vast aerial ocean above, intruders are frequently successful in escaping

Photo by Brown Brothers

Immigration Examination at a Port of Entry.

Courtesy of the United States Bureau of Mines

PREPARING FOR DISASTER: FEDERAL TRAINING IN MINE RESCUE WORK (*See* P. 600).

frontier guards by motor boat, automobile, or aircraft. An innocent looking plane droning away far up in the clouds over some lonely region may really present a critical problem in immigration supervision.

Even the border patrol created in 1924 as a special agency of the Immigration Service to guard against illegal entry is not strong enough to defeat the stratagems of interlopers. Although eighteen thousand aliens were apprehended during the fourth year of its existence in attempts to gain unlawful admission, the net was not close enough to assure strict enforcement. Nor is this a cause for surprise. Since the penalty placed on trespassers for the first offense merely consists of a ride home at public expense, they see everything to gain and nothing to lose in making at least one effort to break through the barrier. A second offense, however, is punishable by a heavy fine or imprisonment or both under an act of 1930.

In view of such circumstances Congress has vested in the commissioner-general of immigration a broad power to deport aliens who gain illegal admission to the United States. To this duty it added in 1918 full authority to expel alien revolutionists, anarchists, advocates of sabotage, violence, and assassination, and all foreigners who aid and abet them. Upon aliens arrested and held for deportation is imposed the burden of showing that they are not in the United States in violation of law. With respect to the facts in such cases the decisions of the commissioner are final, unless, of course, reversed on appeal to his chief, the Secretary of Labor. Under no conditions will the courts go behind the findings of the immigration authorities as to the facts constituting the charge against an accused. In other words emphasis is laid on swiftness in administration rather than on the real or supposed rights of individuals.

Taking full advantage of the legal technicalities, certain federal officers in charge of deportations were guilty of grave injustice when the "anti-red" hysteria swept over the country during and after the World War. Hundreds of aliens were seized, torn from their homes, held in prison, subjected to inquisitorial processes, and hustled, some of them, on ships bound to their native lands without receiving an opportunity to test their legal rights. Often aliens were kept in jails for weeks and then released when nothing could be found to incriminate them. While some undesirable characters and public nuisances were disposed of by this process, innocent persons suffered and the bitterness created by the methods pursued materially offset any benefits obtained. Indeed a number of prominent attorneys, after a careful examination of the facts, were moved to file a public protest against the conduct of the government officials engaged in this work.

Although immigration is limited and guarded, the problem of unemployment in an overcrowded market has not been eliminated. On the contrary owing to the growth of labor-saving machinery there is nearly always present a large body of men and women out of work—at least temporarily. Coupled with this technical displacement of labor is the pressure created by cyclical business depressions, the movement of farmers to the city, and the increasing number of young people seeking opportunities in the urban centers.

With a view to contracting the labor supply, as well as on humanitarian grounds, trade unions have generally supported proposals of law designed to keep children out of mines, factories, and offices until they reach a fair degree of maturity. Jurisdiction over the matter belongs, however, to the states and many of them refuse to adopt high standards in this relation, thus making it difficult for businessmen in the advanced sections to meet the competition of their brethren in backward regions. After a season of agitation advocates of child-labor prohibition finally induced Congress in 1916 to attempt the establishment of an age limit throughout the country in certain fundamental industries, by excluding from interstate commerce the goods of those which employed children below the minimum; but the law was declared unconstitutional by the Supreme Court. A later act directed to the same object, this time in the form of a tax, was likewise held invalid (p. 340). As a last resort, an amendment to the Constitution intended to accomplish this purpose was adopted by Congress in 1924 but failed to secure ratification. The restriction of child labor, therefore, continues to depend entirely on the good will of the respective states.

At all times a considerable part of the prevailing unemployment is due to the fact that the supply of workers is too large in certain industries and districts and too small in others. Obviously this evil is due to a lack of knowledge of the total situation and the absence of machinery for bringing men and jobs together. Although private and state establishments attempt to deal with the problem thus created, their efforts are necessarily limited. The United States constitutes in reality one vast industrial society and nothing short of operation on a national scale can eliminate large maladjustments in the labor market. In recognition of this contingency the Federal Government conducts two types of employment agencies. One is intended to furnish the personnel needed in its own administration while the other serves only private interests. The first is discussed above in the chapter on administration (p. 317). This work, of course, is within the scope of the Government's historical duties. On the other hand the business of aiding people to secure employment in private enterprises and assisting employers in obtaining workmen presents quite different aspects both in policy and performance.

The latter activity is forwarded by the national Employment Service in the Department of Labor. While this undertaking is partly carried on by coöperating state and municipal authorities, federal officials play an important rôle in coördinating local activities along national lines. Reports of employment conditions throughout the country are periodically collected by the Service and distributed in the form of bulletins to guide businessmen and workers alike. But the Service is more than a mere collecting and editing agency. On its own authority it recruits seasonal farm laborers in certain parts of the country and supervises their distribution among the sections requiring their help. In this connection its continuous reporting system also warns interested persons about the existence of surplus labor in some regions and supplies them with information respecting demands for more men in others. Casual farm laborers no longer need "trust to luck" but may now discover the nature of the opportunities ahead before making long journeys to planting or harvest districts in search of work. Still, in spite of the good it does, the Employment Service is severely limited in scope and vigorous efforts have been made in Congress since the financial crash of 1929 to provide it with powers, personnel, and funds adequate to the tasks in front of it—so far in vain.

When all such efforts to adjust supply to demand in the labor world are efficiently made there remains a great deal of unemployment especially in times of business depression. Formerly, as we have said, this evil, with its accompaniments of misery and suffering for millions, was regarded as a visitation of an angry Providence or blind forces which no efforts of mankind could avert. But governments are now beginning to discard the fatalistic view, and schemes for the stabilization of industry and employment are being evolved by statesmen in America as well as abroad. In foreign countries, notably England, a system of allowances, called "doles," has been adopted as a means of tiding idle workers over periods of stagnation. Although the practice, which certainly is open to grave objections, has not met with favor in the United States, high authorities, including President Hoover, have proposed substitutes—large programs of river and harbor improvements, flood relief, public works, and public buildings to take care of the slack in private enterprise. If these undertakings were increased in times of industrial depression, it is argued, work could be extensively provided and the restoration of normal conditions expedited. In fact ever since the panic of 1921 the possibilities of such a scheme have been the subject of serious discussion, never more earnestly than in connection with President Hoover's conference of leaders in industry, agriculture, and labor after the stock market crash of 1929 (p. 642).

Working Conditions

Vital as are the problems of employment, the conditions under which the routine tasks of labor must be performed are certainly of no less concern. While the range of industries over which the Federal Government has jurisdiction under the Constitution is limited in number, their size and nature have called for the enactment of many significant laws in this field. Federal statutes now prescribe minimum standards of various kinds for workers on interstate railways, seamen, and national employees. Ranging from regulation of the sailor's diet in great detail to restrictions on the hours of labor for train dispatchers, such federal legislation shows a tendency to grow in volume. It is also supplemented by measures pertaining to safety in particular industries—to that protection for life and limb so essential in the age of technology, with high speed tools, dangerous machinery, inflammatory materials, and explosive chemicals (pp. 594 ff.).

With an eye to the interests of the public no less than the welfare of the workers involved, Congress has applied certain regulations to nearly all the common carriers of goods and passengers under its control. It has, for example, forbidden railways to require or permit their employees to remain on duty for a longer shift than sixteen consecutive hours, or to return to work after such a stretch of labor before enjoying at least ten hours of rest. Further, Congress has provided that dispatchers and other workers concerned with directing the movement of trains shall not be allowed to be in service for more than nine hours in any twenty-four hour period in places operated continuously, nor more than thirteen hours in places operated in the daytime, save in cases of emergency. This legislation, it should be said, was primarily due to revelations concerning accidents, causing great loss of life among passengers, that had occurred largely because weary workmen had fallen asleep at their posts.

Quite different in origin is the famous Adamson Act of 1916, driven through Congress by the railway unions under threat of a nation-wide strike. This law prescribes that eight hours shall be deemed a day's work and the measure of a day's work for the purpose of reckoning the compensation of all employees on interstate railways (with a few exceptions), who are actually engaged in the operation of trains for the transportation of passengers and property. While considerations of public safety entered into the enactment of the statute in question, its prime purpose was to fix the eight-hour day for trainmen—to establish a fundamental trade union standard as the law of the land in this field. Although a great outcry was raised at the time against it as a form of government intervention not warranted by the requirements of general welfare, the Railway Brotherhoods were determined to win it, either from Congress or the railway companies, by paralyzing transportation if necessary.

As a result of demands scarcely less insistent from the Seamen's Union, Congress has laid down certain labor conditions for vessels coming within its jurisdiction. Since seamen must eat, sleep, and work on shipboard and cannot quit in mid-ocean whenever they are dissatisfied with the facilities furnished, they could with even more propriety call upon the Federal Government for aid in fixing minimum standards. Taking their special situation into account, Congress has enacted an elaborate code of sea legislation, in which the La Follette Seamen's Act occupies a prominent place. It has stipulated that, subject to varying conditions of tonnage and destination, American ships shall provide satisfactory food, water, and clothing for seamen and carry a suitable supply of medicine. With respect to food the law establishes a "minimum diet" of which the following menu for Monday is typical: Water, five quarts; biscuit, one half pound; salt pork, one pound; bread, one and one half pounds; potatoes or yams, one pound; beans, one third pint; rice, one third pint; coffee, three fourths ounce; tea, one eighth ounce; sugar, three ounces; pickles, one fourth pint; lard, one ounce; butter, two ounces; mustard, pepper and salt sufficient for seasoning. If the supply of provisions is cut below this allowance without a just cause, the crew is entitled to additional compensation. As an aid in determining the extent of the reduction, weights and measures must be supplied on request of the crew. If the food or water is inadequate or bad the crew, on reaching port, may complain to a proper federal officer who, upon examination, can require amends. A stock of clothing, tobacco, and blankets must also be kept aboard ship for sale at prices not to exceed ten per cent above the wholesale rates.

Guarantees as to food supply Congress has supplemented by regulations as to living quarters, management, wages, and hours. On long voyages a safe and warm room must be provided for the seamen. Corporal punishment, once a grave abuse on the ocean, is forbidden on board American vessels. Wages must be paid in gold or its equivalent, and cannot be made to depend on the freight carried or on earnings. Part payment in each port is also mandatory. In general a ship of over one hundred tons is required to have two shifts for its sailors and three for the engine-room force while at sea. When in a safe harbor nine hours constitute the maximum legal work day on such vessels; and, in addition, on Sundays and certain other holidays no unnecessary work shall be required of the crew. If perchance an American seaman is destitute in a foreign land, the local consular officer of the United States may require the master of an American vessel to transport the unfortunate derelict to the home port to which the ship is bound, at federal expense and on specific conditions as amended by an Act of 1930.

With respect to its own operations the Federal Government has adopted certain labor standards. In the executive departments the heads must require of all clerks and other employees not less than seven hours' work each day exclusive of Sundays and holidays, and may by special order extend the period without extra compensation. For practical purposes this establishes a seven-hour day for most of the clerical personnel. For the Government Printing Office, the principle of the eight-hour day is laid down; and the same rule applies to laborers and mechanics who are employed by the Federal Government or by the District of Columbia or by any contractor or subcontractor engaged in a public work of the United States or the District of Columbia, including river and harbor improvements. Teeth are put into the law by the provision of heavy penalties for violations. In connection with the leasing of federal mineral lands to private concerns, Congress has declared that the eight-hour day shall be observed by the lessee for workers employed underground. In other words, with reference to matters subject to its jurisdiction, the Federal Government has widely accepted the idea of the limited work day as a normal rule.

In spite of all precautions in the form of safety regulations and appliances and reasonable hours of employment, accidents happen in the best of industrial enterprises. For a long time, however, the Federal Government made no serious attempt to modify the ancient principle of the law, originating in the days of stage coaches, which threw upon every employee all "the necessary risks" of his occupation and allowed him to recover damages for injuries, by a tedious and costly lawsuit, only when the employer had been personally responsible. But at length in 1908 Congress made all railway common carriers, subject to its jurisdiction, liable to an action for damages for death or injury "resulting in whole or in part from the negligence of any of the officers, agents, or employees of such carrier, or by reason of any defect or insufficiency, due to its negligence, in its cars, engines, appliances, machinery, track, roadbed, works, boats, wharves, or other equipment." Furthermore it provided that employees of such concerns are not to be prevented from collecting at least a certain amount of reparation even when they themselves have been guilty of some contributory negligence. Similar rules were later applied to seamen on American vessels subject to federal jurisdiction, who are injured in the course of their duties. Though a decided advance on the previous condition of affairs, federal compensation laws are not yet abreast of the legislation enacted by the more enlightened states which provide accident insurance and make payment automatic under public authority without resort to long and uncertain litigation.

The federal statutes just reviewed left out of consideration a large class of longshoremen and harbor workers, engaged in loading, unloading, and supplying vessels. Under early law these laborers, variously estimated as numbering between two hundred thousand and five hundred thousand, were not protected by state compensation acts because technically speaking they were not operating on property located on state soil. On the other hand they were not sailors and could not come under federal legislation governing damage cases for that group. To remedy this injustice Congress provided in 1927 a system of compensation for longshoremen and harbor workers, on more modern lines than the arrangements for railway employees and seamen, and vested supervision over execution of the law in the United States Employees' Compensation Commission.

For employees engaged directly in federal services the Government has created a compensation project of its own. This scheme is administered by the Commission, just cited, which in the discharge of its duties makes use of medical facilities of the United States Public Health Service. In accordance with the terms of the Act, compensation is allowed in cases involving the death or injury of federal employees in the performance of duties, not due to willful misconduct or intoxication. Persons claiming compensation do not have to file suit in a court of law but are paid automatically when their claims are rightfully established before the Commission.

Compensation alone does not assure the restoration of an injured worker to a place of usefulness in society. If the cycle is to be completed in many cases, he must be prepared for re-employment, should his injuries require it, in some other occupation. Rehabilitation, intended to train him to overcome handicaps due to loss of limb or one or more of his faculties, is essential not only to his happiness but also to relieving the charitable load carried by taxpayers. Naturally the Federal Government cannot perform this function directly except possibly with reference to its own employees. It can, however, lend financial aid to the operation. Accordingly Congress has appropriated a certain annual sum to states which meet fixed requirements relative to the promotion of vocational rehabilitation. In 1930 it renewed for a period of four years the grants originally authorized under an act passed ten years earlier.

Industrial Disputes

Into that sphere in which labor and capital carry on controversies respecting hours, wages, and conditions of employment not fixed by law, the Federal Government frequently enters in various rôles. Over industrial disputes arising in interstate or foreign commerce, of course, it has constitutional authority. Whenever a contest involves the execution of federal law or the discharge of a regular function, such as the carriage of mails, the Government likewise has a direct interest and full warrant for intervention. Nor do labor conflicts within the jurisdiction of a state lie entirely beyond the scope of federal power. If a strike or lockout of this character results in disorders, the President, on appeal from the proper authorities of the state, may employ federal troops. If the struggle concerns persons or corporations of two or more states, the assistance of federal courts in the form of writs of injunction (p. 506) may be invoked, because these tribunals have jurisdiction over suits between citizens of different states. Finally state legislation relative to picketing, strikes, and other trade union tactics may be declared void by federal courts, particularly under the Fourteenth Amendment (p. 510).

Although the interstate character of labor disputes with common carriers gives legal sanction for adopting almost any policy of intervention, mediatory or coercive, Congress, through the Railway Labor Act of 1926, has merely provided for the extension of good offices on the part of the Government, without authorizing the exercise of power to compel either side to abide by its decisions. Disputes between any express, sleeping-car, or railroad company doing an interstate, international, or intra-territorial business and its employees must be conducted in accordance with the Act; but if all efforts fail the drastic methods of the strike or lockout may be brought into play.

The Act in question simply prescribes certain conditions of negotiation. It requires the carriers and their employees to create boards of adjustment and imposes on them the duty of making every reasonable effort to close their controversies by conciliatory methods. The actual settlement of each issue is in the first instance left to private enterprise. To deal with cases of continued disagreement between contestants, however, Congress has created the Board of Mediation, an independent establishment of the Federal Government composed of five members appointed by the President with the advice and consent of the Senate. On appeal from either party or independently the Board may offer its services as a kind of counsellor in the hope that its leadership will bring the disputants to terms without imposing its will on either. Should its mediation fail, arbitration is the next recourse offered by law, although it is not made compulsory; in case the parties cannot agree on all the arbitrators, it is the duty of the Board to name one or more disinterested men itself. If all these processes come to naught, as a last resort, when a dispute threatens substantially to interrupt interstate commerce, the Board may request the President of the United States to appoint an Emergency Board to investigate and report, but even the conclusions of this special agency are not binding on anybody.

With respect to other circumstances in which federal authority may be invoked in industrial disputes, the terms of law are more vigorous. The Constitution provides that the United States shall protect each state against acts of domestic violence, on request of its legislature or, if that body cannot be convened, of the governor. Full power to respond to calls for intervention under this head has been delegated to the President by Congress. Furthermore whenever unlawful combinations or assemblages of persons make it impracticable, in his judgment, to enforce federal laws by the ordinary course of judicial proceedings, he may call upon the militia of any state as well as the Army and Navy for the purpose of curbing resistance and compelling obedience. A notable example of presidential action under this statute occurred in 1894 when President Cleveland sent troops to deal with the Pullman strike in Chicago and guarantee the movement of mails. As a result of federal interference the strike collapsed, causing a great outcry on the part of labor leaders who contended that in reality Cleveland's procedure was unnecessary and a favor to the railways.

In the matter of labor conflicts which are purely local in character and involve neither interstate commerce, nor the Constitution, nor the enforcement of federal laws, Congress of course has no coercive powers. It has, however, realized that many industrial struggles, working injury to all parties concerned, may be prevented or settled by conferences between the disputants arranged by liaison officers offering their services on a purely voluntary basis. Accordingly it has authorized the Secretary of Labor to act as a mediator or to appoint commissioners of conciliation to serve in his stead, if in his judgment the interests of economic peace may require it. Under this sanction a Division of Conciliation has been created in the Department of Labor. Whenever a serious labor controversy arises, agents of the Division may be sent to the scene of disturbance with the idea of establishing friendly relations with the contestants and effecting a settlement through the exercise of judgment and tact, applying no compulsory force whatever. Each year several hundred cases are handled by the Division, often with good results.

Labor disputes coming within the scope of the Division of Conciliation vary so much in nature and in the conditions from which they arise that few generalizations respecting its activities are possible. An example of its work, however, may serve to illustrate the potentialities. On August 10, 1927, a group of men were discharged from the well-drilling department of a large oil concern because they had joined a labor organization. Having summarily ousted these workers the superintendent in charge refused to negotiate with them or to employ members of a trade union on any terms; for him the matter was closed. When in response to this action sympathetic strikes began to loom on the horizon, a representative of the Conciliation Service was dispatched to the seat of the trouble. Finding the superintendent unwilling to yield in the slightest particular, the agent then sought out the higher officials of the company, finally reaching the president. At last he succeeded in inducing the management to repudiate the decision of its field superintendent and to reinstate the men regardless of their union affiliations. With the outcome both the company and the workers seemed satisfied in the end.

If extraordinary conditions arise the President of the United States may himself intervene in industrial disputes which lie entirely outside of federal jurisdiction. For such action Roosevelt set a very notable precedent in 1902. In that year a strike of anthracite coal miners, starting in the summer and running on late into the autumn, paralyzed many industries and threatened whole cities with the menace of a heatless winter. Powerless to do anything themselves, governors and mayors appealed to the President for aid. When he inquired into the situation, he found John Mitchell, leader of the miners, willing to arbitrate the issues at stake in the contest and the mine owners resolutely determined to reject the demands of the men and all outside interference with their policies. At length President Roosevelt came to the conclusion that this state of affairs was intolerable. He, therefore, made preliminary arrangements to have federal troops, if necessary, take possession of the mines and operate them until the strike could be settled. After this preparatory gesture he then invited the contestants to the White House and by dint of hard labor induced them to accept, as a substitute or compromise, arbitration by a commission appointed by himself. In this way the long struggle was brought to a close. Thus President Roosevelt showed what the Chief Magistrate of the nation, using the prestige of his high office, could do in the way of industrial conciliation.

Passing from the relations of Congress and the President to industrial controversies, we now come to the rôle of the federal courts, supported by the armed forces of the Government if necessary to the execution of their decrees. They have, of course, a wide jurisdiction over all cases involving interstate commerce and the enforcement of federal statutes in general, touching labor interests at many points. Under the Constitution they likewise have jurisdiction over suits between citizens of different states (p. 111). Since our great business corporations, which are "citizens" in this connection, usually have plants and offices in various parts of the country, they can as a rule find legal grounds for taking actions against trade unions and petitions for injunctions against strikers into federal tribunals, even though no measures of national law are involved. Accordingly it may be said that the courts of the United States have numerous sanctions for hearing and deciding the causes of interested parties engaged in industrial contests.

Inasmuch as the writ of injunction constitutes a powerful weapon which the federal courts can bring to bear in labor disputes, this famous instrument deserves special consideration here. Such a writ, as explained elsewhere (p. 122), may take various forms. It may be a decree ordering a specified person or corporation to continue the performance of particular acts. Thus the employees of a railway may be commanded to continue handling the cars of a company on which they may wish to bring pressure for one reason or another. Again, an injunction may enjoin a party from altering certain existing conditions in any respect until the merits of the case have been decided. Sometimes the writ is in the nature of a mandate instructing a party to desist from determinate practices, such as picketing, holding public meetings, or committing other wrongs for which no legal remedy is available. In ordinary circumstances anyone who disobeys an injunction may be summarily tried and punished by the judge who granted it.

Against actions of the federal courts in this connection trade union leaders have long protested. As early as 1896 they made the subject an issue in national politics. During the great Pullman railway strike two years before, the federal district court in Chicago issued a general command to all persons concerned, ordering them not to interfere with the transmission of the mails or with interstate commerce in any form. For refusing to obey the decree Eugene V. Debs, director of the strike, was arrested, fined, and imprisoned. Thereupon, through his counsel, Debs claimed the right to jury trial and contended that the federal judge could not impose a penalty which was not expressly provided by statute. On appeal, the Supreme Court upheld the power of the lower court to grant the order in question, and ruled that imprisonment for contempt without jury trial did not violate the principle of due process of law. From that time forward vigorous efforts were made by organized labor to pledge the major political parties to a reform of the law.

In the main the Democrats took a more sympathetic interest in the restriction of injunctions than did the Republican party. After they came into office in 1913 they gave extended consideration to the demands of labor and in enacting the Clayton Anti-trust law (p. 463), the following year, made numerous concessions to it. Since, by an unexpected interpretation, the Supreme Court had held that the Sherman Anti-trust Act applied to trade unions as well as to other combinations in restraint of trade, Congress expressly exempted labor and farmers' organizations from the operation of the legislation against trusts. Taking up the matter of injunctions specifically, it then provided that no restraining order of this character shall be granted by federal courts or judges in industrial disputes involving terms or conditions of work, except to prevent irreparable injury to property or property rights for which the law provides no adequate remedy. Furthermore no such writ shall prohibit persons singly or in concert from ceasing to work or from persuading others in a peaceful manner to take similar action, or from in effect boycotting any party to the dispute, or from peacefully assembling, or from spending money to secure the services of others. Thus workers are given the right to bring a certain pressure to bear on employers by peaceful means without interference on the part of the federal judiciary in the form of injunction. As an additional safeguard against abuses, Congress legalized jury trial in certain contempt cases.

This law, which Samuel Gompers hailed as the "Magna Charta of Labor," in reality made little change in the injunction process, for during the strike of the railway shopmen in 1922, the federal Attorney General, H. M. Daugherty, obtained from the district court of Chicago the most sweeping injunction in the history of industrial disputes. The judicial order in question forbade strikers and their leaders to engage in picketing, or to encourage any person to leave his employment or refrain from entering employment, by "letters, printed or other circulars, telegrams, telephones, word of mouth, oral persuasion, or suggestion, or by interviews to be published in the newspapers, or otherwise in any manner whatsoever." Thus in explicit language the trade union officials were absolutely estopped from issuing any statement instructing members of their organizations to leave their work or persuade others to do so. In short a mere judicial decree made the strike in all of its substantial manifestations unlawful.

The principles applied in the shopmen's case were later

amplified by the federal court for the southern district of Ohio in 1927 in an injunction against the United Mine Workers. In this instance the federal judge, besides forbidding the officers and agents of the trade union in question to resort to violence, commanded them not to do "anything" designed or intended to interfere in any way with the mine owners or their employees or any persons having business with them. Not content with this general interdiction, the court then went on to mention a number of particular actions which were to be construed as definitely proscribed. This list of prohibitions included unlawfully entering upon any property belonging to or controlled by the employers or setting foot on lands adjacent to the mines, whether owned by parties to the dispute or not, and the collection of crowds, for the purposes of intimidation, upon or near any public road or railroad over which men were transported by the mine owners or their agents for the operation of their plants. To make the edict still more effective all interference with the hiring of other workers was declared illegal. Banners and posters intended to insult or overawe strike-breakers with such cryptic remarks as "yellow dog" were put under the judicial ban; these silent sentinels were not to be located on any highway or in any railroad station within a radius of ten miles of the mines. Having generally forbidden the strikers to do anything likely to disturb the business of their former employers, the court, however, enumerated certain forms of picketing which were permissible.

To speak summarily, by repeated judicial decisions the labor clauses of the Clayton Act have been interpreted to mean next to nothing. They do not authorize unions to commit any "unlawful" act; the injunction may be issued whenever any material damage is being done to an employer by his striking workmen; trade unionists may not agitate among non-union employees who have an agreement with their employer not to join a union—a pledge called by labor leaders a "yellow dog" contract; only that kind of picketing is legal which is carried on by individual unionists stationed at or near plants;

trade union officials and "agitators" from the outside cannot interfere in any local controversy; the "secondary boycott" is unlawful, that is, trade unionists cannot strike merely for the purpose of bringing indirect pressure on some other employer engaged in a labor dispute with their fellow members; and finally a trade union still may be sued under the Sherman Act for damages done to an employer in a strike.

Owing to the extraordinary character of such legal developments, organized labor is now urging Congress to enact a new statute governing the issue of injunctions by federal tribunals. Indeed the Senate committee on the judiciary prepared in 1928 a draft of a bill, spread over several pages, defining and limiting the power of the courts in this respect. But lack of interest as well as opposition prevented its passage. Hence the whole issue remains as yet undetermined. Nor can it be settled entirely by Congress, for a large part of the authority enjoyed by the courts in the premises is constitutional in essence and cannot be diminished by mere legislation.

Constitutional also is the power of the federal courts over the attempts of states to restrain the granting of injunctions in industrial controversies purely local in nature. Applying the Fourteenth Amendment, the Supreme Court, in the case of Truax *vs.* Corrigan, decided in 1921, declared invalid an Arizona statute which prohibited the issue of any writ forbidding strikers to abuse employers in strong language, patrol in front of their places of business carrying banners, or otherwise seriously disturb their enterprises. This ruling in effect set aside similar statutes in other states and now controls all state courts in dealing with the question of injunctions. It would seem, therefore, that nothing short of an amendment to the Constitution of the United States or a reversal of the trend in judicial opinion could grant to the states effective authority over the regulation of industrial disputes within their boundaries.

Research Work

If labor questions are to be intelligently treated, central research agencies for the collection and distribution of pertinent information on a national scale are indispensable. While private establishments undoubtedly could do this work, they are usually unstable; they come and go, expand and contract according to the energy of their directors and their ability to raise funds. On the other hand when federal offices perform these useful functions a high degree of permanency is assured. Moreover reports on the subjects investigated can always be obtained by writing to one point—in Washington.

To meet the need for comprehensiveness and continuity in this field, various divisions have been created in the Department of Labor and expressly charged with responsibility for gathering, analyzing, and disseminating industrial data. Among these fact finding bodies the Bureau of Labor Statistics takes first rank. Its duty, as set forth in the law, is to assemble information on all phases of labor and on the means of promoting the material, social, intellectual, and moral prosperity of wage earners throughout the country. In discharging its obligation the Bureau now makes studies covering such fundamental questions as unemployment, wages and hours of work, industrial disputes, the cost of living, industrial accidents, and labor legislation. Shifting its researches as needs arise the Bureau furnishes Congress and other officials, as well as citizens, with important contemporary and historical facts bearing on labor and its problems. In the same Department the Children's Bureau investigates child welfare and naturally comes in contact with child labor in every form—still an important question in the United States. All inquiries related to the formulation of standards and policies tending to promote the welfare of wage-earning women, improve their working conditions, increase their efficiency, and advance their opportunities for profitable employment are placed in charge of the Women's Bureau. Thus the duty of studying and reporting on affairs pertaining to the welfare of women in industry is vested in a permanent institution and a long neglected problem of modern society is given official recognition in the Department of Labor.

CHAPTER XVI

Agricultural Interests

WITHOUT any express constitutional warrant, Congress has created a varied assortment of federal offices to deal with the multifarious problems of agriculture. In practice these agencies have been evolved under pressure from a wide array of interests—such as fruit growers, grain raisers, cattlemen, sugar and cotton planters, truck gardeners, poultry producers, and dairymen. While there is a marked lack of unity among these diverse groups, which is deeply reflected in the establishments and activities of the Government, on one point there has been general accord in the past; production on the land must be increased in quantity and improved in quality. In furtherance of this purpose great blocks of the public domain in the West have been opened up to homestead entry and arid regions reclaimed by extensive irrigation works. Thus the area under tillage has been expanded enormously. Meanwhile the cause of intensive cultivation has received full consideration. Through experiment stations, agricultural colleges, and other educational and research institutions, better and more prolific methods of raising plants and animals have been developed. Within limits and subject to fluctuations in the world market, the processes of aid in enlarging and improving the agricultural output have been to the advantage of farmers.

When, however, they finally found their output so huge as to imperil their earning capacity, owing to the creation of a surplus, a reaction set in. The very Government that had been instrumental in bringing about the increase was called upon to take action in the matter of handling and curtailing the excess. At length in response to continued pleas, the Federal Farm Board was created in 1929 with a view to promoting the fusion of individual farmers into coöperative associations through which the growing and selling of agricultural produce might be subjected to rational control. But this new Board, far from replacing the federal agencies interested in the stimulation of production, was merely added to them. Thus with one hand the Government now seeks to enlarge the annual yield and with the other tries to offset the effects of that policy in the market. It remains to be seen whether a house divided against itself in such a fashion can achieve results of lasting benefit to agriculture.

Increasing Production

In assisting agriculture through research the Federal Government has taken a hint from the pages of history. Recognizing the fact that nature has not bestowed her favors equally on all countries and that crops introduced from distant lands often flourish luxuriantly in new locations, federal agents scour the whole world in search of foreign plants which may prove successful in America. Thus in 1928 in a quest of this kind a party of experts from the Department of Agriculture travelled by airplane, canoe, and afoot through the wilds of New Guinea in places where white men had never trod before. In the course of its wanderings the expedition collected 167 varieties of sugar cane for future study in the United States. One species, towering thirty-three feet in the air, showed particular promise on account of its hardness and straightness. Accordingly a shipment was made by refrigerator steamer across the Pacific and by express from San Francisco to a national experiment station in the eastern part of the country. At the same time a garden of these specimens was planted in nearby Australia from which shoots might be easily taken in case the collection of cane sent to the United States was lost in transit. In economic utility this ransacking of the world has added millions of dollars to the wealth of the country. To cite a single illustration, a small bag of Sudan grass seed brought to the United States

Courtesy of the United States Department of Agriculture

THE QUEST FOR NEW PLANTS: A FEDERAL AGENT ON AN AFRICAN EXPEDITION.

Courtesy of the United States Bureau of Reclamation

RECLAIMING THE DESERT: THE ORLAND IRRIGATION PROJECT.

by the Department resulted in the starting of a new crop estimated as worth more than sixteen million dollars in 1918.

With materials gleaned from all parts of the world at its disposal, the Department carries on a large amount of research work annually. Not only does it conduct laboratories where plant and animal culture is studied but it owns and operates farms where new ideas may be tried out. Since this work is highly specialized it is distributed among several technical bureaus. Thus the Bureau of Animal Industry, through numerous subdivisions, investigates livestock problems; while the Bureau of Plant Industry performs kindred duties with respect to crops. Studies of fertilizers, soil analysis, and similar matters are entrusted to the Bureau of Chemistry and Soils. The Department, however, does not have sufficient facilities for performing all the necessary tests at its own establishments. Accordingly arrangements have been made for tying the numerous state and territorial experiment stations into a supplemental system to fill the gaps in the federal work.

Owing to their wide geographical distribution, the local stations make possible the prosecution of studies under many conditions of climate and soil. And unity is given to their operations by the Office of Experiment Stations in the Department of Agriculture. In the case of the territorial and insular institutions this unity is very real, for here federal control generally takes the form of direct operation and maintenance. With respect to the state experiment stations, however, it is less complete. According to the terms of the law, the latter are merely required to accept a certain degree of national supervision in return for annual grants of money made available by congressional appropriation. In practice, therefore, the Office of Experiment Stations, which exercises this supervision, acts as a coördinator rather than a dictator. It scrutinizes the expenditure of federal funds. It examines and approves plans for coöperation between federal and local agencies in common research projects. It voluntarily gives advice and assistance to the several stations in adjusting their programs of investigation so that they may avoid duplications of effort. In this connection the Office goes over current literature from all parts of the world and distributes digests to stations on application. By such arrangements many widely scattered units employing state, national, and private funds have been grouped into a body which admirably complements the work of the federal establishments.

The results of federal and state research are made available to the farmer through various agencies. They are taught, of course, in the agricultural and mechanical colleges founded principally under the land grant act of 1862 extending national aid to the states in this sphere. Since, however, only a limited number of men and women can attend the higher institutions in person, an extension system has been evolved to reach even those who live in remote places. Under a carefully planned arrangement, local agricultural colleges carry out the work with the advice, financial assistance, and supervision of the Department of Agriculture. Each year approximately five thousand agents visit farming regions and conduct practical demonstrations illustrating numerous phases of rural economics.

But knowledge alone is not enough; those who possess it must have proper tools with which to work. In recognition of this fact the Federal Government supplements its activities in conducting, stimulating, and coördinating research and distributing information by regulating certain supplies of vital concern to agriculture. For example, congressional statutes forbid the importation of, and all interstate traffic in, seeds that are unsound or adulterated. In this way an attempt is made to keep the planting materials of the country up to a minimum level through the machinery of government control. Kindred protection is afforded to the raiser of livestock, for national food and drug legislation forbids the adulteration and misbranding of animal as well as human food. To make effective such safeguards, the Food, Drug, and Insecticide Administration in the Department of Agriculture is charged with the duty of excluding from interstate trade all livestock feed which does not comply with federal standards. Often it blocks the sale of such unhealthful combinations as elevator sweepings and ground limestone offered to farmers by concerns whose zeal for profits outruns their sense of propriety. Thus by providing scientific information and assuring a certain degree of excellence in seeds and feed, the Federal Government seeks to improve the quality and increase the quantity of agricultural production.

At the same time the Government fosters extensive cultivation by opening up new areas for tillage. By 1890 almost all the arable land which had come into its possession with westward expansion had been granted away to individuals and corporations under various measures of Congress, particularly the famous Homestead Act of 1862. No more free farms of rich soil were now to be had for the asking. But there were still left on the public domain huge arid regions which could be redeemed for the plow by irrigation—in the most favorable circumstances an expensive process.

At first the construction of the irrigation projects was left to private parties and to the states, with some national aid, but the technical difficulties and the economic uncertainty of the ventures proved to be serious deterrents. When at length it was found that local and private capital was insufficient Congress was urged to undertake the work with public funds and on a large scale. The war-cry of "make the desert bloom," at government risk, stirred the imagination, rallying several influential interests to the cause. Railroads, keen to haul settlers and freight to regions where there had been little business before, supported the idea. Chambers of commerce and similar bodies, foreseeing big developments in neighborhoods otherwise stagnant, lent their aid. Contractors, eager to embark on profitable engineering enterprises were enthusiastic. Under tremendous pressure, Congress at last authorized the Secretary of the Interior in 1902 to begin irrigation projects on a generous basis. Money was provided from the sale of public lands, royalties from oil leases on the national domain, and certain minor sources —to which were added receipts from the water rights on completed projects—making a kind of perpetual fund for the redemption of waste places.

Administrative duties connected with the irrigation program thus initiated are delegated to the Bureau of Reclamation in the Interior Department. Generally speaking the Bureau does not build units itself; it lets the work on contract to private concerns and merely supervises the execution of plans in accordance with its specifications. Under its jurisdiction reservoirs, drains, and canals are constructed on favorable sites, and water from distant points is distributed directly to ditches on the parched soil to be reclaimed. The land thereby redeemed is sold in small plots to settlers who pay for it in installments, and so contribute to the fund for new schemes.

Within twenty-five years an irrigation system of astonishing magnitude has been created under the Reclamation Acts. The capacity of the storage reservoirs completed by June 30, 1928, and scattered over fifteen states was sufficient to hold a quantity of water which would cover the entire state of Maryland to a depth of two feet. The volume of material in the several dams was six times that contained in the great pyramid of Cheops in Egypt. The length of the canals, ditches, and drains totalled sixteen thousand four hundred miles. But the end was not yet in sight. The Owyhee project, then under construction, called for a dam of 405 feet in height, the tallest in the world at the time. Moreover the giant Boulder Dam proposed for the Colorado River and authorized in 1929 is to outdo all others, towering some seven hundred feet above its base. When completed it is expected to hold back enough water to fill a wading pool one foot deep as large as the state of Maine.

All this vast engineering outlay is, of course, only a means to an agricultural end. Its success, therefore, depends upon the degree to which the settlers on these projects can adapt themselves to the economic environment of their new home

And that adjustment is seriously complicated by the radical differences between the methods employed in tilling ordinary land and irrigated tracts. The farmer operating in an area of normal humidity leaves to nature the task of delivering rain in proper amounts to his plot of land. The water thus falling from the sky is almost pure except for such minor detritus as dust. It descends upon hills and hollows alike.

Now picture this same individual transported to an irrigated district. Here he becomes his own rain-maker. Through ditches he admits to his crops what he considers to be a proper amount of water. If he uses too much they are drowned; if too little they dry up, for marketable products flourish only within certain rather narrow limits of soil moisture. Hence great judgment and care are necessary to prevent either catastrophe. Sometimes, moreover, this water contains chemicals, accumulated by miles of passage on the surface of the earth, which cause reactions to take place in the soil clogging it up and destroying the plants. In any event the farmer must take pains to level off his land, for the ditches will not deliver water up-hill. Ordinarily he must also turn his first crop under to furnish with the necessary plant waste sand that has been baking in the sun for years. Furthermore while making his way in the face of such obstacles, he is called upon to pay for the water he uses as well as his share of the cost of the dams, canals, and other equipment needed in the undertaking.

As in other parts of the agricultural world, the success of settlers on federal irrigation projects varies from place to place. As a whole immense crops have been produced but in a number of cases the collections for water rights are sadly delinquent. To tell the cruel truth, on several works as much as one half the total rentals remained unpaid in 1928 —even though settlers are generally given forty years or more in which to meet construction charges and do not have to pay any interest on the capital investment. A balance sheet of the whole irrigation experiment, based on a searching study of all costs, full interest charges, and receipts, would probably show that a very large part of it, considered from a strictly business standpoint, has been an economic waste.

As a matter of fact in the best of circumstances the perplexities of administration are immense. Since each project is planned to care for a definite acreage, it must be fully occupied unless unduly large charges are to be assessed against actual settlers to pay for expensive waterworks run far below capacity. Even under favorable conditions respecting occupancy, settlers are often reluctant to come or arrive without the capital and experience necessary to success. Ordinarily it costs from fifty to seventy-five dollars an acre to clear away the brush, level the ground, and do the other "pioneering" work preliminary to operation; and in addition the farmer must wait two or three years for his first paying crop. Without substantial resources, therefore, he is sadly handicapped. Hence it is not at all surprising that the Government encountered difficulties in securing full quotas of occupants for its projects and had to announce in 1928 that more than 800 settlers were wanted to put four ten-year-old irrigation districts on a paying basis.

If any evidence were needed to show the existence of grave troubles in the field of irrigation, it can be found in the numerous acts of Congress granting relief to settlers in general and in detail. The Secretary of the Interior has been given broad powers in easing up the financial burdens imposed on land holders in various projects. Under the law as amended in 1930 he may classify certain areas as temporarily unproductive and suspend the payment of all construction charges against them. Should he find any of them to be permanently useless, he may write off the charges as a positive loss to the reclamation fund. Such lands he may sell at public auction or private sale at prices not less than those fixed by independent appraisal. Thus many deficits may be covered up in the accounts of the combined irrigation enterprises of the National Government.

What, then, has been the net result of all this federal work? Some observers are convinced that the services rendered to the West by these projects offset any financial losses which they entail. Others, less optimistic, believe that the time is not ripe for developing arid regions as long as good land elsewhere is going back to brush, especially if the development of such districts is not a strictly paying proposition. In making a judgment, however, it must be remembered that sectional interest is deeply involved. Without irrigation some of the Western states would have very limited agricultural resources or population. Have they a right to be considered for their own sake or should they be allowed to drop back into a minor position in the nation's agricultural plan?

Whatever may be the verdict on these undertakings, the agitation for irrigation in the West continues and carries local governments as well as the federal authorities into action. In response to urgent demands, Congress has provided for lending assistance to certain states engaged in reclamation work of their own. With the approval of the President, the Secretary of the Interior is authorized to set aside portions of the public domain to aid them in their irrigation schemes. As an insurance for efficient performance, however, the law stipulates that the areas so dedicated cannot be formally transferred until the states applying for them have demonstrated their capacity for management by actual construction. To give additional help to local projects, surplus water from federal irrigation works is sold to them under conditions favorable to successful administration.

Fighting the Farmer's Foes

In the preceding section attention was directed to methods by which the Federal Government stimulates the agricultural production of the country both in quality and quantity. But all this effort is not sheer gain for while man attempts to improve farm plants and animals, nature contrives to offset his efforts in many ways by letting loose disastrous forces. Some of these are inanimate, such as frosts, floods, or hurricanes. Others are masses of living creatures of all sizes, shapes, and habits, ranging from mountain lions to tiny worms or ugly fungi. Nor does nature wage her fight against the farmer unaided. Man, by introducing the steamer, the train, the motor-truck, and other means of transportation has enabled the pests of the world to become cosmopolitans. He has assisted nature in spreading destruction in a few years over vast areas which she might not have covered in centuries if artifice had not lent a hand. Having upset a certain balance of things, he is now confronted with the task of restoring it, if he can, by mastering the numerous difficulties he has created. So the Federal Government, through an elaborate organization, is intensively engaged in fighting the farmer's foes including those which technical development has conjured up and distributed as world menaces. Now it wins; now it loses; with great uncertainty as to the future on many battle fronts.

In the struggle to protect agriculture from the ravages of the weather, the Federal Government undertakes a distinct service. It cannot control atmospheric disturbances, but it can and does warn farmers of the approach of such unwelcome visitors as frosts and storms. This function it discharges through the Weather Bureau in the Department of Agriculture. Inasmuch as changes in the weather often involve great areas and the probabilities of snow, rain, or frost in a given region are dependent on conditions at a distance, the Bureau has developed a nation-wide scientific network. As fundamental units in the complex, federal observation stations are located at strategic points throughout the country and are tied into a combination through a central "nervous system" of telegraph wires established in coöperation with the private companies. Over these lines dispatches are rushed from the recording posts to central offices where they are rapidly analyzed and used as the data for predictions. As soon as calculations are completed, forecasts are hurried out to many distribution points where they are made available to the general public. No pains are spared to reach the farmers through radio broadcasting, the press, flags, whistles, and other methods, before it is too late for them to act on the basis of the information furnished.

Owing to their high degree of accuracy in the general run these forecasts have gone a long way toward removing from the farmer's mind his old feeling of helplessness with respect to all of nature's changes. In the old days when unfavorable weather of every type caught him unawares, he had to regard the havoc wrought simply as "hard luck" which could not be avoided. Now, through federal predictions, he can frequently secure warnings of approaching danger sufficiently in advance so that he can take steps to ward off the foe. Thus, for instance, frost signals from the Weather Bureau often enable fruit growers to light up outdoor stoves in time to preserve their orchards from what might otherwise be serious damage. Nowhere is the new spirit of defense against the terrors of storms better exemplified than in the following praise for the work of the Bureau received from a grateful farmer in the South: "We find if your warnings are heeded it saves money and time. Last January we thought maybe you did not know what you were talking about, and lost sixty head of fine cattle, some hogs, and goats [by flood]. This year we listened to your warnings and saved eighty-three head of cattle, fifty head of goats, and seventy-five head of hogs that would have drowned if left in pasture in a river swamp."

Nature attacks agriculture with living things as well as with the inanimate force of the weather. The larger of these creatures—wild beasts—cause a huge economic loss each year to the farmers of the United States through depredations. Some animals, coyotes, wild cats, and wolves for example, are meat eaters and devour livestock. Others, such as rats, prairie dogs, and gophers, live on plant crops. Between the two foes, many branches of agriculture from sheep-raising to corn growing feel the impact of sharp teeth. Together these flesh and vegetable eaters, which respect no man-made laws or boundaries, create a serious problem owing to their modes of operation. Some of them act singly, like the famous "Custer Wolf" which prowled alone among the cattle of a Western state picking out and slaughtering twenty-five thousand dollars' worth of stock before it was itself destroyed. Others descend in great swarms, stripping large areas of crops or decimating flocks almost overnight. Whether acting individually or collectively they are capable of sudden raids followed by equally rapid escapes. On the great plains of the West in particular, it is necessary to have measures of control more drastic than those which can be applied by farmers single-handed.

Through the Bureau of the Biological Survey in the Department of Agriculture, the Federal Government comes to the aid of the farmer in his battle with destructive animals. The Bureau supervises campaigns against pests by means of an experienced field force working in conjunction with existing local agencies. By special arrangements with it, states, counties, producers, and other interested parties not only coöperate in action but help to meet the expenses of eradicating wild creatures in their respective neighborhoods, often bearing a share of the costs running in totals considerably above the grants from the national treasury. The results of such efforts measured in money may be gauged by the fact that work directed by the Bureau in Idaho is estimated to have reduced the losses from ground-squirrel depredation alone by two million dollars annually over an area of one thousand square miles. During the year ended June 30, 1928, campaigns managed by the Bureau netted in the aggregate 35,709 coyotes, 219 mountain lions, 226 predatory bears and numerous other prey. Within the same period over two thousand tons of chemicals were employed in the war on rodents. Ultimately the success of all these undertakings, however, depends upon a nice balance between the conservationists interested in the propagation of wild life and the farmers concerned about the depredations on their property which result in part from such conservation (p. 565).

Going down the scale in size from wild animals to insects, fungi, and bacteria, other enemies of the farmer are to be found in great profusion. These myriads of living things arouse fear not by strength and cunning, like the mountain lion, but by sheer weight of numbers. Although individually small and weak, they are capable of reproduction with amazing rapidity. Hence it is not feasible to destroy them singly; forms of mass destruction must be developed in keeping with their power of multiplication. This is not all. If the farmer had to deal with only a few classes of minute pests the battle would be less serious, but unfortunately for him the number of varieties of insects alone, not to mention fungi and bacteria, almost passes belief. According to careful estimates there are over six hundred and fifty thousand known species of them—one type for every two hundred Americans and, owing to their different characteristics, thousands of methods of warring against them must be devised. In such circumstances the task of identifying and studying the life and habits of the several types, with a view to finding an effective means of attack on each harmful one, is obviously prodigious. But the problem must be squarely faced. If duplication is to be avoided and results are to be obtained with a minimum of effort, a great central research agency must assume charge of this experimental work. It is not surprising, therefore, to find the responsibility has been offered to the Federal Government.

All along the line, the advance on the farmer's little foes is led by the Government. In the Department of Agriculture, two units are responsible for dealing with separate phases of the problem—one in the animal and one in the vegetable kingdom. The first of these, the Bureau of Entomology, the world's largest organization of the kind, is devoted to research into the economic relations of insects to man. The second, the Bureau of Plant Industry, is simultaneously engaged in studies of normal crops and methods of dealing with fungi or other injurious plant growths which assail them. To these agencies a living thing is not just "a bug" or "a fungus" but a distinct challenge. Before they can provide satisfactory means for exterminating a pest, they must make patient studies of its life cycle in the hope of finding its weak points and devising appropriate means of destruction. After the methods thus developed are thoroughly tested they are described in technical pamphlets and made available to the agricultural interests of the country. Moreover, through the good offices of a federal pest survey, constantly in progress, both Bureaus are able to gauge the success of their work in practice as well as to secure warnings of new developments as fast as they appear.

The task of carrying the results of laboratory research into the field where they can be made effective in the war on the farmer's foes is also largely a federal function. In controlling insect and fungus outbreaks the Department of Agriculture directs its efforts into two main channels. First of all it seeks to prevent, within the limits of its power, the further spread of trouble wherever found. If a plague can be localized, then steps to eradicate it may be taken with fair prospects of success. The former object is achieved through federal quarantines established under broad powers granted by Congress. By law the Secretary of Agriculture is authorized to isolate any part of the country in an effort to restrict the spread of pests, regardless of political boundaries; but such action may be taken solely to safeguard the rest of the nation from a malady which has not yet become widely prevalent. To put teeth into embargo regulations, he can issue orders stopping the movement of material objects across a protective line whenever they are likely to scatter hazards. Goods may be halted entirely without respect to the purpose to which they are to be put, no matter whether they are passing in interstate or local traffic. As if to strengthen the ban the use of the mails may be refused to shippers under instructions from the Secretary. In practice, however, the hardships which a severe exercise of such jurisdiction would entail on legitimate business are mitigated through arrangements for the inspection, disinfection, and supervision of commodities with a view to making it possible for them to enter commerce or to continue in transit. Indeed from the beginning safeguards are provided against abuses of authority, for Congress has stipulated that all quarantines must be preceded by hearings at which government officials, interested private parties, and public bodies may discuss the problems involved.

Before a quarantine may be safely lifted, measures of eradication must be taken if lasting benefits are to be achieved. While this phase of suppression is frequently left to the states, certain major outbreaks receive direct attention from the Federal Government. Such was the case when a plague of Mediterranean fruit flies attracted attention in the orchards of Florida during 1929. In the large-scale man and insect war which followed, it was quickly seen that there was serious danger of country-wide infection and that a temporary quarantine would not in itself be sufficient. Although state and local officials early attacked the task of extermination it was soon apparent that they needed help. Accordingly the Federal Government offered its services. Under a large congressional appropriation running into the millions, spent in coöperation with the state of Florida, a small army of five or six thousand men was put into the field to battle with the insects. This force scoured cultivated areas, searched desolate swamps, and destroyed approximately six hundred thousand crates of fruit in its effort to stamp out the pest. Naturally the drastic campaign resulted in great losses to the growers and they in turn urged Congress to assume a part of the cost of the damage done to their groves through federal activities particularly designed to protect the rest of the nation.

Since the conflict between agriculture and its foes is trying in the most favorable circumstances, it is important that farmers should be supplied with the best of destructive materials. Accordingly Congress has enacted a law to raise the quality of their ammunition. Made responsible for the enforcement of this act, the Food, Drug, and Insecticide Administration in the Department of Agriculture conducts tests of insecticides and fungicides found in the market to insure that they are properly labelled and conform to scientific standards. By this means unscrupulous manufacturers are forced out of the general trade in such chemicals.

Financial Assistance to Agriculture

Owing to the small size of their holdings, farmers are at a disadvantage in securing loans on their property as compared with huge industrial concerns. An inquiry made under congressional authority in 1914 disclosed the fact that in parts of the country they were paying ten per cent and even more on borrowed money. Responding to a demand for lower interest rates and easier terms of repayment Congress created, two years later, a nation-wide farm loan system. At the head of the organization stands the Federal Farm Loan Board consisting of the Secretary of the Treasury *ex officio* and six persons appointed by the President and the Senate; while administrative responsibilities for detailed supervision are entrusted to the Farm Loan Bureau in the Treasury Department. The Board issues charters to local lending associations which in its opinion are economically sound and legally constituted. It controls the issue of bonds floated to obtain the funds from which to make loans to farmers and fixes the interest rate. It keeps a check on the complicated structure under its jurisdiction through a staff of appraisers, examiners, and other officials who periodically inspect the condition of the units in the system and scrutinize their transactions. Subject to its authority are two types of local agencies formed to lend money to farmers: private corporations known as joint stock land banks and coöperative societies called federal land banks.

With the approval of the Federal Farm Loan Board, any group of ten or more persons may raise capital and establish a joint stock land bank. Once formed and chartered by the Board such an organization may lend money on farm mortgages and issue bonds to secure resources for that purpose. Every block of bonds sold, however, must be approved as to terms and conditions by the Farm Loan Board and farm mortgages offered in pledge must be deposited with its registrar. Although all joint-stock land banks are subject to supervision in a general way by the Board, each bank of this type is solely liable for its own obligations, so that in case of default the reserves of other institutions cannot be drawn upon to pay its debts. Furthermore, joint-stock land banks need not admit farmers to a share in their government. Essentially they are private enterprises conducted as profit-making concerns, subject to federal control and enjoying the privilege of tax exemption for their securities.

Quite distinct from such undertakings are the agencies for coöperative lending and management, known as federal land banks, which form the second part of the national farm loan system. In the interest of efficient administration the United States, including Alaska and Porto Rico, is divided into twelve districts, each of which is served by a federal land bank with branches reaching down into communities. These banks also issue tax-exempt bonds, with the approval of the Federal Farm Loan Board, to raise money from which to make loans secured by first mortgages on landed property. To furnish a special safeguard for bonds of this class, the law provides that every federal land bank shall be liable for an assessment to meet any default on principal or interest on bonds issued by any one of the twelve institutions. Thus while the country is split up into sections for administrative reasons it is one for purposes of financial stability.

In making loans federal land banks employ two methods. In certain localities, where the Farm Loan Board sees no prospect of getting farmers to unite on a common borrowing program, regular banking concerns are selected as agencies and authorized to act for the federal land banks on a commission basis. Where coöperation is feasible, another method is adopted; ten or more owners or prospective owners of agricultural land who wish to borrow money may form a national farm loan association for mutual aid. When duly chartered by the Farm Loan Board, such an association may lend money on mortgages subject to federal supervision.

In either case provision is made for a certain measure of coöperative management and profit-sharing. Each of the twelve federal land banks is administered by a board of seven directors. Three of them are appointed by the Federal Farm Loan Board; three are elected by the farm loan associations of the district and by the borrowers making use of independent agencies; and one is chosen by the Board from nominees presented by the local parties in interest.

Besides participating in the election of officials, each borrower is an active partner in the land bank of his district, if he operates through an agency, or in an association if he is a member. In order to obtain a loan, he must buy a certain amount of stock in one or the other, as the case may be, and is entitled to dividends when earned. If he carries on his business with an association, he shares in its government and hence indirectly in the administration of the parent land bank. In short, an association is a local coöperative society, engaged in lending money on a profit-sharing principle. A similar theory is applied in the case of the federal land banks themselves. Although outsiders may buy stock in them in the beginning, they are liable under the law to be retired when the component bodies acquire enough money to purchase their holdings.

In spite of all these precautions and the privilege of tax exemption extended to their bonds, several of the joint stock land banks and a few of the federal land banks have encountered grave difficulties during the depression of recent years. In certain cases dishonesty and incompetence in management, permitted by earlier neglect on the part of the Federal Farm Loan Board, have already resulted in receiverships for institutions of the former class; while two or three of the latter have been driven into serious financial straits. In fact unless Congress makes some provision for reorganization, the whole system of joint stock land banks may be forced out of the field of agricultural credit. In most cases their bonds are below par, and it is practically impossible for nine tenths of them to float on favorable terms any additional issues necessary for new business.

Supplementing the above organizations are other types of banks established under acts of Congress to extend short-term credits to farmers, secured by crops and livestock. Such assistance may now be obtained through two classes of institutions. One—consisting of intermediate credit banks, twelve in all—is essentially a national system knit into a single enterprise. The other, serving the same purpose, is composed of national agricultural credit corporations which are primarily private undertakings—separate entities operating independently on their own account without any joint responsibility, subject merely to the supervision of federal authorities.

Each federal intermediate credit bank is located in a city which already has a federal land bank. In reality the two institutions are tied together, for the same directors control both of them. Like the land banks, all credit banks are chartered by the Federal Farm Loan Board. They may discount or purchase from specified institutions, including other banks of the system, obligations that have been incurred for agricultural uses. They may also lend money to any agricultural or livestock coöperative association on products offered as security, up to seventy-five per cent of their market value. In all cases, however, commercial paper held by the federal intermediate credit banks must have a maturity ranging from six months to three years from the date of acquisition; in other words their dealings are in short-term paper. The capital stock of each bank is held entirely by the United States Government which receives all the profits from its operations after the appropriate expenses of administration have been taken out. On the other hand it is not liable for defaults on the part of these organizations.

Additional funds for the operations of the intermediate credit banks are obtained by the sale of debentures subject to the approval of the Federal Farm Loan Board. These obligations are backed by short-term paper put up as collateral and as a further safeguard the total issue of each bank cannot amount to more than ten times its capital and surplus. As in the case of federal land bank bonds, the credit debentures are issued separately by the individual banks but all of the twelve intermediate credit institutions are subject to assessment to fulfill the obligations of any one of them.

Of special importance to agriculture is the provision for securing lower interest rates than were formerly customary. Debentures offered for sale to the public by the intermediate credit banks can in no case bear a rate in excess of six per cent, and the figure is subject at all times to the approval of the Federal Farm Loan Board. In turn the bank of issue is not allowed to charge more than one per cent in addition as a commission on loans. Outside institutions which discount their agricultural paper at an intermediate credit bank cannot add more than one and one half per cent to the rate thus fixed. All in all, then, the farmer does not have to pay over eight and one half per cent interest on his short-term obligations. While this is undoubtedly high it by no means equals the rate which he has often been compelled to pay in times past.

The second group of short-term credit agencies, the national agricultural credit corporations, as we have said, are privately owned and operated. Five or more persons may form such an association and do business with the consent of the Comptroller of the Currency. After they are organized these corporations are subject to the general supervision of the Comptroller much in the same fashion as members of the federal reserve system (p. 365), that is to say, their books are periodically examined by federal agents for the purpose of assuring compliance with the law. Like the intermediate credit banks, the credit corporation may sell debentures, make loans on livestock and crops raised for market, and if its capital is large enough discount agricultural paper for other institutions. Its interest rate, however, is limited only by the law of the state in which it is located and the debentures which it sells are secured only by its own obligations.

Agricultural Marketing

In the previous sections we have seen how the Federal Government helps the farmer in each stage of his operations up to the moment his goods are ready for market. But while the quantity of the output is increased, the quality is improved, pests are destroyed, and money is lent on farms and crops in case of need, produce is often allowed to rot for want of buyers or is sold at a sacrifice price which shakes the very foundations of prosperity. To restore the needed balance, the Government is now making a vigorous effort to strengthen the weakest link in the chain by trying to organize the marketing procedure of the country. The time is not yet ripe to gauge the success of this undertaking. If it should fail, owing to continued over-production, then a fundamental readjustment of the entire program from top to bottom, reconciling supply and demand, will be necessary if a lasting solution of the farm problem is to be effected. But such a readjustment would be revolutionary.

The most significant of all federal efforts to deal with the selling aspects of the farm problem began in 1929 when the Agricultural Marketing Act was passed. By its opening declaration of policy the Act marked a departure from historic individualism in agriculture. Its purpose, as announced, was to run far beyond mere aids in selling, for its sponsors knew full well that control over production was essential to the stabilizing of the industry. By express provision the law is intended to minimize speculation, prevent wasteful methods in distribution, encourage the organization of producers into associations and corporations for self-government, and to assist in "preventing and controlling surpluses in any agricultural commodity through orderly production and distribution," all with a view to eliminating undue fluctuations and depressions in prices. The old day when each farmer produced as much as he could and sold it when he liked is evidently passing.

In trying to accomplish the purposes thus declared, Congress authorized the creation of a revolving fund of five hundred million dollars to be employed in making loans at rates not to exceed four per cent. To administer this huge sum of money, only part of which is available as yet, a Federal Farm Board of nine members has been established. Eight of them are appointed by the President and Senate while the Secretary of Agriculture serves *ex officio* as the ninth. Naturally the work of the new institution is still in its preliminary stages with prospects for many adventures and changes in modes of operation under the pressure of experience. Certain underlying principles, however, are definitely fixed by law as guides to its actions.

To assist the Board in its administrative duties Congress has provided for a number of advisory agencies. Recognizing that agriculture includes such widely diverse occupations as the growing of grapes and the raising of wool, it has authorized the Board to encourage the various private parties interested in any given commodity to select a "trade" committee of their own. Each of these bodies is called into consultation whenever the Board requires technical information with regard to the particular specialty which it represents. Serving primarily in an expository capacity, the committees exercise no administrative functions of significance.

In granting aid under the marketing law the Farm Board does not establish connections with individuals as such. On the contrary it is merely empowered to lend money to well-established agricultural associations, many of which had already been formed before its foundation, in several instances under a favoring act of Congress passed in 1922. Loans made to these economic societies are available for a wide range of purposes. In some cases they are used to strengthen the borrowing organization by financing campaigns for new members. In others they are employed for the benefit of the existing fellowship—in providing facilities necessary to prepare, handle, process, store, and market goods or in operating them after completion. Associations assisted by the Board can also advance money to their affiliated farmers on produce in storage, allowing them more in proportion to the market price than can be obtained through ordinary credit channels (p. 531).

Reaching out all over the country the Farm Board seeks to coördinate the work of the several associations in given lines by furnishing financial aid in forming clearing houses controlled by producers. Intended to eliminate waste in cross-shipping and other transactions, these clearing agencies, it is thought, will effect a more economical distribution of agricultural commodities among the various markets available. The idea, of course, is not new. For a long time such establishments have been operated in Europe to cancel accounts among members with the minimum movement of cash or goods, much after the manner of bank transfers. Just how the American institutions modelled after them will function is still problematical.

The Farm Board goes beyond aiding in the creation of machinery for coöperative marketing; it also attempts to help in maintaining price levels. For this purpose "stabilizing corporations" may be organized to operate in particular commodities with the consent of the Board, granted upon recommendation of the appropriate advisory committees. Each corporation must demonstrate that there is need for its services; it must be owned and controlled by a farmers' coöperative association; and it must be legally incorporated in a state or territory. When duly constituted and approved a corporation may go out into the market in time of depression and buy up stocks of the commodity committed to its charge, no matter by what group of growers they have been produced. If it cannot finance its undertakings, it is entitled to borrow temporarily from the Board. Obviously this is a dangerous authority. And as a safeguard against abuses the law provides that no stabilizing corporation can withhold an article from the market when prices are unduly enhanced and such action would cause distress to consumers in the United States.

As a corollary to its work in this field of stabilization, the Farm Board will insure members of coöperative associations against losses from price declines in produce, provided they are unable to obtain such insurance from private agencies on suitable terms. Into its novel adventure the Government has not plunged without taking precautions. The law does not permit the granting of federal support for any commodity which is not handled in sufficient quantities to command a general market; nor may it be offered unless there is available ample information concerning the yearly price fluctuations of the produce in question on which to base the necessary insurance premiums. When, however, under the stipulated conditions, federal insurance is tendered by the Board, a farmer may haul his crop to the warehouse of his coöperative association and, on payment of a fee, obtain a guarantee which will cover his losses in case the price of his produce should fall before its sale. If it rises, of course, he gains.

Operating often against stabilization in values is the practice of trading in "futures," a form of private speculation. Hence it must be considered in relation to insurance. An operator in wheat, for example, deals in a future when he makes an agreement with a miller to deliver a certain quantity of it six months ahead at a fixed rate per bushel. Having thus sold a future he hopes that when the time comes for delivery wheat will be far below the contract figure so that he can make a large profit. In such a case the trader in futures flourishes in a falling market and is interested in depressing it—the very thing against which the farmer may seek protection under the management of the Farm Board. It is true that the grower's immediate loss is covered under the scheme, but if declines are frequent and sharp, the insurance premium will rise so that the advantages of the system will be materially reduced if not destroyed. Fortunately steps have been taken to prevent raids on the exchanges designed to bring about a depression. In fact the regulation of this type of business enterprise had been started before the Farm Board was established.

The first attempt on the part of the Federal Government to control "futures" was in connection with cotton. In 1916 Congress passed the Cotton Futures Act levying an internal revenue tax of two cents a pound on all contracts for the delivery of cotton at a future date, unless they follow a prescribed form. To escape this impost dealers must draw up agreements containing a definite understanding as to the grade of cotton to be delivered in each case, thus protecting the buyer against the necessity of accepting a quality inferior to that which he expected to receive. The law then merely insures fairness in trading; it does not halt any over-speculation that might injure the farmer. Indeed Senator Rankin pointed out in 1929 that, despite the diminished supply of cotton at the time, prices continued to fall through what he alleged to be extensive manipulations in futures. At all events the subject frequently comes up in Congress, with possibilities of legislation against speculation looming up to supplement the anti-fraud rules now in force.

A more stringent policy has been adopted with reference to grain. By the Grain Futures law passed in 1922 Congress declared that "transactions in grain involving the sale thereof for future delivery . . . are affected with a national public interest." In its concrete provisions this measure is intended to eliminate some of the evils of speculation and private price control, which seriously affect producers and consumers not only in the United States but throughout the world.

Subject to the terms of the Act are all dealers in grain futures whose activities involve the eventual interstate movement of wheat, corn, oats, barley, rye, flax, and sorghum. Such traders are divided by law into two groups. The first consists of producers, such as farmers' coöperative associations, which are permitted to carry on transactions without federal supervision. The second class, which includes all other dealers, is authorized to operate only through duly constituted "contract markets."

Within the meaning of the law a contract market is one which has been so designated by the Secretary of Agriculture after he is convinced that it fulfills certain requirements. To receive his stamp of approval, it must be located in a place where the volume and nature of the grain sold for cash is such as to represent fairly the different qualities of the commodity and where the inspection services furnished by the Department of Agriculture are available for grading. Furthermore the market must be founded and managed by a board of trade in compliance with definite regulations. As a protection to the public each of these bodies is required to keep specific records and to open them at all times to representatives of the Department—a measure aimed at the prevention of secret agreements. In addition every board must take measures to prevent the distribution of false or misleading reports, the manipulation of prices, and the cornering of grain. When once established with federal sanction, the contract market may receive applications for seats on the exchange. But to prevent the formation of monopolies through control over this process, the law requires all admissions to be made on the same terms. If a dealer legally accepted abuses his privileges in the market by attempting to juggle prices or to spread false crop reports, he may be excluded from the right to transact further interstate business. Indeed the entire market may be closed by federal order when found to be generally engaged in unlawful practices.

Despite all the loans in aid of coöperative selling now available, despite all the federal regulation of trading in futures, the prosperity of farmers acting singly or in groups still depends very largely on their own knowledge of market conditions and their ability to take advantage of the right opportunities for selling. At one time information respecting the demand for commodities was obtained by a short trip to town but to-day all this has changed. In 1887 the first car of Southern produce under refrigeration crossed the Potomac River on its way to Northern cities, while during the same year the first refrigerator car filled with California fruits was hauled over the Rockies bound for the East. With the problem of long-distance transportation of perishables successfully solved, the grower found beckoning him a truly bewildering array of buyers, both large and small, scattered throughout the United States and in foreign lands as well. In order that individuals and societies might keep in touch with the new complexities in demand and supply brought about by this revolution, something more was necessary than corner store reports and newspaper accounts arriving from a few scattered points one to three days late. The trader in stocks had his ticker; how was the agriculturist to keep in close touch with the exact state of affairs in his wide realm?

Obviously there was need for nation-wide market and crop news emanating from some unbiased agency not interested in making money through fraudulent reports. Moved by the insistence of farmers the Federal Government at length established an information service to meet their demand, finally placing it under the Bureau of Agricultural Economics in the Department of Agriculture. This Bureau keeps a careful watch on growing crops, collects data on the areas under cultivation, estimates their probable yield, and makes other pertinent calculations. Its findings are then distributed in the form of periodical statements.

The Bureau also follows produce to the doors of buyers. Under its supervision federal market news is sent humming continually over a network of leased wires second only in magnitude to the Associated Press System. Each night the number of cars of fruit and vegetables, to mention only two articles of commerce, in movement on every railroad in the country is secured by the federal service, for the guidance of those interested in supply and demand. Arrivals of carload lots in the several trading centers, prices of commodities at shipping and receiving points, and many other significant facts are ascertained and reported by the Bureau.

But the collection and dissemination of figures on butter, eggs, cheese, and other produce is not enough in itself. Expert analysis and interpretation of market trends is equally imperative. To meet this requirement, the Bureau prepares statistical forecasts indicating what the future holds in store for the farmer, and makes its reviews available in a long line of documents such, for example, as the "Hog Outlook Statement for July." By very elaborate processes, involving over three hundred thousand federal agents, some serving without pay, the Government supplies the farmer's "ticker," informing him when to sell or hold his goods.

Efficient marketing and fair price determination cannot, however, proceed at random; physical standards for commodities are necessary if buyers and sellers are to know what they are talking about. Agricultural produce is in no sense uniform. Apples may be large or small, sweet or sour, red or yellow, juicy or pulpy, worm eaten, bruised or sound, to mention a few variables in a single article. If a customer buys apples in a store he can judge of their quality by actual examination. But the situation is very different, when a New York dealer orders a carload from a California grower whose stock of goods cannot be seen or handled but can only be described in words. Here the merchant and the producer must have some sort of understanding as to the precise nature of the goods in question; otherwise the shipment of an inferior quality is possible, resulting in ill-will and confusion.

Within limited areas understandings of a sort were early established by private arrangement or under state laws; but, since each organization or state applied its own criteria, it was necessary for parties engaged in general commerce to become conversant with many systems of grading, often differing widely from place to place and year to year—a requirement which resulted in hardships for all concerned. Inevitably American merchants began to lodge protests against the varying rules developed by innumerable meddlers, and foreign governments complained about the unsatisfactory condition in which certain American goods were delivered. Out of the extension of the market from the community to the world and out of bitter experience arose a demand for national produce standards, scientifically established, and open to all.

Responding to a justifiable agitation, the Department of Agriculture has undertaken the classification of farm produce. In preparing rules in this field it acts with caution, subjecting them to a process of trial and error extending over several years before attempting to make them obligatory. During the period of tentative evolution, the grades established by the Department are often voluntarily employed by growers and buyers as a common basis for commercial agreements. As a matter of fact purely optional arrangements of this sort have already won wide recognition, particularly in the fruit and vegetable business. After principles of classification have reached an advanced stage of development it is then possible to make them compulsory with a view to wiping out all the conflicting private canons which still remain as sources of disorder in marketing.

With respect to two types of commodities Congress has insisted on binding rules, in the Grain Standards Act of 1916 and the Cotton Standards Act of 1923. Under these statutes all interstate and foreign trade in cotton and grain must now be carried on in accordance with national prescriptions except when the parties to a given transaction prefer to sell by actual sample instead. The application of compulsory grades is executed in practice under federal supervision. Instead of setting up an elaborate force of regular officials, however, Congress has provided for the examination and licensing of private citizens to act as inspectors, with full power to apply federal regulations. After passing tests established by the Department of Agriculture, these agents go into the field and offer their services to merchants and producers. They compare samples taken from shipments of cotton and grain with the federal scheme of classification and decide whether they conform to specifications. For example five varieties of wheat have been established under law: hard red spring, durum, hard red winter, soft red winter, and white; and these are in turn subdivided on the basis of weight, moisture content, percentage of damaged kernels, and foreign matter present. Such are the principles which wheat inspectors must apply.

Naturally no hard and fast lines can be drawn in such business; individual judgment remains an important factor and injustice may be done. Accordingly any party dissatisfied with the decisions of a licensed inspector may appeal to the Secretary of Agriculture and secure an order instructing a regular government official to examine the shipment in dispute. Furthermore, on their own initiative, federal experts occasionally review the findings of licensed inspectors for the purpose of appraising their accuracy. Grading, then, remains in private hands subject to restraints and appeals provided by the Department of Agriculture.

Misunderstanding as to the grades of farm produce involved in transactions is not the only difficulty arising out of the distance between producer and consumer. In the past it was a common practice for commission merchants to make false returns relative to the condition in which perishable commodities reached their destination. Thus a dealer, after receiving a shipment, might write back to the farmer who sent it and tell him that the goods had come in a state of decay which made it necessary to throw them away, whereas actually nothing was wrong with them and they had been sold at regular prices. Again, a buyer might declare that a consignment had spoiled when in reality it was all right but had unfortunately arrived during a "glut" in the market which meant a loss instead of profit, if duly paid for. In either case the grower did not relish a long and expensive trip to headquarters to check up on reports and in fact a trickster could usually assume that the victim would not appear.

Against evil practices of this nature Congress launched in 1927 the Produce Agency Act which forbids dealers in their capacity as agents to throw away, without just cause, perishable goods received from other states or to make false statements relative to the condition of such commodities on arrival. Producers believing themselves defrauded may now secure an investigation at any point by writing or telegraphing to the Bureau of Agricultural Economics. On an appeal made in due course the Bureau will institute an inquiry and furnish a certificate setting forth the facts in the case. Owing to federal supervision, therefore, distance is no longer an obstacle to honest marketing.

A still closer federal control over marketing is assured by the Perishable Agricultural Commodities Act of 1930. Under this law no person can carry on a business as commission merchant, dealer, or broker in perishable agricultural commodities entering interstate and foreign commerce, without a license issued by the Secretary of Agriculture. In granting such privileges the Secretary must have a sharp eye to character and responsibility. Unfair conduct in this branch of business is elaborately defined and forbidden. Any party aggrieved by alleged unfair practices may apply to the Secretary for relief and damages, which may be allowed after hearing and inquiry. If awards are not paid then judicial process may be invoked. In making investigations under the Act, the Secretary has a generous power to summon witnesses, require the production of records, and make inspections. When he finds that holders of licenses have been guilty of violating the law, he may revoke their permits either temporarily or permanently, according to the nature of their offenses. As a guarantee for the regularity of their transactions, all merchants, dealers, and brokers coming within the purview of the Act must keep records and accounts correctly disclosing every transaction involved in their business. In short the operation of marketing perishable commodities is placed almost on a footing with a public utility "affected by public interest" and subject to strict national scrutiny.

Since the prices of American commodities depend so largely upon successful marketing abroad, Congress has attempted, by a special act passed in 1930, to put agriculture on a footing with manufacturing in the quest for outlets. Officers of the Department of Agriculture stationed in foreign countries are now organized into "the Foreign Agricultural

Service of the United States." They may be given the rank of agricultural attachés through the Department of State and assigned to diplomatic missions and consulates, on the same basis as our commercial agents (p. 477). Through these officers, the Secretary of Agriculture is to acquire information regarding world competition and then disseminate it at home. He may investigate farm management abroad, demonstrate standard American commodities, and otherwise promote their sale wherever feasible. No stone is to be left unturned in attempts to dispose of American surpluses in foreign lands.

In its efforts to standardize and organize the whole process of marketing produce, Congress has also provided, by the Warehouse Act of 1916, for the regulation of concerns engaged in the storage of agricultural commodities entering interstate or foreign commerce. Federal control in this sphere is designed primarily to safeguard growers against fraud and discrimination. With this end in view, every person who wishes to operate a warehouse coming within the terms of the Act is required to satisfy the Secretary of Agriculture that his physical plant is adequate and to post a satisfactory bond demonstrating his ability to meet the obligations imposed by law. When approved by the Secretary such places are known as "bonded warehouses." In directing these establishments owners cannot discriminate against anyone offering produce for safe keeping or refuse to take it if they have room for the consignment. To prevent misunderstandings that might work injury to the farmer, all receipts for goods deposited must conform to definite rules. Furthermore any shipments accepted for storage must be graded in accordance with federal standards under the direction of inspectors licensed by the Government. In case any user of a warehouse is aggrieved through the illegal acts or fire losses of the owners, he may sue on the bond put up for faithful performance, which, in certain instances, also includes provision for insurance.

Turning to the economic phases of meat processing and

packing, the Federal Government has undertaken to regulate the marketing of one type of farm produce in great detail. Under the Packers and Stockyards Act of 1921 the supervision of certain facilities employed in interstate and foreign commerce is vested in the Department of Agriculture. Packers coming within this legal classification are subject to severe penalties when found guilty of attempts to monopolize business, manipulate prices, or discriminate unjustly against any person. Owners of stockyards to which the law applies are required to register with the Secretary of Agriculture and, upon request, must furnish bonds guaranteeing the correct discharge of their duties. With respect to all cases involving stockyard rates, practices, or regulations which are alleged to be unjust, unreasonable, or discriminatory, the Secretary enjoys the power of preliminary review and may issue appropriate orders. From beginning to end, therefore, official standards are applied.

It is evident from the activities reviewed in this chapter that the old days of individualistic farming and marketing are rapidly giving way to coöperative efforts. Yet it is equally apparent that many of the functions assumed by the Government produce contradictory results. Especially is there a sharp opposition between the efforts to increase production and devices employed to stabilize prices, balancing demand and supply within reasonable limits. Indeed this is the prime issue in the agricultural controversy and, unless some efficient adjustment can be made in this relation, all other federal enterprises in the field of agriculture, however useful, will merely scratch the surface.

CHAPTER XVII

Natural Resources

From time to time the American nation is confronted with startling figures showing the decline and waste of the natural resources upon which its wealth-producing industries depend for raw materials. Thus Stuart Chase, writing in 1926, declares that half of the native petroleum supply is gone, that the peak of natural gas extraction has already passed, that the use of this "wonder fuel" is drawing towards a close, and that a third of our high-grade coal is exhausted. A similar story is told with respect to certain organic resources such as forests, fish, and fur-bearing animals. Although this gloomy outlook for the future is relieved to some extent by the ability of man to replenish his stock of timber and wild animals if he will, that operation is not possible in the case of minerals and natural gas. Taken as a whole the situation is undoubtedly serious. Nevertheless the nation reads such statistical warnings almost unmoved, trusting that they merely picture a kind of lurid nightmare which will vanish from sight in due course, somehow, some way. Like many a healthy person who takes little care of himself while he is well, the country has long continued to deplete its heritage with relatively little heed for consequences, thus incurring a great risk of finding itself economically sick in the near future.

Waste and the Conservation Movement

Doubtless the drift of industry with the currents of technology and profit-making has been largely responsible for the dearth of interest in conservation. This lack of concern is nowhere better illustrated than in the case of petroleum and natural gas. In the distant past, under conditions widely different from those prevailing in our day, man created a rigid system of property lines in accordance with which title to land generally implied ownership of a particular portion of the earth and all its underlying mineral wealth. With reference to solids, such as coal, this convention may prove to be quite satisfactory, agreeing as it does with existing modes of mining. But petroleum and natural gas, being fluids, refuse to conform to any such arbitrary legal arrangements.

These substances are found in great pockets, or underground "lakes," where nature has erected no barriers against their flow from one point to another across the property partitions established by law. As an inevitable result, a person who owns a small parcel of land containing an oil or gas reserve, may tap the deposit lying under the surface and drain it from the land of his neighbors as well. Against this operation the legal machinery of the country provides no recourse. Hence as a rule, whenever oil and gas are "struck," prospectors flock to the scene, buy land, and begin a race in which the driller or company that is able to operate fastest makes the most money, while landowners who fail to act lose the wealth which lies under their soil. With logical regularity, then, a discovery of oil brings a mad rush, over-production, low prices, and the encouragement of waste on the part of everyone involved. Unless complete control of the whole deposit and all the land above it is vested in a single far-sighted management, regard for the future is thrown to the winds and coming generations are deprived of a birthright. Fortunately, as far as the federal domain is concerned, coöperative administration of oil and gas fields may be authorized by the Secretary of the Interior under an act of 1930.

Nor is man more eager to use to best advantage the plentiful solid resources, such as coal, where there is no peculiar obstacle to individual conservation, such as exists in the case of the fluids. According to Stuart Chase, continual inefficiency in mining has had the effect of throwing away for all time one ton of coal for every ton marketed. The tendency to "skim the cream," by working the richest veins with crude methods, will make it extremely difficult if not impossible to finish the task in the future by extracting the remainder. Thus, while the coal reserves of the United States are immense, a large part of the supply must stay in the ground in the coming years on account of the wasteful processes now followed by many mining concerns. Nor are technical devices much improved when the coal reaches the power plant, for here great losses result from poor firing, lack of modern equipment, and bad management. On the average, Mr. Chase estimates, only four per cent of the heat value of the coal in a given mine is realized in producing power, if the several wastes in extracting and burning are taken into account.

All the other natural resources likewise suffer from misuse and depletion unless proper supervision is exercised. Organic riches, such as forests, fish, and game, though capable of indefinite growth to furnish steady supplies, can only be maintained by scientific administration and coöperation. Unfortunately in these branches of economy also, exploiters frequently engage in destructive harvesting methods, with the inevitable outcome that normal recuperation is either fatefully delayed or prevented entirely.

Closely dependent upon organic matter, especially forests and plant life, is water power which is sometimes thoughtlessly considered inexhaustible. While not absolutely necessary at the present day, its utilization helps to relieve the burden put on solid, liquid, and gaseous fuels in furnishing the country with energy. The greater the shift from steam to hydro-electric plants, of course, the greater the heritage of minerals which may be passed on to the coming generations; but water power itself must be administered in relation to other materials and uses if it is to be kept at a steady level.

These facts technicians have recently been emphasizing and there is already evident a certain rebound from the heedless pioneer spirit which built up the nation's industries at a terrible cost to its material endowment. It is clearly manifest in the "conservation movement," bringing pressure upon the Federal Government and inducing it to take action in the direction of rational management. Conservationists know that leadership must come from Washington. As a great landowner in the West, the Federal Government is in a position to dictate the terms under which coal, oil, timber, and other stores may be taken from its domain. Here it has an opportunity to regulate production and prevent waste on a large scale with complete jurisdiction. But more than this, it can go into the open market and buy up natural resources where they are being mismanaged. For instance in the case of the national forests, described below, vast tracts have been transferred from private to public hands by this means. Nor does its high prerogative stop here. Under its authority over interstate and foreign commerce, including control of navigable streams, federal regulation of water-power development and fishing has been widely extended. Moreover, with the idea of safeguarding the heritage of the country, the Government has undertaken extensive scientific research into the best methods of extracting energy from coal or oil. Its findings are demonstrated both in government plants, ashore and afloat and, by consent, in many private plants. All in all, the influence which Washington now exerts upon the handling of natural resources in the United States is indeed extensive, although far from reaching the extreme form of control to be found in certain foreign lands that have resorted to government monopolies.

Federal Lands — Parks and Minerals

At the beginning of its career as an independent republic, the United States possessed vast areas of unsettled land in the territory beyond the Alleghenies and the Appalachians; and from time to time wholesale additions were made by purchase and conquest. In the course of a century an estate of no less than two million eight hundred twenty-five thousand square miles—an empire almost equal to the entire continent of Australia—has been nationally owned at one time or another. But federal stewardship has been largely temporary, for the Government from the outset has pursued a policy deliberately designed to dispose of its holdings through sale or gift to private parties or to state and local governments. This program has enabled thousands of pioneers to build homes in the West; it has led to rapid exploitation and production; it has afforded an incentive to the construction of railways; and, despite the evils attached to it, has been largely justified by results in the creation of prosperous communities. To-day, however, this process is slowing down partly because the supply of high-grade vacant lands is exhausted and partly through the adoption of a new policy by the National Government—the policy of withholding large tracts from the market. Perhaps, however, this halt is only provisional, for there is now a lively agitation in favor of dividing still more of the public domain among several Western states. Nevertheless for the moment a large remnant of the national estate is still in the possession of the Federal Government—in all about three hundred forty million acres, to which may be added twenty million acres of mineral lands reserved with respect to rights of exploitation after the sale of the surface.

As a result of congressional and presidential action in withdrawing land from sale, this remnant embraces a national forest tract of two hundred fifty thousand square miles, a national park and monument system of almost sixteen thousand square miles, and a number of other scattered units. Although these reservations are occasionally open to limited entry on the part of corporations or individuals for such purposes as the construction of pole lines, grazing, mining, or the operation of park utilities, their transfer to private parties as property in fee simple is not at present contemplated. Some of these districts have been carved out of the great public domain acquired in the winning of the West, while others have since been added by purchase or gift. In certain cases, for example the national parks, Congress has itself created reservations; in others they have been established by presidential order issued under statutory authority.

Realizing that there are many places which merit preservation on account of their great scenic or historic value, the Federal Government has established a chain of national parks and monuments. If the units in this system lie within the national forests, their administration is vested in the Department of Agriculture. Other segments, consisting of historic battlefields or forts, are supervised by the War Department. Still a third agency, the National Parks Service of the Interior Department, has charge of the units found on the national domain outside of the forests. This diversity of control, though at first somewhat confusing, is in reality logical, permitting the management of the various parks and monuments by those branches of the Federal Government which are in the best position to look after them.

To the traveler, of course, the administrative "set-up" is of little consequence, for all the reservations are open to the general public, and most of them are provided with ample facilities to insure the comfort of visitors. And their services to the country are fully appreciated. The popularity of the federal parks and monuments is attested by the fact that more than three million people made use of them during the year ended June 30, 1929. An even greater influx of tourists may be expected on the completion of plans for the establishment of national parks in the eastern part of the United States where larger centers of population are within easy reach.

Doubtless the extensive travel to national parks and monuments is partly due to the diversity of types among them which admits of appeal to almost every taste for outdoor life. Thus a chain of history may be traced from the remains of prehistoric animals in the Dinosaur National Monument through the cliff-dwelling relics in the Chaco Canyon to the ruins of old Spanish missions in the Tumacacori and Gran Quivira National Monuments in the Southwest. Memorials of more recent times are to be found in the restored Fort McHenry, the birthplace of the Star-Spangled Banner, and the Meriwether Lewis National Monument where the body of the famous explorer lies buried. To the geologist, as well as the general sightseer, the Lassen National Park, which contains the only active volcano in the United States, and the Grand Canyon, the world's most astonishing example of erosion, are points of peculiar interest. The nature lover may ramble through regions of geysers, hot springs, and "paint pots" in the Yellowstone National Park, amid trees over thirty feet in diameter in the Sequoia National Park, enjoy beautiful vistas of mountain and waterfall in the Yosemite Valley, or engage in alpine climbing amid the crags and ice fields of Mount Rainier. Yet even these few examples fail to reveal in its true extent the astonishing variety in form to be found in the national parks and monuments administered by the Federal Government, numbering over ninety in all.

Though it now refuses to deed outright to private persons or corporations certain areas of its domain, the Government has adopted a policy of leasing its mineral lands to exploiters. And clues to the commercial value of the various portions of its huge estate are furnished by its geological studies in the field and in the laboratories. Under the Geological Survey and the General Land Office of the Interior Department a thorough-going classification of the public lands is in progress.

In case evidences point to the presence of valuable minerals on public property, the Department of the Interior may issue permits to private concerns, enabling them to carry on further investigations. Once the way is paved for actual mining operations, the Department grants leases to applicants on a royalty basis. From this source a revenue of some importance is derived. Payments made in return for such authorizations amounted to over four million six hundred thousand dollars in the year ended June 30, 1928, of which a part was transferred to the states. Financial return, however, is not the sole consideration. Through its leasing power the Government may exercise a certain measure of supervision over mineral operations on lands which it owns.

While the Government retains control over the mineral wealth in the public domain by means of leases, it is ready and willing to sell outright the surface of certain lands under definite restrictions. In vacant areas which have been classified as non-mineral and open to entry, any person complying with the legal requirements as to age and citizenship may stake out a homestead, on condition of its reversion to the United States in case the occupant fails to till the soil for a fixed period. If the terms of the law are met in full, ownership passes to the homesteader on payment of a small fee. But the westward march of settlement has left little unclaimed agricultural soil of any value so that the staking out of a claim to-day is likely to mean hardship or loss to the adventurer. Certain areas suitable for grazing, timber, stone, or other surface use, are offered for sale through the General Land Office of the Department of the Interior, subject to the reservation that federal ownership of all the mineral rights beneath the soil is specifically retained. Under these rules the top of the ground in districts open to entry may be bought and developed while the mineral wealth beneath lies dormant, awaiting a period of profitable extraction. When the proper time comes, the Federal Government may then lease the mineral deposits to operators on condition that compensation shall be made for all damages to the owners' property in the process of exploitation.

Forests

Forests are highly valuable not only for their direct contribution to the welfare of the nation, but also for their indirect bearing on the preservation of other resources. The primary use made of the forests is, of course, to obtain timber which is as indispensable in daily life as the metals and fabrics. But their utility does not end here, for they serve as reservations for livestock grazing as well as game life. They furnish recreation in the wilds—urgently needed with the expansion of urbanism. They are also necessary for the prevention of soil waste and the maintenance of natural waterways—two related functions. They help to conserve earth by absorbing the rain and compelling it to seep away instead of rushing over the surface and causing erosion. In the process they act as reservoirs, holding back moisture and giving it out gradually, thus checking floods during freshets and preventing the drying-up of streams in seasons of drought.

While these advantages are great they cannot be easily secured, for trees are both perishable and notoriously slow in reaching maturity. For example, white pine requires from twenty-five to thirty-five years to reach a size suitable for fence posts, from thirty-five to forty-five years for wood pulp or fuel, as much as fifty or sixty years for railroad ties, from sixty-five to seventy-five years for poles or piling, and from ninety to one hundred years for saw-logs. Ordinarily, therefore, a businessman cannot expect to plant white pines and live long enough to see them harvested. But tedious development in itself is not an impossible limitation if the obstacles are recognized and plans are made accordingly. It is perfectly feasible to replant cut-over areas with fresh growth for the coming generations at a low cost; although the operation may eat into present profits, it can be made economical over a long term of years.

Since the major portion of the timber area of the United States is in private hands, forestry is at present primarily a private problem. If, then, the owners of such land would take up the burden of replanting, there would be little cause for governmental action. Unfortunately, they have not in most cases assumed the rôle of altruists in the interest of the future, for, according to estimates of the United States Forest Service, the country is sawing timber four times as fast as it is growing. The Secretary of Agriculture has reported that "the greater part of the lumber annually pro-

Courtesy of the United States Forest Service

Slaking Thirst on the Fire Fighting Line in a Federal Forest.

Photo by S. T. Dana, Courtesy of the United States Forest Service

A Phase of Forestry under Private Enterprise.

duced is cut from private lands on which the appearance of new growth is at best a matter of accident, is likely to be long delayed, or may never occur . . . Private initiative cannot be depended upon to secure the requisite conservation." These two statements, pointing towards an exhaustion of our forest wealth, show that public action must be taken before it is too late.

Finding private owners naturally bent on immediate advantages, conservationists have turned to the states as well as the Federal Government for help. The results of their appeals, with respect to separate state action, do not come within the province of this book. National authorities, however, have recognized the possibilities presented by the forestry activities of the states and coöperate with them in many ways, employing local officers as field agents. Joint action has even reached the point where federal money is supplied to furnish nursery stock at, or below, cost to residents of the several states for private planting. Congressional appropriations are also made for extension training in this sphere, including the demonstration of best practices to interested parties. To protect growth already under way, federal aid has been granted to states for the prevention and fighting of fires in both public and private forests. Yet in spite of such efforts the devastation wrought by forest fires in the United States is appalling.

This program of federal aid might be generally satisfactory if all the states were alike intent on conservation and possessed similar supplies of timber. Such is not the case. One half of the standing trees in America are to be found in three states—Washington, Oregon, and California. About ninety per cent of the lumber and wood-pulp business is concentrated in eight or ten states. Regions with great forests, subject to the powerful influence of the lumber companies, are primarily interested in quick returns. On the other hand, the states in which the major portion of the consumers live, are anxious about the long supply. Hence forestry is at bottom a national issue and the Federal Government, on its own account, has become directly involved in it by the establishment of an extensive system of public forests which it can control and operate in accordance with a general plan of conservation.

Land for this system was first secured by the reservation of property already public in ownership; not by purchase. In 1891 Congress delegated to the President the power to set aside as national forests those portions of the federal domain deemed suitable for the purpose. For a number of years, the power thus given was exercised by presidential proclamation, generally on the basis of preliminary examinations into the probable utility of the several regions for tree raising. But the grant of authority to the President has been narrowed and Congress now insists on retaining for itself the sole right to withdraw from sale additional timber lands in certain of the Western states. By 1910 the total holdings reached a huge figure, amounting approximately to one hundred seventy-two million acres. About that time a thorough revision of the boundaries was begun, which finally effected a material reduction of the area in conformity with more careful surveys designed to reclassify the various sections of the national domain on the basis of their true economic character. Constant changes are still being made in the area in reserve.

As long as it relied solely upon the public domain, the Federal Government could establish forests on an extensive scale only in the West where almost all its land was to be found. In the East, where its holdings had always been slight, no system of national reservations could be created by this process. At length, however, the development of the conservation policy burst sectional bounds. In 1911 the beginnings of a truly national program were authorized by Congress in the enactment of the Appalachian Forest Reserve law, providing for the purchase of land for federal forests on the watersheds of navigable streams. Under the terms of this law, a Forest Reservation Commission, consisting of three cabinet officers, two Senators, and two Representatives, now selects suitable sites, which are bought with funds made available by Congress from time to time. A departure from historic precedent, this measure was only accepted by states' rights advocates on the theory that the formation of such forests was necessary to protect navigable waters subject to the jurisdiction of Congress under its power over interstate commerce. But in view of the tremendous areas of watersheds in the country, the significance of the law, even with this limitation, can scarcely be overestimated. Furthermore, it has been widened by an act authorizing the purchase of other lands useful for timber production.

By reservation and purchase, therefore, a wide-spread system of national forests has been gradually built up, covering in all approximately one hundred sixty million acres in 1928—an area almost equal to that of our largest state, Texas. In that year there were thirty-one states in the Union which had national forests, including five hundred ninety thousand acres in Virginia, four hundred fifty thousand acres in New Hampshire as well as smaller regions in states scattered from Maine to Illinois and throughout the South, especially Alabama, Florida, and Georgia. Perhaps the day is not far distant when all the states will have federal forest reservations within their boundaries.

The actual administration of the national timberlands has been vested in the Forest Service, a branch of the Department of Agriculture. With at least one hundred and fifty different tracts under its supervision and confronting a complex of interests pressing for favoritism, the ways of the Forest Service are not smooth. At the outset it is attacked by those conservationists concerned primarily with recreation, such as hiking, camping, or hunting, who urge it to maintain intact large areas for their own enjoyment by forbidding the cutting of timber, the building of roads, or the grazing of domestic animals. Next are the watershed advocates who wish to keep campers out of the woods, owing to the danger of fire and the pollution of drinking water; they insist that the preservation of timber to prevent the erosion of soil and to regulate the flow of water precedes all other considerations. Prospectors in search of mineral wealth further confuse the situation by crossing the paths of all others in their efforts to stake out private claims. Grazers, on their part, are naturally agreed in opposing the care of predatory animals for the enjoyment of hunters. Timber men are divided into factions: some want the forests to stand completely idle with a view to reducing competition in the lumber and pulp business; others wish to purchase and cut trees without regard for grazers, prospectors, or visitors seeking recreations. In such circumstances the forest policy of the Federal Government, unlike that of a private owner who may use his land as he pleases, must preserve a nice balance between rival groups in the interests of "the whole people," however divided.

Naturally the outstanding function of the Forest Service is to administer the timber resources of the nation. In many regions it operates with trees already grown. Yet there are huge areas indicated in current statistics as "national forests" which really consist of denuded land, brush, and burnt-over districts, where nature must receive the aid of science. These handicapped sections the Forest Service attempts to redeem by planting young stock, but not on a scale commensurate with the task at hand. Figures establish the fact. During the calendar year of 1926 there was a striking contrast between the twelve thousand six hundred acres of national forest land redeemed by the Service and the two million one hundred thousand acres needing attention. Indeed the Forester in charge pointed out that the Federal Government was even lagging behind the states, for in the same year two states together produced more young trees for transplanting than the whole national Service. Fortunately the year 1930 saw a prospective change in this state of affairs for by an Act approved June 9, Congress set aside large funds for use in promoting new growth and creating additional nurseries.

The protection of trees, whether young or old, presents a

constant and difficult task to the Forest Service. In large areas particularly, the invasions of plant and insect pests are hard to resist, sometimes making necessary a wholesale cutting of timber to stamp them out. The war on these pests is so common to all organic life that attention is given to it elsewhere (p. 524) as a phase of the national campaign against the enemies of agriculture. Unlike most other crops, forests are peculiarly subject to continual dangers of fire, calling for special precautions. While the acts of man responsible for destruction may be partly eliminated through regulation and education, lightning, that great source of conflagration, cannot be brought under control. In the best of circumstances, therefore, prevention must be supplemented by fighting. To forward this work by giving early alarms, look-outs are maintained by the Forest Service on prominent points in the districts subject to its jurisdiction—survey posts from which watchers continually scan the horizon for the first sign of smoke. Even airplanes are occasionally used, although with limited success. As soon as an outbreak is detected, men and materials are rushed to the scene—wherever possible over broad roads which have been built on the national domain for the double purpose of facilitating a rapid concentration of combat forces and stopping the spread of flames. Some notion of the extent of the operations involved in this enormous responsibility may be gathered from the figures for 1922-26. During that period seven thousand outbreaks occurred annually, on the average, in the national forests, causing a damage of one million five hundred thousand dollars; while the yearly expenditure in contending with them amounted to one million one hundred thousand dollars.

Since the steady production of timber is its prime goal, the Forest Service, in a number of places, seeks to raise regular crops of trees so that local saw-mills and affiliated enterprises may operate at uniform speed with assurances for an indefinite future. In such regions timber is sold to private concerns at an even rate, purchasers being required in some cases to pay in advance for replanting. Neighboring business is thereby stabilized—affording a fine contrast to the haphazard methods, often followed, of cutting and sawing for two or three years until a district is "skinned off" and then shutting down for fifty or a hundred years until a new growth has matured.

Unfortunately, however, a wholesale adoption of continuous production throughout the entire area of the national forest is not possible for the simple reason that it would bring hot protests from the owners of private timberlands. Although the Forest Service turns out millions of board feet every year, it estimates that six times the amount could be obtained, without mortgaging the future, merely by cutting the existing trees as they mature and thus saving them from decay and total loss. Hence the country faces this anomalous situation—private concerns are sawing their timber four times as fast as it grows and devastating huge areas by wasteful methods, while millions of feet of logs rot on the ground in the national reserves. At the same time the public is being taxed to buy and replant denuded areas in order to make provision against the coming shortage. The wisdom of this "economy" is difficult to discern.

National forests are valuable not only for the production of timber but also for the grazing of livestock—a utility not fully appreciated. At first the owners of animals were allowed to turn their herds or flocks into the public domain without paying for the privilege and subject to very little regulation. Gradually, however, the Forest Service has developed a scheme for controlling this practice in order to prevent the destruction of herbage by over-use. It limits the number of animals admitted to a figure determined by the capacity of the land. It also requires the owners to pay a fair price to the Government for their rights and stipulates that they must possess an acreage of their own on which to produce grain for the winter. In the beginning grazers objected to such interference on the ground that it was their concern, not the Government's, if their cattle died of starvation. But the success in the conservation of livestock as a result of the new policy was so marked during occasional "hard" years that most of the objections have been silenced. Although grazing cannot be permitted in certain districts, especially where very young trees are being raised or where predatory beasts are common, the Forest Service nevertheless estimates that the area of land now available is sufficient to feed one third of the cattle in the Western range states. In the season of 1926 about seven and a half million animals foraged in the national forests and there was room for more.

While often subordinate to other phases of utility, the recreational value of the national forests is of genuine significance. It is a splendid release, beneficial to health, for people to camp, hike, or wander in great regions where nature remains substantially untouched; and the automobile has increased its practicability. For the accommodation of such seekers after pleasure and vigor a number of camp sites and trails are provided in the federal forests and certain types of wild game are preserved. With the development and extension of national holdings in the regions of the urban East their recreational features will undoubtedly be increasingly emphasized.

When the best has been said for the achievements of the Federal Government in the supervision of the national domain, it remains a fact that, on a conservative estimate, about one hundred ninety million acres of unreserved and unappropriated federal lands await constructive administration and development. After suggesting that these lands should be turned over to the states in which they are located, for use and management, President Hoover appointed a commission to study the problem and make recommendations for action. Meanwhile Mr. Henry S. Graves, experienced in forestry and kindred fields, proposes a program worthy of full consideration. He would extend a system of grazing control similar to that now applied in the forests to all public land, make charges for this use and turn part of the proceeds into state treasuries, add to the national forests some of the land adjoining, thus allowing a combination in grazing administration, and enlarge the present forest reserves by including additional forests in the neighborhood. Elsewhere he would establish permanent federal grazing reserves under conditions favorable to their development and use. He would effect a consolidation of holdings in convenient areas by making appropriate exchanges with states, railroads, and private owners and would grant certain lands to states where their holdings may be profitably rounded out. In some cases land might be sold to individuals with advantages in economy. Finally Mr. Graves would transfer the administration of the public ranges from the Department of the Interior to the Department of Agriculture which already has a corps of experts trained in range control. In this way vast regions now neglected could be turned to productive purposes, national interests protected, and the states given a share of the proceeds. Undoubtedly here is a great problem awaiting administrative solution and calling for managerial talent of the highest order.

Wild Animal Resources

The conservation of wild animal life serves several ends. Fish furnish amusement for the sportsman, provide a livelihood for commercial operators, and supply an important element in the national diet, valued at over one hundred million dollars in 1928. The preservation of the buffalo, after almost complete annihilation through wholesale slaughter in the course of westward expansion, is of biologic and historic interest. Birds have economic as well as esthetic value, for they bear an intimate relation to the control of insect pests. So the pressure for the rational management of animal resources comes from many groups—sporting, commercial, scientific, historical, esthetic, and dietetic.

Fish may be too quickly depleted unless attention is given to their nurture. In the interior, irrigation ditches draw the young out into the tilled fields where they die; polluted streams destroy aquatic life or make its survival difficult;

hydro-electric dams block the migration of fish while the power machinery tears them to pieces. Still more destructive are the ravages of commercial exploitation. If fishing becomes too intensive, it outstrips the natural rate of propagation, thereby making certain species scarce and bringing economic loss in the long run. An example of this process is to be found in the halibut fisheries of the northern Pacific, off the coasts of the United States, Canada, and Alaska. While operations in these waters are now conducted over an area three times larger and with an equipment two and a half times greater than at the close of the last century, they net annually less than half the former output. Whether this fact is the result of chance or deliberate greed, such a destruction of nature's balance is a clear economic loss to the country.

Fortunately the Federal Government has control over its nationals on board American vessels off the coast and power over navigable inland waterways. It is, therefore, in a position to take vigorous action leading to the conservation of fish and in fact it employs its authority to good advantage in the promotion of that work. To the Bureau of Fisheries in the Department of Commerce are assigned important functions in this relation. Not only does it engage in many forms of research intended to improve the quality and increase the quantity, but it seeks to put to effective uses the ideas which it develops in the laboratory. For the purpose of rearing young fish to restock depleted waters, the Bureau conducts a number of hatcheries of its own and coöperates with the states and private parties in the management of others. During the year closed June 30, 1928, its establishments produced approximately sixty fish or eggs for every inhabitant of the United States, a commentary on the wastefulness of nature in the streams. These supplies are shipped to various points where conditions of survival are favorable. Under a law passed in 1930 a five-year program for the expansion of the experimental and productive work of the Bureau has been inaugurated. Besides furnishing new stock, the Bureau seeks to conserve that already in existence. Great schools of fish are often trapped in closed areas by the rising and falling of rivers during floods. Instead of letting these victims of nature die as the pools in which they are caught dry up, the Bureau operates a "rescue" service which collects such fish and returns them to open waters where they can complete their growth. During the year ended June 30, 1928, one fish for every person in the United States was thus salvaged from destruction, thereby reducing the load which hatcheries must bear.

A further increase in the total output may be obtained by protecting fish during the breeding and rearing season. In recognition of this fact, the United States and Canada entered into a joint agreement in 1924 to control the operation of their nationals in the halibut industry of the Northern Pacific, off the west coast of North America. Under its power to regulate vessels of American registry, Congress has put life into the treaty by making it entirely illegal for American ships to catch halibut for commercial purposes at any time during the season of propagation.

Should the Government go beyond aiding private parties in obtaining an adequate supply of fish and engage directly in commercial operations when business enterprise fails properly to conserve the wealth placed at its disposal? In practice the answer has been in the negative but there is a noteworthy exception. The Pribilof Islands, when acquired with the purchase of Alaska from Russia in 1867, had been for years of immense value as breeding grounds for fur-seals. During the period from 1870 to 1910 they were exploited by two private companies under lease from the Government. At the end of that period, however, the seal herd on the Islands was approaching extinction and the need for remedial measures was pressing. Apparently unable to cope with the evil in any other way, the Federal Government finally terminated the leasing system and assumed the task of reviving the industry on the basis of a national monopoly. As a result of the program thus inaugurated, the herd was built up until it contained in 1929 over a million animals—

five times as many as in all the other herds of the world combined. According to the estimates of the Bureau of Fisheries, now in charge of the Pribilof business, more than forty thousand skins can be taken annually. The yearly output is brought to the United States and sold at public auction.

Once considered "inexhaustible," the supply of wild birds and big game has almost reached the vanishing point in many places where the advancing tide of civilization has upset nature's balance. Thus the buffalo, once so common on the Western plains, has all but disappeared, under the arrow of the Indian and the rifle of the white man. A number of wild fowl, also, have felt the pinch with the advent of drainage projects which destroy their resting or breeding spots in swamps, ponds, and lakes. Consequently, conservationists have pressed the Federal Government to set aside special areas for certain animals, and in compliance with their demands it has established national game and bird reserves in various parts of the country. The major portion of these reserves are administered by the Bureau of Biological Survey in the Department of Agriculture, but some are operated by other agencies in connection with their usual work. The Lighthouse Service, for example, takes care of a limited number of birds in the vicinity of its stations. The Forest Service watches over beavers, deer, and other creatures in the national forests; while the national parks, monuments, and military reservations often furnish selected spots for the harboring of wild life. Some of the reservations are fenced districts where elk, buffalo or other big game obtain their food and roam at will. Several consist of bodies of water on which wild fowl and other birds rest or settle. Under federal care a few of these wild animals have multiplied so rapidly that the authorities in charge cannot handle them, proving the effectiveness of the new conservation policy. Occasionally this "over-protection," if it may be so termed, makes it necessary to sell, give away, or kill surplus animals.

The Federal Government cannot, of course, provide for more than a fraction of the wild life of the country on its own bird and game preserves. Under the pressure of conservationists, however, it has taken steps to extend its supervision to wild animals on lands not federally owned, through the exercise of its jurisdiction over other matters. For example, its power over interstate commerce is employed in some instances to reinforce local legislation. To give an illustration, Congress has made it a federal offense to ship game out of a state if it has been killed contrary to state law (p. 665). And through a system of federal game wardens, the Bureau of Biological Survey undertakes the task of tracking down violations coming under this head by visiting distant points, such as fur warehouses, which lie outside the state in question. In this way federal and state game law officials may take joint action against offenders. National control over the importation of animals from foreign countries is also exercised through the same Bureau with an even more important object in view, namely, that of preventing as far as possible the introduction of harmful creatures. As a case in point the Bureau recently denied a rod and gun club permission to import ten European hares for release in connection with sports near an important apple region where they could easily have become a menace to trees. Realizing that too many pests of this kind have already found entry into the United States, the Bureau is seeking to erect safeguards against a repetition of such evils.

Besides supporting the local game laws and supervising the importation of animals, the Federal Government assumes special responsibilities with respect to certain birds which are differentiated from other creatures by very migratory habits. One authority, E. M. Nelson, of the Bureau of Biological Survey, states that the majority of our wild fowl breed north of the United States and probably ninety per cent of them winter in the southern part of the United States or in Mexico. Birds, then, cannot be truthfully said to be "residents" of any one country or state, subject solely to its jurisdiction; they are actually international travellers.

In coping with this peculiar situation, the United States

and Great Britain have undertaken by formal convention to protect migratory birds as joint wards. In conformity with this agreement federal game laws now control all wild fowl in the United States. Detailed federal regulations, enforced by game wardens of the Bureau of Biological Survey in co-operation with the states, prohibit the sale of these birds on the market, specify the seasons in which they may be hunted, and control the number of animals that may be shot in a day—rules aimed at preventing their extermination. States are not permitted to pass laws of their own dealing with this subject unless their provisions are still more rigorous. Birds, therefore, are granted a degree of federal protection not vouchsafed to other animals, in part a tribute to their value in the destruction of insects.

Since the Bureau of Biological Survey is called upon to administer so many regulations pertaining to animal life, it must necessarily carry on a large amount of research work as an aid in planning. Are the game laws now in force actually maintaining our supply of wild creatures? The answer is found by taking a census as accurately as conditions permit. Is a given animal helpful to man or harmful? Should it be conserved or attacked? To answer these questions in the single case of the English sparrow, the stomachs of approximately eight thousand birds were examined to secure information on their diet and its economic significance. If the animal is found to be injurious, especially to agriculture, methods of control are developed (p. 524). In these and other ways, the Bureau is attempting to appraise the total situation and so achieve the necessary balance between such conflicting groups as insects and birds, fur-bearing animals and sheep. Whether by his conscious effort man can maintain a better order of things than nature preserved, unaided, before the advance of civilization remains to be seen; but research alone can find a way out, if there is one.

Water Power

The National Government has become involved in the utilization of water power as an outgrowth of its attention to collateral problems rather than on account of any direct interest in this great natural resource as such. Nevertheless the contacts established between other phases of its work and the development of hydro-electric enterprises are many and varied, in the aggregate enough amply to justify several forms of intervention. Indeed, for years, the War Department, through its concern with the promotion of navigation on inland waters, has given attention to such obstructions as dams or races likely to interfere with transportation. Under its authority to regulate interstate commerce, Congress has vested in the Department supervisory control over all structures, including water-power plants, insofar as they affect navigation.

Another relation to this utility issue has been established in the West where the Federal Government, as a great landowner, has been called upon to formulate a policy with regard to the use of power sites on the public lands. In this region, through its promotion of irrigation, it has also become interested in the generation of power as a by-product of its supply units. Even the treaty-making clause of the Constitution has been called into play, for questions pertaining to the international division of energy from Niagara Falls have been settled by a compact between the United States and Canada. A still newer form of federal activity in the water-power field has arisen out of the construction of the giant Muscle Shoals plant by the Federal Government during the World War for the manufacture of chemicals of value in munitions. Finally, with the growth of great companies engaged in transmitting electricity across state boundaries, problems in the regulation of interstate commerce are presented to Congress. It is amid such circumstances that federal control over the development of water power has been raised to the dignity of a major economic and political issue.

Despite the number and complexity of the contacts between federal agencies and water-power interests, general legislation covering their relations is of very recent origin. Not until 1920 did the Federal Government undertake the comprehensive regulation of all hydro-electric construction on public lands and on locations affecting navigation. In that year Congress passed the Federal Water Power Act creating a Federal Power Commission composed at first of the Secretaries of War, Agriculture, and the Interior—but under an act of 1930, of five independent members appointed by the President with the consent of the Senate. Among other things the Commission is charged with the duty of developing well-balanced plans for the utilization of all waters affecting navigation or passing through the public lands.

Under this authority the Commission has prepared, in coöperation with other federal agencies and certain states, a number of valuable reports on specific rivers. To insure general conformity with the plans which it adopts, a system of compulsory licensing has been inaugurated. Before any organization, whether a city, state, or private concern, can erect a hydro-electric plant on a site coming within the scope of the Act, it must secure a license for the purpose. Such permits are issued by the Commission only when it is satisfied that the project in question is properly designed. In every case, moreover, preference must be given to states and municipalities applying for the right to construct their own plants, provided the Commission is convinced of their utility. Licenses so issued run for definite terms up to fifty years, on condition that the site is developed within a fixed time; and the right of the Government to recover possession is specifically reserved.

Federal control over licensing and engineering construction, however, does not insure the operation of a completed plant in the public interest. Since a private corporation obtains in effect a monopoly over a given site when it secures a concession from the Power Commission, Congress has taken the position that the public is entitled to require the grantee to make reasonable use of the property in question. Accordingly the Water Power Act provides that the Commission shall regulate the issue of securities, the services rendered, and the rates charged by concerns under its jurisdiction in cases where state regulatory bodies fail to provide adequate control. At first glance it would appear that this leaves little authority in the hands of the Commission but such is not the outcome in reality, on account of local apathy and court decisions.

If electricity from a plant under federal supervision is sold entirely within the state in which it is generated, the Federal Power Commission, as we have just said, has jurisdiction over rates and services only when state regulatory agencies are not endowed with the necessary authority. In point of fact, by 1928, not more than half the states had vested adequate control over regulation in official bodies, so that a large field of work was thereby left under the surveillance of the federal Commission. The law also made similar provisions with regard to the interstate sale of electricity, stipulating that the Commission shall act only when state agencies are unable to provide regulation jointly. Since the courts, however, have declared that the states have no right to regulate the rates for electricity crossing their boundaries, this burden remains, theoretically at least, on the National Government. It is evident, therefore, that the Federal Power Commission is in a position to exercise a large degree of supervision over both state and interstate hydro-electric affairs, but for various reasons it has not yet taken full advantage of its opportunities. With an inadequate staff and apparently slight desire to act, the Commission has done little to regulate the rates of concerns under its auspices, while the states themselves are often either legally disqualified or utterly indifferent.

Up to the present moment federal regulation of electrical utilities has been at best a feeble innovation. Empowered to deal only with hydro-electric plants in certain locations, the Commission possesses no authority over stationary steam, gas, Diesel, or other plants generating electricity, even though their current passes from one state to another. In practice the upshot of this limitation is indicated by the fact that in 1928 only a third of the nation's electrical energy was derived from hydro-electric establishments and that only one third of their output was either under or subject to federal supervision. While the law does not provide for federal surveillance over utilities which are not licensed by the Commission, the increasing inter-connection of steam and water-power plants and the growth of large holding companies controlling many scattered enterprises are creating a problem that Congress cannot wisely evade. Although at this time only approximately thirteen per cent of the electricity generated in the country crosses state lines, the amount involved in the case of individual states exceeds a third in several instances and the supervision of even this small proportion of power production could not fail to affect rates and securities all over the nation. Furthermore the whole range of services and charges is affected by the operations of huge holding companies doing in fact, whatever the theory, an interstate business and as yet uncontrolled by either the states or the Federal Government.

Besides the problems connected with the regulation of private utility concerns, there are questions of public ownership which must be faced. During the World War the United States Government constructed a large factory at Muscle Shoals for the fixation of nitrogen from the air and the production of chemicals indispensable to the manufacture of munitions. Power to operate this factory was derived from a combination of hydro-electric and steam plants capable of supplying enormous quantities of electricity. At the close of the war the disposal of this equipment became a matter of national concern. While the debates over the best methods for placing the plant on a peace-time footing continued in Congress, scientific developments gradually rendered the original chemical works more and more obsolete until to-day they are of doubtful value as they stand. Pending congressional action the chemical plant is idle, while a part of the electricity produced is sold at wholesale rates to a private power company.

Although more than ten years have elapsed since the World War, the final disposal of Muscle Shoals remains uncertain. On the one side it is suggested that the nitrogen project should be abandoned and the power plant either leased to private parties or operated by the Government for the production of electricity. On the other side, it is urged with equal fervor that the manufacture of cheap fertilizers for farmers be undertaken either by a private corporation under contract or by a federal agency created for the purpose. A deadlock of long duration continues over Muscle Shoals.

A second great project calling for federal action arose out of the potentialities of the Colorado River for power and irrigation of vital concern to seven states: Arizona, California, Colorado, Nevada, New Mexico, Utah, and Wyoming. Owing to the extent and variety of the interests involved, both public and private, the enterprise was the subject of many hearings and debates in Congress. Advocates of public ownership insisted that the Federal Government should itself construct the dam and the plant and distribute electric power through state and municipal agencies at a charge calculated to cover merely the cost of production. Their opponents contended that the site should be leased to a private company under federal regulation as to uses of water and rates for electricity. The outcome was a compromise in the Boulder Canyon Project of 1928, supplemented by a compact among certain participating states formally sanctioned by Congress in 1930.

Like all compromises this Act is vague in its terms, shifting a large part of the responsibility to the Secretary of the Interior. Subject to the approval of the states concerned, he is authorized to construct, operate, and maintain a dam and incidental works at Black Canyon or Boulder Canyon on the Colorado River at a cost not to exceed one hundred sixty-five million dollars. The water so impounded he may by contract employ for irrigation, domestic uses, and the generation of electrical energy to be delivered at the switchboard to states, municipal corporations, political subdivisions, and private corporations. The rates which he may charge are to cover expenses of operation and upkeep. In making contracts for the use of water and the generation or sale of electrical energy, the Secretary must always, with due regard to the public interest, give preference to states for use within their borders. Indeed the policy of granting priority to states and municipalities, embodied in the Federal Water Power Act, is expressly reaffirmed in the Boulder Canyon law.

Scarcely was this act signed by the President, when a terrific struggle began over the meaning of its terms. Applications for power filed by public bodies, particularly cities in Southern California, were sufficient to exhaust the entire amount assumed to be available on the completion of the project. Yet established utility concerns already serving constituencies also demanded a share "in the public interest." Beset on all sides the Secretary of the Interior allotted a small portion of the output to private companies, and the remainder to states and cities. About the same time he announced that he would not himself build the power plant as authorized by the Act, but would merely lease the falling water at the dam, thus raising objections among advocates of public ownership who expected him to apply the principle of government construction embodied in the law. In the the summer of 1930 work was at last begun.

The Lands and Rights of Indians

Among the great areas of land subject to federal jurisdiction are the Indian reservations embracing approximately forty-nine thousand square miles, equal in size to the state of New York. The practice of setting aside specific districts of the public domain for the Indians was gradually adopted as the rush of the white man across the continent made impossible their further retreat into the wilderness. In the conflict between modern civilization and tribal custom, this proved to be the only alternative to their extinction or assimilation. Once established the Indian reservations, often rich in mineral resources, timber, and water power, presented thorny problems for the Federal Government, even in the most favorable conditions and with the best of will on the part of its officials.

As soon as the right to a separate tribal existence on the reservations had been granted to the Indians, questions inevitably arose as to how their life should be governed and their property managed. The simplest policy, at least for the moment, was to grant them a certain financial support and allow them to continue in their old ways. In the long run, however, the maintenance of primitive societies with large landed interests in the midst of a highly developed industrial country proved to be exceedingly difficult.

Confronted by this situation the Government has evolved a definite policy looking to the final incorporation of the Indians into American civilization and the conversion of their tribal lands into individual and private property under the American system. The controlling principle of administration in this connection, therefore, is to prepare the Indian for life as a regular citizen of the United States, in the hope that he will find greater satisfaction in adapting himself to the prevailing culture than he has enjoyed in attempting to follow the footsteps of his ancestors now that primitive conditions have disappeared. The social leap thus contemplated is immense and it certainly cannot be made without years of hard effort on the part of the Indian and earnest assistance from the Government. Will it be crowned with success in the end? If it is, then the reservations will close, the Indian will be absorbed into the great melting pot, and a century-old question will be written off the political ledger.

The development of this new program is marked by clear

steps. In 1871 the practice of regarding Indian tribes as nations, by making treaties with them, was abandoned and all Indians and their property were brought directly under the legislative power of Congress. By a series of laws beginning in 1887 the President is authorized to cause parts of reservations to be surveyed and to allot lands in private holdings to individual Indians subject to certain restrictions as to inheritance and alienation. Finally in 1924, after experimenting with the process of gradual naturalization, Congress declared all Indians born within the territorial limits of the United States to be American citizens. Thus legal provision has been made for the possible dissolution of tribal institutions and the absorption of the Indians, with their property, into the neighboring communities.

But the process is slow. Meanwhile, during the transition stage, the Federal Government is administering the vast estates of the Indians, presumably for their benefit, and is seeking to instruct them in citizenship. The management of this business is vested in the Bureau of Indian Affairs in the Department of the Interior, supplemented by the Board of Indian Commissioners, appointed by the President and the Senate, acting as an inspectional and advisory body.

An important task of the Bureau is, of course, the supervision of the Indian Reservations. These tracts, being classed as federal lands, are not subject to the jurisdiction of the respective states within which they lie, but are in effect treated as "colonies." From time to time, as circumstances warrant, allotments of land are made to Indians in severalty. As trustee, the Bureau scrutinizes the leasing of forests, water power, mineral lands, and other natural resources, under acts of Congress, turning the income over to the Indians entitled to it or holding it in trust where collective ownership obtains. When the lands and revenues available for the Indians are not sufficient for their support, and sometimes in accordance with historic treaties, Congress makes additional provisions for them in the form of supplies and grants.

It is needless to say that in connection with the administration of Indian lands and resources, as in the case of the public domain in general, numerous scandals and frauds have occurred. Indeed, if the friends of the Indian are correct in their contentions, he has been the helpless victim of exploitation from the beginning. Yet it would be a mistake to overlook such conscientious efforts as have been made by the Federal Government to conserve the property of the Indians and assure them the benefits of it. In the operation, of course, there is a perpetual strife between the trustees in charge of their interests and white men eager to seize, distribute, and develop their patrimony. And doubtless that struggle will continue until tribal relations are dissolved and all Indians have been assimilated to the general mass of citizens.

For this outcome the Federal Government is preparing them by a system of education. Under authority of congressional acts the President has established schools for Indians, at least for instruction in elementary subjects and agriculture. As a stimulus to attendance, pressure may be brought to bear on parents by withholding rations and allowances for their children of school age who are not actually in classes whenever facilities for education are available in the neighborhood. Furthermore the Bureau of Indian Affairs makes special efforts to secure the enrollment of Indians in state public schools. According to its report for 1929, about sixty-eight thousand Indian children were in educational institutions, and approximately sixteen thousand eligibles were still at large.

Involving a clash between two rival cultures, the education of the Indian is fraught with problems. It became apparent at an early date that many of them, on completing their schooling, were returning home to their tribes where group influences quickly carried them back into their old modes of life. Obviously individualistic education could make little progress under such handicaps. Partly for this reason the practice of partitioning tribal lands into separate holdings was extensively applied on a number of reservations. Then as an additional step in the promotion of independence responsible Indians were given the right to sell their land freely just like other citizens. Thus the magic spell of individual ownership, so foreign to Indian life and so sacred to the white man, was cast over tribal institutions. But the spell did not produce the expected results. It was too easy for an Indian to sell his land to a white man for a small sum in "ready cash" and, after spending his money, seek public support. As a consequence of bitter experience, the Government has drawn a more rigid line between competent Indians and those less enterprising. The former are permitted to sell their reservation property; the latter, while allowed to own separate plots, cannot dispose of them.

As things now stand Indian administration is evidently between two worlds—one dying and the other not yet born. The Federal Government holds vast resources in trust for its wards and seeks to prepare them for outright ownership. But it does not dare to divide all this property at once among the Indians as individuals, give them freedom to sell it as they will, and allow them to take their chances with their white neighbors. Suffering and poverty would follow—as indeed is the case among great masses of other citizens. Yet without dissolving tribal institutions the Government is attempting to educate Indians out of their ancient habits and at the same time is providing them with other aids and props against the buffets of fortune. What proportion of the Indians in the United States, numbering about three hundred fifty-six thousand, can establish themselves successfully as American citizens is a matter of guesswork. Many have undoubtedly proved their capacity for the struggle as farmers, laborers, and professional workers. How soon, if ever, the others can carry the burden is highly uncertain. In such circumstances the policy of the Federal Government with respect to the Indians and their property is based on individualistic hopes tempered by the necessity of recognizing, at least for the moment, the usages of tribal collectivism and the principle of trusteeship.

CHAPTER XVIII

PUBLIC HEALTH, SAFETY, AND MORALS

NOWHERE in the Constitution do the words "health" and "morals" appear. The term "public safety" is there but in its historic meaning—with reference to the maintenance of order, not to security for life and limb in an industrial society. Yet under these heads, in their modern sense, the Government spends each year many times the total budget of the first administration under Washington.

In the development of activities in this sphere is illustrated the flexibility of the original document, the growth of technology, and the upward movement of public opinion from the states to the Federal Government. It is under the power to regulate foreign and interstate commerce, to impose taxes, to appropriate money, and to establish post offices and post roads that most of the laws relative to the subjects of this chapter are enacted by Congress. Only one constitutional provision, the Eighteenth Amendment, falls, though not entirely, within the domain of morals, strictly considered.

Health

Broadly speaking the health functions of the Federal Government may be divided into two groups—the prevention of the spread of disease and the maintenance of hospitals for the sick and injured. In connection with the regulation of foreign commerce, steps are taken to insure the country against the introduction of human diseases by incoming passengers, ships, and commodities. The beginning of this defense—though partly economic in purpose—consists of the total exclusion of immigrants suffering from certain disorders (p. 488). Under specific enactments the following classes of aliens are flatly denied admission to the United States: "All idiots, imbeciles, feeble-minded persons, epileptics, insane persons; persons who have had one or more attacks of insanity at any time previously; persons with constitutional psychopathic inferiority; persons with chronic alcoholism; . . . persons afflicted with tuberculosis in any form, or with a loathsome or dangerous contagious disease; persons not comprehended within any of the foregoing excluded classes . . . certified . . . as being mentally or physically defective, such physical defect being of a nature which may affect the ability of such alien to earn a living."

Originally medical inspection to enforce such legislation was made only at the points of entry in this country. Under this process, as a Senior Surgeon of the Public Health Service has observed, many immigrants who were rejected and deported on arrival returned to their homes broken in spirit and practically pauperized, having sold their possessions and, in many instances, borrowed funds in order to proceed to the United States. The arrangement not only worked hardships on individuals and the steamship companies; it also made more difficult the tasks of the Public Health Service in discharging its quarantine and inspectional duties.

As a remedy for this unsatisfactory state of affairs, federal consular officers were finally directed by act of Congress in 1924 to refuse passport visas, or permits for travel to the United States, to everyone whom they knew to be ineligible for admission or even suspected of being banned by law. By its broad terms the new statute sanctioned the exclusion of "doubtful" persons at the source instead of allowing them to come over and puzzle other government agents on reaching America. In accordance with this provision medical representatives of the federal Public Health Service are now stationed in Ireland, England, Scotland, Belgium, Holland, Norway, Sweden, Denmark, Germany, Czechoslovakia, Poland, and Italy for the purpose of giving physical examinations to applicants for visas and advising our consular officers whether to grant or withhold that privilege.

The mere elimination of unhealthy passengers from ships leaving foreign ports for the United States does not, of course, solve the problem of keeping disease from our shores. Bubonic plague, for instance, is carried by fleas on rats, a roundabout process to be sure but nevertheless one that has been responsible for many disastrous epidemics. If a steamer is infested with these pests, the dread plague may break out on board among the passengers and crew before the ship comes to anchor in American waters. Obviously the proper sanitation of the vessels themselves, at the time of departure from all parts of the world, is highly desirable. But at first glance it would seem that the Federal Government itself could not by any possible action achieve this beneficial end, owing to the fact that its authority does not extend to foreign craft leaving other shores. In reality, however, it is not entirely helpless, for it can prevent the docking of any vessel within its jurisdiction that does not comply with American law, and Congress has acted on this right of control. Consequently shipowners of many countries, rather than have their property subject to penalties on arrival, have wisely chosen to abide by rules adopted for pre-inspecting vessels bound for the United States.

Sanction for this examination system is found in the statute requiring every ship sailing for the United States from a foreign country, with exceptions in the case of a few nearby cities, to obtain a bill of health from the federal consular officer at the point of departure or suffer the consequences when reaching America. The bill of health just mentioned is in substance a document describing the sanitary conditions of the port in question and of the vessel to which it is issued, as well as the state of health among the passengers and crew. For practical purposes it is a guarantee that certain minimum American standards have been met previous to sailing. Since consular officers are not usually experts in this line, they commonly rely, in granting such permits, upon advice from members of the medical staff of the Public Health Service, who are dispatched by the President to certain key centers. As a rule assignments to that duty are made with a view to maintaining a continuous watch on particular danger spots where disease lies dormant but may burst out at any time with volcanic suddenness spreading its menace to the ports of the seven seas.

In weighing the effectiveness of federal health activity abroad as a protection for citizens at home, account must be taken of the interval elapsing between the inspection of men and equipment in foreign countries and their arrival in the United States. Each technical advance diminishing the length of sea voyages not only enables passengers to travel faster but also affords an opportunity for bacteria to spread wider at higher speed. While it once required several weeks for diseases to get over the Atlantic on slow sailing vessels, they may now cross in five or six days on modern liners. Since the incubation period in several cases is greater than the time consumed in the passage, a person infected immediately previous to embarking from Europe can reach the United States before the appearance of any symptoms of trouble. Nor is rapid ocean transportation the only means of such distribution. With airplanes capable of transferring pests at the rate of one or two hundred miles an hour, still more perplexing problems arise. In his zest for rapid movement man must squarely face the consequences. Fortunately technology has provided the public health authorities with at least one weapon for combating the perils arising from this source. Even though passengers may be carried across the Atlantic in five days, news of the outbreak of any epidemic at the port of departure, likely to affect them, may be sent ahead by wireless at a rate of one hundred eighty-six thousand miles a second—a velocity with which germs cannot compete.

To cope more efficiently with difficulties resulting from the rapid spread of disease among the countries of the earth by rail, steamer, and air, several general agencies have been formed and world-wide standards have been evolved by periodical conferences. Apart from the special committee on this subject created under the auspices of the League of Nations, the most noted of these institutions is the International Health Office, having general headquarters in France, with which the United States is affiliated by treaty. For the western hemisphere as a unit, a regional body, known as the Pan-American Sanitary Bureau, has been established in Washington, D.C. With both of these associations federal health authorities maintain constant contact for the exchange of information respecting the outbreak of epidemics in the various ports of the member nations. By such connections quarantine officers are kept currently informed about the communicable diseases prevalent at important points all over the world and are put on their guard against the passengers and crews of vessels coming from zones of danger.

Work in and with foreign countries is merely the first line of defense maintained for the protection of American citizens. On our shores, at many points of entry, quarantine stations serve as the second line of inspection and exclusion. At these domestic posts of scrutiny vessels, immigrants, crews, passengers, and cargo are given a final examination before being admitted to the country.

The goal of quarantine work is to prevent the introduction of disease with the least possible disturbance to normal commercial activities. One of the many means employed is that of testing passengers and crew with the object of discovering whether they are immune to certain outbreaks to which they may have been exposed either on board ship or at the point of departure. This procedure insures a minimum of delay, for those who are not subject to attack need not be detained. On their arrival at quarantine persons coming within the ban of the law are temporarily held for observation and treatment, and those who do not meet the medical requirements for admission to the United States are deported. Vessels infested with rats are fumigated; while baggage is subjected to similar precautions. In short the federal authorities resort to the best practical methods of destroying germs and pests or at least making sure that they do not spread beyond the ship or the narrow quarters of inspection.

Some idea of the magnitude of this preventive health work is afforded by a single statistical statement: during the year ended June 30, 1929, 3,320,959 persons, a number greater than the population of Chicago at the preceding census, were examined by the quarantine officials and 27,867 vessels were inspected.

If the framers of the Constitution intended to confer upon the Federal Government a wide jurisdiction over public health in connection with its control of foreign relations, they certainly did not foresee the need or possibility of extensive national activities in the medical sphere at home. In their day science was in a rudimentary stage; indeed more than half a century elapsed before the first state health board was created—by Massachusetts in 1869. Moreover when they clothed Congress with power to regulate interstate commerce, trade and travel over long distances formed no considerable part of American economy, owing to the primitive condition of transportation and manufacture. In the beginning, therefore, the national legislature deemed it sufficient to instruct federal officers, by an act passed in 1799, to obey the health laws of the several states.

New aspects were given to the problem, however, by technology and science, the introduction of the locomotive and the steamer as well as discoveries pertaining to the causes of disease. Keeping step with the development of commerce and the advance of medicine, Congress has progressively conferred upon federal authorities new functions pertaining to public health in its interstate relations. By numerous laws it has sought to prevent the spread of epidemics among the states by passengers, by the instrumentalities of transportation, and by commodities. While in the ordinary course of things the traveler from one state to another is not subjected to physical examination, except in times of serious epidemics, this does not imply that he is entirely overlooked. On the contrary, whenever a person known to be suffering from a communicable disease wishes to make such a journey he is required by federal law to obtain the consent of the health authorities in the state of departure and also in the state to which he is going. If approval is forthcoming, he is generally confined to a separate room with a trained attendant. As an additional protection to his fellow passengers, the eating utensils and the compartment which he uses are carefully disinfected at the end of the trip.

In the normal course of their business, all common carriers engaged in interstate commerce are compelled, by acts of Congress, to observe certain precautions against the spread of disease. For example, drinking water on board trains must meet federal standards, which, incidentally, are often higher than those of many localities along the line of travel. Only grade A milk can be served to passengers in dining cars; and coaches must be kept clean in conformity with federal regulations. To make sure that the rules are properly observed, representatives of the Public Health Service make periodical inspections. In these and other ways, which escape the notice of the ordinary observer, the health of interstate travelers is safeguarded.

Far more extensive are the health activities of the Federal Government with respect to the manufacture and sale of commodities entering into interstate traffic. Here again the change of jurisdiction from local to national authorities has been the inevitable result of technical developments. For the few fresh vegetables and medicinal herbs produced in nearby gardens, the machine age has substituted an elaborate array of foods and drugs grown in remote regions or prepared in distant factories. While the industrial revolution, by multiplying the average length of haul, has brought an ever mounting percentage of these articles under the commerce power of Congress, it has had another significant effect. It has increased the demand for regulation on the part of the average consumer who, though ordinarily able to judge the value and purity of new potatoes or corn on the cob at the corner grocery, has no way of telling the worth and composition of man-made substances such as jellies, canned goods, or evaporated milk. Left to his own devices he may be easily imposed upon and indeed often has been victimized by dealers willing to exploit his ignorance and his lack of equipment for testing complex compounds. Consequently the necessity for government action designed to insure pure products, truthfully labelled, grew steadily during the nineteenth century with the processes of industry.

And yet it was not until 1906, after the country had been shocked by many scandals in this connection, that Congress took heed of the new situation by passing a comprehensive law intended to provide remedies. The measure, enacted under its power over commerce, covers a wide range of articles. Their number and variety are now so great that a special agency, the Food, Drug, and Insecticide Administration of the Department of Agriculture, has been formed to execute the statute. In broad language the law itself forbids the manufacture and sale of adulterated or misbranded foods and drugs in the sphere of interstate and foreign commerce. But since this general prohibition does not offer a clue to "adulteration" or "misbranding" in specific cases, a series of standards for the determination of purity and composition has been officially formulated to guide manufacturers, dealers, and the public. With respect to most drugs, compliance with federal stipulations merely means a rigid adherence to the terms of the United States Pharmacopœia—the great general directory of medical chemicals. Less easily defined with precision, foodstuffs are controlled by various requirements reached by the Government and manufacturers, usually in coöperation.

Obviously it is not an easy task to establish many of these standards owing to legitimate differences of opinion regarding the true nature of most articles, especially compounds. What, for instance, constitutes "pure" sausage, marmalade, ketchup, or ice cream? What is mayonnaise? What preservatives and coloring matters are injurious to the human system? If definitions were formulated in words broad enough to satisfy everybody they would be well-nigh useless in practice; if narrow they would be irksome to legitimate business. Hence conflicts between manufacturers and federal authorities are continuous, leading frequently to compromises, if critics may be believed, contrary to the public interest. But sometimes it is possible to reach a conclusion that is both technical and just, leaving few if any loopholes for evasion and fraud. As a case in point the following description may be cited: "Oil of Ceylon cinnamon is the lead-free volatile oil obtained from the bark of the Ceylon cinnamon (*Cinnamomum zeylanicum Nees*), and contains not less than sixty-five per cent by volume of cinnamic aldehyde and not more than ten per cent by volume of eugenol."

Nor is the task of applying such scientific standards to actual commodities taken from commercial channels an easy one. The increasing complexity and variety of foods and drugs, multiplying the difficulties of detecting fraud and deterioration, tax the chemist's ingenuity to the limit. For instance, he must resort to ingenious laboratory manipulations to determine whether coumarin, the active principle of the Tonka bean, and caramel, a coloring matter, have been employed to adulterate vanilla extract. Physics likewise comes into play; in order to find a mere trace of some forbidden narcotic substance in an article of trade, the searcher may have to use optical methods, particularly if only one or two small crystals have been obtained for his test. The more perplexing realm of biology must also be invaded; for, to discover whether a product contains certain vitamins, experiments on animals are often necessary, owing to the obstacles in the way of directly isolating and identifying these elusive substances. Evidently, then, the Government is doing more than relieving the consumer of responsibilities; it is daily performing for him highly skilled operations which he is not in a position to undertake for himself.

At bottom the purpose of scientific checks on foods and drugs is threefold—to prevent the sale of articles liable to injure the human body, to block the offering of inferior ingredients under false guises, and to stop the vending of worthless commodities. The first of these functions can scarcely be overemphasized. Disease, agony, and death may result from the use of infected, putrefied or poisoned foods. In fairness to producers and merchants, however, it should be said that unfit commodities are often placed on the counter through mere carelessness or ignorance on their part rather than through design. But, whatever the cause, federal law decrees that such articles must be promptly removed from the market. Doubtless the process can be illustrated best by taking a single case.

Not long ago the attention of a federal inspector in Chicago was drawn to the death of one man in that city and the serious illness of another, presumably as the result of eating some canned onions imported into the United States from a foreign country. At once the inspector secured another container from the same shipment and sent it to the Food, Drug, and Insecticide Administration in Washington for examination. On taking up the inquiry a bacteriologist in that division found nothing wrong about the outward signs of the can or of its contents. The appearance and odor of the onions were normal. Moving to the next stage he began to test their purity by feeding some of them to guinea pigs, and by taking a culture from them with a view to identifying any injurious bacteria. Within a few hours the guinea pigs were dead. And a bacteriological examination of the culture revealed the presence of *B. botulinus,* which produces a highly dangerous toxin responsible for one of the gravest forms of food poisoning known to man, a form that usually causes the death of its victims within a few hours.

Immediately after this startling discovery the Food, Drug and Insecticide Administration telegraphed to its branch stations in sixteen leading trade centers of the United States advising them to locate and remove from the market as quickly as possible every can of the specific brand of commodity in question. At the same time it wired to state and city food and health departments throughout the country definite information concerning the perilous character of this particular shipment. Not yet satisfied, it started an investigation into origins which revealed that the onions had been distributed by a certain New York representative of the foreign packer to many cities and towns in the East and Middle West. Thereupon the federal authorities obtained the names and addresses of all dealers to which consignments had been sent, numbering more than three hundred and scattered all the way from Connecticut to Colorado. Through the efforts of the Administration and local officials, every can of the contaminated product that could be located was impounded, seized, or destroyed.

Adulterated, no less than poisonous, foods come within the prescriptions of the law. Intended as a rule to cheapen the manufacture of products by the addition or use of less expensive materials, adulteration is not an accident but a deliberate expedient employed in the interest of profits. Although it may not affect the wholesomeness of a commodity, it defrauds the consumer by making him pay more for the article than it is worth. It also penalizes honest business by subjecting it to unfair competition.

A few examples of practice, from hundreds that might be cited, illustrate the possibilities of the "art:" chicory and clay molded in the form of coffee berries, colored and flavored to represent coffee but containing no trace of the latter; white stone ground into a fine powder and mixed with wheat flour; vinegar tinctured with sulphuric acid; milk made synthetically and not containing one drop of the genuine substance; artificially colored sawdust ground and added to cayenne pepper. If the watchfulness of the federal authorities and their promptness in seizing adulterated goods tend to reduce the number of such old frauds, the ingenuity of scientific schemers constantly provides new types of cheating to tax their defensive organization and skill.

Allied to the work of the Food, Drug, and Insecticide Administration in the suppression of adulteration are its activities directed towards the elimination of "quack medicines." For centuries worthless "cures" have been manufactured with the design of robbing guileless sufferers in quest of relief. It seems that the hopes of the sick, like those of youth, are eternal, and the country always has an army of "fakirs" to prey upon them. Concoctions "to restore health," of course, are not necessarily harmful, for they may contain nothing but water, sugar, and tea leaves. On the other hand they waste the money of consumers and often give them a false sense of security, leading them to delay in seeking the advice of competent physicians until serious, if not fatal, damage is done. Whenever the federal authorities discover a fraudulent preparation circulating in interstate commerce, they pounce upon it at once and remove it from the market.

Among the products recently withdrawn from the channels of trade by this process are the following items: a cure for pernicious anaemia consisting largely of ground granite; a cure for cancer in the form of a bread and milk poultice; two syrups similar to New Orleans molasses offered as a "sure remedy" for all ailments of the kidneys; and an Epsom-salts compound "guaranteed" to cure diabetes. While, doubtless, individual "initiative" was stifled in the case of the person who ground up rock and sold his victims "tombstones" for internal rather than external use, less acquisitive laymen appreciate this form of federal protection in their interest.

One group of bona fide medicines, distinctly marked off from other types by the peculiarities of its uses and manufacture, calls for a supervision especially strict. This class includes serums, viruses, antitoxins, and related products employed in inoculations against certain diseases. They are obtained by injecting germs into the living bodies of animals and collecting materials created by their life processes. In every case, therefore, great precautions are necessary to secure standard qualities. Unsanitary conditions of preparation or improper testing of strength may result in serious injury to the users. An overdose or underdose or the presence of disease germs in the drug obtained from an unhealthy animal can have fatal consequences.

Awakening to the perils lurking in this branch of pharmacy, Congress enacted in 1902 a law making all such "biologic products" subject to federal control insofar as they enter interstate commerce. In the execution of this statute the newly established National Institute of Health collects samples of these articles in the field and examines them for purity as well as strength. As a further protection to the public, every manufacturer of vaccines is required to procure a license from the Secretary of the Treasury before engaging in interstate business. In checking up the use of permits, federal authorities make periodical inspections of the sanitary conditions under which production takes place. So much for the prevention of disease.

The second great branch of federal health activity—the provision of medical care for certain classes of sick and injured civilians—is entrusted to government hospitals scattered over the United States. Speaking historically, the oldest group of private persons enjoying this service comprises members of the crews of merchant vessels flying the American flag. For this there are good reasons. Often far from home and possessing scanty funds, seamen have a special claim to public assistance. Usually they cannot receive adequate attention on shipboard where medical facilities are limited and space is at a premium. If they go ashore they may readily become a liability to the community in which they land. For more than a century, therefore, federal authorities—now the Public Health Service—have provided free hospitals and free treatment for the sailors belonging to the American merchant marine. And owing to the rapid growth in commercial shipping during recent years, the function has added materially to the expenses and responsibilities of the Government.

Besides the sailors there is a large class of longshoremen and harbor workers entitled to the advantages offered at the hospitals maintained by the Public Health Service. For a long time these laborers were in a sad plight. They were engaged in operations on board boats, such as loading and repairing, which brought them within the scope of marine law and hence excluded them from the protection afforded to fellow workmen on land by the state industrial legislation (p. 501). Yet, although deprived of this benefit, they were not "seamen" and, in case of sickness or injury, they could not turn to federal hospitals for help. Here was an evident injustice, but not until 1927 did Congress, yielding to an insistent agitation, extend to them the medical privileges which it had bestowed upon the crews of the merchant marine in the early days of the republic.

Without any direct sanction like that supplied by the commerce clause of the Constitution, Congress furnishes hospital care for lepers, persons afflicted with a dreadful disease which at one time scourged humanity. For these unfortunates two homes are maintained by the federal Public Health Service. One is located on the Hawaiian Islands to handle cases arising in that territory. The other, at Carville, Louisiana, accepts lepers who voluntarily present themselves, those apprehended under the quarantine laws, and others committed to the institution by state authorities. In 1929 there were 306 patients at Carville taking treatment under federal auspices, with favorable results in a number of instances.

In addition to the above classes of private citizens entitled to the hospital and medical privileges provided by the Federal Government, thousands of public servants enjoy similar benefits. As a matter of right, of course, officers, nurses, and men belonging to the Army and Navy, and war veterans are entitled under certain conditions to care in appropriate institutions. A kindred service is likewise rendered to the civilian employees of the Government injured in the performance of their duties.

In the discharge of its complex and wide-reaching functions, the federal Public Health Service must carry on extensive researches. A large part of this work is concentrated in its National Institute of Health, a novel investigational agency of great promise created in 1930 by a reorganization of the former Hygienic Laboratory. Under the new statute, which marks a milestone in the history of public medicine, provisions are made for the acceptance of private donations in the interests of medical science, and noted specialists outside of the government service may be awarded fellowships in research. In spite of some structural changes the Institute is to continue on an extended scale the studies carried on by its predecessor, the Hygienic Laboratory, in the diseases of mankind—to marshal experts in a war on human suffering.

Under the new order, as before, trained specialists are constantly seeking the solution of medical riddles. Their task is indeed endless. As fast as one difficulty is cleared up, field agents of the Government present new cases for consideration. With unremitting zeal the whole country is scoured for rare diseases in order that they may be investigated and countered by remedial measures before they have a chance to spread. In this way are unearthed important facts which might escape the eye of other scientific groups less eager in their quest for the odd and the unexpected. Thus the Public Health Service ferreted out a strange affliction, Tularaemia, once supposed to be highly exceptional, but now reported from almost every state in the Union. Having "spotted" the disorder, the Service then determined its cause, sought to find out how it was transmitted, and was one of the first health authorities to wage open war against it. As things turned out, its action was not a whit too soon for later inquiries seemed to indicate that the disorder had escaped attention largely because it was so little understood and not on account of its actual scarcity. It is hardly necessary to say that work of this character, done quietly in Washington and in various parts of the United States, is as important as the more spectacular activities to which public attention is regularly called.

Most of the functions described in the preceding pages, except those connected with epidemics, have to do with a normal course of affairs, but it is well to remember that fires, floods, hurricanes, and earthquakes are also common enough to call for vigilant preparedness against disaster. When such a calamity suddenly strikes a community, local health and safety authorities often find themselves face to face with responsibilities far beyond their powers and their equipment. If the crisis is really grave the charitable people of the nation, generally through the Red Cross or some other institution of benevolence, rush money, supplies, doctors, and nurses into the stricken region and Congress may come to its aid with a special appropriation. In furtherance of this work, the Army and Navy likewise render signal service for they are so organized that they can supply a police force, hospital outfits, and food to sufferers on the shortest possible notice. Never laggard in the discharge of its duties, the Public Health Service likewise springs into action and coöperates with official and private agencies in devising measures of control, relief, and rehabilitation.

Public Safety

For convenience, the term public safety is employed here to cover a wide range of federal functions designed to protect life and property against dangerous things rather than dangerous men. As in many other branches, these activities are in the main the outcome of the mechanical inventions and scientific discoveries which have revolutionized the modern world. When people travelled in ox carts or stage coaches at a few miles an hour, they needed little or no guarantee against faulty or obsolete equipment. But in this age of high-speed transit on complicated machines—with automatic couplings, air-brakes, and electric signals, ailerons, carburetors and Diesel engines, the "layman" is incapable of forming a judgment concerning the risk involved in choosing any particular vehicle. Although he may, of course, sue for damages if he is injured in a railway accident, that is little consolation for his pain and losses. Nor is the ordinary employee, outside of his special responsibility, in any better position to arrive at a correct opinion concerning the soundness of the general apparatus with which he works.

Taking into account the requirements of the technical era, Congress has, under its power to regulate interstate and foreign commerce, set up standards of safety for certain common carriers and prescribed the adoption of special devices or practices to protect both the public and its servants. The general provisions of law are supplemented by orders of the Interstate Commerce Commission and other agencies.

As the major operators in this field, of course, railroads are subject to extensive supervision in the interest of security. Locomotive boilers and appurtenances, power brakes, automatic couplers, and automatic train-stop devices on interstate lines must comply with government prescriptions which are enforced through inspection by federal agents. If it does not meet official requirements, any car, locomotive, or other piece of equipment may be ordered out of service pending suitable repairs. In its practical upshot this control produces results. Such at least is the conclusion to be drawn from the figures of the Interstate Commerce Commission, the agency in charge of enforcement. In 1923 it inspected 63,657 locomotives and found sixty-five per cent of them defective. In that year, accidents due to failure of steam locomotive parts numbered 1,348, causing a loss of 72 lives and injuries to 1,560. Five years later, in 1928, of the 100,415 locomotives examined, only twenty-four per cent were reported below standard; the number of mishaps fell to 419, deaths to 30 and the injuries to 463.

In connection with its safety work the Commission is required by law to investigate all serious railway accidents that come to its attention. This function serves a double purpose. "Coroners' inquests" over damaged apparatus develop information of value in drawing up and revising regulations. Even the mere certainty that they will be held acts as a stimulus to the adoption of precautions and the observance of law.

Common carriers by water, especially on the ocean, are or ought to be subject to the same kind of close scrutiny that is given to the railroads. This statement calls for no argument. In fact and fiction the perils of the deep have been brought home to "landlubbers" too often to need description here. Taking cognizance of their unfailing presence, the Federal Government has provided that all American ships engaged in interstate or foreign commerce and those of other nations using our ports must meet certain safety requirements. Some of these regulations limit the number of passengers and crew that may be carried; others dictate the physical equipment of the vessels; and a third group deals with the licensing of officers and crew.

It is well known that the overcrowding of excursion boats has resulted in many horrible disasters in the past. Against such calamities the Government now tries to establish safeguards by sending inspectors to the points from which vessels of this class depart on holidays and other occasions when extraordinary loads are likely to be carried. As their primary concern, these agents seek to prevent ships from taking on board any number of persons in excess of the list for which life-saving apparatus is furnished. During the year 1927–28 the power of exclusion was exercised more than two hundred times by shutting the gates against additional passengers when the fixed limits had been reached.

With respect to the physical equipment of vessels the laws and orders of the Federal Government go into great detail. Boilers on steamships, fire fighting equipment, hulls, steering gear, and innumerable other items must comply with official standards and are subject to periodical inspections. A single example may serve to illustrate the minuteness of the survey. A lifeboat must have on board, among other things, "one box of friction matches wrapped in a waterproof package and carried in a box secured to the underside of the stern thwart;" also "one canvas bag containing sailmaker's palm and needles." Boat drills, fire drills, and tests of the ship's signals are held under the supervision of inspectors. In fact, the number of matters to be checked is so large that a complete description of the specifications for ocean and coastwise vessels alone fills a volume of two hundred and fifty pages.

By no means subordinate to proper equipment is the necessity that every ship should be manned by a competent crew. Here, too, Congress has intervened. Under federal law no marine officers can be placed in posts of authority on American vessels subject to federal control until they pass examinations, set by the Steamboat Inspection Service, showing that they have had the requisite training and experience to qualify them for the responsibility they are to assume. Indeed from the captain down to common sailors entrusted with handling lifeboats, varying degrees of skill are required by statute, and the Steamboat Inspection Service is charged with the task of seeing that proficiency is guaranteed. Yet prolix as is the legislation in this field it falls far short of the highest standards and efforts are continually being made in Congress to bring it abreast the latest scientific knowledge.

Even though all these precautions have been taken, accidents still occur from storms, fires, icebergs, and derelicts (p. 397). To alleviate suffering and reduce material losses from such sources Coast Guard vessels stand ready at all times to assist ships on the high seas as best they may. But it is not only on the ocean far from land that the danger to life and limb exists; it is even greater along shores where rocks, shoals, and similar hazards lie in wait. As an aid to those wrecked on our coasts the Government maintains a string of life-saving stations which serve as headquarters for a patrol of watchmen. When a vessel in distress is discovered, Coast Guard men and equipment are sent to the scene. Employing special boats, rockets, life-lines, and other devices these workers often perform feats of signal bravery in holding losses to a minimum. Nor do their efforts cease when all on board are landed, for sufferers from accidents then receive temporary medical treatment, shelter, and nourishment until they can be carried to the nearest settlements. Through these services the Government, in a sense, helps to make up for defects in vessels, crew, and guides to navigation for which it is also responsible.

From land and sea federal control over transportation has recently spread to the skies above. Not many years ago the passenger who stepped into an airplane for a "hop" had no assurance that the pilot was physically fit or had received adequate training. In addition it was questionable whether the mechanic who had made the last adjustments knew his business or was really more than a mere "tinker." Perhaps he forgot to tighten up the guy wires on the wings or make sure that the landing gear was firmly attached. Perhaps the plane was in reality an assemblage of junk patched together out of spare parts taken from antiquated craft. Whatever the situation, the traveler was never certain that all possible precautions had been taken to safeguard life and limb. In such circumstances accidents were unduly frequent and the much-advertised "air-mindedness" could gain little headway.

With the growth of interstate aviation the Federal Government was moved by accidents and opinion to erect safeguards for the general public in this novel field of transportation. As a result the Department of Commerce now stands between the non-technical passenger and the aircraft business, enforcing certain fundamental regulations touching equipment and management. In accordance with these rules airplane engines are subjected to rigid tests before their design is approved. Planes themselves must be properly built, formally licensed, and periodically inspected. Only mechanics who have demonstrated their expertness can be put in charge of maintenance; only pilots who have proved their ability through physical, written, and flight examinations can be entrusted with operation. To-day, then, by demanding permission to see the licenses of plane and pilot before embarking on an interstate air trip, a mere passenger may make sure that in the judgment of skilled inspectors every precaution has been taken in his interest. Supplemented by investigations of accidents, such official activities have materially reduced the hazards of aviation.

Standard equipment and competent operators, however, do not remove all dangers from transportation. Explosives, gases, and inflammable materials hauled by common carriers offer special perils to all concerned. Within the limits of its jurisdiction Congress has, therefore, made the shipment of dangerous commodities subject to regulation by the Interstate Commerce Commission. According to the directions of this body, high explosives, including dynamite, may not be conveyed on the same vehicle as passengers; and all articles of this general class must be suitably marked, packed, and handled in conformity with specific rules.

Departing from the well-defined channels of interstate and foreign commerce, Congress has employed its power to tax in the interest of public safety. A clear example of such action is afforded by the levy on all matches made with white phosphorus. In the present state of scientific technique this chemical, extensively used in their manufacture, is a menacing poison which may inflict on workers, exposed to it in factories, a distressing and often deadly malady known as "phossy jaw." For more than half a century the evils of the match industry had been well understood but, since they were clearly under state jurisdiction, Congress apparently had no power to deal with them by adopting measures openly restrictive in character. At length, however, in 1912 it struck at them indirectly, as we have just said, by imposing on white phosphorus matches a tax high enough to be prohibitive in effect, and was upheld in a decision of the Supreme Court (p. 340).

Through a second indirect route—under its power to appropriate money—Congress has gone into other questions of security once supposed to be reserved to the states. Sustained by grants from the Treasury, the Bureau of Standards, in coöperation with public and private bodies, has worked out a number of "Safety Codes" covering such subjects as woodworking machinery, logging, and sawmills. On their face these proposals merely set up rules of practice for construction and operation with a view to eliminating physical hazards wherever possible. While they cannot be transformed into federal law and enforced by the Government, they have nevertheless been observed by numerous manufacturers and voluntarily adopted by several state legislatures.

With respect to one particular enterprise over which its explicit jurisdiction does not extend, the Government has gone far beyond the mere suggestion of standards. Stirred by repeated tragedies in mining, taking their dreadful toll in suffering and death, Congress has established a special Bureau of Mines and authorized it to devise rules and instruments for the elimination of risks in this industry. With assistance from many quarters, the Bureau operates along two lines: prevention and rescue. In the former relation it carries on researches in the explosives used in blasting and in the electrical apparatus employed underground in lighting and hauling—both sources of frequent disasters. On the basis of its studies, it has prepared a long list of "permissible" materials and equipment calculated to reduce perils to a minimum. Convinced of their practicality, manufacturers produce them for the market and many mine owners install them in their plants. Thus humanity and rationality march together against ancient foes of mankind.

Notwithstanding many precautions, awful disasters still occur underground, demanding prompt, skillful, and energetic measures of relief. With an eye to efficiency in rescue work, therefore, the Bureau of Mines, aided by the industry itself, has developed special apparatus to cope with gases, fires, cave-ins, and floods. This equipment is installed in railway cars and automobile trucks and held in constant readiness at convenient points in mining regions. As soon as a call for help in a catastrophe reaches the nearest headquarters, the car or truck, with its corps of expert operators, is rushed to the scene of trouble, to help in saving life and property. But even in the most fortunate circumstances a certain interval of precious time must elapse before the Bureau's agents can reach the spot. Therefore, it is important that officials and workers at mines should be trained to grapple at once with calamity of every sort. This first-aid talent the Bureau develops by conducting courses in mine-rescue technique in various parts of the country and since its system was inaugurated over three hundred seventy-five thousand men have been given an opportunity to learn the best practice.

Another outstanding problem in the field of public safety has attracted the attention of the whole country—the prevention of floods and the amelioration of suffering from such disasters. The most conspicuous attempt to forestall such catastrophes is now taking place on the Mississippi. In their eagerness for homesteads, settlers along its banks, singly or with public assistance, have gradually confined the river to a narrower and narrower channel by means of earthen levees. As a rule these dykes serve very well but when a super-flood occurs, the mighty stream pours over its restraining walls and may cover as much as thirty thousand square miles of land. For years individual farmers, city governments, and states attempted to wrestle with such periodical crises without any marked success. Finally, after the great disaster of 1927, Congress, aroused to the necessity for federal action, authorized an expenditure of three hundred twenty-five million dollars to carry out a comprehensive scheme for controlling the waters of the Mississippi. Under the direction of the engineer corps of the War Department, projects for this collective enterprise, to cost almost as much as the Panama Canal, were immediately launched, though not without much confusion and opposition.

Briefly summarized, their plan provides for continuous

Courtesy of the United States Bureau of Mines

FEDERAL AGENTS COOPERATING IN RESCUE WORK AT A FAMOUS MINE DISASTER.

Courtesy of the United States Coast Guard

A Coast Guard Cutter Saving Life at Sea.

dams on both sides of the Mississippi from Cairo, Illinois, to the Gulf of Mexico. Under fairly normal conditions the river will not rise above the height proposed for these barriers and, after they are built, cannot spill over into the rich, populous areas lying on either side below the water level. But when an unusual freshet occurs, an extra outlet must be provided, for the suggested embankments will not suffice. At several places along the Mississippi, therefore, provision is to be made for great "reservoirs" to receive the peak of the flood and hold the surplus until the river subsides. For the special protection of New Orleans, a short-cut from one to two miles wide is planned to drain flood waters away from the city into Lake Pontchartrain. In ordinary years the reservoirs will be dry and, although they are definitely held in reserve for use in case of a super-flood, the land in them may be tilled most of the time. While the scheme seems logically perfect and technically feasible, immense political and economic difficulties stand in the way of execution and the time of its completion is yet indefinite.

The Federal Government does not rest content with its efforts to prevent the evils of floods. Like the good Samaritan it also renders aid after high waters have subsided by granting medical aid (p. 593) and financial assistance to devastated districts. For example in 1930 it appropriated approximately three million dollars for the relief of South Carolina, Georgia, and Alabama under the color of reparations for damages caused to roads and bridges by floods. In the same year, by joint resolution, it authorized the Secretary of Agriculture to make loans to farmers in the storm, flood, and drought stricken areas of Alabama, Florida, Georgia, North Carolina, South Carolina, Virginia, Ohio, Oklahoma, Indiana, Illinois, Minnesota, North Dakota, Montana, New Mexico, and Missouri, wherever he found an emergency at hand, for the purpose of assisting them in purchasing seeds, tools, and other materials. By offering funds for the restoration of inundated regions the national authorities serve, in effect, as a great insurance agency, the fortunate states contributing out of taxes to help cover the losses in afflicted regions. Although this service is limited in scope and founded on no definite principles of accountancy, long practice has established the rule that federal aid is to be expected in the rehabilitation made necessary by great disasters.

Public Morals

On first thought it may seem that public morality is a theme far removed from the topics previously discussed in this chapter but in reality there is a strong tendency to rest it, as far as the law is concerned, more and more on grounds of health and safety. Historically considered, morals are "mores," or manners and habits. In or near the beginning of human society, custom as proclaimed and fortified by tribal leaders was the source of all law and, to this day, it shows a marked propensity to seek the sanction of legislation.

The dividing line between morals and law is not easy to draw. One school of critics claims that too many private habits have become subject to political regulation and that there should be a clear distinction between the rules which a government enforces and those which groups of citizens voluntarily obey as commands of God, convenience, or conscience. Contrariwise, other citizens are inclined to extend the scope of government even so far as to include the general enforcement of "Truth," as they understand it. At times both Catholics and Protestants, where they have been powerful enough, have insisted that the state should make their particular variety of religion legally binding on everybody, strictly applied by civil and ecclesiastical courts.

Although they have generally abandoned their efforts to enforce clerical decrees, owing to the number of sects or for other reasons, all governments are still subjected to impacts from that direction. Catholics believe that divorce is "wrong" and a social menace and insist on legislation forbidding it. Large groups of Protestants accept divorce but support the prohibition of intoxicating liquors. So it goes. In fact a sharp distinction between civil and moral law can only be hypothetical. What any sect or association believes to be "right" or in the public interest, it may try to make mandatory. What the legislator enacts into statutes nearly always carries with it ethical implications.

Nor is it easy to separate morals from mere convenience or practical advantage. Take the matter of intoxicating liquors. Some people favor prohibition because they believe it is "wrong" to drink. Others approve it because they think it makes for sobriety among working people, contributes to safety in the machine age, increases the output of factories and dividends on stocks, and reduces the menace of alcoholism to public health. Still others may be indifferent to the questions of private virtue or public economy and yet favor prohibition because they believe that the old-fashioned American saloon, with its fringe of drunkards and liquor politicians, was a community nuisance, a social and cultural disgrace.

To divergence of opinion over law and morals are added differences about the agency best suited to regulate conduct. It is frequently urged that in any event legislation relative to such matters belongs to the states, that the Federal Government is limited to certain specific concerns enumerated in the Constitution, and that the Prohibition Amendment is a radical departure from original principles and practice. This theory is utterly without historical support. As far as the fundamental law of the land is concerned, it may be said that all groups and classes large enough and powerful enough to compel action by Congress have usually been astute enough to find "constitutional warrant" for whatever they want. In this relation those who merely want "to do good" seldom differ from protective tariff, utility, or labor interests.

Moreover from early times the Federal Government has been forced to deal with issues quite commonly regarded as "moral." For example it was long ago necessary to decide whether the Post Office should carry obscene mail matter—and on no subject under the sun is there more difference of opinion among experts in propriety. Again, in the exercise of its undoubted powers over interstate and foreign commerce, Congress was compelled to deal with problems primarily ethical in character, long before prohibition became a serious national issue. Federal legislation pertaining to the importation of indecent books, to lotteries, to commercialized vice, to the sale of narcotics, and to numerous topics of this class, preceded by years the adoption of the Eighteenth Amendment. Some people favor one type of such legislation and some another; few condemn it all. The distinguished Catholic authority, Dr. John A. Ryan, in the same volume attacks both prohibition and birth control. He would repeal the Eighteenth Amendment as a gross violation of personal liberty, but he would uphold the federal statute forbidding the spread of knowledge respecting contraception. Yet to many other citizens the latter piece of legislation is far more obnoxious than the former. All this is by way of illustrating the difficulties of dogmatism in the domain of law and morals.

Under its power to control the mails the Federal Government has dealt with a number of schemes which are supposed to run counter to public welfare. The use of the Post Office for the promotion of frauds and lotteries is forbidden. All advertising, circulars, and other materials coming under these heads are specifically banned. So too in theory are foreign newspapers containing information on national lotteries, but in practice they are not—at all events unless their primary purpose is to advertise foreign lotteries.

A large amount of matter which does not affect the pocketbook is also shut out of the Post Office. Everything tending to incite to crime is excluded. But psychologists are far from agreement on the extent to which dime novels, detective stories, or newspaper accounts of hold-ups, homicides, and burglaries act as a stimulant to law-breaking. Obviously reading a description of a shocking murder would scarcely transform a police captain into a criminal whereas the absorption of the same tale by a careworn clerk might awaken dreadful potentialities within him. It would seem, then, that the question whether a given publication incites to crime or not is more dependent on the individual who has access to it than on the nature of the material itself. And in reality federal authorities display no little confusion in devising and enforcing laws of this type. They make all kinds of haphazard and illogical decisions in their efforts "to do good."

In the same general class may be placed legislation closing the mails to matter containing libelous, scurrilous, defamatory or threatening statements on the outside of envelopes, wrappers, or post cards where they may be seen by any person other than the addressees. Within this category also come all obscene pictures and publications—presenting many thorny issues for postal officials to decide.

Restrictions of this character are not limited to domestic sale and transportation. Congress has sought to keep all "dangerous and wicked" thoughts and objects out of the country. The Tariff Act of 1930, containing modifications of previous legislation, prohibits the importation of printed matter and drawings advocating treason or insurrection against the United States, resistance to law, or threats of bodily harm to any person in the country, and everything else which is "obscene or immoral." In the past similar provisions had permitted customs officials to seize books and objects at their own discretion, and the works of many classical writers in the Old World, ancient and modern, had been rigidly excluded as "indecent"—Chaucer, Swift, and Montaigne being among the proscribed authors. After a witty and exciting debate in the Senate in 1930 certain changes were made in the earlier law. Under the new dispensation the Secretary of the Treasury is made the supreme censor of imported literature; he may in his discretion "admit the so-called classics or books of recognized and established literary or scientific merit" but only when they are "imported for non-commercial purposes." As a further limit on the sovereignty of customs officials, they cannot destroy "objectionable" books and materials until a federal District Court has passed upon their merits under the law.

Even a subject apparently so remote from the Constitution as sex figures in federal statutes. Indecent matter bearing on it cannot go through the mails or enter the United States from foreign countries. It is unlawful to send by post or through any channels of interstate commerce or to import into the United States information pertaining to birth control or devices connected with that practice. The transportation from state to state or from foreign countries of girls and women for immoral purposes is forbidden by the Mann Act of 1910—a measure directed against commercialized vice and the international white slave traffic.

Well aware that some persons, when denied the use of the mails, may turn to other means of carriage, Congress has, as we have indicated, enacted statutes excluding certain matters from all interstate movement as well as from foreign importation by any process. Lottery tickets and advertisements and prize fight films, strange bedfellows indeed, come under this embargo. While it is not illegal to ship films of vivid encounters in the World War—the bayoneting of soldiers, the blasting of trenches with cannon shot, and the wholesale destruction of life—the tender youth of America are to be protected against insidious pictures of boxing matches.

On the border line between morals and health come alcohol and narcotic drugs. For centuries evils connected with their use have been recognized by governments and efforts have been made, through various devices, to regulate and control them. The Eighteenth Amendment to the Federal Constitution, establishing prohibition, was merely an extreme culmination of a repressive movement which had been going on for more than half a century—a movement recorded in innumerable state and federal acts. When the Amendment was put into force, two thirds of the states and large areas in the others were already "dry" by constitutional amendments, laws, and local option. Moreover, Congress had distinctly favored the prohibition states by restricting the right to transport intoxicating liquors in foreign and interstate commerce.

It is, then, an extension of historic experiments which the Eighteenth Amendment effects: "The manufacture, sale, or transportation of intoxicating liquors within, the importation thereof into, or the exportation thereof from the United States and all territory subject to the jurisdiction thereof for beverage purposes is hereby prohibited. The Congress and the several states shall have concurrent power to enforce this article by appropriate legislation."

Though apparently clear as far as it goes, this Amendment leaves any number of perplexing questions unsettled. What is intoxicating liquor? What limits are implied on private manufacture for personal use? How shall the enforcement officers be chosen? What qualifications must they have? What methods may they employ? What penalties should be imposed for violation? How shall importation from foreign countries where the manufacture and sale are lawful be blocked?

At the time prohibition was adopted it was urged that light wines and beer containing three per cent or perhaps more of alcohol were not intoxicating and, therefore, outside the ban; but Congress, in the famous Volstead Act which went into effect with the Amendment in 1920, settled the debate by including within its scope every liquid "containing one half of one per centum or more of alcohol" and "fit for beverage purposes." Going beyond the express words of the Amendment, the Volstead law forbade even the possession of intoxicants for consumption and declared that its provisions "shall be liberally construed to the end that the use of intoxicating liquors as a beverage may be prevented." It is true that the storage of such goods in one's house for consumption by the family and bona fide guests is not forbidden by federal statute but the burden of proof rests on the owner to show that it has been lawfully acquired. Exceptions are also made of liquors for sacramental, industrial, and medical purposes, but in these cases the manufacture, transportation, and sale are surrounded by many restrictions.

At first the enforcement of the law was placed in the hands of the Commissioner of Internal Revenue, the Attorney General, and their assistants, agents, inspectors, and employees, appointed in the main without reference to civil service requirements and armed with great powers to search persons, premises, and property in their quest for violations of the act. In 1927 a special unit was established in the Treasury Department to enforce prohibition, and all the appointments to the field service were made subject to the provisions of the civil service laws. Dissatisfied with the results of this arrangement Congress transferred, three years later, the enforcement division and its staff to the Department of Justice, where it was reorganized as the Bureau of Prohibition.

Meanwhile demands for a more rigid enforcement of prohibition mounted and in 1929 the Jones-Stalker Act was put on the statute books. The Volstead law had fixed the penalty for the first offense at a fine not exceeding one thousand dollars or imprisonment for not more than six months. The new measure stipulates that the penalty imposed for each offense punishable under the prohibition law shall be "a fine not to exceed ten thousand dollars, or imprisonment not to exceed five years, or both; provided that it is the intent of Congress that the court, in passing sentence hereunder, should discriminate between casual and slight violations and habitual sales of intoxicating liquors or attempts to commercialize violation of the law."

Commenting on the Jones-Stalker law, the Department of Justice called attention to the fact that "by virtue of the prison sentences authorized by the Act the offenses of illegal manufacture, sale, transportation, importation and exportation of intoxicating liquor . . . have been raised to the status of felonies, and therefore, if committed after the passage of the Act, may be prosecuted only upon an indictment or presentment by a grand jury." Desirous of giving the new legislation a fair trial, the Department added that "only good strong cases involving commercialism should be made the basis of these initial tests," and that offenses of a minor character should be prosecuted under such charges as common nuisance and possession.

Although the use of liquors for religious and medicinal purposes has raised difficulties in administrative control, they are slight as compared with the knotty problems connected with the numerous and indispensable industrial applications of alcohol. In the ordinary course of things denaturants are added to prevent the diversion of alcohol into illegal channels. Of necessity these substances must be so constituted that they are not easily removable, do not adversely affect the chemicals with which they are employed in manufacturing processes, and at the same time prevent the use of the liquid as a beverage. Evidently it is no light task for government agents (now grouped under an act of 1930 in the Bureau of Industrial Alcohol in the Treasury Department) to work out formulas which will satisfy these three conditions.

The magnitude of the undertaking is made very evident by the fact that on the average almost two hundred million gallons of industrial alcohol are distilled annually in the United States. In their efforts to keep this liquor from escaping the denaturing process, federal authorities have established a quota of production for each year. By limiting the output to a fixed amount, based on estimates as to the probable lawful need, they have stabilized the entire trade, adjusted supply to demand, and eliminated "over-production" —an interesting result of a unique situation.

Having created a control system for domestic alcohol manufacture, the Federal Government has sought to check the importation of intoxicating liquors. With this end in view it has made treaties with Great Britain, Germany, and several other foreign countries allowing it to inspect their merchant vessels within one hour's sail of the American coast. In substance such an arrangement is merely the application to prohibition of an early statute which gave a similar authority, within a twelve mile limit, to customs officers in actions against smuggling—a law based in turn on British precedents. No effective provision has been made, however, for coöperation in stopping "rum-running" from Canada and Mexico by air, water, and land. Since these countries legalize the manufacture and sale of intoxicating liquors, they naturally assume that the burden of prohibition rests on the United States, not on themselves. To close these long frontiers to "bootleggers" would be in itself a Herculean labor. Nevertheless Canada made a generous concession to American demands in 1930 by passing a law restricting the clearance of liquor-laden vessels from her ports.

The states of the American Union, as well as foreign countries, stand in a peculiar relation to the Federal Government with reference to national prohibition. The Eighteenth Amendment confers upon states concurrent power to enforce its terms by appropriate legislation. And the argument is sometimes made that this provision, by implication at least, lays on the states the duty of helping to carry the Amendment into effect, leaving them virtually no choice in the matter. Against the contention, however, runs a decision of the Supreme Court holding that "concurrent power" is an independent power, at least as far as Congress is concerned. In making its ruling the Court explained that the states may pass prohibition laws not inconsistent with the Eighteenth Amendment but that such statutes "derive their force . . . not from this Amendment but from power originally belonging to the states." H. L. McBain is undoubtedly correct when he says that according to the Court's interpretation the states are "under no obligation, moral or legal, to enact such laws because of the Amendment." They may do so and all except a few states have legislation of this character, often more drastic in its restraints than the national statutes, but still the prime responsibility for executing the Eighteenth Amendment seems to fall directly upon federal authorities. Indeed the extent to which state officers may even coöperate in the enforcement of national prohibition is uncertain. It has been argued from Supreme Court decisions that they are not bound in any way to render assistance.

Undoubtedly no small part of the inefficiency in prohibition enforcement is due to the confusion which exists about the obligations imposed by the Eighteenth Amendment on state and local authorities. In an effort to clear up the muddle, the Bureau of Prohibition issued in 1930 a special memorandum on the subject in which it took the position that the states are equally responsible with the Federal Government in executing the law. It especially emphasized a statement made by the Supreme Court in the case of Rhode Island *vs.* A. Mitchell Palmer, Attorney General, to the effect that the Amendment "binds all legislative bodies, courts, public officers, and individuals . . . and of its own force invalidates every legislative act . . . which authorizes or sanctions what the section prohibits." Since there were then about two hundred thousand state, county, and city peace officers in the United States and only about two thousand federal prohibition officers in the field, the Commissioner in charge of the Bureau insisted that loyal coöperation on the part of the former was absolutely necessary to the success of the experiment.

Oceans of ink are spilt on the subject before us. Nearly everybody has a decided opinion about prohibition, but there is little exact knowledge respecting its legal meaning, its effect on drunkenness, the amount of liquor consumed, or the extent of the violations. If, as claimed, it is a failure, still a repeal of the Eighteenth Amendment seems almost impossible, for the simple reason that the requisite three fourths of the states could scarcely be marshalled in favor of a reversal in policy. According to the present temper of Congress, there does not appear to be much likelihood of a serious modification in restrictive legislation in the near future or the substitution of other methods of control over the liquor traffic. Will the Eighteenth Amendment, like many other laws, including parts of the Fourteenth and Fifteenth Amendments, become a dead letter in states where public opinion does not support it? History can provide illustrations but the coming years must give the answer. The situation leaves little middle ground for those who reject prohibition as a solution but advocate government supervision over the manufacture and sale of intoxicating liquors.

And a kind of middle ground is the only alternative to the continuance of the present state of affairs. Few there are, even among the stoutest opponents of prohibition, who advocate a return to the old-fashioned liquor saloon. It was the bitter experience with this institution that was largely responsible for the adoption of the Eighteenth Amendment. Although some superficial thinkers speak freely of the repeal of the Amendment and the return of the liquor question to the states, anyone accustomed to dealing with facts rather than theories knows that this is an illusory proposition. If the Amendment were repealed the problem of liquor transportation in interstate and foreign commerce would yet remain to vex the counsels of Congress. Since, in our age of large-scale industry, distilling and brewing concentrate in great centers, the distribution of liquor must be made mainly through the channels of interstate commerce. Long before national prohibition was adopted, Congress had been compelled to enact legislation dealing with this issue. If the wet states could rightly protest against forcing prohibition on them, dry states could object with equal warrant to the failure of the former to stop rum running and bootlegging over their borders. A repeal of the Amendment would still leave the liquor question in the federal sphere, no matter what powers were restored to the states.

Although similar difficulties arise in connection with the control of narcotics, there is far less difference of opinion on this subject. Indeed it is generally agreed that governments should put a curb on the free manufacture and sale of such drugs. Without any express constitutional warrant, merely under its power to regulate commerce and to tax, Congress has subjected all traffic in narcotics to strict federal supervision, chiefly through the Bureau of Narcotics. By special legislation it has prohibited their importation in excess of the amount actually needed for lawful purposes as determined by the Government. Violators are punished and contraband goods are seized. Kindred restraints cover shipments to other countries. Before a person can send narcotics (other than opium which cannot be exported at all) out of the United States or its possessions, he must show that the country of their destination is a signatory to the International Opium Convention of 1912 and has adopted adequate regulations dealing with the drug traffic. As an extra safeguard, he must prove that the foreign nation in question is suffering from an actual shortage of narcotics for medical uses and that the goods offered for export are in fact intended for a specified permittee under its jurisdiction.

As a check on the smuggling of narcotics, provision has been made for the international distribution of information relative to the subject. Many countries, including the United States, now coöperate in the interchange of news and evidence, finger-prints, photographs, and other materials dealing with illegal traffic. And for the purpose of expediting these mutual services, an agreement has been reached with various foreign powers whereby ordinary diplomatic methods are discarded and exchanges may take place directly between the enforcing agencies of the several governments.

Within the United States the power to levy internal revenue taxes has enabled the Federal Government to exert a high degree of control over the manufacture, sale, and use of narcotics. All producers of smoking opium, for instance, are taxed three hundred dollars a pound on their output and in addition must furnish a bond of one hundred thousand dollars—a sum certainly large enough to discourage newcomers. Manufacturers, wholesalers, and retailers of narcotics are required to register with the collectors of internal revenue in their respective localities and pay a yearly tax for the privilege of engaging in the business. Every purchaser of any drug on the prohibited list must either show a doctor's prescription for it or receive it while under medical care.

Going far beyond the mere imposition of restraints, in an enabling act of 1929 Congress authorized the establishment of federal farms for the care of drug addicts. To be "eligible" for treatment in one of these institutions a person must have been convicted of violating the national narcotics laws and be a victim of the drug habit. Undoubtedly the new quarters will be quickly filled with unfortunate addicts. According to official estimates, the number of people given to the dangerous use of drugs in the United States ranges from one hundred thousand to one million, and the amount of narcotics smuggled into the country is four times the consumption legally permissible. Although not as spectacular as the conflict over the prohibition of intoxicating liquors, the war against this national menace is certainly not any less significant.

CHAPTER XIX

Measurements and Planning

In the modern age, when the Federal Government engages directly in technical operations on a large scale and regulates those of many private undertakings, an accurate knowledge of pertinent facts and a wide distribution of information among all parties concerned are indispensable to the conduct of affairs. A great society, founded on a national system of production and marketing, depends essentially upon rationality, upon large-scale and coördinated planning carried out in harmony with the known data of physics and social economy. Underlying the whole fabric is the spirit of engineering—the spirit of law as distinguished from chance. Its commands are imperative; get the facts, draw conclusions, make designs to specific ends, and execute accordingly. While this method has decided limitations, due to the fallibility of the human mind and the nature of the available materials, the area of its application to government and private enterprise widens with the advance of science into all fields of economy and conduct. In recognition of this truth, the Federal Government is continually extending the range of its researches and is spreading more broadly the results of its findings. A part of its work, no doubt, is haphazard and fragmentary but every decade sees immense gains in the quantity and excellence of its analytical, statistical, and standardizing operations.

This phase of development is becoming steadily more conspicuous in all technological nations and it is as inevitable as the growth of corporate business itself. There is no use to deny that it runs counter to the fortuitous and individualistic methods inherited from the agricultural age.

Perhaps it is "undemocratic" and "tyrannical" to subject to police supervision the food circulating in interstate commerce. Perhaps it is an interference with individual freedom to force the leading railways to follow one standard time. Few persons, however, who take into account the immense conveniences derived from the confiscation of poisons offered as table delicacies and the rapid through passenger and freight service of the United States, will regard such forms of ordered intervention as cramping the spirit of liberty. If other government manipulations in this field are less obviously beneficial, they may be equally necessary to the creation of an efficient society in which productive work is done with the least friction, lost motion, and waste of materials. Although the theme has received scant attention in treatises on government, its significance can scarcely be overestimated. Mankind's conquest of the future—indeed national survival—will largely depend on the successful application of the scientific method to the affairs of government as well as private enterprise.

As new technical situations have called for treatment, the Federal Government has constructed agencies to handle them with more or less competence and comprehensiveness. From the very foundation of the Republic some recognition has been given to the need for statistical and other operating data. The Constitution itself provides for a decennial census for general uses in addition to the specific purpose of ascertaining the population as a basis for distributing representation and direct taxes. It likewise empowers Congress to fix the standard of weights and measures. Surveying, mapping, and the classification of natural resources, especially on the public domain, were early seen to be indispensable to administration and were undertaken by Congress without explicit authorization. With the growth of natural science and the rise of machine industry, one investigational establishment after another has been created, culminating in the organization of the Bureau of Standards, the greatest governmental research laboratory in the world. While as yet the whole field is imperfectly surveyed, various institutions and offices of the Government have at least plotted out, and to some extent are covering, the three great divisions of data so fundamental in effective nation planning, namely, standards of measurement; the location, configuration, and nature of our physical resources; and the form and tendencies of social phenomena.

Standards

From ancient times people have employed weights and measures as tools for gauging objects about them. Once a relatively simple process, measurement has now become a matter of great complexity, owing to the rise and growth of the machine environment. With the expansion of technology there has been an enormous increase in the variety of materials and devices to be tested, accompanied by a phenomenal development of new units. The invention of electrical apparatus, for instance, has added the ampere, the volt, the ohm, the henry, and the farad to the primitive yard and pound. Modern illumination has brought about the use of lighting units such as the lumen and the standard candlepower.

But technology has done more than multiply the number of measurement types in service; it has sharpened to an astonishing extent the accuracy with which all are employed. Comparing the weight of a nebula in the heavens with a historic unit, science places its mass at 1,100,000,000,000,000,000,000,000,000,000,000,000,000 pounds. At the other end of the scale, research reveals the weight of the negative proton, the wonder-worker of chemistry and radio, as being but .0000000000000000000000000000002 pounds. Nor are these two examples merely oddities. Employing electrical units of recent origin, technicians have succeeded in measuring incoming radio signals so slight that they could be produced continuously for ten years with the energy used by a fly in climbing four tenths of an inch up a wall. The modern art of measurement, then, is not a casual matter, but one of great variety and delicacy.

In order that investigators and producers throughout the country may make comparable tests, there must be provision for a single system of measures by means of which all gauging instruments may be calibrated alike. While the hundreds of private concerns in the United States might conceivably develop the necessary units by common agreement, they have been spared a large part of this difficult task. The Constitution grants to Congress the power "to fix the standard of weights and measures" and in the exercise of this authority it has from time to time promulgated regulations. At the outset it was confronted with the fundamental question whether the metric or the English system should be adopted. Rather than take sides in the controversy so disturbing to ancient custom, Congress chose a middle course by declaring both to be legal for the United States. It also established a statutory table of conversion factors by which measurements can be changed from one system to the other. As a result, the scientific and industrial world, left free to do as it wishes, uses the two side by side. In addition to these fundamental prescriptions, Congress has established many other units for public and private purposes. In this class come standard time, standard gauge for steel plates, standard lime barrels, and standard hampers for vegetables.

Having developed certain principles of measurement the Government is faced with the task of making them effective in the main stream of the country's economic life. This is accomplished through the Bureau of Standards in the Department of Commerce. Within its buildings are housed all the original national units of weights and measures in such a fashion that duplicates may readily be prepared from them. Moreover to the several states accurate copies of the federal standards are sent for application in local administration. But the Government does not rely solely on the states to calibrate commercial apparatus in terms of the legal units established in Washington. The Bureau of Standards also

Courtesy of the United States Geological Survey

A Field Party from the Geological Survey Mapping in the Grand Canyon.

Courtesy of the United State's Bureau of Standards

BUREAU OF STANDARDS EQUIPMENT FOR TESTING RAILWAY SCALES.

places its equipment at the disposal of the public directly by supplying a continuous testing service. For a small fee it will check against the national standards innumerable articles, including surveyors' steel tapes, thermometers, watches, and water current meters. Upon completion of the examination, these devices are returned, accompanied by a certificate indicating the amount of error discovered in them. Through this process distant derivatives of the United States standards are constantly being gauged by the Bureau with a view to detecting inaccuracies accumulated in the course of their manufacture and use. Supplementing its distribution of secondary standards to local governments, the federal testing service thus spreads widely accurate copies of the national units.

Besides acting as a reference agency for checking instruments voluntarily submitted to it, the Government has the duty of enforcing standards of measurement in certain divisions of general commerce. If, for example, the label on a container coming under the Food and Drug Act (p. 585) states that there is more of a given material in the package than is actually there, federal agents may seize the goods on the ground of misbranding. But most of the enforcement work falls upon the states. Responsibility for the prevention of fraud in such matters as retailing gasoline, potatoes, and fish, is left entirely to local authorities. Still even here federal assistance is forthcoming. Since there is great variation in the enforcement methods pursued by the several states, the Bureau of Standards sponsors an annual conference of their weights and measures officials in the interests of uniformity and efficiency.

Going far beyond the establishment of units of measurement, such as pounds, ohms, and yards, and their enforcement, the Federal Government has undertaken the definition of quality standards for many complex articles entering into modern commerce. Compelled to apply tests to the commodities bought for its own purposes, it has developed a large number of "Master Specifications" which describe in detail the composition, durability, and other properties of the various types of goods used by federal agencies (p. 371). Since these Master Specifications have been developed to a high degree of perfection with the aid of the great research facilities of the United States Government, less well-equipped organizations naturally turn to them as authorities. Gradually states, cities, and other communities have found it advantageous voluntarily to adopt federal standards as guides in their purchasing rather than to attempt the formation of duplicates on their own account. Accordingly many copies of the Master Specifications are printed for the convenience of public and private buyers wishing to adhere to them on a strictly optional basis.

As consumers become interested in and apply standards to their transactions, producers are also compelled to give heed. Already many manufacturers announce with pride the conformity of their goods to recognized federal principles. To give a single illustration, a large industrialist who makes soap for the general market has specifically labelled his commodity in the following terms: "This Liquid Soap is guaranteed to comply with the United States Government Specification No. 27, for Liquid Soap, as adopted by the Federal Specifications Board, on June 20, 1922 when tested by method shown in circular of the Bureau of Standards No. 124. Copies of specification and method of testing will be sent gratis upon application." Thus an activity originally intended to help the Federal Government alone has been expanded into one of broad usefulness to the nation, substituting exactness for guess work throughout wide ranges of production and distribution.

Under various acts of Congress regulating interstate commerce, the Federal Government has also created specifications to control the sale of certain goods, entirely apart from its own supplies. The Secretary of Agriculture, in particular, is authorized to adopt for various foods and drugs "definitions" with which interstate trade must comply or lay itself open to prosecution (p. 585). The grain and cotton grading laws, administered by his Department, afford still other instances of obligatory standards of quality applicable to important items in the national market (p. 541). With the tremendous growth in the interstate shipment of commodities brought about through mass production, mandatory federal specifications, such as these, exert a salutary influence on business transactions throughout the country.

Although the Federal Government can compel business men to observe certain commodity standards whenever they seek to sell materials to it or in case they are engaged in certain forms of interstate commerce, its powers do not cover the whole realm of trade. As a means of supplementing its legal authority, however, the Government has embarked upon a policy of assisting in the development of other specifications on a purely voluntary basis. Thus the Bureau of Standards encourages the several trades to call conferences for the purpose of adopting definitions to control the actions of their respective members. When a meeting is able to reach the desired agreements, the Bureau then makes a canvass of all other interested concerns to discover how many of them will adhere in practice to the recommendations of the convention. If a satisfactory majority engaged in the particular business consents to abide by the stipulations, the rules are printed and issued by the Government as "commercial standards" for the trade in question. From time to time the Bureau likewise makes general surveys of various industries, from which the Department of Commerce compiles a list of "willing-to-certify" manufacturers—those who will guarantee their goods to comply with the "commercial standards" whenever they are asked to do so by purchasers.

On the other hand, business may be impeded by the existence of too many standards as well as too few. If, for example, a dealer or manufacturer is called upon to handle forty-nine regular sizes of a given commodity when nine would serve the requirements of the trade, he is subjected to needless costs. Such a superfluity of units compels him to maintain unnecessary stocks of different dimensions, for which an elaborate storing and accounting system must be devised. Furthermore, since several sizes of an article are sometimes made with the identical factory equipment, an adjustment of machinery must occur for the production of each type, and this consumes both time and money. If the number of standard shapes turned out at a plant can be cut down to the minimum, therefore, burdensome changes by hand may be avoided and automatic machinery installed. There is, apparently, much to be gained and little to be lost through such simplifications.

Proceeding on this assumption the Bureau of Standards has undertaken to act as a coördinating agency for the purpose of bringing producers, consumers, and traders together and inducing them to eliminate by united effort needless and profitless variations in size and shape. Through educational campaigns, important groups of enterprises are urged to form associations and inquire into the number and relative sales-values of the many types of goods they handle. On the basis of its experience in this activity, the Bureau of Standards has stated that such "studies of many fields show that eighty per cent of the business in almost any line of goods is done on twenty per cent of the varieties in which that line is offered." If research indicates that conditions of this nature exist in any particular trade, a conference of leaders is then called, under Bureau auspices, to adopt "simplified practice recommendations," designed to cut out little used but expensive variant patterns. Thereupon the Bureau makes a canvass of the whole industry by mail to determine what proportion will accept and employ the new standards. If the men in responsible charge of eighty per cent or more of the volume of business in the given branch agree to follow the suggestions, the new regulations are printed by the Bureau as a unit in its series of "Simplified Practice Recommendations" and made available for general distribution.

So far the results achieved through the actual application of simplified practice recommendations published by the Government amply justify its work. By this process, for instance, the sizes of milk bottles have been reduced from forty-nine to four, of hospital bed-widths from thirty-four to three, and of vitrified paving brick from sixty-six to five. Accompanying the phenomenal curtailment in the number of patterns on the market, a large saving in dollars and cents is reported. By way of illustration, leaders in certain industries affected by the process estimate the following savings in a single year: "reinforcing bars, five million dollars; metal laths, two million dollars; lumber, two hundred fifty million dollars." In a theoretically perfect economic order standardization would be applied in the production of ordinary commodities from top to bottom, eliminating all waste and cutting costs of production to a minimum. How many millions are yet lost annually by inefficiency in this sphere there is at present no way of estimating.

Surveying and Mapping

Surveying is the art of collecting statistics on the configuration of the earth's surface while mapping is the art of their graphic presentation. Both operations apply to geographical areas certain arbitrary man-made measures established by the several governments of the globe. A few of these have received the common sanction of many peoples, the latitude and longitude lines which serve as the guiding network for all large surveys being reckoned among such international conventions. Others are merely of local significance. The United States, on its own part, has promulgated a legal foot and mile for use throughout the country. And in the enforcement of this regulation, as we have already seen, the Federal Government offers, for a small fee, to compare the measuring devices of surveyors with national standards, thereby assuring a high degree of uniformity in American surveys and maps.

But the Federal Government did not develop standards of surveying measurement solely to help private parties and local communities. Entirely apart from such intent, the

United States was compelled to establish these units as a basis for its own extensive operations. At its very inception the Government was confronted with a mapping enterprise of the first magnitude—the exact plotting of its own boundaries. And with the rapid expansion westward to the Pacific, resulting in the addition of new territories, that task was immensely increased. Nor is the work complete at the present day. Two commissions, one composed of representatives of the United States and Canada, the other of delegates from Mexico and the United States, are permanently in charge of determining and marking the borders of the three countries. These bodies are constantly at work conducting new surveys and maintaining the established lines in suitable condition. In this connection they erect and repair monuments and clear the trees and brush along the frontiers so that customs and immigration officers may have unmistakable guides in enforcing laws. Moreover the Rio Grande River, forming part of the Mexican border, does not submit to official decisions after they are made, for that unstable stream shifts its channel at irregular intervals causing disturbing changes of nationality in the land along its banks. Here constant watching and re-surveying are necessary.

Within the confines of the United States numerous federal problems require surveying and mapping for their solution. Outstanding among them has been the huge task of laying out territories for temporary administration and breaking public lands into convenient holdings for sale or lease. As an important supplement to its work in delimiting the surface of these areas, the Government has undertaken the classification of the mineral wealth lying underneath. Thus geological inquiries are made to reveal the presence of coal, oil, phosphate, and other resources in order that fair prices may be fixed for the disposal of the tracts which still belong to the Government. Apart from the public lands open to entry, there are reservations—national forests, national parks, game refuges, Indian holdings, and military camps—which all require surveying and mapping. Then there are additional burdens due to the fact that federal authority is constantly invoked in disputes over land titles relative to former federal grants, to public works, such as Mississippi flood control, and to innumerable waterway and harbor improvements. Hence, besides making surveys good for indefinite periods, the engineers of the Government are kept busy traversing old ground and dealing with new problems.

While maps of standard accuracy and on standard scales were being prepared by federal agencies in connection with surveys of national boundaries, waterways, and the public domain, engineers realized the need for similar maps covering sections of the country to which the National Government did not have direct title. True, maps issued by state and local authorities were available but these usually had decided drawbacks. Regions handicapped by lack of funds did not engage in intensive charting although these very sections were often of particular concern to engineers planning new developments. Furthermore maps were made on various scales, sometimes showing too little detail to be of practical service or revealing errors due to the absence of checks imposed by a common national standard. The heights of mountains and other geographical configurations were frequently referred to arbitrary spots chosen separately by the officials in charge; and, since these starting places were at various points above sea-level, no one could tell by looking at a map how high a given mountain actually was above the surface of the ocean. More system was urgently needed. For good reasons, therefore, the National Government was called upon to iron out the inequalities and imperfections in mapping which the smaller units seemed unable to clear up by coöperation among themselves.

Responding to insistent pleas for a "geographical census" of the United States on a single, comprehensive plan, the Federal Government has been engaged for many years in plotting the whole country. Under the Coast and Geodetic Survey of the Department of Commerce a preliminary network of carefully measured lines has now been thrown over many large sections. At strategic points in this huge net, "bench marks," or permanent signs, are placed for the assistance of the technical public. Through the use of these marks engineers are saved a great deal of time and effort in making local and minute surveys. For example, the designer of a water-supply system wishes to know whether a given lake is above or below a certain distant city. If it is sufficiently above, he can rely on gravity to carry the water; if it is below, he must install pumps. Without definite directions, he would have to spend days or weeks in surveying and making calculations in order to ascertain this simple fact; but on account of the services already rendered by the Federal Government, he merely has to locate the official markers nearest to the lake and the city. By writing to Washington, he can obtain the geographical position and elevation of these points of reference.

From the bench marks established by the Government in the manner just described, the Geological Survey of the Interior Department carries on detailed mapping operations. In the undertaking it is aided by the Coast and Geodetic Survey, local governments, railroad companies, and other bodies. The final product of this topographical work is a series of maps of the United States, on standard scales, which show not only natural objects but such works of man as highways and buildings. For the guidance of ships an additional set of charts is prepared indicating marine channels and dangers (p. 396). When completed, the individual maps are offered for sale to the general public at a nominal price. Collectively they form an atlas of great commercial importance.

In making its "geographical census" of the country, the Federal Government does more than merely show the configuration of the surface of the earth; it also analyses the resources of the nation. A special survey, conducted by the Department of Agriculture in coöperation with other agencies, investigates the nature and extent of various soil formations. Results are then made available to farmers, engineers, and others in the form of pamphlets containing detailed soil maps combined with sufficient descriptive matter to make them clear. A second type of surface study is carried on by the Geological Survey with respect to the water resources of the United States. Through the operation of numerous stream-gauging stations, it continuously records the flow of rivers in many states. The data so assembled are of high service to engineers in the design of water-works, bridges, power plants, and river improvements.

Leaving the more conspicuous ground materials behind, the Geological Survey burrows deep into the earth. It makes investigations of oil fields, coal beds, rock formations, mineral deposits, water tables, and other subterranean phenomena. The information thus secured furnishes a guide to quarrymen, engineers in search of strong foundations, miners and prospectors. Owing to their broad scope such researches serve a remarkably wide range of economic interests. More than that; they supply a fairly accurate picture of the nation's material endowment upon which all productive industry rests.

If the geographical census of the Federal Government is to be of maximum value to the public, however, an accounting must be rendered of varying forces which make it impossible for surveying and mapping to become a static art. One of the most perplexing of these variables is the constant change in the electrical properties of the earth, which causes the needle of the ordinary magnetic compass to shift its direction not only from place to place but from year to year. Whenever an earlier survey must be retraced, therefore, both the old and the new compass positions are essential to accuracy. To supply such information the Coast and Geodetic Survey has established a nation-wide recording system for the preservation of magnetic data. Through periodic observations at a number of select stations scattered over the country, a watch is kept on the wanderings of the compass needle and a record is preserved for the benefit of engineers and scientists alike.

A second variable, which certainly requires no introduction, is the earthquake, a natural phenomenon that not only changes the altitude and position of land but occasionally creates or destroys lakes, river beds, and islands. Wherever they are prevalent, such disturbances inevitably have a profound effect on all surveying and mapping operations. In order that its work may be conducted with due regard to them, the Coast and Geodetic Survey collects data by means of special instruments, located in the United States and outlying possessions, which indicate the time, place, and extent of these deep-seated commotions.

Federal Statistics—Population

Through its surveying and mapping operations the Government is able to describe in detail the natural theater of mountains, rivers, rocks, minerals, and soil which constitute the United States as a geographical unit. But the background is not enough. The people themselves and their activities must also be brought into the picture if the scene is to be complete and effective national plans are to be made and executed. Aware of this imperative the Federal Government, from its very foundation, has carried on economic and sociological studies with the object of interpreting American civilization and its patterns to the people and their official representatives. And the task is not an easy one, for the complexity of modern life is so great as to prevent many relationships from being readily apparent. Sharp eyes are needed to discover the effects of urbanization on agriculture, of invention on unemployment, and of mass production on the problems of distribution. Yet just such discernment and disclosures are essential to an understanding of the materials with which governments must work. Statistics reveal operations, trends, characteristics, and possibilities. Without them all is guesswork. In human affairs as well as in nature, there are movements, laws, and forces. If they are less evident and tangible, still the statesman must reckon with them. At all events statistics of humanity in its varied relations furnish him with some guidance and often with dictation.

Numerous federal agencies are employed in making mathematical surveys of persons and objects. Outstanding among them is the Bureau of the Census in the Department of Commerce which conducts studies in more fields of human activity than any other federal institution and is consequently the best known in this sphere. Supplementary services engaged in gathering statistics usually operate with reference to their particular specialties. A few examples may be offered by way of illustration. The Bureau of Labor Statistics, in the Department of Labor, collects information on wages, hours of work, employment, strikes, and cost of living, all closely interwoven with its work in the promotion of labor interests (p. 511). Through the Office of Education, the Department of the Interior assembles data on the number of children in school, the cost of their training, and other salient facts connected with the general subject. Several independent branches of the Government, of which the Interstate Commerce Commission is typical, also contribute their share of statistics, the Commission itself tabulating earnings of railway, telephone, and telegraph companies over which it has supervisory power.

From the nature of things the methods used by the different federal services in collecting data are various. The most accurate of all, obviously, is the employment of special agents to interview personally those who can furnish the desired information but who might not otherwise take the trouble to report. In conducting the general census of 1930, therefore, approximately one hundred thousand enumerators were sent out to canvass the country. But this process has one serious drawback—its expense. Consequently other means are utilized in certain cases. Federal figures on marriage and divorce, for instance, are secured from officers of state and local governments, not by direct recording and reporting. On the other hand there are many fields where even local governments cannot render effective aid. Fortunately, however, private groups will often respond generously to calls for assistance in the form of questionnaires, supplying facts without charge. In this fashion a considerable volume of current business statistics is assembled on the understanding that the Government will not divulge firm names when such action might reveal important clues to competitors. Composite pictures of many fields of work are thus obtained at low cost.

Despite its extent and diversity, the statistical research of the Government is mainly centered about certain large topics which stand out in bold relief. Undoubtedly one of the most fundamental is the nature and composition of the population of the United States. Indeed the Constitution specifically provides for a decennial census of the people, on the basis of which popular representation in Congress can be adjusted from time to time. Under the American system, then, such a periodical survey is imperative. But the regular census goes far beyond mere head counting. As taken in 1930 it recorded, among other things, data on the relationship of each person to the head of the family, sex, color or race, age, marital condition, age at first marriage, literacy, place of birth, mother-tongue, whether naturalized, whether able to speak English, occupation, whether a veteran of the United States forces, whether unemployed, and whether attending school or college at any time since September 1, 1929.

In large part the value of all such population measurements depends upon the accuracy with which they reflect the great movements of peoples that seriously affect our national existence and economy. Certainly increases or decreases in the number of inhabitants by regions and groups as well as throughout the country are among the important changes to be watched and recorded. The Government also takes pains to secure, in addition to the regular census returns, careful vital statistics from which the ratio of births to deaths, so fraught with meaning for the future, may be computed. In reaching final conclusions these figures must also be studied with reference to a disturbing force—immigration. For the purpose of meeting this requirement, the Government makes available figures on the number of persons entering and leaving the United States. Taken together, then, the federal vital and immigration statistics present a fairly clear picture of the growth and changes in population, so important for many aspects of nation planning.

Not content with recording numbers, ages, and increases in the population, the Government also surveys some aspects of its cultural organization. Since America is a land of many races no study of the people would be complete without the collection of statistics on their national origins. The existing Immigration Act, to mention only one practical application of such data, is founded on the figures relative to nationality assembled and interpreted by the Government. Secular and religious training, as well as racial characteristics, enter into the heritage within which statesmen must operate. Consequently the Government gathers facts on literacy and education, so closely related to planning and production. Intimately associated with this background of schooling are the spiritual beliefs cherished by the people. And through its census of religious bodies by creeds, the Government is prepared to make at least a partial answer to the persistent query of the day—what is happening to religion?

Interwoven with the cultural characteristics of the people are their economic conditions and activities, likewise pertinent to all phases of calculation and planning. In this relation the Federal Government collects and analyses more or less completely a multitude of data bearing on occupations, with special emphasis on the movement from rural to urban districts and shifts from trade to trade. With less completeness it furnishes, at least collaterally, information on the distribution of wealth. Surveys of home ownership, tenancy, and farm mortgage indebtedness throw light on this subject. It is further illuminated by studies of incomes reported for taxation and the earnings of corporations, supplemented by data bearing on the lower wage groups, brought together by the Departments of Labor and Agriculture. Still it must be said that, with reference to this branch of social economy, the statistical materials of the Federal Government are far from exhaustive or satisfactory. It is easier to discover in its voluminous reports the prices of hogs over a period of years than the true course of economic development among all classes of the population.

When a fair picture of the nation's social composition has been obtained, one may well ask: To what extent is the system of national economy, public and private, operating efficiently and commanding the support of the people, as measured by the statistics of crime, delinquency, and insanity? Unfortunately here, as in the case of the distribution of wealth, the data collected by the Federal Government are sadly inadequate. From time to time the country is disturbed by cries about a "crime wave" or a "decline of morality and stamina," but in reality no comprehensive figures are available for answering the questions raised.

In a large measure this paucity of materials is due to the fact that most of the statistics on crime, delinquency, and insanity are collected by state and local governments, generally on the basis of widely diverse principles of classification. They are frequently imperfect besides. The Federal Government, it is true, reports crimes committed against its own laws as well as the number of persons in its institutions for the criminal and insane. And to supplement this material it also periodically gathers figures on the inmates of state and local institutions.

Yet at best they are unsatisfactory. Owing to the deficiencies in such returns and the great need for more exhaustive information, the Committee on Uniform Crime Records of the International Association of Chiefs of Police has prepared a manual on uniform crime-reporting for general use throughout the country. It has also induced the Division of Identification and Information in the federal Department of Justice to widen the scope of its coöperation with local police authorities and undertake the continuous collection and publication of criminal statistics. Until more responsibilities of this character are assumed by the Federal Government, leading questions pertaining to crime and delinquency in the United States must go unanswered.

Statistics of Industry and Agriculture

For reasons sometimes regarded as more practical, the Government covers very thoroughly every phase of the nation's material economy. Several federal agencies are constantly engaged in gathering information bearing on industry and agriculture as going concerns. The first step in this work consists in the collection of data relative to the nature and extent of the physical plant now in operation. In this connection the Government makes studies of such items of industrial equipment as mines, factories, railroads, electrical machinery, and power houses. Similarly agriculture is gauged by means of reports on the area of farm land under cultivation, tools, and other forms of capital employed. These studies, then, reveal the nation's capacities for turning out wealth.

Are these potentialities properly realized? To answer this question the Government assembles statistics on every department of production, with which the figures on capital equipment may be compared. Thus the periodic output of hides, skins, and leather, boots and shoes, coal and oil, knitted underwear, locomotives, fertilizers, wool, and tractors, to mention only a few, is all recorded in the reports of federal agencies. In order to measure fluctuations in the flow of goods from factory and field to market, the Government also makes comparative studies of production, showing trends over long stretches of time.

On the basis of such figures and the known possibilities of technology, competent engineers maintain that the annual output of wealth could be increased enormously, making undeserved poverty as obsolete as famines, if the problem of distribution could be more effectively handled. Although the theme lies outside the immediate scope of this volume, it is undoubtedly true that there is great lost motion in the methods at present employed in the marketing of goods, accounting in part for high prices and a reduced buying power among the mass of the people. Although we have elaborate reports on foreign commerce (p. 475), there is a dearth of data on this domestic theme. In point of fact, studies of distribution costs have not kept pace with studies of production costs. At last awakened to this neglect the Federal Government decided to undertake, in connection with the census of 1930, a comprehensive survey of the methods and machinery used in transferring commodities from the producer to the consumer.

So far we have dealt with the general classes of statistics gathered by the Government but have paid little attention to the specific agencies responsible for each type. Fortunately the reader need not burden his mind with this detail as the Department of Commerce publishes an annual *Statistical Abstract of the United States* which contains summary tables on important subjects secured from many places widely scattered. If the desired information is not in the *Abstract*, it may be easily found, for the Department will put any inquirer in touch with the appropriate public or private sources whence it obtains its supply. This service, rendered by its Bureau of Foreign and Domestic Commerce, is supplemented by the facilities of a translating staff which furnishes materials printed in foreign languages and referring to points outside the United States. Thus a coördinating agency has been created to gather data from all over the world and present them to the public in convenient form.

The Dissemination of Information

The collection of information, so essential to nation planning in gross and in detail, is only one part of the process. To be effective, each special group of data must be made available at the proper time and to the proper persons, official or private, and in such a form that it may be made the foundation of decisions and actions. This function the Federal Government also assumes to a limited extent and, in discharging it, employs all the usual channels—the printed word, the radio, motion pictures, and lectures by competent authorities. Its immense publishing undertakings are carried on by the Government Printing Office, an independent establishment under the direction of a Public Printer appointed by the President and Senate, but subject to supervision by a body of six Congressmen known as the Joint Committee on Printing. In this Office, business of great magnitude is transacted. The annual production of books, pamphlets, and circulars alone totals over one hundred million copies. In addition to publications for general circulation, the Office turns out huge quantities of post cards, money orders, and forms for the convenience of the Government in its administrative work. To achieve such wholesale results, use is made of the latest machinery operated by a force of approximately four thousand employees. Indeed the honor of being the largest printing house in the world is claimed for the Government Printing Office.

For the benefit of those who wish to obtain its publications easily and rapidly, the Government Printing Office conducts a bookstore in Washington, D. C., under the direction of the Superintendent of Public Documents. By writing to the Superintendent in care of the Government Printing Office, a reader may obtain a catalogue covering federal publications in any field in which he may be interested. As a special service to those desirous of keeping up-to-date, a weekly list of current issues is also supplied by the Office. In looking through these catalogues the inquirer will find numerous books and pamphlets listed as free and, since the Government carries them through the Post Office without charge, a post-card will bring them to his door. For other materials a small charge is made, sufficient to cover the cost of printing. By eliminating authors' royalties and all the expenses of advertising, remarkably low prices are quoted on most of the government publications.

Government books and pamphlets are also made generally available by several federal agencies acting on their own responsibility. Thus copies of the *Congressional Record* and public documents in specified quantities are furnished free to Congressmen who may in turn distribute them among their constituents through the mails. The same policy has been adopted with respect to the many bulletins for farmers provided by the Department of Agriculture and dispatched under congressional direction. Naturally, of course, the Senators and Representatives, in their laudable desire to keep in close touch with the voters at home, are very helpful in securing a wide-spread circulation of public papers.

As an aid to the spread of official information the publications of the Government Printing Office are regularly sent to many libraries where the general public reads. By special act members of Congress are empowered to designate certain institutions in their respective districts as "depositories." Such libraries, now numbering about five hundred, are entitled to receive automatically all issues from the federal press without charge other than transportation costs. But since the vast mass of books and pamphlets annually tendered to them often exceeds their shelf room, almost all the depositories have chosen to accept only selected portions of the material put at their disposal. And in view of the fact that none which they accept may be lawfully discarded, a still greater curtailment in this method of distribution is inevitable in the near future. Nevertheless, for the reader who has occasion to examine many federal documents, the nearest official library is usually found to be the most satisfactory place to work.

For the benefit of private citizens and officials the Government maintains in Washington a great national depository, the Library of Congress, an institution freely open to the public, even to the most casual reader. To this library are sent samples of all books copyrighted in the United

States, together with the thousands of government publications. Here also are housed many extremely valuable originals of famous American letters and documents safeguarded for future generations. To supplement these treasures, agents of the Library are constantly occupied in making transcripts of unpublished foreign papers bearing on American history thus enriching the stores of domestic materials. In addition to books and manuscripts, the library finds room for charts, photographs, music sheets, and similar copyright items in great profusion. Containing over six million works, the Library of Congress is now the largest in the western hemisphere, and is frequented by thousands of investigators from every part of the country. Although its collections cover all fields of knowledge it renders particular service in the various branches of American politics and government.

Complementing the Library of Congress as an agency for the dissemination of information is the Smithsonian Institution, founded prior to the Civil War as the result of a bequest from James Smithson, an Englishman. Working in the realm of material things rather than in that of books, this organization gathers objects of scientific and cultural interest from all quarters of the globe. The specimens collected and the investigations made by its field parties afford a fund of data to be studied by its staff and made the basis for numerous technical treatises. But its activity is not confined to pure research, for interesting items are placed on display where the general public may have ready access to them without charge. Almost any taste may be satisfied in this way. Ship-models, the transatlantic plane *The Spirit of Saint Louis,* precious jewelry, famous paintings, living birds, and reptiles are all housed where they may be easily seen. Thus the reader in the Library of Congress has only to take a short walk if he would enliven the printed page by an inspection of the exhibits of the Smithsonian Institution nearby. In furnishing this contact with reality the latter agency renders a signal service to students.

With the development of the motion picture industry, federal activity in the dissemination of information entered a new field. Taking advantage of the educational possibilities afforded by the screen, several governmental agencies make and issue films under their own auspices. The Department of Agriculture, for example, has produced many interesting reels showing various phases of its work, such as the fighting of forest fires, the grazing of livestock, and the introduction of plants from foreign lands. Through coöperative arrangements with private concerns, the Bureau of Mines has also developed an extensive film library comprising about fifteen hundred separate pieces. The pictures thus prepared by federal agencies, now constituting a valuable source of general and technical information, are lent on a large scale to schools, clubs, business, civic, and other bodies at a nominal sum covering the costs of transportation. Some idea of the extent of this service may be gathered from the fact that, according to estimates, more than one million five hundred thousand people have seen the films of the Bureau of Mines alone. Enthusiasts have claimed great things for visual education and the Government of the United States has not been remiss in utilizing the new medium of instruction.

Yet, in spite of its extensive activities in the dissemination of information, the Government cannot be said to have attained an efficiency of one hundred per cent in this relation. It does not even employ all the methods obtaining in private business. Since it has rejected the policy of making profits out of its operations, it does not advertise its wares widely, like other publishers, expecting a return in increased sales; nor does it make a practice of distributing its works through the innumerable bookstores scattered over the country. Watchful and interested individuals, it is true, obtain important government documents as soon as they come from the press, but it is largely by chance that ordinary citizens become aware of the highly valuable materials made available by the federal agencies.

How many persons, for instance, about to build houses, know that the Federal Government offers them a useful pamphlet on "How to Own Your Home," which describes methods of financing, the issuance of building permits, the planning of rooms, and the hiring of contractors? A still more striking illustration is a story related not long ago of the United States Geological Survey. In one of its printed documents, it described a large gold supply easily accessible near Nome, Alaska, and gave full directions for finding the spot. But nobody paid any attention to its report, even on gold! Later some casual prospectors, who had not heard of the official document, drifted into the region in question, panned the precious sand, and soon found themselves on the road to wealth. Every year state and local authorities re-investigate topics that have already been well covered in federal studies to be had for the asking or at a nominal price. Obviously some kind of clearing house for the translation of information into the dynamics of action is one of the real needs of the Federal Government.

Coördination and Planning

From the preceding pages it is apparent that all the interests and activities of public and private economy are more or less successfully reflected in the statistics and reports of the Federal Government—the condition and drift of manufacturing, agriculture, railways, and mining, the wages of labor, the extent and uses of natural resources, the finances and functions of the Government, and the ebb and flow of foreign trade. As each agency engaged in the collection and compilation of data presses deeper into its particular field, especially in seeking the causes of movements, it comes into contact with the researches of other agencies. For example, a quest for an explanation of the trend in the transportation business leads the investigator into the statistics of agriculture and manufacturing. This is inevitable, for the various branches of economy are interrelated—dependent upon one another for their efficient functioning and their prosperity. From the interconnections thus mathematically revealed comes a recognition of the necessity for coördination—conscious planning and coöperation in all divisions for the purpose of developing and maintaining high productive capacities so vitally associated with the national standard of life. And this concept is in keeping with the science of technology which is essentially rational in its methods, that is, insists on substituting system, forecast, and control for chaos and rule of thumb; law for chance.

While the need for such social engineering is continuous and springs from the highest requirements of national economy realistically conceived, it is dramatically emphasized and thrust upon popular attention in times of business depression when the lack of organization is most apparent, when millions suffer from "overproduction" and maladjustment. It is one of the paradoxes of machine civilization that penury for workers often accompanies a surplus of wealth. Poverty and misery are common to other types of society, but there they spring from famines, floods, and pestilence, not from a plethora of riches. For a long time, as we have said above (p. 469), industrial panics were viewed in the spirit of primitive mythology as the visitations of angry gods, not in the spirit of man's new and amazing instrument—technology. To believers in ancient mythology, there appeared to be no way of escaping the evils of cyclical disasters—bankruptcies, reduced dividends, unemployment, destitution among working people, disruption of families, increase in crime, and other grave social disturbances. But in the course of time, economists, after inquiring into the causes of business cycles, began to suggest methods for avoiding them, for stabilizing production through a better coördination of public and private operations.

Recognition was given to this concept in the Federal Reserve Act of 1913, especially its provisions for the expansion and contraction of credit, with a view to stabilizing manufacturing and agriculture. Again in 1921 official notice was taken of the new economic trend, when President Harding, disturbed by the financial crash of the previous year, called a national conference on unemployment—a conference composed of "men representative of all sections, predominately those who can influence the action of employing forces and who can influence public opinion." In sponsoring this affair, Herbert Hoover, then Secretary of Commerce, stated that "the object of the conference will be to inquire into the volume of needed employment and the distribution of unemployment, to make recommendations as to the measures that can properly be taken in coördinated speeding-up of employment by industries and public bodies during the next winter and in addition a broad study of the economic measures desirable to ameliorate the unemployment situation and give impulse to the recovery of business and commerce."

In the course of the conference, national responsibility for finding a remedy for industrial crises was taken for granted. Although he deplored attempts to give relief through the public treasury, President Harding declared that "there are no problems affecting our national life and the welfare of the American people which we cannot and will not solve. . . . And all America has never failed when committed to a common cause." While taking a similar attitude toward "paternalism," Secretary Hoover stated that "the Administration has felt that a large degree of solution could be expected through the mobilization of the fine coöperative action of our manufacturers and employers, of our public bodies and local authorities." In the conference itself a number of concrete measures were proposed: an expansion of public construction, changes in the seasonal practices of certain enterprises, part-time employment by manufacturers wherever possible, and a curtailment of the profit-seeking motive in keeping with "the requirements of safe business practice."

In order to continue the interest thus begun, Secretary Hoover appointed two committees to carry on investigations related to the objects of the conference. One of them inquired into seasonal operations in construction industries and recommended a long list of changes in historic customs—changes designed to eliminate ups and downs in building activities. Under the general supervision of the second committee, a private organization, the National Bureau of Economic Research, made an elaborate study of business cycles and unemployment and the general character of recent economic changes. Among other things, these reports urged a more extensive coördination of public and private statistical agencies for the purpose of securing more accurate and exhaustive data bearing on the subject of national economy. The last of the documents resulting from this conference was published in 1929, just in time to greet another great crash on the stock market, foreboding the usual business depression.

Within a few days after this collapse, President Hoover summoned to the White House outstanding leaders in manufacturing, transportation, agriculture, utilities, and labor organizations and asked them to adopt measures calculated to keep economic enterprises running on an even keel. But it appeared that industrial managers alone could not solve the problems presented by the crisis. Hence official help was invoked and promised. Attention was again directed to the fact that our governments, national, state, and local, are extensive builders and buyers of commodities, and it was again insisted that they should come to the aid of business by expanding their special operations. In the name of the Federal Government, a swift enlargement of the construction program was announced, and at the same time President Hoover called upon the governors of the forty-eight states for assistance in pushing public undertakings. Immediately telegrams of approval poured in upon the President and with extraordinary unanimity official reënforcement was promised from all quarters.

From beginning to end, President Hoover's appeal to state governors illustrated the close connection between business and government and the new economics. "With a view to giving strength to the present economic situation," he said, "and providing for the absorption of any unemployment which might result from present disturbed conditions, I have asked for collective action of industry in the expansion of construction activities and in stabilization of wages. As I have publicly stated, one of the largest factors that can be brought to bear is that of the energetic yet prudent pursuit of public works by the Federal Government and State, municipal and county authorities.

"The Federal Government will exert itself to the utmost within its own province and I should like to feel that I have the coöperation of yourself and the municipal, county and other local officials in the same direction. It would be helpful if road, street, public building and other construction of this type could be speeded up and adjusted in such fashion as to further employment.

"I would also appreciate it if your officials would canvass the State, municipal and county programs and give me such information as you can as to the volume of expenditure that can be prudently arranged for the next twelve months and for the next six months and inform me thereof."

During the wide-spread discussion of President Hoover's policy, one note of serious criticism was heard. With unmistakable relevance it was urged that public works construction could not be started over night, especially by state and local governments; that plans and specifications had to be prepared; that official sanction had to be secured, in some cases even by popular vote on a referendum; that bonds had to be floated and contracts let; and that these legal operations required weeks, if not months, of time. From this it was argued that preparations for the crisis should have been made years before it occurred. Recognizing a certain validity in such contentions, President Hoover announced in November, 1929, the creation of a continuing council of business leaders charged with the duty of keeping informed on the trends in national economy and bringing about the coöperation of all parties in order to hold production on an even base. While insisting that government and business should be considered as separate entities, the President proceeded on the theory of planned national economy rather than on the assumption of fatalistic helplessness common to classical economic doctrines. And business leaders, while repeating the historic formula of "no government in business," welcomed government aid in staving off industrial depression—aid designed to prevent a shrinkage in profits as well as in production and employment. Evidently much water had gone under the bridge since the great panic of 1837 when President Van Buren thought that he could do nothing but let the storm wear itself out.

Implicit in the criticisms cited above is another, no less important. There is danger, in hasty and unplanned action, that "makeshift undertakings" may be started—buildings that are not really needed or public works that will add high maintenance charges to the original costs without enlarging the productive capital of the country. There is a limit to the amount of wealth that can be diverted to dead, if beautiful and convenient, enterprises. Since heavier taxes must be laid to pay the new bills, it is by no means certain that the burden may not ultimately exceed the relief; may not in the long run add to the depression rather than relax it. To counteract possible tendencies in this direction, it has been proposed that, in times of business distress, a portion of the public funds devoted to debt reduction be diverted to public works, thus for the time being avoiding, in part at least, an increase in taxation. But at best this is a temporary expedient. Nothing can take the place of long-time planning and the projecting of public works calculated to increase the active capital equipment of the nation. There is little doubt that, in view of the beginnings already made, this aspect of national economy will finally receive the popular consideration which its potentialities deserve.

CHAPTER XX

Federal Relations with the States

In our emphasis on federal functions there is danger of forgetting that the system established by the Constitution includes states within its embrace. Popular theories accentuate the danger. It is the fashion of orators to speak of the National Government and the states as "sovereign within their spheres," the former possessing enumerated powers and the latter all reserved rights. In reality, as we have said (p. 64), no sharp distinction can be drawn; in letter and spirit the Constitution contemplates a general political organization involving the states from the base to the top of the structure. While conferring powers on the national authorities, it imposes restraints on the states; and the definition and enforcement of these limitations are functions of the Federal Government in fact, whatever logic may say. Moreover, with the spread of railroads, motor transportation, highways, scientific knowledge, public health activities, and education, Congress is multiplying its provisions for cooperating with state agencies, encouraging the creation of state organs, subsidizing them, subjecting them to national standards, and scrutinizing their administrative performances.

The Theoretical Boundaries

In their nature and their operations the states are limited by the powers which the Constitution confers on the three branches of the Federal Government. In one case "exclusive" authority is given expressly to Congress; namely, in respect of legislation over the District of Columbia and other places purchased by the consent of state legislatures for the erection of forts, arsenals, dockyards, and other needful buildings. In other cases, the exclusive jurisdiction of Congress is clearly implied, because the states are definitely estopped from acting in connection with the subjects covered. For example, the power to coin money and regulate the value thereof is assigned to Congress and at the same time states are forbidden to coin money, emit bills of credit, or make anything but gold and silver coin a tender in payment of debts. In still other cases, the right of the states to act is obviously denied by the very language employed in conferring a specific prerogative on Congress. For instance, Congress is authorized "to establish a uniform rule of naturalization" throughout the United States. "This," says the *Federalist,* "must necessarily be exclusive, because if each state had power to prescribe a distinct rule, there could be no uniform rule." The opinion thus expressed has been confirmed by the Supreme Court.

If many questions of power are well settled there is still a "border line" of uncertainty at which practice and judicial rulings must constantly be determining whether the states are entirely excluded from acting in specific ways on subjects placed under the jurisdiction of the Federal Government. In this connection, the commentator, Story, has laid down a rule of interpretation. "Wherever," he says, "the power given to the general government requires that, to be efficacious and adequate to its end, it should be exclusive, there arises a just implication for deeming it exclusive. Whether exercised or not in such a case makes no difference. . . . In cases of implied limitations or prohibitions of power, it is not sufficient to show a possible or potential inconvenience. There must be a plain incompatibility, a direct repugnancy, or an extreme practical inconvenience leading irresistibly to the same conclusion." The significance of this language lies in its very vagueness. With reference to innumerable practical matters, therefore, nothing precise can be said about many of the powers which may be interpreted as belonging exclusively to Congress and hence withdrawn from the states. The needs of each age must be reconsidered in the light of what appears to be incompatible, repugnant, and extremely inconvenient. So much for the flexibility of the "exclusive" powers of the Federal Government.

Even in a wide range of operations in which the authority of Congress is not exclusive, namely, in which the states possess a "concurrent power," the latter are materially limited in the exercise of the rights they enjoy. This makes still more indefinite the boundary between local and federal jurisdictions. Both Congress and the states, for instance, have the power to tax; they may even tax the same objects, let us say, incomes. Yet, by judicial interpretation, states are forbidden to tax "the instrumentalities of the Federal Government," and hence the incomes of its officers derived from their salaries. Again Congress can make laws on bankruptcy; but, subject to their limitations or in the absence of congressional action, the states are free to legislate in this connection.

To some extent federal statutes in such concurrent spheres supersede state statutes; how far and in what degree, as Story remarks, is a question of "delicate nature." With good reason, therefore, does he conclude that "it would be impracticable to lay down any universal rule as to what powers are, by implication, exclusive in the general government, or concurrent in the states; and in relation to the latter, what restrictions either on the power itself, or on the actual exercise of the power, arise by implication. In some cases, as we have seen, there may exist a concurrent power, and yet restrictions upon it must exist in regard to objects. In other cases the actual operations of the power only are suspended or controlled when there arises a conflict with the actual operations of the Union. Every question of this sort must be decided by itself upon its own circumstances and reasons." Since this summary by the learned Justice of the Supreme Court has been confirmed by later opinions of that high tribunal, the good ship Federal Union is evidently afloat on the sea of experience and each generation must make its own chart.

Specific Federal Limitations on States

Nevertheless certain general principles in the form of positive limitations on the states are laid down in the Constitution, and they must be considered in connection with any survey of the federal system. These rules, as expounded from time to time, bind the states and if necessary will be enforced by the appropriate department of the Federal Government, especially the judiciary. All ideology aside, that Government, in particular the Supreme Court, determines for practical purposes the nature of the Union, at least with reference to the powers of the states in it. If "sovereign" in their sphere, as the orators say, their dominion is positively restricted and is subject to contraction or expansion under interpretation.

The first group of limitations on the states pertain to their taxing power. States cannot lay ordinary imposts and duties upon exports and imports. They may, it is true, levy such taxes to defray expenses incurred in the execution of inspection laws, but always subject to the control of Congress.

Duties on imports, said the Supreme Court in the case of Brown *vs.* Maryland, include levies not only on the operation of importation itself, but also on the commodity imported. "When the importer has so acted upon the thing imported that it has become incorporated and mixed up with the mass of property in the country, it has, perhaps, lost its distinctive character as an import and has become subject to the taxing power of the state; but while remaining the property of the importer in his warehouse, in the original form or package in which it was imported, a tax upon it is too plainly a duty on imports to escape the prohibition in the Constitution." Thus foreign commerce is evidently protected against all impediments in the form of taxes devised by state governments.

Analogous to this provision is the rule which forbids any

state to lay a tonnage duty without the consent of Congress. States may tax the ships of their citizens as property valued as such; but it is clear and undeniable, the Supreme Court has held, "that taxes levied by a state upon ships and vessels as instruments of commerce and navigation are within that clause of the instrument which prohibits the states from levying any duty of tonnage without the consent of Congress; and it makes no difference whether the ships or vessels taxed belong to the citizens of the state which levies the tax or to the citizens of another state, as the prohibition is general."

Turning to purely internal affairs; no state can lay a tax on the property, lawful agencies, and instrumentalities of the Federal Government or franchises granted by it. This principle is not expressly incorporated in the Constitution. It was derived by Chief Justice Marshall, with his usual logic, from the nature of the federal system itself. The power to create implies the power to preserve; the power to tax is the power to destroy, and if wielded by a different hand is incompatible with the power to create and preserve; therefore if the states could tax federal instrumentalities, they could destroy a union which was meant to be indestructible. According to this doctrine, states cannot tax branches of a United States bank, federal bonds, or federal property, or by taxation "retard, impede, burden, or in any manner control the operation of the constitutional laws enacted by Congress to carry into execution the powers vested in the General Government." Even bonds issued under its auspices, not for its direct use but to obtain money to be lent to farmers, are declared to be federal instrumentalities exempt from state taxation.

However, the strict doctrine laid down by Marshall has been modified to mean that the states merely cannot interfere with a federal instrumentality in such a manner as to impair its efficiency in performing the function for which it was designed. A state, for example, cannot tax federal bonds, but it may tax the buildings and other property of a national bank chartered by the Federal Government. "It is manifest," the Supreme Court says, "that exemption of federal agencies from state taxation is dependent not upon the nature of the agents or upon the mode of their constitution, or upon the fact that they are agents, but upon the effect of the tax; that is, upon the question whether the tax does in truth deprive them of power to serve the Government as they were intended to serve it, or does hinder the efficient exercise of their power. A tax upon their property has no such necessary effect. It leaves them free to discharge the duties they have undertaken to perform. A tax upon their operations is a direct obstruction to the exercise of federal powers."

In another important department of economy the states are still more severely restricted. They cannot regulate or in any way seriously interfere with interstate commerce. To be sure they may pass laws relative to local matters which to some extent bear on commerce of that character. For example, the Supreme Court sustained a law of Kentucky providing for the inspection of illuminating oils and imposing a penalty upon persons selling oil branded as unsafe by state officers; this statute was evidently in the interest of public safety, although it certainly interfered with the right of citizens of other states to sell oil freely in that commonwealth. Likewise a quarantine law of Louisiana was upheld, in spite of the fact that it incidentally restricted freedom of interstate movement. States may prohibit the running of freight trains on Sundays, forbid the employment of color-blind engineers on interstate as well as local trains, require the heating of cars, regulate speed within city limits, and compel the guarding of bridges and the protection of crossings. But legislation of this type must be clearly intended to afford local police protection. If it passes beyond that object it is likely to be set aside by judicial process as a trespass on the authority of Congress.

State actions which, beyond question, constitute invasions of federal power over interstate commerce may likewise be illustrated by concrete cases. A law of Minnesota requiring the inspection of all meat twenty-four hours before slaughtering—in substance a pure-food measure—was declared invalid by the Supreme Court because it necessarily prevented the importation of meat from other states where, of course, no such scrutiny could be enforced by Minnesota officials. To cite a more explicit example, Illinois passed an act regulating railway rates within the state; when it attempted to apply the rule to a shipment starting in Illinois and destined to another state, the Supreme Court of the United States by proper process interfered, and declared that control over such a shipment from beginning to end was vested exclusively in Congress. Again, a state cannot impose a tax upon all freight carried by a railway, but it can levy on its franchise, using its total income, including receipts from interstate and foreign commerce, in determining the taxable valuation.

When a state comes to that high prerogative historically associated with all governments, control over the monetary system, it confronts insurmountable barriers. Here it is, for all practical purposes, powerless. It may charter and regulate state banks, but it cannot coin money, emit bills of credit, or make anything but gold and silver coin legal tender in the payment of debts. Although theoretically it may authorize a state banking association to issue notes for circulation, the exercise of this right is really prohibited by an act of Congress, in effect in 1866, laying a ten per cent tax on such currency. On account of the weight of the tax, state banks simply cannot issue notes at all.

Even in the matter of criminal legislation—a subject peculiarly reserved to them, the states are limited by provisions of the federal Constitution. No state can pass any bill of attainder; that is, a measure which inflicts punishment upon some person without ordinary judicial trial. Fully aware that this expedient had been frequently employed for partisan designs by the British Parliament, the framers of the Constitution firmly resolved to prevent all such abuses of legislative authority in the United States. Nor can any state pass an *ex post facto* law: that is, one which prescribes a penalty for an act which was legal when committed; or imposes a penalty in addition to that in force when the act was committed; or changes the rules of evidence to the serious disadvantage of an accused person, allowing conviction on testimony less rigorous than was required at the time of his alleged offense. Framed to protect citizens from punishment by legislative acts having retroactive operation, the *ex post facto* limitation applies only to criminal legislation.

Federal Protection of Private Property

More extensive than these restrictions on what may be called the "normal" legislative powers of the state are the provisions of the Constitution curbing its right to interfere with the use and enjoyment of private property. In explicit language the original Constitution stipulates that no state shall pass any law impairing the obligation of contracts. Now the obligation of a contract, as judicially interpreted, is the body of law existing at the time the agreement is made, defining and regulating it and making provision for its due enforcement. For example, one Crowninshield, on March 22, 1811, gave a note for a sum of money to one Sturges; shortly afterward the legislature of New York, in which the note was dated, passed a bankruptcy act; somewhat later Crowninshield became a bankrupt, paid Sturges a portion of what he owed, and then claimed the right to be discharged from the remainder of his obligation under the terms of the new law. On appeal the Supreme Court declared invalid the New York bankruptcy measure, insofar as it applied to debts contracted *before* its passage, on the ground that such retroactive legislation was a clear impairment of the obligation of contracts.

As employed in the Constitution, the word "contract" has a far wider meaning than in ordinary law. It covers not only agreements between private parties with respect to property but also grants, charters, and franchises issued by a state to individuals and corporations. In one of its most celebrated cases, decided in 1819, the Supreme Court firmly established the broader interpretation by holding that a charter granted to Dartmouth College by the King of England was a contract which New Hampshire, as his successor in interest, was bound to honor on securing its independence. Having announced this ruling the Court then declared that a law of the state in question designed to control the College and its funds was void as an impairment of the obligation of the contract. Under a literal application of such a doctrine, a state legislature having once granted a privilege to a person or corporation would be bound to maintain it unimpaired forever if no specific provisions were made in the grant as to time limitations or other conditions.

The Supreme Court, however, has refused to extend the term "contract" to several forms of agreement between a state and its citizens. An appointment to a public office even for a fixed period at a definite salary is not a contract and a legislature may abolish the position without impairing any obligation. From the category of contracts are also excluded such measures as a legislative grant of power to a municipal corporation and a bounty law offering to pay from the public treasury a specific rate on the production of certain commodities. If judicial interpretations were less generous the states would be seriously hampered whenever they attempted to repeal any law under which property rights and claims have been established.

In its practical operation, moreover, the contract clause has been limited in another direction. By one early school of thought the term "obligation" was construed to place certain eternal principles of property privilege forever beyond legislative reach, but this view did not prevail. As we have seen, obligation was finally defined as the body of law existing and controlling a contract at the time it is formally made. Hence the Supreme Court, in applying the clause, declares a law invalid only when it is retroactive; that is, when it impairs contracts made before its passage. Therefore, if a state provides in its constitution or laws that all future charters and franchises granted under its authority may be amended or repealed, it thereby makes the very reservation a part of the obligation of such contracts and thus leaves the legislature free to alter or abolish them without running counter to this historic provision of the Constitution.

Taking the hint from early judicial decisions the states now safeguard, by precautionary measures, their right to control privileges once granted; hence, it is no longer possible for private corporations to secure, either honestly or by corrupt means, priceless concessions and then defend them against withdrawal or modification by taking shelter under the sacredness of contract. In their general tenor the provisions freeing state legislatures from the strangling effect of this clause are illustrated by the following extract from the constitution of Wisconsin: "All general laws or special acts, enacted under the provisions of this section [dealing with corporations], may be altered or repealed by the legislature at any time after their passage."

Yet there is in truth more shadow than substance to such declarations, for the Fourteenth Amendment, adopted in 1868, has radically altered their legal effect by forbidding states to deprive any person of life, liberty, or property without due process of law. The state may still rescind charters granted to corporations, if it has previously reserved the right, but it cannot revoke them in such a manner as to deprive stockholders of their property without due process. In other words, a legislature may extinguish a corporation but cannot touch the tangible rights which the latter has developed under its franchise.

As time has proved, the most significant phase of federal control over the activities of states in their various relations is authorized by the Fourteenth Amendment. For practical purposes, this clause of the Constitution places in the hands of the federal judiciary a veto power over local legislation on nearly all important economic matters. According to the first section of that Amendment, no state can make or enforce any law which abridges the privileges or immunities of citizens of the United States; no state may deprive any person of life, liberty, or property without due process of law, nor deny to any person within its jurisdiction the equal protection of the laws. In order to understand the full import of the several terms employed in this brief but highly important legal declaration, it is necessary to examine them in the light of judicial decisions, for in themselves they furnish only a slight clue to the restraints which they provide.

At the outset, what are the privileges and immunities of citizens of the United States which cannot be abridged by a state? One school of publicists, represented by Professor John W. Burgess, contends that it was the purpose of the men who framed this sentence to nationalize civil liberty in its broadest sweep; in other words, to deprive states of the power to violate any of the privileges and immunities established against federal interference in the first ten amendments to the Constitution.

The Supreme Court of the United States, however, has taken a more restricted view of the language in question. It has held that the only privileges and immunities guaranteed to a citizen by the Fourteenth Amendment against state infringement are a few elementary personal rights which he enjoys as an American—for example, to petition the National Government, share its offices, transact business with it, and use its navigable waters. General rights to life, liberty, and the pursuit of happiness are still within the control of the states, as before the adoption of the Amendment.

Over this discussion with respect to privileges and immunities, it is not necessary to tarry long. The truly vital part of the Fourteenth Amendment is the brief sentence which forbids any state to deprive any person of life, liberty, or property without due process of law. The term "life," as Professor Burgess says, is "self-defining." The word "liberty" is elusive at best. It is scarcely to be taken in a philosophical sense but still the Supreme Court seems inclined to the view that it includes "freedom of speech, religion, and allied civil liberties." In declaring unconstitutional an Oregon law requiring all children to attend the public schools, the Court asserted that the act "unreasonably interferes with the liberty of parents and guardians to direct the upbringing and education of children under their control." One Justice has ventured to say that liberty embraces the right to enjoy generally "those privileges long recognized at common law as essential to the orderly pursuit of happiness by freemen." At all events it is broad enough and vague enough to confer on the Supreme Court jurisdiction over almost any state laws which it wishes to invalidate. The term "property" is likewise highly cryptic; it is not limited to tangible goods having exchange value, but extends to innumerable vested rights legally acquired.

Of none of these things may any person be deprived without due process of law; but what is due process of law? The Supreme Court has steadily refused to define the phrase in concrete terms, and it is not possible to make any satisfactory generalization. It may be safely argued, however, that due process, as prescribed by the Fourteenth Amendment, does not require the use, by the state, of all those legal procedures, such as indictment by grand jury and trial by petit jury with unanimous verdict, established in the first ten amendments to the federal Constitution. Due process of law, said the Court in one case, is "a course of legal proceedings according to those rules and principles which have been established in our system of jurisprudence for the protection and enforcement of private rights." And in another case, it declared that there are certain immutable principles of free government which control the law of every state. In other words, the Court appears inclined to hold that a law of a state may be invalidated under the due process clause if it transgresses certain general theories of government and economics entertained by a majority of the judges.

In such circumstances, therefore, the best way of ascertaining the upshot of this phrase is to examine its application to specific classes of state acts. Considered in relation to due process these laws fall into two groups: they are either procedural or substantive; that is, they either pertain to methods to be followed by the government in trying criminals, laying taxes, and performing other "normal" administrative duties or they pertain to control over the conduct of people and the ownership and uses of property.

Taking up procedural matters first, we may ask: "What is due process of law in criminal cases?" An example will illustrate the answer in general terms. A law of California provided that a person could be prosecuted for felony after examination and commitment *without* indictment by a grand jury. Under this act one Hurtado was charged with the crime of murder on mere information and, after jury trial in the ordinary manner, was found guilty and condemned to death. Was this procedure constitutional? The Supreme Court replied that due process of law under the Fourteenth Amendment was different from that under the Fifth Amendment; that the California statute was valid; and that "any legal proceeding enforced by public authority, whether sanctioned by age and custom, or newly devised in the discretion of the legislative power in furtherance of the general public good, which regards and preserves these principles of liberty and justice [lying at the basis of all our civil and political institutions] must be held to be due process of law."

Due process of law in civil matters has also been defined in a similar spirit by the Supreme Court. In one pertinent case it held that the Fourteenth Amendment did not guarantee trial by jury in suits at common law in state courts but merely required conformity to a set course of judicial proceedings. In other words, any method which provides for reasonable security, full notice, and a satisfactory protection to the substantial rights involved in such suits may be regarded as complying with the stipulations of that Amendment.

With respect to taxation the Supreme Court has been inclined to allow the states the same latitude. Whenever a tax is laid according to the valuation of property, due process merely requires general notice to owners and public hearings affording them a chance to contest their liability; personal notice is not necessary. Not even the right to be heard is indispensable to due process in the imposition of poll and license taxes, specific taxes on things, persons, or corporations, and many other kinds of taxes.

In dealing with such procedural and administrative questions, the courts are merely handling technical phases of law, in the main, although of course their decisions frequently concern life and liberty in vital relations. Here they have long lines of precedents to guide them and their usual practice is to uphold state legislation which does not depart too arbitrarily from historic traditions. In this connection they do not often have to consider large issues of public policy.

But when we pass from problems of correct procedure in trials at law and in ordinary administration to the subject of federal control over state legislation touching property directly, we find that the due process clause involves the whole range of psychology, sociology, and economics. Did the framers of the Fourteenth Amendment intend to permit state and local legislatures to regulate the rates and services of public utility corporations—water, gas, and electric plants? The hours of women in factories? The wages of children? The conduct of strikes in labor disputes? If so, subject to what limitations? In answering these questions, the federal courts do not deal with obvious technicalities of law but rather with broad questions of public interest. Here their decisions will depend more on their sympathies and preconceptions than on any inescapable mandates of legal reasoning.

However, in considering the validity of state and local laws regulating public utilities, the Supreme Court pursues certain broad principles developed under the Fourteenth Amendment. First of all, state governments may control within limits the rates and services of such concerns, but in so doing they must make provision for a judicial review of the cases arising out of the action. In the end, the determination of every important issue in this sphere is vested in the judiciary headed by the high tribunal at Washington. Even though appeals may not be made against their rulings, official bodies engaged in utility supervision must always operate with due reference to the precedents and dicta of the federal courts.

In the second place, whenever it tests the legality of a state measure restricting the charges of utilities, the Supreme Court applies a rule of "reasonableness." Broadly speaking, this means that in the absence of a special contract the rate fixed in each instance must be high enough to permit the company in question to earn a "fair" return on its "capital." If such earnings are not assured then the concern is deprived of its property without due process of law, in violation of the Fourteenth Amendment. While the theorem may seem clear at first glance, it will be found on examination to raise many complex problems. In calculating the "capital" on which a "fair" return must be allowed, what elements are to be considered? The actual cost of the property? Cost plus good will? The cost of reproduction to-day, which may be almost double the original outlay? The value of the plant as determined on the basis of prudent investment? Its selling value, which may be due to high earning power under exorbitant rates?

To the questions thus presented, the Supreme Court has made no clear-cut answers. On the contrary it has vibrated to and fro among the various elements encountered in evaluating utility property. Indeed it has been inclined to include all rather than to emphasize some of them. In one case, for example, it contended that, in order to fix a fair value, "the original cost of construction, the amount expended in permanent improvements, the amount and market value of its stocks and bonds, the present as compared with the original cost of construction, the probable earning capacity of the property under particular rates prescribed by statute and the sum required to meet operating expenses, are all matters for consideration and are to be given such weight as may be just and right in each case." As if this sweep were not broad enough, the Court added, "We do not say that there may not be other matters to be regarded in estimating the value of the property." On another occasion, it declared that a company was entitled to the benefit of any increase in the value of its property, but immediately countered by remarking, "We do not say that there may not possibly be an exception to it, where the property may have increased so enormously in value as to render a rate permitting a reasonable return upon such increased value unjust to the public." Not content with covering past and present factors in its calculations, the Court has insisted that "An honest and intelligent forecast of probable future values made upon a view of all the relevant circumstances is essential." In such language as this are to be found the "principles" which the Supreme Court applies in deciding whether, in any particular state or local action on rates, the capital of the utility company concerned has been fairly evaluated.

When, by some mysterious process, a conclusion is reached respecting the true capital of a company, there remains another vital question. What is a fair return on it? Here, too, the Supreme Court has not adopted any definite rule. In the Baltimore case, decided in 1930, it declared confiscatory a rate that allowed a company to earn only about six per cent on its capital, in which was included a large sum representing easements granted to it by the city free of all charges. Judging from the general run of decisions eight or ten per cent would be somewhere near the Court's idea of a "fair" return, although neither of these figures has been established as the minimum. Moreover in this connection it should be noted that the percentage allowed is applied to the entire capital of the company, when as a matter of fact one half or three fourths of its funds are usually secured from bonds on which it may pay only five or six per cent. By such a process of judicial calculation the company's actual earnings on its mere stock may be lifted, under the fair return theory, to fifteen or twenty per cent.

Even if definite rules bearing on valuation and rate return were established, all the problems arising in this field under the due process clause would not be solved. Suppose a company's failure to earn a fair dividend is not due to the low rate allowed by the state but to inefficient management. What then? Suppose it charges up to operating expenses money spent in propaganda, perhaps for higher rates, as has sometimes been the case. What if it pays enormous salaries to superfluous officials or extravagant fees to holding companies for advice? It is not necessary to go further to show that under the Fourteenth Amendment the Supreme Court exercises a vast and elusive power over all the states and communities in the American Union. It is also evident that in this relation the Court is called upon to decide issues purely technical in character and to assume functions of great economic intricacy in restraining the "sovereignty" of the states. If, as was claimed in the debate in the Senate over the appointment of Charles E. Hughes as Chief Justice, in February, 1930, the Court is inclined to be tender to the utility companies as against the public, it must be admitted that owing to the present confusion in law and opinion the tendency is not surprising.

In the field of labor legislation, as well as utility regulation, the states often come into conflict with the due process clause of the Fourteenth Amendment (p. 510). When, for example, New York several years ago passed an act limiting the hours of labor in bakeshops to not more than ten a day or sixty a week, the Supreme Court, in the celebrated Lochner case, intervened; it declared the measure invalid on the ground that it was an unreasonable, unnecessary, and arbitrary interference with liberty of contract—the liberty to purchase and sell labor being within the protection of the Fourteenth Amendment.

Whether this ruling is good law to-day is an open question. At the time it was the subject of much adverse criticism on the ground that it blocked enlightened and progressive legislation passed to protect the health and safety of working people. And as judges died and public opinion changed, the Supreme Court seemed inclined to take a broader view of the matter. In fact, several years after the Lochner case, it upheld laws providing compensation for persons injured in industries, an act of the Oregon legislature fixing the hours of labor, regardless of sex, in manufacturing establishments at ten per day, and an Oregon law relative to minimum wages for women and minors. In the case last named, however, the Court was divided four to four (Justice Brandeis not voting) and the law was thus sustained by a narrow margin, indicating a turn in the liberal tide. Shortly afterward more conservative judges were appointed and in 1925 the Court declared void the minimum wage law of Arizona, with only one judge dissenting.

When it deals with other phases of the labor question, the Supreme Court has usually been very strict in its views. It declared invalid a Kansas statute making it a misdemeanor for an employer to threaten to discharge an employee on account of membership in a trade union. As fourteen other states had similar laws, which were thus automatically set aside at one stroke, the range of the judicial decree was stunning to labor leaders. More significant yet was a decision rendered in 1921 invalidating another Arizona law—one forbidding the issue of injunctions in labor disputes in certain cases (p. 510).

Notwithstanding the prohibitions of the Fourteenth Amendment, the states retain, under judicial interpretation, their "police power," and may in fact do many things that interfere with life, liberty and property. But the Court refuses to define the term police power, reserving to itself the right to determine at the proper moment whether a particular act comes within that sphere or not. Doubtless a broad interpretation of this very elastic phrase would give a state sanction for passing any legislation designed to promote general welfare as opposed to special privilege. Indeed, the Court once said that the police power includes full authority "to prescribe regulations to promote the health, peace, morals, education, and good order of the people, and to legislate so as to increase the industries of the state, develop its resources, and add to its wealth and its prosperity." If applied by a court in sympathy with enlarging state control over private rights in the name of general welfare, such a generous theory might almost nullify the provisions of the Fourteenth Amendment.

However that may be, a state, under its police power, may do many definite things. It may, for example, restrict dangerous and objectionable trades to certain localities; it may provide for dividing cities into zones; it may regulate, to a limited extent, railways and other common carriers; and it may fix the hours of women and children in certain industries.

If it be said that after all relatively few state laws are set aside by the Supreme Court under the various constitutional clauses cited above, the answer is that it is not their number but their significance which counts. Moreover cases of this character are now increasing. That is not all. Whenever an act of one state is declared void, legislation of the same type in all the other states falls to the ground with it and future experiments of a kindred nature are barred. When doctrines are laid down in connection with the valuation of public utilities or the regulation of their rates, legislatures throughout the Union must take note of these instructions from high authority. In short, owing to the broad and indefinite character of the restraints imposed on them by the Federal Constitution, the states are not entities but are in fact, whatever pleasing hypothesis may be adopted, wards of the Supreme Court.

Federal Coöperation with the States

The difficulties of drawing an absolute dividing line between the powers and functions of the states on the one side and those of the Federal Government on the other are increased in our age by the multiplication of citizen activities which completely transcend political boundaries. Owing to the growth of corporations controlling industries in many states and selling goods throughout the country, it is almost impossible to separate the business transacted in any one community from the general mass of national undertakings.

Furthermore, railways, telephones, the telegraph, and the radio cut across all geographical borders and, as in the case of corporate manufacturing, make it hard to discover sharp distinctions between intrastate and interstate traffic. In public health a similar situation arises, for modern science shows that human maladies, particularly contagious diseases, are not confined to localities, but spread far and wide without respect to political "sovereignties." Nor is it possible to say that in social relations the affairs and policies of one state do not concern those of its neighbors. Low labor standards in one section affect adversely life in other sections; illiteracy in one region tends to lower the level of civilization in other parts of the Union.

If, therefore, commentators on the Constitution and judges were unable to fix definite lines of law between state and federal powers before the advent of the railway and radio, it is not surprising that they are even more bewildered amid the social complexity of our own time. Besides, in some cases where fairly clear divisions have been established by the Constitution, it has been found expedient to bridge the gaps by federal and state coöperation, occasionally by the establishment of a kind of third government, a joint institution, to which functions are entrusted by mutual consent.

An extreme form of coöperation is to be found in the few instances in which states in effect assign to the Federal Government functions that clearly belong to them under the Constitution, and the Federal Government in turn attempts to give force to state laws throughout the Union. The shift of function from state to nation is nowhere better illustrated than in the case of aeronautics. Under its power to regulate commerce the United States Government licenses aircraft and pilots engaged in flights of an interstate character. Confronted with the problem of supervising local aviation—a matter entirely subject to her own jurisdiction, the state of New York had to establish a separate system of control for intrastate flying or extend the federal licensing system to include that branch of traffic. After a brief debate the state adopted the latter course in a law of 1928 which requires all planes and pilots flying within her borders to possess federal licenses even if their operations are purely intrastate—a rule now in force in a majority of the states. In other words in this relation the Federal Government for practical purposes sets the standards and makes the law for a state without violating its rights or amending the Constitution. Here the need for engineering uniformity based on rational principles simply cuts across mere political boundaries—an action significant for the future when the true nature of our technological society will be more clearly discerned.

A shift of authority also occurs occasionally in the other direction—in the validation of state law throughout the Union by federal action. Coöperation in the conservation of wild life affords an example of this reverse process. The states, under the Constitution, possess the power to prescribe the conditions under which game may be killed, and the Federal Government has no authority in this connection, except over migratory animals. Congress, however, has agreed to accept state game statutes as binding in all shipments under its jurisdiction. It is now a criminal offense against the United States for any person to deliver to a common carrier or for a common carrier to accept for transportation to another state wild animals killed in violation of local laws. Consignees in other states are also forbidden knowingly to receive such game, under penalties. In taking this action the Federal Government has really made state game legislation, no matter what its nature, obligatory with respect to the interstate commerce of the entire nation. Here the Government assumes the rôle of special policeman for the states.

Still a third type of federal and state relations is illustrated by a law of 1929 which divests goods, wares, and merchandise produced or mined by convicts of their interstate character in certain cases. Upon arrival in any state or territory commodities of this nature shall be subject to the effect and operation of the laws of such state or territory just as if produced within its borders and shall not be exempt therefrom by reason of being introduced in the original package or otherwise. In 1934, when this measure goes into force, the shipment of prison-made goods from one state to another can be put under the ban in interstate commerce. The upshot is that Congress has placed a substantial check on prison labor within states—a matter outside of its normal jurisdiction—and deprived them of another one of their historic "rights."

Coöperation between the two governments is not limited to shifts of functions which in reality enable one to invade a field monopolized in theory by the other. In certain cases, as we have said, the law of the Constitution admits of concurrent federal and state jurisdiction with relation to the same matter. Thus the states, under their police power, can establish quarantine stations and promulgate rules in the interest of public health for the protection of their citizens; while Congress may take similar steps to safeguard the nation against diseases entering from abroad or passing from state to state. There are no legal reasons, therefore, why two quarantine systems, one federal and one state, cannot exist side by side. In our early history a state quarantine régime prevailed, with federal officers assisting under orders in the execution of local regulations just as if they were statutes of Congress.

In time, however, the confusion resulting from conflicting rules led to the establishment of federal quarantine institutions apart from those of the states, the two schemes operating simultaneously. Under the new arrangement, federal authorities helped to enforce all state quarantine laws which they deemed adequate; but if they considered local provisions too lenient they applied the stricter federal rules. Experience with this dual arrangement revealed that there was little to be gained from it and that the national quarantine methods were as a rule technically superior. Accordingly in 1893 Congress provided that in certain circumstances state stations might be taken over by the Federal Government for incorporation into its organization whenever the states were willing to surrender them for that purpose. At present all quarantine plants at American ports are under the control of the federal Public Health Service. Here, then, is a case in which coöperation between the two governments finally resulted in the assignment of all rights over foreign quarantine to one of them. Rationality in effect created an exclusive monopoly out of a concurrent jurisdiction.

In addition to lending sanction to transactions in which functions are carried out jointly by the two governments or are shifted from one to the other, the Constitution allows Congress to appropriate money for operations over which it has no express powers whatever (p. 65). Under this authority, the Federal Government deals with many matters which fall within the competence of the states, at least according to historic tradition. Its activities thus undertaken may be divided into two broad classes. The first embraces research and standardization; the second, financial aid to the states, under administrative supervision.

In our technical age when all governments, from the rural community upwards, must constantly deal with highly complicated scientific questions, research and the development of standards are absolutely necessary to efficient procedure. The problems involved, though they may be handled locally, are not local in their intrinsic nature. Hence from year to year, the Federal Government has assumed new responsibilities in this relation. Education, for example, except in the case of the Indians and the territories, is not a federal function; nevertheless the National Government maintains an Office of Education which makes special studies, collects data, issues publications, and gives advice and counsel to state and local authorities. Somewhat in the same way, the Department of Labor compiles statistics, analyzes laws, and disseminates information relative to labor questions falling entirely within state jurisdiction. Even more striking is the work of the Bureau of Standards which carries on investigations in various fields of science, evolves regulations, and makes them available to local as well as federal officials. Some of its standards, for instance those dealing with heat and light units and model ordinances for zoning cities, have been adopted by many states as binding within their respective jurisdictions. As soon as new scientific questions arise and begin to receive local consideration, the interest of the National Government is usually enlisted and its powerful assistance invoked.

Such extensions of federal functions into fields of primary concern to the states have, as we explained in Chapter XIX, a high significance for nation planning in the large. Modern science makes rapid strides in every field. It is expensive to experiment. It is difficult to keep up with the sweep of events. So there arises the question: How can we make available to the humblest official in the most out-of-the-way place the results of the best thought, the greatest scientific achievements, bearing on his problems? Except in rare instances such results are beyond the reach of local authorities. If each of the forty-eight states makes its own inquiries, there will be an immense duplication of effort. Indeed, this is what happens regularly. Often there are many state commissions engaged in investigating the same problem. Hence, it seems reasonable and natural that the National Government should come into the field with its larger financial power and wider prestige and place at the disposal of state and local governments the fruits of the most advanced scientific research.

The second type of responsibility assumed by the Federal Government under its power to appropriate money for general purposes, namely, that of rendering financial and administrative assistance to states, runs still deeper into national economy. It involves the distribution of wealth as well as research and the establishment of standards. The costs of governmental services are mounting, and the states, especially those with slight economic strength, find it increasingly difficult to carry their burdens. Moreover the sources of public revenue are not local, but national, in their connections. For example, Smith owns a small farm in Indiana;

it is taxable for local purposes; but it is mortgaged to Jones in New York, who receives in interest a considerable share of the proceeds of the farm. Is it just to put the whole burden of local improvements on local property irrespective of circumstances? A large part of modern wealth is intangible, namely, stocks, bonds, and mortgages related to property scattered throughout the Union and it has become increasingly difficult for states and localities to tax such wealth for their own needs. The national income levy reaches it more easily and surely and, judging by the decisions of Congress, a majority of the American people believe that only through federal taxation can the funds be effectively secured to raise the standards of public service for the whole country.

The practice of granting subsidies to states from the federal Treasury is not new. By numerous laws beginning with the Land Ordinance for the Northwest Territory in 1785 and running down to our own time, Congress has made grants, particularly from the sale of public lands, to the states for schools, roads, and canals. The most outstanding of the earlier measures was, perhaps, the Morrill Act of 1862, which set aside for the benefit of each state, in proportion to its representation in Congress, an enormous block of the national domain and provided that the proceeds were to be devoted to the maintenance of one or more colleges engaged principally, but not exclusively, in teaching branches of learning related to agriculture and the mechanical arts. This Act, although attacked by a Senator from Virginia as "an unconstitutional robbery of the Treasury for the purpose of bribing the states," attempted to impose no federal control over them in the use of the money. Congress simply made the gift and trusted them to employ it wisely. Later amendments to the Act, however, went into some detail as to the management of the land-grant colleges, and authorized the withholding of the allotment of any state which did not comply with the terms of the concession, subject to an appeal to Congress.

With a view to improving the work already started in this field, Congress began in 1887 to make an annual lump sum appropriation to each state to assist in the development of an agricultural experiment station in connection with the agricultural college. In 1906 it materially increased the appropriation and laid down additional rules for the use of the money. Nine years later it took another step in the direction of closer control by reorganizing, in the Department of Agriculture, the administrative division charged with the duty of supervising the agricultural colleges and experiment stations. At the present time the whole field of relationships created by these subsidies is covered in minute regulations reached by agreement between state and federal authorities. In fact the coöperation is close, continuous, and helpful to both parties. Federal supremacy is unquestionable, because funds can be withheld if rules are not complied with, but resort to this drastic action is seldom if ever necessary.

Enlarging its historic interest in the subject, Congress commenced, with the Smith-Lever Act of 1914, to make appropriations for extension work in agriculture to be undertaken by the Department of Agriculture and the state agricultural colleges. At the outset a small lump sum was assigned to each of the states and the remainder of the annual allotment was distributed among them on the basis of their respective proportions of rural inhabitants; in other words, farming population, not geographical units as such, was used as the standard to measure needs. Even more striking was the additional provision that national funds should not be given to any state until it accepted the terms of the Act and appropriated or otherwise secured a sum equal to that granted to it by federal law. Under this Act the agricultural extension work of the entire country is conducted according to broad and uniform principles adopted by the Secretary of Agriculture and the state college officials.

Not content with its efforts on behalf of agricultural education Congress undertook, by passing the Smith-Hughes Vocational Education Act of 1917, to promote technical train-

Courtesy of the United States Department of Agriculture

An Agricultural Extension Agent at Work in the South.

Photo by Brown Brothers

A Case for Federal Highway Aid.

ing. In substance it appropriated money from the federal Treasury to assist the states in teaching trades, industrial subjects, and home economics. At the same time it kept an eye on general supervision by arranging for the execution of the Act under the direction of a Federal Board for Vocational Education composed of the Secretaries of Agriculture, Commerce, and Labor, the Commissioner of Education, and three citizens representing manufacturing and commercial, agricultural, and labor interests.

If education, primarily a state function, can receive assistance from the federal Treasury and be brought to some extent under national administrative control, why not forestry, a branch of economy also within the jurisdiction of particular states, except where the Federal Government holds domains of its own? In spite of vigorous protests on constitutional grounds, Congress decided that action was imperative in this field and in 1911 it passed the Weeks Act which made appropriations for the purpose of enabling the Forest Service in the Department of Agriculture to coöperate with any state or group of states, when requested, in protecting the forested watersheds of navigable streams against fire. Though falling nominally under the power of Congress to regulate interstate commerce and hence navigable waters, this Act in effect established a system of coöperative forest protection by a combination of federal and state administrative authorities (p. 555).

With this extraordinary precedent accepted, it was comparatively easy for Congress to find warrant, in its authority over post roads if nowhere else, for enacting the Highway law of 1916 (p. 408). By a bold stroke it inaugurated the practice of granting immense sums of money to the states for road building programs and established close federal scrutiny over both construction and maintenance. Under the terms of the Act, modified by later amendments, uniform scientific specifications have been forced upon state highway engineers, common working agreements have been formulated by federal and state officers, conferences of state highway officers have been held under national auspices, and to cap the climax states which forbid their governments to appropriate money for such public improvements are in effect ordered to change their constitutions! Under the control and stimulus of the Federal Government the highway legislation of the states has been multiplied many times in volume and raised to high standards in quality, and incidentally they have been induced to incur enormous debts.

If by advancing into the fields of education, forestry, and highway construction Congress "invades the sovereignty" of the states, it certainly goes still deeper into that reservation by legislation which virtually incorporates their militia forces in the national army. Doubtless Thomas Jefferson and Patrick Henry would be astounded and alarmed by the very idea. Nevertheless, by the National Defense Act of 1916, extending principles laid down thirteen years earlier, Congress has, to all intents and purposes, made the militia of each state a cog in the military machine of the Union. In this case, as in others, federal aid is extended; and federal standards for equipment, drilling, administration, and service are strictly applied. The very name "militia" has been dropped and the term "National Guard" substituted for it. Thus the ancient symbol of independence, armed force, passes from the states to the nation. Once it was contended that militiamen were obligated to fight only within the borders of the country and in defense of its territory; in 1917 they were swept into the Expeditionary Army and sent across the seas.

It may be argued, of course, that all these measures represent merely an extension of old practices duly authorized by the Constitution. From the beginning, it is true, Congress in disposing of federal lands has assisted the states in promoting education, constructing roads, and undertaking local improvements. It might also seem reasonable to say that the National Government, having immense forests of its own to protect, could form coöperative relations with certain states in forestry affairs without making a radical departure from established policy. As far as mere financial help goes this appears sound enough, but the newer legislation listed above has actually entered the domain of state and local government and really creates new organs of administration which are neither federal nor state in a strict sense. The end is not yet. There are in addition to the statutes already cited two more laws which by no stretch of the imagination come within any of the enumerated powers of Congress as laid down in the Constitution.

The first, the Industrial Rehabilitation Act of 1920, as given a new lease of life in 1930, provides federal aid in restoring to civil employment persons injured in industry or any legitimate occupation. As Dr. A. F. MacDonald points out, "the number of workers disabled every year in the course of industry exceeds the total number of American soldiers incapacitated during the entire course of the World War." In recognition of this startling fact Congress, by the Act just mentioned, offers the incentive of monetary aid to the states to induce them to do justice by "the soldiers of the hammer and plowshare as well as the soldiers of the sword." Within a year after its passage thirty-five states had accepted the provisions of the statute and begun work under federal supervision.

The second of the newer laws, the Sheppard-Towner Act of 1921, also went deeply into social legislation—an undoubted function of the states—by appropriating federal money to their account with the design of promoting the welfare of mothers and infants at the time of childbirth. Although attacked as unconstitutional, it was sustained by the Supreme Court in the case of Massachusetts *vs.* Mellon in 1923. When the act was allowed to lapse in 1929, the reason was a lack of funds, not a failure in legality. The precedent stands.

Under laws enumerated in this section millions of dollars are appropriated annually to the states in aid of activities which were once generally regarded as outside the sphere of the National Government. This is perhaps not the most salient feature. Under these laws the states benefiting from federal grants must themselves make appropriations usually equal in amount and in some cases greater; hence the effect of federal initiative is to compel states to raise money for new undertakings or at least increase their expenditures for old functions. That is not all. Before receiving their allotments from the national Treasury the states in question must enact a large and varied body of legislation conforming to federal standards. Moreover we now have the strange anomaly of state officers on federal pay-rolls and federal officers on state and local pay-rolls. And we see state and federal officers conferring in Washington and making administrative agreements binding on their respective governments.

Indeed without any explicit statutory sanction whatever numerous federal agencies coöperate with state authorities in enterprises of bewildering variety. In a single year the Public Health Service aided Maryland in planning a county anti-mosquito campaign; detailed a federal sanitary engineer to a midwestern city for the purpose of examining the local water supply; conferred with a state food research laboratory staff in regard to certain chemical tests; assisted two Southern states in the conduct of a thyroid survey; helped the six New England states in the development of a uniform rabbit control law; and made, together with the state of Washington, a study of the public health work and needs of the city of Seattle. Without any difficulty this list of coöperative activities could be extended to include every Department of the Federal Government and almost all types of local enterprise.

In exploring the administration of a single state, Arkansas, in 1930, A. E. Buck, an authority on the subject, encountered federal assistance in the form of financial grants or official coöperation, or both, in the following branches of its work: road construction, equipment and management of the militia, county health work, civilian vocational rehabilitation, agricultural and home economics extension, vocational education, maintenance of the land-grant college, collection of crop statistics, plant-disease and pest-quarantine control, eradication of tuberculosis in cattle, hog cholera control, extermination of cattle tick, forest fire prevention, promotion of forestry, conduct of free employment service, special studies of ground waters, topographical surveying, and stream gauging. In some divisions expenditures from the federal Treasury ranged from two to five times the outlays from state and local sources. In all of them serious difficulties would arise if national support, economic and technical, were entirely withdrawn.

Whatever may be said on the point of constitutionality, federal coöperation with the states offers one solution to the old problem of centralization *versus* decentralization in administration. If the actual direction of all the activities cited above were concentrated in Washington and even county farm-extension agents were appointed by the President, an immense machine would be created, a gigantic bureaucracy, in other words. Now, such a bureaucracy is itself a formidable interest. It tends to harshness, dogmatism, and routine, and puts a check on local spirit, initiative, and ingenuity. On the other hand if all communities were left to themselves, some of them would inevitably sink to low levels in education, health, and culture. How to combine local energy with high national standards, to stimulate the weak without oppressing the strong, is really the problem at which the Federal Government is working in the extension of its functions. By distributing money automatically among the states on the basis of population, area, and other factors and by requiring them to bear their fair share of each burden, the gravest evils in subsidies, especially favoritism, can be avoided. By a skillful adjustment of relations between the supervising federal authorities and the state executive officials, scientific standards and individual initiative may be united. At all events here is a phase of national evolution which will deserve the most careful study during the coming years. It is here that the nature of American government and economy may be transformed.

Interstate Relations

In addition to controlling the individual states and co-operating with them in discharging various functions, the Federal Government exercises certain supervisory powers over their relations with one another. By a specific provision the Constitution guarantees to the citizens of each state the privileges and immunities of the citizens in the several states, and the federal judiciary enforces the pledge by proper processes. In substance this means that there are certain great legal rights necessary to free migration throughout the American empire, to the successful conduct of business and industry, and to the enjoyment of property, which no state may take away from a citizen of another commonwealth coming within its borders. It means also that no state may confer civil rights on its own citizens and at the same time withhold them from citizens of other states. It does not imply, of course, that if A. of Illinois goes into Indiana, he can carry with him all particular privileges which he had in the former state, but simply that he will be entitled to those advantages at law which are enjoyed by citizens of the latter state.

A concrete illustration is afforded by the case of Ward *vs.* Maryland. By a law passed in 1868 the legislature of Maryland provided that all non-residents must take out licenses before offering for sale, in certain districts, goods not manufactured in the state. Without procuring such a license, Ward, the plaintiff in the case, a resident of New Jersey, sold within a forbidden region commodities produced outside of Maryland. He was accordingly arrested for violating the act in question, but set up the contention that it was invalid under the federal Constitution. When the case came up on appeal the Supreme Court of the United States agreed with him and ruled that the statute was in fact repugnant to the section which provides that the citizens of each state shall be entitled to all privileges and immunities of citizens in the several states.

A kindred arrangement for facilitating intercourse among the several states, especially in the conduct of legal business, is furnished by the clause of the Constitution which declares that full faith and credit shall be given in each state to the public acts, records, and judicial proceedings of every other state. Congress has provided by law the form in which legal transactions shall be authenticated, and has ordered that, when they are so verified, such faith and credit shall be given them in every court within the United States as they have by law and usage in the courts of the state from which they are taken. In practice the system operates as follows. A. brings suit on a debt against B. in a court in Ohio, of which state they are both residents; after trial, the court decides that B. owes A. one thousand dollars and gives judgment accordingly. B. thereupon moves into New York, taking his property along, before it can be attached for the debt. When A. in quest of his money goes after B. into New York, it is not necessary for him to bring another suit in that state in order to get the proper process to recover the amount due him. All he has to do is to show in the New York court of proper jurisdiction the authenticated judgment of the Ohio court. B. may contend that the records are not correctly transcribed, or that the court which rendered the original opinion did not have jurisdiction, but he cannot secure a reopening of the case on its merits. He is bound in New York by any decision properly rendered against him in Ohio.

Another phase of interstate relations, the extradition of criminals, long an international practice based on treaty arrangements between independent countries, is covered by the federal Constitution. An explicit provision stipulates that any person charged with crime, fleeing from justice and found in another state, shall be delivered up for trial on demand of the executive authority of the state in which the alleged offense was committed. This language Congress has amplified by an act declaring that on proper application, "it shall be the duty of the executive authority of the state to which a fugitive has fled" to cause him to be seized and handed over to the agent of the state making the requisition. But the words "it shall be the duty" have been interpreted by the Supreme Court as merely announcing a moral, not a mandatory, obligation. "The act," explains the Court, "does not provide any means to compel the execution of this duty, nor inflict any punishment for neglect or refusal on the part of the executive of the state; nor is there any clause or provision in the Constitution which arms the Government of the United States with this power." Hence the governor of a state may use his discretion in every case brought to him for consideration and decline to accede to a requisition if he sees fit to do so.

The detailed process to be followed in the rendition of criminals is prescribed in federal legislation. In addition most states have statutes providing that an accused person can be arrested when information of the charge against him is duly received, and held until the official demand is made. Let us suppose that A. commits murder in Ohio and escapes into Indiana. As soon as his place of refuge is discovered, the authorities of the community in which the crime occurred will call for his arrest, and he will be taken into custody by the police or the sheriff of the locality where he is found. A regular charge will then be lodged against him in Ohio, if this has not been already done, either in the form of an indictment by grand jury or an affidavit made before a magistrate. Thereupon the governor of Ohio will issue to the governor of Indiana a formal request for the surrender of A., appending to it a certified copy of the aforesaid indictment or affidavit. If the governor of Indiana finds that the papers are regular and that A. is in fact a fugitive from Ohio and was there at the time the alleged murder took place, he will, in the ordinary course, issue an order for the surrender of the accused to the agent sent from Ohio to assume charge of him. On the other hand, if for any reason whatever the governor refuses to accede to the demand, the issue is closed, for no appeal can be taken to any other authority against his decision.

CHAPTER XXI

Territories and Empire

The founders of the American system, in giving the name "United States" to our country, contemplated a union of equal states, each inhabited by an English-speaking population, enjoying self-government, and sharing the benefits of the federation on the same terms. They did provide, of course, for the organization of territories, but only as potential states held in temporary tutelage. Therefore in the acquisition of Hawaii, Porto Rico, the Philippines, Guam, Tutuila, and the Virgin Islands, the Government of the United States made a break with its historic policy; it undertook to rule other races and nationalities that in some cases at least could not possibly be assimilated to the social order established by the Fathers. As a matter of fact these acquisitions were made in the course of our commercial and naval expansion without much thought as to the larger political consequences. It was not until they were actually brought under the flag that a fierce debate arose as to the significance of the action and their probable future.

On the whole the types of opinion represented in this debate may be roughly classified in the following fashion. There are some who maintain quite frankly that the United States can profit commercially by the ownership, development, and exploitation of imperial domains just as the powers of Europe have done for centuries. If the hope proves illusory, the motive is clear and calls for no explanation. At the other extreme are those who claim that the government of "subject races" violates the principles of the Declaration of Independence—the right of self-determination so proudly announced by America, involves the United States in expensive military enterprises, and leads to grave international complications. Still a third group of citizens take a more sentimental attitude toward the problem; they speak of "the white man's burden," meaning his duty to educate and civilize backward and primitive peoples. It was this view which President McKinley voiced when he said of the Philippines: "There was nothing left for us to do but to take them all, and educate the Filipinos, and uplift and civilize them, and by God's grace do the very best we could by them as our fellow-men for whom Christ also died." Doubtless in the practice of colonial administration, all motives are mixed; the desire to do good is mingled with eagerness to make money out of commerce. At all events the United States now controls numerous dependencies and protectorates. And for weal or woe, therefore, the American people are confronted with the problem of managing imperial dominions scattered from the Caribbean to the Indian Ocean.

The Legal Powers of the National Government Over Its Possessions

Strange to say, especially in the light of American expansion, the Constitution of the United States makes no express provision for the acquisition of territory, and at the time of the Louisiana purchase the question was raised whether the Federal Government really had the power to buy that domain. President Jefferson had grave misgivings on the subject and thought that an amendment was necessary to authorize any such addition to the original Union. Since that was impracticable in the circumstances, he gave up the idea, but he confessed to a friend: "The executive, in seizing the fugitive occurrence which so much advances the good of their country, have done an act beyond the Constitution. The legislature, in casting behind them metaphysical subtleties and risking themselves like faithful servants, must ratify and pay for it, and throw themselves on their country for doing for them unauthorized what we know they would have done for themselves had they been in a situation to do it."

On the other hand, those among Jefferson's supporters who took a broader view of the matter insisted that there was full constitutional warrant for the action; that the Federal Government enjoyed the undoubted right to acquire territory under its treaty-making power. In time this view prevailed. Several years later the Supreme Court sanctioned it by declaring that "the Constitution confers absolutely on the Government of the Union the powers of making war and of making treaties; consequently that Government possesses the power of acquiring territory either by conquest or by treaty."

All possessions, however acquired, are governed by Congress under a clause of the Constitution giving it authority to dispose of and make all needful rules and regulations respecting the territory or other property belonging to the United States. The nature of the jurisdiction thus conferred has been the subject of a conflict which has furnished a long and stirring chapter in the constitutional history of the United States.

What clauses of the Constitution actually control the national authorities in the administration of territories? It requires no very subtle analysis to discover that certain provisions are designed to restrain the operations of the Federal Government within the states. But do all the limitations in behalf of private rights contained in the Constitution, especially in the first ten amendments, run into the territories and control the Federal Government there? In his famous opinion in the Dred Scott case, Chief Justice Taney answered in the affirmative, and declared that Congress could not abolish slavery in any territory because in so doing it would deprive slave-owners of their property without due process of law. Many years later the Supreme Court confirmed this judgment by holding that the Seventh Amendment, prescribing a unanimous verdict in common law trials, was binding on both Congress and the territorial assemblies. In other words, according to these opinions, the inhabitants of territories enjoy the rights proclaimed in the amendments which restrict the governing power of Congress. So things stood at the close of the nineteenth century.

Then suddenly a new aspect was given to the old theme

when the Hawaiian Islands and the Philippines were acquired, for it was obviously impossible to apply there all the elaborate principles of Anglo-Saxon jurisprudence laid down in the federal Constitution. Confronted by this dilemma the Supreme Court cut the knot by bold strokes. In a series of decisions, known as the "Insular Cases," involving many technical points, it held, in effect, that the Constitution may be divided into two parts, fundamental and formal; that only the fundamental parts control the federal authorities in the government of territories; and that the Supreme Court will determine, from time to time, as specific cases arise, what parts of the federal Constitution are fundamental and what parts are formal. Thus we may say, with a judge of a lower federal court, that, for practical purposes, "the territories of the United States are entirely subject to the legislative authority of Congress. They are not organized under the Constitution, nor subject to its complex distribution of powers of government as the organic law, but are the creation exclusively of the legislative department and subject to its supervision and control. The United States, having rightfully acquired the territories and having become the only government which can impose laws upon them, has the entire domain of sovereignty, national and municipal, federal and state. It may legislate in accordance with the special needs of each locality, and vary its regulations to meet the circumstances of the people." Under this liberal interpretation of the Constitution, Congress may establish and maintain virtually any form of government in the insular possessions.

The Government of Districts, Territories, and Possessions

In practice the actual administration of the districts, territories, and possessions not organized into states assumes different forms according to local circumstances. This is inevitable, owing to the wide variety in the areas, economy, races, population, resources, and public interests involved. Some regions are governed in part by local legislatures and enjoy a large measure of autonomy; some are placed under the control of federal officers; and others are in effect as much subject to marine law as if the inhabitants were on board a ship.

Among the classes of regions directly subject to congressional authority the District of Columbia, the seat of the Federal Government, occupies of course a unique position. The District was originally accepted by Congress in 1790 as a cession from Maryland and, reckoning subsequent modifications, now consists of about seventy square miles. After several experiments in the administration of the municipality through the agency of a mayor and council had been tried and found wanting, Congress made a radical departure in 1878 by destroying the last vestiges of popular representation. At the present time the supreme legislative power of the District is assumed by Congress itself, which has by rule set aside certain days to be devoted to the business of the community. The executive authority is vested in a board of three commissioners—two civilians appointed by the President and Senate and one military officer detailed by the President. Besides carrying on important administrative activities, this body makes ordinances relating to public health, safety, and welfare.

Popular government, with varying qualifications for voting, has been granted to four territories and possessions of the United States. The first of these, Alaska, secured from Russia by purchase in 1867, remained under direct administration from Washington until 1912 when a large measure of home rule was conceded. The second, Hawaii, was annexed by a joint resolution of Congress in 1898 and accorded representative institutions two years later. In the Philippines, acquired by conquest from Spain in 1898, government has passed through various stages. At the outset a military system was organized; this was followed shortly by a civil régime consisting of a governor and a commission; in 1907 a representative body was installed; and finally by the Jones law of 1916 the senate, as well as the lower chamber, was made elective. A somewhat similar course was pursued in the case of Porto Rico, likewise wrested from Spain in 1898. After a brief period of military rule, Congress arranged in 1902 for the establishment of a legislature with one popular chamber; fifteen years later it provided that the upper house also should be chosen by duly qualified voters. Notwithstanding the diversity in their history these four territories and possessions have now achieved substantially the same form of government.

The executive power in each of them is vested in a governor, appointed by the President with the concurrence of the Senate of the United States. In every case the law-making functions granted by Congress are exercised by a legislature composed of two chambers—a senate and a house of representatives, both elected by local voters. In exchange for the governors sent from the United States to serve as administrative heads, the territories and possessions send agents, called delegates or resident commissioners, to represent them in Congress at Washington. These spokesmen are chosen by popular vote, except in the Philippines where the legislature makes the selection. But the exchange, of course, is not entirely equal for, while the governors have great powers, the delegates and commissioners in the House of Representatives have none. True, they may speak on affairs that concern them; but they do not enjoy the right to vote in that body.

The government of the Virgin Islands, purchased from Denmark in 1917, represents a transition stage between direct rule by federal officers and the type of local autonomy just described. As in the case of the four systems mentioned above, the governor of the Virgin Islands is chosen by the President and Senate; but in this connection the power of the President is wider, for he selects many more subordinate officials. Legislative functions are delegated to colonial councils—two in number, one for each of the municipalities into which the Islands are divided. Some of the members of these bodies are locally elected by popular vote while the remainder are appointed by the governor—a procedure quite different from that followed with respect to the territories and possessions already considered. Furthermore no official agents are sent from the Virgin Islands to represent them in Congress.

At the bottom of the scale in local autonomy are a few American possessions governed directly by federal officers without the intervention of a legislative assembly in any form. The most important of these are the Panama Canal Zone, obtained by a treaty from the Republic of Panama in 1904, Guam, secured by arrangements with Spain in 1898, and Tutuila with neighboring islets, finally acquired in a settlement with England and Germany in 1899.

Administrative power over the Panama Canal Zone is vested in a governor appointed for a four-year term by the President with the consent of the Senate; all other officials attached to the Zone are also chosen by him or under his authority and hold office at his pleasure. Most of the laws and ordinances for the strip are made by executive decree, subject to the right of Congress to change them, if it sees fit, by specific enactment. The chief business of the Zone authorities is the all-important function of maintaining and operating the Panama Canal and its adjuncts, such as the Panama Railway (p. 379).

Still less subject to political influences are the governments of Guam and American Samoa, for they are carried on by naval officers under presidential supervision. In both places the local commander of the armed forces of the United States acts as the supreme authority, with power to frame laws and ordinances and compel obedience to them. In this fashion the civil and military governments are combined in a single head, which is not surprising in view of the fact that the islands are of significance chiefly as naval bases or coaling stations. Nevertheless an agitation for the establishment of a separate civil administration appears from time to time, urging the emancipation of the local inhabitants from what objectors call "naval despotism."

Besides the regions just enumerated there are several minor

islands lying in the Pacific Ocean, which are claimed by the United States. But this mere show of authority does not always settle the question of ownership since title to certain of these regions is hazy, to say the least. Thus an American ship, *St. Mary's,* took formal possession of Jarvis Island, in the Pacific, in 1858, and the Government thereafter listed it as American soil. About thirty years later the British ship *Cormorant* also laid claim to the same spot in the name of Great Britain without paying any attention to prior assertions of right. At the present time, therefore, both nations apparently control the identical tract and a dual sovereignty seems to exist.

Nevertheless several minor Pacific islands are definitely under American jurisdiction. A number of them are of no importance; for example, Baker's Island, less than two square miles in area, which in 1914 had no fresh water, trees, or inhabitants. Others in a similar plight have since become useful to cable systems and fishermen. A few contain guano, a valuable fertilizer; and as a consequence controversies over the right of user have arisen on different occasions. To arrange for settling arguments of this character Congress has enacted legislation dealing with stray bits of insular territory. As a rule its measures simply grant to the President the power to determine whether in fact American sovereignty extends over the areas at issue and permit the discoverer of an island on which guano is found to exploit the deposit under the provisions of maritime law. In effect, then, a number of fragments of land are governed as if they were vessels on the high seas, a fitting system when their size is considered. In addition the statutes generally provide that, after the removal of the guano, the President may surrender all authority over them, on the assumption that barren wastes might as well be opened to "annexation" by others more interested in space than value.

Unlike England and other leading world powers the United States does not have a central "Colonial Office" for the administration of its possessions. Instead, Congress has given three separate agencies varying degrees of control. Continuing practices adopted in connection with the former continental territories, the Department of the Interior exercises a limited supervision in Alaska and Hawaii. The Navy Department holds complete sway over two islands, Guam and Samoa, which, as we have said, are chiefly valuable as naval bases and are administered as such. This Department also takes a hand in the government of the Virgin Islands which afford the Navy another important strategic center. Through its Bureau of Insular Affairs, the War Department handles problems of finance, personnel, and information connected with the Philippine Islands and Porto Rico. Owing to the evident dissipation of responsibility in imperial matters, it is not surprising that proposals are continually being made for the establishment of a single colonial office or division. Indeed a bill combining in one authority the functions discharged by the Navy, War, and Interior Departments in the various possessions was introduced in Congress during 1927 but it failed of passage, leaving the question of centralization still pending.

Protectorates

Apart from the regular possessions of the United States, in which permanent government has been established under federal authority, there are certain regions, especially in the Caribbean, where American control is sporadically exerted over nations nominally recognized as independent. Whenever the acts of such countries are deemed to be contrary to "American interests," the President may send armed forces to the scene of trouble for the purpose of assuming some degree of temporary supervision (p. 281). During occupancy then, these states are limited in their "sovereignty" by the necessity of satisfying the requirements of officials representing the United States. To districts over which dominion of this nature is exercised the vague term "protectorate" is applied; they are theoretically free but they must always conduct their affairs with an eye to pleasing the guardian power and at any moment they may come under its suzerainty.

American intervention of this sort assumes a number of forms. In 1905 President Roosevelt, by executive action, took over the customs houses of Santo Domingo, and stationed war vessels in Dominican waters to give point to the argument. In 1911 an American warship was sent to Nicaragua, a loan arranged, and a treaty drawn, reciting "the benevolent intentions" of the United States and putting the customs service in the hands of a presidential appointee. When, in spite of three urgent messages from President Taft, the Senate declined to ratify the agreement, military forces were landed in Nicaragua and business was restored to a normal course. In 1915 marines were dispatched to Haiti and American supremacy was established there, incidentally involving the death of more than two thousand natives who, for one reason or another, got in the way of the operation. In 1916 Admiral Knapp—"to maintain domestic tranquility"—took possession of Santo Domingo and declared that "republic" subject to the military protection of the United States. In 1921, after some American marines had smashed the office of the *Tribuna* in Managua for printing critical articles, the minister of the United States requested the local Nicaraguan government to set apart adequate space outside the capital for drill grounds, a dance hall, and a moving picture theater, to be used by American officers and men, and also to designate special liquor saloons for their convenience. In 1925 American troops intervened to halt riots against high rents in the Republic of Panama. In 1928 American marines supervised the presidential elections in Nicaragua—guarding the booths and counting the ballots.

At the present moment there are no United States forces in Santo Domingo, the last contingent having been withdrawn in 1924, but the customs service is still in charge of an American receiver. After the election mentioned above, Nicaragua was started in the direction of another experiment in independence, with a few marines to help. Although Haiti

Photo by Brown Brothers

United States Marines Train Native Constabulary in Santo Domingo.

Photo by Brown Brothers

THE INSULAR BUILDING IN MANILA: A SYMBOL OF AMERICAN OCCUPATION.

is still under an American military officer as high commissioner, his tenure is to be cut short. In 1930 President Hoover sent a special commission to this republic with instructions to make an inquiry into the situation, and on the strength of its report he announced that steps would soon be taken to aid the natives in establishing their own government, that the marines would be gradually withdrawn, and that diplomatic representation would be substituted for direct supervision over their affairs. Yet, whether American authorities actually exercise sovereign powers over them or not, various independent Caribbean states are in fact American protectorates, for intervention on the part of the United States is always potential.

In the case of one protectorate, the island of Cuba, the authority of the United States has been formally sanctioned by agreement. In the joint resolution of Congress demanding the withdrawal of Spain from Cuba in 1898, it was publicly declared that the United States disclaimed any intention of exercising sovereignty, jurisdiction, or control over the Island except for the pacification thereof; and it was furthermore asserted that when this task was accomplished the government of the Island would be left to the people. However, in 1901 a provision, known as the "Platt Amendment," was incorporated in the army appropriation act, which directed the President to turn the control of Cuba over to the inhabitants as soon as they established a regular government and expressly recognized in their constitution, among other things, the right of the United States to intervene under certain circumstances, particularly to maintain order.

And this stipulation is by no means theoretical. In the summer of 1906, when an armed uprising was fomented by discontented natives, repeated appeals from American citizens in Cuba induced the President to act under the Platt Amendment. Military forces were immediately sent to the Island, and responsibility for the entire administration was assumed by an American officer representing the authority of the United States. After an occupation lasting until January, 1909, the government was turned over to the native president and congress, duly elected in the preceding November.

In spite of periodical interventions, the actual acquisition of additional territory in the Caribbean regions has been avoided. True, the power of the President to dispatch American marines to these places is sufficient to give him a large measure of continual control; but he generally exercises it in "friendly coöperation" with some of the native politicians rather than in the form of conventional conquest. An anomalous situation has thus arisen. The President may direct movements of troops which really constitute hostilities but he cannot declare war or make treaties—actions necessary to the transfer of land to the United States. Congress alone holds the power to make an official war, and it has not yet seen fit to lend formal approval to military excursions in the Caribbean regions. Nor is it probable that the Senate, which controls the ratification of treaties, would approve annexation, except under special circumstances. Indeed, as American publicists have repeatedly pointed out, presidential supervision permits the easy erection of tariffs against such protectorates for the benefit of American industry while affording practically all the advantages of formal possession besides, especially security for life, trade, and property.

Problems of Imperial Policy

In accordance with Anglo-Saxon traditions, the territorial possessions of the United States beyond the seas have been acquired by what are sometimes termed "accidents of history," rather than as a result of deliberate policy formulated by the people and their representatives in Congress. While it is true that some of the leaders high up in the Republican administration which managed the war with Spain early intended to take advantage of the occasion to annex remnants of the Spanish Empire in the Atlantic and the Pacific, this object was not widely advertised or admitted. Certainly it could not be said to have been the solemn resolve of the American people. On the day these fragments of territory came under the American flag public opinion was sharply divided and the controversy has continued to the latest hour. With respect to some of the possessions described above, therefore, especially the Philippines, imperial policy has fluctuated with the changing winds of domestic politics. Shall these "gifts of fortune" be finally accepted or shall they be granted independence?

So far as Guam and Porto Rico are concerned, there seems to be no real question, for these islands are generally regarded as permanent and integral parts of the United States. In the case of Cuba, a curious situation exists; independence was granted to this republic on the assumption that the Monroe Doctrine and a "protectorate" over it would prove ample safeguards for American interests. The Philippines, however, occupy an intermediate position between these two extremes; they are neither nominally independent nor is their status as a part of the United States irrevocably determined. Since they stand in this unique relation, the question of their independence remains the most fundamental problem in American imperial policy.

At first glance, to be sure, the issue of Philippine independence appears to be settled, for many authoritative expressions of opinion on the part of outstanding political leaders in the United States definitely point to it as a goal. In 1900 the Democratic party platform denounced the Republican administration for placing this country "previously known and applauded throughout the world as the champion of freedom, in the false and un-American position of crushing with military force the efforts of our former allies to achieve liberty and self-government." By way of a pledge the platform then urged ultimate independence. In 1904 Elihu Root said that the Philippines might eventually be given the same status as Cuba. In 1908 President Roosevelt expressed the hope that they could, within a generation, "decide for themselves whether it is well for them to become independent." As Secretary of War, William H. Taft declared that American policy "must logically reduce and finally end the sovereignty of the United States" in the islands. To clinch the matter the Jones Act of 1916, in reorganizing the Philippine government, solemnly announced that "it is . . . the purpose of the people of the United States to withdraw their sovereignty over the Philippine Islands and to recognize their independence as soon as a stable government can be established." So far as mere declarations of intention are concerned, then, American policy definitely hints at independence, at least in some remote day.

A more careful analysis, however, shows that these expressions of opinion simply set up a final goal, without indicating clearly how or when it is to be reached. True, the Jones Act only postponed Philippine independence until the formation of a stable government is assured; but what is a stable government? General Woods characterized it as one "under which capital seeks investment at normal rates of interest." Indeed he went further and said that a stable government must be strong enough to defend itself. Applying these tests of stability to our own nation, critics cite a number of repudiated state debts, repeated business panics, high and low interest rates fluctuating with the market, records of a costly civil war, and proof that foreign troops even invaded our national capital in the War of 1812. If the Philippines must comply with General Woods' standards, their independence is a distant contingency. After all, the real crux of the matter does not lie in verbiage but in the fact that, notwithstanding strong pledges, many leaders in both political parties apparently intend to keep the Philippines as a permanent possession of the United States. Since the Federal Government has the power not only to name the terms under which independence is to be granted but also to define them and decide when compliance with them has been reached, it is obvious that the question may long remain to vex American politics.

Of course the issue is not solely one of political ethics. There are business and strategic questions involved in the status of the Philippines. Large amounts of American capital are invested there and opportunities for economic development lie ahead. Furthermore, the Islands are an important element in the maintenance of American naval strength in the Far East. They afford a base for the protection of our enterprise in China. In short, American occupancy serves notice on the powers of the world that the United States is not to be ignored in any partition of privileges and trade in the Orient.

Such at least are the contentions of those who insist that the United States should hold the Philippines permanently. But are the arguments sound? Are there not countervailing risks which more than offset the gains? No proof is forthcoming to show that the Philippines "pay" in an economic sense. It is true that individual capitalists and merchants make large profits from business in that part of the world but no figures are available to prove that the costs of supervision and naval protection met by the taxpayers of the United States do not exceed by far the gains of private citizens from Philippine industry and trade. This is a phase on which politicians are strangely silent. If the Philippines pay, the question may be properly asked: "Whom?" As to national defense, they are an element of weakness, not of strength. It has been said on good authority that in case of a war with any first-class power in the Pacific, the American Navy would not even attempt to defend the Philippines. If they were seized by such a power, would the people of the United States pour out blood and treasure in endless streams to recover them? There is the real issue—and obvious as it is, it receives little consideration from those who vaguely discuss what is called "Philippine independence."

Finally, there are the imponderables. No small part of the rivalry with Japan and the imperialist movement in that country is due to the American occupation of the Philippines. As a Tokyo publicist has put it, the Japanese have felt about the

American advance into Asiatic waters very much as Americans would feel if Japan occupied one of the Caribbean Islands. On the other side are democratic forces. Asia is aflame with revolt against "imperialist domination." Ever since the outbreak of the World War the spirit of independence has been growing in India and has now reached menacing proportions. Whatever the outcome, Great Britain can no longer continue to rule that country on the old terms. The Dutch are having their popular troubles in Java. China is both revolutionary and nationalist. Korea stirs restlessly. And Russia encourages all such uprisings. Repeatedly the Philippine legislature has resolved in favor of complete independence; if such action can be discounted as politics, it certainly is an expression of the regular representation of the Islands. Evidently those who are thinking of the Orient in terms of the McKinley age are out of touch with the course of events. Roosevelt's "big stick" can only be used successfully on heads that are empty.

Closely allied with the question of colonial status is that of the protective tariff in relation to the overseas possessions of the United States. By a curious line of reasoning, the Supreme Court has held that Porto Rico and the Philippines are not parts of the United States within the meaning of the revenue acts, and hence Congress has full power to fix the duties levied on commodities passing in both directions. Thus it may place a high tariff on any products coming from these possessions while forcing them to admit American goods free of all charges, an action against which local residents would have no recourse. A case in point is the existing tariff relation with the Philippines. Commodities arriving in the United States from these Islands must pay a duty unless eighty per cent or more of the material of which they are composed is of native or American origin or both. On the other hand all goods entering the Philippines from the United States are exempt from customs levies. Thus coffee, brought into the United States from South America, may be roasted and shipped to the Philippines free of duty while the same commodity imported into those Islands and prepared there is subject to tax if sent to the United States. The effect of such arrangements has been to increase the percentage of American imports into the Philippines from seven in 1899 to fifty-five in 1925. The tariff, then, is a vital element in colonial policy. This was vigorously emphasized in the struggle over the revenue bill of 1929–30 when American producers demanded protection against Philippine sugar, tobacco, hemp, and other commodities, going so far in some cases as to advocate independence as a means of justifying a higher barrier between the United States and the Islands.

While the external trade of the possessions has been extensively regulated by Congress through customs legislation, certain policies relative to internal industry have also been evolved. Since all the territories and dependencies, except Alaska, are tropical or semi-tropical in nature, local economy may be entirely upset by the establishment of great plantations for producing sugar, rubber, and other commodities adapted to large-scale operations. Should corporations, owned and operated by absentee capitalists in America, be given free rein in these sections regardless of native interests? Should they be allowed to accumulate immense holdings of land and turn small farmers into hired laborers? Or should a check be put upon them to insure reasonable contentment among the inhabitants, advance their own well-being, and thus forestall serious internal troubles?

In conformity with the practice of other imperial nations, which have discovered that the costs of colonial disorders sometimes more than offset the profits of exploitation, laws have been passed setting the maximum size for land holdings in certain of the possessions under the American flag. In the case of Porto Rico, Congress, as far back as 1900, restricted the amount of land to be owned by any agricultural corporation to five hundred acres. But, since the statute specified no penalties, it has not been enforced and the natives' soil is rapidly passing into the possession of American capitalists. In a report made to Congress in 1916, President

Wilson listed 477 flagrant violations which time had failed to remedy. In reality the act has become a dead-letter although undoubtedly it could be carried into execution by vigorous effort. In the Philippines the local legislature has enacted measures restricting all holdings carved out of the public domain to 2,530 acres. Apparently the Philippine law has been more effective than that applicable to Porto Rico in preventing the accumulation of great plantations but since it covers only the public lands its scope is materially restricted.

Difficult problems of citizenship as well as economy have arisen in connection with American possessions. On the acquisition of Alaska many Russians came under the jurisdiction of the United States. Following the surrender of Porto Rico and the Philippines, the status of Spanish citizens had to be determined. After the purchase of the Virgin Islands, numerous Danish subjects were found on American soil. The situation has been further complicated by the large native population of Indians, Negroes, Malays, and other races ranging all the way from wild tribes to settled farmers and merchants. To meet this wide variation in local conditions different expedients have been adopted in dealing with the question of nationality.

In some cases United States citizenship has been generally bestowed. Thus the inhabitants of Alaska, except certain uncivilized tribes, became American citizens unless they preferred their Russian connection. A similar policy was later applied to Porto Rico and the Virgin Islands. In the former, all Spanish citizens, including of course the natives, and in the latter all Danish citizens, were allowed to retain their old allegiance; then by subsequent acts those who had not so elected were granted American citizenship. In each of these cases the nation which surrendered its sovereignty over the possession in question continued in existence so that the inhabitants could, if they saw fit, remain loyal to their mother country. On the other hand when the Hawaiian Islands were annexed the former government, namely, the Republic of Hawaii, was extinguished. Whether they liked it or not "all persons who were citizens of the Republic of Hawaii on August 12, 1898," were declared to be citizens of the United States, that is, transferred as a body to the new régime.

By way of contrast, the people of the Philippine Islands have been accorded no such privilege; they are merely entitled to local citizenship. All inhabitants of these Islands who were Spanish subjects on April 11, 1899, were permitted either to retain their old allegiance or to become citizens of the Philippines; and the Philippine legislature has been authorized to make regulations pertaining to the naturalization of other persons. Thus the Filipinos hang between two worlds. They are not citizens of the United States even though they enjoy its protection when traveling; nor are they citizens of an independent country. Apparently also, Filipinos resident in the United States cannot become naturalized Americans under the law as it now stands. Whether this position is a stepping-stone to full American rights or to independence the future alone will determine. In a still more curious plight are the inhabitants of American Samoa. Although they had been ruled by American naval officers for more than a quarter of a century, their country was not formally annexed until 1929 and then they were not declared to be American citizens. What are they? Law and diplomacy make no answer.

Closely associated with the problem of citizenship is that of immigration from the possessions. Naturally citizens of Alaska, Hawaii, and other regions in which full American rights have been conferred wholesale may freely enter the United States. Philippine citizens and natives of Guam enjoy the same privilege. By adopting this policy America has thrown open her doors to races which would be excluded if her flag did not fly over them. Thus while immigration from England, Germany, and other quota countries is sharply restricted, in the interest, it is said, of preserving American nationality, immigrants from imperial possessions, certainly less readily assimilable, may come without restraint. Already the peculiarity of this arrangement has become apparent. Riots involving Filipino laborers on the Pacific Coast have forcibly directed public attention to it recently and raised a demand for new forms of restriction. Like the agitation over the tariff, the discussion of this question has strengthened the movement for granting independence to the Philippine Islands. Whether Congress could withdraw the citizenship conceded to inhabitants of other possessions and raise immigration bars against them is highly doubtful in view of constitutional provisions, but nevertheless hints of that expedient may soon be heard. In any case empire involves problems of race no less than of national defense and commerce.

Imperialism has created a situation of serious delicacy. On the one side there is a rising pressure in the United States for economic expansion, made manifest by the growing emphasis on export trade, the quest for new investment opportunities, and the search for additional raw materials, especially oil. On the other side there is an evident increase in the natural resentment entertained by Latin-American and Philippine patriots against "Yankee intrusion," intensifying ancient antagonisms and disturbing the cordial relations necessary to free intercourse. Disorders and irregularities in certain Caribbean countries are of constant occurrence, endangering legitimate business in every department, not only of the United States but of European countries as well. And unless efforts at stabilization are made in the New World, the imperial powers of the Old, following their historic traditions, will intervene on behalf of their nationals, thus putting in jeopardy the Monroe Doctrine with all that is implied in such a peril (p. 736). In these circumstances it seems impossible for the United States merely to hold aloof and allow revolutions and uprisings to run their inevitable course. But there is another alternative available, namely, coöperation with the stable governments of Latin-America rather than independent interference in all cases calling for the maintenance of order. Indeed this policy is now urged upon the

President by American publicists of great distinction and time may prove that it is both wise and practical. Good intention, as Burke said long ago, is an excellent medicine in critical times.

Such good intentions, however, involve statecraft in foreign affairs, broadly conceived in the light of our modern age, when national interests are geared by swifter transportation, intercourse, and communications into the mesh of world relations. Beyond all doubt, irresistible technology has set a new stage for imperial policies—one which makes obsolete most of the traditional practices in this sphere, especially since popular ferments even in darkest Africa may baffle crude force of the historic type. Whether imperialism "pays" involves more than a calculation of immediate profits; the World War, which grew largely out of imperial rivalries and ambitions, certainly swept away the gains accumulated by long years of colonial exploitation; and conflagrations of that nature must be taken into the reckoning when balance sheets are struck. Many signs seem to indicate, therefore, that the pursuit of trade by the rational process of commodity exchange under coöperative conditions offers a far better method than conquest for augmenting "the wealth of nations" and the happiness of mankind.

CHAPTER XXII

Nature and Conduct of Foreign Relations

There was a time, not so long ago, when international relations were comparatively simple and diplomacy was primarily a graceful art. In those days kings were states, commerce was small in volume, travel and migration were slight, and raw materials, such as coal and iron, seldom if ever entered into political calculations. In that age the relations of independent governments were essentially personal; the business of the diplomatic agent was to effect favorable alliances between monarchs and to counteract royal combinations dangerous to the sovereign for whom he spoke. Suavity in manner and skill in insinuation were the first requisites for the ambassador, because his operations were limited almost entirely to the narrow circle of the court to which he was accredited. Intimacy with a courtier or a lady of the royal retinue was more important than a knowledge of political economy. How to shine in ceremonial and to carry on deft intrigues was the chief concern of the ambassador. Such was the world in which the traditions of diplomacy were established.

The Revolution in Diplomacy

Since the art was first developed, however, a revolution has taken place in governments and in the relations of nations. For monarchies have been substituted democracies in most countries of the Western civilization. Kings no longer speak for peoples; that task is generally committed to ministers responsible to parliaments or to elected presidents. The day has passed when a fortunate alliance can be made through the good offices of the queen's first lady-in-waiting. Whole classes, capitalistic or socialistic, rather than fickle princes, must be taken into account by the diplomat. He must cultivate politicians of various parties, financiers, heads of great industrial corporations, and in these later days, in some countries at least, outstanding labor leaders.

While governments have been shifted to a popular base, the relations of peoples to one another have altered even more fundamentally. Nations are no longer isolated entities represented by rulers who may make or break official intercourse at will. Underlying the whole fabric of modern civilization is a network of physical, economic, social, and cultural connections. Railways, steamships, telegraphs, cables, and wireless communications unite homes, offices, industries, and farms in a universal web. The daily papers give great spaces to news from abroad as well as to domestic events; foreign offices often hear of incidents through the press before they receive reports from their ambassadors. Economic ties multiply with physical affiliations. Through the growth of trade, millions of individuals in various countries are brought into constant and direct contact with one another. They exchange goods, borrow and lend money, form business and banking corporations for world-wide operations. The bonds, stock, and other obligations of governments, municipalities, corporations, and individuals in every quarter are held by investors in all parts of the globe. Investment trusts representing the financiers of a score of nations buy and sell the securities of the governments and industries of as many different peoples. Cartels and agreements respecting the manufacture and sale of vital commodities, such as iron, steel, and rubber, are frequently made among the industrialists of two or more countries. Now a Bank for International Settlements, a world super-bank, representing the central financial institutions of the leading powers and largely emancipated from political control, is transacting business in every part of the earth.

Social, cultural, and scientific intercourse likewise cuts across the boundaries established by governments. Trade unions and socialistic parties are organized internationally and carry on diplomatic relations of their own. The republic of science and letters is international. By its intrinsic nature machine industry tends to give uniformity to the civilization of all races and nations, breaking down the picturesque costumes and customs of provincial communities. Humanitarian interests now draw the women of the world together. Traveling has become a major concern of intelligent persons. Once foreign tourists were regarded as intruders; now they are cordially welcomed by railway companies, hotel-keepers, and merchants as national benefactors. Only by war and drastic official control can these associations be broken. In time of peace they are continuous and largely independent of political institutions, although they assist in setting the tasks and determining the policies of cabinets and presidents. For example, the Government of the United States does not recognize or maintain diplomatic connections with Soviet Russia, but American citizens go to observe its institutions and American businessmen carry on commerce with its agents. Russian communists, though excluded by law, are freely admitted to the United States by the federal authorities, provided they come to buy and sell goods; Russian literature circulates through bookshops and Russian films are seen at the movies.

With these startling changes in governments and economy has gone a revolution in the nature and substance of diplomacy. The relations of countries are no longer spasmodic; they are continuous and fundamental to prosperity and convenience; they call for constant legislative, judicial, and administrative action. For instance the international carriage of mails by land, air, and water goes on day and night from year to year; the rules for the conduct of this huge enterprise are made by a periodical international postal congress held under the authority of the International Postal Union; administrative officers take charge of the distribution of postal revenues among the countries participating in the Union; and innumerable questions arising under the terms of the agreements are judicially decided. By no mere exchange of diplomatic notes, politesse or subterfuge, could this immense world undertaking be managed. A kind of super-government must of necessity assume charge of it. As we shall see, no less than twenty distinct international unions have been formed to make rules for and administer as many different branches of international economy; and there is a marked tendency to bring such operations under the auspices of a single international government—the League of Nations.

Amid these new circumstances the ambassador is less of a courtier and more of a sociologist; less of an intriguer and more of a propagandist. Judging by recent diplomatic revelations, he may still purloin papers and employ spies, but he has other more important functions. Fundamentally the duties which come within his purview are now economic in character, not personal. Whether Jones, Smith, or Brown is foreign minister makes little difference in the matters to be treated; they involve the adjustment of conflicts over trade, tariffs, investments, immigration, raw materials, and colonies —the promotion of business enterprise (Chapter XIV). Naturally, therefore, the information necessary to the correct handling of such incidents cannot be derived from court gossip but only from a study of social and economic conditions—movements in commerce and rivalries in trade. Statistics are more useful than rumors; an accurate survey of world economy is a surer guide than whole portfolios of reports from detectives.

Yet it must not be thought that the conduct of foreign affairs is a mere matter of commercial arithmetic. It is still, as ever, related to vital questions of policy and destiny. Nations may be destroyed by foreign wars no less than by internal decay. Whether they survive in the modern world depends on their prowess in avoiding unnecessary enmities, no less than on the ingenuity and strength of their engines of defense. It was, in part at least, the skilful labor of Benjamin Franklin at the court of Louis XVI which brought France to the aid of the United States in 1778 and assured, if it did not actually gain, American independence. To the dexterity and persistence of Charles Francis Adams, as minister to the Court of St. James', was largely due the refusal of the British government to lend open aid to the Southern Confederacy in the fateful days of the Civil War. It was with respect to strategic national ends that the British Foreign Office assiduously cultivated the friendship of the United States between 1898 and 1917. Though science and machinery have erected a new stage for world economy, diplomacy is still the art by which large and fateful policies are realized in international dealings—a modern art conditioned and served by novel instrumentalities.

Broadly speaking, those responsible for foreign affairs have five prime functions to perform. They must accumulate and interpret information about the economic, political, and social conditions of the countries with which they carry on relations. On the basis of such information, they must promote national interests, by amicable adjustments if possible. With reference to potential armed conflicts they must prepare for victory by making an advantageous alignment of allies, friends, and neutrals. During the course of war they must watch every contingency liable to thwart national triumph. And at its close the burden of formulating the terms of peace falls upon them. To some extent their work is determined by geographical and commercial factors, historical traditions, and public opinion. But in a large measure they direct emergencies by their handling of information and episodes.

Clearly, then, diplomacy may work for war or for peace. It may order events in such a fashion as to make war inevitable. It may dissipate enmities that threaten to eventuate in armed contests. If America avoids taking part in the world conflagrations that may arise in the future, diplomacy can help to accomplish the consummation devoutly to be wished. If, in the long flow of time, America becomes involved in a terrible conflict with a combination of foreign foes and is brought face to face with ruin on land and sea, that circumstance, too, will be laid at the door of diplomacy.

Leadership in Foreign Affairs

Although the Fathers of the Republic well understood the significance of diplomacy, the Constitution which they framed does not specifically explain how and by whom the foreign affairs of the United States are to be conducted. It provides, to be sure, that the President shall have the power to make treaties, but with the advice and consent of the Senate, two-thirds of the members present concurring. It likewise declares that he shall appoint ambassadors, consuls, and other public ministers, but here too the approval of the Senate is required. Any other authority over foreign relations accrues to him from his general position as chief executive and from the provision that he is to receive the ambassadors and ministers of foreign countries accredited to the United States. Evidently the framers of our fundamental law intended to make the Senate a kind of council on foreign affairs.

Out of these meagre constitutional provisions and out of practice has been evolved the rule that the President is the official representative of the nation in foreign affairs. It would be improper, therefore, for a foreign government to address a dispatch to Congress or for Congress to send a message directly to the head of another nation. Yet in this relation, some distinctions must be noted. On various occasions Congress has condemned by resolution the policy of some other country; for example, the treatment of the Irish by Great Britain or the Jews by Tsarist Russia. It has also called upon the President publicly to negotiate or abrogate certain treaties.

Moreover the Senate may reject treaties negotiated by the President, and thus actually repudiate the program which he has formally announced as the official policy of the United States. It has done so more than once. When in the autumn of 1918 the Republicans carried the congressional elections, Theodore Roosevelt in a kind of message to the world declared that President Wilson was no longer the true representative of the country in foreign affairs. "Our allies and Mr. Wilson himself should understand," he said, "that Mr. Wilson has no authority whatever to speak for the American people at this time. His leadership has just been emphatically repudiated by them. The newly elected Congress comes far nearer than Mr. Wilson to having the right to speak for the purposes of the American people at this moment." In the end the treaty which President Wilson signed in Paris was defeated and his leadership authoritatively denied. If in fact the President is the official spokesman in foreign affairs, what he says may be flung to the winds. Hence he always operates under the shadow of a vast uncertainty. When other governments deal with him in this capacity they must reckon with the actual limitations on his powers and may indeed take advantage of the very weakness of his position.

Nevertheless it is the President, rather than Congress, who officially formulates the chief principles of American foreign policy. He can do this in messages to Congress; for example, Monroe's famous doctrine enunciated in 1823. He can do it in dispatches to foreign chancelleries; in this way President Wilson built up a program with respect to Germany's submarine warfare which finally led to an armed conflict. Or he may give his views to the world in public addresses.

Although in theory the President is supposed to send his official communications to other powers through the State Department, in fact he adheres to no such rule. He may and often does write directly to American ministers abroad—and in effect to foreign governments. He may employ special agents to represent him. President Roosevelt sent a personal envoy to Tokyo in 1905 to enter into a secret understanding with the Premier of Japan and later he instructed Senator Lodge to convey to King Edward VII important information regarding American policy. President Wilson not only gave Colonel E. M. House a "roving commission" as his representative in Europe, but crossed the sea himself to take part in drafting the Treaty of Versailles. In 1929 the world witnessed at a distance the extraordinary spectacle of the President of the United States and the Premier of Great Britain carrying on conversations about international relations of the highest importance while strolling in Virginia forests. Although the President cannot as a rule give force to his measures without the coöperation of one or both houses of Congress, he can within broad limits shape American foreign policy and compel the world to give heed.

In this connection, the administrations of President Wilson are unique in our history. Owing to peculiar conditions, foreign affairs during that period involved questions running deep into national life. The World War and the peace which marked its conclusion raised international problems more serious than any hitherto confronted by a President. Moreover, Wilson had a decided concept of his duties as the leader of his party as well as national spokesman, and he was unwilling to share his gravest responsibilities with any subordinate in his Cabinet. It happened also that he had slight confidence in the capacity of William Jennings Bryan. Temperamentally the two men were as far apart as the poles. On Bryan's resignation as Secretary in 1915, President Wilson elevated to the post, Robert Lansing, a former counselor in the Department of State, who enjoyed no political prestige and thus could command no party support against his superior.

Amid these circumstances the conduct of foreign affairs really passed from the State Department to the White House. In his notes directed to foreign governments, especially the Central Powers, President Wilson announced policies of fateful consequence and, as the submarine crisis developed, he steered the Government into a course which inevitably led to war. After America entered the world conflict, Wilson received official missions from the powers associated with the United States and settled matters of vital concern by first-hand negotiations. At the close of the war, he went in person to the Peace Conference at Paris, against the protests of his Secretary, and assumed full responsibility for all American policies and decisions. He visited England, France, and Italy, made public addresses on delicate questions, and in fact appealed to the people of those countries for support in realizing the great principles which he had laid down—especially the Fourteen Points in which he had defined American war aims. Overshadowed in everything, the Secretary of State, Robert Lansing, sank into the background; he tells us that the President failed to answer many of his communications and neglected to inform him about matters of prime importance. On one occasion the Secretary was placed under the embarrassing necessity of asking Chinese delegates at the Conference to inform him about the President's position on a certain point. Shortly after his return to the United States, Lansing was rather curtly dismissed by the President on the ground that he was wanting in loyalty and the spirit of harmonious coöperation.

Under President Harding the situation was radically different. There were, no doubt, foreign problems of major concern to be considered, but he did not choose to solve them himself. Instead of selecting a pliant subordinate as Secretary of State, he appointed Charles E. Hughes, one of the most powerful personalities in the Republican party, whose opinions could not be ignored on any account. Then he gave the Secretary empire over his own department. When the conference of great powers assembled in Washington in 1921, the President contented himself by opening its first session with a few appropriate generalities and left the serious business of leadership with Secretary Hughes. In doing this, of course, he did not abdicate; he chose to work with his Secretary rather than to become the master of ceremonies and realities.

The Department of State

In the organization of the Department of State the position of the President as official spokesman of the nation is expressly recognized. The act of Congress creating it provides that the Secretary shall perform such duties as the President may entrust to him relative to correspondence, commissions, and instructions to the public ministers and consuls sent out from the United States and also pertaining to negotiations with the public ministers from foreign governments and princes. In other words the Department of State, besides assuming certain functions connected with the publication of domestic laws and with interstate relations, is to transact such foreign business as the President may assign to it and, as a matter of course, pursue the policies which he lays down.

Thus the Department is the legal organ of communication between the President and other countries and is recognized as such by foreign powers, for it is to the Secretary of State that they address their formal notes to the Government of the United States. When the French minister here, in 1793, directed a letter to the President in person, the Secretary made a ruling to the effect that it was not proper for diplomatic representatives to institute correspondence immediately with the chief executive. Yet it would be a great mistake to lay too much stress on this ceremony. Many questions, as we have seen, are taken up directly with foreign powers by the President either through his special agents abroad or through their representatives in Washington. About the only safe generalization is that the State Department serves as the federal agency through which foreign business is ordinarily transacted.

In a peculiar sense the Secretary of State is the President's personal selection; the Senate would scarcely dare to reject any nomination he might make for that office. Usually, as we have said, the Secretary is a figure of great importance in the President's party—a man acceptable to the voters behind the administration. Many of the leading characters in American history have held the place: Jefferson, John Marshall, Madison, Monroe, John Quincy Adams, Webster, Seward, John Hay, William Jennings Bryan, and Charles

E. Hughes, for example. Seldom has a Secretary been chosen from among the officials who have grown up in the service. President Wilson's transfer of Robert Lansing from the office of counselor in the State Department to the headship was an exception which illustrates the general rule. Frequently it happens, however, that the Secretary is drawn from the diplomatic ranks; Jefferson was serving as minister in Paris when President Washington called him home to take charge of the Department; John Hay was promoted from the American embassy in London. Generally some outstanding figure in domestic politics is made head of the Department because he is too influential to be passed over, not on account of his special knowledge of foreign affairs. Wilson selected Bryan partly for the reason that he simply could not be ignored and partly to enlist his support for a legislative program in Congress. Perhaps it is fair to say, therefore, that the weight of a Secretary in the actual direction of foreign affairs will depend mainly on his prowess, his experience, and the circumstances of his appointment.

To take care of the enormous mass of business that passes through its hands and to provide expert counsel for the Secretary, the Department of State is organized in great divisions, each headed by a specialist. Six of them, as their titles imply, cover the issues arising in particular regions: Far Eastern Affairs, Latin-American Affairs, Mexican Affairs, Western European Affairs, Eastern European Affairs, and Near Eastern Affairs. Other divisions or offices deal with passports and visas, so important for travelers, with foreign service buildings, and with consular business. Records are in charge of the chief of the bureau of indexes and archives and the historical adviser. Two divisions have jurisdiction over matters of foreign service administration and personnel under civil service regulations (p. 719).

In spite of liberal provisions for certain activities of the Department, Congress has failed to make grants of money commensurate with the significance of its work. It is the duty of that Department to wage peace, just as it is the duty of the War and Navy Departments to wage war; and if peace is the avowed principle of the Federal Government, as often declared by the Presidents, if the renunciation of war as an instrument of national policy under the Kellogg Pact of 1928 (p. 741) is a reality rather than a fiction, then the State Department ought to have adequate financial support to secure competent servants and to collect the complicated information necessary for the intelligent management of international relations. In recognition of this fact, President Hoover, in his Armistice Day speech of 1929, declared that the Department "must be strengthened and supported as the great arm of our government dedicated to peace," and again, in his first message to Congress, he urged a material increase in appropriations for this purpose.

While much emphasis has rightly been laid on the Department of State as the organ of communication between the United States and foreign countries, it should be remembered that it is not the sole branch of the Federal Government which has agents abroad. The War and Navy Departments have their representatives in all important countries—military and naval attachés—theoretically affiliated with American embassies and legations but practically enjoying a general commission to find out all they can and report directly to their respective heads at home. An attaché's secret communication to his chief may be far more valuable than an ambassador's long dispatch. Though supposed to observe military and naval affairs primarily, the most active of the attachés cover a wider range—not overlooking politics and opportunities to sell goods. Equally alive to its interests the Department of Commerce maintains a host of foreign trade agents scattered throughout the world—some independent, others connected with embassies and legations. The Department of Labor has its immigration officials in many foreign ports of embarkation; the Treasury its tariff investigators; the Department of Agriculture a number of experts in its field; and Justice a police force engaged in tracking down criminals. Only the Post Office and the Department of the Interior, it seems, are not regularly represented abroad in some capacity.

Diplomatic and Consular Representatives in Foreign Countries

The representatives of the United States in foreign countries who come immediately under the direction of the State Department fall into two general groups: diplomatic and consular.

According to ceremonial ranking, the first of these groups is divided into four classes: ambassadors, envoys and special commissioners, ministers resident, and *chargés d'affaires.*

For over a century the United States did not send ambassadors; it was represented abroad only by agents falling within the second, third, and fourth classes. It thus came about sometimes that a minister of the United States was compelled, on public occasions, at receptions, and in interviews with foreign officers, to step aside in favor of the representative of some small nation, who happened to bear the title of ambassador. Though all European courts did not follow a rigid system of precedence, American ministers often received treatment which they deemed humiliating to the spokesmen of so great a nation. Accordingly in 1893 Congress provided that our representative to any foreign country should have the same rank as the representative of that country to the United States. Therefore, whenever a nation sends an ambassador to us, we return the honor. Indeed on one occasion at least, in the case of Turkey, the President took the initiative in the negotiations which resulted in the elevation of rank. In every new case, however, the consent of Congress is now necessary.

All diplomatic representatives of the United States are nominated by the President and appointed by and with the advice and consent of the Senate. In spite of the thorough knowledge and experience which ought to be required of those who enter the diplomatic service, our official agents, especially ambassadors and ministers, are often selected without regard to such qualifications, in exchange perhaps for political service and large contributions to campaign funds. As Secretary Hay once remarked, "A quiet legation is a stuffed mattress which the political acrobat wants always to see ready under him, in case of a slip." Besides, owing to the small salaries paid and the expenses of entertaining, only rich men can afford to take the post in many capitals. The term of office is uncertain and liable to be brief; for, whenever a shift of party occurs at Washington, many changes take place in our representation abroad. There is no automatic arrangement for prolonged tenure of office throughout this division of federal activities, beginning with the lower grades of the diplomatic service and ending with a position at the head of one of the foremost embassies in Europe; but, as we shall see below (p. 719), by the Rogers Act of 1924 provision is made for a permanent group of "foreign service officers" from which the President makes many appointments, chiefly to posts of minor importance.

In choosing diplomatic officers, the President always ascertains in advance whether any particular appointee is personally acceptable to the government to which it is proposed to send him. After his confirmation, the ambassador or minister is given a formal letter of credence, and on arriving at his post he at once enters into communication with the authority in charge of foreign affairs. Ordinarily he is received in audience by the head of the government to which he is accredited, with the ceremonials dictated by the custom of the country.

A diplomatic mission abroad may be closed by various methods. An ambassador or minister may exercise his constitutional right of resigning at pleasure, or he may be recalled by the President. In an extreme case, his retirement may be requested, or he may even be summarily dismissed, by the government of the country in which he is stationed—sometimes a signal of a crisis, if not a war.

Every diplomatic officer enjoys, under the rules of international law, several peculiar privileges and immunities. Any injury or affront to him is an offense against the country which he represents and the principle of international comity. The house in which he resides is under particular safeguards; it may not be entered or disturbed by anyone against his will. He is entitled to special protection while traveling on land or sea. He and his official family, including even his domestic servants, are exempt from arrest—in short, from all criminal and civil processes at all times.

The functions of the diplomatic agent may be given in the language of a report made by the Department of State many years ago. According to this document the duties of an ambassador or minister are not confined to the transmission of instructions from his Government. Official communications, indeed, constitute a relatively unimportant part of his business. He should cultivate friendly personal relations with the officers of the country to which he is sent, so that on proper occasions he may have easy access to them and, having thus gained their confidence in advance, may converse freely with them. It is, therefore, necessary for him to adapt himself to the mode of life of the official classes in the nation to which he is assigned. To do this, he must study its sensibilities, prejudices, form of government, and spirit of public affairs. When issues arise between the United States and its government, he must endeavor to adjust matters as informally and genially as possible, without resorting to official representations or discussions. Thus, the real successes of diplomacy are usually not heralded far and wide, and are unknown save to the few immediately involved in them. As the report concludes, a diplomat does his duty by discharging innumerable daily obligations that attract no attention; and he may be regarded as successful just in proportion to the constant tranquility which he is able to maintain in the relations of his Government with the country in question.

Moreover, long practice has established a certain code for the general guidance of the diplomatic representative.

He is not supposed to act as an agent for the collection of private claims against private persons and companies abroad, but as a matter of fact he does, often on instructions from the Department of State, press the claims of American creditors against the government to which he is accredited. This is the essence of so-called "dollar diplomacy." While theoretically he is not primarily concerned with the advancement of American commercial interests, in fact more than one ambassador has devoted himself largely to that form of enterprise. It is the duty of the diplomatic officer scrupulously to abstain from interfering in local political controversies. It is not deemed advisable for him to make public addresses except on ceremonial occasions, and even then he should be extremely cautious in referring to politics in any form. With decided emphasis, this principle was asserted by the House of Representatives in 1896 in a resolution censuring our ambassador to Great Britain for a speech made in Edinburgh in which he criticized the protective tariff in the United States rather severely.[1]

Anyone who wishes an intimate view of an ambassador at work can find it in the remarkable letters of Walter Hines Page, written during his service at the Court of St. James'. They reveal the serious as well as the lighter labors of an ambassador from day to day. In one of his letters, dated December 22, 1913, he makes the following summary somewhat in a humorous vein:

> If you think it's all play, you fool yourself; I mean this job. There's no end of the work. It consists of these parts: Receiving people for two hours every day, some on some sort of business, some merely to

[1] Every American diplomatic representative abroad has a staff of assistants, varying in number according to the quantity of business in the country to which he is accredited. The first secretary of an embassy or legation should be a man of long diplomatic experience, well acquainted with the officials and the customs of the country in which he resides. Owing to his special qualifications, he assumes, as *chargé d'affaires ad interim,* all the duties of a minister in case of the absence of that official. He enjoys also the privileges and immunities of a diplomatic representative in international law. There is a tendency to attach more importance to the office of secretary of a legation, and to make that branch of the public service more attractive. There are usually two or three additional secretaries and a number of clerks and interpreters.

"pay respects," attending to a large (and exceedingly miscellaneous) mail; going to the Foreign Office on all sorts of errands; looking up the oddest sort of information that you ever heard of; making reports to Washington on all sorts of things; then the so-called social duties—giving dinners, receptions, etc., and attending them. I hear the most important news I get at so-called social functions. Then the court functions; and the meetings and speeches! The American Ambassador must go all over England and explain every American thing. You'd never recover from the shock if you could hear me speaking about Education, Agriculture, the observance of Christmas, the Navy, the Anglo-Saxon, Mexico, the Monroe Doctrine, Co-education, Woman Suffrage, Medicine, Law, Radio-Activity, Flying, the Supreme Court, the President as a Man of Letters, the Hookworm, the Negro—just get down the Encyclopædia and continue the list! I've done this every week-night for a month, hand running, with a few afternoon performances thrown in. I have missed only one engagement in these seven months; and that was merely a private luncheon. I have been late only once. I have the best chauffeur in the world—he deserves credit for much of that. Of course, I don't get time to read a book. In fact, I can't get time to keep up with what goes on at home. To read a newspaper eight or ten days old, when they come in bundles of three or four—is impossible. What isn't telegraphed here, I miss! and that means I miss most things.

I forgot, there are a dozen other kinds of activities, such as American marriages, which they always want the Ambassador to attend; getting them out of jail when they are jugged (I have an American woman on my hands now, whose four children come to see me every day); looking after the American insane; helping Americans move the bones of their ancestors; interpreting the income-tax law; receiving medals for Americans; hearing American fiddlers, pianists, players; sitting for American sculptors and photographers; sending telegrams for property owners in Mexico; reading letters from thousands of people who have shares in estates here; writing letters of introduction; getting tickets to the House Gallery; getting seats in the Abbey; going with people to this, that and t'other; getting tickets to the races, the art-galleries, the House of Lords; answering fool questions about the United States put by Englishmen. With a military attaché, a naval attaché, three secretaries, a private secretary, two automobiles, Alice's private secretary, a veterinarian, an immigration agent, consuls everywhere, a despatch agent, lawyers, doctors, messengers—they keep us all busy. A woman turned up dying the other day. I sent for a big doctor. She got well. As if that wasn't enough, both the woman and the doctor had to come and thank me (fifteen minutes each). Then each wrote a letter! Then there are people who are going to have a Fair here; others who have a Fair coming on at San Francisco; others at San Diego; secretaries and returning and outgoing diplomats come and go (lunch for 'em all); niggers come up from Liberia; Rhodes Scholars from Oxford; Presidential candidates to succeed Huerta; people who present books; women who wish to go to court; Jews who are excited about Rumania; passports, passports to sign; peace committees about the hundred years of peace; opera singers going to the United States; artists who have painted some American portraits,—don't you see?

As we have said, the United States is also represented abroad by consuls, who are primarily commercial agents and perform a large number of routine duties. Consuls are divided into three classes: consuls-general-at-large—traveling representatives who inspect the consulates of the United States throughout the world; consuls-general, who supervise the entire consular systems of particular countries or large regions of the same; and consuls, stationed at innumerable points in every civilized country of the globe. To these three groups may be added vice consuls and consular agents who act as representatives within particular districts under the direction of the regular consul.

Consuls are appointed by the President with the approval of the Senate, subject to the rules of the merit system provided by the Foreign Service Law discussed below (p. 719).

The specific powers and duties of the consular officer are enumerated in the "Consular Regulations of the United States." First and foremost, he is a commercial representative. He must certify the invoices of goods intended for exportation to the United States; and to do this correctly he must have a wide knowledge of the character and value of the commodities produced in his circuit. He must, furthermore, be an expert with respect to every detail of our tariff system in order that he may coöperate with officials at home in securing a correct valuation of imports and in preventing violations of the customs law. An equally important responsibility placed upon the consul is that of reporting trade opportunities and aiding in the extension and increase of

American business—a function considered in detail elsewhere (p. 476).

In connection with shipping the consul has many obligations. When an American vessel touches at a foreign port, the master must deposit his register with the local consul of the United States, and before clearing he must secure the return of his papers. The consul has a limited jurisdiction over disputes between the masters, officers, and men of American ships; he hears the complaints of American seamen and gives relief to them when they are in distress. Upon all matters entrusted to his control, he is expected to make periodical reports to the State Department in Washington, some of which are edited and transmitted to the Department of Commerce for publication.

To crown it all the consul has numerous functions of a miscellaneous character. He administers oaths, takes depositions, authenticates public documents, acknowledges deeds and other instruments, acts as a witness to marriages which occur in the consulate, and administers, under certain circumstances, the property of citizens of the United States dying abroad. In some countries, notably China, Siam, and Persia, our consuls exercise, to a greater or less extent, legal jurisdiction over American citizens within their respective districts. This practice originated in the great differences formerly existing between the law and procedure of many nations and those of the United States—differences which made American citizens unwilling to submit their causes to native tribunals. It once obtained in Japan but, owing to the modernization of Japanese law, it has been abolished there. Now China demands the same emancipation from foreign intervention.

The Development of the Personnel for the Foreign Service

Owing to the technical knowledge required for the discharge of diplomatic and consular duties, it was long evident that the use of the foreign service to reward party workers was open to pointed objections. In 1906, therefore, the consular branch was placed under civil service rules and three years later similar principles were applied to the lower ranges of the diplomatic scale. Finally by the Rogers Act of 1924 the two divisions were merged into one, known as "the United States Foreign Service." This Service is divided into classes and provision is made for admission by examination and for promotion from the lower to the higher stages on the same basis. Members of the Service may be assigned to duty in either branch at the discretion of the President. A Personnel Office and a board of examiners in the Department of State supervise the administration of the Act, and a Foreign Service School gives probationary instruction to candidates who have passed the preliminary examinations. Theoretically the power of the President and Senate to appoint consular and diplomatic officials according to the provisions of the Constitution remains intact, but in practice a large proportion of the selections are now made under the civil service rules. Already many ambassadors and ministers, all to countries of minor rank, have been taken from the "career men," as the members of the Service are called, and precedents are set for a more extensive use of the system.

This reform, of course, has not escaped criticism—some of the most trenchant coming from so distinguished a personage as former Vice President Dawes. Few there are, it is true, who can deny the importance of having trained and experienced men in the consular service and in the lower grades of the diplomatic service, where matters of marked complexity must be handled; but there is cogency in the argument that ambassadors and ministers to the great nations should be selected from citizens of wider business and political experience and larger economic independence than are usually to be found among civil employees even of long standing. More recently citations of favoritism and discriminations affecting consuls have been lodged against officials in charge of examinations and promotions, apparently with some reason. When, however, concessions are made to the critical, it cannot be denied that the Rogers Act of 1924 marks a signal step forward in the development of a more efficient consular and diplomatic personnel. If dangers lurk in the creation of a permanent bureaucracy, the President may break the routine by selecting at will from among citizens of affairs not subjected to its discipline, particularly when international situations calling for special qualities arise. It will not be forgotten that the diplomats who got Europe into the World War were all "trained" and "seasoned;" so-called "shirt sleeves" diplomacy could not have done much worse.

The Treaty-making Power

The Constitution of the United States provides that the President, by and with the advice and consent of the Senate, two thirds of the Senators present concurring, may make treaties; and that treaties so adopted under the authority of the United States shall stand as the law of the land. No express limitations whatever are placed on the treaty-making power; and the question has been raised whether the National Government in negotiating treaties with foreign countries may deal with subjects not entrusted to its jurisdiction by the federal Constitution.

With respect to this point Jefferson laid down four rules: a treaty must concern foreign nations; the treaty-making power is intended to comprehend only those matters which are usually covered by treaty and cannot be otherwise regulated; the rights reserved to the states are excluded from the scope of the treaty-making authority, for the President and Senate ought not to be allowed to do, by way of treaty, what the whole Federal Government is forbidden to do in any way; and finally the President and Senate should not negotiate treaties on topics of legislation in which participation is given by the Constitution to the House of Representatives. Confirming Jefferson's strict interpretation, the Supreme Court once said that whenever an act of Congress would be unconstitutional as invading the reserved rights of the states, a treaty to the same effect would likewise be invalid.

However, in practice these severe limitations are not recognized. Indeed, the courts have sustained a number of treaties relative to matters which are ordinarily handled by state governments and are entirely outside the immediate scope of federal legislative power. For example, several years ago a Russian died in Cambridge, Massachusetts, leaving personal property, and according to the law of that commonwealth a local officer undertook to settle the affairs of the deceased. Thereupon the Russian consul for the district intervened and claimed that, by a treaty between his country and the United States, he had the right to administer the estate in question. On appeal to the courts his contention was upheld and the legality of the treaty expressly declared.

It is also maintained on good authority that the Federal Government can intervene in the administration of the criminal law of a state whenever the treaty rights of foreigners residing within its jurisdiction are involved. In a message bearing on this point President Harrison once said: "It would, I believe, be entirely competent for Congress to make offenses against the treaty rights of foreigners domiciled in the United States cognizable in the federal courts. This has not, however, been done, and the federal officers and courts have no power in such cases to intervene, either for the protection of a foreign citizen or for the punishment of his slayers." Notwithstanding the suggestion, Congress has not yet seen fit to provide special protection for aliens asserting rights against the states under the cover of treaty stipulations (p. 80).

Undoubtedly the power of the Federal Government to make treaties pertaining to matters which are clearly within the sphere of state legislation raises many perplexing questions, and will require far more earnest consideration as our relations with other people increase. An excellent example of the importance of the problem was afforded several years ago by a long dispute over the exclusion of certain Japanese from the regular public schools of San Francisco, which,

Japan claimed, was an infringement of treaty provisions. There is no doubt that federal authorities as such have no power whatever to interfere with the public schools of a state; it may prescribe such conditions of admission as it sees fit, subject perhaps to the due process clause of the Fourteenth Amendment (p. 655). President Roosevelt, however, declared that the action of San Francisco did violate the treaty rights of the Japanese in America and by a firm stand in the case brought about a settlement. Several years later a similar issue was raised by a law in California designed to prevent all aliens "not eligible for American citizenship" from owning or leasing land in that state. Japan took the position that this law also ran counter to privileges guaranteed by treaty to her citizens, but the Supreme Court of the United States placed an opposite interpretation on the act in question, and sustained it, without settling the issue of the treaty-making power itself.

About the same time, another phase of the subject was examined by the Court in a case involving a treaty with Great Britain framed to prevent local hunters from indiscriminately killing migratory birds which make seasonal flights between Canada and the United States. In this instance a state, Missouri, protested against the restriction, claiming that control over wild game within its borders belonged to the state legislature and not to the President and Senate in the exercise of their treaty-making power. But it was overruled. In a clear-cut decision the Supreme Court supported, against the pleas of the state, the validity of the limitation imposed by the treaty on its ordinary authority.

Hence it may be said that while there are theoretically some limits on the treaty-making power, they cannot be defined in the abstract. Beyond question, the President and Senate may conclude with foreign countries agreements touching domestic matters over which the Federal Government normally has no jurisdiction. Such provisions have been sustained by the courts. But this does not imply that the judiciary would not intervene if some vital issue of American life or property were adversely affected by a formal treaty with a foreign government—a remote contingency perhaps.

The Negotiation of Treaties

In the negotiation of treaties, as well as executive agreements and conventions (p. 275), the President has a choice of many devices. He may go abroad and take part in the operation himself as did President Wilson when he participated in the formulation of the treaty that concluded the World War. He may commit the undertaking to the Secretary of State; he may employ an ambassador, minister, or *chargé d'affaires,* or, if he likes, he may select a commission or some private person peculiarly fitted for the task by skill or acquaintance with the language and customs of the country with which the transaction is to be effected.

The extent to which the Senate under its right to advise and consent may participate in the actual drafting of treaties is by no means settled. On the one hand, it has been maintained that it is the constitutional privilege of the President to direct this phase of the work without any interference from the Senate, and that he is merely bound to submit the final document to that body for action. On the other hand, it is claimed by eminent authorities that the Senate should share in treaty-making at all stages, and may even advise the President to undertake a particular negotiation.

Certainly the framers of the Constitution believed that the President should consult the Senate at various steps in the procedure. President Washington once stated to a Senate committee that in all such affairs even oral communications were necessary. He contended that in the course of the business there must naturally arise many issues requiring not only consideration but sometimes an extended discussion which would make written exchanges tedious and unsatisfactory. Early in his first administration, he visited the Senate to lay before it papers relating to the preparation of a treaty with an Indian tribe. He made a brief statement and then put several queries to the members, inviting them to reply in the form of affirmation or negation. Somewhat perplexed by the situation the Senate postponed action on these questions, but finally drew up answers to them.

Although Washington later ceased to make personal visits to the Senate, he frequently directed messages to it asking its advice in connection with the exercise of his treaty-making powers. For example, on one occasion he sent to the Senate three questions relative to the terms of a certain convention. However, he did not always follow this practice, and his successors have seen fit to do so only under exceptional circumstances.

Finding himself in a ticklish position on the issue of the Oregon boundary dispute, President Polk, in 1846, laid before the Senators a draft of a treaty suggested by the British envoy proposing an adjustment of the difficulty, and asked their advice about the decision to be reached in the case. Although he was undoubtedly actuated by peculiar political reasons on this occasion, he justified his conduct by a reference to the practice of President Washington. Thus another precedent was set in favor of executive coöperation with the Senate in the negotiation of treaties.

In later times it became a custom for the Secretary of State to consult influential Senators, especially the members of the committee on foreign relations, as to the advisability of opening conferences with the representatives of foreign powers on particular problems. John Hay, when Secretary of State, frequently asked Senators what they thought of various propositions, whether the subject matter was a proper one for negotiation, and whether other provisions should be incorporated. Senator Bacon expressed the belief that Secretary Hay conferred with many Senators either in writing, or in person, respecting a general arbitration treaty while it was in process of negotiation. Mr. Bacon further said: "I recollect distinctly the Alaskan treaty. Time after time and time after time Mr. Hay, then Secretary of State, conferred with Senators, and, I presume, with all the Senators, as to the propriety of endeavoring to make that treaty and as to the various provisions which should be incorporated in it, recognizing the delicacy of the situation; and the provisions of that treaty were well understood by members of the Senate and approved by members of the Senate before it was ever formulated and submitted to Sir Michael Herbert."

Beyond all question it is wise for a President to be sure of senatorial consent, if possible, before he commits himself to an agreement with a foreign power vitally affecting American life and policy. The constitutional rule requiring the approval of two thirds of the Senators present for ratification nearly always makes it necessary for him to go outside his own party for support. If the opposition can make an issue out of a treaty, it will almost certainly do so. For this reason the two-thirds rule has been the despair of more than one Secretary of State. It has often blocked administrations in their efforts to carry out important policies in the foreign sphere. As Woodrow Wilson remarked on this point in his *Congressional Government,* published many years before his entrance into public life: "The President really has no voice at all in the conclusions of the Senate with reference to his diplomatic transactions. . . . His only power of compelling compliance on the part of the Senate lies in his initiative in negotiation, which affords him a chance to get the country into such scrapes, so pledged in view of the world to certain courses of action, that the Senate hesitates to bring about the appearance of dishonor which would follow its refusal to ratify the rash promises or to support the indiscreet threats of the Department of State."

Long after he wrote these lines, President Wilson dramatically illustrated their truth during his conflict with the Senate over the treaty of Versailles. In the negotiation of that instrument he assumed full responsibility. He did not include among his associates on the peace commission any Senators, either of his own party or the opposition. And on his return with the document, he simply called a senatorial conference and explained to it in more or less detail the various sections of the historic paper. Had he limited the settlement to mere terms of peace, his Republican foes might have hesitated to prevent the formal ending of the war, but he insisted on including in it the Covenant of the League of Nations, involving important changes in future international relations. Even if the Covenant had been acceptable in all respects, the opportunity would have been too good for his critics to neglect. At all events, his treaty went down to defeat in the Senate. Profiting by this experience President Harding put two Senators, a Republican and a Democrat, on his delegation at the Washington arms conference of 1921–22 and President Hoover followed this example in making up the American commission for the London conference of 1930. Discretion in this relation is evidently the better part of valor.

For practical purposes, therefore, we may say that the Senate often insists upon being consulted informally during the course of treaty negotiations; otherwise its approval may not be forthcoming. It does more. It sometimes seeks to originate transactions with foreign countries; and a claim to the right of sharing in such initiation is occasionally made by the House of Representatives. For example, the two chambers once adopted a resolution requesting the President to open negotiations with foreign powers with a view to making arbitration agreements providing for the peaceful settlement of international disputes. With the suggestion the President later complied. Congress even passed an act in 1902 advising the President relative to the terms it wished to see incorporated in a treaty. In reality he cannot ignore the possible action of the House of Representatives in the case of any treaty calling for an appropriation or legislation to put it into effect. This truth was forcibly demonstrated when Alaska was purchased from Russia in 1867. After the treaty had been duly signed and ratified, it required a great deal of maneuvering to secure from Congress the money which the United States was bound to pay in consummation of the bargain.

In this sphere, as in so many others, the spirit of coöperation, barter, and compromise is necessary. However independent in theory the several branches of the Government may be, none of them can proceed entirely without reference to the will and purposes of its neighbors. The generalization applies to treaties as well as to the enactment, interpretation, and enforcement of laws. Doubtless great inconveniences arise from the fact that the President cannot make international agreements on his own authority but must submit them all to the Senate. Still, unless we are to believe in executive infallibility, mistakes equally serious might be made if he did not have to ask for senatorial approval.

After the terms of a treaty are all adjusted with a foreign power, the final draft is laid before the Senate, and it may be approved, amended, or rejected. Like nominations to federal offices, such agreements were once generally acted upon in an "executive session," which was supposed to be secret. But in practice, the transactions were invariably reported by the newspapers in more or less accurate detail, and controversies arising in this connection led in 1929 to the adoption of a Senate rule providing for open sessions unless otherwise specifically decided (p. 166). A treaty rejected by the Senate may be returned to it by the President for reconsideration.

When a treaty is approved by the Senate, it is sent to the President, who ordinarily completes the process by the formal exchange of ratifications with a representative of the foreign country in question. If he sees fit, however, he may refuse to take the final step, and thus prevent a duly signed and sanctioned treaty from going into effect. This power of stopping the procedure rests on the assumption that, through agents of the Federal Government abroad, the President has access to sources of information closed to the Senate, and may discover at a late hour reasons for not seeing the business through to the end.

If a treaty is substantially amended by the Senate, the President may abandon it altogether or he may induce the foreign power concerned to accept the proposed change and bring about the concluding ceremonies of ratification. Often the Senate approves a treaty with "reservations" more or less vital in character. On some occasions such declarations really amount to material alterations in the original instrument and make necessary renewed negotiations with the country or countries involved in the transaction; at other times reservations merely exclude certain American rights from the scope of the treaty or interpret its provisions with more precision or make some high-sounding announcement pleasing to American ears. In cases of this nature the President and the foreign powers engaged in negotiations must decide whether the Senate's action is important enough to call for a reopening of the whole matter. When a treaty is at last completed, it is made a part of the law of the land by an official proclamation. It is enforced by the appropriate authorities and applied by the courts in the same way as any act passed by Congress.

Once consummated, how may a treaty be broken if it does not provide for its own termination? Under international law, each party to the contract may put an end to it by formally denouncing it subject to consequences. What branch of the United States Government can exercise that power? History gives a confused answer. One precedent indicates that the President may do it on his own authority; another, that he may take such action with the approval of Congress in a joint resolution; and a third, that Congress may abrogate a treaty in effect by legislation. Ordinarily, a treaty which has the appearance of permanency and contains no word as to its life will be modified or nullified by the substitution of a new agreement through the regular channels of negotiation. Arbitrary action in the form of outright denunciation by one party is generally viewed as contrary to international courtesy. Discretion, if not manners and morals, suggests that changes be made by the process of conciliation and bilateral understanding, which takes into account all rights and susceptibilities.

Secret Diplomacy

Owing to the scandalous revelations which followed the outbreak of the World War, secret diplomacy has been widely condemned as a peril to world peace. Those revelations showed that each of the two groups thrown into mortal combat had been bound together by secret treaties, agreements, and "conversations" and that the war itself was the immediate outcome of this "conspiracy against mankind." All the important understandings had been made by diplomats and governments without taking the respective peoples into their confidence, without telling the whole truth to the parliaments and the masses that were to pour out blood and treasure to fulfill commitments reached behind their backs. Not until the revolutions in Russia, Germany, and Austria tore open hidden archives did the belligerent nations know to what lengths their diplomats had gone in pledging them to fight and die for causes and on conditions of which they knew little or nothing. At once the cry went up that "secret diplomacy" was a leading cause of wars, a danger and disgrace to humanity. Giving voice to such sentiments, President Wilson put at the very head of his program of Fourteen Points the following principle: "Open covenants of peace, openly arrived at, after which there shall be no private international understandings of any kind, but diplomacy shall proceed always frankly and in the public view." And this creed was incorporated in the Covenant of the League of Nations.

In the United States President Wilson's doctrine was received with great enthusiasm as in accord with American principles. It was pointed out with pride that all treaties negotiated by the President and Senate are published and laid open to the world. But slight attention was paid to the fact that treaties are not the only form of obligation reached with foreign powers. Little or no reference was made for instance to the Gentlemen's Agreement reached with Japan in 1907, the terms of which were not revealed until long afterward. Nor was it known at the time that President

Roosevelt had previously come to a secret understanding with Japan and Great Britain respecting affairs in the Orient (p. 277). It is true that this "conversation" did not bind anyone except the President himself, but the same could be said of the exchanges made between the governments of England and France which united them against Germany—exchanges which Sir Edward Grey, who approved them, pronounced "obligations of honor," in the same breath in which he told the House of Commons in 1914 that it was free to decide whether to fulfill them or not. If treaties cannot be kept under lock and key in the United States, diplomacy certainly can be as secret as the President and the State Department choose to make it.

After the post-war furor over "secret diplomacy" had died away, a calm examination of the new doctrine revealed perils even in "open diplomacy." On second thought it was discovered that ambassadors who carry on clandestine negotiations may seek peace as well as war and that airing the wrangles now kept behind closed doors might make the relations of nations worse rather than better. Equally questionable is the assumption that if all the issues in debate between governments were made public the masses would consistently oppose war and advocate settlement by conciliation and arbitration. Certainly the amount of wrath stirred up by congressional debates over the immigration bill of 1924, as contrasted with the calm settlement of the Japanese exclusion question by President Roosevelt seventeen years before, seemed to indicate that a popular forum is not always the best place to adjust disputes.

If diplomats must publish all they say, then they will inevitably talk for "home consumption," which usually means that they must make stiff-necked demands and appeal to chauvinistic sentiments. Moreover the question can be properly asked: How can we tell when open diplomacy is really open? At best people can only know what their government lays before them as the official view and cannot possibly penetrate into the inner recesses of council chambers. Nor can diplomats be prevented from speaking with one another at dinner tables and over tea cups. Finally, since many questions involve highly technical matters, it is not always possible to present them in simple form for popular debate. Hence, in spite of its excellent appeal, there are material limits on open diplomacy, and risks in it as well.

Open diplomacy is no guarantee against militarism. Democracies may be as warlike as aristocracies when foreign policies are submitted directly to them for decision. Napoleon counted on manhood suffrage to support his imperial projects and his endless campaigns. It is sometimes said that enfranchised women, socialists, and organized labor are the consistent opponents of war and friends of peace. American admirals have repeatedly brought such charges. But there is little evidence in history to bolster up any such argument. If wars were once the trade of princes, that is no longer the whole truth.

Yet the wide-spread distrust of secret intrigues and the agitation over the subject of open diplomacy have undoubtedly had an influence on the conduct of international relations. The fate of nearly all the diplomats who arranged the World War has given caution to those who would follow their ways, were it still feasible. Severely taught by the revelations of the old chicanery, the press has become more canny and more skeptical about official statements and denials. Governments have grown somewhat circumspect. If many of the important sessions of the Washington conference of 1921–22 were held behind closed doors, others were wide open and the grand results were laid before the world in the form of treaties and documents.

It would seem, therefore, that no fixed rule can be laid down respecting the conduct of diplomacy. Wise governments do not make commitments for which there is no popular foundation; and to win that support they do well to formulate policies and understandings which will in the long run promise security rather than adventures. As in so many other cases the problem is one of intelligent discretion on the part of officials and watchfulness on the part of the public. A wider distribution of knowledge concerning the forces at work in international affairs is more important than additional regulations on the technique of diplomacy.

American Foreign Policies

Although in diplomacy, as in law, general propositions do not decide concrete cases, certain fundamental doctrines have received the sanction of the Government of the United States and are supposed to control the conduct of its foreign relations. In fact they have almost taken on the form of dogmas to be applied in that sphere. It is true that they are vague and that their meaning is doubtful. Not long ago an association which investigated one of them by sending questionnaires to leading authorities asking for definitions reported that no consensus of opinion could be reached about its precise character. Nevertheless these doctrines appear constantly in the headlines. They roll out in the periods of orators. They are popular shibboleths approved by millions of citizens who could not give a ten-word account of the inner significance of a single one. But under the cover of their authority important decisions have been reached, precedents established, and commitments made. Every analysis of American foreign affairs must take them into consideration.

First among these doctrines is the dogma of "isolation." It originated in the eighteenth century, before steamships, cables, and the radio had narrowed the oceans and American commercial relations had multiplied in the remotest corners of the earth. The sources of this concept are usually traced to opinions expressed by Washington in his Farewell Address, in which he advised his countrymen to extend their commercial activities, but warned them to have as little political connection with Europe as possible. "Europe," he said, "has a set of primary interests which to us have none, or a very remote, relation. Hence she must be engaged in frequent controversies, the causes of which are essentially foreign to our concerns. Hence, therefore, it must be unwise in us to implicate ourselves by artificial ties in the ordinary vicissitudes of her politics, or the ordinary combinations and collisions of her friendships or enmities. . . . It is our true policy to steer clear of permanent alliances with any portion of the foreign world."

However, the very commercial interests which Washington urged his countrymen to develop in the world's markets have been steadily drawing the nation into the current of world politics. Indeed from his time to our own, the United States has vigorously defended American enterprise in various parts of the globe. Practice frequently belies theory. When the Pasha of Tripoli, discontented with the tribute paid to keep him in good humor, chopped down the American flag, President Jefferson immediately ordered warships to the Mediterranean. By a display of power, the Pasha was driven to terms. A few years later the Dey of Algiers grew restive, complained about the small amount of money which he received, and expelled the American consul-general and American citizens from his territory. At the close of the War of 1812, Congress passed an act for the protection of American commerce against Algerian corsairs; Bainbridge and Decatur, with two squadrons, were dispatched to the scene of trouble, and in a little while the Dey capitulated, agreeing not to levy any more tribute on the United States. Thus by vigorous action the American Government helped to rid the Mediterranean of freebooters.

Again, in 1843, after Great Britain had battered down the Chinese wall of exclusion, the President sent Caleb Cushing to China to obtain for the United States those commercial privileges which had been so recently extended to the British. It was due to American initiative that Japan was opened to Western trade. In 1853 Commodore Matthew C. Perry, in command of a small squadron, and bearing a special message from the President, demanded as a right, not as a favor, "those acts of courtesy which are due from one civilized nation to another;" and by pursuing a stern policy he was able to wring a treaty from the Japanese government in 1854.

The Civil War and reconstruction, arousing as they did such terrible passions at home, obscured foreign affairs for a time in the public mind, but not in the mind of the Government. The thunder of American guns mingled with the roar of British cannon in the bombardment of Kagoshima, undertaken in 1864, to punish the Japanese for firing on a small American ship in their waters. Eight years later American power was established in the Samoan Islands on the strength of a mere commercial arrangement concluded by a naval commander. As early as 1869 President Grant negotiated a treaty for the annexation of Santo Domingo and, though the Senate rejected it, he continued to advocate the idea until the last day of his second administration. Long before the Civil War, the Department of State warned European countries that the United States would not permit any of them to seize the Hawaiian Islands; concessions for a naval station there were obtained in 1887; and the first attempt at direct annexation was made in 1893—five years before the Spanish War was supposed to have made the United States a "world power." That war, therefore, was merely an incident in a long chain of events which were widening the commercial interests of America.

After the conflict with Spain, as before, the Federal Government participated in world affairs. It joined England, Germany, Japan, and Russia in sending troops to China in 1900 to suppress the Boxer Revolt. It sent representatives to the conference at Algeciras in 1906, where a futile attempt was made to adjust European rivalries over Morocco. It took a prominent part in The Hague conferences of 1899 and 1907, when the representatives of nearly all countries considered, if they did not adopt, plans for the reduction of armaments. As a kind of general warning, President Roosevelt ordered a fleet around the world to remind all nations, if they needed a reminder, that America was aware of the nature and uses of the sea power.

In a few years the World War broke in upon the peace of both hemispheres. America was drawn into the vortex as she had been a hundred years before when Europe was devastated by the Napoleonic struggles; and at the conclusion President Wilson, in a quest for permanent peace, urged the country to join the League of Nations. Then a great cry against European entanglements arose; the treaty providing for the League was defeated in the Senate; and the country swung over to isolation—a violent opposition to European "involvements." Under President Harding, separate treaties were made with Germany and Austria, and invitations to take part in the numerous conferences, held with a view to composing the affairs of Europe, were all declined. American troops were withdrawn from the Rhine and the Old World was left to adjust its own fortunes without American official coöperation.

Nevertheless the very same administration, soon after its installation in 1921, called a conference of nine leading powers at Washington to stop the growing rivalry in naval armaments (p. 752). It helped to devise and then entered what amounts to a league of the Pacific nations, in an effort to maintain the *status quo* in that great theater of commercial enterprise. It bound the United States to England, France, and Japan in a "four-power treaty" which pledged the contracting parties to respect the insular territories of one another in the Pacific and to take counsel whenever the possessions of any one of them are threatened. It concerted with the other governments on a settlement of the troubled estate of China. It agreed to a reduction of naval armaments and the maintenance of a fixed ratio in battleships with the chief rivals, England and Japan. These things accomplished, President Harding then urged the country to join the World Court formed under the League of Nations.

While these political events have been taking place the economic ties binding America to the world have grown more numerous and stronger. Americans now play the rôle of bankers to all nations; the bonds of every country are bought and sold on the New York stock market. The American merchant marine and navy have risen from third or fourth rank to rival those of the Mistress of the Seas. American commerce increases. American capitalists hunt and obtain concessions in all the backward places of the earth. American gunboats steam through the muddy current of the Yangtze serving notice that the Government at Washington never sleeps. If the ancient objections to "entangling alliances" are still valid, the theory that the United States can, in its own interest, refuse to take part in world adjustments becomes more doubtful every day. Without being involved in any alliances it has been drawn into the two world wars fought since the opening of the nineteenth century. It can formulate no important policy without affecting the European balance of power. It cannot safely curtail its expenditures for national defense without reaching an agreement with competing countries. No shift can be made in European affairs without affecting its destiny. Hence the creed of isolation which once seemed convincing, unless wisely interpreted, may be employed to defeat its own purpose, namely, the maintenance of national security.

The second fundamental dogma of American foreign policy is the Monroe Doctrine. It originated during the turmoil of Spain's colonial revolutions, partly because the United States really feared the growth of despotism in Europe after 1815, and particularly because American merchants were actively seeking to share the trade of the former Spanish colonies. During her dominion over them Spain had systematically endeavored to monopolize the business of her American possessions; thus the United States and England—the two commercial nations especially eager to develop their interests in Latin-America—were legally excluded from a rich field of enterprise. When in 1808 the Spanish-American colonies began their long struggle for independence, they tasted at last the sweets of freedom. As soon as the conflict started American and English merchants were quick to seize the opportunity of opening up profitable relations with these new states and equally quick to resent all thought of their return to Spanish sovereignty.

Spain, of course, was loath to surrender her colonies and the lucrative traffic with them; but when, in 1820, she was preparing an expedition to put down the independence movement in America, a serious revolution broke out within her own borders and quickly spread over into Italy. At once, Metternich, the conservative Austrian diplomat, invited Russia, Prussia, France, and England to unite in suppressing the development of "revolt and crime." In 1822 the representatives of these countries met at Verona to discuss their common concerns and decide, among other things, what should be done to help Spain. At this congress an attempt was made to devise a plan for aiding her in reconquering her rebellious colonies, although as a matter of fact most of the powers were really in no position to afford military support for the scheme. England, however, refused to agree to cooperate, owing to the liberal spirit prevailing among her people in part, but more especially because her economic interests were certainly on the side of the Spanish colonists with whom she had developed a paying trade.

The United States occupied about the same economic position; and, in view of what seemed a possible intervention in American affairs by despotic European governments, President Monroe, in his message to Congress of December, 1823, called attention to the impending dangers, adding these significant words: "We owe it therefore to candor and to the amicable relations existing between the United States and those powers to declare that we should consider any attempt on their part to extend their system to any portion of this hemisphere as dangerous to our peace and safety. With the existing colonies or dependencies of any European power we have not interfered and shall not interfere. But with the governments who have declared their independence and maintained it, and whose independence we have on great consideration and on just principles acknowledged, we could not view any interposition for the purpose of oppressing them or controlling in any other manner their destiny by any European power in any other light than as a manifestation of an unfriendly disposition toward the United States." In the same message in which this doctrine was announced, there appeared another significant declaration, called forth by a recent decree of the Russian Tsar, claiming the northwest shore of North America down to the fifty-first parallel. With regard to this contention President Monroe said flatly, "that the American continents, by the free and independent condition which they have assumed and maintain, are henceforth not to be considered as subjects for future colonization by any European powers."

In the course of time the principles laid down in this message were officially interpreted to mean that the United States, while observing the existing rights of European nations in this hemisphere, would oppose any intervention interfering with self-government in any country on this side of the Atlantic whose inhabitants had cast off European rule. When a dispute between Great Britain and Venezuela over the boundaries of their respective territories reached an acute stage in 1895, Richard Olney, then Secretary of State under Cleveland, declared that the United States did not propose to help relieve any Latin-American state of its obligations under international law and did not intend in any case to prevent any European government directly interested from enforcing such obligations or inflicting punishment for a breach of them; but he added that the United States would not permit any European country or combination of countries "forcibly to deprive an American state of the right and power of self-government and of shaping for itself its own political fortunes and destinies." The strong stand taken by President Cleveland on this interpretation of the Monroe Doctrine kindled the war spirit; but fortunately the dispute was finally settled by arbitration. Again, a few years later, when Great Britain, Italy, and Germany brought force to bear upon Venezuela for the satisfaction of claims, President Roosevelt stated: "The Monroe Doctrine is a declaration that there must be no territorial aggrandizement by any non-American power at the expense of any American power on American soil. . . . We do not guarantee any state against punishment, if it misconducts itself, provided that punishment does not take the form of the acquisition of territory by any non-American power."

Along with this interpretation of the Monroe Doctrine, as a limitation on European power and influence in the western hemisphere, has gone a correlative theory that the United States must accept, to some degree, responsibility for the conduct of the Latin-American countries which are to be defended against European aggrandizement. This correlative principle President Roosevelt announced in 1904: "If a nation shows that it knows how to act with decency in industrial and political matters, if it keeps order and pays its obligations, then it need fear no interference from the United States. Brutal wrong-doing or impotence which results in the general loosening of the ties of civilized society may finally require intervention by some civilized nation, and in the western hemisphere the United States cannot ignore its duty." Although this assertion by Roosevelt was challenged in a publication by J. Reuben Clark, issued under the auspices of the State Department in 1930, and placed outside the true scope of the Monroe Doctrine, it still stands as an authoritative precedent.

If we put aside all rhetoric and get down to the meat of the matter, we find that the Monroe Doctrine in fact, as Professor David Y. Thomas points out, covers the following elements: European powers are forbidden to take any territory in the western hemisphere; the smaller states in Latin-America, especially in the Caribbean region, must pay all debts owed to foreign bankers, not overlooking, of course, American creditors; the Government of the United States is likely to intervene in one form or another to secure the discharge of such debts; the protection of the Panama Canal and American islands in the West Indies brings the entire Caribbean region within the sphere of our national supremacy; the extensive commercial and industrial interests of American capitalists in Mexico and Central America will be protected by our Government; and "Pan-Americanism will be favored," that is, there will be friendly coöperation between the United States and the powers to the southward as far as that is compatible with the safety and economic advantage of the United States. If in a strict sense, as often urged, the Monroe Doctrine merely concerns American relations with Europe, no such clean-cut conception is possible in practice, for it is seldom feasible to separate the direct dealings of the United States with Latin-American countries from the interests of European nationals in these transactions.

It is proper to add, moreover, that Latin-American states look upon the Monroe Doctrine with mixed feelings. Whenever they are engaged in a controversy with some first-class European power, they are usually happy to seek the shelter of that historic protection. But ordinarily most of their leaders regard the Doctrine as a mere subterfuge which excludes European powers from territorial aggression in the western hemisphere while permitting the United States to buy or annex or assume a protectorate over any desirable territory, such as the Virgin Islands, the Panama Canal Zone, Haiti, Santo Domingo, and Nicaragua. Naturally the statesmen of the United States and those of Latin-American countries do not always see eye to eye on matters of policy in this connection.

Fortunately, however, a new spirit of coöperation is already manifest in two conventions signed at the Pan-American Conference assembled in Washington in 1928—one providing for the compulsory arbitration of legal disputes and the other for conciliation in the case of other controversies not submitted to arbitration. Neither of these agreements makes any reservations respecting the rights of the United States under the Monroe Doctrine and if they are ratified by the Senate they will substitute law and moderation for force in Latin-American international relations whenever the peace of the two continents is threatened.

While placing a bar against European political interference in Latin America, the Government of the United States insists upon an "open door" for American business enterprise in all parts of the world. This third doctrine of foreign policy, which seems to have been suggested by Great Britain, was first given significant application by John Hay, as Secretary of State, in the dispute among the world powers over China at the turn of the nineteenth century. It was embodied in a note to the interested governments suggesting coöperation in seeking "a solution which may bring about permanent safety and peace to China, preserve Chinese territorial and administrative entity, protect all rights guaranteed to friendly powers by treaty and international law, and safeguard for the world the principle of equal and impartial trade with all parts of the Chinese empire." Bearing mainly upon the so-called "backward countries," this doctrine means that other industrial nations, in attempting to establish "protectorates" and "spheres of influence," must not adopt exclusive measures to the detriment of American economic interests, but must open the door to American capital and trade on the basis of an equality of rights and opportunity. In this sense it has been repeatedly emphasized by the State Department in dealing with places as far from the United States as Mesopotamia, Turkey, and Java.

In order of time, the last great principle of American foreign policy, officially proclaimed, is that the conduct of international relations shall proceed on the basis of peace. This doctrine is incorporated in the Kellogg Pact of 1928—duly ratified by the Senate—to which all the leading powers of the earth, including Russia, are now signatories. By Article I of this pact, the high contracting parties "solemnly declare in the names of their respective peoples that they condemn recourse to war for the solution of international controversies and renounce it as an instrument of national policy in their relations with one another." In Article II they "agree that the settlement or solution of all disputes or conflicts of whatever nature or of whatever origin they may be, which may arise among them, shall never be sought except by pacific means."

The sweeping language of this agreement, however, is restricted by reservations. Under its terms, as explained by the signers, nothing "restrains or compromises in any manner whatsoever the right of self defense;" and as every country now claims that its wars are fought solely for such reasons, the loophole seems big enough for any eventuality. Furthermore, according to interpretations, resort to war by one party "would automatically release the other parties from their obligation to the treaty-breaking state." Agreements to resort to arms arising under the Covenant of the League of Nations also stand unimpaired. Likewise the defensive alliances concluded between France and certain powers in Eastern Europe are in effect excluded from the scope of the Pact. By way of a supplement, the British Government has declared that the renunciation of war does not apply to those regions of the world which have a special interest for British peace and safety. According to a tacit understanding, the Monroe Doctrine is not affected by this "outlawry of war." Hence it is difficult in speaking of this dogma of foreign policy, as of the others, to say just what it may mean in any concrete case of controversy and conflict. Nevertheless, subject to qualifications, the Government of the United States has renounced war as an instrument of national policy, has pledged itself to seek the solution of all disputes by pacific means, and by the Washington and London compacts on naval construction (p. 752) has set its face against the competitive race in armaments so certain to lead to armed conflict in the end.

In signing the London treaty, President Hoover laid special emphasis on the conciliatory aspects of the achievement. "It will renew again," he said, "the faith of the world in the moral forces of good will and patient negotiation as against the blind forces of suspicion and competitive armament. . . . It will mark a further long step toward lifting the burden of militarism from the backs of mankind and speed the march forward of world peace. It will lay the foundations upon which further constructive reduction in world arms may be accomplished in the future." So, to the long line of official declarations on the American policy of peace is added another avowal in the same tenor.

International Government

Thus far American international problems have been treated as if they involved only specific cases handled in the negotiations of diplomatic and consular officers at home and abroad. Important as are actions of this character, they by no means cover the whole field of foreign affairs. Under the newer spirit of coöperation between countries, which springs out of commitments to world peace and the pressure of technological development, a second method of managing their relations has been evolved. As the thirteen states left in the wake of the American Revolution joined in creating the Federal Government to deal with various common problems, so a higher integration of nations into limited world governments has occurred. In a somewhat similar manner several international organizations have been established by treaties drawn up in conventions, composed of representatives speaking for the interested states, and properly ratified. The super-governments thus formed are not occasional diplomatic assemblies, but permanent bodies which take over from the contracting parties definite phases of their work that are international in scope. As a great power, the United States has inevitably been drawn into the web of agencies which now envelops the earth, and has helped to give direction to this form of unification.

The most general international government in existence to-day is the League of Nations, a product of the World War. By the ratification of the peace treaty with Germany at the close of that conflict, or through subsequent arrangements, fifty-four countries have bound themselves together in the League and have assigned to it certain functions in connection with their common relations. In its fundamental structure the League is composed of three bodies: a permanent secretariat, located at Geneva; an Assembly consisting of one delegate from each country, dominion, or colony included in the association; and a Council embracing representatives of France, Germany, Great Britain, Italy, and Japan and representatives of nine other states, chosen by the Assembly.

The obligations accepted by the powers included in the League are numerous and important. They all agree to respect and preserve, as against external aggression, the territorial integrity and the existing political independence of each member. They bind themselves to submit to arbitration or inquiry by the Council every dispute which cannot be adjusted by diplomacy. Should any member disregard its agreements, its conduct would be considered an act of war against the entire association, and the members would be bound to cut off the trade of the disobedient state. The Council would then recommend to the affiliated governments the appropriate military measures. In accordance with the terms of the original Covenant, the League has taken steps to formulate a scheme for the reduction of armaments and has established a Permanent Court of International Justice. It has also created numerous important committees to study and report on issues of great international consequence.

To the League of Nations the United States bears a peculiar historical relation. President Wilson was largely instrumental in the establishment of this association and expected that the United States would join it; but the Senate, by refusing to ratify the Treaty of Versailles, failed to take that step. Besides rejecting President Wilson's program, the Government of the United States, under President Harding, adopted a policy of coolly ignoring communications from the Secretary-General of the League. Not until the new organization had been in operation for many months did the Department of State choose a more courteous course and at least reply to letters, if formally and negatively. When, however, the League commenced to hold conferences dealing with serious problems in which the United States was obviously concerned, the Federal Government began to send official representatives to act "in an unofficial and consultative capacity." Later, for this somewhat curious action, was substituted the practice of authorizing regular representatives to attend particular conventions held under League auspices. For example, in 1927, the Government of the United States was officially represented at four meetings of this character—on economic affairs, transit and communications, import and export prohibitions and restrictions, and preliminary disarmament arrangements. Speaking as Secretary of State, Charles E. Hughes declared that there was no more difficulty in dealing with the League than with the nations separately in connection with matters in which the United States has an interest.

Carrying forward the principle enunciated by Secretary Hughes, President Hoover indicated his willingness to "coöperate with the League's endeavors to promote scientific, economic, and social welfare, and secure limitation of armaments." In 1929 the Senate set important precedents by ratifying two conventions drawn up by the League with respect to abolishing slavery and controlling restrictions on international trade. As a matter of fact the United States officially participated in the meeting at which the latter agreement was formulated. Moreover during the same year, American delegates took part in conferences on other international questions held under League auspices, including one on the equitable treatment of foreigners and foreign business. In recognition of its obligations, the Federal Government even made a contribution towards the League's expenses in connection with certain arrangements to which it was a party. Although such transactions involve no commitment to the political guarantees of the League of Nations, they show that the United States is prepared to work with it in adjusting some international relations of high significance.

Indeed, since more and more of the international business once handled in special assemblies is naturally passing under the jurisdiction of the League, the United States must negotiate with its agencies or take the impossible position of insisting that separate institutions shall be set up for its particular benefit.

A second international association, known as the Pan-American Union, has been established to deal with problems arising in North and South America. Covering a smaller portion of the globe, it naturally has less authority than the League of Nations, measured in terms of membership and responsibility. Nevertheless it has potentialities for peace and stability in the two Americas. The governing board of this Union consists of the Secretary of State, representing the United States, who acts as president, and delegates chosen by the member countries of the western hemisphere. Conferences are held from time to time at which resolutions and conventions are adopted for subsequent ratification by the affiliated nations. Already treaties thus formulated provide for a specific degree of protection to copyrights, patents, and trade marks and for the submission of international disputes to arbitration and conciliation (p. 740). The Union also endeavors to promote closer cultural and commercial relations among the several members by maintaining at Washington a central office which serves as a clearing house for the collection and dissemination of information and acts as a secretariat.

While the League of Nations is the only world association political in nature, a number of special international institutions have been created and endowed with limited functions. Thus there are two judicial bodies for hearing disputes that arise between nations. The first of these, the Court of Arbitration, was founded at The Hague as a result of a conference held in 1899. It consists of a large panel of judges, chosen by the nations participating in the convention, from which a tribunal is selected for each case when it comes up. With respect to methods, the Court seeks to adjust conflicts between nations by effecting compromises rather than by rendering decisions under the forms of international law. Consequently it is not a permanent body but is constituted anew for each occasion and its procedure is more conciliatory than judicial in the strict sense of the word. Although the signatory nations, of which the United States is one, are not compelled to submit any controversies to it, they may do so voluntarily.

The second international judicial body is the World Court, a product of the League of Nations. It is a permanent tribunal of judges elected by the Assembly and Council of the League from among the distinguished jurists of the world. Its seat is also at The Hague where sessions are held regularly every year. To this Court certain nations are bound by treaty to bring all international disputes of a specified character. Other countries, that have not so strictly committed themselves, may voluntarily and by agreement lay before it causes over which they have differences of opinion. In either case the World Court considers the issue with reference to the ever-growing body of international law, and renders its decisions on the basis of the legal merits involved, thus differing from the Court of Arbitration mentioned above.

Although the World Court was founded by the League of Nations, governments not affiliated with that association were invited to join it, and the United States had to take the question under consideration. After a long and acrimonious discussion, the Senate in 1926 ratified a proposal to accept, with numerous reservations touching American rights. When these restrictions were found to be unsatisfactory to the other contracting parties, a substitute project was worked out under the supervision of Elihu Root representing President Coolidge. Duly signed, this agreement is now in the hands of President Hoover awaiting transmission to the Senate for its final approval.

Besides the connections just described, the United States is represented in more than twenty special international executive bodies created by treaty. Some of these institutions are primarily concerned with the collection and dissemination of technical information. The International Bureau for the Publication of Customs Tariffs, as its name implies, belongs to this class. So too does the International Prison Commission which handles data relating to the prevention and repression of crime and to prison systems. Other governmental agencies of an international character seek to secure uniformity throughout the world in specific matters. Thus the International Bureau of Weights and Measures is responsible for the development and maintenance of the universal metric standards of length and mass with which the national standards of the several contracting countries are compared. It also determines certain physical constants and fixes their numerical value. In this way the Bureau prevents the endless confusion which would result from differences in the systems of nations—a confusion which would seriously affect the nature of competitive bidding on goods bought and sold in the general market. In the absence of such arrangements international trade could not be conducted on a rational basis.

Other international bodies assume regular administrative burdens; such, for instance, as the Universal Postal Union (p. 423). A few operate equipment in international undertakings; for example, the International Ice Patrol in the Atlantic Ocean, consisting of vessels managed by an American personnel under international treaty, is engaged in promoting safety of life at sea quite irrespective of the flags which steamers may fly. The expenses of its maintenance are shared by the chief beneficiaries (p. 397).

In the case of the International Joint Commission organized by Canada and the United States in 1909, the actual regulation of certain proceedings in both countries by a common governmental agency has been tried with success. This body is composed of three members from each power, six in all. Any person who desires to use or to divert specified waters along the boundary between the two countries must first secure its approval. In making decisions, it can go beyond a mere verdict on a proposal; it may also lay down the rules under which the particular development is to take place and supervise their enforcement. Already about fifteen problems have come before it for settlement and under its auspices works have been speedily undertaken that otherwise would have involved a long exchange of "messages" between the diplomatic officers of the two governments. The larger possibilities of such technical cooperation are emphasized by the fact that the conclusions on all the issues mentioned above have been unanimous.

Thus foreign policy, conforming inevitably to growing intercourse and communication as facilitated by technology, tends to run in channels of peace and rationalization, while the war machine invented in days of simple and isolated economies grinds away on its ancient bearings, usually accompanied by belligerency. It would seem, therefore, that the next adjustment which looms on the horizon of civilized nations is that of subordinating force to the continuing requirements of business enterprise and cultural interchange. New situations inexorably bring new relations in human affairs.

CHAPTER XXIII

The War Machine

No function of government has been more completely revolutionized by technology than warfare. Not a phase of that ancient art—equipment, drill maneuvers, or combat methods—remains untouched by machinery, power, and chemistry. Its history, of course, dates from the dawn of the world when cave men fought with clubs and stones; it comes down to the latest hour when the echoes of the most awful conflict ever waged are still ringing throughout the earth, and feverish preparations for future struggles are going forward almost unabated amid all the efforts to establish peace on a firm footing. During the long state-building process, it has been one of the most powerful, if most terrible, factors in social evolution. Even the United States, traditionally a land of peace, was born in a revolutionary war for independence and has been four times engaged in armed contests with foreign powers, to say nothing of its own Civil War and minor clashes with Indians, Mexicans, Filipinos, Haitians, Chinese, and Russians. But whatever its rôle in the past, war has entered a new stage since its instrumentalities have been basically altered by science and invention and its consequences made ruinous to the life of nations founded on modern means of communication and transportation.

In the presence of the dreadful phenomenon of war, minds react in different ways. There are those who regard it as a noble occupation, productive of idealism and good. Thus said Treitschke, the German political philosopher: "Without war no state could be. All those we know of arose through war, and protection of their members by armed force remains their primary and essential task. War, therefore, will endure until the end of history, as long as there is a multiplicity of states. The laws of human thought and human nature forbid any alternative; neither is one to be wished for. . . . It is war that fosters the political idealism which the materialist rejects. What a disaster for civilization it would be if mankind blotted its heroes from memory. . . . To appeal from this judgment to Christianity would be sheer perversity, for does not the Bible say that the ruler shall rule by the sword and again that greater love hath no man than to lay down his life for his friend? . . . God above us will see to it that war shall return again, a terrible medicine for mankind diseased." Among large classes of all countries this faith in war as a nursery of virtue still remains.

At the other extreme are the pacifists, who contend that war is a stupid, brutal, and degrading way of disposing of international disputes, that it never settles any question on the basis of right, and that it leaves in its wake nothing but hatred, suffering, debts, and disorder. Between the extremes are those who believe in defending our country against aggression, but think vaguely about the subject, hope that war will never occur again, fear that it may, and insist on a certain degree of preparation for it without reference to any particular exigency.

Where is the truth to be found? What are the standards by which to measure the military and naval needs of the country—the material equipment necessary merely to defend it against armed assault? These questions, though vital to the whole issue, are seldom asked, much less discussed. Certainly they can only be answered by reference to national ideals and ambitions, for the degree of military preparedness needed by a nation is determined by its geographical location, the power of its potential enemies, and by the character of the foreign policy which it pursues. Separation of ends and means is a fundamental mistake. The stubborn reality of this statement is illustrated by the experience of Great Britain between 1906 and 1914. During that period her Foreign Office was carrying on secret negotiations with France and Russia which bound the British government by ties of honor to come to the aid of those two countries in case of a war with Germany; and yet the British people knew nothing of these pledges and no adequate military preparations were launched by responsible statesmen to support their own commitments. To be sure, arrangements were made to land English troops on the Continent, but only a handful of soldiers were organized for the undertaking.

On the whole it can be safely said that, like the British, we have never had a consistent theory of national defense aligned clearly with our diplomacy. Menaced by no formidable neighbors along our land boundaries, we have been content with a small standing army. Until the growth of our industries brought a high pressure for foreign markets and the Spanish war added imperial domains, little attention was given to the upbuilding of the navy. Previous to that conflict, when our territory was nearly all compact and on the North American continent, it was thought that good coast defenses would suffice. But the development of commerce and the acquisition of insular possessions from Spain changed the whole face of things. It then became clear that it would be necessary to have a large navy to defend the new territories in two oceans in case of a war with a first-rate European or Asiatic power.

Thereupon naval appropriations began to rise rapidly. By 1912 the United States stood next to Great Britain in the amount spent annually for defense on the high seas. A few years later the extinction of Germany's fleet in the World War left America the second naval power in the world. Moreover, the rapid launching of battleships between 1914 and 1921 and the adoption of an elaborate program for new construction indicated that the United States would soon have the greatest navy on earth. Then came the Washington conference (p. 735) which halted for a term of years the race for supremacy in capital ships, gave Great Britain and America equality in such vessels, and placed Japan next in rank. This adjustment was followed by the London Conference of 1930 at which the United States, Great Britain, and Japan reached a restrictive agreement respecting battleships, airplane carriers, cruisers, destroyers, and submarines, subject to the right of any of the three powers to increase its allotted tonnage if its "requirements of national security" are materially affected by the construction of a fourth party outside of the understanding. Yet none of these efforts at stabilization have substantially allayed anxiety over preparedness or brought disarmament appreciably nearer. If they have reduced somewhat the tension of competitive building, they have not established international confidence.

Neither our rapid naval development nor our attempts to check it by international agreements have been accompanied by a clear definition of the responsibilities to be assumed by the people of the United States on the world stage. Do they intend to retain the Philippines and take an active part in the quarrels and unrest of the Orient? Then one military and naval policy is appropriate. Do they intend to draw back on the Hawaiian base? Then another is fitting. Do they propose to support American capitalists and merchants through thick and thin in their search for foreign markets? If so, the nature of the military requirements is apparent. It is not necessary to give more illustrations of the fundamental fact that the character and strength of military and naval forces should be determined with reference to the foreign policy which the people intend to pursue.

In spite of the obvious nature of such reflections no philosophy of war in its relation to diplomacy, world economy, national destiny, or ideals of the good life has ever been formulated in the United States. It is true that years ago Admiral Alfred Thayer Mahan, in many volumes, traced the historical relation of the sea power to the rise and growth of nations and that Major General Emory Upton, in a work on the military policy of the United States, demonstrated the haphazard character of past preparations for national defense; but these works, though excellent in themselves, do not attempt to cover the whole domain of war as a phase of social evolution. No American writer has conceived, in this connection, any great work comparable to the technical masterpiece of General Von Clausewitz, *Vom Kriege* (concerning War) or the analysis of the subject in Heinrich von Treitschke's *Politics*. Nor can it be said that the Government or people of the United States have pursued with consistency any particular theory or program, or have brought their thinking in this sphere into harmony with action or action into harmony with reasoned policy.

This state of affairs is due, of course, to many circumstances and cross-currents of opinion. Historically war was once primarily the craft of princes, feudal aristocracies, and professional soldiers. When the American colonies were being founded, the middle classes of England were finally breaking the military might of the monarch and his feudal supporters. Although mercantile classes, no less than their predecessors, have employed armed force as an instrument of economic advancement, war has not been to them a major interest or sport or calling. It has been, on the contrary, an incident to the pursuits of peace. And it was from mercantile and agricultural classes that the American colonists were drawn. If they waged war against the Indians and French on many occasions, it was not because they consciously regarded fighting as a virtue to be pursued for its own sake, but rather because they looked on it as a necessity associated with winning land and economic opportunities.

On the whole, the Fathers of the Republic believed that war was principally a wicked trade of princes and tyrants, and that the United States, by keeping out of the brawls of Europe, might steadily enjoy peace as a national blessing. If, being practical men, they took into account the possible recurrence of war and made ample provision in the Constitution for defense, they did it with reference to the chances of life, not in praise of war as a manly exercise. By and large, the creed of peace, scorned by feudal aristocracies as the craven ethics of commercial huckstering, became a kind of national tradition, although nearly every generation after the establishment of independence passed through an armed conflict. Even while condemning pacifists privately as weaklings, cowards, and near-traitors, President Roosevelt never publicly exalted war as a virtue in itself but only when waged for a "righteous" cause. President Wilson branded it as an evil and called on the nation to help him "end war." It is not surprising, therefore, that some haziness exists in the American mind on the subject of armed combat and its uses in world economy.

Owing to the strength of this heritage it is assumed in some quarters that military preparation and action in the United States are connected merely with "national defense," not with war as an instrument of policy in general. Here too theory and practice are confused. Nothing in the Constitution lends any color of sanction to this view of military utilities. Congress has the power to declare an aggressive war as well as any other kind. It opened hostilities on Spain in 1898, not because that country had any idea of attacking the United States, but for the purpose of carrying into effect certain resolutions with regard to Spain's colonial possessions. Only during recent years has the notion got abroad in wide circles that a deliberate war on a neighboring country for reasons of state is immoral.

Perhaps this is due to the disillusionment that followed the recent world conflict, especially the eagerness with which the participants accused their enemies of being criminally responsible for it and proclaimed their own innocence. At all events it caused such a great agitation that the leading nations of the world signed the Kellogg Pact in 1928 (p. 741) renouncing war "as an instrument of national policy," outlawing it as such, and admitting it only as a means of defense. In the light of what is said above it is questionable whether the Kellogg Pact is strictly constitutional, whether the President and Senate by treaty can in fact renounce or take away from Congress the power to employ war for any purpose it chooses—a power which it certainly enjoys under the Constitution and has more than once exercised. Yet the Kellogg Pact has established as an official creed the rule that war is to be used only to defend the country against assaults.

However this new rule may influence the future direction of foreign affairs, it has had no effect on military preparations for coming contingencies and all except those pacifists who make peace a matter of conscience generally agree that such safeguards shall provide for "adequate defense." No other phrase falls more frequently from the lips of the army and navy authorities. Statesmen who speak warmly in favor of peace always supplement their declarations by repeating it. Yet the slogan which passes current as if it were hard money is never closely scrutinized. Defense must be adequate, but adequate to what purpose, against what foreign power or association of powers? Although it is popularly assumed that "America can whip creation," even the most optimistic advocate of this doctrine can scarcely hope to provide means sufficient to cope with any possible combination of countries that might be aligned against the United States. Hence in the most extensive preparations there inheres a large measure of uncertainty and inadequacy. Indeed, on analysis, the word "adequate" becomes about as hazy as a fog.

Nor is the term "defense" self-explanatory. Defense of what? Defense of the people residing in the continental United States? Defense of all the races and nationalities inhabiting American dependencies in the Caribbean and the Far Pacific? Defense of American citizens in China or any other country on the globe where disorders are likely to do damage to their persons and property? Defense of American merchant vessels on the high seas and in all the ports of the world? Defense of American investments wherever they may be endangered? Although a former Secretary of the Navy once declared that the arms of the Government must be strong enough to hold all these territories, persons, things, and intangibles within their embrace, it cannot be said as yet that this theory has been formally adopted as a national resolve. If it were accepted, nothing very precise would be settled, for it covers too many imponderable factors and, besides, nobody knows what it implies in terms of war machinery. Defense of national territory is fairly definite, but military protection for persons and property in foreign lands is not so easy to calculate. As a matter of fact the Government of the United States has renounced, by a treaty made at the Washington conference, the right to fortify the Philippine Islands and accordingly the provision of "adequate defense" for them, whatever that may mean.

To make matters more complicated, neither defense nor attack—even where possible enemies are agreed upon and the persons and things to be protected are well known—is an exact science. No doubt military preparations must bear some material relation to natural configuration: rivers, mountains, and seas, but inventiveness continually introduces new mechanical devices which rapidly render obsolete the best calculations concerning these aspects of nature. The airplane, for example, scorns the highest mountain barriers and the widest rivers. Tradition and accepted practice at a given moment prescribe certain military equipment and maneuvers but, as the surprising developments of the World War demonstrated, hopes respecting the efficiency of fighting gear can be rendered futile almost over night. Owing to their hidden potentialities, science and invention have revolutionized the character of historical warfare with its established organization and routine methods. A man with a test tube in a distant laboratory may upset the designs of the most competent general at the battle front. At no time has warfare, with its variable human factors, been a question of mere mathematics; in the modern age its claim to precision has become still more dubious.

It is not only research and mechanical inventions that have introduced bewilderment into the "science of national defense." Modern wars are conflicts of civilizations as well as of military engines. Railways, industries, finance, newspapers, education, religion, propaganda, and even art are all involved in it. Strength at the front depends upon organizing abilities behind the lines, upon capacities of endurance among the people, upon ideas circulating among them. The conduct of a civil government may undermine, even inadvertently, the strength of its military forces. In turn the methods of the military director may destroy the faith and economy of those upon whom he depends for support. The great care which the belligerents in the World War took to formulate moral "aims" designed to encourage their friends and disconcert their foes is proof that thought, no less than machines, figures in armed combats, especially in this age of universal literacy, education, and democracy.

It is scarcely necessary to cite additional illustrations to show that war and preparations for war involve more than mere problems in military engineering. Both hang fundamentally upon the activities of private citizens at home and abroad, especially in commerce and finance, and upon the tactics pursued by the Government. Until policy is clearly defined military men cannot make their reckonings with any degree of accuracy. On the other hand, if they are given a free rein in accumulating engines of war, they may in fact so change the attitude of foreign countries as to work a revolution in the position of the civil government in spite of its intentions. An excellent example of this operation is afforded by the action of the naval party in Germany before 1914 in building up a competition with Great Britain which accelerated, if it did not produce, the radical shift in the European balance of power that finally overwhelmed the Central Empires. Military and civil policy evolve together; they are parts of the same thing. Decisions in both spheres are full of fate.

Since, then, the degree of preparedness should depend upon the character of the Federal Government's foreign policy and complicated social situations, it is obviously impossible for American military and naval officers to claim any special authority on the subject. At best their expertness is limited to machines. It is their business to determine, as well as they can, what engines of war are necessary for defense and offense under specific circumstances. It is the business of the American people to decide what kind of foreign tactics is to be pursued. Unfortunately there has never been and is not now a coördination of armed forces with diplomacy. Whether we have one, two, or three hundred thousand men in the national army or a small or large navy is determined largely by sentiment, tradition, interested lobbies, and guesswork. Doubtless the War and Navy Departments conduct their studies and make their preparations on general assumptions as to possible wars with certain potential foes, but they do not know just how the diplomatic operations of the Government will turn out in the long run. Neither does Congress or the President. Those who know most speak with the least assurance.

Relation of Civil and Military Authority

Fearing military control, the founders of the American Republic sought to establish firmly the supremacy of civil authority. "The liberties of Rome," explained the *Federalist,* "proved the final victim to her military triumphs; and the liberties of Europe, as far as they ever existed, have, with few exceptions, been the price of her military establishments. A standing force is therefore a dangerous, at the same time that it may be a necessary, provision. On the smallest scale it has its inconveniences. On an extensive scale its consequences may be fatal. On any scale it is an object of laudable circumspection and precaution." In their great fear of the army during the Revolution the leaders of the movement almost lost the war by failing to make adequate provisions for its support. And when they framed the Constitution they took great care to assure civilian dominance or, to speak more precisely, the supremacy of Congress and the President over the military branch of the Government.

This supremacy is asserted in numerous provisions. The right to declare war is vested in Congress alone. Likewise the power to raise and support armies is entrusted entirely to it, with an express condition that "no appropriation of money to that use shall be for a longer term than two years." To Congress is granted by the Constitution full authority to make rules for the government and regulation of the land and naval forces, to arrange for organizing, arming, and disciplining the militia of the states, and to provide for calling forth the militia to execute the laws of the Union, suppress insurrections, and repel invasions. In a word, the size of the military and naval forces, their structure, and their use in war are to be determined by Congress. Finally, a civil officer, the President, is made commander-in-chief of the Army and Navy in war and peace. And repeatedly in the course of American history, Presidents have endorsed and emphasized civilian supremacy. Jefferson made it a special point in his first inaugural address. Long afterward, Coolidge, in an address at the Naval Academy, referred to this essential American tradition and laid stress on it anew, lest it be forgotten.

Yet a declaration of abstract principle does not easily dispose of all concrete cases that arise in adjusting the relations of civil and military authorities. Although the armed forces of the United States do not form a caste founded on a feudal aristocracy, they are, in a way, an estate in themselves. Members of Congress, Presidents, and heads of departments come and go; army and navy officials are permanent. Necessity, if not professional interest, compels them to be alert in demanding men and supplies, for they are in constant peril of being forced by popular excitement into a war without preparations adequate to its exigencies. This has happened more than once in American history and soldiers have paid in blood and tragedy for civilian neglect. Experience no less than ambition, therefore, leads military and naval officers to consolidate their energies and to insist upon the continual enlargement of the resources at their command. Like every other class, they likewise strive for an increase in the powers, honors, and emoluments of their division.

Still, in the absence of outside support, the military authorities of the United States would ordinarily have little strength as against the civil branches of the Government. Their weight in numbers and direct economic pressure is not great. But enlisted on their side are powerful private interests—industrialists who annually sell millions of dollars' worth of munitions, chemicals, airplanes, ships, and other war materials to the Government. Partly out of patriotism and partly for practical reasons, these capitalists subscribe to private societies engaged in propaganda for increased armaments, and sometimes, it seems, employ agents of their own to promote policies likely to multiply their profits. For example, an investigation initiated by the Senate on motion of President Hoover in 1929 showed that three important corporations, which did a lucrative business building warships for the Government, had hired a professional agitator to represent them at the Geneva conference on the reduction of armaments, two years before, and had made large expenditures with a view to securing congressional aid for the mercantile marine—an auxiliary arm of naval defense. Inevitably such incidents make it difficult for Congress to differentiate between military proposals founded on the merits of the situation and those which arise from interested machinations. It is on this ground that many advocates of civilian supremacy demand that the Government manufacture its own munitions without profit to anyone, or at least "take all the profits out of war."

The relations of civil and military authorities are not only complicated by the difficulties of preparation. They are usually badly strained in time of war over problems of command and direction. "No politics in war" is one of the most popular slogans in military circles and, if by this is meant that the petty job brokerage common to vulgar intrigue should be entirely shut out, its force cannot be gainsaid. But in the truer sense of statesmanship, politics cannot be excluded from war without peril. It is easy, of course, to cite horrible examples of political interference with strategy, especially from the experience of the Civil War, but mere illustrations do not prove the case. An armed conflict, as we have said, calls into play other forces than those of military engineering; in fact, all the social and economic energies of civilization. Command at the front cannot be separated from management behind the lines. And the training which fits an army officer for his special operations does not necessarily fit him for mobilizing material and sentimental resources; indeed, by its emphasis on mechanical routine, it often fails to reckon with many of the vital human factors involved. Moreover military officers must be appointed, promoted, and demoted by someone. If this function is entrusted to military men alone, then politics is simply transferred to the army; there is no way of assuring the automatic rise of the highest competence to the top. Nor are combat operations themselves of such a purely technical character that military officers can divine their mysteries with mathematical infallibility.

For every case of civilian blundering in preparations and wars can be cited a similar instance of military blundering. This proposition is demonstrated with adequate proof in the work on the German Republic by Arthur Rosenberg already cited (p. 18). There he shows that in the old German system the selection and promotion of military officers were kept entirely separate from parliamentary politics and vested in the Supreme Commander, the Kaiser, subject only to advice from army circles. During the World War the military authorities of Germany actually took over the direction of the civil government as well as all strategy of combat. And the history of their conduct in this crisis is a history of great mistakes in every department. As a matter of fact the military leaders differed among themselves as violently as did the civilians with regard to measures to be taken in their own field. In the end they lost the war and were overthrown by revolution. War is a branch of sociology, not a mere engineering science. Hence there is more hope for national security in civilian supremacy than in military dictatorship.

The Peace Footing

In making provisions for military operations the authority of Congress is practically unlimited. There are no restrictions of any moment on its power to prepare, call citizens to the colors, incur debts, build ships, spend money, and commandeer the economic resources of the country. Likewise the scope of the President's sovereignty as commander-in-chief under the Constitution and under acts of Congress is free from any substantial restraints so far as the exigencies of war are concerned.

The armed forces of the United States are divided into two branches: military and naval. The former consists of three general divisions: the Regular Army, the National Guard (formerly the state militia), and the Organized Reserves. Under acts of Congress the strength of the Regular Army is kept at approximately one hundred twenty-five thousand men on the average. On the other hand the number of men in the National Guard depends on the fluctuating enlistments in the local contingents which compose it. Although each of the states maintains a certain control over its own section of the National Guard, all the militiamen are organized, equipped, and disciplined in accordance with standards fixed by federal laws and are subject to the constant supervision of the War Department. At any time the Guard of every state may be called into national service and it is, therefore, for practical purposes a part of the federal military system. Since the total enrollment of the National Guard at present is about one hundred eighty thousand, it brings the active land forces of the Union up to approximately three hundred thousand men. Supplementing the Regular Army and the National Guard are the Organized Reserves, with two wings: the Officers' Reserve Corps and the Enlisted Reserve Corps, both composed of men who have received a minimum training prescribed by the War Department. Besides its officers and enlisted men for ordinary naval duties, the United States Navy has a special branch, known as the

Marines, available for service on land and water. All of these divisions of the armed forces of the United States are recruited by volunteers in time of peace.

To supply officers for the Army a Military Academy is maintained at West Point; while a Naval Academy at Annapolis performs a similar service for the Navy. For advanced work the Government conducts the Naval War College at Newport and the Army War College at Washington, D. C. In choosing men for West Point and Annapolis provisions are made for preventing favoritism to any section of the country or any single class. Moreover civilian control over practically the whole selective process makes it impossible for either the military or naval authorities to confine the choice of men to their own circles, and prevents the erection of a hereditary caste. As a guarantee against centralization the great majority of the admissions to both institutions are distributed among states, congressional districts, and territories, and in these instances the selection is determined by a Senator, Representative, or territorial delegate as the case may be. As a guide he may prescribe a competitive examination or he may use his own discretion. Other appointments are made by the President and the Vice President. Then come special arrangements. Under recent legislative enactment, a number of places in each institution are allotted to the sons of veterans who were killed in action or died of wounds or diseases contracted in the World War. Finally, with a view to encouraging students taking military training elsewhere, certain openings are made at West Point for "honor graduates" from colleges and other institutions offering military courses under United States Army officers and for men selected from the enlisted ranks of the Regular Army and the National Guard.

Supplementing the historic institutions for educating army and navy officers is a nation-wide system of military training designed to reach civilians through colleges, universities, other institutions of learning, and citizens' camps. This work is divided between a Senior and a Junior Reserve

Officers' Training Corps. The former branch includes colleges and universities which grant degrees and private military schools. Higher institutions deriving benefits under federal land grants must give military instruction; elsewhere it is voluntary. Under the head of the Junior Reserve Officers' Training Corps come other public and private educational institutions, including high schools.

Theoretically the aim of these arrangements is to prepare the youth of the nation, through the schools, for military service in times of emergency. In furtherance of the purpose the Government invested, during the academic year of 1929–30, over two and one half million dollars in training approximately one hundred thirty thousand young men and boys scattered among the universities, colleges, and high schools of the country. Although the extent of the system appears impressive, on analysis doubts about its efficiency have arisen in Congress. R. A. Collins, for example, speaking in the House of Representatives on January 10, 1930, declared that "In its anxiety to attract all these young men the Army has discontinued bayonet work and many other unpleasant features of the training. Every effort is made to attract the boy to join for what he can get out of it personally—free uniforms, rifles to shoot, horses, military circuses, and so forth."

Mr. Collins then went on to cite instances showing that cavalry horses were provided for college polo matches, that pretty girls were made honorary officers of units, that the training was made a substitute for gymnasium exercises in graduation credit from high school, and that other inducements having no relation to military discipline were offered. He felt, therefore, that such a policy "brings back the romance to military service which was so greatly damaged by the experience of that generation which saw the mud of the trenches in the World War," without forwarding the cause of genuine preparedness. Besides giving students little insight into the nature of actual service, such as that demanded of the American soldiers who went through the holocaust of the World War, the reserve-officer system, according to Mr. Collins' figures, fails to hold their interest after they have been "disciplined" at public expense. Out of the 147,402 enrolled in the Reserve Officers' Training Corps in 1929 only 5790 felt the lure of the service strongly enough to join the Organized Reserves subject to call in time of war. This fact, it is urged, shows that "the War Department is wasting money on boys who are too young for serious military work."

Indeed it must be confessed that these elaborate provisions for subsidizing the National Guard and introducing military training into colleges and schools are largely makeshifts. They are due in part to the eagerness of the states to shift to the Federal Government a portion of the burden of supporting their own militia and in part to the defeat of all schemes for universal military service at the close of the World War. Doubtless the rejection of these proposals sprang from popular fear of huge military establishments and their possible consequences as illustrated by the plight of Europe. But whatever may be said for the existing military arrangements of the United States as "the best that can be obtained in the circumstances," they certainly cannot be characterized as ideal. What then is the alternative?

In the present stage of social evolution, force is necessary to preserve order and defend the national heritage. How shall it be provided? Besides the schemes already discussed there is universal service, illustrated, for instance, by the Swiss militia army, founded on a democratic basis, relying fundamentally on a rank and file drawn impartially from the whole body of males between the fixed age limits and subjected to regular and continuous discipline for a definite period. Such an army is not likely to be the tool of despotism, like the *janissaries* of ancient Rome. It does not interfere with the ordinary processes of national education. It is economical because the money spent on it produces results rather than hopes or mere volunteer reserves. It combines some of the best features of the American militia, as historically defended, with the possibilities of adequate discipline. But if the recent legislation of Congress is a correct gauge of popular temper, the people of the United States are more inclined to maintain the present aggregation of expedients than to make a drastic reorganization of the whole foundation of national defense.

In matters of administration, the Army and Navy of the United States are under the control of the Departments of War and Navy respectively, subject always to the President of the United States, who in peace and war is commander-in-chief of the armed forces of the country. The Secretaries of these departments are nearly always civilians without practical military or naval experience. They are political officers, men of the President's party, appointed by him with the consent of the Senate. It is their prime duty to form a connecting link between the technical men on the one side and the civil government on the other. In addition to supervising the establishments committed to their charge, they must prepare estimates of expenditures and lay before Congress plans for maintaining and improving the efficiency of the fighting machine.

The distribution and movement of the land forces in time of peace are determined partly by legislation dividing the country into military departments and divisions; the assignment of the naval forces is likewise subject to acts of Congress; but the President has a large discretion in this relation. He may order troops, battleships, and various war craft to ports in any quarter of the globe or, as did President Roosevelt in 1907, send a fleet on a voyage around the world. The exercise of such personal authority is of great significance, whether it is a matter of preparing for eventualities, demonstrating foreign policy, or precipitating hostilities.

The United States on a War Footing

No idea of the military potentialities of the Federal Government can be gained, however, from a mere survey of the Constitution and the laws designed for times of peace. American military power in action can only be understood in terms of the measures employed in an actual conflict, such as that waged with the Central Powers of Europe in 1917–18.

That titanic struggle gave a new aspect to war, its requirements, and its dreadful possibilities. In previous contests, the armies in the field and the civilians engaged in making supplies for them included only a part—usually a small part—of the total populations concerned. In the World War, whole nations were mobilized. It was estimated that from three to twenty adults were required to keep a single man on the firing line. If we take the most conservative figure and recall that the grand total of men in the United States army (including the marines) at the moment of greatest strength, on the day of the armistice, was 3,703,273, we see what a modern war involves in terms of civilian strength to sustain it. It means that virtually the whole nation must be in the ranks or at work in support of the armed forces on land and sea. As President Wilson said: "In the sense in which we have been wont to think of armies, there are no armies in this struggle. There are entire nations armed. . . . It is not an army that we must shape and train for war; it is a nation."

For the purpose of meeting this extraordinary situation, Congress discarded the practice of relying on volunteers to supply the necessary recruits. After associating the National Guard with the Regular Army for immediate action, it adopted early in the war the principle of compulsory enrollment. It placed under liability to serve all male citizens and all male persons (not alien enemies) who had declared their intention to become citizens, making certain exceptions in the case of public officers, ministers, and a few other groups. It then fixed the age limits to extend from twenty-one to thirty inclusive—later from eighteen to forty-five. All men within this classification were required to register. Quotas were assigned to the several states and territories according to population. And from the official lists were chosen by lot the number of men needed for the war.

To make easier the burden of the men called to the colors, Congress organized a scheme of financial assistance. It provided for the payment of allowances to their families and to those relying in whole or in part upon their earnings. It established a project for compensation covering all cases of disability or death. These arrangements for automatic grants were then supplemented by a system of relatively inexpensive insurance which permitted members of the armed forces to make further provisions for themselves and their dependents against hazards.

While drawing upon the man power of the nation for war on a vast scale, the Federal Government likewise mobilized its economic resources. The President was given full authority by Congress to requisition and fix the price of supplies for the army, to prescribe regulations governing marketing, to determine the price of wheat, coke, and coal, and, if necessary, to take possession of and manage factories, mines, packing houses, and other plants essential to war purposes. By a special proclamation the President placed the railways immediately under government control, and designated the Secretary of the Treasury to act as director-general. This executive stroke Congress supported by passing a law laying down the conditions under which the Government was to operate the railroads for the period of the war and not to exceed twenty-one months following the return of peace. A short time afterward the express, telephone, and telegraph systems were taken over by the Government. Coastwise and high-seas shipping was likewise placed entirely at its disposition and an Emergency Fleet Corporation was created to rush the building of ships. These positive measures were amplified by legislation which forbade the deliberate destruction of necessaries for the purpose of enhancing prices, the restriction of production, the committing of waste, and attempts to monopolize commodities. By the Sabotage Act heavy penalties were laid on all persons who willfully destroyed war materials or interfered with their production.

To carry into effect this policy of material mobilization, numerous federal agencies were erected. The War Industries Board, a planning commission, was empowered to bring essential industries under government control, speed up their output, distribute the orders for supplies among concerns best fitted to fill them expeditiously, and coördinate these functions in such a fashion as to prevent waste, duplication, and delay. A subdivision of this establishment, the Priorities Board, was charged with the duty of guiding industries and public officials in "the production, supply, and distribution of raw materials, finished products, electrical energy, fuel, and transportation," and of prescribing rules for assuring preference to those materials and activities necessary to meet the pressing war needs of the Government, always in the ratio of their importance. In order to bring international trade within the circle of organized economy and conserve military resources, Congress created the War Trade Board and made it responsible for supervising commerce with foreign countries. The enforcement of provisions for mobilizing food and fuel supplies was committed to the Food Administration and Fuel Administration respectively.

In connection with marshaling and administering labor forces, three important agencies were established. The Employment Service, in the Department of Labor, opened employment offices throughout the country, enrolled eligible men and women, and aided in placing them in useful positions, especially in the war industries. To the War Labor Policies Board, in the same Department, was entrusted the task of evolving principles to be applied in determining wages, hours, and working conditions in public and private enterprises connected with emergency production. But despite these efforts of the Government to assure satisfactory terms of employment, strikes and disputes interfered with business in many parts of the country. Accordingly there was created in

April, 1918, a War Labor Board, to which was committed the function of adjusting controversies arising between employers and employees in war industries. Although the Board had no power to compel capitalists and workmen to accept its decisions, it could bring heavy pressure to bear on them, for the President of the United States had full authority to seize the factories of employers who would not yield and to deprive strikers of their immunity from the draft if they refused to abide by awards officially made. A hint to the wise was often effective.

It was not only physical and material resources that were brought under strict official supervision during the war. Public opinion and the agencies connected with it—the press, churches, schools, colleges, and universities—were also mobilized. An Espionage Act, approved June 15, 1917, provided heavy penalties for everyone who attempted to communicate to any foreign nation information to the injury of the United States, who willfully made or conveyed false statements with intent to interfere with the operations of American forces or promote the success of their enemies, or who willfully sought to cause disloyalty, insubordination, mutiny, or refusal of duty among members of the Army and Navy of the United States. Extending these principles beyond strictly military requirements, the Sedition Act, approved May 16, 1918, penalized all persons "who use abusive language about the Government or institutions of the country, who advocate or incite any curtailment in the production of war materials, and who by word or act favor the cause of an enemy country." Even the postal service could be closed by the Postmaster General against any person who tried to use the mails for "seditious" purposes. To prevent indirect communication with the enemy, a Censorship Board was set up and granted full power to scrutinize letters, telegrams, and messages directed to neutral countries. Then a special propaganda was instituted under a Committee on Public Information which furnished literature bearing on the aims, ideals, and accomplishments of the Government and spread millions of books, pamphlets, and leaflets to the four corners of the earth.

Although the duty of waging war is laid primarily upon Congress and the President, the coöperation of the state governments is an important factor in the actual conduct of hostilities. During the conflict with the Central Powers, the various states of the Union created councils of defense to help in carrying out federal policies. They enacted laws touching military education, aid to soldiers and their dependents, and espionage. They promoted the formation of local organizations to assist federal officials in administering the draft laws, conserving food, and sustaining a favorable public opinion.

Speaking summarily, no power over the possessions and opinions of citizens deemed necessary for the successful prosecution of the war was withheld from the duly constituted authorities. The farmer's wheat, the housewife's sugar, coal at the mines, labor in the factories, ships at the wharves and on the high seas, trade with friendly countries, the vast national railway system, banks and stores, private riches, lands, and houses—all were mobilized and put under the obligations made imperative by the requirements of war. Never before were labor and capital, industrial and natural resources, public opinion and private conduct so completely subjected to governmental direction in a common undertaking. Never before was war waged on such a scale with all the engines of power that human will and intelligence could command.

In organizing and carrying forward this great war enterprise, the Federal Government, of course, made enormous expenditures which had to be met by taxation and by the sale of interest-bearing bonds. When the proposition to raise the armed forces by selective draft was presented, it was greeted by the contention that "wealth as well as men should be conscripted." In a strict sense this meant that the entire cost of the conflict should be laid immediately upon the possessors of large fortunes and incomes and that no debts should be incurred for future generations to pay. In practice Congress adopted a middle course. The total outlays of the Government, apart from debt charges and postal operations, between the declaration of war on April 6, 1917, and October 31, 1919, are estimated by the economist, Davis R. Dewey, at approximately thirty-five billion five hundred million dollars, including loans to Great Britain, France, and other associates in the war. Of this total about thirty-two per cent was met by revenues from taxation and kindred sources and sixty-eight per cent from loans.

In devising its great war-revenue measures, Congress departed from the principle of "ability to pay." It increased the indirect duties on consumption in many directions—for example, on tickets to places of amusement, the sale of automobiles, tobacco, soft drinks, and "luxuries." On the other hand, however, it imposed heavy and progressive taxes on incomes rising steadily in percentage with the amount of the income, graduated taxes on inheritances based on similar principles, and excess profits taxes on corporations and partnerships. "This," says E. R. A. Seligman, "is the high-water mark thus far reached in the history of taxation. Never before in the annals of civilization has an attempt been made to take as much as two-thirds of a man's income by taxation."

Notwithstanding the burdensome taxes laid on personal incomes and on the earnings of business enterprises, notwithstanding official efforts to control prices in the public interest, enormous profits were made out of the war. Of this there can be no doubt. Many speeches were delivered on the subject in Congress setting forth indubitable facts, although the attempts of a few members to secure a scientific and comprehensive analysis of all the pertinent data were consistently blocked. Important materials for such a study, of course, lay in the tax returns of the Treasury Department, but they were not all brought out into daylight. It was only after a hard struggle on the floor that the Senate carried in 1918 a resolution calling upon the Treasury for a list of all corporations which had reported earnings of fifteen per cent or more on their capital stock in 1917, with comparative tables showing their profits for 1916.

In compliance with this resolution, the Treasury, in July, 1918, stated that approximately fifty-five thousand corporations had made fifteen per cent or more on their capital stock in 1917 but supplied figures for only thirty-one thousand five hundred of this number. Thus in spite of specific instructions, it withheld some of the information requested by the Senate. Furthermore only a few copies of its report were printed so that the document did not enter into general circulation. Yet incomplete as the figures were, they revealed huge profits in nearly every line of industry and increases in the gains of 1917 over those of the previous year in a large majority of the industries covered by the survey. According to another reckoning from general tax returns, all corporations in the United States combined made between January, 1916, and July, 1921, a clear profit of thirty-eight billion dollars over and above all federal charges, including those on excess profits—a sum more than equal to the total war expenditures of the Government between 1917 and 1919.

Revelations of this character provoked an outburst of protests and led to a demand for effective provisions against repetition of the experience. The American Legion, in urging upon Congress the enactment of a universal draft law as a preparation for future wars, advocated a general measure which will place "at the disposal of the Government without profit to any one person, the men, money, and material resources of the nation." Both the leading political parties endorsed the sentiment. President Coolidge declared in 1926 that "any future policy of conscription should be inclusive, applicable in terms to the entire personnel and the entire wealth of the whole country." But nothing has been done to translate this theory into legislation. Many who want to conscript men, do not wish to "frighten capital" by heavy taxes. Others who favor "conscripting wealth" do so because they think it will help to prevent wars. Indeed

Photo by Brown Brothers

Preparing for War in the Machine Age: a Federal Armament Factory.

it might act as a deterrent. [illegible]ce for various reasons, Congress has not yet been able [illegible] agree upon a bill that will satisfy claims from all quarters. It was not until after a long debate that the sponsors of the idea could carry a resolution in 1930 authorizing the President to appoint a commission to inquire into the possibility of taking profits out of war and report a project by the close of the following year.

Discussions of the issue, at any rate, serve to emphasize the fact that war and preparations for it are costly. They were costly in the old days of small armies and simple engines of destruction. They are many times more expensive in these days of embattled nations and massed economic power. Even before the World War revealed the financial significance of armed conflicts under the régime of modern technology, the Government of the United States spent about seventy-two per cent of its total annual outlay in getting ready for war and in discharging obligations arising out of past hostilities; while approximately twenty-eight per cent was devoted to the civil functions. During the fiscal year ending June 30, 1920, ninety-three per cent of the billions paid out of the federal treasury went for army and navy maintenance, pensions, interest on the debt, and other purposes connected with military affairs. In the same period only one per cent was spent for what Dr. E. B. Rosa, of the Bureau of Standards, classified as scientific and educational functions unrelated to warfare.

The Care of Veterans

The occupation of the soldier and sailor is admittedly highly dangerous and involves elements of great sacrifice. Men who risk their lives in battle, as well as their dependents likewise liable to hardships, are therefore entitled to particular consideration from the nation they help to preserve. Recognizing the unusual character of this service, the Federal Government early inaugurated a policy of making financial and other rewards to its veterans and to certain classes of their relatives. [illegible] equal appropriateness war nurses, whose skill and lab[illegible] e indispensable in such large-scale hostilities, are also brought within the scope of this legislation. While the entire responsibility might theoretically devolve on the National Government alone, the widespread desire to render tribute to patriotic valor knows no political boundaries. So the states often supplement national schemes and voluntarily assume a part of the burden.

The outstanding feature in the existing federal program of assistance for veterans and related classes is the pension system through which the Government of the United States makes periodical payments of money to those coming within the range of the law. In the course of time certain principles—highly complicated in detail—have been evolved in this connection. All men released at the close of each war are not automatically pensioned. The number is too large and those who are able-bodied when mustered out can usually take care of themselves.

In practice, therefore, the Government directs its attention at the end of a conflict to providing for honorably discharged members of the service whose earning power has been adversely affected by injuries or sickness arising from military duties and for the dependents of the men who lost their lives. At the initial stage the Government undertakes to make allowances to all persons in these categories in proportion to disabilities or the nature of the dependency—paralleling the policy generally pursued in industry in workmen's compensation projects.

As time thins the ranks and wage earners become infirm on account of advancing years, the scope of the scheme is widened to include those who are suffering from disabilities no matter how acquired, unless by willful misconduct, and their dependents. Outstanding examples of this type of pension are afforded by two Acts of 1930 dealing with veterans of the Spanish War and the World War—the former carried over a veto by President Hoover. Under the first of these measures all Spanish War veterans and nurses with a record of ninety days' service who are suffering from any mental or physical disability that incapacitates them for performing manual labor are entitled to a pension proportioned, within limits, to the degree of their inability to earn a livelihood. The second pension act applies similar principles to World War veterans who are afflicted by at least a twenty-five per cent disability and whose income for the year preceding their application is so low as to exempt them from the payment of a federal income tax.

A third stage is reached at a still later period when the number of possible claimants is further reduced. At this point the range of the pension system is widened to include practically all veterans of the war in question and their dependents, irrespective of disabilities however incurred. For instance an amendment to the Civil War pension acts, passed in 1930, allows seventy-five dollars a month to veterans of that conflict and forty dollars a month to their widows—with certain exceptions. Those veterans who are seriously disabled are paid at the rate of one hundred dollars a month. Finally it should be said that such universal provisions are supplemented by congressional grants to particular groups and individuals who are outside the scope of the general laws or are believed to be deserving of extraordinary consideration. Between 1897 and 1928 approximately sixty-six thousand special acts of this character were put on the federal statute books.

The pension, using the term in its broadest sense, is not the only recognition given by the Federal Government to those who serve it in arms. At the close of the World War a wide-spread agitation arose in favor of paying a bonus or "adjusted compensation" to all soldiers and sailors enlisted for that conflict, whether they saw fighting or not, whether they were injured or not. With a good deal of justification it was said that they had offered their lives to their country while civilians had made profits out of its necessities or had received the highest wages ever paid in the history of American industry. At all events the issue was carried into

Congress and at length in 1924 a bill was passed granting compensation to veterans of the War who had conducted themselves honorably, at the rate of $1.25 per day for overseas service and $1.00 per day for home service. This was in fact a form of "conscience money" and was not, like the pension, related either to disability or age. Those entitled to small sums under the law were paid outright in cash and those whose allowance ran to more than fifty dollars obtained it in the form of life insurance certificates. The total cost of the adjusted compensation act as of October 1, 1928, was placed at approximately three and one half billion dollars.

Still a third type of federal financial aid to former soldiers and sailors has been developed in recent times. Veterans of the World War are now given the right to take out a limited amount of life insurance under the auspices of the United States Government. The rates charged on these policies are low, for the Government assumes the cost of administration and all the extra risks involved in insuring persons liable to premature death on account of injuries or other disabilities incurred in service. In other words the veterans are put on the same footing as the civilians who did not go to war and may secure insurance at ordinary commercial rates. Under this scheme they have an additional advantage; excess earnings of the Government accruing from the insurance system are distributed among the policy-holders. Furthermore, in case of need, a veteran has the privilege of securing loans on his policy through local banks or the Veterans' Bureau of the United States Veterans' Administration. On October 1, 1928, life insurance amounting to about three billion dollars was outstanding, demonstrating the significance of this feature of federal assistance.

Finally, the Federal Government makes institutional provisions for the afflicted. Veterans of the World War who suffer from ailments incurred as a result of that conflict are specifically entitled to medical treatment free of charge at a number of designated hospitals and coöperating agencies.

Besides this, the veterans of the several wars have at their disposal a number of federal institutions under the Veterans' Administration. The National Homes for Disabled Volunteer Soldiers, outstanding examples of this class, accept honorably discharged soldiers, sailors, marines, and nurses who have seen service and are so infirm or disabled that they cannot earn a living. Admirably functioning as auxiliaries to the miscellaneous federal institutions are many state homes, locally supported and managed, to which veterans are admitted usually under very generous regulations.

Although formerly scattered among various agencies of the Federal Government, the management of this complicated system of pensions, compensation, and relief has now been concentrated by executive order under an act of 1930 in a single Veterans' Administration, headed by a chief appointed by the President and the Senate. Thus the Pension Bureau formerly in the Department of the Interior, the soldiers' homes previously attached to the War Department, and the Veterans' Bureau, an independent establishment, are united under one head to eliminate overlapping and duplication. As President Hoover stated in giving effect to the new law, this was "one of the most important steps taken in the reorganization of the Federal Government," and should contribute materially to the efficiency of administration.

As may be imagined from the above legislative outline, the cost of veterans' aid has been and still is enormous. According to conservative figures the outlay for this purpose between 1792 and 1930 reached a total of more than fifteen billion dollars and the end is not yet in sight. Approximately eight hundred million dollars is now spent annually on the veterans of the World War, with prospects for rapid increases in the near future. Actuarial authorities estimate that the last of these veterans will live until about 1997 and that many dependents will survive them. Hence payments for pensions and the maintenance of hospitals and homes will remain a duty of the Federal Government until the turn of the century—even if future wars do not indefinitely extend the obligation.

In the best of circumstances the formulation and administration of pension and compensation systems, it cannot be denied, are accompanied by perplexing difficulties. To do equal justice to all veterans similarly situated is far from easy. To prevent waste and fraud—as demonstrated by the frightful scandal in the Veterans' Bureau a few years ago—calls for almost superhuman watchfulness. It requires no special capacity, to be sure, to provide by law that those who suffer from "a ten per cent disability" shall receive a fixed sum per month and that the amount shall be increased by stages *pro rata* up to a one hundred per cent disability. But the determination of the degree of infirmity in every case is left to fallible officials, subjected always to heavy pressure from interested parties, and exact justice to all applicants is well-nigh impossible. Moreover Congress is constantly besieged to widen the scope of each law and increase the payments allowed under it. Schemes for showing favoritism to special groups can be readily cloaked by a sentimental appeal to patriotism. With due respect to all the obligations fairly involved it may be safely said that this branch of federal activity is constantly in need of public scrutiny and competent direction to assure equal treatment for veterans of every class and scrupulous efficiency in operation.

DEPARTMENT OF STATE

Secretary of State.
Undersecretary.
Assistant Secretaries.
Office of Foreign Service Personnel.
Economic Adviser.
Historical Adviser.
Divisions:
- International Conferences and Protocol.
- Current Information.
- Treaty.
- Far Eastern Affairs.
- Latin-American Affairs.
- Western European Affairs.
- Near Eastern Affairs.
- Mexican Affairs.
- Eastern European Affairs.
- Passport Control.
- Foreign Service Administration.

Commercial Office.
Foreign Service School.
Visa Office.
Bureau of Accounts.
Bureau of Indexes and Archives.

DEPARTMENT OF THE TREASURY

Secretary of the Treasury.
Undersecretary.
Three Assistant Secretaries.
Commissioner of the Public Debt.
Bureaus:
- Narcotics.
- Industrial Alcohol.
- Mint.
- The Budget.
- Farm Loans.
- Engraving and Printing.

Comptroller of the Currency.
Treasurer.
Commissioner of Internal Revenue.
Public Health Service.
- National Institute of Health.

Coast Guard.
Commissioner of Accounts and Deposits.
Secret Service Division.
Customs Service.
Supervising Architect.
Division of Appointments.
Division of Supply.
General Supply Committee.

D

Secret
Assista
Chief c
- Pe
- Mi
- Op
- Su
- Wa

Arms:
- Inf
- Ca
- Fie
- Co
- En
- Air
- Sig

Trainin
Adjutan
Service
- Ins
- Ju
- C
- Ch
- Ch

Bureaus
- Inst
- Mil

Current
Industria
Procur
Organize

BIBLIOGRAPHICAL NOTE

Primary Sources

Copies of the Constitution of the United States annotated as to Supreme Court decisions are available in many works, notably the *Rules of the House of Representatives.*

The general and permanent statutes of the United States are to be found in *The Code of Laws of the United States of America, in Force December 7, 1925* (Government Printing Office) and the *Supplements,* published periodically bringing federal legislation up to date.

Annual and special reports of the several Departments, agencies, and establishments can be secured by writing directly to the chief officer. Access to the huge mass of documentary material published by the Federal Government may be obtained through catalogues issued under the auspices of the Superintendent of Public Documents, Washington, D. C. On receipt of an inquiry, he will send a catalogue of materials bearing on any subject published by the Government.

For current affairs *The United States Daily,* published privately in Washington, is simply indispensable. Composed entirely of official reports, statements, and papers and well-indexed, it keeps citizens abreast the latest developments in the National Capital.

Chapter I

Although there is a library of works on the influence of technology on economics, no comprehensive study of its relation to government has ever been made. For brief surveys: H. L. McBain, "Government," in *Whither Mankind* (1928), and L. W. Wallace, "Engineering in Government" in *Toward Civilization,* (ed. by C. A. Beard, 1930). There is a useful small German work, S. Hartmann, *Technik und Staat.* For the difficulties of government by the masses in the machine age, R. Michels, *Political Parties* (1915), chap. ii. C. D. Burns, *Government and Industry.* A vast mass of raw materials is contained in reports of the various establishments of the Federal Government, especially those which have to do with the regulation and promotion of economic interests. For theories relative to the economic aspects of politics, C. A. Beard, *The Economic Basis of Politics,* and *Economic Origins of Jeffersonian Democracy;* C. M. Walsh, *Political Science of John Adams* (1915); A. Ireland, *Democracy and the Human*

Equation (1915). There is a huge literature on "intelligence testing." An excellent introduction is C. Spearman, *Nature of Intelligence* (1927). For witty and penetrating reflections under this head, W. Lewis, *The Art of Being Ruled* (1926). For citizenship in the new conditions, S. Eldridge, *The New Citizenship,* a suggestive study in the organization of public opinion; F. G. Wilson, "The Pragmatic Electorate," Political Science Review, Feb., 1930.

Chapter II

The various chapters of this volume are illustrations of the way in which the simple words of the Constitution can be stretched to cover a bewildering number of governmental enterprises. The older commentaries by Kent and Story are still useful. For a modern commentary, W. W. Willoughby, *On the Constitution of the United States,* 3 vols., 2nd ed. For the case of Marbury *v.* Madison, J. A. C. Grant, American Political Science Review, August, 1929, pp. 673 ff.; A. J. Beveridge, *Life of John Marshall,* Vol. III, chap. iii. Illuminating comments on the psychological process of judges, A. Lief, *The Dissenting Opinions of Mr. Justice Holmes;* Beveridge, *op. cit.,* Vols. I and II, dealing with the education and views of John Marshall previous to his elevation to the bench; for the case of the appointment of Justice Holmes, see *Selections from the Correspondence of Theodore Roosevelt and Henry Cabot Lodge,* Vol. I, pp. 517 ff.; also the *Congressional Record,* February–May, 1930, for debates in the Senate on the appointment of Charles E. Hughes and J. J. Parker. For the function of criticism in the development of public law, F. J. Goodnow, *Social Reform and the Constitution;* F. Frankfurter, *Mr. Justice Holmes and the Constitution* (1927). There is no complete history of the amendments to the Constitution. H. V. Ames, *Proposed Amendments to the Constitution of the United States,* is excellent but does not cover the recent period. For the Fourteenth Amendment in particular, B. B. Kendrick, *Journal of the Joint Committee of Fifteen on Reconstruction.* H. L. McBain, *The Living Constitution* (1927), best brief analysis; C. Warren, *The Supreme Court in United States History;* J. A. Smith, *Spirit of American Government* (1907) and *Growth and Decadence of Constitutional Government* (1930).

Chapter III

For the general student, J. W. Burgess, *Political Science and Constitutional Law* (2 vols.), is still excellent, though not up to date. Valuable summaries of judicial decisions by R. E. Cushman are published periodically in the American Political Science Review, giving clues to the latest opinions.

On the separation of powers, F. J. Goodnow, *Politics and Administration* and H. J. Ford, *Rise and Growth of American Politics* (1898).

Civil liberty: Z. Chafee, *Freedom of Speech* (1920) and *An Inquiring Mind* (1928); W. Lippmann, *American Inquisitors* (1928); B. N. Cardozo, *Paradoxes of Legal Science* (1928); G. Seldes, *You Can't Print That* (1929); *Report on Illegal Practices of the United States Department of Justice* (National Popular Government League, Washington, D. C.); J. A. Ryan, *Declining Liberty* (1927); L. Post, *The Deportations Delirium of 1920.*

Judicial supremacy: article cited from A. T. Hadley, The Independent, April 16, 1908.

Suffrage and citizenship: E. M. Borchard, *Diplomatic Protection of Citizens Abroad* (1927); A. J. McCulloch, *Suffrage and Its Problems* (1929); J. L. Tenny, *All about Naturalization* (1926); J. T. De Bolt, *Naturalization of Aliens* (1924); F. A. Cleveland, *American Citizenship as Distinguished from Alien Status* (1927); W. Weinstein, *Immigration Laws and Rights of Aliens* (1926).

Chapter IV

H. F. Bruce, *American Parties and Politics;* R. Michels, *Political Parties* (1915), on European methods primarily but illuminating for American affairs; J. K. Pollock, *Party Campaign Funds* (1926); H. M. Rocca, *Corrupt Practices Legislation* (1928); R. C. Brooks, *Political Parties and Electoral Methods* (1924); M. R. Carroll, *Labor and Politics* (1923); A. N. Holcombe, *Political Parties of Today* (1924), indispensable for the economic composition of parties and factions; F. R. Kent, *The Great Game of Politics* (1923), by an observant journalist; M. Ostrogorski, *Democracy and the Organization of Political Parties* (1902), the second volume devoted to American politics; K. H. Porter, *National Party Platforms* (1924), historical collection; P. O. Ray, *Introduction to Political Parties and Practical Politics;* S. A. Rice, *Farmers and Workers in American Politics* (1924); E. A. Robinson, *Evolution of American Political Parties* (1924); E. M. Sait, *American Parties and Elections* (1927); C. A. Beard, *American Party Battle* (1928); S. Lewis, *Party Principles and Party Politics* (1928); S. Lewis, *Readings in Party Principles and Practical Politics* (1928); C. E. Merriam and H. F. Gosnell, *American Party System* (1930); J. W. Davis, *Party Government in the United States* (1929); E. R. Sikes, *State and Federal Corrupt-Practices Legislation* (1928); W. B. Graves, *Readings in Public*

Opinion (1928); W. Lippmann, *The Phantom Public;* L. H. Jenks, ed., *The Future of Party Government* (1929). For a penetrating criticism of loose notions about democracy, T. Geiger, *Die Masse und Ihre Aktion* (1926), a sociological study.

Chapter V

C. W. Bunn, *Brief Survey of the Jurisdiction and Practice of the Courts of the United States* (1927); J. N. Claybrook, *Federal Courts* (1928); F. Frankfurter and J. M. Landis, *Business of the Supreme Court* (1927); W. F. Willoughby, *Principles of Judicial Administration* (1929); J. A. Bent, *Independent Judiciary* (1925); C. N. Callender, *American Courts* (1927); J. H. Ralston, *Study and Report for American Federation of Labor upon Judicial Control over Legislatures as to Constitutional Questions* (1923); J. Dickinson, *Administrative Justice and the Supremacy of Law in the United States* (1927); C. Warren, *The Supreme Court in United States History;* F. Frankfurter and N. Greene, *The Labor Injunction* (1930). For political controversies over judicial authority, C. Warren, *Congress, the Constitution, and the Supreme Court* (1925); C. G. Haines, *American Doctrine of Judicial Supremacy;* C. A. Beard, *The Supreme Court and the Constitution;* F. E. Melvin, *Judicial Bulwark of the Constitution.* A. Langeluttig, *The Department of Justice of the United States.* M. Spahr, *Supreme Court on the Incidence and Effects of Taxation* (1925); C. Warren, *Supreme Court and Sovereign States* (1924); H. W. Jessup, *Bill of Rights and Its Destruction by Alleged Due Process of Law* (1927); F. J. Stimson, *American Constitution as It Protects Private Rights* (1923).

Chapter VI

There has been no fresh survey of the organization of Congress in recent times. The chapters in Bryce, *American Commonwealth,* are still illuminating if old. They should be supplemented by reference to works on party government cited in the bibliography for Chapter IV. H. C. Lodge, *The Senate of the United States* (1921); L. Rogers, *The American Senate* (1926), especially valuable for study of working methods; W. Wilson, *Congressional Government,* old but suggestive; R. Luce, *Legislative Principles* (1930); J. R. Commons, *Proportional Representation* (1907); H. C. Remick, *The Powers of Congress in Respect to Membership and Elections* (1929, Princeton, privately printed). M. A. Mussman, "Changing the Date for Congressional Sessions and Inauguration Day," American Political Science

Review, Feb., 1924, pp. 108 ff. E. C. Griffith, *The Rise and Development of the Gerrymander* (1907), a brief history of the gerrymander to about 1850. G. H. Haynes, *The Election of Senators* (1906), a study of the former system and of the arguments for and against popular election.

Chapter VII

M. E. Dimock, *Congressional Investigating Committees* (1929); E. J. Eberling, *Congressional Investigations* (1928); A. C. McGown, *Congressional Conference Committee* (1927); G. R. Brown, *Leadership of Congress* (1922); R. Luce, *Congress; an Explanation* (1926); C. Warren, *Congress, the Constitution and the Supreme Court* (1925); D. J. Ettrude (comp.), *Power of Congress to Nullify Supreme Court Decisions* (1924); P. De W. Hasbrouck, *Party Government in the House of Representatives* (1927); L. Haines, *Your Servants in the Senate* (1926); H. C. Lodge, *Senate of the United States* (1921); E. M. Phelps (ed.), *Revision of Rules of the United States Senate* (1926); L. Rogers, *American Senate* (1926); E. B. Logan, *Lobbying* (Annals of the American Academy of Political and Social Science, Vol. CXLIV); E. P. Herring, *Group Representation before Congress* (1929); J. M. Landis, "Constitutional Limitations on the Congressional Power of Investigation," Harvard Law Review, 1926, Vol. 40, pp. 153–221. M. P. Follett, *The Speaker of the House of Representatives* (1904), a history of the speakership. H. B. Fuller, *Speakers of the House* (1909), a general historical sketch of the development of the office. L. G. McConachie, *Congressional Committees* (1898), a detailed study of the procedure and work of committees in Congress and their influence on legislation.

Chapter VIII

J. B. Bishop, *Our Political Drama* (1904), for conventions and campaigns; E. Stanwood, *History of the Presidency* (1928), in various editions, for campaigns and platforms; L. Overacker, *The Presidential Primary* (1926); C. E. Merriam and L. Overacker, *Primary Elections;* L. H. Cannon, *Presidential Election Statistics,* 1900–1924 (1928); J. Hampden Dougherty, *The Electoral System of the United States* (1906), a history of the electoral college and a study of its defects, with suggested remedies; G. J. Schulz, *Election of the President of the United States by the House of Representatives* (Library of Congress, 1925).

Chapter IX

Insight into the substance of presidential power is to be gained from a careful study of the letters and papers of Roosevelt and Wilson and their official biographies. J. B. Bishop, *Theodore Roosevelt and His Times* (2 vols., 1920); R. S. Baker, *Life and Letters of Woodrow Wilson* (in progress); *Selections from the Correspondence of Theodore Roosevelt and Henry Cabot Lodge* (2 vols., 1925); C. Seymour, ed., *The Intimate Papers of Colonel House* (4 vols., 1926–28). E. S. Corwin, *President's Removal Power under the Constitution* (1927); E. H. Wriston, *Executive Agents in American Foreign Relations* (1929); E. M. Phelps (comp.), *Single Six-year Term for President* (1925); E. Berman, *Labor Disputes and the President of the United States* (1924); J. P. Comer, *Legislative Functions of National Administrative Authorities* (1927); J. Hart, *Ordinance Making Powers of the President of the United States* (1925); H. White, *Executive Influence in Determining Military Policy in the United States* (1925); W. Bondy, *Separation of Governmental Powers;* C. E. Morganston, *Appointing and Removing Power of the President* (Govt. Doc.); for significance of the Myers case, see J. Hart, American Political Science Review, August, 1929, pp. 657 ff.; C. A. Berdahl, *War Powers of the Executive in the United States* (Illinois Studies in the Social Sciences, IX, 1921). E. C. Mason, *The Veto Power* (1891), a historical discussion of the presidential vetoes; description of the procedure; and the political significance of the power.

Chapter X

G. A. Weber, *Organized Efforts for the Improvement of Administration in the United States,* survey of various inquiries and schemes pertaining to the efficiency of government, federal and state. L. M. Short, *Development of National Administrative Organization in the United States,* valuable for historical growth of federal functions. L. Mayers, *The Federal Service,* a study in personnel administration. G. C. Thorpe, *Federal Departmental Organization and Practice* (1925). W. F. Willoughby, *Principles of Public Administration,* a study of principles and problems. The chief bureaus and establishments of the Federal Government have been covered in great detail in sixty-two volumes, called *Service Monographs of the United States Government,* published under the auspices of the Brookings Institution in Washington, D. C., beginning in 1918. They are indispensable for the study of federal administration in detail, even the volumes which are now out of date on account of changes made by law and practice. For the Civil Service Commission, see D. H. Smith, *The United States Civil Service Commission* (1928) in the above series. J. P. Comer, *Legislative Functions of the National Administrative Authorities* (1927). M. F. Halloran, *Romance of the Merit System* (1929). C. R. Fish, *The Civil Service and the Patronage* (1905), a history of the patronage system and civil service reform.

Chapter XI

A. P. Comstock, *Taxation in the Modern State* (1929); A. Handy, *Inheritance and Other Like Taxes* (1929); H. G. Brown, *Economics of Taxation* (1924); H. W. Peck, *Taxation and Welfare* (1925); E. R. A. Seligman, *Essays in Taxation* (1925) and *Shifting and Incidence of Taxation* (1926); A. W. Mellon, *Taxation* (1924); W. F. Willoughby, *National Budget System* (1927); E. W. Kemmerer, *ABC of the Federal Reserve System* (1928); C. S. Tippetts, *State Banks and the Federal Reserve System* (1929); W. R. Burgess, *Federal Reserve Banks and the Money Market* (1927); J. S. Lawrence, *Wall Street and Washington* (1929); P. M. Warburg, *The Federal Reserve System* (2 vols., 1930); A. E. Buck, *Public Budgeting* (1929), including sections on federal budgeting; R. Forbes, *Governmental Purchasing* (1929), brief treatment of federal purchasing included; H. P. Seidemann, *Manual of Accounting and Reporting for the Operating Services of the National Government* (1926); C. O. Hardy, *Tax-exempt Securities and the Surtax* (1926); D. H. Smith, *Office of Supervising Architect* (1923); W. F. Willoughby, *The National Budget System* (1927), with suggestions for its improvement; W. F. Willoughby, *The Legal Status and Functions of the General Accounting Office* (1927).

Chapter XII

Inland waterways: H. G. Moulton, *Waterways versus Railways* (1926); H. G. Moulton and C. S. Morgan, *St. Lawrence Navigation and Power Project* (1929); F. A. Collins, *Our Harbors and Inland Waterways.*

Merchant marine: L. W. Maxwell, *Discriminating Duties and the American Merchant Marine* (1926); G. R. Putnam, *Lighthouses and Lightships of the United States* (1917).

Railways: F. H. Dixon, *Railroads and Government* (1922); L. H. Haney, *A Congressional History of Railways* (1910); W. M. W. Splawn, *Consolidation of Railroads* (1925) and *Valuation and Rate*

Regulation; American Academy of Political and Social Science, *Railroad Consolidation* (1929); H. S. Perry, *Federal Intrastate Railroad Rate Regulation* (1926); J. M. Herring, *Problem of Weak Railroads* (1929); D. P. Locklin, *Railroad Regulation since 1920* (1928); J. Bernhardt, *Interstate Commerce Commission* (1923); W. S. Holt, *Bureau of Public Roads, Its History, Activities and Organization* (1923); American Academy of Political and Social Science, *Aviation* (1927); S. O. Dunn, *Government Ownership of Railways* (1915); L. M. Short, *Steamboat-Inspection Service* (1922); G. A. Weber, *The Hydrographic Office* (1926); L. M. Short, *Bureau of Navigation* (1923); D. H. Smith and F. W. Powell, *The Coast Guard* (1929); G. A. Weber, *Coast and Geodetic Survey* (1923); G. Weiss, *The Lighthouse Service* (1926); W. S. Holt, *Office of the Chief of Engineers* (1923).

Chapter XIII

L. Rogers, *Postal Power of Congress* (1916); D. C. Roper, *United States Post Office* (1917); E. W. Kemmerer, *Postal Savings* (1917), historical and critical. G. A. Schreiner, *Cables and Wireless and Their Rôle in the Foreign Relations of the United States* (1924); *Government Control and Operation of Telegraph, Telephone, and Marine Cable Systems, 1918–1919* (Govt. Doc., 1921).

Chapter XIV

C. J. Doyle, *Tyranny of Government in Business* (Utility Assn., 1927); W. B. Harrison, *Attack on Individual Enterprise;* C. D. Thompson, *Objections to Public Ownership Answered* (1925); H. A. Van Dorn, *Government Owned Corporations* (1926); J. Viner, *Dumping* (1923); D. R. Dewey, *Financial History of the United States* (1922); T. W. Page, *Making the Tariff in the United States* (1924); F. W. Taussig, *Selected Readings in International Trade and Tariff Problems* (1921); F. W. Taussig, *Tariff History of the United States* (1923); American Academy of Political and Social Science, *Tariff Problems of the United States* (1928); G. C. Henderson, *Federal Trade Commission* (1924); W. W. Thornton, *Treatise on Combinations in Restraint of Trade*—The Sherman Act, Clayton Act, Federal Trade Commission Act, Webb-Pomerene Act (1928); F. L. Vaughan, *Economics of Our Patent System* (1925); E. L. Graham and F. W. Harris, *Patents, Trade-Marks, and Copyrights* (1921); J. Klein, *Frontiers of Trade* (1929); H. F. Fraser, *Foreign Trade and World Politics* (1926); B. H. Williams, *Economic Foreign Policy of the United States* (1929) ; G. A. Weber, *The Patent Office* (1924) ; L. F. Schmeckebier and G. A. Weber, *Bureau of Foreign and Domestic Commerce* (1924) ; J. Bernhardt, *The Tariff Commission* (1922), of great historical value; W. S. Holt, *Federal Trade Commission* (1922) ; E. W. Crecraft, *Government and Business* (1928).

Chapter XV

F. P. Cavanaugh, *Immigration Restriction at Work Today* (1928) ; R. D. McKenzie, *Oriental Exclusion* (1928) ; J. J. Davis, *Selective Immigration* (1925) ; H. P. Fairchild, *Immigration* (1925) ; R. L. Garis, *Immigration Restriction* (1927) ; I. A. Hourwich, *Immigration and Labor* (Viking Press, 1922) ; M. V. Safford, *Immigration Problems* (1925) ; G. M. Stephenson, *History of American Immigration 1820–1924* (1926) ; W. Weinstein, *Immigration Laws and Rights of Aliens* (private, 1926) ; L. F. Post, *Deportations Delirium of 1920;* M. R. Carroll, *Labor and Politics* (1923) ; G. A. Weber, *Employees' Compensation Commission* (1922) ; J. Bernhardt, *Railroad Labor Board* (1923) ; also *The Division of Conciliation* (1923) in the Department of Labor; G. A. Weber, *The Women's Bureau* (1923) ; F. Frankfurter and N. Greene, *The Labor Injunction* (1930) ; D. H. Smith, *Bureau of Immigration* (1924) and *United States Employment Service* (1923).

Chapter XVI

R. P. Teele, *Economics of Land Reclamation* (1927) ; F. H. Newell, *National Efforts at Home Making* [irrigation] (1924) ; C. L. Benner, *Federal Intermediate Credit System* (1926) ; C. Eliot, *Farmer's Campaign for Credit* (1927) ; H. P. Willis, *Federal Farm Loan Systems* (1924) ; C. T. Brues, *Insects and Human Welfare* (1920) ; A. Wilson, *Insects and Their Control* (1929) ; J. E. Boyle, *Farm Relief* (1928) ; E. R. A. Seligman, *Economics of Farm Relief* (1929) ; P. H. De Kruif, *Hunger Fighters* (1928) ; H. B. Price, *Federal Supervision of Grain Inspection* (1922) ; T. D. Hammatt, *Future Trading in Grain;* U. G. Houck, *Bureau of Animal Industry of the United States Department of Agriculture:* its establishment, achievements, and current activities (1924) ; G. A. Weber, *Plant Quarantine and Control Administration* (1930) ; also *The Bureau of Entomology* (1930) ; J. Cameron, *Bureau of Dairy Industry* (1929) ; M. Conover, *Office of Experiment Stations* (1924) ; W. S. Holt, *Federal Farm Loan Bureau* (1924) ; M. Conover, *The General Land Office* (1923) ; G. A. Weber, *Bureau of Chemistry and Soils* (1928); J. Cameron, *Bureau of Biological Survey* (1929); F. W. Powell, *Bureau of Animal Industry* (1927), and *Bureau of Plant Industry* (1927); G. A. Weber, *Food, Drug, and Insecticide Administration* (1928), *and The Weather Bureau* (1922).

Chapter XVII

B. H. Hibbard, *History of the Public Land Policies* (1924); J. Ise, *United States Oil Policy* (1926); R. S. Yard, *Our Federal Lands* (1928); R. S. Yard, *Book of the National Parks* (1928); M. A. Rolfe, *Our National Parks* (1927); J. Cameron, *Development of Governmental Forest Control in the United States* (1928); J. E. Johnsen (comp.), *Federal and State Control of Water Power* (1928); J. G. Kerwin, *Federal Water-power Legislation* (1926); L. Meriam and others, *Problem of Indian Administration* (1928); L. C. Kellogg, *Our Democracy and the American Indian* (1920); J. C. Malin, *Indian Policy and Westward Expansion* (1921); D. H. Smith, *The Forest Service* (1930); M. Conover, *The Federal Power Commission* (1923); J. Cameron, *National Park Service* (1922); H. S. Graves, "The Public Domain," New York *Nation,* August 6, 1930.

Chapter XVIII

J. A. Tobey, *National Government and Public Health* (1926); R. D. Leigh, *Federal Health Administration in the United States* (1925); G. A. Weber, *Food, Drug, and Insecticide Administration* (1928); H. W. Wiley, *History of a Crime against the Food Law* (1929); R. L. Dorr, *Drink: Coercion or Control?* (1929); E. Boole, *Give Prohibition Its Chance* (1929); H. Feldman, *Prohibition* (1927); W. G. McAdoo, *Challenge* (1928); H. L. McBain, *Prohibition Legal and Illegal* (1928), for the law of the subject; P. Odegard, *Pressure Politics,* a study of the war on the saloon; D. L. Colvin, *Prohibition in the United States* (1926) historical; L. F. Schmeckebier, *Public Health Service* (1923).

Chapter XIX

Brief general introduction to social statistics, A. L. Bowley, *The Nature and Purpose of the Measurement of Social Phenomena* (1915); more advanced works, E. E. Day, *Statistical Analysis,* and S. A. Rice, *Quantitative Methods in Politics* (1928); L. F. Schmeckebier, *Statistical Work of the National Government* (1925); W. S. Holt, *Bureau of the Census* (1929); H. M. Muller, ed., *Government Fund for Unemployment* (1929); V. A. Mund, *Prosperity Reserves of Public Works* (1930); L. S. Lyon, *Hand-to-Mouth Buying: a Study in the Organization, Planning, and Stabilization of Trade* (1929); C. O. Hardy, *Credit Policies of the Federal Reserve System* (1930), announced); L. F. Schmeckebier, *Government Printing Office: Its History, Activities, and Organization* (1925); G. A. Weber, *Bureau of Standards* (1925); *Business Cycles and Unemployment* (Report of the President's Conference on Unemployment, 1923); C. Kehr, *Nation Plan;* a basis for coördinated physical development of the United States of America; with a suggestion for a world plan (1926).

Chapter XX

Most of the writings on states' rights are stump speeches in disguise. For beautiful historical illustrations, see H. V. Ames, *States Documents on Federal Relations* (1906). For the general reader a brief summary of the limitations imposed on states by the federal Constitution, J. W. Burgess, *Political Science and Comparative Constitutional Law,* Vol. I, pp. 201 ff., which can be readily supplemented by a later commentary such as W. W. Willoughby, *On the Constitution of the United States* (1929). W. Thompson, *Federal Contralization* (1923), descriptive and argumentative. Judicial review of state utility regulation is well covered by W. E. Mosher, ed., *Electrical Utilities: the Crisis in Public Control* (1929). For federal financing of state enterprises: A. F. Macdonald, *Federal Aid: a Study of the American Subsidy System* (1925); J. E. Johnsen, ed., *Financing State Highways.* R. L. Mott, *Due Process of Law* (1926), a conservative view of the principles applied by the courts in cases involving this concept.

Chapter XXI

On the economics of imperialism: P. T. Moon, *Imperialism and World Politics;* R. W. Dunn, *American Foreign Investments;* S. Nearing and Freeman, *Dollar Diplomacy;* H. Motherwell, *The Imperial Dollar* (1929); L. Denny, *We Fight for Oil* and *America Conquers Britain;* J. A. H. Hopkins and M. Alexander, *Machine-gun Diplomacy* (1928).

Atlantic operations: J. E. Thomson, *Our Atlantic Possessions* (1928); L. H. Jenks, *Our Cuban Colony* (1928); K. Mixer, *Porto Rico* (1926); V. S. Clark and Associates, *Porto Rico and Its Problems* (1930), a comprehensive survey of public and private economy.

Latin-American relations: J. F. Rippy, *The United States and*

Mexico, 1821–1924 and *Latin America in World Politics* (1928); J. B. Bishop, *The Panama Gateway;* W. S. Robertson, *Hispanic-American Relations with the United States.*

The Pacific theater: F. F. Bunker, *Hawaii and the Philippines* (1928); R. M. C. Littler, *Governance of Hawaii* (1929); W. C. Forbes, *Philippine Islands* (1929); D. C. Worcester, *The Philippines, Past and Present* (1930); ed. by J. R. Hayden; M. M. Kalaw, *Self-Government in the Philippines* (1919); R. L. Buell, *Philippine Independence* (N. Y. Foreign Policy Assn., 1930), an excellent summary guide to the problem, with references to literature in foot notes.

L. F. Schmeckebier, *The District of Columbia* (1928), government and administration, and *Government and Administration of the District of Columbia* (1929), with suggestions for changes.

Chapter XXII

On the substance of diplomacy: J. Bakeless, *Economic Causes of Modern War* (1921); P. T. Moon, *Imperialism and World Politics;* A. Bullard, *American Diplomacy in the Modern World* (1928).

Organization of diplomatic machinery: T. H. Lay, *Foreign Service of the United States* (1925); H. K. Norton, *Foreign Office Organization* (1929); W. T. Stone, *Administration of the Department of State* (1929); G. Hunt, *The Department of State* (1914), historical and descriptive; J. M. Mathews, *The Conduct of American Foreign Relations* (1922).

International organization: P. B. Potter, *Introduction to the Study of International Organization* (1928); J. S. Bassett, *The League of Nations;* D. Myers, *Nine Years of the League of Nations;* P. C. Jessup, *The United States and the World Court* (1929); R. L. Buell, *International Relations* (1929); C. E. Martin, *The Politics of Peace.*

Treaties: E. S. Corwin, *Treaty Power versus State Power;* D. F. Fleming, *Treaty Veto of the American Senate* (1930).

American foreign policy: D. Y. Thomas, *One Hundred Years of the Monroe Doctrine;* J. T. Shotwell, *War as an Instrument of National Policy* (1929) for the Kellogg Peace Pact; J. H. Latané, *History of American Foreign Policy* (1926); for an excellent general bibliography on international relations, P. T. Moon, *Syllabus on International Relations,* pp. 239–276; for current affairs, C. P. Howland, *Survey of American Foreign Relations;* for the Orient, T. Dennett, *Americans in Eastern Asia* (1922) and *Roosevelt and the Russo-Japanese War* (1925), pp. 112–116, for the secret understanding between Roosevelt and Japan; bibliography, pp. 340 ff.

Chapter XXIII

On the rôle of war in history, J. T. Shotwell, *War as an Instrument of National Policy,* pp. 3–38; E. Upton, *The Military Policy of the United States* (Government Document). J. M. Palmer, *Statesmanship or War* (1927); W. H. Glasson, *Federal Military Pensions in the United States* (1918); M. K. Reely (comp.), *Selected Articles on Disarmament* (1921); J. E. Johnsen (comp.), *Selected Articles on National Defense* (1928); H. White, *Executive Influence in Determining Military Policy in the United States* (1925); A. E. McKinley, *Collected Materials for the Study of the War* (1918); W. F. Willoughby, *Government Organization in War Time and After* (1919); L. T. Beman (comp.), *Military Training Compulsory in Schools and Colleges* (1926). Congress authorized in 1930 a comprehensive inquiry into the operations of the pension system, which should produce a mass of valuable data on the subject.

MOTION PICTURES

Since this volume emphasizes technology in relation to government it seems fitting that the bibliography should pass beyond the printed word and take into account the mine of realistic information to be found in motion-picture films. For this reason a list of such pictures is added to the table of books. Although there are numerous catalogues of educational reels in circulation, few if any of them have been organized with reference to any logical study of government. Hence the selected titles which follow have been grouped according to the chapters of this book as far as possible. For educational institutions equipped with projectors the cost of films need not be large because many of the reels listed below may be rented free of all charges, except transportation, from the governmental agencies mentioned. All films included here are on 35 mm. stock. Numbers in brackets indicate the private agencies producing and distributing films, for which a key is given on the last page.

Chapter VII

Congressional Tour of Inspection (from New York through Panama Canal to Alaska), 7 reels, Signal Corps, War Department (reference No. domestic 394).

Chapter VIII

Inauguration of President Herbert C. Hoover (the ceremony and parade on March 4, 1929), 2 reels, Signal Corps, War Department (reference No. domestic 787).

Chapter IX

President Woodrow Wilson's Trips Abroad, Signal Corps, War Department, several reels in sets as follows: A. E. F., 505, *His Arrival in Paris, Dec. 14, 1918,* 1 reel; A. E. F., 592, *He Goes to England, Dec. 26, 1918,* 2 reels; A. E. F., 727, *He Visits Italy, Jan. 3, 1919,* 1 reel; A. E. F., 913, *His Trip through Belgium, and Return to the U. S., June and July, 1919,* 2 reels.

Chapter X

The Department of Agriculture, Commerce, etc. (detailed explanation of the functions of the Departments), 2 reels [4].

Chapter XI

The Federal Reserve System (functions and operations of Federal Reserve Banks. Some animation), 1 reel [14].

Chapter XII

The Panama Canal (its construction and operation), 2 reels, Signal Corps, War Department (reference No. domestic 720); *The Road Goes Through* (National forest and federal aid highway work in the West), 1 reel, Department of Agriculture (reference No. 113); *Lighting the Sea Lanes to N. Y. Harbor* (tracing the course of an incoming vessel guided by aids to navigation), 1 reel [11].

Chapter XIII

U. S. Army Transport Cableship Dellwood (Army laying the Alaska Cable), 2 reels, Signal Corps, War Department (reference No. domestic 448); *Operations on the Cableship Dellwood* (repairing Alaska cable), Signal Corps, War Department, 1 reel (reference No. domestic 579); *Uncle Sam's Stamp Factory* (How stamps are made for the Post-Office Department), ¼ reel [1], [13].

Chapter XIV

Our Navy in Near East, 2 reels, Recruiting Bureau, U. S. Navy (reference No. 203); *Checking the Imports* (activities of the Customs Service), 1 reel [11].

Chapter XV

Immigration to the United States (important waves of immigration and causes; contributions made by immigrants to U. S.), 1 reel [10].

Chapter XVI

Story of Federal Reclamation, 2 reels, Bureau of Reclamation, Interior Department; *Settlement on Federal Reclamation Projects,* 2 reels, Bureau of Reclamation, Interior Department; *Cotton's Worst Enemy—The Pink Bollworm* (insect pests), 1 reel, Department of Agriculture (reference No. 71); *Poison* (Work of Insecticide and Fungicide Control of the Government), 1 reel, Department of Agriculture (reference No. 133); *Halting Foreign Plant Foes* (Quarantine against plant diseases), 1 reel, Department of Agriculture (reference No. 131); *Exploring the Upper Air* (Weather Bureau work), 1 reel, Department of Agriculture (reference No. 198); *Production's Pulse* (crop reporting of the Federal Government), 1 reel, Department of Agriculture (reference No. 197); *Naturalized Plant Immigrants* (important crops introduced by the federal plant explorers), 3 reels, Department of Agriculture; *Corn and the Borer* (European corn borer control and national quarantines), 1 reel, Department of Agriculture; *Construction and Economic Results* (Reclamation work), 2 reels, Bureau of Reclamation, Interior Department.

Chapter XVII

National Bird Refuges, 1 reel, Department of Agriculture (reference No. 49); *When Elk Come Down* (protection of elk in national forests), 2 reels, Department of Agriculture (reference No. 47); *Harvesting Uncle Sam's Timber* (supervision of lumbering in national forests), 2 reels, Department of Agriculture (reference No. 151); *Pack Train Trip through the Washington National Forest* (scenic film), 1 reel, Department of Agriculture (reference No. 170); *Future Forest Giants* (reforesting national forest lands), 1 reel, Department of Agriculture (reference No. 179); *Grazing in National Forests,* 1 reel, Department of Agriculture (reference No. 185); *The Forest Ranger's Job* (in national forests), 1 reel, Department of Agriculture (reference No. 186); *Forest Fire!* (Fighting forest fires in national forests), 1 reel, Department of Agriculture; *Arizona's Grand Canyon,* 1 reel, National Park Service, Interior Department; *Know Your National Parks,* 2 reels, National Park Service, Interior Department; *The First Americans,* 2 reels, Indian Service, Department of the Interior.

Chapter XVIII

Keeping Out Bad Food (inspection of imported foods by the Government), 1 reel, Department of Agriculture (reference No. 130); *The Honor of the Little Purple Stamp* (federal meat inspection), 1 reel, Department of Agriculture (reference No. 129); *The Mississippi River Flood of 1927,* 3 reels, Signal Corps, War Department (reference No. domestic 654); *When a Man's a Miner* (Work of the Bureau of Mines in mine safety told in story form of a young man and his sweetheart), 4 reels, U. S. Bureau of Mines (reference No. 103); *Let's Finish the Job* (treatise on the Eighteenth Amendment), 5 reels [8].

Chapter XIX

Pan and Ceres in the Movies (illustrative bits from the motion-picture work of the Department of Agriculture), 1 reel, Department of Agriculture (reference No. 218); *Old Jake Wakes Up* (trick photography showing nightmare with 10-foot corn borers, etc., intended to arouse interest in pest control among farmers), 1 reel, Department of Agriculture.

Chapter XX

Helping Negroes to Become Better Farmers and Homemakers (Agricultural-extension work), 2 reels, Department of Agriculture (reference No. 214); *The Family Goes to College* (Utah Agricultural College and its work for farmers), 2 reels, Department of Agriculture.

Chapter XXI

Philippine Snapshots (views in Manila and outlying Provinces), 1 reel, Signal Corps, War Department (reference No. domestic 691);

Hello Hawaii, 1 reel, Recruiting Bureau, Bureau of Navigation, U. S. Navy (reference No. 130); *Outposts of Old Glory,* 1 reel, Recruiting Bureau, U. S. Navy (reference No. 127); *Alaskan Revelations* (glaciers, birth of an iceberg, vegetation, icefields), 1 reel [2]; *Cruising to Alaska* (scenes of the country), 1 or 2 reels [6]; *Washington, D. C.* (view of city from Washington Monument), 1 reel [5]; *Rambles in Porto Rico* (scenic beauty), 1 reel [11], [13]; *Sunny Porto Rico* (impressions of life in the island), 1 reel [11]; *Hawaii the Beautiful* (miscellaneous scenes of the islands and their industries), 1 reel [7]; *Aloha Land* (Hawaiian scenes), 1 reel [3]; *Civilizing the Philippines* (Island life under the United States), 1 reel [9]; *Paradise of the Pacific* (Samoan scenes), 1 reel [9].

CHAPTER XXII

The Signing of the Peace Treaty at Versailles (at close of the World War), 1 reel, Signal Corps, War Department (reference No. A. E. F. 914); *Icebergs* (The International Iceberg Patrol at work), 1 reel [12].

CHAPTER XXIII

Flashes of Action (action film of the World War), 4 reels, War Department, Signal Corps (reference No. "Special"); *New Glory for Old* (task of sending army overseas and maintaining it during the World War), 8 reels, Signal Corps, War Department (reference No. "Special"); *Cadets in the Making* (West Point pictures), 1 reel, Signal Corps, War Department (reference No. domestic 780); *Annual Field Maneuvers—Ordnance Specialists School,* 2 reels, Signal Corps, War Department (reference No. domestic 535); *Sharks of the Navy* (submarine work), 1 reel, Recruiting Bureau, Bureau of Navigation, U. S. Navy (reference No. 121); *Wings of the Fleet* (Naval Aviation), 2 reels, Recruiting Bureau, U. S. Navy (reference No. 206); *Anchors Aweigh* (activities of all units of the fleet), 2 reels (reference No. 208), Recruiting Bureau, U. S. Navy; *Life in the Marine Corps,* 1 reel [14]; *Upkeep and Disposal of Uncle Sam's Ships* (Naval problems), 1 reel [11].

AGENCIES DISTRIBUTING FILMS

United States Government, Washington, D. C.: Department of Agriculture, Office of Motion Pictures of Extension Service; Department of Commerce, Motion Picture Section of Bureau of Mines;

Department of the Interior, Reclamation Service, National Park Service, and Indian Service; Department of War, Army Pictorial Service in Office of the Chief Signal Officer; Department of the Navy, Navy Recruiting Bureau (South and Whitehall Streets, New York City, N. Y.).

Private: [1] Bray Productions, Inc., Educational Department, 729 Seventh Avenue, New York City, N. Y.; [2] Carter Cinema Producing Corp., 551 Fifth Avenue, New York City, N. Y.; [3] Church Film Co., 1108 Boylston Street, Boston, Mass.; [4] Fox Film Corporation, 850 Tenth Avenue, New York City, N. Y. (many branches); [5] Harcol Motion Picture Industries, 610 Baronne Street, New Orleans, La.; [6] Northern Pacific Railway, St. Paul, Minn.; [7] Pathé Exchange, Inc., 35 West 45th Street, New York City, N. Y.; [8] Phoenix Photoplay Exchanges of America, 130 West 46th Street, New York City, N. Y.; [9] Sanford Educational Film Service, 730 South Wabash Avenue, Chicago, Ill.; [10] Society for Visual Education, 327 South LaSalle Street, Chicago, Ill.; [11] Spiro Film Corporation, 161 Harris Avenue, Long Island City, N. Y.; [12] University Film Foundation, 11 West 42nd Street, New York City, N. Y., 25 Divinity Ave., Cambridge, Mass.; [13] Wholesome Films Service, Inc., 42 Melrose Street, Boston, Mass.; [14] National Council of Y. M. C. A., Motion Picture Division, 120 W. 41st Street, New York City, 1111 Center Street, Chicago, Ill.

INDEX

Accounting Act, 1921, 352.
Adams, Charles Francis, 704.
Adams, Pres. John, 9–10, 36, 37, 110, 283.
Adams, Pres. John Quincy, 60, 242.
Adamson Act of 1916, 498.
Adee, Asst. Secy., 302.
Administration, increase in burdens of, 6 ff.; organization of federal, 295 ff.; President as head of, 264 ff.; and appointing powers, 267 ff.; relation with legislature, 288 ff., 330 ff.; its social environment, 327 ff.; tax and debt, 348 ff.; supplies and buildings, 370 ff.; and law enforcement, 135 ff.; *see* Judiciary, Civil Service, and functions such as Transportation, Communications, &c.; and state relations, 663 ff.
Admiralty cases in fed. jurisdiction, 112.
Adulteration of food, 588–589.
Aeronautics Branch, Dept. of Commerce, 414.
Agrarian interests, 85, 86, 368–369.
Agrarian Senators, 183.
Agrarian states, 86, 156, 163, 456.
Agric. experiment stations, 515, 670.
Agricultural interests, 513–545; Fed. Farm Board, 513–514; Govt. research, 514–516; experiment stations, 515, 670; disseminating information, 516; agricultural colleges, 516; regulation and improvement of farmers' supplies, 516; Food, Drug, and Insecticide Administration, 516–517, 527; reclamation by irrigating—*see* irrigation; protecting farmer against weather hazards, 522–523; Weather Bureau signals and forecasts, 523; pests—*see* pests.

Financial aid, 528–533; Natl. System headed by Fed. Farm Loan Board, 528; admin. by Farm Loan Bureau, 528; joint stock land banks, 528–529; federal land banks, 529; loan methods, 529; borrowers' cooperation, 530; difficulties in management, 530–531; other types of farm-credit banks, 531–532; interest rates and debentures, 532; short-term credit agencies, 532;

Fed. org. of agric. marketing, 532–545; Ag. Marketing Act of 1929, 533; its purposes, 533; funds for, 534; admin. by Fed. Farm Board, 534; advisory agencies, 534; loans to ag. organizations, 534; aid to producers' clearing houses, 535; in maintaining price levels, 535; "stabilizing corporations," 535; insurance against losses, 536; trading in "futures," 536–537; Govt. control of futures —cotton, grain, 537; "Contract Markets," 538; preventing secret agreements, cornering, other abuses, 538.

Distribution of information to farmers, 539; Bureau of Ag. Economics Service, 539; analysis of market trends, 540; quality criteria for produce established, 540; classification of produce, 541; Grain and Cotton Standards Acts, 541; inspectors of cotton and grain, 541–542; dealers' tricks, 542; penalized under Produce Agency Act, 542–543; Perishable Agric. Commodities Act, 543; export markets, 543; Foreign Agric. Service, 544; Warehouse Act, 544; meat processing and packing, 545.
Agricultural Marketing Act, 533.
Air Commerce Act of 1926, 416.
Air mail service, 417, 427.
Air rates, interstate, fed. regulation of, 418.
Air traffic—fed. licenses for intrastate, 664–665. *See also* transportation—by air.
Airships, 418–419.
Airways, marking of, 413, 414.
Alaska—roads, 410; administration of, 683, 687; 696; purchase of, 724–726.
Alaskan Railway, 375.
Alcohol, industrial use of, 609. *See also* prohibition problem.
Aldrich, Sen., 171.
Algeciras conference, 1906, 734.

Algerian Corsairs, 733.
Algiers, Dey of, 733.
Aliens—marriage of or to, in relation to citizenship, 74; their naturalization, 75; ineligibles, 75; examples of exclusion, 76–78; their rights, 79–80, and disabilities, 81; cases of exclusion at port of entry, 300. *See also* immigration.
Ambassadors—judicial cases pertaining to, 111, 112, 113; apptd. by Pres., 268, 705; functions, 714–717. *See also* diplomatic and consular service.
Amendment to Const. proposed, for congressional supervision of primaries, 100.
Amendments to Constitution, 22, 30, 39; ratification of, 40–41; criticisms of amending process, 41–43; 19 amendments severally considered, 43–51; first ten, 43–45; 11th, 45–46; 12th, 46–47; 13th, 47; 14th, 47–48; 15th, 48; 16th, 49–50; 17th, 50; 18th, 50; 19th, 50–51.
Am. Assn. of Engineers, 310.
Am. Assn. of Railway Executives, 214.
Am. Bar Assn., 20.
A. E. F., 672.
Am. Fed. of Labor, 213, 214, 325, 326, 484, 487.
Am. Legion, 213, 774.
Am. Railway Express Co., 406.
Am. Tel. and Tel. Co., 435.
Anarchists excluded, 487.
Animal life, wild—depletion of, 548; conservation of, 562–567; purposes, 562; depletion of fishes, 562–563; Fed. action conserving, 563 ff.; restocking, shipping, 563; "rescue" of trapped fishes, 563–564; protection during propagation, 564; halibut industry, 564; conservation of seals, 564–565; wild birds and big game conservation, 565–567; land and water preserves for, 565; Fed. game wardens, 566; joint state and fed. action, 565–566; joint action with Gt. Britain to protect migratory birds, 566–567, 722; Bureau of Biol. Survey research work, 567.
State laws conserving, made binding throughout Union, 665.
Animals harmful to agriculture, 523–528.
Antitoxins, 589–590.
Appalachian Forest Reserve law, 556.
Appointing power of President, 68, 267–271, 291. *See also* diplomatic and consular service.
Area coördination of federal departments, 311–312, 373.
Arizona law as to injunctions in labor disputes invalidated, 662.
Armaments, Geneva conference on reduction of, 1927, 761.
Army, 265; "Regular," 763, 764, 768. *See also* war *and* World War.
Army cable to Alaska, 437.
Army engineers—in control of admin. of inland and coastal waterways, 378, 385, 386; work in preventing floods, 600–601.
Army Radio Net, 445.
Army War College, 764.
Articles of Confed., 21, 145, 449.
Asiatic aliens, 75, 80. *See also* immigration.
Atlanta Penitentiary, 141.
Attainder, 651; of treason, 60.
Atty.-General, 137–144, 264, 265, 608.
Aviation, 413–419. *See also* air mail service, air traffic, *etc.*

Bacterial pests, 525–527.
Bail, excessive, 62.
Bainbridge, Admiral, 733.
Baker's Island, 686.
Baltimore case on confiscatory rates, 660.
Bank for Internatl. Settlements, 333, 701.
Banks, natl., 29. *See also* money and banking.
Barge and rail transportation, 381.
Bell, Alex. Graham, 433.
"Bench marks," 626.
Benton, Sen., 204.
Berger, Victor L., 153–154.
Beveridge, Sen., 260.
"Big-navy scandal," 1929, 256.
Bill of Rights, 335.
Bingham, Sen., 457, 458.
Biology—*see* technology.
Birds, wild, conservation of, 565–567; treaty with Gt. Br. protecting migratory, 566–567, 722.
Birth control, 604, 606.
Bismarck, 106–107.
Black Canyon project, 572.
Blackstone, 20.
Blaine, James G., 230, 240.
Blockade during Civil War, 280.
Board of Estimates, 354.
Board of Indian Commrs., 575.
Board of Mediation, 503.
Board of Parole, 144.
Board of Tax Appeals, 349.

Board of Temp., Prohib., and Public Morals, 214.
Boats, public safety on, 595; *see* shipping.
Bolsheviki, 11, 25, 107, 280.
Book censorship by customs officials, 605–606.
Border protection, 138–139.
Botanical Garden, 295.
Boulder Canyon Project, 572.
Boulder Dam, 518.
Bounties, 462.
Boxer rebellion, 281, 734.
Brandeis, Justice, 116, 662.
British Foreign Office, 704, 752.
British mandate over Mesopotamia oil regions, 478.
Brown, Walter F., 309.
Brown *vs.* Maryland, 648.
Bryan, William Jennings, 85, 132, 230, 234, 235, 236, 297, 707.
Bryce, James, 51, 83, 152, 211.
Buchanan, Pres., 244, 254.
Buck, A. E., 674.
Budget Act, 1921, 293–294, 352.
Budget system, 350–360; Bureau, 352; President's relation to, 353–357; how Budget is prepared, 353–354; Board of Estimates, 354; adoption of annual Budget, 354–355; its results, 356; check on law-making, 357, 359; dominion of Director, 358–359; powers of Gen. Acctg. office, 359–360.
Bureau of Agricultural Economics, 539, 543.
Bureau of Animal Industry, 515.
Bureau of Biological Survey, 524, 566, 567.
Bureau of the Budget, 311, 312; Director, 322; 352, 353, 354.
Bureau of the Census, 629.
Bureau of Chemistry and Soils, 515.
Bureau of Education—*see* Office of Education.
Bureau of Engraving and Printing, 314.
Bureau of Entomology, 525.
Bureau of Foreign and Domestic Commerce, 477.
Bureau of Indian Affairs, 575, 576.
Bureau of Industrial Alcohol, 609.
Bureau of Insular Affairs, 687.
Bureau of Investigation, 138.
Bureau of Labor Statistics, 511, 629.
Bureau of Lighthouses, 374, 394, 395, 414, 565.
Bureau of Mines, 599, 638.
Bureau of Narcotics, 612.
Bureau of Naval Intelligence, 481.
Bureau of Plant Industry, 515, 525.
Bureau of Prisons, 141–142.
Bureau of Prohibition, 138, 608.
Bureau of Public Roads, 409–410.
Bureau of Reclamation, 518.
Bureau of Standards, 371, 373, 599, 616, 618–622, 775.
Bureaucracy, *see* administration; 675; 720.
Burgess, Prof. John W., 71, 422, 655.
Burr, Aaron, 46.
Business, federal promotion of, 447–483; early Am. theories, 449; *laissez faire,* 449, 450; Hamilton's program, 449; limits of govt. activities, 450; their origin in businessmen's demands, 451; business methods in Fed. Govt., 451–452; tariff, 452–461 (*see* tariff); bounties, 462.
  Anti-trust legislation, 462; Sherman Act, 463; Clayton Act, 463–464; Fed. Trade Comm. and "unfair" domestic competition, 464–468; its operation, 465 ff.; interprets law to define unfair practices, 466; investigates and reports, 467; enforces law, 467–468; Govt. help to business during depressions, 469.
  Trade-marks, 469–471; patents 471–472; copyright, 472–474; *see also* commerce, foreign.
Busses, motor, 410.

Cabinet, English, 91, 184.
Cabinet, President's 25; not originally planned for, 261; under Washington, 261–262; its meetings, 262–264; members chosen by President, 268.
Cable lines, 436.
Calhoun, John C., 85.
Calif. law on prosecution without grand-jury indictment, 657.
Campaign expenditures, 95–99; laws controlling methods of collection, 96–97; amounts, 97; purposes, 98; publicity, 98; control of committee outlays, 98–99; scandals, 99; weaknesses in existing legislation, 99–102; primary and election expenses, 99–100, 102; corruption, 100; kinds of expenditure exempt, 100; outlays of candidates' friends, 100; party deficits, 101; weak enforcement, 101–102; needed revision of corrupt practices acts, 102.
Campaign, presidential, 232–238; directed by national committee, 232–

235, expenditures, 233–234; "literature," 234–235; press, 235; speeches, 235; radio, 236–237; work in doubtful states, 237–238.
Canal Zone—*see* Panama Canal Zone.
Candidates' expenditures—*see* parties (campaign expenditures).
Cannon, Speaker, 186, 260.
Cape Cod Canal, 381.
Capital, fair return on, Supreme Court decisions, 658–660.
Caribbean islands and regions—armed forces sent to, 281; Am. capital loaned to, 477–478; 480, 482, 739. *See also* territories, U. S.
Carlyle, Thomas, 104, 106.
Caucuses in Congress, 180–183.
Censorship—*see* freedom of press and speech *and* book censorship.
Censorship Board, 771.
Census, 630; of 1920, 147; of 1930, 629, 630.
Certiorari, writ of, 113–114.
Chafee, Prof. Zechariah, 57.
Chart of admin. organization, facing 307.
Charters, states' obligations in respect of, 652–654.
Chase, Stuart, 546, 547, 548.
Chemistry—*see* technology.
Chicago's lowering of Lake Michigan, 384–385.
Child labor, 340, 494–495.
Children's Bureau, 511.
China, 5; open to American trade, 474; Am. capital in, 477, 478; 693, 735, 741.
Chisholm *vs.* Georgia, 45.
Choate, Joseph, 341.
Circuit Courts, 118.
Citizenship, 73–81; by birth, 74, or naturalization, 75; affected by marriage, 74; ineligibility to, 75; method of naturalization, 75–76; examples of exclusion from, 76–78.
Civil Service, 315–323; examinations, 318; appointments, 319; promotions, 319–320; removal, 320; pay, 321–322; Classification Act, 322–323.
Civil Service Act, 267, 315, 320, 324; Commission, 295, 315–326; reform, 91.
Civil War—in relation to 13th Amendment, 47; to 14th, 47–48; to 15th, 48; taxation controversy as a cause, 335; taxes levied during, 338; specie currency during, 364.
Clark, J. Reuben, 739.
Clark, Sen., 161.
Classification Act, 322.
Clausewitz's *Vom Kriege,* 754.
Clay, Henry, 230.
Clayton Anti-trust Act of 1914, 463, 464, 465, 472, 507, 509.
Clerical, Administrative, and Fiscal Service, 314.
Clerical-Mechanical Service, 314.
Cleveland, Fredk. A., 308.
Cleveland, Pres., 230, 231, 240, 254, 265, 275, 286, 504, 738.
Coal—waste of, 547–548; conservation of, 549.
Coal industry, 15.
Coal strike of 1902, 252, 505–506.
Coast and Geodetic Survey, 304, 396, 415, 625, 626, 628.
Coast Guard, 138, 304, 397, 437, 596–597.
Cochran, Bourke, H., 175, 176.
Cole Act of 1929, 410.
Collective naturalization, 75.
Collins, R. A., 765–766.
Colorado River for power and irrigation, 572–573.
Commerce Court, 110.
Commerce, foreign—promotion of, 474–483; recent growth of, 474; compiling and distributing information about, 475, provided for by statute, 475–476, and assisted by consuls, 476, 479; Foreign Comm. Service, 477; foreign loans, 477–478; aid to Am. citizens developing nat. resources in foreign countries, 478–479; exporters protected at home by Webb Act, 479–480; other aids to commerce, 480; Navy, 480; its services, e.g., in Near East, 481; other armed intervention—e.g., in Mexico, 482; Govt. supervision of foreign loans, 482.
Comm. on Economy and Efficiency, 308, 352.
Comm. on Uniform Crime Records (of Internatl. Assn. of Chiefs of Police), 632.
Commr. of Internal Revenue, 608.
Commissioner-General of Immigration, 312, 491.
Committee on Public Information, 771.
Committees, Natl. (party), 232–235.
Common law cases before Supreme Court, 114.
Communications Comm., proposed, 446.
Compensation, industrial, 500–502; laws, 500–501.
Competitive examinations for office in England, 316–317.

Comptroller General, 272, 295, 359, 360.
Comptroller of the Currency, 365, 532.
Comptroller of the Treasury, 462.
Confiscatory taxation, 336.
Congress—as interpreter of Constitution, 24; 37, 38, 39, 50; its powers limited by Constitution, 52 ff; as regards personal liberty, 54–63; and property, 63–64; authority to make laws, 65; relation to Federal judiciary, 109; authorizes "judicial conference," 119; 125.
Its structure, 145–172; House, 146–155 (*see* House of Representatives); Senate, 155–164; special session to revise tariff, 162; privileges of Congressmen, 164–165; salaries, 164; exemption from arrest, 164; freedom of speech, 165; instruction of, by states, 165.
Its organization and rules, 166; open and closed sessions, 166–167; attendance, 167; summoning citizens for testimony, 168; long and short sessions, 168–169; dates of seating new members, 169; special sessions, 169–170; comparison of two houses, 170; influence of Senators, 170–172; complex functions, 173; regulated by Constitution, 174; its varying interpretations of Constitution, 175; amount and variety of business, 177; "public" and "special" bills, 178; "pork-barrel" legislation, 178–179; "log-rolling," 179; process of selecting measures to be discussed, 179; directing machinery of party, 180; party conferences, 180–181; caucuses, 180–183; leadership, 183–188; President's influence, 189; causes of insurgency, 189–190.
Committees, 190–196; standing committees enumerated, 191; appointments to committees, 192; "seniority rule," 193; bills going to committees, 193–195; criticism of committee system, 195–196.
Procedure, 197–201; debate, 198; action on bills, 199–200; rules, 201–207; filibustering, 202; length of debate, 204; minority action, 206; agencies for getting information, 207–211; Congressional commissions, 207–208; inquiries into acts of corporations, 208; of federal departments, 208–209; of private citizens, 210; debates not informative, 211; pressure on Congressmen, 212; lobbying, 212–219; leading lobbies named, 213–214; family and social lobbies, 215–216; instance of public-utility propaganda, 216–218; proposed legislation to control lobbying, 219.
In relation to President, 257, 260, 261, 264, 266, 267, 269, 270; to removal power, 271–273; its authority in foreign affairs, 273–279; in connection with President's war powers, 279–281; its adjournment in connection with "pocket veto," 285; authority over Comptroller General, 295; relation to admin. depts., 295 ff., 330–331; power of taxation—*see* taxation; appropriation—*see* finance; tax imposed on ships of countries that penalize ours, 393; power to estab. post roads, 421, and mails, 422; aid to early telegraph, 433; in relation to tariff, 455; its acts in promotion of business enterprise, 468; authority in labor disputes, 502–503; action in regard to natl. forests, 556; in setting up safety standards for common carriers, 594; eliminating mining risks, 599; forestalling floods, 600–602.
In relation to 18th Amendment, 607–614; on prison labor, 666.
Sole authority over insular possessions, 682; its part in foreign affairs, 705; Roosevelt on its leadership in Wilson's admin., 705–706; its regulation of land and naval forces, 760.
Congressional districts, 148–150.
Congr. Joint Comm. on Reorganization of Govt. Depts., 309.
Congr. Joint Comm. on Salaries and Grades, 322.
Congr. Library—*See* Library of Congress.
Congressional Record, 168, 169, 198, 199, 200, 636.
Conservation—*See* natural resources.
Constantinople, Am. tobacco interests in, 481.
Constitution, U. S., 20–51; paramount in U. S. politics, 20; origin, 21; interpretation, 22 ff.; by Supreme Court, 23; by Congress, 24; by President, 25; by political leaders, 25; its framers, 4, 21, 26; interpreting intentions of framers, 26–28; of ratifiers, 29–30; interpreting amendments, 30; other methods of

interpretation, 30 ff.; as a written document, 38–39; amending process, 39 ff.; ratification of, 40–41; objections to process, 41–43; its amendments severally considered, 43–51; first ten, 43–45; 11th, 45–46; 12th, 46–47; 13th, 47; 14th, 47–48; 15th, 48; 16th, 49–50; 17th, 50; 18th, 50; 19th, 50–51; its restraints on government—*see* Federal Government *and* States; its departmental separation of federal powers, 67–71; its principles covering citizenship and suffrage, 73–81; covering alien residents, 79–80.

On the judiciary, 109; 112; on Supreme Court, 113; on powers of federal courts to decide constitutionality, 124; 127, 129; on elections to House, 150–151; on qualifications of Representatives, 151–152; on elections to Senate, 155; 165, 171, 173.

On the presidential office, 246–250; no provision for admin. depts., 295.

On taxing power of Congress, 335 ff.; not always clear, 336–337.

Its separation of Fed. and State powers, 645 ff.; 14th Am. on charters, 654; on states' power to make laws abridging personal liberty, 654–656, or touching public utility property, 658–659.

No provision for acquiring or administering overseas territories, 681–682; its provision for diplomatic service, 705; for treaty-making, 720.

Constitutional Convention, 27–29, 124, 246.

Constitutionality of statutes, 123–127; controversies arising from decisions on, 127–135. *See also* Supreme Court.

"Consular Regulations of the U. S.," 717.

Consuls—judicial cases pertaining to, 111, 112, 113; apptd. by Pres., 268, 705; functions, 717–718; commercial services, 717; obligations as to American Shipping, 718; other duties, 718. *See also* diplomatic and consular service.

Contempt of court, 123; imprisonment for, without jury trial (Debs case), 507; 508.

Continental Congress money, 363.

Contraception information, 604; devices, 606.

Contract, obligation of, state laws impairing, 652–654.

Convention, national—its composition, 221–224; apportionment of state delegates, 221; inequalities, 222; method of choosing delegates, 222–223; direct primary, 223–224; confusion in primary laws, 224.

Procedure, 224–229; purposes, 225; opening scenes, 225–226; committee reports, 226–227; platform, 227; nominations, 227–228; voting, 228–229; candidates notified, 229; candidates' qualifications—historical review, 229–232.

Cooley, Judge, 38, 79.

Coolidge, Pres., 84, 123, 232, 268, 271, 283, 286, 291, 309, 342, 343, 760, 774.

Coördination, under Budget Bureau, 311–312; interdepartmental, 312–313.

Copyright, 472–474.

Corporations in actions within fed. jurisdiction, 112; *see also* business.

Corrupt election practices, 98 ff.; revised legislation needed, 102–103.

Corrupt practices Acts, 99 ff.

Cortelyou, George B., 329.

Corwin, E. S., 341.

Cotton Futures Act, 537.

Cotton Standards Act of 1923, 541.

Counterfeiting, 137, 139.

Court of Arbitration, 746–747.

Court of Claims, 117 footnote, 272, 426.

Court of Customs Appeals, 349.

Courts, Federal—*See* judiciary *and* Supreme Court.

Couzens, Sen., 446.

Criminal procedure stipulated by Const. 61–62.

Criminal trials—supremacy of federal law, Justice Strong quoted, 66–67; 657.

Crowninshield-Sturges bankruptcy case, 652.

Cuba, 689–690, 691.

Cuban Sugar Lobby, 215.

Cultural heritage and environment, their effect on government, 4.

Currency, 85; forging of, 139. *See also* money and banking.

Cushing, Caleb, 733.

Custodial Service, 314.

Customs duties, 342, 370. *See also* taxation.

Customs Service, 138.

Cutting, Sen., 102.

"Dairy legislation," 339–340.

Dartmouth College case, 33; charter case, 653.
Daugherty, Atty.-Gen. Harry M., 210, 508.
Daugherty, Mally S., 210.
D. A. R., 213.
Davis, Jefferson, 85.
Dawes, Vice Pres., 205, 719.
Debs, Eugene V., 422, 507.
Debt, national, 349–350.
Decatur, Admiral, 733.
"Defense" an ambiguous term, 756–757.
Democracy, influence of technology on, 5 ff.; modern controversy respecting, 9 ff.; and intelligence, 12 ff.; *see* parties.
Dem. natl. convention, 1896, 131; plank in platform on federal interference, 132.
Dem. party, 85; changed tariff platform, 86; 131, 365.
Dennett, Tyler, 278.
Dept. of Agriculture, 310, 373, 409, 483, 514 ff.; 636, 638; its foreign agents, 711.
Dept. of Commerce, 313, 441, 461; collects data about foreign trade, 476, 477, 483; its regulation of aircraft equipment, 597; its agents abroad, 711.
"Dept. of Education and Welfare," proposed, 309.
Dept. of the Interior, 518, 687.
Dept. of Justice, 119, 135; organization, 137–138; 608; its foreign police, 711.
Dept. of Labor, 138; its control of immigration, 491, 495; officials abroad, 711.
"Dept. of National Defense," proposed, 309.
Dept. of the Navy, 309, 687; representatives abroad, 711; 759, 767.
"Dept. of Public Works," proposed, 310.
Dept. of State, 478, 482, 483, 706; its character and functions, 708–712; organization, 710; appropriations for, 710–711; the War and Navy attachés, 711; in relation to League of Nations, 744–745.
Dept. of the Treasury, 139; act establishing it, 261, 264; 352, 353; its investigators abroad, 711; 773, 774.
Dept. of War, 309, 374, 386, 568, 600; representatives abroad, 711, 759, 767, 779.
Depts., Govt., their powers as stipulated by Constitution, 67–71.
Depts., Govt., administrative, 295–332; enumerated, 296; heads, 296–301; their competence, 297–298; work, 298; appointing power, 299; regulation of deptl. affairs, 299; relation to Congress, 299–300; to courts, 300–301.
Their organization, 301–305; permanent secretaries, 302; subdepts. and bureaus, 302–303; spoils system, 303–304; changed method of choosing division heads, 304–305; indep. boards, comms., etc., 305–307; their "quasi-judicial" character, 306.
Shortcomings of admin. org., 308–310; overlapping, conflict, 309; plans to correct, 309–311; existing coördinations, 311–313; grades of employees, 314–315; Civil Service, 315–323; fed. pension system, 321; partisan and political activities, 323–325; unions of employees, 325–326; need for scientific treatment of problems of Fed. employment, 326; social environment of Admin., 327; in Europe, progressive polit. career, 328; in U. S. promotion to private business, 329; examples, 329–330.
Relation of Admin. to Congress, 330–331; scandals old and recent, 331–332.
"Depositories," local, for Govt. printed matter, 636.
Dewey, Davis R., 773.
Diplomacy—open and secret, 277; revolution in, 700–703; its functions, 703–704; secret, 729–732; its responsibility for wars, 729; Wilson's plea for "open covenants," 729; various secret understandings, 729–730; perils in open diplomacy, 730–731. *See also* diplomatic and consular service.
Diplomatic and consular service, U. S.—representatives apptd. by Pres., 268, 705, 712; its organization, 712–718; qualifications for, 712–713; method of apptg., 712–713; privileges and immunities, 713–714; ambassadors' functions, 714–717; Page's description of, 715–716; consuls' duties, 717–718; training of personnel, 719–720; Foreign Service School, 719; Rogers Act, 720. *See also* diplomacy *and* foreign relations.
Director of the Budget, 352, 357, 358, 359.

Director of Railways, 406.
Directorships, under Clayton Act, 464.
Disarmament conference, Washington, 735.
Diseases, aliens with certain, excluded, 488; *see* public health.
District Courts, fed., 117.
District of Columbia, admin. of, 683.
Division of Conciliation (Dept. of Labor), 504, 505.
Div. of Eastern European Affairs, 710.
Div. of Far Eastern Affairs, 710.
Div. of Identification and Information (Dept. of Justice), 138, 632.
Div. of Latin-American Affairs, 710.
Div. of Mexican Affairs, 710.
Div. of Near Eastern Affairs, 710.
Div. of Western European Affairs, 710.
"Doles," 496.
Dominican Republic—*see* Santo Domingo.
Dred Scott case, 28, 38, 128–131, 681.
Drug addicts, fed. farms for care of, 614.
Drug smuggling, 613.
Drugs, pure—*see* public health.
"Due process of law," 656 ff.; in criminal and civil cases, 657; in taxation, 657–658; in public-utility legislation, 658 ff.; Supreme Court decisions touching, 658–661; in labor legislation, 661–662; 722.

Earthquakes, Govt. data on, 628.
Economic basis of party system, 84.
Economic changes, their effect on political organism, 5.
Economic enterprises, regulation of, in Supreme Court jurisdiction, 113, 114.
Education, Office of—*see* Office of Education.
Education, state institutions of, assisted by federal aid, 669–670.
Edward VII, King, 260, 706.
Efficiency Bureau, 322.
Eighteenth Amendment, 30, 41, 42, 578; quoted, 607; its operation—*see* prohibition problem.
Election of President—*see* pres. election.
Election of Senators by direct vote, 50.
Elections, use of money in, 99–100, 102.
Electoral votes, casting of, 239–241; const. method prescribed, 241; counting of, 241–242; conditions for decision, 242.
Electors, pres., 25–26, 46, 220; how apportioned and chosen, 238–239.
Eleventh Amendment, 45–46.
Emancipation of slaves, 280.
Emergency Fleet Corp., 387, 769.
Eminent domain, 64.
Employment of prisoners, 142.
Employment Service of Dept. of Labor, 495–496, 770.
Engineering—*see* technology.
English competitive examinations for office, 316–317.
Enlisted Reserve Corps, 763.
"Entangling alliances," 733, 735, 736.
Equity cases in fed. jurisdiction, 112.
Esch-Cummins Transportation Act of 1920, 400, 404, 405.
Espionage Act—1917, 57–58, 60, 771.
Estates General, 1789, 335.
Exclusion from Congress—*see* House of Representatives *and* Congress.
Executive, the—*see* President.
Executive Mansion, 288.
Experiment stations, agricultural, 514, 515.
Ex post facto laws, 60, 651–652.
Excises, 342; *see* taxation.
Extradition of criminals, 677–678.

Far East, 277–278, 693 f., 735, 741.
Farewell Address, Washington's, 243, 732.
"Farm Bloc," 183.
Farm Bureau Federation, 213.
Farm relief, 87. *See* agricultural interests.
Farmers—*see* agricultural interests.
Farmers' Union, 213.
Fascism, 11, 249.
Fed. Aid Road Act of 1916, 409.
Federal aid to states—*see* states.
Fed. banking—*see* money and banking.
Fed. Board of Hospitalization, 311.
Fed. Business Assns., 312.
Fed. Council of Churches, 214.
Fed. employees—*see* Civil Service *and* Depts., Govt.
Fed. Employees' Union, 213.
Federal employment services, 318–319, 495–496.
Federal Farm Board, 369–370, 513–514, 528, 534, 535, 536.
Fed. Farm Loan Board, 306, 528, 529, 530, 531, 532.
Fed. Farm Loan Bureau, 370, 528.
Federal Government—constitutional

restraints on, 52 ff.; to protect personal liberty, 54–63; alleged violations during World War, 62–63; restraints in behalf of property rights, 63–64; has only delegated powers, 64; its laws *vs.* state laws, 65–66; jurisdiction of its courts, 66–67; powers of its three departments, 67–71. *See also* Congress, President, judiciary, *and* Depts., Govt.

Federal land banks, 529.

Fed. pension system, 321.

Fed. Power Comm., 307, 569, 570.

Federal Public Health Service—*see* Public Health Service.

Fed. Purchasing Board, 372.

Fed. Radio Comm., 441, 442, 443.

Fed. Real Estate Board, 311.

Fed. Reserve Act, 259, 365 ff., 640.

Fed. Reserve Board, 365 ff.; system, 349, 365 ff.

Fed. Specifications Board, 371, 372.

Fed. Trade Comm., 208, 216, 306, 461, 464–468; Act, 465, 467, 472.

Fed. Traffic Board, 311.

Fed. Water Power Act, 569, 570.

Federalist, 26, 33, 68, 84, 124, 155, 246, 247, 248, 288, 345, 646, 759.

Federalist party, 10, 24, 37, 56, 84, 111, 175.

Federalist-Whig-Republican party, 84, 85.

Fifteenth Amendment, 48, 78, 79.

Fifth Amendment, 54.

Finance, Federal—taxation, 333–349; debt, 349–350; appropriations, 350 ff.; Taft Commission on Economy, 352; Budget Bureau Created, 352 (see Budget); money—*see* money and banking; expenditures for supplies and bldgs., 370–375; Fed. Govt. a large purchaser, 370–371; how purchases are systematized and standardized, 371; Fed. Specifications, 371; Board, 371–372; coördination, 372; Gen. Supply Committee's work, 372–373; purchases tested, 373; construction and operation of bldgs., 373–374; Supervising Architect, 374; some work done by contractors, 375.

Fingerprint collection, Dept. of Justice, 138.

First Amendment, 55.

Fish, depletion of, 548, 562–563; conservation of, 549, 563–564.

Flexible tariff—*see* tariff.

Floods, 593, 600–602.

Food Administration, 770.

Food, Drug, and Insecticide Administration, 516–517, 527, 585, 587, 589.

Foods, pure—*see* public health.

Foraker, Sen., 260.

Ford, Henry, 161.

Ford, Henry Jones, 70, 165.

Foreign Affairs—Pres.'s power in, 273–279. *See also* foreign relations.

Foreign Agric. Service of the U. S., 544.

Foreign Commerce Service, 477.

Foreign relations, 14, 700–749; changes in, and in diplomacy, 700–703; new economic functions of ambassadors, 703; their influence, 703–704; functions of dipl. officials, 704; Pres. as leader of diplomacy, 705–706; his direct communications with ministers abroad, 706; Wilson's trip to Paris, 707–708; his unique attitude to for. affairs, 707–708; Dept. of State, 708–712; foreign representatives of other Govt. Depts., 711.

Organization of foreign service, —*see* diplomatic and consular service; negotiating and making treaties—*see* treaties; secret diplomacy —*see* diplomacy.

Dogma of "isolation," 732–736; U. S. increasingly drawn into world politics, 733; examples past and present, 733–734; involved in world war, 735; disarmament conference, 735; "four-power treaty," 735; economic ties with world, 735–736.

Monroe Doctrine—*see* Monroe Doctrine; "open door," for Am. business, 741; other nations' "spheres of influence," 741; Kellogg Pact, 741–743.

See also internatl. govt.

Foreign Service Act, 717.

Foreign Service School, 719.

Foreign vessels, freight and passenger carriage on, by coastal water routes, 382.

Forest Reservation Comm., 556–557.

Forest service—*see* U. S. Forest Service.

Forests—depletion of, 548; utility of, 553–554; slow growth, 554; forestry largely a private problem, 554–555; Fed. coöperation with Conservationists, 555; fire-fighting, 555; public forests, 556; Appalachian forest reserve law, 556; For-

est Res. Comm., 556–557; purchase of new sites, 557; natl. laws admin. by Forest Service, 557–560; its difficulties, 557–558; functions, 558 ff.; trees planted, 558; protected, 559; pests, lightning, fire, 559; loss by fire, 559; crops for saw-mills, 559–568; grazing of livestock, 560–561; recreational value, 561; new program proposed for use and management, 561–562.
Forging, 139.
Ft. Leavenworth Penitentiary, 141.
"Four-power treaty," 735.
Fourteen Points, Wilson's, 283, 708, 729.
Fourteenth Amendment, 30, 47–48, 49, 54, 78, 79, 80, 502, 510, 654 ff.
Framers of Const., 4, 21, 26; interpreting their intentions, 26–29; conception of pres. office, 246–250; 336, 345, 449, 452, 679.
Franchise—*see* suffrage.
Frankfurter and Landis on the Supreme Court, 114, 115.
Franklin, Benj., 703.
Free mail, 430.
Free silver issue, 227.
Freedom of press and speech—55; in war, 56–58, 280; what it consists of, 58–59.
Frick, H. C., 259.
Fruit flies, Mediterranean, 527.
Fuel Administration, 770.
Fungus pests, 525–527.
"Futures," Govt. control of, 537.

Gallatin, Albert, 377.
Game—waste of, 548; conservation of, 565–567. *See* animal life, wild.
Garfield, Pres., 230, 231, 345.
Gary, Ind., steel dispute, 265.
Gaus, John M., 323.
General Accounting Office, 359, 360.
General Land Office, 552, 553.
General Supply Committee, 372.
Gentlemen's Agreement with Japan, 729.
Geodetic Survey—*see* Coast and Geodetic Survey.
Geological Survey, 330, 552, 627, 639.
Georgia and the 11th Amendment, 45.
German aliens in quota, 489.
German army, 18, 762.
Gerry, Elbridge T., 149 footnote.
Gerrymandering, 149, 150.
Gillett, Sen., 134.
Gold standard, 367.
Gompers, Samuel, 508.
Goodnow, Frank J., 39, 70.
Government, *see* democracy, technology, and parties.
Govt. depts.,—*see* depts., Govt.
Govt. Printing Office, 295, 500, 635–636.
Grain Futures Act, 537.
Grain Standards Act of 1916, 541.
Grand jury indictment, 61.
Grant, Pres., 231, 286, 734.
Grass seed, Sudan, 514–515.
Graves, Henry S., 561, 562.
Gray, Justice, 36.
"Great Brass Brain," 396–397.
Great Britain—her experience in defensive preparations, 751–752; amount of money spent on naval defense, 752.
Great Lakes, their level lowered by Chicago's action, 384–385.
Great Society, the, 5.
Greenback party, 86, 195.
Grey, Sir Edward, 730.
Grundy, Sen., 163, 457.
Guam, 685–687, 691, 697.
Guano, islands containing, 686.

Habeas corpus, 44, 61, 121–122, 280.
Hadley, Arthur T., 72.
Hague conferences, 734.
Haiti, 281, 688.
Halibut industry, 564.
Hamilton, Alex., 10, 29, 55, 56, 84, 124, 247, 285, 288, 293, 449.
Hanna, Sen., 171, 233.
Harding, Pres., 37, 182, 231, 232, 265, 275, 291, 297, 331, 357, 380, 640, 641, 708, 726, 735.
Harrison, Pres. Benj., 240, 270, 282, 287, 297, 721.
Harrison, Pres. Wm. Henry, 231, 270.
Hawaii, 683, 687, 696–697, 734; roads, 410.
Hay, Secy., 710, 713, 724, 741.
Hayburn's case, 70.
Hayes, Pres., 240.
Hay-Pauncefote Treaty, 382.
Higginson, H. L., 259.
Highways—*see* transportation.
Hill, Sen., 132, 230.
Hinds' *Parliamentary Precedents of the House of Rep.*, 201.
Hoar, Sen., 161.
Holmes, Justice, 34, 36–37; his labor decisions, 36; on freedom of speech, 56; on Schwimmer case, 77; 116.
Homestead Act of 1862, 517.
Hoover, Pres., 4, 37, 140, 162, 230, 231, 250, 253, 256, 257, 271, 286, 294, 342, 344, 356, 430, 456, 457, 477, 641, 642, 643, 689, 711, 726, 742, 745, 747, 761.

Hopkins, Sen., 156.
House, Col. E. M., 259, 278, 706.
House of Commons, speaker of, 186.
House of Representatives, 25, 48, 50, 57, 60, 146–155; its number based on population, 146 ff.; congressional districts, 148–150; former assignment of state quotas, 148; proportional representation, 150; election methods and dates designated by Congress, 150–151; Constitutional qualifications for members, 151–153; member a resident in his district, 152; House's power of exclusion, 153; disputed elections, 154–155; length of term, 155; caucuses, 180–183; leadership, 183–188; committees (*see* Congress); procedure, 197, 198; action on bills, 199–200; rules, 201; filibustering, 202; length of debate, 204; minority action, 206; its emergency function in acting on electoral vote, 242; its election of Jefferson and of J. Q. Adams, 242.
Its power of taxing, 344–345; process of tariff revision, 346–348; appropriations, 351; share in treaties, 726.
Hughes, Chief Justice, 37, 58, 133–134, 258; as Secy. of State, 297, 708, 745.
Hygienic Laboratory, 313. *See also* Natl. Inst. of Health.

Icebergs—patrol, 397, 398; warning by radio, 444.
"Identical notes," 276.
Identification and Information—*see* Div. of Ident. and Information.
Illinois railway-rate act, 651.
Illiterates excluded, 487.
Immigration—early fostered by Congress, 486; importation of contract labor under 1864 law, 486; protests from unions and others, 486; present statutory exclusions—contract labor, 486–487; Orientals, illiterates, 487; "dangerous" aliens, paupers, diseased, etc., 488; quota system under 1924 Act, 488–491; Commissioner's duties, 491; exam. of immigrants at home consulates, 491; at entry port, 492; doubtful cases, 492; devices for illegal entry, 492–493; penalty, 493; deportation, 493–494; during and after World War, 494.
Problems connected with imm. from U. S. insular possessions, 697–698.
Immigration Act of 1924, 300, 488 ff., 631.
Immigration Service, 493.
Impeachment, 111, 271.
Imperial policy, U. S., 679–680; problems of, 690–699. *See also* territories, U. S.
Imposts, 342.
Inauguration, President's, 243–245.
Income tax—law of 1894, 38, 131; amendment to Const., 49–50; 86, 87, 108.
Indep. Natl. party—*see* Greenback party.
Indians, lands and rights of, 573–577; difficulties arising from reservations, 574; new Fed. policy of training Indian in American citizenship, 574–575; allotment of private lands, naturalization, 575; Bureau of Indian Affairs, Bd. of Ind. Commrs., their work, 576; problems in Indian education, 576–577; varying capacity among individuals, 577.
Indictment by grand jury, 61.
"Indirect taxes," 336.
Industrial disputes—*see* labor.
Industrial interests—*see* business.
Industrial risks and compensation, 500–502.
Industrial Rehabilitation Act of 1920, 673.
Inferior courts, 110, 113, 117.
Inheritance tax, 86, 337.
Injunction, writ of, 122–123, 506–510; in labor disputes, 662.
Inland Waterways Corp., 380, 381.
Inoculation, products used in, 589–590.
Insect pests, 525–527.
Insurgency in Congress, 189–190.
"Insular Cases" decided by Supreme Court, 682.
Insular territories and possessions, U. S., 74, 383, 410, 515. *See also* territories, U. S.
Intelligence of masses, 11.
Intelligence tests, 11–12.
Interdepartmental Board of Ocean Mail Contracts, 312–313.
Interdepartmental Patents Board, 311.
"Interests," industrial, etc., at Washington, 6, 212 ff.
Internal revenue—*see* taxation.
Internal Revenue, Commr. of, 608.
Internatl. Assn. of Chiefs of Police, 632.

Internatl. Bureau for the Publication of Customs Tariffs, 748.
Internatl. Bureau of Weights and Measures, 748.
Internatl. govt., 743–749. *See* League of Nations, World Court, Pan-American Union, Court of Arbitration, Postal Union.
Internatl. Health Office, 582.
Internatl. Ice Patrol, 748.
Internatl. Joint Comm., 748.
Internatl. Opium Convention, 613.
Internatl. Postal Union, 423, 702, 748.
Internatl. Prison Comm., 748.
Internatl. Radiotelegraph Conference, 1927, 440.
Interpretation of Constitution—*see* Constitution.
Interstate Commerce Act, 400.
Interstate Commerce, 115, 208, 259, 295, 306; railways, 400–408; motor transport, 411, 412; mails, 426; telegraph and telephone, 434, 435, 436; the radio, 446; safety standards for common carriers, 594; shipment of dangerous commodities, 598; state interference, 650–657.
Intracoastal Waterway, 378.
Intrastate transp'n rates, 404.
Irrigation projects, funds procured, 517–518; administration by Bureau of Reclamation, 518; various projects, 518; benefits to farmer, 518–519; poor coöperation, 519; other problems, 520, 521. *See also* water power.
Ishii, Ambassador, 276.
Islands belonging to U. S.—*see* insular territories *and* territories, U. S.
Isolation, U. S., dogma of, 275, 732–736.

Jackson, Pres., 37, 230, 231, 254, 286, 303.
Japan, 260, 276, 277–278; open to American trade, 474; as related to Philippine question, 693–694; 721–722.
Japanese ownership of land in California, 722.
Jarvis Island, 686.
Jay, Chief Justice, 109, 293.
Jefferson, Thomas, 9, 32, 44, 46, 55, 56, 59, 85, 110, 124, 125, 242, 243, 250, 286, 377, 680, 710, 720, 760.
Jefferson's *Manual of Parliamentary Practice,* 201.
Johnson, Albert, 358.
Johnson, Pres., 271.
Johnson, Sen., 57.
Joint Committee on Printing, 635.
Joint Comm. on Reclassification, 320.
Joint stock land banks, 528–529.
Jones Act of 1916, 683, 692.
Jones Merchant Marine Act, 13, 14.
Jones, Senator James K., 131–132.
Jones-Stalker Act of 1929, 608.
"Judicial conference" authorized by Congr., 119.
Judiciary Acts, 1789 and 1925, 113.
Judiciary, federal, 28, 35; supremacy of, 71–72; protection of property rights, 72–73; heightened importance, 109; relation to Congress, 109–110; appointments to, 111; jurisdiction, 111–112; structure, 113; business, 113–117 (*See also* Supreme Court); District Courts, 117; Circuit Courts, 118; "judicial conference," 119; protests against its interference in local affairs, 127–135; its responsibility for enforcing laws, 135; enforcement machinery, 135–144; jurisdiction over cases involving labor interests, 506–510. *See also* Supreme Court.
Junior Reserve Officers' Training Corps, 765.
Jurisdiction of fed. courts, 111–112; of Supreme Court, 113.
Jury system, 119.
Jury trial, 61.

Kagoshima, bombardment of, 734.
Kansas law on discharging union employees, 662.
Kellogg Pact, 711, 741, 755, 756.
Kentucky law providing for oil inspection, 650.
Knapp, Admiral, 688.
Knowlton, Atty. Gen., 36.
Korea, 277, 694.

La Follette, Sen., 171, 181, 331.
La Follette Seamen's Act, 498.
Labor—unemployment, 494–495; natl. Employment Service, 495; supply and demand, 496.
Working conditions, Fed. control of, 497–502; railway men, 497; seamen, 498–499; Fed. employees, 499–500; industrial risks and compensation, 500–502; federal, 501; Public Health Service, 501.
Research work in labor problems needed, 511; Bureau of Labor Statistics, 511; Children's Bureau, Women's Bureau, 511.
Labor, Dept. of—*see* Dept. of Labor.

Labor, organized, its connection with Fed. Govt., 484–485; with immigration, 486–491, 494; with child labor, 494–495.

Industrial disputes, Fed. Govt.'s part in, 502–510; grounds for Fed. intervention, 502; Railway Labor Act, 503; Board of Mediation, 503; arbitration, 503; President's intervention, 502, 504, 505–506; powers of Congress, 504; Division of Conciliation, 504–505; its work, 505; fed. judiciary's part, 506–510; writ of injunction, 506–510, 662; concessions to labor in Clayton Act, 507–508, 509; injunction against striking railway shopmen, 508; against miners, 509; labor's demand for new statute governing injunction, 510; Kansas law about discharge for union membership, 662; Arizona law on injunction in labor disputes, 662.

Labor, prison, 142–143.

Labor legislation, state, in conflict with "due process" clause, 661–662.

Labor supply, 494.

Laissez faire theory, 447, 449, 450.

Lake Erie, Huron, Michigan, Ontario, 385.

Lane, Franklin K., 263, 329.

Lansing, Secy., 276; resignation, 263, 707, 708, 710.

Lansing-Ishii Agreement, 276.

Latin-America—*see* Monroe Doctrine.

Law enforcement, 135 ff.

Law Enforcement and Observance, Natl. Comm. on, 140.

Laws, fed., interpreting Constitution, 24.

League of Nations, 582, 703, 743–746; its org., 744; obligations of member Powers, 744; history of U. S. relation to, 744–746; coöperation with, 745–746; Covenant, 726, 729, 742.

League of Women Voters, 213–214.

Lenin, 104, 107.

Leper hospitals, 591.

Library of Congress, 211, 295, 636–637.

Lifeboats and other safety apparatus on vessels, 595–596.

Life-saving service, 398.

Lighthouse Service—*see* Bureau of Lighthouses.

Lighthouses, 377, 395.

Limited government established by Constitution, 52–53.

Lincoln, Pres., 34, 37, 56, 84, 107; on Dred Scott case, 129–131; 231, 250, 253, 262, 280, 297.

Lippmann, Walter, 17, 104, 105, 106, 107.

Liquor traffic, 30, 136. *See also* prohibition problem.

Livestock—problems of, investigated by Bureau of Animal Industry, 515; Conservation of, 560–561.

Lloyd George budget, 35.

Lobbies, 212–219.

Local option, 607.

Lochner working-hours case, 126.

Locomotives, Fed. inspection of, 594.

Lodge, Sen., 35, 171, 251, 252, 260, 706.

"Logic" in interpreting Constitution, 30–32.

"Log-rolling," 179, 351.

London Conference of 1930, 742, 753.

Longshoremen and harbor workers, compensation system for, 501.

Lorimer, Sen., 161.

Louisiana Purchase, 75, 680.

Louisiana quarantine law, 650.

Luce, Robert, 358.

Lusitania, 275.

Macaulay, T. B., 103.

MacDonald, Dr. A. F., 673.

Machine age, its effect on government, 4. *See* technology.

Macmahon, Prof. Arthur, 303.

Madden, Martin B., 356, 359.

Madison, Pres., 6, 11, 28, 68, 84.

Magna Carta, 308, 335.

Magnetic compass, continuous readings of, 627.

Mahan's *The Influence of Sea Power on History,* 753.

Mail Equipment Shops, 314.

Mails. *See* postal services.

Maine, State of, on Dred Scott case, 129; election date, 151.

Maine, U.S.S., 274.

Manchester school of political economists, 448.

Mandamus, writ of, 122.

Mann, James R., 154.

Mann Act, 606.

Maps, Govt., for ships, 396; for aviation, 415, 416; general, 625–627.

Marbury *vs.* Madison, 27, 125.

Maritime cases in fed. jurisdiction, 112.

Marshall, Chief Justice, 24, 27, 31, 33, 36, 37, 56, 125, 649.

Marshall, Vice Pres., 232.

Mass. *vs.* Mellon, 673.

Masses, 9–15; their capacity for gov-

ernment, 10–11; intelligence as determined by "tests," 11–12; considered in relation to new technological demands, 12–15; to political problems, 16–17; Carlyle and others on ignorance of masses, 104–105.
"Master Specifications," 619–620.
Matches, phosphorus, 340, 598.
Mayers, Dr. Lewis, 317.
McAdoo, W. G., 329.
McBain, H. L., 610.
McGrain *vs.* Daugherty, 210.
McKinley, Pres., 36, 84, 231, 251, 257, 274, 474, 680.
McKinley Act—*see* Tariff Act of 1890.
Measurements and planning in Fed. Govt., 615–644; Const. provision for, 616; Bureau of Standards, 616; standards of meas., 617–623; new scientific meas. units, 617; fixing legal standards, 618; enforcing them in U. S. economic life, 618 ff.; public testing service of Bur. of St., 619; compulsory standards in commerce, 619; "Master Specifications" for goods used by Govt., 619–620; private adoption of these M. S., 620; control of goods sold, 620–621; interstate comm. regulations, 620–621; voluntary adoption by trades of Govt. standards, 621; costliness of too many sizes in trade, 621–622; B. of St. as simplifying and coörd. agency, 622; "Simplified Practice Recommendations," 622; examples of results, 622–623.
Surveying and mapping, 623–628; purpose of Govt. surveys, 623–624; border determination, 624; dividing public lands, 624; inquiries into minerals on public lands, 624; maps, 625; bench marks, 626; marine charts, 626; analysis of soil formations, 626–627; of oil beds, coal beds, mineral deposits, 627; record of magnetic data, 627; of seismic data, 628.
Population statistics, 628–633; what they reveal, 628; agencies for making surveys: Bureau of the Census, B. of Labor Statistics, Office of Educ., etc., 629; personal interview to collect data, 629; questionnaires, 630; census data, 630; vital statistics, 630; cultural organization data, 631; religious census, 631; analysis of economic data, 631–632; data on crime, delinquency, etc., 632.
Statistics of industry and agriculture, 633–634; *Statistical Abstract of the U. S.* presenting all data, 634.
Govt. Printing Office, 635; its bookstore, 635; other sources of Govt. printed matter—*Congr. Record* bulletins, etc., 636; "depositories," 636; Library of Congress, 636–637; Smithsonian, 637; motion picture films lent, 638.
Coördination of Govt. fact-finding agencies, 639–640; scientific planning, 640; information for dealing with public crises, 641; unemployment and depression, inquiries into, 641–642; Hoover program, 642–643; anticipating economic crises, 643–644.
Meat processing and packing, 545.
Merchant Marine Act of 1920, 383, 389, 390, 391; of 1928, 391, 393, 419, 428. *See also* shipping.
"Merit system," 304, 315, 317.
Merriam, Charles E., 323.
Mesopotamia, Am. oil interests in, 478.
Metric system and English, both legal, 618.
Mexican War, 274.
Mexico, 281, 482.
Michels, Robert, 12, 104.
Military Academy, West Point, 764.
Militia, state—*see* Natl. Guard.
Milk, quality of, served on trains, 584.
Mineral lands, Federal, 552.
Minimum wage laws, 662.
Mining, elimination of risks in, 599–600.
Minnesota law requiring meat inspection, 650–651.
Misrepresentation in business, under Trade Comm. Act, 467–468.
Mississippi River floods, 600–602.
Mississippi River Improvement, 378, 600–601.
Mitchell, John, 505.
Monetary system during the Am. Rev., 363; Civil War, 364.
Money and banking, 360–370; volume of currency, 361; beneficial margin of manipulation, 361–362; materials for money, 362; issuance of paper money, 362–363; Bank of the U. S. issue, 364; state bank issue, 364; Fed. Reserve Law, 365; organization of Board, 365; functions, 366; its control of bank-note currency, 366; districts, 366; local banks, 366–367; currency compromises,

367; Fed. Res. notes from member banks, 367; their retirement, 368; distribution of profits, 368; attacks on it by agrarian interests, 368–369; its restrictions criticized, 369.
Money factor in party politics, 92–103; revenues to machine, 92–93; expenditures, 95–99; scandals, 99; weakness of legislation controlling, 99–102.
Monroe Doctrine, 283, 691, 698, 706, 736–740; its origin, 736–738; subsequent interpretation, 738–740; Venezuelan dispute, 738–739; our interest in Latin-America, 739; real meaning of M. D., 739–740; Latin-American attitude towards, 740; Pan-Am. Conference, 740; M. D. not affected by "outlawry of war," 742.
Monroe, Pres., 231, 737.
Montesquieu's "Spirit of Laws," 67, 68.
Morals—*see* public morals.
Morley, John, 104.
Morrill Act of 1862, 669.
Morris, Gouverneur, 10, 28.
Morse, Samuel F. B., 433.
Motor busses, 410.
Motor transport, 410–412.
Motor trucks, 411–412.
Muscle Shoals plant, 568, 571, 572.
Mussolini, 11, 15, 104, 107.
Myers, Jefferson, 428.
Myers *vs.* U. S., 272.

Napoleon, 106.
Narcotic Drug Act, 340, 613.
Narcotics, 612–613.
Natl. Advisory Health Council, 313.
Natl. Bureau of Economic Research, 642.
Natl. Catholic Welfare Council, 214.
Natl. Chamber of Commerce, 214.
Natl. Comm. on Law Enforcement and Observance, 140.
Natl. Defense Act of 1916, 672.
Natl. Fed. of Fed. Employees, 325.
Natl. Food Products Assn., 443.
Natl. Grange, 213.
Natl. Guard, 672, 763, 764, 766, 768.
Natl. Homes for Disabled Volunteer Soldiers, 779.
Natl. Inst. of Health, 592.
Natl. parks, 551–552.
Natl. Parks Service, 551.
Natl. Pop. Govt. League, 213.
Natl. Woman's Party, 213.
Natural gas—waste of, 547.
Natural resources, conservation of, 257, 546–577; waste of petroleum, natural gas, coal, 546–548; of forests, fish, game, 548; of water power, 548; conservation movement led by Fed. Govt., 549; Fed. lands, formerly sold, now being held, 550; amount and character, 550–551; natl. parks and monuments, 551–552; mineral lands leased, 552–553; non-mineral sold with restrictions, 553; forests—*see* forests; wild animal life—*see* animal life, wild; water power—*see* water power; lands and rights of Indians—*see* Indians.
Naturalization, 75–78.
Naval Academy, Annapolis, 764.
Naval Communications System, 445.
Naval officers, on mail-contract ships, 393.
Naval War College, 764.
Navy, 265, 480–481, 483.
Navy League, 213.
Near East, 478, 481.
Nelson, E. M., 566.
New Guinea sugar cane, 514.
New Republic, The, 256.
Newberry, Truman, 99, 157–158, 161.
Newfoundland fishing rights, 260.
Niagara Falls, internatl. division of its power, 568.
Nicaragua, 688.
Nicaragua canal, proposed, 379.
Nineteenth Amendment, 50–51, 79.
Non-quota immigrants, 489–490.
"No-party man," 89.
Norris, Sen., 133, 158, 458.
Northern Pacific R.R., 398.
Nullification, doctrine of, 65–66.
Nullification Ordinance of S. C., 66.

O'Fallon rate case, 402.
Office of Education, 302, 667.
Office of Experiment Stations, 515.
Officers' Reserve Corps, 763.
Officers, "superior" and "inferior," 267 ff.
Oil—*see* petroleum.
Oil interests, American—in Mesopotamia, 478; in Mexico, 482.
"Oil scandals," 209, 210, 331.
Oleomargarine, 340.
Olney, Secy., 738.
"Open door" policy in immigration, 486; for Amer. world-trade, 741.
"Opinions," Supreme Court, 116–117.
Opium, 613.
Oregon boundary dispute, 724.
Oregon public school law unconstitu-

tional, 655–656; laws fixing hours and wages, 662.
Organizations, private industrial, function in modern govt., 17–19.
Organized Reserves, 763, 766.
Orientals excluded, 486, 487.
Ostrogorski, 89.
Overcrowding of prisons, 141–142.
Overlapping functions of fed. depts., 309–313.
Overman Act, 266, 280, 296.
Owyhee dam, 518.

Pacific Ocean, U. S. power in, 693.
Packers and Stockyards Act of 1921, 545.
Page, Walter Hines, letter describing ambassador's "job," 715–717.
Palmer, Atty-Gen., 611.
Panama Canal, 375, 378, 379, 382, 685, 739.
Panama Canal Zone, 383, 685.
Panama Railway, 685.
Panama, Republic of, 688.
Pan-American Conference, 740.
Pan-American highway, proposed, 410.
Pan-American Sanitary Bureau, 582.
Pan-American Union, 746.
Panic of 1921, 496.
Paper money, 362–363.
Parcel post, 425.
Pardoning power of President, 282.
Parker, Judge, rejected for Supreme Court bench, 134.
Parliament, English, 20, 53, 154, 156, 165, 174, 180, 336.
Parliamentary régime contrasted with our system, 249.
Parole system, 143, 144.
Parties, political, 25; 82–108; their *raison d'être,* 82–84; historic composition, 84–86; modified by social changes, 85; threatened by independent parties, 86–87; party structure and membership, 87–88; sources of party power, 89–95; organization, 90–91; "spoils system," 91–92; revenues from candidates, contracts, private interests, 92–93; socio-psychological factors in party power, 93–94; propaganda, 95; aid to voters given by party machine, 95; campaign expenditures—*see* campaign expenditures; party sensitive to public opinion, 103–108; party leadership disrupted, 162–163.
Patent cases, 115.
Patent Office, 265, 471; *Official Gazette,* 470.
Patents, 471–472; criticisms of system, 472; proposed bill, 472.
Paupers excluded, 488.
Peace Conference, Paris, 707.
Penal reform, 141–144.
Pa. Mfrs.' Assn., 457.
People's Lobby, 213.
Pension Bureau, 779.
Pensions, 70, 776–778.
Perishable Agric. Commodities Act, 543.
Permanent Conference on Printing, 311.
Permanent Court of Internatl. Justice, 744.
Perry, Commodore Matthew C., 734.
Personal liberty as guaranteed by Constitution, 54–63; principles violated during World War, 62–63; under state legislation, 655–656.
Personal rights under jury system, 120.
Personnel Classification Bd., 322 f.
Personnel Office (Dept. of State), 719.
Pests dangerous to agriculture, 523–528; wild beasts, 523–524; insects, fungi and bacteria, 524–527; insecticides, etc., 527–528.
Petition, right of, 59–60.
Petroleum—waste of, 546–547; conservation of, 549.
"Phantom public" (Lippmann), 105.
Philippines, 277, 383, 474, 683, 687; problem of independence, 691–694; tariff in, 694–695; land holdings, 695–696; citizenship, 696, 697; 753, 757.
"Phossy jaw," 598.
Physics—*see* technology.
Picketing, 507, 508, 509.
Pierce, Pres., 231.
Pipe-lines—oil, 400, 407–408.
Plant explorers, 514, 515.
Platt Amendment, 689.
Platt, Sen., 171, 269.
"Pocket veto," 284.
Poisonous foods, 588–589.
Police forces, fed., 139.
Political economy—English classical, 447–448; in America, 449–450.
"Political offices" not under Civil Service, 316, 317.
Polk, Pres., 274, 724.
Polygamists excluded, 488.
Polygamy, 54.
Poole, Commr., 392.
Population distribution—its effect on process of amending Constitution,

officers, nurses, men, of Army and Govt., 592; Natl. Inst. of Health, 590, 592; researches of its field agents, 592–593; assistance in great disasters—floods, etc., 593; Red Cross, 593.
Public Health Service, 304, 313, 501, 579, 581, 584, 590, 591, 592, 593, 674.
Public lands, power sites on, 568. *See also* natural resources (Fed. lands).
Public morals, 602–614; relation of law and morals, 602; differences of opinion on moral issues, 603, 604; on agencies for regulating conduct, 603; Fed. Govt.'s action in moral issues, 603 ff.; forbids mailing of obscene, fraudulent, defamatory, crime-inciting matter, 604–605; importing of obscene books, 605–606; mailing or importing contraceptive information or devices, 606; prize-fight films, 606; Mann Act, 606; Fed. reg. and control of narcotics, 606.
Prohibition—*see* prohibition question; narcotics, 612–614.
Public opinion, political party sensitive to, 103–108.
Public policy, cases pertaining to, in Supreme Court jurisdiction, 114.
Public Printer, 635.
Public safety, 593–602; risks to travelers on common carriers, 593 ff.; safety standards set up by Congr. and Interst. Comm. Comm., 594 ff.; on railroads, 594–595; on vessels in interstate and foreign commerce, 595; on excursion boats, 595; safety equipment of vessels, 595–596; competent crews, 596; Coast Guard aid in accidents, 596–597.
In air travel, 597–598; regulations for equipment and operation of planes, 597; pilots' competence, 597–598.
Regulation of shipment of dangerous and inflammable materials, 598; tax on white phosphorus matches, to restrict "phossy jaw," 598; Bureau of Standards' "Safety Codes" for machinery, 599; elimination of mining risks, 599–600; aid in mining accidents, 600.
Forestalling of floods, e.g., Mississippi, 600–601; aid in flood relief, 601–602.
Public utilities—*see* Supreme Court *and* water power.
Pullman strike, 132, 504, 507.
"Quack medicines," 589.
Quarantine at entry port, 579, 582–583; La. law upheld by Supreme Court, 650; confusion due to conflicting fed. and state rules, 666–667; plant, 526–527.
Quay, Sen., 171.
Quota, immigration, 488–491; exceptions, 489–490.

Radio, fed. problems connected with, 437–446; difficulty of control, 437–438; confusion in wave-lengths, 438; reg. of transmitting stations, 438; property rights in secret messages, 438; propaganda uses, 439; commercial use, 439; wireless relations with foreign countries, 440–441; Intern'l Radiotel. Conference, 441; domestic jurisdiction of Congress, 441; Fed. Radio Comm., 441–442; supervision of broadcasting, 442–443, question of licensing advtg. over radio, 444; fed. use of radio, 444; examples of precedence, 444; radio plants as part of natl. defense, 445; Army and Navy nets, 445–446; weather forecasts to farmers, 522–523.
Radio, pres. campaigns revolutionized by, 237.
Radio Service, 441.
Railway Brotherhoods, 213, 498.
Railway employees, legal working hours of, 497; Adamson Act, 498.
Railway Labor Act of 1926, 503.
Railway strike—threatened, 1922, 265; Pullman in Chicago, 1894, 132, 504, 507; of shopmen, 1922, 508.
Railways—fed. aid to, 398–399; abuses in management of, 399; legislative reforms, 400; Transp. Act of 1920, 400–401; Interstate Comm. Comm., 400, 401 ff.; rates, 401–405; disputed points, 402–405; valuation, 403; cases of discrimination, 403–404; Supreme Court decisions, 404; proposed consolidation under fed. control, 405–406; express business, 406.
Safety of travelers on, fed. supervision and investigation, 594–595; accidents, 595.
Randolph, John, 29.
Ratifiers of Constitution, 28, 29.
Ratio, battleship, 735.
"Re-capture clause," 405–406.
Reclamation Acts, 518.
Reclamation projects—*see* irrigation.
Reclassification Bill of 1923, 322, 326.

Reconstruction Era, 69.
Red Cross, 593.
Reed, Speaker, 167, 204.
Refrigerator cars, 538–539.
Regular Army, 763, 764, 768.
Religion—power of Congress to enact laws respecting, 54; as ground for refusal to bear arms, 77–78.
Representatives—*see* House of Representatives.
Republican-Democratic party, 85.
Rep. natl. convention of 1860, 53.
Rep. party—divided on tariff, 86; 131; defense of Supreme Court, 132; tariff plank in 1908 platform, 454; Rep. tariff board, 1909, 454; carried 1918 congressional elections, 705.
Reservations, Indian, 573–574.
Reservations, Govt.—*see* animal life, wild, *and* forests *and* Indians.
Reserve Officers' Assn., 213.
Reserve Officers' Training Corps, 764–765, 766.
Retroactive legislation, 652.
Revenue—*see* taxation.
Revenue bills, 63, 193; act of 1894, 336.
Revolutionists excluded, 487–488.
Rhode Island *vs.* A. Mitchell Palmer, 611.
Right of assembly and petition, 59–60.
Rights, personal—*see* personal rights *and* personal liberty.
Risks, industrial, 500–502; in modern travel—*see* public safety.
Roads, federal aid in constructing, 672. *See also* Federal Aid Road Act *and* Bureau of Public Roads.
Roberts, Brigham H., 153.
Rocco, Signor, 11.
Rogers Act of 1924, 713, 719, 720.
Rogers' *The American Senate,* 205.
Roosevelt, Pres., 35, 209, 222, 223, 230, 231, 243, 251, 252, 253, 254, 257, 258, 260, 276, 277, 289, 308, 325, 506, 688, 691, 694, 705, 706, 722, 730, 734, 738, 739, 755.
Root, Elihu, 691, 747.
Rosa, Dr. E. B., 775.
Rosenberg's *Die Entstehung der Deutscher Republik,* 18, 762.
"Rotten borough" system in England, 156.
Rousseau, 145.
Ruling classes, their "wisdom," 10–17.
"Rum-running," 610.
Rural free delivery, 424.
Russia, intervention in, 58, 280.
Russo-Japanese War, 260.
Ryan, Dr. John A., 604.

Sabotage, advocates of, excluded, 488.
Safety Codes of Bureau of Standards, 599.
Samoa, 685, 687, 697, 734.
Santo Domingo, 276–277, 281, 482, 483, 688–689, 734, 740.
Savings banks, postal, 370, 425.
Schwimmer, Rosika, 76–77.
Science—*see* technology.
Scientific management, 455; as applied to Fed. Govt., *see* measurements and planning.
Scientific method, 8.
Seals, conservation of, 564–565.
Seamen's Act, 498.
Seamen's Union, 498.
Seamen's working hours, food, etc., 498–499.
Secret diplomacy, 729–732, 751–752.
Secret service agents, 139.
Secy. of Agriculture, 534, 538, 542, 543, 544, 545.
Secy. of the Interior, 517, 520, 521.
Secy. of Labor, 487, 490; since 1913 a trade-union man, 491; 492, 493, 504.
Secy. of the Navy, 313, 393, 481, 767.
Secy. of State, 264, 476, 483; character in Wilson's admins. 707–708; leading Secs. listed, 709–710; his part in treaty negotiations, 724–725. *See also* Dept. of State.
Secy. of the Treasury, 306, 313, 315, 349, 351, 365, 374; his complex functions as head of Fed. finance, 370; 460–461, 483; 769.
Secy. of War, 756, 767.
Sedition Acts, 154; of 1798, 55, 60; of 1918, 57, 159, 280, 771.
Seismological data, Govt., 628.
Seligman, E. R. A., 773.
Senate, 57; its treaty-making power, 69; 155–164; membership in relation to population, 156; qualifications, 156; exclusions, 156–159; 17th Amendment, 159; effects of popular election on it, 160–163; length of term, 163–164; party conferences, 180–183; leadership, 183–184, 188; committees (*see* Congress); procedure, 197; action on bills, 199–200; rules, 201; length of debate, 205.
Powers relating to taxation, 344–346; to appropriation, 351; to diplomatic service, 705, 712; to

treaties, 705, 720; to treaty negotiations, 723–728; investigation at time of Geneva conference on armaments, 761.
Senators—exclusion of, due to excessive primary expenditures, 100, 157–158, 161. *See also* Senate.
Separation of Govt. powers, 67–71, 246, 247, 260, 261, 288 ff.
Serums, 589–590.
Seventeenth Amendment, 50, 159; its effect on the Senate, 160.
Seward, William H., 297.
Shaw, G. B., 104.
Shearer, W. B., 256.
Sheppard-Towner Act of 1921, 673.
Sherman Anti-trust Act, 209, 247, 462, 465, 507–508, 510.
Sherman, John, 230, 298.
Shipping, and govt., 13, 14, 85; federal loans to, 369; subsidies, 387; mail contracts, 392, 427; inland, 382 f.; in foreign trade, 386 ff.; sanitation, 580 ff.; public safety, 595 ff.; consular jurisdiction, 718; taxation, 649–650.
Shipping Board, 387, 389, 390.
Shreveport, La., discriminated against by Texas, 403–404.
Simplification of sizes in mdse., 621–622.
"Simplified Practice Recommendations," 622–623.
Sinclair, Harry, 101.
Sixteenth Amendment, 49–50, 133, 342.
Slavery, 34. *See also* Dred Scott case.
Smith, Alfred E., 230.
Smith-Hughes Vocational Educ. Act of 1917, 670.
Smith-Lever Act of 1914, 670.
Smithsonian Institution, 637.
Smoot, Reed, 156–157.
Smuggling, 136, 138; of liquor, 610; of narcotics, 613.
Southern states and 14th Amendment, 48–49; 221, 222.
Sovereignty of the states—*see* states.
Spanish War pensions, 286.
Speaker of the House, 167, 182, 184, 185, 186, 192.
Specie currency, 362.
Speyer, James, 259.
"Spoils system," 91, 303–304.
Standard Oil Co., 407.
Standards—*see* measurements and planning.
State authorities and prohibition enforcement, 610–611.
State govts., Supreme Court's power over acts of, 125; their coöp. with Fed. Govt. during World War, 772.
State property and instrumentalities not taxable, 338.
States—their powers under Constitution, 64; their laws in conflict with federal, 65; controversy over their rights, 65–67; judicial cases involving, 111–112; their quotas in House of Representatives, 146–149.
Constitutional restraints on, defined by Fed. Govt., 645–646; "concurrent" powers of, 647; specific fed. limitations, 648–652; state powers of taxation defined, 648; no duties on imports, 648; tonnage duties, 649; no tax on Fed. property, etc., 649–650; no reg. of interstate comm., 650–651; no control over monetary system, 651; limits to their criminal legislation, 651; no *ex post facto* laws, 651–652.
Constl. restraints on passage of laws impairing oblig. of contracts, 652; wide meaning of "contract," 652–653; charter obligations, 652–654; right to rescind charters, 654; veto power of fed. judiciary over local legislation, under 14th Amendment, 654–655; Sup. Court definition of "liberty," 655–656; ambiguity of term "property," 656.
"Due process of law," 656; defined as in criminal cases, 657; in civil, 657, in taxation cases, 657–658; in legislation on public-utility rates, working hours, strikes, etc., 658; Supreme Court on valuation of public-utility property, 658–660; fair return on, 660; "due process" clause in labor legislation, 661–662; hour and wage laws upheld and invalidated, 661–662; states' "police power," 662–663.
Fed. and state coöperation, 663–675; e.g., fed. licenses for intrastate air traffic, 664–665; fed. action validating state law throughout Union, e.g., conservation of wild life, 665; fed. law on interstate shipment of prison-made goods, 666; concurrent fed. and state jurisdiction, 666; confusion due to conflicting rules of fed. and state quarantines, and how settled, 666–667; fed. standardization of local activities, e.g., education, 667–668; results of fed. research at disposal of states, 668.

Grants from fed. treasury for aid to states, 668–669; for schools, roads, canals, 669; Morrill Act, 669; for agric. exp. stations, 670; Smith-Lever Act for extension work in agric., 670; Smith-Hughes Vocational Educ. Act, 670–671.

Grants in aid to forestry, 671; to build roads, 671–672; Federal Aid Road Act of 1916, 671; state militia now Natl. Guard, 672; aid to persons disabled in industry, 673; Industrial Rehabilitation Act, 673; Sheppard-Towner Act giving fed. aid to mothers in childbirth, 673.

Conditions under which above aid is given to states, 673–674; their own appropriations, and legislation meeting fed. standards, 674; examples of fed. coöp. with states, 674–675.

Interstate relations, 676–678; rights of citizens of one state in another, 676; Ward *vs.* Md. case, 676; credit of each state's acts, etc., in other states, 677; extradition of criminals, 677–678; extradition procedure, 678.

Their rights in conflict with treaties, 720–722.

States' rights controversy, 65–67.
Statistics, 628–634.
Stephenson, Sen., 161.
Stock market crash of 1929, 496, 497.
Stockyards, 545.
Stone, Justice, 403.
Story, Justice, 112, 422, 646, 647.
Strong, Justice, 66.
Subprofessional Service, 314.
Sudan grass seed, 514–515.
Suffrage—Negro, 47–48, 78; woman, 50–51, 79, 87; rights, qualifications, etc., 78–79.
Sugar cane, New Guinea, 514.
Supt. of Prisons, 141.
Supt. of Public Documents, 635.
Supervising Architect, Office of, 374–375.
Supreme Court—as interpreter of Constitution, 23; personnel, 36 ff.; final tribunal in states' rights controversies, 66–67; relations with Congress, 69; 70; its supremacy over other Government departments, 71; as defender of private property, 72; on naturalization cases, 77; 109; jurisdiction, 113–114; effect of narrowing its obligatory jurisdiction, 114; types of operations, 115–116; procedure, 116; "opinions," 116–117; on constitutionality of statutes, 123–127; its acts provocative of political controversy, 127–135; suggested reforms of, 135; action in Newberry case, 157, 224; in Daugherty case, 210; Chief Justice administers presidential oath, 244; on President's duties, 264; 306; on income taxes, 337; on taxes for federal revenue, 339; on taxes as penalty, 340; on railway rates, 402, 403, 404; on pipe-lines, 407; on motor busses and trucks, 411–412; on mails, 422; on child-labor law, 494; on Debs case, 507; on strikers' activities, 510; on import duties, 648; on prohib. enforcement, 611; on powers of states—*see* states; on valuation of public-utility property, 659–660; on labor legislation, 661–662; general effects of its decisions in cases involving states, 663; sustains Sheppard-Towner Act of 1921, 673; on rights of a citizen in a state not his own, Ward *vs.* Maryland, 676; on extradition, 678; on "Insular Cases," 682; on treaty-making, 720–722.
Surgeon General, 313.
Surtax, 343.
Surveying, Govt., 623–625.
Swiss militia army, 766.

Taft, Pres., 37, 222, 223, 236, 252, 259, 270, 272 (as Chief Justice, on Myers case), 289, 297, 308, 347, 352, 477, 478, 692.
Taney, Chief Justice, 24, 28, 34, 37; on Dred Scott case, 128, 129, 681.
Tariff, 85, 86; revision, 162, 346–348, 456–459; "flexible," 1929 controversy over, 257, 456; on sugar, 294; 452–462; Dem. view, for revenue only, 452–453, abandoned 1928, 453; questions as to nature and extent of protective tariff, 453–461; infant industries, 453; determination of a "scientific" tariff, 454; Rep. tariff board, 1909, 454; Dem. tariff bill, 1913, 454; "cost of production" theory, 454; depends on efficient mfg., 455; determination of rates, 455; by Congress or Pres.? 455–456; "flexible," 456; Tariff Act of 1930, 456–458; debates on it, 457–458; revision a continuous process under Tariff Comm., 459.

"Unfair" foreign competition and

bounties, 459–462; unjust foreign discrimination against U. S. goods, 460; "dumping" mdse. on foreign markets, 460; duties and powers of Tariff Comm., 461.
In Porto Rico and Philippines, 694–695.
Tariff Act of 1890, 455, 462; of 1894, 462; of 1922, 456; of 1930, 156, 456–458, 605.
Tariff Comm., 456, 458, 460.
Tax, income—*see* income tax.
Taxation—complex significance of, 333–334; taxable objects, 334; classes taxed, 334; taxing power of Congress, 335, limited by Const., 336; Supreme Court decisions on ambiguities, 336–337; no tax on state property, etc., 338; for revenue, 339–340; on child labor, 340; customs duties, 341, 342; on incomes, 341–342, 343; inheritances, 342, 343–344; on consumption, 342.
Laws originate in House, 344–345; Senate's powers, 345–346; tariff revision process, 346–348; administration of taxes and debts, 348–350; by Treasury Dept., 348; customs and int. rev. districts, 348–349; special tribunals for appeals, 349; revenues held at Treasury and in Fed. Res. banks. 349.
"Taxation without representation," 335.
Taylor, Pres., 231, 286.
Technology, influence on government, 4 ff.; on social organization, 6; on forms of property, 6; on increase in government functions, 6–7; on government personnel, 7; on methods, 8; relation of, to democracy, 13–16; in Supreme Court cases, 114–115; in law enforcement, 135–136, 140; business of Congress, 173; presidential influence, 255–256; influence on choice of division heads, 304–305; in departmental reorganization, 310; civil service, 314; revolution in transportation, 370 ff.; shipping, 386 ff.; highways, 408 ff.; aviation, 413 ff.; wire communications, 433 ff.; radio, 437 ff.; trade-marks and patents, 469 ff.; conditions of labor, 497 ff.; agricultural research and education, 514 ff.; irrigation, 517 ff.; weather observation, 521 ff.; war on farmers' foes, 524 ff.; conservation of resources, 546 ff.; water power, 568 ff.; public health, 578 ff.; public safety, 593 ff.; weights and measures, 617 ff.; surveying and mapping, 623 ff.
Telegraph and telephone, 433–437; Morse, 433; Bell, 433; fed. assistance, 434; reg. by Interstate Comm. Comm., 434–436; consolidation, 435; cable lines, 436–437.
Tenth Amendment, 65.
Tenure of Office Act, 69.
Territories, U. S.—underlying principles of their acquisition, 680–681; legal powers of Natl. Govt. over, 680–682; no provision for in Const., 681; under juris. of Congress, 681; const. rights of states applicable to territories, 681; question complicated by acquis. of Hawaii and Philippines, 682; Sup. Court decisions on Insular Cases, 682.
Admin. of, 682–687; Dist. of Col., 683; pop. govt. in Alaska, Hawaii, P. I., Porto Rico, 683–684; governors and legislatures, 684; Virgin Isl., 684–685; Panama Canal Zone, 685; minor islands, 686; supervision of above by Depts. of Interior, Navy, War, 687.
U. S. protectorates in Caribbean, etc., 687–690; Santo Domingo, 688–689; Nicaragua, 688; Haiti, 688; Cuba, 689.
Problems of U. S. imperial policy, 690–699; independence, 691–694; polit. points involved, 692; business and strategic points, 693; rivalry with Japan, 693–694.
Tariff in overseas territories, 694–695; policy with regard to large land holdings, 695–696; citizenship problems, 696–697; immigration, 697–698.
Third term, presidential, doctrine and practice, 243.
Thirteenth Amendment, 47, 48.
Thomas, Prof. David Y., 739.
Thomas, Sen. Elmer, 8.
Timber—*see* forests.
Tolls on water routes, 381.
Tonnage taxes on foreign ships, 393–394.
Trade-marks, 469–471.
Trade unions—*see* unions.
Transportation, 376–419; inland and coastal waters, 377–386; early importance, 377–378; new aspects today, 378; admin. controlled by Army engineers, 378; projects enumerated, 378–379; Panama Canal, 379; expenditures on proj-

ects, 380; use, 380; costs of canal *vs.* rail transp., 381; upkeep of water routes, 381; tolls, 381; Panama Canal tolls, 382; freight and passenger carriage by foreign vessels on coastal waters, 382; bridges, dams, etc., 383–384; other encroachments on waterways subject to Congr. legislation, 384; dumping, floating logs, 384; water diverted for city use, 384; e.g., Chicago and Lake Michigan, 384–385.

Foreign trade, 386–394; dearth of U. S. ships at opening of W. War, 387; many at close, 387–388; Shipping Board, 387, 389, 390; subsidies, 388–389; Merchant Marine Act of 1920, 388, 389, 390; of 1928, 391, 392, 393; mail contracts, 392–393; foreign discriminations against U. S. merchant ships, 393; our tax on foreign ships, 393–394, 450.

Aids to navigation, 394–398; charting and marking, 394; buoys, towers, etc., 394–395; lights, 395; Lighthouse Bureau, 394, 395; guidebooks and maps, 396; tide tables, 396; "Great Brass Brain," 396–397; iceberg patrols, 397, 398.

On land, 398–413; fed. development of railways, 398–399; abuses in financing and operating, 399; reforms, 400; Transp. Act of 1920, 400–401; Interstate Comm. Comm., 400, 401 ff.; rates, 401–405; disputed points, 402–405; problems of valuation, 403; cases of discrimination, 403–404; Supreme Court decisions, 404; proposed consolidation under fed. control, 405–406; express business, 406; oil pipe-lines, 406–408; highways and motor tr., 408–413; Fed. Aid Road Act, 409; Bureau of Public Roads, 409–410; proposed Pan-American Highway, 410; fed. reg. of motor busses and trucks, 410–413; rate conflicts, 411–412.

By air, 413–419; fed. airways, 413–414; lighting, 414; marking, 414–415; maps, 415; airports, 416; mails, 417; fed. control of rates, 417–418; airships, 418–419.

Transportation Act, 115, 400, 404, 405.

Treason defined in Constitution, 60; its penalties, 61.

Treasury, Dept. of the—*see* Dept. of the Treasury.

Treaties—power to make, 69, 274 ff., 720–723; given by Const. to Pres. and Senate, 720; Jefferson's rules, 720; treaties in conflict with rights of states, 720–722; e.g., with Russia, 721; and with Japan, 721–722.

Negotiating, 723–729; Pres.'s action, 723; confers with Senate, 723–724; Secy. of State's action, 724–725; terminating treaties, 728.

Treaty—with Dominican Republic, 1905, 276–277; "four-power," 735.

Treaty of Versailles, 707; rejection of by Senate, 725–726; 744.

Treitschke's *Politics,* 750, 754.

Tripoli, Pasha of, 733.

Truax *vs.* Corrigan, 510.

Tularaemia, 592.

Tutuila—*see* Samoa.

Twelfth Amendment, 46–47.

Unemployment, 494, 495, 496, 641–642.

"Uniform" taxes, 336–337.

Union membership as ground for discharge of employee, Kansas Law on, 662.

Unions, their opposition to prison labor, 142; to child labor, 494. *See* labor, organized, *and* Am. Fed. of Labor.

Unions of Fed. employees, 325–326.

United Mine Workers, 509.

U. S. Bank, 265.

U. S. Employees' Compensation Comm., 501.

U. S. Forest Service, 310, 554, 557, 559, 560, 561.

"U. S. Govt. Master Specifications," 371.

U. S. Pharmacopœia, 585.

United States Reports, 117.

U. S. Shipping Board, 313.

U. S. Steel Trust, 209, 330.

U. S. Veterans' Admin., 778, 779.

U. S. *vs.* Insurgents, 60.

Universal Postal Union, 423, 702, 748.

Upton, Maj. Gen. Emory, 753.

Vaccines, 589–590.

Van Buren, Pres., 644.

Vanderlip, Secy., 301.

Vare, William S., 158.

Venezuelan controversy, 275, 738.

Veterans, care of, 775–780; pension system, 776–777; bonus, 777–778; U. S. Govt. life insurance, 778; institutions for disabled, 778–779; cost of aid to veterans, 779; problems, 780.

Veterans' Bureau, 209, 296, 331, 778, 779, 780.

Veto power, 69, 284–287.